Special Edition

Using
Microsoft
Internet
Explorer 3

Special Edition

USING
MICROSOFT
INTERNET
EXPLORER 3

Written by Jim O'Donnell, Eric Ladd, and Mark Brown

Special Edition Using Microsoft Internet Explorer 3

Credits

PRESIDENT
Roland Elgey

PUBLISHER
Joseph B. Wikert

PUBLISHING MANAGER
Jim Minatel

EDITORIAL SERVICES DIRECTOR
Elizabeth Keaffaber

MANAGING EDITOR
Sandy Doell

DIRECTOR OF MARKETING
Barry Pruett

ACQUISITIONS MANAGER
Cheryl D. Willoughby

ACQUISITIONS EDITORS
Doshia Stewart
Philip Wescott

PRODUCT DIRECTOR
Mark Cierzniak

PRODUCTION EDITOR
Maureen A. Schneeberger

COPY EDITORS
Chuck Hutchison
Gill Kent

PRODUCT MARKETING MANAGER
Kim Margolius

**ASSISTANT PRODUCT
MARKETING MANAGER**
Christy M. Miller

TECHNICAL EDITORS
David Medinets
Matthew Brown
Joe Risse
Bill Bruns

TECHNICAL SUPPORT SPECIALIST
Nadeem Muhammed

SOFTWARE RELATIONS COORDINATOR
Patricia J. Brooks

ACQUISITIONS COORDINATOR
Jane K. Brownlow

EDITORIAL ASSISTANT
Andrea Duvall

BOOK DESIGNER
Ruth Harvey

COVER DESIGNER
Dan Armstrong

PRODUCTION TEAM
DiMonique Ford
Amy Gornik
Kay Hoskin
Darlena Murray

INDEXERS
Ginny Bess
Tim Tate

Composed in *Century Old Style* and *ITC Franklin Gothic* by Que Corporation.

To my parents, Robert and Beth Ladd.
—Eric Ladd

To Mom and Dad, Jean and Jim O'Donnell; I guess those trips to the library paid off.
—Jim O'Donnell

About the Authors

James R. O'Donnell, Jr., Ph.D., was born on October 17, 1963, in Pittsburgh, Pennsylvania (you may forward birthday greetings to **odonnj@rpi.edu**). After a number of unproductive years, he began his studies in electrical engineering at Rensselaer Polytechnic Institute. Jim liked that so much that he spent 11 years there getting three degrees, graduating for the third (and final) time in the summer of 1992. He can now be found plying his trade at the NASA Goddard Space Flight Center. He's not a rocket scientist, but he's close.

Jim's first experience with a "personal" computer was in high school with a Southwest Technical Products computer using a paper tape storage device, quickly graduating up to a TRS-80 Model II. His fate as a computer geek was sealed when Rensselaer gave him an Atari 800 as part of a scholarship. After a long struggle, Jim finally chucked his Atari (sniff, sniff) and joined the Windows world. When he isn't writing or researching for Que, or talking on IRC (Nick: JOD), Jim likes to run, row, play hockey, collect comic books and PEZ dispensers, and play the best board game ever, Cosmic Encounter.

Eric Ladd is an Internet consultant living and working in Washington, DC. Prior to doing Internet work, he was a mathematics instructor at Rensselaer Polytechnic Institute in Troy, New York, where he earned his B.S. and M.S. degrees in mathematics. Eric had never been published until he was introduced to the good people at Que, who have put him to work on such titles as *Running a Perfect Web Site with Windows*, *Running a Perfect Netscape Site*, and *Special Edition Using the World Wide Web, 2nd Edition*.

Away from the computer, Eric enjoys reading, baking, running, playing ice hockey, and watching *Animaniacs*. He is currently looking to adopt a Boxer (or two!) from a reputable breeder in the DC area. If you know of one, or just want to say hello, please drop him a line at **erl1@access.digex.net**.

Acknowledgments

Both Eric Ladd and Jim O'Donnell would like to thank the editors and staff at Que for their encouragement and support during this project. Special thanks in particular to Mark Cierzniak, Maureen Schneeberger, and especially Doshia Stewart, for their sound advice, unwavering patience, and continued support.

Additionally, Eric is appreciative of the moral support from all the folks from "that place he used to work at." Specifically, thanks to Lona, the world's coolest cubemate; to Bill, for getting him started with this whole writing thing in the first place; to Bob, for encouraging him to have a life; to Patrick, for hosting the daily Menu Lady sessions; to Cat, for all of the impersonations and sound effects; to Chad, for showing him the wisdom in getting out early; and to Puru, Joan, Carolyn (Alanis?), Michelle, Adam, Juan, Carla, and José. You guys made the time spent under the big pink W worth it.

Eric is also grateful to his family for the understanding when he "disappeared" during the month of April. Thanks to Mom and Dad in Ilion and to Brenda in San Diego.

Jim wants to thank his family; Mom and Dad instilled a love of books, both reading and writing, that continues to this day. Jim would like to extend his thanks to Tobin (it's all your fault!), to his roommates, friends, and teammates (go DC Strokes and DC Nationals!), and an extra special thank-you and IRC *BIG HUG* to Dimas, Tygrr, HotThang, CoCaCola, and the rest of the Soho/IRC bunch for their friendship and help. Hey guys, it's "after the book!" (What, Cheryl? You want me to write another one? Sigh…)

Finally, Eric and Jim would both like to thank the Microsoft Corporation for *not* releasing a third beta of Internet Explorer 3!

We'd Like to Hear from You!

As part of our continuing effort to produce books of the highest possible quality, Que would like to hear your comments. To stay competitive, we *really* want you, as a computer book reader and user, to let us know what you like or dislike most about this book or other Que products.

You can mail comments, ideas, or suggestions for improving future editions to the address below, or send us a fax at (317) 581-4663. Our staff and authors are available for questions and comments through our Internet site, at **http://www.mcp.com/que**, and Macmillan Computer Publishing also has a forum on CompuServe (type **GO QUEBOOKS** at any prompt).

In addition to exploring our forum, please feel free to contact me personally to discuss your opinions of this book: I'm **mcierzniak@que.mcp.com** on the Internet.

Thanks in advance—your comments will help us to continue publishing the best books available on new computer technologies in today's market.

Mark Cierzniak
Product Director
Que Corporation
201 W. 103rd Street
Indianapolis, Indiana 46290
USA

Contents at a Glance

Table of Contents

II │ Mastering Microsoft Internet Explorer

III | Using Helper Applications

VII | Appendixes

Internet Fundamentals

Introduction

The World Wide Web, though originally intended for the exchange of research data, has become part of the daily lives of millions of people. You, like many others, might get on the Web at work to research topics relevant to the tasks you need to complete or to check out what your competitors are up to. At home, you have probably already seen television ads that include a company's Web site address. Indeed, the marketing arms of many companies are scrambling to develop an online presence for their firms, guided by Internet content providers and advertising agencies. You, or someone you know, may have already created a home page and put it up on the Web for public consumption.

In a sense, consumption of information is at the heart of activity on the Web. But to be a Web information consumer, you need a program that allows you to access the Web and to move among the many sites you'll find there.

Enter Microsoft Internet Explorer 3. Internet Explorer has always been available to Windows 95 and Windows NT users, and Microsoft makes Internet Explorer upgrades freely available on its Web site. As its features improved over versions 1.0 and 2.0, Internet Explorer quickly acquired a significant share of the graphical browser market. Microsoft's deal with America Online (AOL) earlier this year will bring Internet Explorer to millions of new users who were otherwise accustomed to AOL's own browser software. And now, with the release of version 3.0, Internet Explorer is even more versatile and useful than before.

That means, of course, there's more to learn—like JavaScript, the new scripting language based on Sun Microsystem's Java and ActiveX Controls, which allow "live" content to be displayed in the Internet Explorer window without launching helper applications.

To assist you in your discovery of what Internet Explorer has to offer, we present *Special Edition Using Microsoft Internet Explorer 3*. This book gently guides you through all the steps to get Internet Explorer installed and working to its full potential on your machine. ■

Who Should Use This Book

This book is intended for anyone and everyone who wants to get the most out of Internet Explorer and the World Wide Web. In particular, users of Windows 95, Windows NT, and AOL will find this book of value since they already have free access to Internet Explorer.

New users will find information on how to obtain, install, and configure Internet Explorer. Intermediate users will discover tips, tricks, and techniques to make Internet Explorer even more fun and useful. And advanced users will learn the nuts and bolts of Internet Explorer operation, including how to use powerful new features like the JavaScript scripting language and ActiveX Controls.

How This Book Is Organized

Special Edition Using Microsoft Internet Explorer 3 is organized into six logical sections.

Part I, "Internet Fundamentals," explains what the Internet and World Wide Web are, and what they are likely to become in the future. It explains how the Web is organized and how it works, and how you can get your computer hooked up to the Net.

Part II, "Mastering Microsoft Internet Explorer," talks you through loading and configuring Internet Explorer. This section also tells you how to navigate on the Web using links, online search engines and indexes, and favorite places. You'll learn how to create your own customized start page—a trend being implemented on many sites—on the Microsoft Network. You'll also find information on how to use online forms, including a discussion of security. The section wraps up with information on using Internet Explorer to access Internet services other than the World Wide Web, like e-mail, FTP, Gopher, and UseNet news.

Part III, "Using Helper Applications," guides you through the process of finding and configuring Internet Explorer helper applications for audio, graphics, and video. You'll also be introduced to Virtual Reality Modeling Language (VRML), learn how it fits into the Web, and how to view it using Internet Explorer helper applications. NetMeeting, Microsoft's exciting new Internet collaboration platform, is discussed in detail. Adobe Acrobat and other portable document formats are also covered, as are compressed files and how to deal with them.

Part IV, "Building World-Class Web Pages for Internet Explorer," gets you started with HyperText Markup Language (HTML), the language used to create Web pages. You'll learn how to create links and use advanced graphic techniques like imagemaps to make your Web pages more engaging. You'll even learn about Microsoft extensions to HTML and proposed future HTML commands. You'll discover how to work with the Web's most advanced page development tools, including Microsoft's set of Internet Assistants that complement the Microsoft Office suite of programs. Finally, you'll see how to make your pages more dynamic by using HTML forms and CGI scripts.

Part V, "Building World-Class Web Sites and Servers for Internet Explorer," builds on the knowledge you gained in Part IV, tying together Web page creation techniques with good user interface advice to help you build an excellent Web site. You'll also read about the Microsoft Internet Information Server, the software package that delivers Web pages to browsers like Internet Explorer.

Part VI, "Advanced Internet Explorer Customization," delves into the depths of Internet Explorer's most powerful new features, with chapters on Sun's Java language for C, C++, and JavaScript. This section finishes with a discussion of ActiveX Technologies, Microsoft's approach to incorporating "active" content into Web documents.

The appendixes in Part VII finish out the book with information on how to load and configure Internet Explorer for Windows 3.1 and what's on the CD-ROM.

The Book's CD-ROM

Inside the back cover of this book you'll find a CD-ROM containing several megabytes of helper applications, links, tips, and programs that will help you get the most out of Internet Explorer.

On the CD

Whenever we mention a program in this book that is included on the book's CD, you'll see this icon in the margin. Keep an eye out for it.

Conventions Used in This Book

This book uses various stylistic and typographic conventions to make it easier to use.

Keyboard shortcut key combinations are joined by plus signs (+); for example, Ctrl+X means to hold down the Ctrl key, press the X key, and then release both.

Menu items and dialog box selections often have a mnemonic key associated with them. This key is indicated on-screen by an underline on the item. To use these mnemonic keys, you press the Alt key and then the shortcut key. In this book, mnemonic keys are underlined, like this: File.

This book uses the following typeface conventions:

Typeface	Meaning
Italic	Variables in commands or addresses, or terms used for the first time
Bold	Text you type in, or addresses of Internet sites, newsgroups, mailing lists, and Web sites
`Computer type`	Commands, HTML tags, directory names, or filenames

N O T E   Notes provide additional information related to the topic at hand. ■

 Tips present short advice on a quick or often overlooked procedure. These include shortcuts that can save you time and assist you along the way.

CAUTION
Cautions alert you to potential pitfalls or dangers in the operations discussed.

 TROUBLESHOOTING

What is a troubleshooting section? Troubleshooting sections anticipate common problems you might encounter while following the procedures in the book. The solution provides you with practical suggestions for solving these problems.

▶ **See** these cross-references for more information on a particular topic.

Sidebar
Longer discussions not integral to the flow of the chapter are set aside as sidebars. Look for these sidebars to find out even more information.

## CHAPTER 2

The World Wide Web and Internet Explorer 3

The explosive proliferation of Internet usage and Web browsing have led many new users to freely exchange the terms Internet and World Wide Web, as if they are the same entity. Well, let's begin by setting the record straight—the Internet and the World Wide Web are not the same!

Internet is a collective term used to describe an interconnection of worldwide computer networks. Operating on the Internet are a variety of computer services such as e-mail, UseNet newsgroups, FTP, Telnet, Gopher, and the World Wide Web. While only a part of the Internet, the growth of the World Wide Web has been explosive. By the end of 1995, it is estimated that there will be more than 13,000 Web servers worldwide, displaying more than ten million Web pages.

Before learning all about Microsoft's Web browser, Internet Explorer 3, to help give you an overall better idea of how we've gotten this far and what's going on behind the scenes, this chapter covers the history and operation of the Internet and the World Wide Web. ■

How did the Internet get started, and how does it work?

In this chapter, you'll read a description of the evolution, structure, and operation of the Internet that helped make it what it is today.

What is the World Wide Web?

Learn about the part of the Internet called the World Wide Web (WWW), and how it allows you to access multimedia from around the world.

What are URLs?

Learn what Uniform Resource Locators (URLs) are and how they are used to locate resources on the Internet and the World Wide Web.

What's new in Internet Explorer 3?

Microsoft has added an impressive amount of capability to the newest version of its flagship Web browser. Some of its new functions are outlined here.

N O T E   Throughout this chapter, you will see references to certain publications such as RFC-1738 or RFC-1173. RFCs (Request For Comment) are informational documents that describe policies, procedures, and protocols on the Internet. If you're interested in reading the in-depth discussions that have taken place on various aspects of the Internet (from "soup-to-nuts" as the saying goes), this is your ticket. RFCs can be referenced from various locations on the Internet, but to save you the time of locating them, here's one reference point: **http://www.uwaterloo.ca/uw_infoserv/ rfc.html**. ▪

Who Uses the World Wide Web

The World Wide Web is one of the most accessible places because it is accessible to virtually anyone worldwide who has access to a computer and a modem. For this reason, the Web has literally become "the kiosk for the entire planet." Because of the potential for getting a message to a very large and diverse audience, it's no wonder that there are now more than ten million Web pages available for your viewing, all posted on the Web in just the last three years.

As mentioned earlier, the initial release of Mosaic for Windows was one of the keys to the success of the Web because Mosaic on the "common" PC made the Web accessible to the masses of ordinary PC users.

So who are these masses of ordinary PC users who have posted those 10 million Web pages? The answer is literally anyone and everyone. Major corporations, small businesses, government agencies, politicians, social organizations, historical societies, and a burgeoning industry of would-be Web authors are among those who have Web pages they are trying to get you to view.

Many Web authors are simply trying to supply information over the Web, but more often, you will see businesses advertising their presence and products, advertising their services, or directly trying to sell you their wares.

When you look out on the Web, you will see Coca-Cola, CNN, and the Virtual Quilt home page, just as an example of some of the diversity you'll find (see figs. 2.1, 2.2, 2.3).

FIG. 2.1
The Coca-Cola home page is one of thousands of pages devoted to advertising non-computer related products.

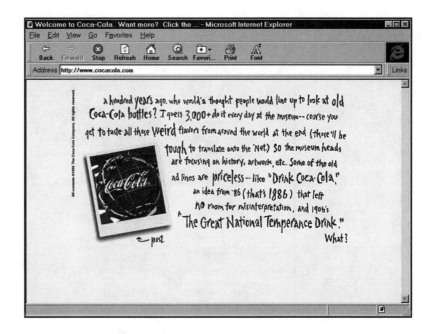

FIG. 2.2
The CNN Interactive home page gives you access to news and information gathered by the Cable News Network.

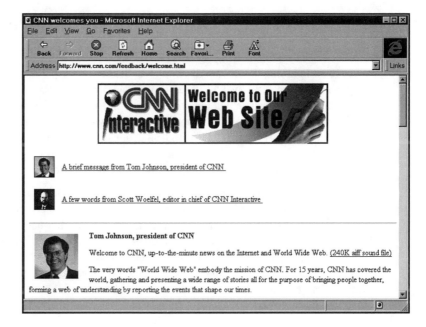

FIG. 2.3

The Virtual Quilt home page—this is an example of one of the many pages devoted to crafts and hobbies.

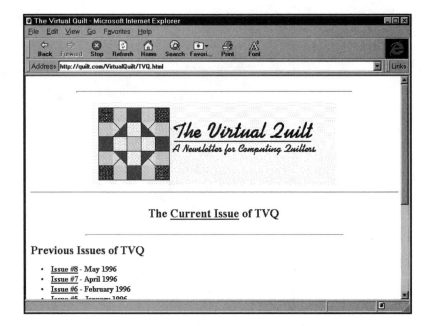

Understanding the Evolution of the Internet

To understand how the Internet functions, you need to know something of its history.

In the 1960s following the Cuban Missile Crisis, the RAND Corporation, America's foremost think tank, first proposed the idea of a decentralized computer network spanning this country. The proposal envisioned linking together military and academic computers in a network that could survive a nuclear attack. The key to this design was to decentralize the control and authority of this network, so that failure or destruction of one or more segments of the network would not result in the network's collapse. This design could only be accomplished if multiple pathways existed between each computer (node) on the network.

The original proposal, released in 1964 by RAND staffer Paul Baran, simply stated that each node in the network would be equal in status to all other nodes. Each node would have the authority to originate, pass, and receive messages from any other node. The messages would be broken down into smaller, standardized units for transmission called *packets*. Packets would be individually addressed to their destination node, and because each node would be capable of passing or forwarding (or routing) packets along the network to the designated address, each message was guaranteed to reach its destination. The network's multiple pathway design ensured that there would always be one or more pathways available for message transmission.

Creation of the Early ARPANET

In the late 1960s, the RAND Corporation, MIT, and UCLA experimented with the concept of a decentralized, packet-switching computer network, as did the National Physical Laboratory in

Great Britain. In 1968, the Pentagon's Advanced Research Projects Agency (ARPA) began funding a project in the U.S. By the fall of 1969, the infant ARPANET came into being with its first four nodes:

- An SDS SIGMA 7 at UCLA
- An SDS940 at the Stanford Research Institute
- An IBM 360 at the University of California at Santa Barbara
- A DEC PDP-10 at the University of Utah

The early tests conducted on ARPANET proved highly successful. Scientists at the test institutions were able to transfer data and share computer facilities remotely. By 1971, ARPANET expanded to 15 nodes, and included links to MIT, RAND, Harvard, CMU in Pittsburgh, Case Western Reserve, and NASA/Ames. By 1972, there were a total of 37 nodes on ARPANET. In 1973, the first international connection to ARPANET was made to the University College of London and to the Royal Radar Establishment in Norway.

Despite the fact that the early makeup of ARPANET consisted of connections between this country's most prestigious research institutions and that the earliest proposals for ARPANET stressed its importance as a means of allowing remote computing, the main traffic on ARPANET in its early days did not fit its intended role. At first, scientists were using it to collaborate on research projects and exchange notes on work. But, very quickly, it became the equivalent of a high-speed, computerized "party-line." Many of its users were sending personal messages and gossip, and eventually using it mainly to just "schmooze."

Growth and Change of ARPANET in the '70s

Nevertheless, despite what it was being used for, ARPANET and the concept of a packet-switching, decentralized network were a huge success. During the 1970s, this decentralized structure made expansion easy and resulted in tremendous growth. Its decentralized structure, vastly different from corporate computer networks at the time, allowed connection of virtually any type of computer as long as it could communicate using the packet-switching protocol NCP, Network Control Protocol (the forerunner to TCP/IP, Transmission Control Protocol/Internet Protocol).

As early as 1974, Vint Cerf and Bob Kahn, both of the National Science Foundation (NSF), published their first specifications for a transmission control protocol, which was being used by other networks to attach to the ARPANET by 1977.

TCP/IP, released into public domain, differed from NCP in that it converted messages into packets at the source, and then reassembled them back into messages at the destination. *IP*, or *Internet protocol*, was used to establish the addressing for the packet, and was able to ensure that packet addressing guided packets through multiple nodes and, more importantly, across multiple networks even if the standards differed from ARPANET's early NCP standard. TCP/IP was the impetus in the late 1970s and early 1980s that led to further expansion of ARPANET, because it was fairly easy to implement on most any computer and allowed easy expansion from any existing node.

By 1983, ARPANET (which, by then, was commonly referred to as the Internet because of the vast array of interconnected computers and networks) officially dropped NCP and replaced it with the more advanced and more widespread TCP/IP, which had been officially adopted by the Department of Defense (DOD) the year before.

Expansion in the '80s and '90s

The 1980s was a period of tremendous growth for the Internet. The pattern established in the U.S. of interconnecting remote computer systems via a decentralized network was spreading worldwide, and many of those foreign computer networks wanted to become connected to the U.S. network. The Internet's reach was broadened by the inclusion of the following:

- **EUnet**—the European UNIX Network, in 1982
- **EARN**—the European Academic and Research Network, in 1983
- **JUNET**—the Japanese UNIX Network, in 1984
- **JANET**—the Joint Academic Network in the United Kingdom, in 1984

It was also during the 1980s that the major players in this country, through funding from the National Science Foundation, established the NSFNET—five supercomputing centers at Princeton, CMU, UCSB, UIUC, and Cornell that loosely became known as the "Internet backbone in the U.S." The original speed of NSFNET in 1986 was a blazing 56 Kbps. In less than two years, the continued expansion of the Internet and demand for computing services led to an upgrade of the NSFNET backbone in 1988 to T1 speed (1.544 Mbps). In 1987, there were more than 10,000 host computers interconnected on the Internet. By 1989, the number of hosts reached 100,000.

The 1990s and the Coming of the Web

The 1990s saw continued expansion of the Internet along with the invention of several Internet services and programs. In 1990, Archie was released by Bill Heelan, Alan Emtage, and Peter Deutsch. In 1991, the NSFNET backbone was upgraded to T3 status (44.736 Mbps), and Brewster Kahle invented WAIS. Also in 1991, Paul Lindner and Mark McCahill of the University of Minnesota released Gopher, followed in 1992 by the release of Veronica from the University of Nevada. 1992 was also the year that the number of host computers on the Internet broke the one million mark.

▶ **See** "Accessing Other Internet Services with MS IE" for the rundown on Gopher, Veronica, and other Internet Services, **p. 223**

But by far the greatest advancement to the Internet in the 1990s (some might even say in its entire existence) was the creation of the World Wide Web. In November of 1990, Tim Berners-Lee of CERN created the first Web server prototype using a NeXT computer. The Web as an actual functioning system did not go online until 1992. In February of 1993, the alpha version of Mosaic was released by the National Center for Supercomputing Applications (NCSA). By September 1993, the first working version of Mosaic was released and WWW traffic was already one percent of NFSNET. By October 1993, there were already 200 Web servers in operation.

In the years following, Internet and Web expansion continued at even greater levels. Actual statistics on the number of host computers and Web servers are hard to measure because they change almost daily. A good guess on the number of host computers on the Internet (averaged from several sources) as of June 1995 would be about 6.5 million, with the largest concentration, as you might expect, to be in the United States.

Internet Administration

The Internet, despite its initial development, support, and funding by ARPA and NSF, does not really belong to anyone, even though it has had a number of agencies and groups "overseeing" its operation. In 1979, ARPA first established the ICCB (Internetwork Configuration and Control Board). The ICCB was replaced in 1983 by the IAB (Internet Activities Board). In 1987, the NSF contracted with Merit Network, Inc. to manage the NSFNET backbone. Ordinarily, the management of the Internet would not warrant much mention, except that in 1993 NFS began laying the plans for a new U.S. Internet backbone as a total replacement for NSFNET. The new backbone went into operation in 1995 as Internet traffic was transitioned from the NSFNET, which ceased backbone operations on April 30, 1995. The new backbone is composed of the following:

- A very high-speed Backbone Network Service (vBNS) OC3 line (155 Mbps) funded by NSF; its use is restricted to organizations requiring high speeds for scientific calculations or visualizations
- Four regional Network Access Points (NAPs) located in San Francisco, Chicago, New York City, and Washington, D.C. that interconnect the vBNS, other backbone networks, both domestic and foreign, and network service providers
- A routing arbiter (also funded by NSF) that arbitrates high-speed and low-speed bandwidth requests

Hypertext and Hypermedia Concepts

With an understanding of how the Internet has grown and evolved to its present state, understanding what URLs (Uniform Resource Locators) are and how they function is key to understanding how the Internet and the Web function and how Internet resources are located and accessed.

URLs are a very convenient method of identifying the location of devices and resources on the Internet. As defined in RFC-1738, all URLs follow this format:

<scheme>:*<scheme-dependent-information>*

Some examples of *<scheme>* are **http**, **ftp**, and **gopher**. This scheme tells you the following:

- The application you are using
- What type of resource you are trying to locate (for example, a Web page, a file, or a Gopher menu or document)

■ What mechanism you need to access the resource (for example, a Web browser, an FTP utility to download the file, or a Gopher client)

The ***<scheme-dependent-information>*** usually indicates:

■ The Internet host making the file available

■ The full path to the file

A more recognizable pattern for most users is:

scheme://machine.domain/full-pathname-of-file

Here you see the scheme describing the type of resource separated from the computer and its Internet address by two slashes (//) and then the Internet address separated from the path and file name by one slash (/). URLs for http, FTP, and Gophers generally fit this pattern.

To make this example a bit clearer, let's use a real-world URL as an example. The URL for my home page is **http://www.rpi.edu/~odonnj/index.html**. Figure 2.4 shows you how my home page appears.

FIG. 2.4

Welcome to my home page!

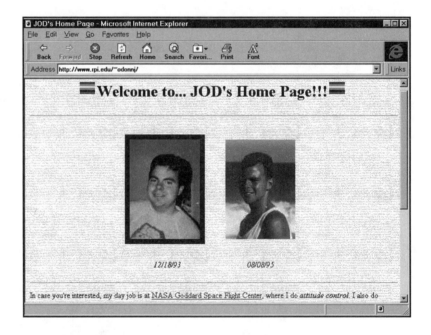

Here's the scheme for this URL broken down into its component parts:

■ **http:**—indicates that you are using the HyperText Transfer Protocol to access the resource, which usually means you want to use your Web browser

- **www.rpi.edu**—identifies the host computer and its Internet address (its domain name, to be precise)
- **/~odonnj/index.html**—identifies the path and filename on the host computer for the desired resource

Most Web pages follow this scheme. You may have noticed that when accessing http, FTP, or Gopher URLs, the "full pathname" sometimes ends in a single slash (/). This is used to point the URL to a specific directory instead of to a specific file. In this case, the host computer will usually return what is called the *default index* for that directory. In http, the default index file is usually named **index.html**, but can also be named **home.html**, **homepage.html**, **welcome.html**, or **default.html**.

How the Domain Name Service Works

So, let's say you're sitting in front of your PC in Pittsburgh (or anywhere for that matter) and decide to visit my Web page. You start Internet Explorer, and enter **http://www.rpi.edu/~odonnj/** (you can leave out the **index.html**, since that is the default index file on my server) in the location window, press Enter, and in a few seconds my home page appears. How did your Web browser use the URL to find it?

One of the key components responsible for helping Internet Explorer run on your computer and locate my home page file, **index.html** (which is stored on the Web server of my service provider) is a program, or, more precisely, a series of programs called the *domain name service.*

Here's how the domain name service, or DNS for short, works its magic. When you initially set up your connection to your Internet service provider, you were asked to enter the IP address of your DNS server. The IP address you entered, which your service provider supplied you with, looked something like the IP address shown in figure 2.5.

FIG. 2.5
When setting up your Internet connection, you'll need your IP address, as well as that of a domain name server.

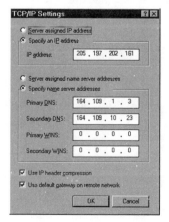

N O T E   An IP address is a unique number, in the format ***nnn.nnn.nnn.nnn*** (where ***nnn*** is a number between zero and 255) that is assigned to every physical device on the Internet. Your service provider is assigned a block of IP addresses (by the InterNIC Registration Services) that are, in turn, assigned to each user who is provided access to the Internet. Your provider either assigns you a permanent IP address that doesn't change; or each time you log in to your provider, you are assigned a dynamic IP address, which could be any number in your provider's assigned block of IP address numbers. ▇

When you enter the URL for my home page, **http://www.rpi.edu/~odonnj/**, Internet Explorer parses the domain name from this URL according to the URL scheme explained previously. The domain name Internet Explorer gets from this URL is **rpi.edu**. Internet Explorer, working in conjunction with Windows and your TCP/IP protocol stack, passes the domain name, **rpi.edu**, to your domain name service.

You may have noticed that domain names often end in **.com**, **.edu**, or **.org**. These identifiers are used with the domain name to help identify the type of domain. The most common identifiers are shown here, along with examples of each:

- ▇ **.com** for commercial organizations, for example, **microsoft.com**, **ibm.com**, **fedex.com**
- ▇ **.edu** for educational institutions, for example, **psu.edu** for Penn State Univ., **cmu.edu** for Carnegie-Mellon Univ., **rpi.edu** for Rensselaer Polytechnic Institute
- ▇ **.gov** for government agencies, for example, **whitehouse.gov** for the White House, **fbi.gov** for the FBI
- ▇ **.mil** for the military, for example, **army.mil** for the Army, **navy.mil** for the Navy
- ▇ **.org** for nonprofit organizations, for example, **red-cross.org** for the American Red Cross, **oneworld.org** for Save the Children Fund
- ▇ **.net** for network service providers, for example, **internic.net** for InterNIC, **si.net** for Sprint International

There are also identifiers for countries:

- ▇ **.uk** for United Kingdom
- ▇ **.ca** for Canada
- ▇ **.ch** for Switzerland (Confoederatio Helvetica); you may have noticed that the domain name for CERN is **cern.ch**
- ▇ **.li** for Liechtenstein
- ▇ **.cn** for China
- ▇ **.jp** for Japan
- ▇ **.br** for Brazil

TIP The lack of a country identifier usually indicates the domain is in the United States.

Your domain name service in one sense is a very large database program running on one of your service provider's computers (other computers are running other services such as mail service, news service, and FTP to name a few). When the domain name is passed to the domain name service, the DNS returns the corresponding IP address.

N O T E If, by some chance, your DNS does not contain the domain name, your DNS will attempt to locate the IP address by requesting the domain name from another DNS, in this case a centralized DNS containing **.com** domain names. If the domain name is still not located, the DNS will finally return an error message indicating the requested domain name does not exist. ■

In the previous example using my home page, the domain name **rpi.edu** is passed to your DNS, and your DNS should return 128.113.1.7. The IP address is not only used for identification, it is also used to route the request to the appropriate host computer. The starting sequence of this IP address, 128., routes the request to North America. Additional routers connecting various Internet segments in North America, and containing routing tables for the segments they connect, eventually route the request to Troy, New York, and to RPI. Once the request arrives at the domain **rpi.edu**, it is routed to the appropriate host computer, using the host part of the name, **www**, and finally to the appropriate directory path until the file **index.html** is located.

> **CAUTION**
>
> Sometimes when you are looking up a URL in your Web browser, you will get an error message that the domain couldn't be found. This is usually a sign that you have mistyped the domain name, but not always. It is also possible that the DNS that you are using is not operating correctly. You can verify this by trying some other domains, or trying the same one again later.

Because the request for **index.html** was made using http, the host computer, a Web server, returns the requested file for display by the requesting client, which in this case is Internet Explorer, a Web browser.

The Web Metaphor Hypertext Links

Now you have an understanding of how URLs work, and how URLs are used to help route files to the computers that request them. Figure 2.6 does a good job of illustrating Internet connections in the U.S. and how requests to various host computers could possibly be routed over the various interconnected Internet segments.

Part
I
Ch
2

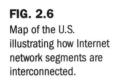

FIG. 2.6
Map of the U.S.
illustrating how Internet
network segments are
interconnected.

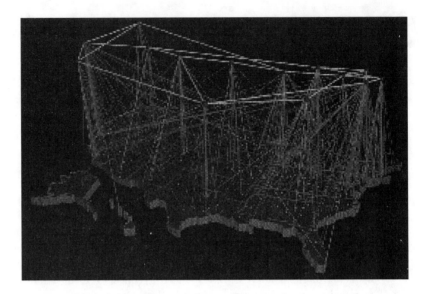

The World Wide Web is a means of supporting hypertext across the Internet. *Hypertext* is simply text that contains links, and these links provide additional information about certain keywords or phrases. Links are just what they sound like, and on Web pages, these links are used to connect one page (or file) to another page. You can use the home page of a friend of mine as an example of Web page hypertext links. Figure 2.7 shows the two links from his home page. These links are references to two different versions of his next Web page, one with lots of graphics and one with only a few.

 T I P You can easily identify links when using Internet Explorer because links will appear as either blue or magenta underlined text.

Selecting the full graphics link will send another request from your PC across the interconnected segments of the Internet to the Web server, requesting the file **main/index.html**, which is the filename of the full graphics Web page. The URL for the full graphics page is included in this link. In a few seconds, the page shown in figure 2.8 appears.

Scroll down this page and you will see additional links to more Web pages. Some of these links are to the same Web server, but you can eventually follow links to servers all over the country.

N O T E Internet Explorer 3 will let you see the URLs in links even before you select the link. Use your mouse and place the pointing finger Internet Explorer 3 cursor on the link without clicking your mouse. Look down at the status bar and you'll see the URL for that link. ■

FIG. 2.7
Links from Damone's home page.

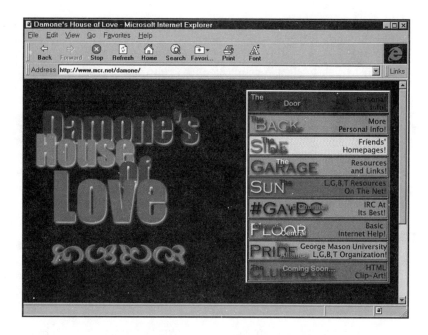

FIG. 2.8
Damone's "full graphics" Web page.

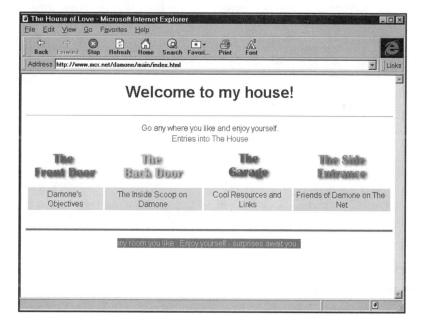

You should now have a much better understanding of how the hypertext metaphor applies to the Web and to Web pages. You can see that the World Wide Web resembles a spider's web with connections from any one point or Web page, branching outward to various other connection points or other Web pages, which in turn can also contain connections to even more Web pages.

Other Internet Services Accessed Through the Web

In the past year or so, many Web browsers have exceeded their original purpose of simply displaying HTML pages. Many Web browsers are becoming all-purpose Internet tools that can also be used for accessing non-Web Internet services such as FTP, e-mail, newsgroups, and Gophers.

FTP

FTP, short for *file transfer protocol*, is an Internet protocol that allows you to upload or download text or binary files. FTP is most often used to download files from an archival storage site. In the past few years, numerous FTP sites have sprung up all over the Internet as repositories for shareware, freeware, and general PC utilities and various support files.

It has also become fairly common for computer hardware and software manufacturers to set up FTP sites for customer support. These FTP sites are stocked with software updates and hardware support drivers, which are free for customers to download.

FTP sites that are used for hardware and software support are usually advertised so users who need access to their contents can easily find the sites and the files they store. Unfortunately, many FTP sites do not fall in this category and largely remain unknown, except when passed from user to user, or when these sites are included in a list of FTP sites in books like this. Fortunately, there is another way to locate files on FTP sites. In 1990 Peter Deutsch, Alan Emtage, and Bill Heelan created a program they called Archie, which can be used to locate files stored (or archived, hence the name Archie) on FTP sites.

Until you become more familiar with using Archie servers, go to this Web site for a listing of FTP sites you might find helpful: **http://hoohoo.ncsa.uiuc.edu/ftp/** (see fig. 2.9).

For more information on FTP and how to use this protocol, especially in Web browsers, see Chapter 12, "Accessing Other Internet Services with Microsoft's Explorer."

▶ **See** "Downloading Files Using FTP" to learn about how to download files via the File Transfer Protocol, **p. 224**

E-mail and UseNet Newsgroups

E-mail, short for electronic mail, is a simple system designed to allow the sending and receiving of messages across a network. For most of its history on the Internet, e-mail has been used primarily by businesses and academicians, but in the past few years a large percentage of e-mail messages have been created and read by individuals.

FIG. 2.9
The Monster FTP
Sites List.

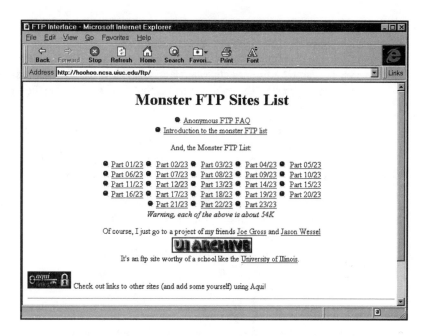

E-mail access is another traditional non-Web service that Web browsers are starting to encroach on. E-mail was one of the earliest services available on the Internet, having been invented in 1972 by Ray Tomlinson to send messages across the early distributed networks. E-mail today, probably the widest used of all Internet services, is still used primarily for sending messages, but an increasing percentage of e-mail messages now include some sort of file attachment.

UseNet newsgroups are strikingly similar in operation to e-mail, since both involve sending messages that often have file attachments, and like e-mail, newsgroup functionality is also starting to turn up in Web browsers. The first UseNet newsgroup was set up in 1979 by Tom Truscott and Steve Bellovin using UUCP (UNIX-to-UNIX Communication Protocol) between Duke University and the University of North Carolina.

E-mail and UseNet both suffered early on from the same problem—how to attach a non-text file to a text-based message—but there are now several different ways to achieve this. For more information, see Chapter 10, "E-Mail with Internet Explorer and Microsoft's Internet Mail Client," and Chapter 11, "Reading UseNet Newsgroups with Internet Explorer."

Gophers

Accessing Gopher servers is another non-Web function being taken over by Web browsers. Gopher servers, or simply Gophers, first appeared on the Internet in 1991, and were originally created and released by the University of Minnesota by Paul Lindner and Mark P. McCahill (Gophers were named after the UM mascot, the Golden Gopher).

Gophers are similar in operation to FTP sites in that they are established as repositories for files. Gopher files, however, are largely academic and informational text documents, and are meticulously arranged by subject under a hierarchical menu structure. Accessing a Gopher server to search for documents by subject is similar to using a Web search engine such as Lycos or WebCrawler. The only problem is that Gophers differ in the subjects they contain documents for.

To solve this problem, developers at the University of Nevada in 1992 devised a Gopher database search program, which they dubbed Veronica. Veronica works to create its database of Gopher documents and menus like the robot search tools used in many Web search engines. It continuously scans Gopher servers to see what menus and documents are being stored.

If you want to see how Gophers and Veronica work, point your (Gopher-functioning) Web browser to **gopher://gopher.lanl.gov/1**. You can also get more information on Gophers in Chapter 12, "Accessing Other Internet Services with Microsoft's Explorer."

▶ **See** "Finding Information on Gopher Servers" for a guide to using the Gopher Internet service, **p. 226**

The Future of the Web

The Web, just like the Internet, is still growing and, more importantly, still evolving. As you might expect, numerous groups and organizations are developing new projects to assist in the evolution of the Web, most notably, the World Wide Web Consortium, or W3C for short, at CERN in Geneva, Switzerland. The W3C has posted on its Web server a list of some of the projects it currently has under development. If you want more information on these projects, go to **http://www.w3.org/hypertext/WWW/Bugs.html** to see the entire listing. The following sections are a sampling of some of the projects. Some of these new features are at least partially supported in Internet Explorer 3.

HTML Style Sheets

The HyperText Markup Language (HTML) is language used to create pages on the World Wide Web. The HTML language offers the author a lot of control over what information he or she presents, but until recently, not nearly as much control over its final appearance. That's because, since there are so many Web browsers operating on so many different platforms, HTML allowed each Web browser to render information a little differently. A new capability being added to HTML will change that, giving Web authors a lot more control over the final appearance of their documents. This capability is known as an HTML *style sheet*.

Most high-end word processors have some sort of style sheet capability, as do some HTML editors, but there is no HTML standard for style sheets. There are several proposals for how to implement HTML style sheets along with examples from some of the W3C members. This is a very active discussion forum, and much of the information and proposals can be found at **http://www.w3.org/hypertext/WWW/Style/Welcome.html**.

▶ **See** "Basic HTML" for an introduction to the HyperText Markup Language, **p. 365**

SGML and the Web

SGML, Standard Generalized Mark-up Language, is, in many ways, the parent language of HTML. The HTML standard is based on SGML. This relationship is another discussion hot button at W3C. The focus of the discussion is on extending HTML to encompass more of the SGML standard language. To get more information on this discussion and project, take a look at **http://www.w3.org/hypertext/WWW/MarkUp/SGML/**.

Internationalization of Character Sets

This will likely be one of the hot areas to watch for future HTML and Web development. Everyone agrees now that the Web has a severe bias toward English and the western-European/Latin writing system. There are several factors that have contributed to this bias, primarily 7-bit ASCII.

> **N O T E** ASCII is the American Standard Code for Information Interchange. The 7-bit ASCII code, which most computer manufacturers recognize, allows for the creation of only 128 characters and symbols, which does not include foreign or non-Latin-based characters. There are several 8-bit character sets that allow for 256 characters, but there is no agreement on which one will be universally accepted. ■

Currently, the greatest concentrations of Internet computers and domains are in the U.S. and Western Europe (see fig. 2.10).

FIG. 2.10
Internet domain
concentrations
worldwide.

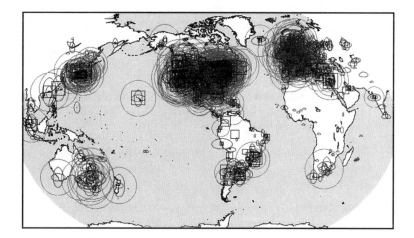

With the Internet spreading into more countries that do not use the standard Western character set (the ISO-8859 Latin-1 8-bit character set), there is pressure to approve a 16-bit character set (which would permit a total of 65,536 characters) standard, which will provide character sets for Eastern Europe, Asia, and the Pacific rim.

For more on this discussion, see **http://www.w3.org/hypertext/WWW/International/**.

Virtual Reality

This is a hot topic, not just at W3C, but all over the Web. Virtual reality (VR) is considered the next step for multimedia on the Web, and there are several proposals for how best to handle 3D VR graphics. Much of the discussion extends to how best to implement VR on the Web—should it be through *Virtual Reality Mark-up Language* (*VRML*), should it be through PostScript extensions, or should a new VR platform be done "from the ground up?" The discussion in W3C can be found at **http://www.w3.org/hypertext/WWW/Bugs/ GraphicalComposition.html**.

For more information on VRML and how VRML is implemented, see Chapter 18, "Using VRML and ActiveVRML."

Emerging Technologies

Several emerging technologies that could have an impact on the Web and the Internet in the next few years are just on the horizon—specifically ISDN and cable modems.

ISDN *Integrated Services Digital Network* (*ISDN*) simply stated is digital telephone. ISDN's main advantage over the current analog telephone system is speed. With ISDN, your connection to the Internet will be 4 1/2 times faster (128 Kbps) than the current top speed that uses analog telephone lines and 28.8 Kbps modems.

ISDN's main drawbacks now are availability and cost. As of November 1995, ISDN was available to only about 70 percent of available telephone service areas in the U.S., with the heaviest concentrations in the Northeast. Also, many Internet service providers are not set up to provide ISDN connections to their subscribers but are scrambling to offer it.

The other drawback is cost. Each of the regional Bells in the U.S. has established a separate pricing scheme for ISDN service. Through Bell Atlantic, there is a one-time installation charge of only $169, but there is a monthly charge of $39, plus an online charge of $0.02 per minute per channel ($0.04 per minute if you're multiplexing the two 64 Kbps channels into one 128 Kbps channel). Other Bell service providers have dropped the online charge but charge upwards of $500–$700 for installation.

The other cost for ISDN is in the equipment. Equipment prices are dropping as more companies begin offering ISDN equipment, but costs for an NT-1 terminal adapter are still in the $300–$500 range.

Cable Modems The other emerging technology, which many experts feel is still several years away, is what is being called *cable modems*. Cable modems are, in effect, two-way digital communications lines tied in over the same line used for cable TV. With many cable TV operators upgrading their service line to fiber optic, the potential here is for communications connections to the Internet in the 1–10 Mbps range.

Cost will be another factor driving this technology as well, both for the user and the provider. Early speculation for cable modems estimate prices in the $500–$700 range. Also, cable operators will have to install fiber optic hubs and routers at an estimated cost of $2,000–$5,000 for every 30–50 users.

Obviously, there are problems associated with both of these technologies, but once these are solved and either (or both) of these technologies is more widespread, the Internet backbone could begin to face serious bandwidth constraints. Apparently, this concern is being addressed. In April 1995, the NFSNET backbone was phased out and replaced with a new "very high-speed Backbone Network Service" (vBNS). The vBNS is currently running at 155 Mbps. In 1996, it is scheduled to be upgraded to operate at 622 Mbps. While no mention is made of upgrading other segments of the Internet backbone in this country, this example clearly shows that bandwidth concerns remain a high priority.

Exploring the WWW with Internet Explorer 3

Microsoft has managed to come a long way in a very short time with their Web browsers, with the release of Internet Explorer 2 in December, 1995 and Internet Explorer 3 in the Spring and Summer of 1996. With Internet Explorer 3, Microsoft has added support for the HTML 2.0 specification, most of the Netscape enhancements to HTML, and a large amount of the proposed HTML 3.0 and 3.2 specifications. Because Internet Explorer 3 is free, is a part of Microsoft's Windows 95 operating system, and is beginning to be provided by many Internet providers, Microsoft has the fastest growing share of the Web browser market.

Internet Explorer 3 pushes the limits of a Web browser even further by incorporating new features such as ActiveX Technologies, ActiveX Controls, and support for Java, JavaScript, and Visual Basic Script, to give Web authors a great many ways to add interactivity and continually evolving exciting content to their Web pages.

The following gives a cursory overview of some of the new features you'll be seeing in Internet Explorer 3. All of these features are explained in greater detail in later chapters.

Improved Browsing Performance

In addition to the other new features Microsoft is adding to its Internet Explorer 3, users will also notice improvements in speed and performance. Microsoft has made improvements to speed up multiple, simultaneous loading of text, images, and files. Caching, including caching from CD-ROM-based media, is quicker. And most importantly, to prepare for more widespread use of multimedia on the Web, Microsoft has also created a new level of support for audio and video types utilizing dynamic code modules called *add-ins* or *plug-ins*, which will integrate better with the core browser application than previously with helper applications.

Enhanced Security

With Internet Explorer 3, Microsoft has introduced a range of services meant to make transactions over the World Wide Web safer, and more secure. These services range from support for authentication and code signatures meant to make downloading software over the Internet secure—by making sure you only get what you want from whom you want it—to Microsoft's Private Communication Technology (PCT) protocol, meant to make it possible to perform private transactions over the Internet, whether they be financial, proprietary, or otherwise confidential.

Internet E-mail

In previous versions of Internet Explorer, you were forced to use Microsoft Exchange, which is overkill for most private users' needs, or a third-party program to send and receive e-mail through the Web browser. With Internet Explorer 3, Microsoft has introduced a new Internet Mail Client that makes sending and receiving e-mail much easier.

With the Internet Mail Client, you can do the following:

- Archive e-mail messages in a personalized folder structure
- Maintain an address book of your e-mail correspondents
- Read and compose e-mail messages offline, saving on connection costs

▶ **See** "E-Mail with Internet Explorer and Microsoft's Internet Mail Client" for everything you need to know about using the Internet Mail Client, **p. 183**

Enhanced Newsgroup Capabilities

Internet Explorer 3 comes with a new Microsoft Internet News Client. This UseNet newsreader gives you access, through a newsserver usually maintained by your Internet Service Provider, to the thousands of UseNet newsgroups. In addition, Microsoft also maintains a newsserver of its own, **msnews.microsoft.com**, which hosts newsgroups devoted to giving support and information about the complete range of Microsoft products.

As a MIME-compliant news reader, the Microsoft Internet News Client allows you to embed binary files—graphics, executables, Zip files—right into your postings. The news reader also supports multiple news servers.

▶ **See** "Reading UseNet Newsgroups with Internet Explorer" for a complete description of Internet Explorer's new newsgroup capabilities, **p. 201**

Java

Internet Explorer 3 also incorporates support for Sun's Java object-oriented programming language. If you haven't encountered Java *applets* (small applications) on the Web, chances are you will as more and more Web site administrators are turning to Java to produce small, portable Web applications. Java is well-suited for use on the Web because Java applets are platform independent, meaning that the same Java application will work with your Internet Explorer 3 browser regardless of whether it has been written on a PC under Windows 95, on an Apple Macintosh, or on a Sun Sparc workstation running UNIX. If you're curious about Java and how it is being used on the Web (or how Sun is promoting its new programming language), Sun has set up an informational site at **http://www.javasoft.com/about.html**. (Internet Explorer 3's support for the Java programming language is presented in detail in Chapter 31, "Sun's Java and Internet Explorer," and Chapter 32, "Java for C++ Programmers.")

Frames

Internet Explorer 3 fully supports the Netscape enhancement of frames, permitting the Web page author the ability to split the screen into two or more independent dynamic or static frames. This permits the developer to place a static Web page element in one frame, such as a toolbar, title screen, or copyright notice, while at the same time allowing the user to browse the page using the dynamic frame. Users who are familiar with spreadsheet programs that allow you to split a worksheet into multiple windows will immediately understand and appreciate the concept and functionality that frames will add to Web pages.

JavaScript and Visual Basic Script Scripting Languages

Another new feature Microsoft has included in Internet Explorer 3 for developers is support for Netscape's JavaScript, as well as is its own scripting language, Visual Basic Script (VBScript). These scripting languages give developers the ability to script certain events, actions, and objects. (See Chapter 34, "JavaScript," and Chapter 35, "Visual Basic Script," for more on these topics.)

Extended Capabilities through ActiveX Controls

A central part to Microsoft's Internet Explorer 3, and its whole Internet strategy, is its ActiveX Technologies. Through the use of what they call ActiveX Controls, an outgrowth of Microsoft's Object Linking and Embedding (OLE) standard, new capabilities can be continually added to Internet Explorer 3, and any other compatible software. This is essentially Netscape's plug-in concept, but taken one step further. Not only can Internet Explorer's capabilities and functionality continually evolve to include access to both past and present information and technology, but these new capabilities can be simultaneously developed for other application, as well. Microsoft plans to make its Windows 95 and its entire suite of desktop applications a part of this technology.

▶ **See** "Microsoft's ActiveX Technologies" for an overview of Microsoft's ActiveX Technologies, and what they will mean for Internet Explorer 3, **p. 591**

Part

I

Ch

2

Internet Basics

Getting a connection to the Internet can seem to be an overwhelming problem. Hundreds of Internet service providers (ISPs), many different types of connections, different levels of support, and different pricing plans are available. How are you supposed to sort through all of it so that it makes sense?

In this chapter, we tackle the major issues related to getting connected to the Internet and show you how to evaluate the various considerations. ■

What kind of Internet connection do you need?

In this chapter, you learn what types of connections to the Internet are available, and what might best suit your needs and your budget.

What services are available, and how much do they cost?

Learn about the different types of Internet services, what each provides to you, and get an idea of their relative cost.

How should you choose an Internet service provider?

This chapter discusses the different factors you should take into account when choosing an Internet service provider.

How do you set up Windows 95 for PPP?

Learn how to set up Windows 95 for an Internet connection using the Point-to-Point Protocol (PPP), the most common connection method over the telephone line.

TCP/IP Basics

Before we dive into the details of setting up an Internet connection, we need to discuss a few details of the protocols that make the Internet work. To understand all the issues involved with an Internet connection, you need to understand the basics of TCP/IP, domain names, and IP addresses.

The History of TCP/IP

The suite of widely used protocols known as *Transmission Control Protocol/Internet Protocol* (*TCP/IP*) has become increasingly important as national networks such as the Internet depend on it for their communications.

In the mid-1970s, the U.S. Department of Defense (DOD) recognized an electronic communication problem developing within its organization. Communicating the ever-increasing volume of electronic information among DOD staff, research labs, universities, and contractors had hit a major obstacle. The various entities had computer systems from different computer manufacturers running different operating systems and using different networking topologies and protocols. How could information be shared among all of them?

The Advanced Research Projects Agency (ARPA) was assigned to resolve the problem of dealing with different networking equipment and connection schemes. ARPA formed an alliance with universities and computer manufacturers to develop communication standards. This alliance specified and built a four-node network that is the foundation of today's Internet. During the 1970s, this network migrated to a new, core protocol design that became the basis for TCP/IP.

No matter what version of Internet Explorer you are running, they all require a TCP/IP protocol stack to be present in order to communicate with the Internet. TCP/IP is the "language" that computers on the Internet use to speak to each other.

Domain Names

With millions of computers on the Internet, how do you specify the one that you want to interact with? You must know the name of the computer, just as you must know the name of someone you want to send a letter to. These names are specified by a convention called the *domain name service* (*DNS*).

A domain name typically gives a hierarchical structure for a computer or group within an organization. The portion of the name to the far right, the domain field, provides the most general category. The United States has eight domain fields, which are listed in Table 3.1.

Table 3.1   Listing of U.S. Domains

Domain	Description
arpa	ARPANET members (obsolete)
com	Commercial and industrial organizations
edu	Universities and educational institutions
gov	Non-military government organizations
mil	Military
net	Network operation organizations
org	Other organizations
us	United States ISO domain

When you hook up to the Internet, you are a part of some domain, whether it is your own domain or that of your company or service provider. You also give your computer a name to identify it as part of your domain. For dial-up accounts with an Internet service provider, you can usually pick the host name for your computer yourself.

Let's look at an example. Assume that you have a personal account through a fictional Internet service provider named SpiffyNet. SpiffyNet's domain name is **spiffy.net**. SpiffyNet allows you to pick the name for your computer, so in a fit of creativity, you choose to call your computer **viper**. Thus, the full host and domain name of your computer would be **viper.spiffy.net**.

IP Addresses

Just as you have a name to identify a computer, your computer also has a number that uniquely identifies it to the rest of the world. This number is known as the *IP address* of your computer. Let's look a little closer at how IP addresses work.

An IP address is a 32-bit value that is divided into four 8-bit fields, each separated by a period. This means that the address would look something like 192.1.5.1. Each computer has exactly one IP address for each physical interface that it has connected to a network.

N O T E   In networking terminology, an 8-bit field is known as an *octet*.

The IP address of a computer is divided into two parts: a network section, which specifies a particular network, and a host portion, which identifies a particular machine on the network. Five categories of IP addresses are now based on the type of network address. They are called Class A through Class E.

In a Class A address, the first octet has a value between 1 and 126, and the network portion consists of the first octet. This obviously limits the number of Class A networks to 126; however, each network can have more than 16 million computers. Class A networks are limited to major corporations and network providers.

Class B networks use the first two octets to specify the network portion and have the first octet in the range of 128 to 191. This leaves the last two octets free for the host ID. The Class B network space provides for 16,382 network ID numbers, each with 65,534 host IDs. Large companies and organizations such as universities are typically assigned Class B addresses.

Class C addresses use three octets to specify the network portion, with the first octet in the range from 192 to 223. This provides for more than 2 million different Class C networks but only 254 hosts per network. Class C networks are usually assigned to small businesses or organizations.

In Class D addresses, the first octet is in the range from 224 to 239 and is used for *multicast transmissions*, Internet transmissions that are sent to many clients simultaneously.

Class E addresses, with the first octet in the range of 240 to 247, are reserved for future use.

When computers communicate using TCP/IP, they use the numeric IP address. DNS names are simply devices that help us humans remember which host is which and what network it's connected to. Originally, when the Internet was first formed, the number of hosts was very small. As a result, each host had a complete list of all host names and addresses in a local file. For obvious reasons, this system quickly became unwieldy. When a new host was added, it was necessary to update every host file on every computer. With the explosive growth of the Internet, the host files also grew quite large. The mapping of DNS names to IP addresses is now accomplished via a distributed database and specific software that performs the lookup.

Static Versus Dynamic IP Addresses

As you've probably figured out by now, your computer must have an IP address to communicate on the Internet. How does it get the address? Well, in most cases, it is assigned by your ISP when you set up your account. Even if you are setting up a whole network of computers, your ISP will probably handle everything for you.

For direct Internet connections, the IP address of your computer is permanently assigned to you. It never changes. These addresses are known as *static IP addresses*. Most Internet service providers, however, use a scheme known as *dynamic IP addressing*.

Because most ISPs typically have many more dial-up customers than they do modems, only a fraction of their dial-up customers can be online at any given moment. Only being able to support a limited number of users online usually isn't a problem, unless they all want to sit in front of their computers and run Internet Explorer 24 hours a day! In short, this means that an ISP can "recycle" IP addresses by assigning them only when your system dials up to connect to the service. This way, ISPs can get by with far fewer IP addresses than if they were statically assigned.

How does this limitation affect you, the network user? First, you have to configure your networking software differently depending on whether you have a static or dynamic IP address. Second, you just can't do a few things if you have a dynamic IP address. Specifically, because your IP address is dynamic—it changes every time you log in—your host name cannot be registered in a domain name service database along with your IP address. Basically, this restriction prevents anyone out on the Internet from being able to initiate contact with your computer. You can't run an FTP server or a Web server if your computer has a dynamic IP address. Similarly, some commercial database services limit access to specific IP addresses based on subscription. Obviously, if your IP address is changing all the time, this scheme doesn't work.

While these limitations don't really affect a lot of people, they can be a real problem if you really want to run an FTP or Web server. Some ISPs charge extra for static IP addresses—sometimes a lot extra! If having a static IP address is a real issue for you, make sure that you check with your ISP before signing a service contract.

Part
I

Ch
3

Types of Internet Connections

Depending on how much money you want to spend, you can get many different levels of connection to the Internet. These connection levels primarily differ in the amount of data you can transfer over a given period of time. We refer to the rate at which data can be transferred as the *bandwidth* of the connection.

Internet connections fall into two categories: dial-up and direct connections. A *dial-up connection* uses a modem to dial another modem at an Internet service provider, perform some connection sequence, and bring up the TCP/IP network. A *direct connection* uses a dedicated, data-grade telephone circuit as the connection path to the Internet. Let's look at these connections in a bit more detail.

Dial-Up Connections

When you sign up for a dial-up Internet account, you use a modem to dial a telephone number for an Internet service provider. After the modems connect, your computer performs some type of login sequence, and the computers start to communicate via TCP/IP.

 For Internet Explorer to be usable with a dial-up connection, you should have at least a 14.4 Kbps modem. A faster modem, such as a 28.8 Kbps model, is recommended. Internet Explorer can be used with slower modems, but probably won't be worth your time.

The login sequence that your system performs depends on the requirements of your particular ISP. Most of the time, these login sequences are automated by using a script file. (For more information on script files, see "Setting Up Windows 95 for PPP" later in this chapter.)

We use a bit of smoke and mirrors when we refer to "starting TCP/IP networking." What this really means is telling the remote system that you want to start communicating via TCP/IP instead of just via ASCII terminal emulation. The way this is accomplished via a dial-up connection is by using a protocol such as PPP.

PPP, the Point-to-Point Protocol, and SLIP, the Serial Line Internet Protocol, allow you to use TCP/IP communications over a dial-up connection. While either of these protocols works for serial TCP/IP, most ISPs are migrating to PPP because it is newer and has more robust features. For this discussion, we are assuming you use PPP.

The way you start PPP varies depending on your ISP. In some cases, it starts automatically for you when you log in. In other cases, you may have to execute a command from a login shell on the ISP. Still another way is to make a selection from an interactive menu. It really depends on your ISP.

Direct Connections

The other major way of connecting to the Internet is through a direct connection. This method is typically used by large offices and companies to tie their internal networks into the Internet. Quite simply, it requires a lot of money.

A direct connection consists of a dedicated, data-grade telephone line that runs between your location and your service provider. Depending on the bandwidth of this line, the charges from your phone company can be several thousand dollars per month! In addition to this charge, you also have the recurring monthly charge from your ISP, which can also be very expensive. Add to that the cost of the network hardware required, and this option quickly prices itself out of reach of individuals and small companies.

But let's assume that you have the money to set up a direct Internet connection. How do you do it, and what does it buy you? Well, mainly, it gives you the ability to have a large pipe into the Internet through which to pump data, the ability to assign IP addresses to a whole network of computers, and static IP addressing. As for setting up the connection, most established ISPs have a setup package in which they order your phone line, provide the hardware, register your domain name, and get your IP addresses for you—all for a flat fee. Check with the ISP of your choice for more information.

Types of Services

Now that we've got the basics out of the way, let's look at what services you can get from an ISP. Most ISPs provide dial-up and direct connect services, with a whole menu of services that you can select from.

Dial-Up IP

For most ISPs, the basic level of dial-up IP gives you PPP-based, dynamic IP addressing on a public dial-up number. This number is connected to a modem bank and rotates to the next available modem when you dial in—if a modem is available. For some ISPs, busy signals can be a common problem, especially during the prime evening and weekend hours.

Some ISPs provide a couple of levels of service above the basic dial-up PPP account. For example, you may be able to pay an additional fee to dial into a restricted number that has a better user-to-modem ratio. For even more money, the ISP may provide you with a dedicated dial-up line—a phone line that only you can dial in on. Deciding what type of dial-up account you are going to need is important because it is one of the primary factors that affects the cost of your Internet service.

E-Mail

If you've managed to get this far and set up an Internet connection, you probably want e-mail, right? By using a dial-up PPP account, you can almost always read and send e-mail via the Post Office Protocol (POP). To do so, you get an e-mail client program, such as Eudora, for your PC and configure it with your e-mail account information and the IP address of your network mail server. If you have a dial-up account, your network mail server is a computer located at your ISP's offices.

NOTE E-mail is transferred between systems on the Internet using a protocol known as the *Simple Mail Transport Protocol*, or *SMTP*. POP is the protocol that a local e-mail client program uses to retrieve mail from a mail server. ▓

Most personal dial-up accounts provide you with at least one e-mail address. Some ISPs even provide as many as five different addresses for personal or family accounts. Other ISPs make you pay an additional monthly charge for extra e-mail IDs. Business accounts usually have a fixed number as well. If you have more than one person who will be using e-mail from your system, you might want to shop around to see what the ISP policies on multiple e-mail addresses are in your area.

News

Just as with e-mail, if your Internet service provider gives you access to UseNet news, you can probably read and post news from your PC by using a newsreader that supports the *Network News Transport Protocol* (*NNTP*). To do so, you simply configure your newsreader with the names or addresses of your mail and news hosts—the computers that you exchange e-mail and news with. Most ISPs provide UseNet news as part of the basic dial-up PPP account service.

Part

I

Ch

3

Shell Access

Another service that is often available with a dial-up account is *shell access*. This term refers to the ability to access a command line processor on the remote ISP system.

> **N O T E** Because most ISPs use a UNIX system to provide Internet access, and UNIX command line processors are known as shells, the term *shell access* has become rather common. ▦

Your ISP may or may not provide shell access as part of your basic network package. Most people can get by fine without having shell access. It is useful for accessing your account over the Internet, via Telnet or FTP from another location, as well as performing tasks such as compiling C code. But if you are just running Internet Explorer from home, you can probably survive without it.

> **CAUTION**
>
> Be aware that some ISPs sell a "shell-access-only" account as a dial-up account. Typically, you cannot run PPP or SLIP from this type of account. Because Internet Explorer needs TCP/IP to run, you need to make sure that you get the right type of service from your ISP.

Web Servers

The Web is a hot item—obviously, or you wouldn't be reading a book about Internet Explorer! Another service that is provided by many ISPs is access to a Web server. Web servers allow you to put home pages on the Web so that they can be accessed by people with Web browsers such as Internet Explorer 3. Figure 3.1 shows an example of a Web page.

> **N O T E** Don't confuse Internet Explorer with a Web server. You can still surf the Net by using Internet Explorer even if you don't have Web server access. ▦

Having access to a Web server means that you can write Web pages in HTML and make them available on the Web. Many ISPs provide their personal account customers the ability to create personal Web pages. Businesses usually have to pay an additional fee for the service.

> **N O T E** Companies that have a direct connection to the Internet can simply set up their own Web server on one of their own machines. ▦

If your ISP doesn't provide Web server access, don't give up hope. Many companies provide Web services alone, without providing any type of interactive access to the Internet. Basically, you pay a monthly fee to have the Web provider's site place your pages on the World Wide Web. These Web service providers also typically offer consulting and design services to help you create effective Web pages.

FIG. 3.1
Que, the publishers
of this fine book,
maintain a Web site
featuring information
about its complete line
of books.

Virtual Domains

If you are setting up a business account, you may want to use your own domain name, instead of simply using the name of your ISP. A domain name that is actually a directory on an ISP's server is commonly called a *virtual domain*.

To set up a virtual domain, you must register your domain name with the Network Information Center (NIC). The NIC acts as the clearinghouse for all Internet domain names. You can reach the NIC by Telnet at **rs.internic.net**, on the Web at **http://rs.internic.net**, by e-mail at **question@internic.net**, or by telephone at 703-742-4777. You must fill out a domain name registration template and submit it to the NIC. Currently, the NIC charges a fee of $100 to register a domain, and $50 per year to use the domain. The $100 fee covers the first two years.

As part of the registration process, you must provide information about which network name servers advertise your domain name. In short, this means that you have to find an ISP that provides virtual domains and have it enter your domain name in its name server.

As with everything else, most ISPs charge an additional fee for supporting virtual domains. If you require this service, make sure that you shop around and ask questions.

Finding an Internet Service Provider

With the explosive growth of the Internet, you now can choose from lots of ISPs. The services, cost, and customer satisfaction of ISPs vary widely. Some are terrible, a few are wonderful, but most fall somewhere in the middle.

National Providers

You can divide ISPs into categories based on whether they have a national presence or they are mainly a local company. If you think about this concept, any ISP has a national presence in the sense that it is connected to the Internet and can be reached from anywhere. What we are referring to is the ability to contact the ISP via a local telephone call. Several of the larger ISPs have local dial access in many different locations, effectively making them national providers.

Using a national provider presents both pros and cons. The company is usually larger—not a basement operation—and it usually has competent technical support people working for it. Also, national providers usually have a better uptime percentage than local providers and also have a better price structure. On the other hand, because national ISPs tend to be larger, reaching a technical support person when you have a problem may be harder. You may find that their policies are less flexible than local providers and that they are less willing to make exceptions and work with you. If you are setting up a business connection, your ISP's office may be hundreds or thousands of miles away. If you are the kind of person who values working with a local company, this distance could present a problem for you.

Regional and Local Providers

Local and regional providers are ISPs that serve a regional market, instead of having a national presence. Like national providers, these providers present both pros and cons here, too. You will probably find that local providers are more flexible on their services and policies. For business, you can usually meet face to face with someone in the office to discuss your Internet needs. On the down side, the service quality of local ISPs tends to be less reliable. Sometimes these companies are very small operations, with limited hardware and technical support. You may find that connecting is difficult because of busy signals during certain times of the day.

Local and regional ISPs are notorious for expanding their customer base faster than their hardware will support it. When their servers get overloaded, response creeps to a crawl and uptime suffers. Phone lines are continually busy. If this problem happens to an ISP, it has to respond immediately; otherwise, its systems will become unusable.

Private Information Services

Many people belong to private national information services such as CompuServe or America Online (AOL). Increasingly, such services are beginning to provide full access to the Internet, and can be an attractive option for their subscribers who want to start accessing the Internet and the World Wide Web. They are typically able to provide their users with extensive technical support in setting up their Internet connections. However, Internet access through these information services tends to be a lot more expensive than going through an ISP. Unless you have a specific need for one of the proprietary services that CompuServe, AOL, and so on provide, you are probably better off going with a dedicated Internet service provider.

Service Levels and Cost

As you have seen, you must consider several issues when selecting an ISP. The level of service you need is probably the main thing that affects the cost of your connection.

Dial-up modem connections in the general public modem pool are usually cheapest. A restricted modem group is more expensive. A dedicated dial-up line costs even more. Direct connections via leased lines are among the most expensive.

In addition to service level, many ISPs offer different connection pricing plans. Some plans give you a fixed number of connect hours per month and charge you for extra hours. Other plans may give you unlimited hours during a certain time period and charge you for hours outside that window. Still other plans give you unlimited connect time for your fee.

Before you choose an ISP, take time to evaluate how you are going to use the service and what level of service you need. Check with computer users in your area to see if they can recommend a local service or a national service that works well.

Internet Explorer 3 and Windows 95

You can use Internet Explorer 3 a couple of different ways to connect to the Internet. The easiest way is probably to connect using Microsoft's TCP/IP, as it is built in to Windows 95. You can also use a third-party TCP/IP package. In this section, we look at how to set up Internet Explorer 3 to run under Windows 95.

Setting Up Windows 95 for PPP

By using Internet Explorer 3 and Windows 95, you're already ahead of the game a little because Windows 95 includes support for PPP, which is what enables Internet Explorer 3 to access the Internet. Assuming that you have an account already set up with an Internet service provider, configuring Windows 95 so that it provides you dial-up PPP support is not too difficult.

You need several bits of information to configure PPP for Windows 95 correctly. Your ISP should provide all this information when you set up your account. If you don't know some of these items, contact your ISP for help. You need to know the following:

- The username that you use to log in to your ISP
- The password for your ISP account
- The telephone number for your ISP
- The host name for your computer
- The network domain name for your ISP
- The IP address of your ISP's default gateway or router
- The IP subnet mask of your ISP's network
- The IP address of your ISP's DNS name server(s)
- Whether you have a static or dynamic IP address
- The IP address of your computer, if you have a static address

After you gather all the preceding information, you're ready to start installing PPP for Windows 95. You might not have installed all the components for PPP when you installed Windows 95, so you need to check to see what's already there and install the ones that are missing.

Dial-Up Networking, the Dial-Up Adapter, and TCP/IP

The dial-up networking and dial-up adapter items are necessary to set up a dial-up account to the Internet. Make sure you have your Windows 95 installation media handy throughout this process. For simplicity, let's assume that you are installing from the Windows 95 CD-ROM. To see whether dial-up networking is installed, follow these steps:

1. Click the Start button, and choose Settings, Control Panel.

2. Double-click the Add/Remove Programs icon.

3. Select the Windows Setup tab. The section of the Add/Remove Programs dialog box that allows you to install or change various components of Windows 95 then appears.

4. Select the Communications option.

5. Click the Details button. The Communications dialog box then appears showing the current configuration of your Windows 95 communications system.

6. Make sure the Dial-Up Networking entry is selected. If it is not selected, select it and click OK.

Now that the dial-up networking package is installed, you need to check for the dial-up adapter. Basically, this program allows Windows 95 to use your telephone to make a network connection. To see whether the dial-up adapter is installed, follow these steps:

1. Click the Start button, and choose Settings, Control Panel.

2. Double-click the Network icon. The Network dialog box appears. Here, you can configure your network setup.

3. Select the Configuration tab. This portion of the Network dialog box allows you to add new network protocols and adapters to your Windows 95 environment (see fig. 3.2).

4. Look for TCP/IP and Dial-Up Adapter in the list.

FIG. 3.2

The Network dialog box allows you to configure your Internet connection environment.

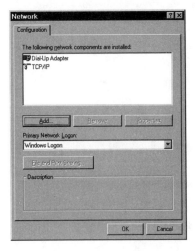

Follow these steps if you don't see the Dial-Up Adapter in the Configuration tab of the Network dialog box:

1. Click the Add button. The Select Network Component Type dialog box then appears. Here, you tell Windows 95 what sort of networking item you want to add to your computer.

2. Double-click Adapter. The Select Network Adapters dialog box appears. You want to add the Dial-Up Adapter so that you can use dial-up networking.

3. Scroll the Select Network Component Type box on the left until you see the Microsoft entry.

4. Select Microsoft from the Select Network Component Type scroll box. Choose Dial-Up Adapter from the Network Adapters scroll box on the right.

5. Click OK.

Follow these steps if you don't see TCP/IP in the Network dialog box:

1. Click the Add button to add the protocol to your computer.

2. Double-click Protocol. TCP/IP is a networking protocol, and that is what you need to add. Clicking this option opens the Select Network Protocol dialog box.

3. Scroll the Manufacturers scroll box on the left until you see the Microsoft entry.

4. Select Microsoft in the left scroll box, and then choose TCP/IP in the Network Protocols scroll box on the right.

5. Click OK.

At this point, you should see both TCP/IP and the dial-up adapter in the Network dialog box. Select Dial-Up Adapter and click Properties. The Dial-Up Adapter Properties dialog box appears. Select the Bindings tab. Then verify that the TCP/IP box is selected (see fig. 3.3).

FIG. 3.3
Make sure that the TCP/IP protocol is bound to your dial-up adapter so that you can use Internet Explorer 3.

Part
I

Ch
3

Dial-Up Scripting

Some Internet service providers require additional steps, beyond just logging in, to begin your PPP connection. If yours is like this, you will probably want to create a script that handles logging you in to your ISP's system. This way, you can just double-click an icon and have Windows 95 dial your ISP, log you in automatically, and start PPP. You'll come back to scripting in a bit, but first you need to verify that the Dial-Up Scripting program has been installed. To do so, follow these steps:

1. Click Start and choose Programs, Accessories.
2. Look for an entry for the Dial-Up Scripting tool.

Follow these steps if the Dial-Up Scripting tool isn't installed:

1. Click the Start button, and choose Settings, Control Panel.
2. Double-click the Add/Remove Programs icon.
3. Select the Windows Setup tab. Remember, on this tab you add components to your Windows 95 system. We need to install the Dial-Up Scripting tool from your Windows 95 CD.
4. Click the Have Disk button. Clicking this button tells Windows 95 that you need to install something from the CD.
5. Enter the path to the Dial-Up Scripting program on your Windows 95 CD. For example, if your CD is drive G:, you enter **G:\admin\apptools\ dscript**.
6. Click the OK button.

Entering the Address Information

At this point, you should have all the drivers and other programs installed so that you can configure TCP/IP with your network information. A couple of steps in this section depend on whether you have a static or dynamic IP address, so pay attention. To enter the address, follow these steps:

1. Click the Start button, and choose Settings, Control Panel.
2. Double-click the Network icon. The Network dialog box appears.
3. Select the TCP/IP Protocol entry and click the Properties button. The TCP/IP Properties dialog box appears.
4. Select the IP Address tab (see fig. 3.4).

FIG. 3.4

If you have a static IP address, enter it here. Otherwise, check the Obtain an IP Address Automatically box.

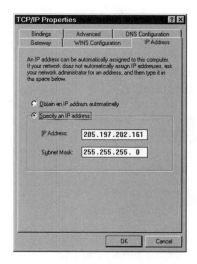

5. If you have a static IP address, select the Specify an IP Address option, type your IP Address into the box, and enter your subnet mask into the Subnet Mask box.

6. If you have a dynamic IP address, choose the Obtain an IP Address Automatically option.

7. Choose the WINS Configuration tab and select Disable WINS Resolution.

8. Select the Gateway tab, type the IP address for your ISP's gateway or router in the New Gateway box, and then click the Add button, as shown in figure 3.5.

FIG. 3.5

Add the IP address of your ISP's gateway computer here; this machine connects your computer to the Internet.

9. Select the DNS Configuration tab and choose the Enable DNS radio button (see fig. 3.6).

FIG. 3.6

The information in this box configures your computer to use your ISP's domain name server(s).

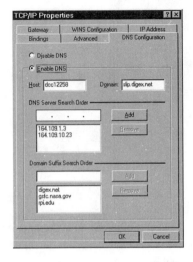

10. Type the host name of your computer in the Host box.

11. Enter the domain name of your ISP in the Domain box.

12. In the DNS Server Search Order section, enter the IP address of your ISP's DNS server. Press Add.

13. Type the domain name for your ISP in the Domain Suffix Search Order section, and then click the Add button. You can add other frequently used domain names here as well. By doing so, you can specify their addresses and URLs using host names only.

14. Double-check all your entries, and then click OK.

15. At this point, Windows 95 asks you to reboot your computer. Click Yes.

Your Windows 95 environment should have support for dial-up networking, TCP/IP, and the Dial-Up Scripting tool. Now you're ready to establish your first Internet connection.

Setting Up a Connection Icon

Now you're almost ready to log on. The *connection icon* is the icon that you use to initiate your PPP connection. To start configuring it, double-click the My Computer icon on your desktop. Next, double-click the Dial-Up Networking icon, and then double-click the Make New Connection icon. A wizard box then appears, as shown in figure 3.7.

FIG. 3.7

Microsoft's Internet Connection Wizard leads you through the steps of setting up and configuring a dial-up connection.

This wizard helps you set up a new connection entry. To do so, simply follow these steps:

1. Enter the connection name that you want to use into the dialog box.
2. Click the Configure button. A dialog box with the properties of the modem you selected appears.
3. Select the General tab in the Properties dialog box (see fig. 3.8).
4. In the Maximum Speed box, set the port speed for your modem. In general, 57600 is a good setting. This is because most modems will automatically set their connection speed as fast as they can go, so you want to set the port speed to be higher than this.
5. Make sure that the box marked Only Connect at This Speed is not checked.
6. Open the Connection tab so you can set the connection preferences that your ISP expects (see fig. 3.9). If you don't know them for sure, set Data Bits to 8, Parity to None, and Stop Bits to 1. This is a good set to try.

FIG. 3.8

The General tab allows you to configure the communications port your dial-up connection will use.

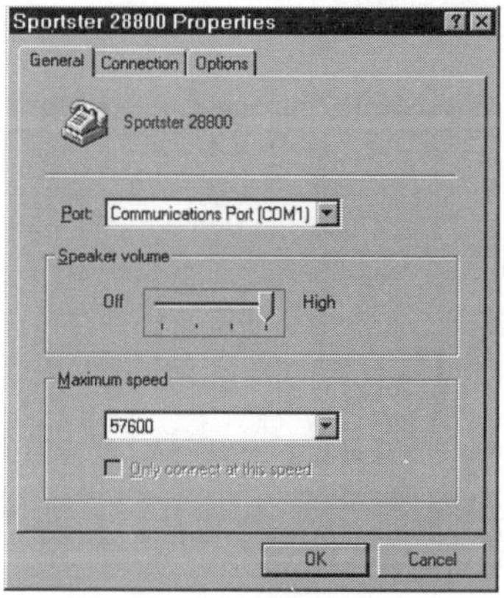

Part

I

Ch

3

FIG. 3.9

The Connection tab configures Windows 95's communications software to communicate correctly with your ISP.

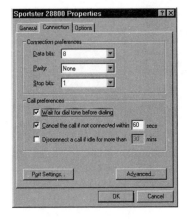

 T I P   If your modem doesn't dial when you attempt a connection, call waiting or some other phone system option may be keeping your modem from recognizing the dial tone. Try unchecking the Wait for Dial Tone before Dialing box to try to correct this problem.

7. If you are not going to use a script to automate your login process, select the Options tab in the Properties dialog box. From here, you can have PPP open a login window for you so that you can manually log in to your server (see fig. 3.10).

8. Click OK, and then click Next in the Wizard dialog box.

9. Enter the area code and phone number of your ISP in the dialog box, and click Next.

10. Click Finish.

FIG. 3.10

The Options tab enables you to get a terminal window if you need to enter information manually during the connection process.

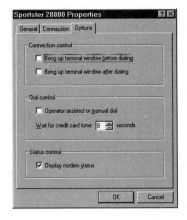

At this point, you should see a new connection icon, with the name that you specified, on your system. You just have a couple more steps to do before it's ready to use:

1. Right-click your connection icon. A pop-up menu for the connection icon appears.

2. Choose Properties from the pop-up menu.

3. Click the Server Type button. The Server Types dialog box appears (see fig. 3.11).

FIG. 3.11
The Server Types dialog box allows you to configure the correct communications protocol.

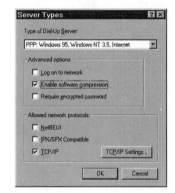

Part
I

Ch
3

4. Select PPP from the drop-down list box.

5. Verify that the TCP/IP box in the Allowed Network Protocols section is checked, and make sure that the Log on to Network box is not selected.

6. Click OK.

7. Click OK again.

You're done configuring TCP/IP! If you want to set your modem to redial automatically, you can do so by choosing the Settings option from the Connections menu in the Dial-Up Networking folder.

Basic Scripting

As mentioned earlier, using a script to automate your login process makes your job a lot easier. You can start your connection session and run to the fridge while Windows 95 retries your ISP dial-up line and logs you in! Also, scripting is very easy. You can think of a script as telling Windows 95 what to look for from the ISP server. Just as you might look for a login: prompt to type your username, you can have your script do the same thing. The Dial-Up Scripting tool is the way you create scripts to control your dial-up network session (see fig. 3.12).

FIG. 3.12

The Windows 95 Dial-Up Scripting tool gives you an easy way to create a script to automate your PPP login process.

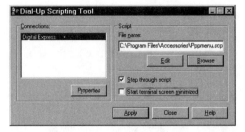

To make a script, follow these steps:

1. Click the Start button, and choose Programs, Accessories.
2. Select the Dial-Up Scripting tool. Its dialog box appears.
3. Click the Edit button to start editing a script.

All scripts start with the following line:

```
proc main
```

They end with the following line:

```
endproc
```

Between these two statements, you enter the commands that tell Windows 95 what to transmit and what to wait for. You need to know three basic commands to write a script: `transmit`, `waitfor`, and `delay`.

The `delay` statement causes your script to wait for a specified number of seconds. For example, the following line causes the script to pause for three seconds:

```
delay 3
```

The `waitfor` statement makes the script wait until the specified string is received. For example, the following line waits for the string `"ssword"` to be received by your system:

```
waitfor "ssword"
```

The third statement, `transmit`, transmits a string to the remote system. It does not automatically send a carriage return at the end of the string. To send a carriage return, you need to transmit the string `"^M"` to the remote system. Here is an example of a script:

```
proc main
delay 1
transmit "^M"
delay 1
transmit "^M"
delay 1
```

```
transmit "^M"
waitfor "name>"
transmit $USERID
transmit "^M"
waitfor "ssword>"
transmit $PASSWORD
transmit "^M"
waitfor "enu:"
transmit "3"
transmit "^M"
endproc
```

 TIP Using only the last part of a string in a waitfor statement is usually a good idea, in case the first character or two get garbled by the network. For example, you should use waitfor "ssword>" instead of waitfor "password>".

The preceding script waits for one second and then sends a carriage return to the remote system. It then repeats this sequence two more times. The script then waits for the string name from the remote system. It sends the contents of the special variable $USERID, which contains the user ID that you enter when you start the network connection program. It follows the user ID with a carriage return.

The script then waits for the ssword> prompt from the remote system and sends the contents of the $PASSWORD variable. This variable contains the password that you enter when you start the network connection program. It follows the password with a carriage return. It then waits for the string enu:, and sends the number 5 and a carriage return. This will select option "5" from the ISP's connection "menu:", which, in this case, initiates a PPP connection. That's all there is to it!

Once you have written your script, save it with the .SCP extension. Then, in the Dial-Up Scripting tool, select the network connection that you want to attach the script to and click Apply. Your script is now associated with that network connection and will be executed automatically any time you run that particular network connection.

You can also select the Step through Script checkbox to be able to step through the script one line at a time to debug it. By selecting the Start Terminal Screen Minimized checkbox, you see no terminal box displaying the progress of your script. Uncheck this box if you want to watch your script execute as it runs.

You've done it! You're ready to connect to the Internet. Just double-click your connection icon, and you get the Connect To dialog box, shown in figure 3.13. Click the Connect button, and you're on your way to the Internet.

Dunce, a Handy Connection Tool

Here's one last word about a handy little tool that no dial-up connection user should be without: the *Dial-Up Networking Connection Enhancement*, or *Dunce*. This program is currently at version 2.0.2, and can be found at **http://www.cjnetworks.com/~vecdev/vector/**.

One thing you'll find when you want to establish an Internet connection is that while Windows 95's dial-up scripting and other configuration options allow you to automate the connection process almost completely, you still have to click the Connect button in the Connect To dialog box (refer to fig. 3.13). And, if your ISP's phone number is busy, and you want to try to reconnect, you have to click the Connect button again.

FIG. 3.13

Once you've set up your dial-up connection, just click the Connect button to initiate the Internet connection process.

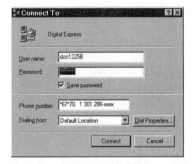

The main function of Dunce is to click that Connect button for you, thus allowing you to automate the connection process completely after you have double-clicked your connection icon. Figure 3.14 shows the main configuration box for Dunce. In addition to clicking the Connect button automatically, you can configure Dunce to redial automatically if the number is busy, reconnect automatically if disconnected, and minimize the Connected dialog box automatically.

FIG. 3.14

Dunce is a handy tool for completely automating your Internet connection process.

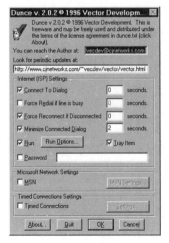

In addition, by enabling and clicking the Run Options button to open the Run Options dialog box, you can configure Dunce to run up to four other programs automatically at various stages of the connection process (see fig. 3.15). For example, while connecting, we have Dunce run *Duca* (the *Dial-Up Connection Alarm*), available at **ftp://ftp.coast.net/SimTel/win95/ commprog/duca9505.zip**.

FIG. 3.15

Dunce allows you to run up to four programs automatically during different phases of the Internet connection process.

Duca plays a sound once an Internet connection is established. After the connection is established, you can also use a mail monitoring program, Qbik Mail Monitor, available at **http:// nz.com/NZ/Commerce/creative-cgi/special/qbik/mail.htm**. ●

Mastering Microsoft Internet Explorer

## CHAPTER 4

Loading and Configuring Internet Explorer

In Chapter 2, "The World Wide Web and Internet Explorer 3," you learned about the history of the World Wide Web, its uses, and the direction in which it is developing. The Web has become one of the most common methods of finding specific information about any topic under the sun. Internet Explorer, the World Wide Web browser with the fastest growing market share, is used by many households and businesses connected to the Internet.

When considering using any product, you try to look at all the options available so you can get the best value for your investment of time and money. The fact that Internet Explorer is rising in popularity so quickly, is developed and supported by Microsoft, the largest software company in the world, and is free, may assist you in making the decision to use Internet Explorer. ■

How do I download and install Internet Explorer 3?

Find out how to load Internet Explorer from the CD-ROM accompanying this book, or directly from the World Wide Web.

How do I get on the Web for the first time?This chapter provides a "quick start" guide for connecting Internet Explorer to the World Wide Web.

Where do I get support for Microsoft products?

Microsoft offers a variety of ways to get support for Internet Explorer and their other products—this chapter discusses some of them.

Downloading Internet Explorer 3 from the Internet

On the CD

In addition to being available on the CD-ROM that comes with this book, Microsoft's Internet Explorer is available on the Internet through Microsoft's Internet Explorer Web site (see fig. 4.1). Internet Explorer is freeware, and can be downloaded by pointing your current Web browser at **http://www.microsoft.com/ie/**.

FIG. 4.1
Microsoft's Internet Explorer Web site is the source for Internet Explorer software.

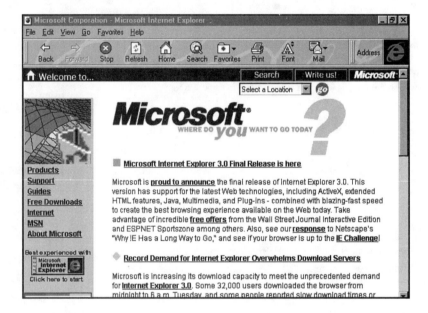

TIP

It is always best to download files into a temporary directory. By creating a temporary directory to receive your download, you can extract the compressed file into that directory without moving it. Using a temporary directory also makes clean-up a snap. All you have to do is delete the temporary directory and you are done.

The copy of Internet Explorer that you just downloaded, either from the CD-ROM or from the Internet Explorer Web site, is in a self-extracting executable file. Double-click it from Windows Explorer, or run it from a DOS window. This extracts the installation and setup files. At this point, you can install Internet Explorer as explained in a following section "Installing the Internet Explorer 3 Web Browser." Remember to look at your temporary download directory, rather than the CD-ROM, when you are looking for the setup program to start the installation.

TIP

The World Wide Web is a very dynamic environment these days, and Web browsers change as fast as everything else. After you install Internet Explorer 3 from the CD-ROM, you might want to visit the Web site listed above and make sure you have the latest Internet Explorer revision.

N O T E   Time is always of the essence in today's hurried society. We constantly rush to get to work on time, pick up the kids after school, fix and eat dinner, and, hopefully, catch up on weekend projects looming over our heads on Wednesday.

It is always nice to start a new project with some idea about the amount of time that it is going to involve. The following table shows the average download time I experienced when transferring this file several times while preparing this book. These times should be close to what you will experience, although you should not worry if your times are a bit longer or shorter.

Connection Type	Total Transfer Time
14,400 modem	20 minutes
28,800 modem	9 minutes (at least a 24,000 baud carrier)
57,600 network	6 minutes
T1 cable	3 minutes

Loading Internet Explorer 3

Of course, you have to install the program before you can catch that first wave. But don't worry; Microsoft has included an Installation Wizard that guides you through the entire installation process. Internet Explorer has a few system requirements that you must have to complete the installation and run the program effectively. If your system is able to run Windows 95, though, it should support Internet Explorer 3.

Installation Requirements

The minimum requirements for installing and running Internet Explorer 3 are the same as those for Windows 95, with the addition of a LAN or SLIP/PPP connection (hardware, software, and service provider) to the Internet.

> **CAUTION**
>
> It's always a good idea if your system exceeds the minimum requirements to run Internet Explorer 3 under Windows 95. Keep in mind that you need more hard drive space if you keep a large list of sites you have visited or if you download lots of images and other files. Also, the faster your system is—faster processor, video hardware, storage devices, and Internet connection, and more memory—the better your performance will be.

Installing the Internet Explorer 3 Web Browser

The installation process is relatively quick and painless. Because Microsoft uses an Installation Wizard to walk you through the Internet Explorer installation, most of your questions are answered right on-screen. If you experience problems during the installation, you can find some help through one of the means listed in the section titled "Receiving Technical Support from Microsoft," later in this chapter.

To install Internet Explorer 3, follow these steps:

1. Close any Windows or DOS programs that are running. You need to do this because sometimes other programs use files or memory that Internet Explorer 3 needs to use during the install process.

2. Place the CD in your CD-ROM drive and copy the self-extracting file to a temporary directory on your hard drive (for example, `C:\TEMP`).

3. Run the self-extracting file in the temporary directory. The file will extract itself and automatically begin the installation process of Internet Explorer 3.

4. Click OK to start the installation of Internet Explorer 3. First, the Installation Wizard is installed. Once the Wizard's initialization is complete, an introduction appears. Click Next.

5. Internet Explorer 3 will be installed into a specific destination directory on your hard drive, overwriting any previous versions that exist there. Click Next to begin the installation process.

N O T E If you still want to be able to use a previous version of Internet Explorer—Internet Explorer 2, for instance—before installing Internet Explorer 3, rename that Internet Explorer executable. It should be found as the following:

`C:\PROGRAM FILES\PLUS!\MICROSOFT INTERNET\IEXPLORE.EXE`

Rename it to something like `IE20.EXE`, and create a shortcut to it in the usual way. Now, after Internet Explorer 3 is installed, you will still have access to the older version. ▧

6. The needed files are now installed in the appropriate places on your hard drive. The scales shown during installation enable you to keep track of its progress. When the installation is complete, the Wizard creates the desktop icon called "The Internet" for Internet Explorer 3.

7. When you see the short message letting you know that the installation was successful, click OK. A prompt asking you to read the `README.TXT` file should appear. Choose Yes or No. Now you have Internet Explorer 3 installed, and almost ready to use.

N O T E The `README.TXT` file is full of useful information giving some basic pointers on where to get more information if you encounter problems using Internet Explorer 3. Although it does not provide very much helpful information for individuals that are first-time users of Internet Explorer 3, it may help some old pros fix a new problem. ▧

8. As is true whenever adding new network drivers or installing new protocols, the last step needed before you can use Internet Explorer 3 is to reboot your computer. The installation process made the necessary changes in the Windows 95 Registry and other parts of the system to use Internet Explorer 3, but to make those changes part of your active session requires a reboot. After you have done this, Internet Explorer 3 is ready to go!

Getting on the Web for the First Time

The World Wide Web is considered one of the best places to get information on any subject, at any time. To reach this large body of information, you first need to connect to the network of computer systems that makes up the Internet. Use the information in the following sections to connect to your Internet service provider or to your company's network. If you have problems attaining these connections, Chapter 3, "Internet Basics," provides you with more detailed information.

Connecting to Your Service Provider

Although the term *service provider* usually refers to a dial-up SLIP or PPP connection, you can also use a standard TCP/IP LAN connection. There are specific details in Chapter 3, "Internet Basics," that discuss how to set up a working Internet connection. The following section covers only the basic steps in the setup process for Windows 95.

Making a LAN Connection   When using a local area network (LAN) to connect to the Internet, you must make sure that your computer is correctly configured to use the specific type of network to which it is physically attached. You have to know the specific type of network card that your computer uses and the names of the drivers that are required to run your card. Once you have this information, you must load those drivers, or tell your computer to do it automatically for you each time it starts, before you can connect to the network. The following steps guide you through the process of getting these drivers loaded and running properly:

1. Open the Control Panel and select the Networks icon.

2. On your Network Properties screen, make sure that you have a TCP/IP protocol loaded for your network card.

N O T E   This protocol needs to be configured with the following information:

- Your network IP address

- The address of your Internet gateway

- The address of the Domain Name Servers (DNS) used by your facility

Complete the configuration by choosing Properties and filling out the forms on the tabbed dialog box that appears. See Chapter 3, "Internet Basics," for detailed information on how to configure these settings. ■

3. Choose the OK button to exit this screen once you have ensured that the proper drivers are loaded.

4. Double-click the Internet icon on your desktop.

Internet Explorer 3 finds your network and travels through it and out onto the Internet to find the home page for the Microsoft Network. Once you are there, you can travel across the Net to anywhere.

Part

II

Ch

4

TROUBLESHOOTING

Every time I open Internet Explorer 3, I get an error message telling me that I have a Winsock error. Generally, you get this error when you do not have your TCP/IP protocol properly loaded. Go back to the Control Panel's Network Properties dialog box and ensure that the appropriate TCP/IP and network drivers for your network card are loaded. If you have selected the wrong network card, you will load inappropriate drivers and receive this message. If you just installed your network drivers, you must restart your computer for them to load. Windows 95 does not automatically load the drivers into your computer's memory after you install them.

Making a SLIP/PPP Connection   Very few home users and relatively few businesses have a direct connection to the Internet, which leaves the majority of the world connecting to the Internet through a SLIP or PPP connection and a modem. Because Internet Explorer 3 does not provide you with a dialing program, you have to use the one that comes with Windows 95, or another third-party dial-up connector. Before you attempt to use Internet Explorer 3 the first time, check your dial-up program. It will save you time in the long run. Follow these steps to do so:

1. Open the Control Panel and select the Networks icon.
2. Check to ensure that you have the dial-up adapter and a TCP/IP protocol loaded for that adapter.
3. Open the Start menu and choose the Programs option, and then choose the Accessories option. This opens the Accessories pop-up menu on which you will find an icon labeled Dial-Up Networking. This is the utility that dials your phone connection for you.

Internet Explorer 3 automatically starts the dial-up networking client, which calls your service provider and establishes a connection. Depending on how you have installed the dial-up client, you might have to manually enter your name and password. When you establish your connection, all the features of Internet Explorer 3 are available.

Selecting a Start Page

We have all heard about creating personal home pages that reflect our hobbies and interests. Internet Explorer 3 uses the term "start page" to designate its point of entry onto the Web when the program is first started. When you first run Internet Explorer 3, you may see the Microsoft Network's home page on its Web server appear automatically. As you use the World Wide Web, you will probably find yourself returning to one page time after time. Sometimes you will go there three and four times a day to retrieve information. When you find yourself visiting a site this frequently, you may want to make it Internet Explorer 3's entry point into the world of the Web. It may be your personal home page or the introductory document for your company's Web server. There is more information on how to use the home page in Chapter 6, "Finding Information on the Web."

To change Internet Explorer 3's start page, simply follow these steps:

1. If it is not already running, start Internet Explorer 3 by double-clicking its desktop icon.
2. Load the Web page that you want to use for your start page, whether it be a local file or a Web page out on the World Wide Web.
3. Open the View, Options menu and choose the Navigation tab from the Options dialog box that appears (see fig. 4.2).

FIG. 4.2
Internet Explorer 3 allows you to select what Web page is displayed when you start it up.

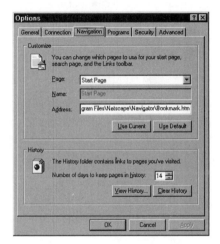

4. Make sure the drop-down menu shows Start Page.
5. Click the Use Current button, and the current Web page will now be your start page.
6. Choose OK to save your selection, and the next time you start Internet Explorer you will see the site that you selected.

You do not need to worry about selecting a start page that does not include links to every site you visit often. Internet Explorer 3 includes a very advanced favorite places feature that allows you to keep a list of the sites that interest you.

▶ **See** "Creating Favorite Places" for an explanation of how to set up and use favorite places, p. 126

Saving and Printing Copies of a Web Page

Because the Web is used as a source of information on a myriad of topics, you often need to keep a copy of the material that you read. Sometimes you need to incorporate some of this information in another document, or you may simply need a hard copy to give to someone else. In either case, Internet Explorer 3 allows you to retain that Web site permanently with a click of your mouse.

Saving an HTML File for Future Reference   All Web pages are created from a text file that has special key commands stored in it that the Web browser reads. These codes allow you to

Part
II

Ch
4

see graphics, colorful backgrounds, bold text, and brightly colored links to other sites. You can save a copy of the original HTML file for future reference by following these steps:

1. Open the File menu and select Save As File.
2. The Save As dialog box appears, which allows you to direct Internet Explorer to save a copy of the HTML code to a directory of your choosing.
3. Select the directory in which you want to save this page.
4. Place your cursor in the File name field and enter a name for this HTML document.
5. Choose Save. You have now saved a copy of this World Wide Web page that you can view at any time without actually connecting to the Internet.

Because you are saving pages, you need to look at them at least every once in a while. The following steps assist you in reading a saved HTML document.

1. Open the File menu and choose the Open option, or press Ctrl+O.
2. The Open dialog box appears. Click the Browse button and then find the file that you want to open.
3. Click your mouse pointer on the name of the file that you want to open.
4. Choose OK.

Internet Explorer opens the file, allowing you to continue working with that Web site. You do not have to retrace your steps, you can forge ahead finding the information you need to complete your tasks.

CAUTION

Be aware that quite often Web pages reference and load in images or other information from other sites on the Web. At best, that will mean that when you save such a document to disk and then view it, the graphics that it included will not be displayed, being replaced by a placeholder.

Sometimes, however, you can load a local file that contains absolute URL references. When Internet Explorer loads this local Web page, it will then try to load the other URLs, and may try to initiate an Internet connection to do so. This makes it difficult to view a document offline. You can click the Stop button on the toolbar to stop this.

▶ **See** "URL References" for a description of the format and use of URLs, **p. 80**

Printing Web Pages   Sometimes you simply need to capture the information that is on a Web page in the fastest way possible and you do not necessarily have to be able to look at it in electronic form. That is where Internet Explorer 3's printing feature enters the picture. To print Web pages, follow these steps:

1. Open the File menu and select the Print option, or press Ctrl+P.
2. Select the name of your printer from the Name drop-down list.
3. Set the number of Copies and the Print Range options to meet your needs.
4. When you're done setting up the printer, choose the OK button.

A window appears telling you that your document is being retrieved from the main Web site and that it is being formatted for the printer. This process should only take a few moments, and you can resume your search of the World Wide Web.

 TIP If you end up with a stack of printed pages and you're not sure where they are from, you will find the URL for that Web page located in the upper right corner of the printout. This URL also allows you to go back to that site to get more or updated information.

Displaying Information on a Web Page

Internet Explorer allows you to look at a Web page in a couple of different views. The first, and most common, is through the browser with all the HTML tags activated. This is the way you are going to automatically see all sites when you first jump to them.

Another method involves looking at the text file that makes up the body of the Web page. This is viewing the document source, and it is useful if you want to know how the Webmaster at that site achieved a specific look in her Web page. Of course, if you are just starting to program with HTML, you will want to look at a lot of Web sites in this view. It helps you learn the language, and the conventions that are used when writing HTML documents.

To view the source document of any Web page, open the View menu and select the Source option. This opens a document viewer—in this view, you see the source code that is interpreted by the Web browser to create the graphical pages that you see on your screen.

Part

II

Ch

4

Internet Explorer Configuration Options

Now that you have Internet Explorer 3 up and running, there are some additional configuration options that you might want to become familiar with. Some of these increase the capability and utility of the Web browser, and some allow you to exert greater control over what parts of the Internet and the Web can be accessed. And, of course, some of the options allow you to tailor the "look and feel" of Internet Explorer to your wants.

Accessibility and Multi-Language Support

Internet Explorer supports the accessibility of the Web browser to people with disabilities and to non-English speakers, through its support for alternative fonts and different character sets. Internet Explorer supports the use of large fonts to make it more convenient for people with vision disabilities. Also, by clicking the International button on the General tab of the View, Options window, you may specify an alternative character set to allow for use in other languages.

Security

The built-in security features of Internet Explorer are designed to enable you to tailor the amount of risk you are willing to take when downloading software and information from the Internet. As shown in figure 4.3, you can determine how much warning Internet Explorer will give you when it is exchanging information with sites that it doesn't feel it can trust. Underlying this is a security system that allows trusted sites to identify themselves.

FIG. 4.3

Internet Explorer's software safety settings allow you to determine how much risk you are willing to accept when downloading software and information from the Web.

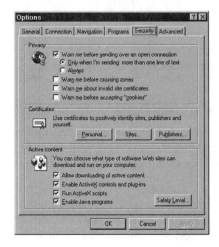

▶ **See** "Interactive Pages and Secure Online Transactions" for more information on Internet security, **p. 153**

Internet Ratings Support

Internet Explorer supports Internet ratings, which allows you to determine what Internet sites may be accessed with your Web browser. For people with children who have access to their computer, this provides control over what the children are able to see. Various settings exist, under the Advanced tab of the Options dialog box, in the ratings categories of:

- Language
- Nudity
- Sex
- Violence

By selecting a supervisor password and creating a setting for each category—for instance, the language category can be set to allow only inoffensive slang, mild expletives, moderate expletives, obscene gestures, or explicit or crude language—you can control which Web sites are allowed to be viewed (see fig. 4.4). While all sites are not yet rated—at this point, rating is a voluntary exercise—rating is becoming more and more common. Also, the Web browser can be set to not be allowed to view unrated sites.

Toolbar Configuration

The Internet Explorer toolbar is considerably configurable, depending on how much screen area you have and on your personal preference. In addition to being able to turn it off completely by selecting View, Toolbar, you can also determine how much relative space is taken up by its three parts—the button bar, the drop-down Address area, and the Links area. Figure 4.4 shows my preferred configuration, with the Links slid out of the way. If you have more screen area, or like to see the toolbar in all of its glory, it'll look something like that shown in figure 4.5.

FIG. 4.4

By supporting industry-standard Internet ratings, Internet Explorer allows you to determine what Web sites your browser can access.

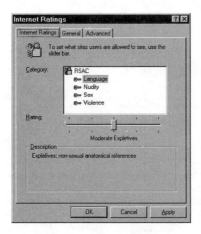

FIG. 4.5

The Internet Explorer toolbar can be configured in a variety of ways.

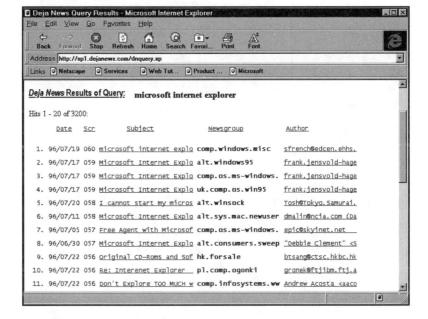

However, unlike toolbars that you might be used to, there are no configuration options hidden in the menus to allow you to customize this. Instead, you just grab the different parts of the menu with the mouse, and drag them in the appropriate direction. For instance, to slide the Links out or slide them out of the way, grab and drag the the toolbar where it says Links (see fig. 4.6). To shorten the toolbar by removing the text labels, grab it at the bottom and slide it up.

FIG. 4.6
By simply sliding the toolbar around, you can place it in a configuration that you like.

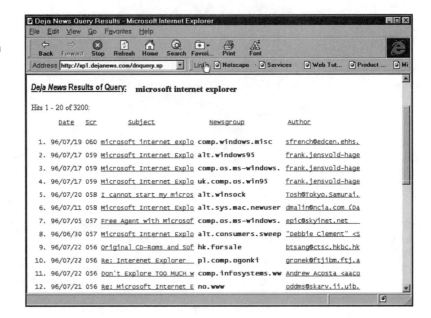

Administration Kit

For Internet service providers interested in redistributing Internet Explorer to their customers or businesses interested in using it in a corporate intranet, Microsoft offers the Internet Explorer Administration Kit. This kit allows ISPs and businesses to configure and tailor versions of Internet Explorer especially for their situation. They can create special versions of the Web browser with default settings for start and search pages, security and ratings settings, and even customize the animated graphic used to show browser activity in the upper right side of the browser window. Information about the Administration Kit, along with details on how to get it and how to get permission to redistribute Internet Explorer, is available through the Internet Explorer Web site at **http://www.microsoft.com/ie**.

Getting Help for Microsoft Internet Explorer 3

There are a variety of ways to get support if you have problems using Internet Explorer. This book will probably tell you everything you will normally need to know to get your Web browser up and running. But, if you run into a problem that you need additional help for, there are a variety of resources, both from Microsoft and otherwise, to help you solve it.

Receiving Technical Support from Microsoft

Microsoft provides its users many different options for getting technical support, including UseNet newsgroups, World Wide Web pages, online help, documentations, and frequently asked question lists.

Referring to Microsoft's Help System   Microsoft's help system uses a series of linked HTML pages and standard Windows Help pages, some of which are located on your local computer, while others are located at Microsoft's Web site. The Help menu in Internet Explorer pops up Windows Help pages (see fig. 4.7). These pages include a great deal of online help and information to enable you to configure and use Internet Explorer. You can generally answer most, if not all, of your questions by reading these documents.

FIG. 4.7
Internet Explorer comes with an extensive set of Windows Help pages.

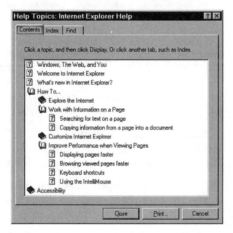

Using Microsoft's World Wide Web Pages   Microsoft uses its Internet Explorer Web site to provide much of its product support. This Web site is located at **http://www.microsoft.com/ie/** (refer to fig. 4.1).

From this page, you can connect to a variety of services that Microsoft provides. Microsoft maintains a variety of support and feedback pages that collect useful information that you might need after you have installed Internet Explorer and are trying to use it. When you get to this page, you are greeted with product FAQs, search engines, and a list of the services Microsoft provides for its Internet line of products (see fig. 4.8). You simply need to find the most appropriate services for the product you have questions on, click its link, and continue down your path to a completely working product.

FIG. 4.8
A Frequently Asked
Questions (FAQ) list
gives you access to
some common
troubleshooting
information.

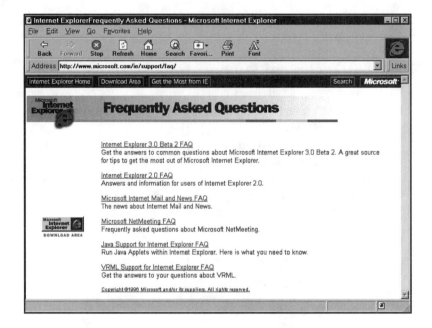

The Web site contains layers upon layers of information. If you see a topic that might be helpful, jump to it and read it. If the site does not contain the information you are looking for, choose Back and continue on to your next option. You never know when a document is going to provide you with that one clue that solves your problem. Hey, even if it didn't solve your problem today, it may keep you from having another problem in the future.

On other thing that you can do from the Microsoft Internet Explorer Web site is register your copy of Internet Explorer (see fig. 4.9). As Internet Explorer is a free product, this registration is completely voluntary, and is used by Microsoft to keep track of who is using their products. By registering, you can also sign up to receive product upgrade notices, and Microsoft's online newsletter, WinNews.

Getting Help from UseNet Newsgroups

As mentioned earlier, UseNet newsgroups are one of the best ways for people with common interests to get together. There are several different ways that these can be used to find out information about Microsoft Internet Explorer.

Conventional UseNet Newsgroups   There are several UseNet newsgroups available through most news servers that contain discussions of the World Wide Web in general, and Web browsers in particular. Reading and posting queries to these groups might be a good way for you to find out answers to problems you might be having with Internet Explorer 3. The following lists some useful ones:

- **comp.infosystems.www.browsers**
- **comp.infosystems.www.browsers.ms-windows**

- comp.infosystems.www.misc

- comp.infosystems.www.users

FIG. 4.9
Registering your
released version of
Internet Explorer allows
you to receive e-mail
updates of product
upgrades.

Microsoft's News Server   Microsoft maintains a UseNet news server that has many different newsgroups that discuss its products. This news server is **msnews.microsoft.com**, and some of the relevant newsgroups are listed as follows:

- **microsoft.public.internetexplorer**—This is for discussion on Microsoft's Internet Explorer Web browsers (see fig. 4.10).

- **microsoft.public.internet.mail**—This is for discussion on the Microsoft Internet Mail client.

- **microsoft.public.internet.news**—This is for discussion on the Microsoft Internet News client.

The newsgroups are a good way to exchange information with other users of Microsoft's products. Also, Microsoft representatives frequently drop in and are able to answer questions are the use or availability of different pieces of Microsoft software.

▶ **See** "Reading UseNet Newsgroups with Internet Explorer" to find out how to access UseNet news through Internet Explorer, **p. 201**

UseNet Newsgroups Search Services   There are a couple of services available through the World Wide Web that allow you to search for UseNet newsgroups and/or UseNet articles about a specific subject. One of the best of these is the Deja News service.

Part
II

Ch

4

FIG. 4.10

Microsoft maintains a UseNet news server that hosts discussions about many Microsoft-related topics.

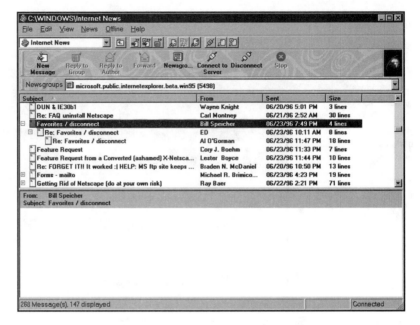

The Deja News system is very easy to use. It is located at **http://www.dejanews.com/**. The following steps enable you to search its entire message database for information specific to your problem with Internet Explorer:

N O T E Please remember that vocabulary and spelling are very important. You may refer to "e-mail" in a search, while someone else calls it "email," and another individual uses the phrase "Internet mail." Your search will not find the messages left by those other individuals. To do a thorough exploration, you need to search on as many different phrases and spellings as you can to get the broadest range of information out of your search. ■

 Access Microsoft's Internet News and Internet Mail Clients by clicking the Mail & News icon located on the toolbar (refer to fig 4.11).

1. In Internet Explorer 3, enter **http://www.dejanews.com/** as the URL you want to visit.
2. Enter your search criteria, such as "Microsoft Internet Explorer," and choose the Find button, as shown in figure 4.11.

Your screen now changes to a listing of all the messages and UseNet newsgroups that are currently discussing Microsoft Internet Explorer. This screen should be similar to the one shown in figure 4.12. You can read the UseNet discussions by double-clicking the highlighted message subject.

FIG. 4.11
The main Deja News search screen is configured to perform a search for Microsoft Internet Explorer.

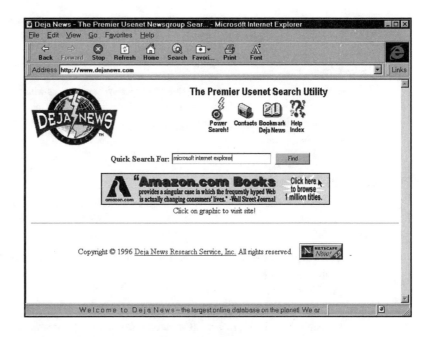

FIG. 4.12
Deja News service lists the most recent discussions about Microsoft Internet Explorer that it can find.

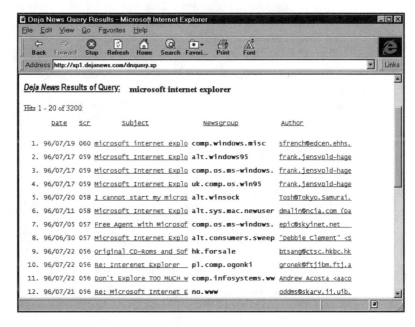

N O T E If you would like more details on using UseNet newsgroups with Internet Explorer 3, please see Chapter 11, "Reading UseNet Newsgroups with Internet Explorer." To go directly to a UseNet newsgroup, type the address preceded by **news:** in the URL field at the top of your Internet Explorer screen.

For example, if you want to look at the **comp.infosystems.www.browsers.ms-windows** newsgroup, place your cursor in the URL field on your main Internet Explorer screen and type **news:comp.infosystems.www.browsers.ms-windows**. Press Enter to tell Internet Explorer to search for that address. ▪

General Troubleshooting

There are more "little" problems experienced every day than all the technical support departments across the country could fix. So when you do have to call or write for technical support, have the following information handy to help the process along:

- **The version of the software you are using.** This narrows down the list of known problems so the support specialist can quickly switch gears to help you best with your product version.

- **A short description of the problem.** For example, "I am able to connect to my service provider, John Doe's Internet Connections, but once I start Internet Explorer 3, I constantly get the error message `Internet Explorer is unable to locate server: www.yahoo.com. This server does not have a DNS entry. Check the server name in the location (URL) and try again.` With this information, the technician will know if your dial-up PPP connection is working properly, allowing him or her to narrow down the possible sources of your problem. They will also know the error messages that you are receiving in case this is a known problem they can fix in just a few minutes. When Technical Support personnel have to dig for information on a problem, it needlessly takes more of your time and causes you and them more frustration than the problem is worth.

- **The name and version of your operating system.** If you are running a product designed for Windows 3.1 under Windows 95, you may be having a known conflict with the operating system.

- **The type of Internet connection you are using: SLIP/PPP or LAN.** If you have a SLIP/PPP connection, know the brand and speed of your modem, and the name of the TCP/IP stack you are loading. If you have a LAN connection, know the name of the TCP/IP stack you are loading, the type of network card you are using, and the type of connection your network has to the Internet (e.g., T1 cable, 57600 baud line, etc.).

- **If you tried other Internet applications, such as Ping or Telnet, and whether they work properly.**

■ **Know when the problem first started, and whether you recently added any new software to your computer around that time.** Sometimes installing new software makes your old software not run properly. Many software packages come with their own versions of hardware drivers, and a new software package will often overwrite the version of the driver installed and used by a previously installed package.

Knowing this information in advance helps the technician to diagnose your problem, get you off the telephone, and back onto the Web faster. Without this type of information, you will be extending the time involved in solving your problem. Technical support personnel are highly trained individuals that really know their job. Remember that they are people, too, and can't read your mind, nor can they see your computer screen. They are dependent on your descriptions of a situation, or a screen to direct them to a solution. By providing them with as much information as you can, you are helping yourself and all the other people who are waiting on the phone lines. ●

Part

II

Ch

4

Moving Around the Web

One of the fascinating features of the World Wide Web, the aspect that makes "Web surfing" possible, is the sheer diversity of information, organized in an intuitive rather than logical way. The Web is not like an encyclopedia, calmly presenting its information from A to Z. It's free-form, not linear. It more closely matches how people think: jumping from topic to topic as we see fit, as opposed to having order forced upon us.

Thus, the metaphor of the "Web" itself is born. Like a spider's web, the Web reaches out across the world, join-ing computer to computer and node to node. By getting out there on the Web with a Web browser such as Internet Explorer, you can trek through a vast landscape of infor-mation, one bit linked to another to another. These links are, in fact, what the Web is all about, and they represent one of the most important things you need to know about the Web. For example, you need to know that you can jump from one Web page to another by clicking a link. You also need to know some other ways to get to a Web page without using links. ■

How do hypertext links work?

In this chapter, learn how hypertext links are used in Web documents to link information together across the Internet.

What can hypertext links do?

Learn about the different things that hypertext links can do in an HTML document, such as directing you to information within a Web page, at the same Web site, or across the Internet.

How do you configure Internet Explorer 3 to work with links?

Learn how to configure the way Internet Explorer 3 renders and works with hypertext links.

Understanding Links

By now, you've noticed the cross-references in this book. They serve a similar purpose as links on a Web page—albeit a little low-tech. They refer you to other places in this book that might be useful or interesting to read. Without these references, you would have to resort to flipping through the pages looking for what you need.

Links on a Web page are even more vital. You have all the pages of this book right in front of you. At least you would know where to start looking. On the other hand, you have no idea where to find all the Web pages on the Internet. And it has too many to keep track of, anyway. Therefore, links are the only reasonable way to go from one Web page to another related Web page.

N O T E *Hypertext* and *hypermedia* are two terms you frequently hear associated with the Web. A hypertext document is a document that contains links to other documents—allowing you to jump between them by clicking the links. Hypermedia can contain more than text; it can contain multimedia such as pictures, videos, and sounds, too. In hypermedia documents, pictures are frequently used as links to other documents. ■

A link really has two different parts. First is the part that you see on the Web page—called an *anchor*. The other part tells Internet Explorer 3 what to do if you click that anchor—called the *URL reference*. When you click a link's anchor, Internet Explorer 3 loads the Web page given by the link's corresponding URL reference. You learn about both parts of a link in the following sections. You also learn about the different resources to which a link can point.

Anchors

A link's anchor can be a word, a group of words, or a picture. Exactly how an anchor looks in Internet Explorer 3 depends largely on what type of anchor it is and how the person who created the Web page used it. You can have only two types of anchors, though: text and graphical. You learn about both types in this section.

 When you move the mouse cursor over a link's anchor, the cursor changes from a pointer to a hand.

Text Anchors   Most text anchors look somewhat the same. A text anchor is one or more words that Internet Explorer 3 underlines to indicate that it represents a link. Internet Explorer also displays a text anchor using a different color than the rest of the text around it.

 Click and drag a link's text anchor onto your desktop. You can return quickly to that Web page by double-clicking the shortcut.

Figure 5.1 shows a Web page that contains several text anchors. In particular, notice how the text anchors on this Web page are embedded in the text. That is, they aren't set apart from the text but are actually an integral part of it. Clicking one of these links loads a Web page that is related to the link. You can find many text anchors used this way.

FIG. 5.1
Text anchors are often included directly in the text; Internet Explorer makes them a different color and underlines them.

Text anchors —

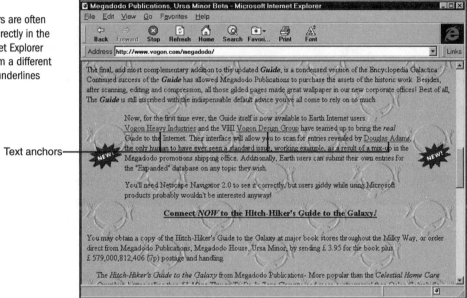

Figure 5.2 shows another Web page with several text anchors. These anchors aren't embedded in the text, however. They are presented as a list or index of links from which you can choose. Web page authors frequently use this method to present collections of related links.

Graphical Anchors A graphical anchor is similar to a text anchor. When you click a link's graphical anchor, Internet Explorer 3 loads the Web page that the link references. Graphical anchors aren't underlined or displayed in a different color, however, though they are usually given a border the same color as text anchors. And no two graphical anchors need to look the same, either. The look depends entirely on the picture that the Web page's author chose to use.

T I P Right-click a graphical anchor, and choose Save Picture As to save the image in a file on your computer.

Part
II

Ch

5

FIG. 5.2

Text anchors can also be presented in HTML lists and tables.

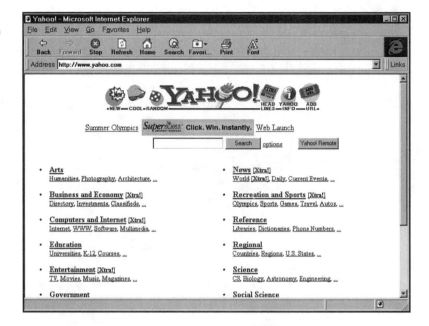

Versatility is the strong suit of graphical anchors. Web page authors effectively use them for a variety of reasons. Here are some examples of the ways you might find graphical anchors used on a Web page:

- **Bullets**—Graphical anchors are frequently used as list bullets. You can click the picture to go to the Web page described by that list item. Frequently, the text in the list item is also a link. You can click either the picture or the text.

- **Icons**—Many Web sites use graphical anchors in a similar manner to the way Windows 95 uses icons. They are common on home pages, and represent a variety of Web pages available at that site. Figure 5.3 shows a Web site that uses graphical anchors in this manner. Click the ProShop icon to open the ProShop Web page, for example.

- **Advertisements**—Many Web sites have sponsors that pay to advertise on the site. Sponsorships keep the Web site free to you and me, while the site continues to make money. You usually find advertisements, such as the one shown in figure 5.4, at the top of Web pages. Click the advertisement, and Internet Explorer 3 loads the sponsor's Web page.

FIG. 5.3

GolfWeb's home page uses graphical anchors to represent a variety of pages you can load.

Graphical anchors used as icons

FIG. 5.4

Many of the Web services pages, such as this one by Excite, pay for themselves with advertising.

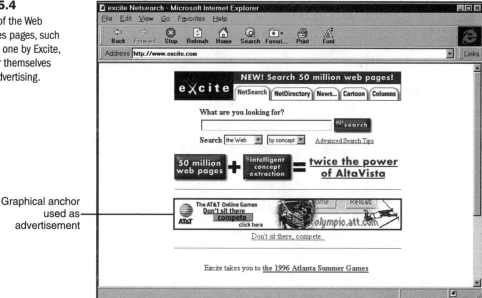

Graphical anchor used as advertisement

Part

II

Ch

5

URL References

The other part of a link is the URL reference. It is usually the address of the Web page that Internet Explorer 3 loads if you click the link. Every type of link, whether it uses a text or graphical anchor, uses either a relative or absolute reference. You learn about each type in this section, but when you're surfing the Web, it really doesn't matter which type of URL reference a link is using—as long as Internet Explorer 3 loads the Web page you want.

Relative References   A URL reference to a file on the same computer is also known as a *relative reference*. It means that the URL is relative to the computer and directory from which Internet Explorer 3 originally loaded the Web page. If Internet Explorer 3 loads a page at **http://www.mysite.com/page**, for example, then a relative reference to **/picture** would actually refer to the URL **http://www.mysite.com/page/picture**. Relative references are used to refer to Web pages on the same computer. Figure 5.5 shows a Web page that contains relative references to other Web pages on that site.

FIG. 5.5
Microsoft's home page contains many relative references to other Web pages at Microsoft.

The primary reason Web authors use a relative reference rather than an absolute reference is convenience. Just typing the filename, instead of the entire URL, is much simpler. This way, moving Web pages around on a server is also easier. Since the URL references are relative to the Web page's computer and directory, the author doesn't have to change all the links in the Web page every time the files move to a different location.

N O T E Web authors also can combine the convenience of a relative reference with the completeness of an absolute one, through the use of the HTML <BASE> tag. Using the preceding
example, a Web author could specify the following in the <HEAD> section of the HTML document:

`<BASE HREF="http://www.mysite.com/page">`

Then all URLs in the body of the document could be given relative to that base URL. The effect is
similar to relative references, with the additional flexibility of being able to specify a base URL different
from the one the current document is in. ■

▶ **See** "The Base URL" for a description of the use of the <HEAD> section <BASE> tag, **p. 371**

Corporate Bulletin Boards

Many corporations such as Hewlett Packard have created corporate bulletin boards that their
associates view with Web browsers such as Internet Explorer 3. These Web pages aren't on the Web,
however. They're stored on the companies' internal network servers. They contain a variety of
information that is useful to their associates such as the following:

- Meeting schedules and meeting room availability
- Announcements about corporate events
- Information about policies and benefits
- Recent press releases and financial statements
- Technological information

You can easily create a bulletin board for the corporation you work for, too. Part V, "Building World-
Class Web Sites and Servers for Internet Explorer," shows you how to build pages for the Web. The
only difference between that and building a corporate bulletin board is in the type of information you
choose to include on the page.

Absolute References   A URL reference that specifies the exact computer, directory, and file
for a Web page is an absolute reference. Whereas relative references are common for links to
Web pages on the same computer, absolute references are necessary for links to Web pages on
other computers.

T I P   Hold your mouse cursor over a link and look at Internet Explorer's status line to see its URL reference.

N O T E You learn about HTML (Hypertext Mark-Up Language) in Chapter 20, "Basic HTML." If you're
curious about what a link with an absolute reference looks like in HTML, however, here's a
sample:

`<A HREF="http://www.yahoo.com/">Yahoo</A>`

The first part of this link, the bit between the left (<) and right (>) brackets, is the URL reference. The
word Yahoo is the text anchor that Internet Explorer underlines on the Web page. The last part ends
the link. ■

Part
II

Ch
5

What Types of Resources Links Can Point To

Links can point to more than just Web pages. They can point to a variety of files and other Internet resources, too. A link can point to a video, pictures, or even a plain text file, for example. It can also point to an FTP server, Gopher server, or a UseNet newsgroup. Table 5.1 describes the other types of things a link can point to and shows you what the URL looks like.

Table 5.1 Resources to Which a Link Can Point

Type	Sample URL
Web page	**http://www.mysite.com/page.html**
Files	**file://C:/picture.bmp**
Multimedia	**http://www.mysite.com/video.avi**
E-mail	**mailto:odonnj@rpi.edu**
FTP	**ftp://ftp.mysite.com**
Gopher	**gopher://gopher.mysite.com**
Newsgroup	**news:alt.fan.que**
Telnet	**telnet://mysite.com**

How To Move Around the Web

You didn't buy this book to learn how to load a Web page in Internet Explorer, sit back, and look at it all day. You want to surf the Web—jumping from Web page to Web page looking for entertaining and useful information.

In fact, surfing is such an important part of the Web that both Internet Explorer and the Web itself provide many different ways to navigate. You can use the links and imagemaps—graphics with embedded hypertext links—that you find on a Web page, for example. You can go directly to a Web page if you know its URL. You can also use some of the more advanced Internet Explorer features such as favorite places and frames. In this section, you learn how to use those features to move around the Web like a pro.

Clicking a Link

You learned about links previously in this chapter. They are the primary method you use to go from the Web page you're viewing to another related Web page. All these links are provided by the Web page's author, and are usually accurately related to the context in which you find them.

Figure 5.6 shows a Web page with both text and graphical links. You can click the Big Yellow graphic to go to its Web site. If you use a text link, the next time you see it, its color will change, indicating that you've been there before. This color-changing helps you keep track of the links you haven't visited, so you don't waste any time.

FIG. 5.6
The Microsoft Network home page has both text and graphical anchors for navigating through its Web pages.

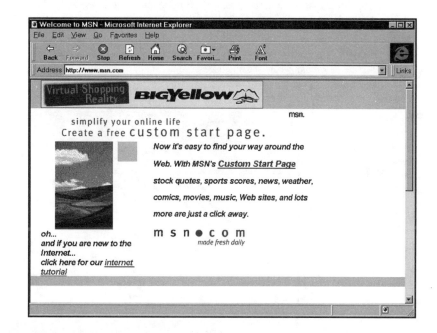

Client Pull on the Web

You may eventually run across a Web page that says something like "We've moved" or "This Web page has a new location." It displays a link that loads the Web page at its new location if you click it. If you wait long enough, however, Internet Explorer may automatically load the Web page at its new location.

Client pull is the technology behind this behavior. Client pull allows the Web server to tell Internet Explorer 3 to reload the current Web page or load a different Web page after a set amount of time. One of the most common uses for client pull is the situation described previously. It's also used for simple sequences of Web pages, however, that work just like slide shows.

Clicking an Imagemap

Imagemaps are similar to graphical anchors, in that if you click an imagemap, Internet Explorer 3 loads another Web page. Imagemaps can load more than one Web page, however, depending on what part of the image you click. The image itself usually indicates the areas you can click to load a particular Web page.

Part
II

Ch
5

Figure 5.7, for example, shows the imagemap that **Windows95.com** uses at its Web site. Each region of the imagemap is clearly defined so that you know where you need to click, and you know what Web page Internet Explorer 3 will load as a result. Click the Win95 Magazine icon, and Internet Explorer 3 loads a Web page containing the latest issue of the *Windows95.com* online magazine. Click the 32-bit Shareware icon, and Internet Explorer 3 loads the shareware Web page.

N O T E   Incidentally, the Windows95.com Web page is enhanced especially for Internet Explorer. If you browse the site and have a sound card and speakers hooked up, get ready for a great background, MIDI sound to play as well! ■

FIG. 5.7

The Windows95.com home page uses an imagemap to navigate through the different parts of its Web site.

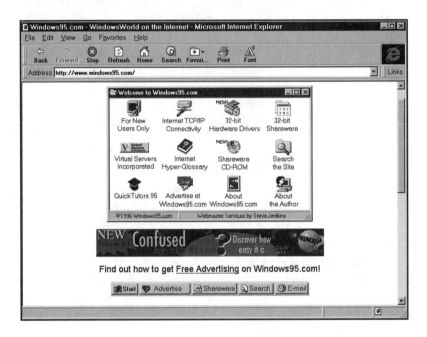

▶ **See** "What Are Imagemaps?" for a description of HTML imagemaps and how to use them, **p. 458**

A common use for imagemaps and graphics images arrayed in a row using tables in a Web page is button bars. *Button bars* are similar to the toolbars you've used in Windows 95 and other windowing environments. They don't appear to click in and out like buttons, however. They are, after all, just graphics. You find them at the top or, more frequently, the bottom of Web pages. Figure 5.8 shows the button bar from the Windows95.com Web site. Notice that each area you can click is clearly defined. You can click different areas to load different Web pages. You can click the Search button to search the Windows95.com, or you can click the Shareware button to check out their shareware collection.

FIG. 5.8
Graphical button bars are popular navigation aids many Web authors include in their Web pages.

T I P If you're having trouble deciphering a button bar, look for text links just below it.

Going Directly to a Resource

Which came first, the link or the Web page? If the only way you could load a Web page was by clicking a link, you would never get anywhere. If a friend gives you a URL, for example, you need a way to tell Internet Explorer 3 to open that Web page without having to use a link. That's why Internet Explorer 3 lets you go directly to a Web page by specifying its URL in the location bar.

T I P URLs are case sensitive. If you can't open a Web page, check for strangely capitalized letters such as **http://www.MywEbsiTe.com**.

Figure 5.9 shows the Internet Explorer location bar with the drop-down list open. Type the URL of a Web page in Internet Explorer's location bar, and Internet Explorer loads the Web page. Internet Explorer keeps the addresses of all the Web pages you've opened this way in the location bar's drop-down list. It keeps this list from session to session, too. That way, you can always go back to that site by dropping down the list and clicking the Web page's URL.

Part
II

Ch
5

FIG. 5.9
The drop-down list keeps track of the Web sites you have visited during the current session.

T I P You don't have to type the **http://** part of a URL in the location bar because Internet Explorer 3 adds it for you.

N O T E Internet Explorer 3 gives you a lot of feedback about what's happening after you click a link or open a URL. The Internet Explorer 3 logo seems to rotate in the upper right corner as it transfers a Web page or file, for example. It also updates the status bar with information that helps you keep track of what Internet Explorer 3 is doing. ■

Moving Forward and Backward

After you've clicked a few links and opened a few Web pages, you may want to go back to a Web page you looked at earlier. Maybe you forgot something you just read, or something didn't seem that interesting then, but it does now. Internet Explorer 3 provides the following two useful features for looking at previously viewed Web pages:

- **The history list**—This keeps track of all the Web pages that you've visited during the current session. You can get at the history list by choosing Go, which shows the most recent Web pages that you've loaded in Internet Explorer (see fig. 5.10). Or, you can get the history list by choosing the Open History Folder at the bottom of the history list. Choosing this option shows the History folder (see fig. 5.11). You can scroll through the list and double-click a Web page to open it in Internet Explorer.

FIG. 5.10

The checkmark in this menu indicates the current Web page.

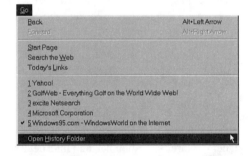

FIG. 5.11

Opening the History folder shows you a history of all of the sites you've ever visited (since the last time you emptied the folder).

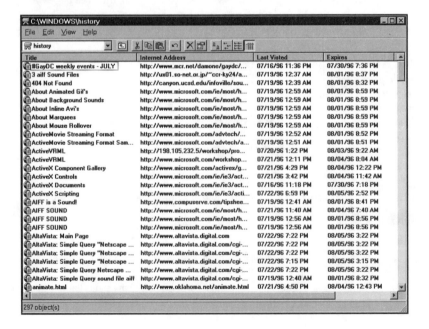

■ **The Forward and Back buttons**—These move you up and down the history list shown in figure 5.10. If you click the Back button, Internet Explorer 3 loads the previous page from the History list. If you click the Forward button, Internet Explorer 3 loads the next one. Once you've reached the bottom of the list, the Back button is disabled. Likewise, when you reach the top of the list, the Forward button is disabled.

 To completely empty your History folder, choose View, Options, select the Navigation tab, and click Clear History.

Going to Your Start Page

If you start feeling a bit lost, getting your bearings is sometimes easier if you go back to your start page—starting over. Internet Explorer 3 lets you configure a start page that it uses for two purposes:

■ Internet Explorer 3 loads your start page every time it starts.

■ At any time, you can click the Home button on the Internet Explorer 3 toolbar to return to your start page.

 Configure your start page to point to a file on your local computer. Then your start page always loads quickly.

To change your start page in Internet Explorer, follow these steps:

1. Load the Web page that you would like to be your start page into Internet Explorer.

2. Choose View, Options from the Internet Explorer main menu. The Options dialog box appears.

3. Click the Navigation tab (see fig. 5.12).

Part

II

Ch

5

FIG. 5.12
Internet Explorer allows you to change the Web page that is loaded when you click the Home or Search toolbar buttons, or any of the Quick Links.

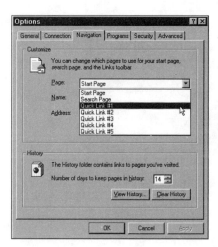

4. Select Start Page from the drop-down list box, and click the Use Current button, or type the URL in the Address field.

5. Click OK to save your changes.

 T I P You can use the same procedure to change the page that is loaded when you click the Search button on the toolbar, or the Links buttons.

N O T E Microsoft usually uses the term *start page* to refer to the first Web page your Web browser opens—another term that many people also use for this is *home page*. The term *home page*, though, also has another meaning. Many people refer to the opening page of a Web site as that site's home page. Hewlett Packard's home page contains links for computers and peripherals, for example. ▧

Quick Links

Internet Explorer 3 also features a row of toolbar buttons called Links. When clicked, these buttons can quickly connect you to a variety of Web sites. The default collection of links takes you to various places on the Microsoft Web site. However, in the same way that you can change the start and search pages, you can also change each of these links. Figure 5.13 shows an example of configuring the first link. After it is changed, the first link on the Links section of the toolbar will take me to my home page (which, on my system, is different than my start page).

FIG. 5.13
Internet Explorer allows you to configure the five buttons in the Links area of the toolbar to quickly send you wherever on the Web you would like to go.

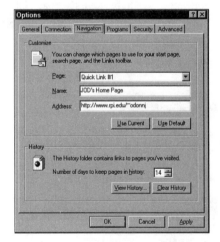

Saving Web Pages as Favorite Places

The easiest way to get back to a Web page that you visit frequently is to use Internet Explorer 3's Favorites menu. By using favorite places, you can save and organize links to your favorite Web pages. Choose Favorites, Open Favorites Folder from the Internet Explorer 3 main menu, or click the Favorite Places toolbar button to open the favorites list (see fig. 5.14).

▶ **See** "Internet Explorer Favorite Places" for an explanation of how to use Microsoft's favorite places, **p. 123**

FIG. 5.14

Open a submenu or click a Web site to load it in Internet Explorer.

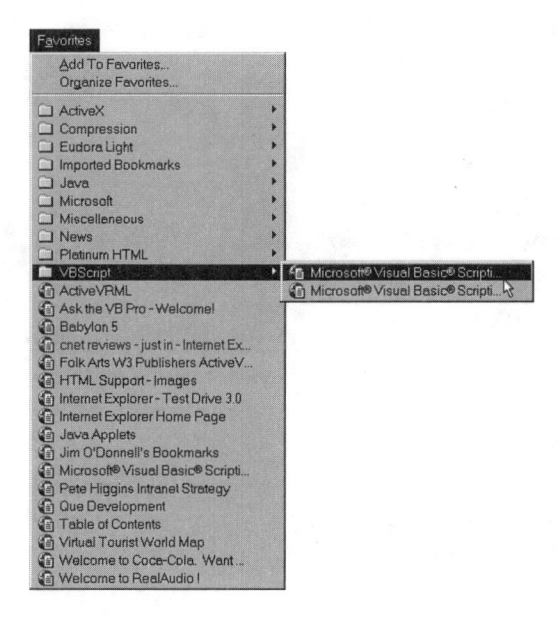

Navigating a Web Site with Frames

Frames, a feature originally introduced by Netscape, are supported by Internet Explorer 3. They allow you to split the Internet Explorer 3 window into multiple sections. Each frame on the window can point to a different URL. Figure 5.15 shows a Web page that uses a frame to present a button bar that's always available to you. Note that Microsoft has itself enhanced Netscape frames, giving the Web author more control over the appearance of each frame. In figure 5.15, you can see three frames, but the Web author has chosen to leave out the telltale gray borders normally present.

Many Windows 95 programs divide their windows into panes. They do so to make the organization of the windows' contents more obvious. A program that performs searches might have two panes: one to display a list of general topics and another for the entry of more specific information. Internet Explorer 3 frames can serve a similar purpose, as well.

Part
II

Ch
5

FIG. 5.15

At this site, the showcase site for the capabilities of Internet Explorer 3, the Volcano Coffee Company banner and the table of contents at the left are always available, regardless of what is being shown in the lower right frame.

Frames

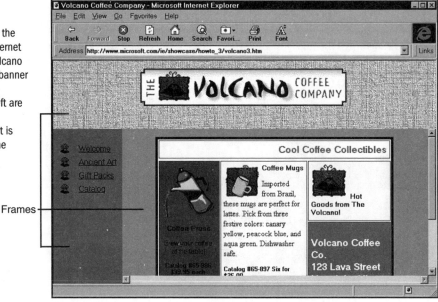

Getting Around Faster

If you're using a 14.4 Kbps or slower modem, you may eventually become frustrated with how long it takes to load some Web pages. Many Web pages have very large graphics that take a long time to download. Unfortunately, the use of large graphics is becoming more common as Web authors take it for granted that everyone on the Internet is using at least a 28.8 Kbps modem.

TIP Many Web sites provide links to text-only versions. Look for a text link that says "Text Only."

If you're having trouble with slow connections, Internet Explorer 3 provides a few features that make Web pages containing too many graphics more tolerable:

■ You don't have to wait for the entire Web page to finish loading before you can click a link. Click the Stop button, and Internet Explorer 3 stops transferring the Web page. If you change your mind and want to reload the page, click the Reload button. Also, most of the text links are available before Internet Explorer 3 has finished transferring the images for the Web page. You can click any of these links. Internet Explorer 3 stops loading the current page and starts loading the Web page referenced by the link.

■ Most of your time is spent waiting for inline images to load. The irony is that the images on many Web pages aren't really worth the time if you have a slow connection. If you don't want Internet Explorer 3 to load inline images automatically, make sure the Show Pictures box under the General tab in the Options dialog box is not checked. If you want to view a particular image, and you've disabled showing the pictures, click the image placeholder. Figure 5.16 shows what a Web page looks like when it's loaded without inline images. Notice that Internet Explorer 3 displays placeholders where it normally displays the images. Internet Explorer 3 also displays alternative text to help you figure out to what the link points. Figure 5.17 shows the same page with all the images loaded.

FIG. 5.16
You can click one of the placeholders to either load the Web page it refers to, if it's a graphical anchor, or to load the image.

Placeholders—

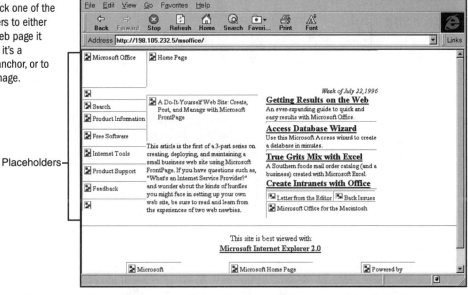

FIG. 5.17
When the inline images are loaded, the Web page looks much more complete but has much the same information.

Part

II

Ch

5

Changing the Way Internet Explorer 3 Works with Links

Internet Explorer 3 gives you a bit of control over how it displays links. It lets you choose whether they're underlined and what color it uses to display them.

Underlining Links

You learned previously in this chapter that Internet Explorer 3 underlines a link's text anchor on a Web page. You can change that. Here's how to configure Internet Explorer 3 so that it doesn't underline a link's text anchor:

1. Choose View, Options from the Internet Explorer 3 main menu. The Internet Properties dialog box appears.
2. Click the General tab.
3. Deselect Underline links, and click OK.

Beginning with the next Web page that Internet Explorer 3 loads, text anchors are not underlined. You can still figure out where the links are, however, because they are displayed in a different color than the text around them.

Using a Different Color for Links

If you don't like the colors that Internet Explorer 3 uses for links, you can change them. If the default colors are hard to tell apart on your computer, for example, you may want to change the colors so that you can easily see the links. You can change the colors Internet Explorer 3 uses for a text link's anchor, by selecting the General tab from the Options dialog box. By clicking the two buttons for Visited links and/or Unvisited links, you can change their colors.

Beginning with the next Web page that Internet Explorer 3 loads, it will display text anchors in the selected color, depending on whether or not you have visited them recently. The period of time considered "recently" can be set by selecting the Navigation tab in the Options dialog box and setting the number of days under Number of Days to Keep Pages in History. ●

Finding Information on the Web

You've probably heard some of the staggering numbers associated with the rise of the Internet and the World Wide Web: 40 million global users increasing by millions each month, millions of Web pages containing countless documents—hundreds of new servers popping up almost daily. How do you navigate through such a vast amount of information? How do you separate the wheat from the chaff (and you can find plenty of both)? What you need is a map. But the Web is so vast and changes so quickly that a map in the usual sense would still be too big to be useful and would almost immediately be out of date.

What you really need is a new kind of map, one that changes continuously with the changes in the Web, and one that gives you the tools to find the information you need on the map. And, in response to that need, the Web has a multitude of services, indexes, and search engines that accomplish just that. If you want to find out what's new on the Web, what's "cool," or information about a specific topic, you have a variety of ways to do it with

How do you specify a start page?

In this chapter, you learn how to change the page that Internet Explorer 3 loads when you start up, and the advantages of the different kinds of start pages.

How can you find what's new and "cool" on the Web?

Learn how to find the new things, the best, and the worst that the World Wide Web has to offer.

How to perform category searches with subject-search tools

Find out how to search through different category databases for information on a given topic, general or specific.

How to find information using the Internet search engines

Discover different search engines to look up information on the Internet, whether it be on Web pages, UseNet newsgroups, or other Internet sources.

The Start Page

What Microsoft calls the *start page* is simply the first Web page that you see when you launch Internet Explorer 3. By default, it is the Microsoft Network Web site, but you have the option of changing your start page to just about any Web page on the Internet you want, as well as to a local (on your computer) HTML file.

> **N O T E** When you upgrade from Internet Explorer version 2 to 3, it is installed in the same directory
> (`C:\Program Files\Plus!\Microsoft Internet`). This way, you retain your current
> start page settings, as well as your Favorite Places folder and any shortcuts you have in your Start
> menu or on your desktop. If you've not yet installed Internet Explorer 3, your start page is set to the
> Microsoft Network Web site. For more information on downloading and installing Microsoft Internet
> Explorer 3, see Chapter 4, "Loading and Configuring Internet Explorer." ■

▶ **See** "Loading Internet Explorer 3" for the steps needed to get Internet Explorer 3 running on your system, **p. 57**

One advantage of using the term "start page" to refer to the initial Web page loaded when you start up your browser is that it leaves the term "home page" free to be used for what has become its other meaning. You may also have seen the term *home page* used in a general sense to describe the main, or first, Web page of other people's and organizations' Web sites on the Internet. This page is also sometimes referred to as the *index page* or *default page* for that site.

Selection of a start page is personal, and it depends on how you use the Web. Whether your interests are business or pleasure—or both—you'll have little problem finding a Web page out there to suit your needs as you begin each browsing session. You do, however, need to know some important things about the start page:

- You can return to your designated start page at any time by clicking the Open Start Page button on the Internet Explorer 3 toolbar.

- The Microsoft Network's own home page (**http://www.msn.com**) isn't bad to use as a start page, especially if you're new to the Web.

- Internet Explorer doesn't load your start page from cache on startup (though it does cache after loading), so expect lag time if you set your start page to a heavily accessed server or URL that has specific time constraints.

- If you copy the source file for a Web page from another site and use it as your start page (loading it off your hard drive), you don't see any changes or updates from the original Web site.

- If you're converting over from Netscape Navigator to Internet Explorer 3, you can set your Navigator bookmarks file as your Internet Explorer start page; this way, you can access your Navigator bookmarks using Internet Explorer 3 (see fig. 6.1).

FIG. 6.1

Using your Netscape Navigator bookmarks file as your Internet Explorer 3 start page is a great way to convert over to using Internet Explorer.

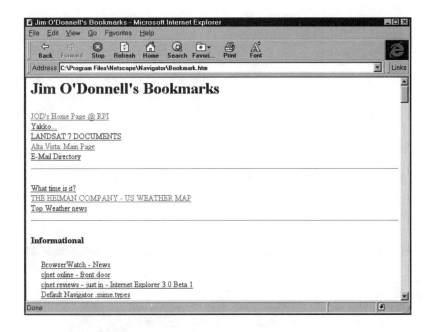

- You can set your start page to bring up any number of files, including Windows 95 applications, helper programs, plug-ins, and Java applets.

Let's look at this process in a bit more detail.

The Open Start Page Button

Clicking the Open Start Page button once takes you to your start page at any time during a browsing session. You can think of the Open Start Page button as a shortcut containing only one hyperlink—a very important link with which you begin your Web session. Loading that page from the Open Start Page button is a bit different, though, than loading it at the start of a session, because of the way Internet Explorer 3 stores the start page in its cache.

Regardless of how you have your cache configured, the first time you load in your start page it does not use the files on your hard drive's cache. Internet Explorer 3 always travels to that first URL, updates the Web page, and then caches its contents in memory. This process is especially important if your start page is an Internet Web site, rather than a local file. Since Internet Explorer 3 must download all the files from your start page without the speed and support of the cache, connecting to a heavily used site or a Web page with a slow server can be frustrating.

N O T E Internet Explorer 3 uses its cache as a configurable. See Chapter 4, "Loading and Configuring Internet Explorer," for more information on how to set up your cache. ■

Part
II
Ch
6

Fortunately, when you click the Open Start Page button and your start page is loaded other than at startup—unless you've designated otherwise—it acts as a regular URL and uses the files from your cache.

The Open Start Page button is a little deceptive—it's a bit more powerful than it lets on. Though you can't move it, assign a macro to it, or change its appearance, you can use it to launch a number of Windows 95 files, as well as files that use a helper application, plug-ins, or Java applets. You will see more about that in a moment. For now, let's take a close look at some of the benefits of using Internet Explorer's own (default) home page as your start page.

Using the Microsoft Network Home Page

The default start page for Internet Explorer 3 takes you to the Web site of the Microsoft Network, located at **http://www.msn.com/** (see fig. 6.2).

FIG. 6.2
The Microsoft Network Web site gives access to a wide variety of information, software, and services, both within and without Microsoft .

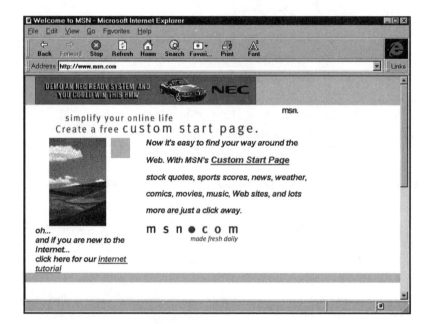

The Microsoft Network Web site offers a variety of resources and features a clickable image map with the following options:

- **Microsoft Products**—This option gives information about the wide range of computer software products from Microsoft.

- **Product Support**—This option is a good link to follow if you have questions or need information about a Microsoft product.

- **Software Downloads**—This option gives you access to a wide range of downloadable software—applications, utilities, drivers, macros, and so on.

- **Tutorial**—Clicking the Tutorial link gives you access to Microsoft's Internet tutorial.
- **Searches**—This option sends you to the Microsoft page that gives you access to a collection of Web search engines, such as Excite, Infoseek, and Yahoo. These search engines are discussed later in this chapter.
- **Services**—This option contains groups of links to other Web sites with many useful services in such categories as financial information, phone and address lookup services, and writer's reference information, among others.
- **Links**—This option is Microsoft's version of the Netscape What's Cool! Web site, giving links to sites that folks at Microsoft consider noteworthy in a collection of different topics.
- **About MSN**—This option gives information about the Microsoft Network.

N O T E   Reloading the Microsoft Network home page is faster than ever because the main imagemap that contains the most important links is now stored in your cache. For more details on client-side imagemaps, see Chapter 24, "Using Imagemaps."

▶ **See** "Client-Side Imagemaps" for information on using client-side imagemaps, and their advantages over server-side ones, **p. 466**

A unique feature of the Microsoft Network home page supported by Internet Explorer 3 is the ability to customize the page to include a variety of links that you choose.

▶ **See** "Customizing the Microsoft Network Start Page" to learn all about how to set up customized Web pages from sites that offer them, **p. 140**

Finding New and "Cool" Web Sites

Users of Netscape Navigator are familiar with its directory buttons, specifically the What's New! and What's Cool! buttons. While Internet Explorer 3 doesn't have these buttons, you can certainly browse these Web sites (and even install them as Internet Explorer Favorite Places). Also, a host of other Web rating services keep lists of the newest and best that the Web has to offer. Some places even keep track of the "Worst of the Web."

What's New on the Web   To access the Netscape What's New! Web page in Internet Explorer, go to **http://home.netscape.com/home/whats-new.html**.

Once there, you see an assortment of new Internet resources, archived monthly. This site is an excellent place for introducing you to new Web sites; it gives you a good feel for just how fast the surface of the Web is spinning. Also, Netscape is interested in hearing about any new Web sites that you would like to tell them about. A typical What's New! page looks like the one shown in figure 6.3.

Part II

Ch 6

FIG. 6.3
This list of the latest sites is compiled by the folks at Netscape.

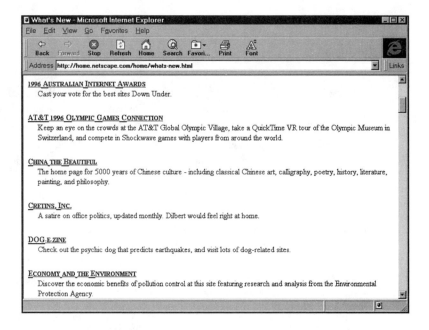

Another list of new sites is also maintained by Yahoo, home of one of the longest-running search engines on the Web. The Yahoo What's New site is available by clicking the What's New button at the Yahoo Web site, located at **http://www.yahoo.com/** (see fig. 6.4).

FIG. 6.4
The Yahoo new Web pages site contains an extensive list of new sites and allows you to view them listed by category.

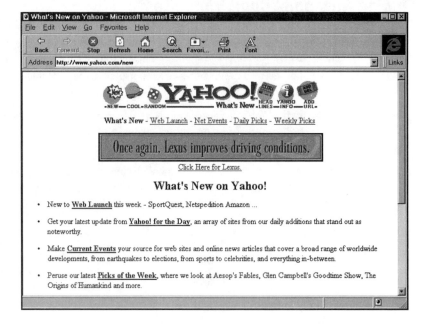

Notice that the Yahoo site offers a little more coverage and organization, enabling you to look at a greater number of Web sites, and also offering them to you listed by category.

TIP Want some other examples of What's New sites? To keep up with the latest software on the Net, point your browser to Stroud's WSApps List at **http://www.frontiernet.net/cwsapps/** and Tucows at **http://www.tucows.com/**. Both of these sites are meticulously maintained and updated daily, include reviews of the newest and best programs, and have direct links to FTP sites to download the freeware and shareware.

What's Cool on the Web   In addition to the Links option on the Microsoft Network Web page, shown in figure 6.2, which gives a list of quality Web sites as selected by Microsoft, both Netscape and Yahoo also maintain lists of "what's cool." The Netscape site is at **http://home.netscape.com/home/whats-cool.html**.

The Yahoo site is also available through their Web site. Note that, as with the new Web sites listing, the Yahoo list has greater coverage and greater organization than the one from either Netscape or Microsoft.

Worst of the Web   Just as the newest, best, and most innovative Web sites are noticed and promoted, so too are the ones at the other end of the spectrum. A number of ratings services—most of them with tongues firmly planted in cheeks—seek out and honor those Web sites that are so bad that they're good. An example is Mirsky's Worst of the Web, located at **http://mirsky.com/wow/** (see fig. 6.5).

FIG. 6.5
To see Web sites so bad that they're good—like a good B movie—visit Mirsky's Worst of the Web.

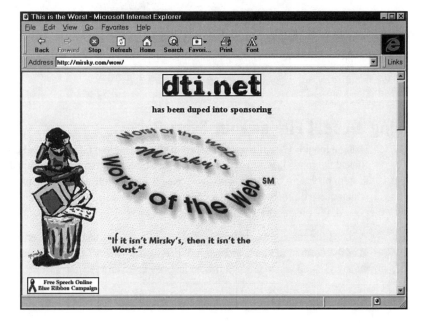

Part
II

Ch
6

Using Another Start Page

As comprehensive and customizable as the Microsoft Network Web page is, you'll probably, at some point, find another you like better. You may discover that you change your start page as your needs change. You can set your start page to load any valid, accessible URL on the Internet. And doing so is as easy as a few clicks. Just remember to watch out for slow servers or heavy Web sites—otherwise, you'll become more intimate with the Stop button than you probably want to be.

To change your start page settings, load the URL of the page you want to use, and choose View, Options. The Option dialog box appears. Select the Navigation tab (see fig. 6.6). Make sure the drop-down list box reads Start Page, and then click Use Current. Your start page is then set to the current page. To return to the default, the Web page for the Microsoft Network, click the Use Default button.

FIG. 6.6
This dialog box allows you to change the start page Internet Explorer 3 loads when it is first run or when you click the Open Start Page button.

Using a Local File as Your Start Page

Using a local HTML file on your hard drive as your start page offers some distinct advantages. A local file loads fast and always loads (barring a badly fragmented hard drive or other local system problem). Again, a heavily accessed site sometimes means loading a remote start page, which takes quite awhile. And, even if you specify a URL on the Web that's not heavily accessed, the site's server may possibly be down.

Perhaps the most important advantage to a local start page, however, is the control it gives you over the content of your start page. Write your own start page, and you can include exactly what you need and want—your own favorite links and graphics.

Finding the Internet—On Your Own Computer

When we talk about a local file, we're talking about a client-side file. If your computer is capable of only connecting to other computers but cannot be accessed by any other machines, it is a *client*. If your computer can be accessed by other machines via the Internet or any network, it is referred to as a *server*.

Part of the evolution of the Web is its move toward an environment where its computers can be both clients and servers. As technologies like ISDN, wireless systems, coaxial cable, and optical fiber evolve—as bandwidth increases—a stronger server base emerges. Still, applications run much faster on your own system than if the bytes are moving through a data link. And, however quickly they grow, the faster access speeds will never be faster than your computer's processor.

The need for a large client-based cache that's updated only at user-specified intervals makes a lot of sense, then, while larger storage devices allow the server to make more interactive, snazzier content available to everyone else out there. This is especially feasible now, when storage devices (hard drives and CD-ROMs) sell for a tiny fraction of what they did a decade ago. For both clients and servers, the ready availability of electronic storage results in less reliance on the bandwidth of the connection.

What does this mean? It means that in the future, in order to support new ways of finding and using the information and resources on the Internet, you'll store more and more HTML (Web) pages, graphics, videos, audio, applets, and so forth on your own computer. As directories and indexes evolve, and as search engines and the like become more intelligent, interactive, and flexible, you'll need more and more of your own client computing power and storage to make your search for information as painless and fun as possible.

Downloading a Web Page To Use as a Start Page Of course, to specify a local file for your start page, you've got to have a file. One option is to create your own HTML page and use it as your start page.

N O T E Controlling just how you want to display your start page is an exciting idea—and a lot easier to do than you may realize. Part IV of this book shows you how to design and create your own Web pages. ■

Another option is to save the source code to any one of the millions and millions of URLs your browser can access. If you spend even a few minutes a day on the Web—and you may spend far more time than that—you'll have already lost count of the number of Web pages you've visited. Just point your browser to the Web page you want to save and follow these steps:

1. With the page you want saved displayed in Internet Explorer 3, open the File menu and choose Save As File. The familiar Windows 95 Save As directory box appears.
2. Select the directory or subdirectory where the file will reside using the Save in drop-down menu.
3. Enter a name for the file.
4. Select the file type in the Save as Type drop-down menu. In this case, you want source option.
5. Click the Save button, and the file will be downloaded to the location you specified.

Part
II

Ch
6

To verify that the page was downloaded successfully, go ahead and load it into Internet Explorer 3. Click in the location bar, and type in the filename of the file you just saved. Your copy of this Web page is then loaded. You may notice, too, that your copy of the Web page has changed. Any inline graphics or other URL references contained in the Web page are not downloaded.

TIP If you don't want to type in the full filename, just enter the drive letter—**C:**, for example—and Internet Explorer 3 gives you a Windows 95 Explorer window through which you can browse to find your file.

Selecting a Local File as Your Start Page   Loading a local file as your start page follows the same procedure as specifying any other URL. First, load the local file into Internet Explorer 3, and choose <u>V</u>iew, <u>O</u>ptions. The Options dialog box appears. Select the Navigation tab, and click the <u>U</u>se Current button making sure that Start Page shows in the drop-down list box.

This procedure is the one you would follow to specify your old Netscape Navigator bookmarks file as your Internet Explorer 3 start page, a good way to make the transition from one Web browser to the other. If you used the default installation for Netscape Navigator, you can load its bookmarks file by entering **C:\Program Files\Netscape\Navigator\Bookmarks.html** into the location bar.

Starting Other Files with Your Start Page

As you learned earlier, if the Web page you saved from the Internet has any graphics or other media besides text, you get a surprise when you load that file—Internet Explorer 3 does not load in the other media with your start page. The reason for this is simple.

The file you saved, of course, is an HTML file. Within the file are references to other files—graphics files—that were stored at the original server you downloaded from. The *tags*—the codes that HTML uses to display a document—within the HTML page gave the location of these files so that Internet Explorer would know where to find them when displaying the page.

Unfortunately, when you saved the HTML file, Internet Explorer did not save the graphics as specific files in the same directory, nor did it do anything to change the code so the references would be renamed to work correctly on your hard drive. You can fix the problem in two ways:

- Return to the Web page at its original URL. Right-click each graphic within that page one at a time, and use the Save Target <u>A</u>s option to save each picture to the same directory that holds the HTML file.

- Open up Internet Explorer's cache subdirectory in Windows Explorer and find the files, which are saved in the directory under their original filenames. Copy each file to the same directory you used for your HTML file.

If this process sounds a bit complicated, don't worry; it is a lot easier than it seems. And, if you're new to HTML document writing, this process will make a lot more sense after you read Part IV of this book to learn how graphics are referenced in HTML files. But, since HTML is not much more difficult than using your favorite word processor, you shouldn't have much trouble.

Launching Helpers, Plug-Ins, and Other Files

As you become experienced with the Web and begin to see some of its exciting new ways to deliver information, you may want to spruce up your start page with other applications. Though using a video or audio file to start your Web session isn't very practical (remember, though, the file is also tied to your Open Start Page button, and you can click the button any time you choose), you may find a plug-in or Java applet works better than a regular HTML page, depending on your particular needs.

For example, if you play the stock market and an available Java applet updates a small spreadsheet to keep you informed of the daily averages, you may want to begin each session with this important information. Or you may want to start off your Web session in three dimensions—using a VRML plug-in, you may intuitively find your favorite links quicker, easier, and a lot more fun. With the functionality and level of interactivity that Java and VRML promise to offer the Web, the possibilities are endless.

▶ **See** "Configuring a Helper Application" for information on how to configure Internet Explorer 3 to use helper applications, **p. 244**

▶ **See** "Using VRML and ActiveVRML" for a primer on the Virtual Reality Modeling Language (VRML), **p. 325**

▶ **See** "Sun's Java and Internet Explorer" to learn about Internet Explorer 3's support for Sun's Java language, **p. 607**

Run Your Other Windows 95 Apps from the Open Start Page Button

You can specify a number of other local files in Windows 95 to load from your Open Start Page button. More specifically, since Internet Explorer 3 communicates directly with the registry in Windows 95, it recognizes file extension associations located there—with the exception of executable files—and loads the associated application that supports your file. (Actually, Internet Explorer 3 also recognizes the executables directly, but you have to disable the Octet-stream MIME that still doesn't work exactly right. The result is not worth the effort.)

For example, if you want to launch a Microsoft Word document (and, by association, Microsoft Word) from your Open Start Page button, you can simply enter **c:\directory\subdirectory\filename.doc** into the location bar, where **c** is the name of the drive the file is located in. Then you can set this document as your Internet Explorer 3 start page.

Internet Explorer 3 recognizes the file extension and has Windows launch Microsoft Word along with the document. Of course, it loads not only when you click the Open Start Page button but also loads at your start page every time you start Internet Explorer 3.

Part

II

Ch

6

Net Directory: Searching the Internet by Subject

Without question, using Internet Explorer 3 and the World Wide Web is the way of the immediate future on the Internet, and it's an amazing tool for gathering information. The Web metaphor, in fact, with its links spiraling out into the unknown, is an ingenious method of information retrieval—if only because it mimics the way most humans think—relationally.

But sometimes information on the Net can feel a little disorganized. Especially when you're on a deadline or sick of surfing to find something. If you've ever used Gopher for information retrieval, then maybe you're feeling a bit nostalgic. Can't the Web be organized somehow?

You can use a wide variety of Web directory pages to search the Internet by subject. Using these pages, you are almost guaranteed to save hours of surfing frustration more than once in your Web life. What do we mean by *directory*? Directories generally provide an editorial service—they determine the best sites around the Web and include them in categorized listings to make finding information easier. Some directories actually combine two features: a directory of categorized sites and a search engine for searching both the category listing and the Internet.

A number of directories are available. The most familiar is Yahoo, known by many as the most outstanding attempt at organizing the Web yet. The following are descriptions of Yahoo and some of the other Web page directories:

- **Yahoo**—This directory is the grandfather of Internet guides. Easily the most comprehensive attempt at creating a table of contents for the Internet, Yahoo lets you get directly at listings of Web sites by category. Internet users send submissions to Yahoo, whose editors screen the sites for suitability. Many sites aren't covered in Yahoo, but many of the quality sites are.

- **The McKinley Internet Directory**—This directory lists a database of World Wide Web, Gopher, FTP, Telnet, and newsgroup and mailing-list links that are divided into categories. The database is searchable, and the sites are rated by an editorial team.

- **Point**—This directory offers reviews of what they consider to be the top five percent of Internet sites. Sites are also allowed to submit their own selling copy, which is edited.

- **World Wide Arts Resources**—This directory offers a digital outlet for more than 2,000 artists. This index page for the arts features links to galleries, museums, arts sites, an antiques database, and arts-related educational and governmental sites.

- **World Wide Web Servers**—This directory offers a huge listing of Web servers. United States servers are listed by state.

- **Virtual Tourist**—This directory is similar to the World Wide Web Servers information but is presented as a clickable graphical map.

The Yahoo Directory

The Yahoo Internet directory was created in April 1994 by David Filo and Jerry Yang, two Ph.D. candidates in Electrical Engineering at Stanford University, as a way to keep track of their personal interests on the Internet. The directory grew quickly in popularity after they made it available to the public and spent more and more time organizing sites into their hierarchy. In early 1995, Netscape Corp. invited Filo and Yang to move their files from Stanford's network to computers housed at Netscape.

Using Yahoo is a little like shopping for the best Internet sites. Instead of blindly following links to different Web sites, hoping that you'll eventually come across one that's interesting, you deal with Yahoo's pages for a while. As you move deeper through Yahoo's menu-style links, you get closer to Web sites that interest you.

 Although Yahoo's primary role is as a directory for the Web, it also offers access to breaking Reuters NewMedia newswire stories. If you're a newshound, click the Headlines button at the top of Yahoo's index page.

First, you need to get to Yahoo. As you learned earlier, Yahoo is at **http://www.yahoo.com/**.

Starting at the top-most level, you choose the category of Web site you're interested in seeing—for instance, Computers and Internet.

 You might want to make Yahoo one of your Internet Explorer favorite places, your start page, or your Internet Explorer search page (you'll learn how to set it in the section "The Internet Explorer 3 Search Button," later in this chapter).

▶ **See** "Creating Favorite Places" to find out how to use Microsoft's Favorite Places menu to remember Web sites, **p. 126**

From there, it's as easy as clicking your way through the hierarchy as you get closer and closer to the type of site you're trying to find. In figure 6.7, for instance, we've moved down the line a little bit, having chosen to view Entertainment, Television Shows, all the way down to Babylon 5. Now you can see a listing of different pages on that topic, each with a small summary of what they contain.

FIG. 6.7
Digging a little deeper into Yahoo gets you closer to the Web sites you're seeking.

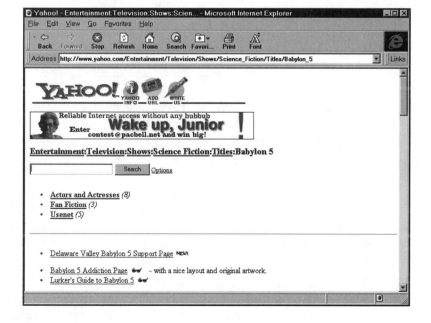

Part

II

Ch

6

How Yahoo Works   What you first notice about the Yahoo directory is its top categories. These categories, determined by the folks who designed Yahoo, are the basic structure of the table of contents approach. But how do you get your Web site included in this hierarchy?

Web site creators decide what category they feel is most appropriate for their Web site's inclusion in the directory. Once you get to the part of the directory you'd like your site to appear in, you click the Add URL button at the top of Yahoo's interface. You're then asked by Yahoo to fill out a Web form with information on its site, the URL, a contact's address, and other tidbits (see fig. 6.8). After reviewing the entry, Yahoo's staff decides if the site merits inclusion.

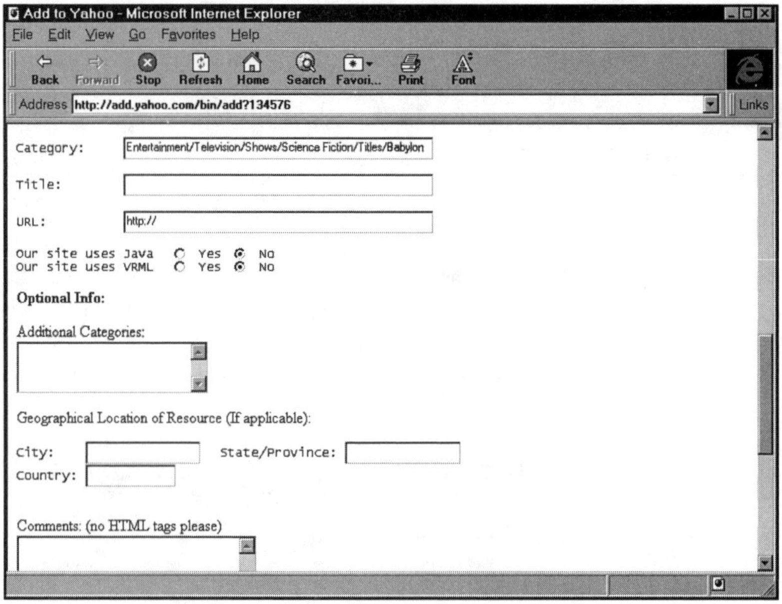

FIG. 6.8

Submitting your own Web site for inclusion in the Yahoo directory.

Why is this important? Two reasons. First, whether you're a Web user or a Web creator, it's significant to recognize that being included in the Yahoo directory is something of a make-or-break proposition. That's not to say that you can't have a successful site if you're not in the Yahoo directory (or that it will be successful just because it does get included). But being in the Yahoo directory does, at least in a sense, suggest that you've arrived.

Second, it's important to note that being in the Yahoo directory is something you generally have to seek actively. These sites, then, want to be accessed. A lot of these sites are high-traffic areas with broad appeal; in fact, a good percentage of them are commercial sites. That is by no means always bad, but you should recognize that it is a limitation to what you'll find using the Yahoo directory.

Searching with Yahoo   Clicking through the directory isn't the only way to get at Yahoo's listed sites. You also can use a basic search engine that uses keywords to find interesting pages for you. Where do you do this searching? From Yahoo's main index page, you enter a search phrase in the text box that sits above the category listings.

The search phrase can simply be a few keywords to help Yahoo limit the search. Using this search engine takes some experimentation (as it does with all the Internet search engines), and we'll discuss that in the section "Net Search: Searching on the Interent," later in this chapter. This simple search from the Yahoo index page assumes you want to find all the keywords you enter. By default, it searches the names, URLs, and descriptions of all its Web pages.

What results from this search is a list of possible matches in Yahoo's database, with hypertext links to the described pages (see fig. 6.9). It gives you an opportunity to look at a number of different pages that may or may not include the information you're seeking.

FIG. 6.9
On the Yahoo search results page, each of these results is actually a link to the site that's being described.

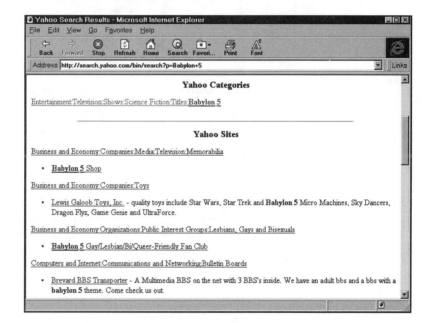

The McKinley Internet Directory, Magellan

Offered by the McKinley Group, Magellan is another Internet directory and search service (see fig. 6.10). You can find Magellan at **http://www.mckinley.com/**.

It offers a listing of over 1,000,000 sites—30,000 of which are reviewed, evaluated, and rated Web, Telnet, Gopher, and FTP sites. Like Yahoo, Magellan allows you to search its database directly for links that match certain keywords. You can also access the staff's recommended sites through a hierarchy of menus.

Magellan isn't quite identical to Yahoo. It's both less and more of a directory than Yahoo is. While searching is more tightly integrated into the directory portion of Magellan, it does offer more description and recommendations than Yahoo does—at least for a limited number of sites.

Part
II

Ch
6

FIG. 6.10

From Magellan's index page, you can search over 1,000,000 sites or browse around 30,000 reviewed sites.

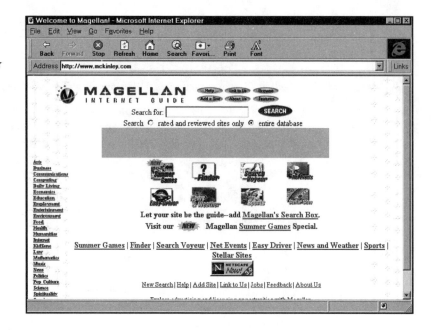

Browsing the Magellan Directory   If you're looking for some of the best possible sites on the Internet, choose the Browse Categories link on Magellan's index page. You get a listing of categories to choose from, much like Yahoo's directory. Eventually, you'll dig deep enough to find some sites that have been reviewed by the McKinley Group staff (see fig. 6.11). Here, you'll see that many of the sites have been given a star rating to let you know how useful and impressive that particular site is.

Notice also that you can limit the number of reviewed sites that appear in the listing by entering keywords at the top of the page and clicking the Focus Search button. Doing so results in fewer listings in a particular category—most of which, hopefully, will include information that interests you.

Searching Magellan   As mentioned previously, you can also search Magellan for interesting Web sites. To begin a search, enter a search phrase in the text box on Magellan's index page, and click the Search Magellan button. That's it! The results of your search will appear in your browser window.

Point

Point is another widely recognized repository of Internet site reviews. Claiming to have links to the "top five percent" of Internet sites, Point is a great place to find some quality sites on the Web (see fig. 6.12). To see a directory of the reviews that Point has to offer, click once on the Top 5% Reviews graphic in the middle of Point's index page interface. Point's index page can be found at **http://www.pointcom.com/**.

FIG. 6.11
After choosing a category and executing a search, you can look at the results or focus the search further.

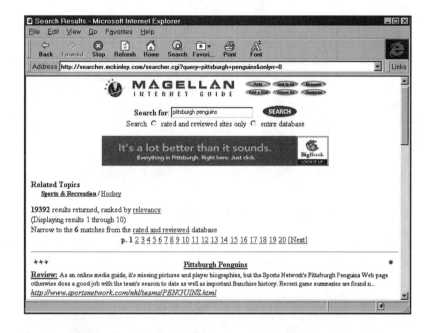

FIG. 6.12
Point offers reviews of what it considers to be the best Internet sites in various categories.

Part
II

Ch

6

The reviews can sometimes be a little irreverent, fun, and pointed (no pun intended!). Internet sites can also submit their own descriptions, which are duly edited. You search the reviews using keywords via the Point Search feature. If you want to submit your site for inclusion in Point's listing, you use the Submit feature.

N O T E Point Communications, which puts out the Point directory and ratings, has been acquired by Lycos, one of the premier search engines on the Internet. According to the Point index page, this acquisition gives you access not only to the top five percent of sites but, through Lycos, access to 90 percent of all the Internet sites around the world. You learn more about Lycos in the section "Net Search: Searching on the Internet," later in this chapter. ▪

The Best of the Rest

Other Internet directories are available besides the ones discussed in this chapter. They're a little more specialized, but, if you're interested, you may find tons of links to the kinds of sites you want to visit.

World Wide Arts Resources For anyone interested in the arts, World Wide Arts Resources offers access to galleries, museums, an antiques database, related arts sites, as well as arts-related educational and governmental sites. The directory also presents the digital work of over 2,000 artists. A variety of resources, which have been actively compiled for well over a year now, are available within the directory. The World Wide Arts Resources page can be found at **http://wwar.com/default.html**.

For example, if you are looking for the work of a particular artist, then use the Artist Index. Other resources include Art Galleries & Exhibits; Museums, for international listings; USA Museums, which features a 20-page preview and has categorized both the museums and what is available at those museums; Important Arts Resources, which lists related arts sites; and Arts Publications, which features both electronic and conventional publications.

World Wide Web Servers The World Wide Web Servers directory is a huge list of available Web servers from the CERN educational institution. You can access it through **http://www.w3.org/pub/WWW/**.

The servers are presented alphabetically by continent, country, and state. Clicking the top level country, for instance, lets you "drill-down" to the next geographic level, where you find listings of individual servers according to region.

North America is subdivided into states, which are listed alphabetically. Also available is a listing of federal government servers for North America. The directory is actually a listing of HTTP (HyperText Transmission Protocol) servers whose administrators have sent requests to **www-request@w3.org** and other sites.

Virtual Tourist The Virtual Tourist is similar in content to the World Wide Web Servers directory but is presented in a visually appealing clickable map (see fig. 6.13).

When you click a specific area of the map, another screen appears to help you narrow down your search for geographically sited Web servers. The Virtual Tourist is at **http://www.vtourist.com/webmap/**.

N O T E Information about individual countries and states is not provided by Virtual Tourist. That sort of information is evidently available in The Virtual Tourist II, which is operated in cooperation with City.Net. The Virtual Tourist II can be found at **http://www.vtourist.com/vt/**. ▪

FIG. 6.13
Virtual Tourist offers a
clickable map listing of
Web servers around the
world.

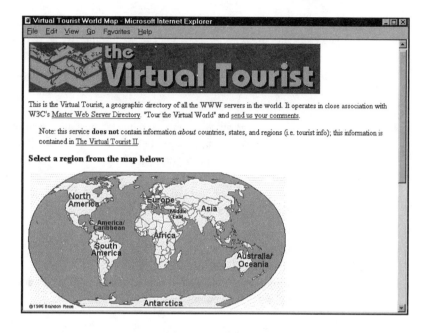

Net Search: Searching on the Internet

Like the search-by-subject directories discussed in the preceding sections, other sites that allow you to search aspects of the Internet in other ways also exist. Although some of these services overlap with the directories we discussed in the preceding section, you may find that all of these sites are more oriented toward searching—and less interested in editorializing. For the most part, these search engines are here to help you find keywords in titles of Web pages. You don't see many reviews in these pages. You do, however, see hundreds of results to your queries—chosen from among millions and millions of possible Web pages.

A number of useful search engines offer a variety of search techniques; for example, some search headers and document titles, some search their own extensive indexes of Internet documents and pages, and others rummage through the Internet itself.

The different search options available in Net Search are discussed in the next section. Here are some of the more popular engines:

■ **Infoseek Search**—This engine allows you to search the Web using plain English or keywords and phrases. Special query operators let you customize your search. Results include the first few lines from each Web site—often making it clear how your keyword is used and, thus, whether a site is actually interesting to you.

■ **The Lycos Home Page**—This extremely comprehensive search engine reportedly features a database of millions of link descriptors and documents. The engine searches links, headings, and titles for keywords you enter. It also offers different search options.

Part

II

Ch

6

- **WebCrawler**—This engine lets you search by document title and content using words you enter into the search box. It's not as comprehensive as Lycos, but it's a quick and easy way to find a few hundred sites that match your keywords.
- **Deja News Research Service**—This engine allows you to search UseNet newsgroups in, what the company claims is, the world's largest UseNet news archive. A variety of search options are available.
- **Excite**—This engine allows you to search a database with over one million Web documents. You can also search through the past two week's worth of classified ads and UseNet news. Internet site content quality evaluations are also available through Excite.
- **W3 Search Engines**—This engine offers a variety of topics and subjects from the University of Geneva, although the list is not updated as often as the more mainstream search engine databases.
- **Alta Vista**—Alta Vista, operated by Digital Equipment Corporation, gives you access to over 30 million Web pages and millions of UseNet news articles. It is simple to use, but also offers sophisticated search and ranking options for advanced searches.
- **CUSI (Configurable Unified Search Interface)**—This engine features a single form to search different Web engines, provided by Nexor U.K.

How These Search Engines Work

Each one of these search services on the Net Search page is designed to give you access to a database of information related to Internet sites around the world. Some are Web-specific (such as Lycos and WebCrawler) while others, such as Infoseek and Excite, allow you to search not only Web pages but also UseNet newsgroups, online publications, and other archives of information.

What all of these search engines do have in common is that they require you to come up with keywords to facilitate the search. There's definitely an art to this search—the more you try it, the more you'll see that it takes some patience and creativity. Let's discuss some of the basic concepts.

The key to a good search is good keywords. What you're trying to do is come up with unique words or phrases that appear only in the documents you want to access. For instance, one thing to definitely avoid are common terms such as *www, computer, Internet, PC, Mac*, and so on. These terms come up time and again on pages that may or may not have material that interests you. Also consider that words like *Mac* not only appear in words like *Macintosh* but also in *Mace, Mach, Machine, Macaroni*, and so on. You'll probably get a lot of bizarre results with such a common keyword. Articles and common English words like *a, an, the, many, any*, and others are generally unnecessary.

Most of these search engines also give you a choice of Boolean operators to use between keywords (AND, OR, NOT). Take care that you understand how these operators work. If you enter them yourself (in the search phrase text box), then an example might be **Windows AND shareware NOT Mac**.

This search results in pages that discuss shareware programs for Microsoft Windows, while it eliminates pages that include the word *Mac*, even if they also discuss Windows shareware. Remember that AND and NOT are used to limit searches; OR is used to widen them. Notice, for instance, that **Ford OR Mustang** generates many more results than either **Ford AND Mustang** or **Ford NOT Mustang**.

Presumably, the first returns only pages that have references to both, while the second returns pages that do reference *Ford* but do not reference *Mustang*.

Infoseek Search

Infoseek is a very popular search engine that generates not only search results but also offers the first few lines from pages to help you determine if a Web site may have what you need before you leave Infoseek to view it. While this capability can often save you time, the way Infoseek reports its results (a maximum of 100 results, ten to a page) can take a little while to flip through. Infoseek, therefore, is really designed for digging deep for a subject—perhaps when you've had less luck with other search engines. You can access Infoseek at **http:// www.infoseek.com/**.

This way, you can quickly get to the Infoseek index page, which offers a text box for entering your search criterion and also includes a quick directory of popular sites (see fig. 6.14).

FIG. 6.14

Infoseek allows you to enter search criteria or look through different topics.

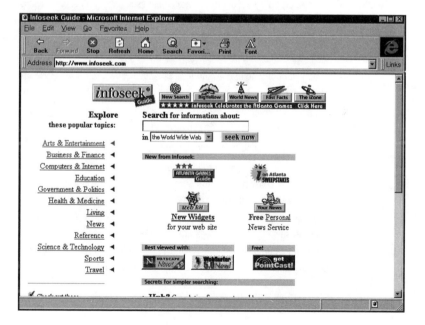

Part

II

Ch

6

Infoseek is very easy to search. Simply enter keywords in the text box and click the Search button. Infoseek assumes an AND between each of your keywords, although it returns pages that don't include every keyword. Capitalization is important, though, so capitalize only words that you want recognized as proper nouns.

Infoseek offers this ability to search the Internet as a free service to the Internet community; however, free searches are limited to 100 results per search, and they don't cover the breadth of services that Infoseek offers. Infoseek's commercial searching accounts may end up being something that interests you, and more information is provided on their Web site.

Advanced Infoseek Searches

At its most basic, Infoseek is a quick and easy way to search the Internet. In fact, it's one of the few search engines that doesn't offer an advanced page with more control over the results. What you see is basically what you get with Infoseek. That is, at least, until you dig a little deeper. Then you realize that you can do some customizing to your searches. It all takes place in your search phrase (what you enter in the text box). The following guidelines may help you get faster, and more reliable, results:

- Before authorizing any search for documents on the Internet, make sure no misspelled words and typographical errors appear in the text box.

- Don't use characters such as an asterisk (*) as wildcards.

- In Infoseek, unlike some other search engines such as Lycos, don't use Boolean operators such as AND and OR between search words because it looks at all words as search terms.

- When searching for documents, try both word variations (plural, adjective, and noun forms of the same word) and synonyms.

- If you want both the upper- and lowercase occurrences of a term, use only the lowercase word in the search text box.

- You need to separate capitalized names with a comma (for example: **Bill Gates, Microsoft**). You can also use a comma to separate phrases and capitalized names from each other.

- Quotation marks and hyphens can be used to identify a phrase.

- You can use a plus sign (+) to distinguish terms that should appear in every document. The + appears at the beginning of the term, with no space before the first letter of the first word (for example: **+skiing Colorado, Utah**).

- As an alternative to a plus sign, you can use a minus sign (−) to designate phrases or words not to be included in any document. This capability is useful if you have a word that is often used with another word in unison, but you want only documents containing the word and not both words to be retrieved (for example: **desktop − computer**).

Lycos

Lycos is a comprehensive and accurate search engine that is also very popular. It consists of a huge catalog with over 34 million URLs. As a result, you may find it often too busy to let you use it, especially during peak business hours. However, it is worth the wait.

Lycos was developed at Carnegie-Mellon University in Pittsburgh. In June 1995, Lycos Inc. was formed to develop and market the Lycos technology. Lycos Inc. says that Lycos will remain free to Internet users, although, as a commercial venture, it will gain revenue from advertising and licensing the Lycos catalog and search technologies. Non-exclusive license holders of the Lycos technology already include Frontier Technologies and Library Corp., as well as Microsoft Corporation for use in the company's newly introduced Microsoft Network online service. Lycos is located at **http://www.lycos.com/**.

Searching with Lycos   The Lycos interface is similar to Infoseek's in that you can just enter words and click the Search button. However, Lycos includes more options and contains a much larger database of indexed Web documents. You can begin by going to the Lycos Web site. There, you find the Lycos index page, where your search begins. A simple Lycos search works just like most of the other search engines. Enter your search keywords in the text box, and click the Search button. Lycos finds any pages or documents matching any of the words you type into the search box.

For a more advanced search, choose the Search Options button next to the text box on Lycos's index page. Now you're presented with a new page, where you can spend a little more time tailoring your search (see fig. 6.15).

FIG. 6.15

The Lycos Search Options page allows you to specify a more advanced search.

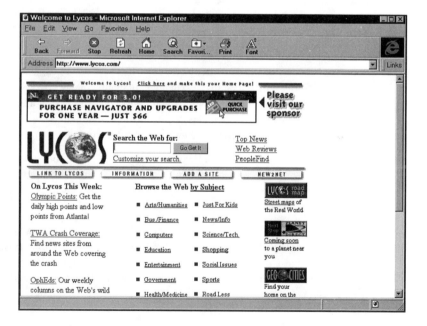

On this page, you can take a little more control of the search phrase. For instance, if you enter a number of keywords, and you want to expand the search to show pages that match any of your keywords, pull down the first Search Options menu and choose Match Any Term. You can also choose to match a certain number of keywords with this same menu.

Part

II

Ch

6

TIP If you're unsure how a keyword is spelled, type in a couple of different ways you think it might appear, and then choose to match the number of terms that you know are spelled correctly. For instance, entering **Heron Hearon Huron senate candidate** and then selecting to match three terms would give you a good chance of finding information about this public figure whose name you may not know how to spell.

The second Search Options pull-down menu allows you to specify if you want close or not-so-close matches. If you are really just fishing for some leads as to where to concentrate your next search, make sure the Loose Match option is selected from the second Search Options menu. If you are pretty sure of the search criteria you typed in the query box, then select Strong Match. A number of choices appear in between, each becoming about 20 percent more lenient as you move down the list.

Lycos offers two Display Options pull-down menus. One dictates how many results are displayed on the page, and the second determines the level of detail for the specified search.

Although Lycos always allows you to access all the *hits* that resulted from your search, obviously all of them cannot be displayed at once. You can choose to display between ten and 40 links on a page at any one time. You do so using the first of the two Display Options pull-down menus. To specify how many search results are displayed on the page at any one time, pull down the first menu and select the number you want to see.

The second pull-down menu lets you determine the level of information detail to be displayed about each search result. This menu has three levels of detail, each one on the list being a little more detailed than the one above it. The level of detail you specify will probably change with each search you do, depending on the documents you are seeking and the research you are trying to accomplish. If you don't specify any level, the default Standard Results takes the middle ground, reporting with a reasonable amount of detail.

How Lycos Works So how does Lycos manage to cover so much ground on the Internet? Actually, Lycos has three parts, all of which are interconnected, and each requires the others to work properly. The first part of Lycos is made up of groups of programs, called *spiders*, that go out and search the Web, FTP, and Gopher sites every day.

The results are added to the second part of Lycos, the "catalog" database, which contains such things as the URL address of each site found, along with information about the documents found at that site, the text, and the number of times that site is referenced by other Web addresses. As a result of the advanced search performed by the spiders, the most popular sites are indexed first. Whatever information and new sites are found by the spiders is added to the existing catalog.

The final element is the search engine itself. It's the real strength of the system for the end user (you) because it can manage to access all this information so smoothly and accurately. The engine sorts through the catalog and produces a list of hits according to your search criteria, listed in descending order of relevance. This means that, according to the search engine, the best and most accurate hits are at the top of the Lycos results list. So, the deeper you dig into Lycos's results, the less likely you are to find what you want—at least, according to Lycos.

WebCrawler

WebCrawler is one of the best search engines on the Web, not least because it is so easy to use and very fast. It is owned and maintained by America Online, which provides it as a public service to the Internet community. It's a great search engine to use when you're fairly sure that what you're looking for will appear in the title of a Web page. WebCrawler searches only titles of Web pages, not all text, and its interface is designed to be as uncomplicated as possible (see fig. 6.16). You can find WebCrawler at **http://www.webcrawler.com/**.

FIG. 6.16
WebCrawler allows for easy searching and quick results.

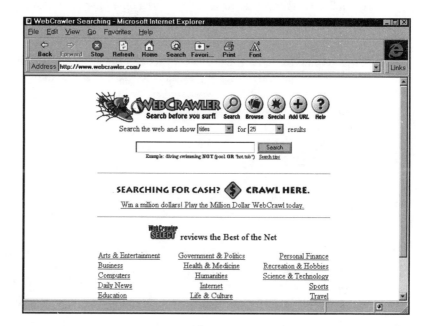

 T I P WebCrawler is also a great way to start out on a directed surfing expedition—that is, when you're not searching too closely. If you want to see 500 hits with the word *Microsoft* in the title, you'll find them the most quickly and easily with WebCrawler.

Instead of searching the entire World Wide Web for instances of your typed keywords, WebCrawler searches its own index of documents. This makes for quicker searches, although, with documents and pages being added to the Web at such an astounding rate, newer resources can be missed.

The result of your WebCrawler search is a list, with each item on the list underlined and colored indicating that it is a hypertext link you can click to retrieve that page from the Internet.

Down the left side of the search results is a list of numbers, with one number corresponding to each item on the list. The highest number is next to the first item on the search results list. It indicates that the first item is the most relevant according to your search keywords, which is the reason that the numbers (from 100 to 001) are called *relevance numbers*. As you move down the list, you notice that the number along the left side decreases for each item on the list—indicating that each of these pages offers fewer occurrences of your keywords than the previous item.

With a large search, not all the results are necessarily displayed on the first page. In fact, WebCrawler limits the results to ten, 25, or 100, depending on how many pages you specified in your search criteria. But if WebCrawler finds, for example, 500 pages that correspond to your search keywords and you chose to view 25 at a time, only 25 are going to be shown on the Internet Explorer screen.

Having a limited number of hits shown on-screen doesn't mean you can't view the rest of the search results. To view the next 25 items in the resulting search list, click the Get the Next 25 Results button under the resulting list, and the next 25 items in the search are displayed. Keep clicking this button until you have viewed all the items in the list, if you need to see them. But don't forget, the further down the list you go, the less relevant the search results, according to your keywords.

Other Search Engines

A variety of other search engines are available on the Internet. These engines tend to be either more specialized—focusing on searching UseNet newsgroups instead of the entire Internet, for instance—or simply convenient ways to access the search engines we've already talked about.

Deja News Research Service   If you want to search UseNet newsgroups exclusively, then the Deja News Research Service is the place for you. Currently claiming over four gigabytes of searchable data, Deja News is updated every two days. You can even follow an entire newsgroup thread by just clicking the subject line when it appears at the top of your screen.

To get to the search engine page, go to **http://www.dejanews.com/**. Then click the Search link on Deja News' index page. The Deja News query form page appears (see fig. 6.17).

For the simplest search, just type search words into the text box, click the Find button, and use the default options. However, for the best results, you should customize your search a little by following these steps:

1. Type your search words into the text box. You don't need to worry about capitalizing words because the search engine isn't case sensitive. The engine automatically assumes that an OR appears between multiple words.

2. Choose the maximum number of hits you want retrieved by checking either 30, 60, or 120 in the Maximum Number of Hits option. The default is 30. If more than the number specified is returned, a link appears at the bottom of the screen allowing you access to the next set of hits.

3. The amount of information retrieved about each site is determined by the Hitlist Format option. Click Terse for less information or Verbose for more.

4. The Sort By option lets you emphasize score, group, date, or author.

FIG. 6.17

Just enter words and click Find for simple searches. You can perform more complex queries from this page as well.

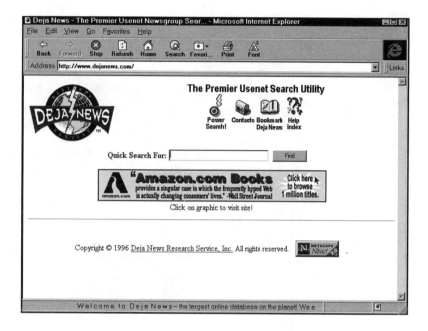

N O T E *Score* is just another way to say *relevance number,* as discussed earlier. The score is how Deja News determines how close each result is to your search phrase. ◼

5. You can choose between default Boolean operators using the Default Operator: OR or AND option.

6. Use the Power Search option if you want to use a filter to narrow down your search. A filter can be used to specify a date range if you want only postings from a specific author or if you know which newsgroups you want to retrieve.

7. The age of the record can also be a factor in your search. If you want newer postings, check the Prefer New box, or if you want older ones, check the Prefer Old box. In addition, you can use the Age Matters option to tell Deja News how important it is that a message is relatively recent or a few months old.

Some groups are not included in the indexing, such as **alt.***, **soc.***, **talk.***, and ***.binaries**. Deja News says that this exclusion is either because they contain a large volume of postings that are mostly flames, or else they don't lend themselves well to text searchings, such as binary groups.

In any event, Deja News is worth using if you want to search the enormous number of UseNet newsgroups available. Reportedly, as many as 80 MB of traffic is posted on newsgroups each day! Newsgroups can be very useful for retrieving information if you know how to search and where to look.

Excite   Excite allows you to search through more than a million Web documents and the past two week's worth of UseNet newsgroups and classified ads. The user interface is as simple as other search engines available (see fig. 6.18). Excite is located at **http://www.excite.com/**.

FIG. 6.18

The Excite database lets you search Web documents, UseNet newsgroups, and classified ads.

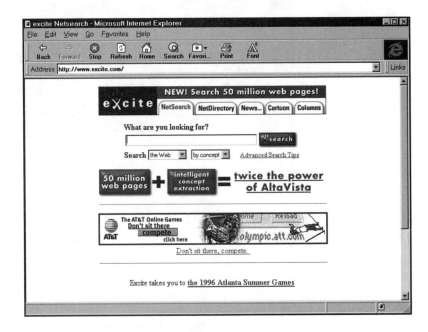

Searching Excite is only slightly different from the other search engines. You start by selecting the type of search you want Excite to carry out—click the Enter Keywords box if you want documents retrieved using regular keywords. You can also click the Enter Words Describing a Concept box if you want the search engine to retrieve documents that seem to involve a subject that's related to the words you typed in the search box and not just those documents that contain those words.

After you type in your keywords, you can choose from another set of checkbox options. Check Web Documents if you want Excite to search its database of Web documents. Check UseNet Discussion Groups if you want to search through the last two week's worth of UseNet messages, or select Classifieds if you want Excite to search the last two week's worth of classified advertisements.

Excite uses both color-coded icons and percentage-style scores to indicate the relevance of retrieved results. When a red icon appears at the beginning of the result line, that is an indication that Excite thinks it's a good search match. On the other hand, a black icon means that it may not be such a good match. The colors are a quick way for you to identify good matches at a glance.

The percentage is a better way for you to identify the relevance of a search result, relative to the next search result. Obviously, the higher the percentage score, the better the match—at least in Excite's eyes.

The title of each result depends on whether it is a Web page or site, or a UseNet article. If it is a Web page, the page's title is displayed, or (if no title exists) it may just show the URL. If it is a Web site, then an Excite editor-selected site title is displayed. With UseNet listings, things are different. If a UseNet group is indicated, the name of the group is displayed. If a UseNet article is referenced, its Subject text is shown.

Excite also offers NetReviews (some of the best Web sites as chosen by the Excite staff) along with its database of Web pages and UseNet newsgroups. In fact, that's the reason that you'll find Excite both on the Net Search and Net Directory pages. To access these reviews, click the NetReviews tab on the Excite index page.

W3 Search Engines   In fact, many more searching services are available on the Internet than we've even begun to touch on in this chapter. While Infoseek, WebCrawler, and Lycos are some of the largest and most popular, they may not always be the best for what you need to find. If you're not having much luck with the big name engines, head over to the W3 Search Engines page.

The W3 Search Engines page is basically an interface to many different types of search engines around the world. You can search information servers (Web and Gopher, primarily), UseNet news, publication archives, and software documentation. You can even use these pages to search for people on the Internet in a variety of ways.

To use the individual search engine, just type in your search words in its text box and click the Search button next to that engine's description. Notice that you really don't have many options for these engines, but using it is a convenient way to initiate simple searches for many different services. The W3 Search Engines can be accessed at **http://cuiwww.unige.ch/ meta-index.html**.

Alta Vista   Alta Vista is a search engine maintained by the Digital Equipment Corporation at **http://www.altavista.digital.com/**.

Alta Vista is one of the newer, and more exciting, search engines on the Web. Digital has combined an extremely thorough data collector, named Scooter, with an easy-to-use search interface that also allows sophisticated, advanced searches and ranking critera, to make a very useful search engine for both Web pages and UseNet newsgroup articles.

CUSI (Configurable Unified Search Interface)   The Configurable Unified Search Engine (CUSI) allows you to check related resources quickly, without retyping search keywords.

This configurable search interface for a variety of searchable World Wide Web resources was developed by Martijn Koster in 1993 and is now provided as a public service by Nexor, which can be contacted at **webmaster@nexor.co.uk**, and found at **http://web.nexor.co.uk/ public/cusi/cusi.html**.

CUSI offers a search text box for both manual Web indexes and robot-generated Web indexes, such as Lycos and WebCrawler.

The Internet Explorer 3 Search Button

Just as you can set your start page in Internet Explorer 3, you can set the search page that will be loaded when you click the Search button on the toolbar. The default Search page, shown in figure 6.19, is actually a front end that allows you to access a variety of the search engines discussed in this chapter.

FIG. 6.19

The default search page for Internet Explorer 3 takes you to a site on the Microsoft Network that offers access to a variety of other search engines.

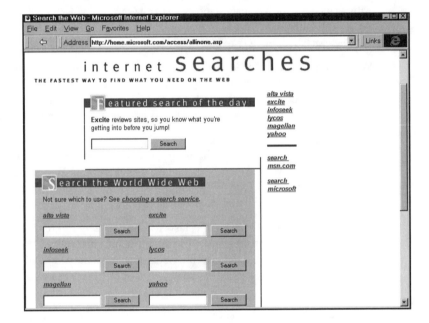

If you are not satisfied with this search page, you can set a new page in much the same way as setting a new start page. Just load the Web page that you want to use as your search button. Then choose View, Options. The Option dialog box appears. Select the Navigation tab. Select Search Page from the drop-down list box, and click the Use Current button. ●

Internet Explorer Favorite Places

The World Wide Web is an immense collection of documents. When you explore the Web, you get that heady feeling that comes from blazing new trails and learning new things. You feel like you could go for hours (and maybe you do!), but, alas, a time always comes when you need to sign off and face reality. As harsh as that may be, something else can be even more difficult: sitting down at your next Web surfing session and thinking "Gee, I really liked that science fiction site I saw the last time I was on...but I can't remember the URL!"

Internet Explorer can help you to record the URLs of your favorite sites as you explore the Web. You can store the URLs in a simple list or even in folders, if you like. Then later, when you want to go back to one of these URLs, you need only select it from your list—much easier than trying to commit URLs to memory.

In the context of Internet Explorer, these recorded URLs are called *favorites*. This chapter discusses how you can use Internet Explorer's Favorites menu to store and organize the URLs of sites you plan to revisit. ■

What features Internet Explorer has to support lists of favorites

Internet Explorer can store your favorites in a list or in folder and gives you quick access to them by both menu options and a toolbar button.

How to add an URL to your list of favorites

Once you've found a site you like, adding it to your list of favorites is as simple as a few keystrokes.

How to organize your favorites into folders

If you've used the Windows Explorer, you'll find it easy to use Internet Explorer's folder structure for arranging your bookmarks.

How to change the name and URL associated with an existing favorite

Sites change frequently, sometimes moving to a new URL. You can update a favorite's URL to reflect such a move.

How to use First Floor's Smart Bookmarks to check your favorite sites for content updates

Smart Bookmarks proactively monitors your favorite sites and lets you know when something has changed.

What Are Favorite Places?

The World Wide Web is a tapestry of millions of different documents and sites, all linked via references from other sites and documents. It is no surprise, then, that help was considered necessary for those people exploring the links.

Because of the complexity of Web URLs, having to remember and manually enter every page's address each time you wanted to view it would be incredibly tedious. And while you can save a document or image on your local drive so as not to have to connect to it over the Internet, you will likely have a great many remote pages that you will want to access on a regular basis, because they will be continually updated with new information by the remote site's administrator.

Favorites take away that tedious task of having to write down or otherwise save each page's or document's URL address. When you add an item to your Favorites list, you are making a record of that item's address on the Internet, along with a description of that item, and placing it in a pull-down list that you can quickly access from the Internet Explorer menu bar.

When you want to go to that site or document or graphic, you just pull down the Favorites list, and select the item. Internet Explorer automatically retrieves the item's URL and tries to access the address. Chances are, you will be able to access the item without any problems, although with the Internet being a global network, difficulties do sometimes occur.

 T I P If a link doesn't work, one reason may be that the filename on the remote server has changed, or it has been moved to another directory. Instead of using the entire URL, type in a truncated version listing just the main server address. That should get you into the remote server from which you can rummage around and look for the old file.

The Technical Details of Storing Favorite Places

If you like to know the specifics, here's a quick tutorial on how Internet Explorer stores favorites information:

In Windows 95 and NT, the URL of each favorite is stored in its own file in the C:\WINDOWS\FAVORITES folder. If an author has given a document a title (which shows up at the top of the Internet Explorer window), and you record that document as one of your favorites, the file's MS-DOS name is the document's title (possibly compressed down to eight characters) followed by a .URL extension. In the absence of a title, the file's MS-DOS name is the document's URL (again, possibly compressed and with reserved characters changed to dashes) followed by the .URL extension. Thus, if you add the document titled Stock Quotes whose URL is **http://www.stocks.com/** to your Favorites list, the URL would be stored in a file named STOCKQ~1.URL. If the document doesn't have a title, it is stored in a file named HTTP--~1.URL.

Inside the file, the URL is stored in the following format:

```
[InternetShortcut]
URL=http://www.stocks.com/
```

Knowing this, you could make your own favorites without Internet Explorer's assistance by creating a simple text file in the preceding format that includes the URL of the favorite that you want to record.

The Favorites Menu

Most of the activity that goes into storing and accessing Internet Explorer favorites occurs from the Favorites menu (see fig. 7.1). The top part of the menu (above the menu separator bar) gives you the option of organizing your favorites or adding the page you're currently looking at to your list of favorites.

FIG. 7.1

The Favorites menu lets you add and organize favorite URLs quickly and easily.

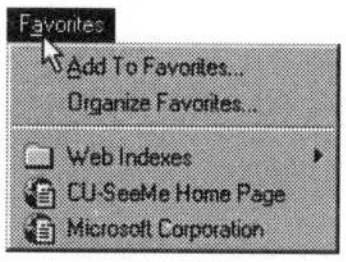

The bottom part of the Favorites menu (below the separator bar) is a listing of favorites currently stored. If you've organized any of your favorites into folders, the topmost folders in your hierarchy show up here. Holding your mouse cursor over a top-level folder reveals a list of favorites and subfolders stored under that top-level folder (see fig. 7.2).

FIG. 7.2

Holding your mouse cursor over a top-level folder gives you a list of the favorites in that folder.

Internet Explorer also furnishes you with a toolbar button that gives you access to your favorites. Figure 7.3 shows that when you click this button, you get the same options you get when you open the Favorites menu.

FIG. 7.3

The Favorites button on the Internet Explorer toolbar replicates the options found under the Favorites menu.

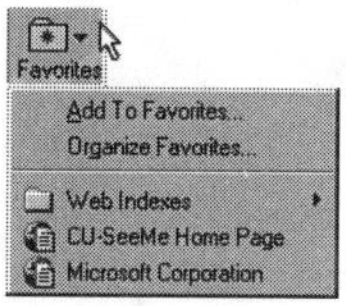

Part

II

Ch

7

In addition to the Favorites menu or Favorites toolbar button, a few other tools are available to help you manage your list of favorite URLs. They are covered as the chapter progresses.

Creating Favorite Places

When you find a Web page that you really like, adding it to your list of favorites is easy. With the page in the Internet Explorer window, you simply follow these steps:

1. Choose the Favorites menu or click the Favorites toolbar button.

2. Choose the Add to Favorites option.

3. The Add to Favorites dialog box will ask you to confirm the addition (see fig. 7.4). Click OK if you want the favorite placed in the top level of the Favorites folder.

FIG. 7.4

The Add to Favorites dialog box asks you to confirm an addition and lets you place the new favorite in the Favorites folder or one of its subfolders.

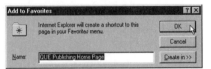

4. If you want the favorite stored in a subfolder, click the Create in button in the Add to Favorites dialog box to reveal an expanded version of the box that displays the available subfolders (see fig. 7.5). You can choose to store the favorite in one of the subfolders or create a new subfolder to store it in.

FIG. 7.5

An expanded version of the Add to Favorites dialog box lets you place the new favorite in a subfolder or create a new subfolder for it.

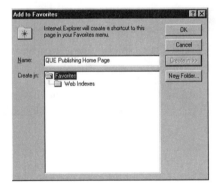

That's it! The page is added to your list of favorites.

Another way to do the same thing is to use the context-sensitive menu produced by right-clicking your mouse. You can add a page to your list of favorites by right-clicking at a point on the page where no hyperlinks and no graphics appear. The menu you see in figure 7.6 then opens. Select the Add to Favorites option from this menu, and follow the steps outlined previously to add the favorite.

FIG. 7.6

You can also add to your list of favorites by using the context-sensitive menu you get when you right-click.

Organizing Favorite Places

As you accumulate a large number of favorites, organizing them into logical groupings makes sense. Groups of related favorites are stored together in *folders*. Figure 7.7 shows a fair-sized list of favorites. Many of them are related and, over the course of this section, you'll see how to arrange them into folders.

FIG. 7.7

In this list of favorites, some are candidates for grouping into folders.

To begin the organization of your favorites, you need to first make some folders to put them in by following these steps:

1. From the Favorites menu, choose Organize Favorites. The Organize Favorites dialog box appears.

2. Right-click a blank spot in the Organize Favorites dialog box to produce a context-sensitive menu.

3. Move the mouse cursor over the New option to reveal a list of new items that you can create (see fig. 7.8).

NOTE The Personal folder you see in figure 7.8 is automatically put there by the Windows operating system. It is meant for storing favorites as well as other documents produced by Microsoft software. ■

Part

II

Ch

7

FIG. 7.8

Right-clicking in the Organize Favorites dialog box lets you create new folders for storing your favorites.

4. Click Folder once. By clicking this option, you can edit the folder's name. Type in an appropriate descriptive name for the folder.

You can repeat the preceding steps to create and name as many new folders as you need. Figure 7.9 shows three newly created folders that can be used to organize your list of favorites.

FIG. 7.9

The favorites in this list can be organized into three new folders.

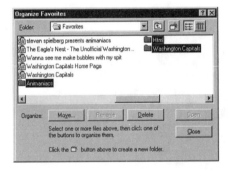

Once the new folders are created, storing favorites in them is as easy as dragging and dropping. Follow these steps to move a favorite into one of the folders:

1. Select Favorites, Organize Favorites. The Organize Favorites dialog box appears.

2. Click the favorite that you want to move.

3. While holding down the left mouse button, drag the selected favorite to the folder you want to store it in (see fig. 7.10).

FIG. 7.10

You can move favorites into folders by dragging them to the desired folder and dropping them there.

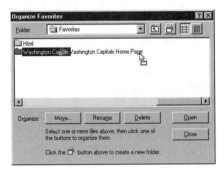

4. Release the left mouse button to place the favorite in the folder.

After repeating these steps for each of the favorites in the list, you're left with the screen you see in figure 7.11. To get to one of the favorites now, you have to double-click one of the folders to open it and reveal its contents. Figure 7.12 shows the favorites in the Animaniacs folder.

NOTE If you don't like dragging and dropping things, you can use the Move option in the Organize Favorites dialog box to move a favorite from one place to another. ▩

FIG. 7.11
The Favorites folder with all favorites organized into subfolders.

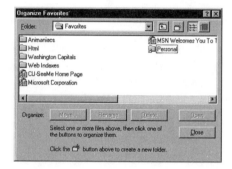

FIG. 7.12
Double-clicking the Animaniacs folder reveals the favorites that it contains.

Changing Favorite Place Properties

World Wide Web sites are always changing. Site administrators may remove pages whose content is out of date, or they may change the URL of a page if the site is reorganized. Changes like these mean that you will inevitably have to make changes to your list of favorites. Internet Explorer makes this process easy.

Deleting a Favorite

If a favorite page has been removed from a Web site, you should remove it from your Favorites list. Deleting is almost as straightforward as adding a favorite. To delete a favorite, follow these steps:

1. Select Favorites, Organize Favorites. The Organize Favorites dialog box appears.

2. Choose the favorite you want to delete. You may have to open one or more subfolders.

3. Click the outdated favorite, and then click the Delete button.

4. Click Yes in the Confirm File Delete dialog box.

 TIP If you're a fan of context-sensitive menus, you can right-click the outdated favorite and choose the Delete option instead of performing step 2 in this process.

Editing a Favorite

Sometimes favorites are moved to new URLs by Web site administrators because of server changes or site reorganizations. Additionally, you may find that you want to give a favorite a name of your choosing rather than use the one the Internet Explorer assigns. Either instance requires you to be able to edit a favorite's information. Both types of changes are discussed in the next two sections.

Changing a Favorite's URL   If a favorite page has moved to a new URL, you can edit the existing favorite and update the URL information. To update a favorite on your list, you do the following:

1. From the Favorites menu, choose Organize Favorites. In the Organize Favorites dialog box, locate the favorite that needs updating.

2. Right-click the favorite to be changed.

3. Choose the Properties option from the context-sensitive menu. A Properties dialog box like the one in figure 7.13 appears.

FIG. 7.13

You can change a favorite's properties in this dialog box.

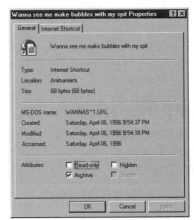

4. Click the Internet Shortcut tab in the Properties dialog box.

5. Update the Target URL field to reflect the new URL of your favorite, and click OK to save the change (see fig. 7.14).

FIG. 7.14
You can enter updated URL information for a favorite in the Target URL field.

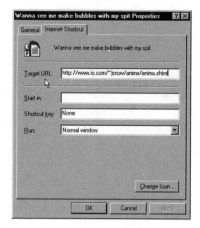

Changing a Favorite's Name   Changing the name of a favorite or a folder that contains favorites is easy. You simply follow these steps:

1. From the Favorites menu, choose Organize Favorites. Locate the favorite or folder in need of a new name in the Organize Favorites dialog box.
2. Click the favorite or folder and then click the Rename button.
3. Type in the new name for the favorite or folder, and press Enter.

N O T E   When editing the name of a favorite or folder of favorites, you are essentially changing a file or directory name. If you've used Windows Explorer to change file and directory names, you'll probably find that the process of changing names of favorites and folders of favorites in Internet Explorer is similar to what you do to change file and directory names in Windows Explorer. ■

Sharing Favorites with Others

In the course of your Web exploration, you'll very likely compile an impressive list of favorites. Once this happens, you'll discover that people with similar interests may become interested in acquiring your list. Conversely, you may find a friend who has a good list of favorites that you want to get your hands on. Can Internet Explorer users easily share their favorites?

The answer is yes. Because favorites are stored in text files, it's just a matter of exchanging the files. You can do so any number of ways. You can copy them to a disk and give the disk to the user who wants your favorites. You can also send them to another user by e-mail by making each favorite file an attachment to your message.

 If you're getting favorite files from someone else, make sure you place them in the C:\WINDOWS \FAVORITES folder because it is the default location that Internet Explorer looks to for favorites.

Part
II
Ch
7

Using First Floor's Smart Bookmarks

First Floor Software has extended its smart bookmarking technology to work with Internet Explorer. First Floor's program Smart Bookmarks gives you another way to store and organize favorite sites plus a means of automatically monitoring them for changes. This last section looks at Smart Bookmarks and how you can use it with Internet Explorer to make your Web exploration as efficient as possible.

Downloading and Installing

You can download an evaluation copy of Smart Bookmarks 2.0 from First Floor's Web site. Just point Internet Explorer to **http://www.firstfloor.com/eval.html** and follow the instructions. You'll need to fill out a short registration form and agree to the terms of First Floor's software license before being given access to the link to the downloadable file.

N O T E If you're using Windows 95 or Windows NT, you should download the 32-bit version of Smart Bookmarks 2.0. This version of Smart Bookmarks requires a 32-bit TCP/IP stack to run properly. Both Windows 95 and NT have 32-bit stacks that you can set up.

If you're using Windows 3.1, you should download the 16-bit version even if you have Win32s installed. ■

Download the self-extracting archive file—either `sb1620.exe` for the 16-bit version or `sb3220.exe` for the 32-bit version—into a temporary directory and then run the file to install Smart Bookmarks. An InstallShield Wizard will walk you through a fairly standard installation process. The one point where you need to be on your toes is when you see the Select Your Web Browser dialog box (see fig. 7.15). Smart Bookmarks is able to work with many different browsers, so you need to tell the installation program that you want Smart Bookmarks to work with Internet Explorer.

FIG. 7.15

You configure Smart Bookmarks to work with Internet Explorer during installation.

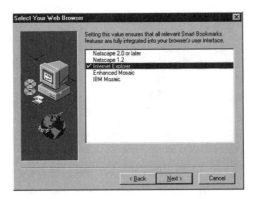

Once the installation is complete, you need to reboot your computer for the new settings to take effect.

Starting Internet Explorer with Smart Bookmarks Installed

Once Smart Bookmarks is installed, it will be launched every time you start Internet Explorer. At startup, you'll only see the Internet Explorer window because the Smart Bookmarks window is minimized. Click the Smart Bookmarks icon on the taskbar to reveal the window you see in figure 7.16.

FIG. 7.16
Clicking the minimized icon displays the full Smart Bookmarks window.

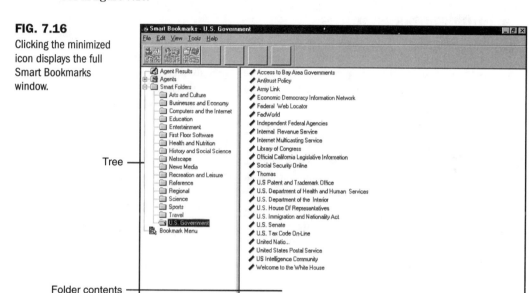

Some people find it distracting to have Smart Bookmarks run at the same time Internet Explorer does. If you're such a person, there's a simple way to tell Smart Bookmarks not to start with Internet Explorer. To do so, follow these steps:

1. Choose Tools, Preferences. The Preferences dialog box appears.
2. Select the Options tab in the Preferences dialog box (see fig. 7.17).

FIG. 7.17
You can deactivate Smart Bookmark's automatic startup in the Options tab.

Part

II

Ch

7

3. Uncheck the Load With the Browser checkbox.

4. Click OK.

Note that you can also change the browser you want Smart Bookmarks to work with from the Options tab of the Preferences dialog box, as well.

Smart Bookmarks Features

Smart Bookmarks lets you save and organize your favorite places just like you can with the Internet Explorer Favorites menu. What makes it worth its $24.95 license price, though, is its ability to automatically check your favorite sites for content changes. These automatic checks—called *agents*—are even customizable so you can check an entire site once a day or portions of a site every hour. The last few sections look at this and other useful Smart Bookmarks features.

The Smart Bookmarks Main Window   The Smart Bookmarks Main Window is what you saw in figure 7.16. If you've used the Windows Explorer in Windows 95, the Smart Bookmarks window will seem like familiar terrain. The left side of the window shows the tree which contains your agents, results from agent searches, and a host of different folders. Smart Bookmarks comes preloaded with more than a dozen different bookmark folders. The contents of each folder are shown in the right side of the main window. To jump to a bookmarked site, all you need to do is double-click its bookmark on the right side of the window.

You can add your own bookmark folders to the tree in one of two ways:

■ Choose File, New and then select Folder to reveal the Folder dialog box (see fig. 7.18). The folder's name is what will be displayed in the window. The folder descriptions and keywords are used for Smart Bookmarks' searches of your catalog of bookmarks.

FIG. 7.18
When you create a new folder, you give it a name, a description, and search keywords.

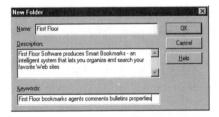

■ Right-click your mouse in the right side of the window and select New, Folder from the context-sensitive menu that pops up. This brings you to the same Folder dialog box you see in figure 7.18.

Agents   Agents are the automatic searches that Smart Bookmarks will perform on bookmarks for sites. When you create a new agent, an Agent Wizard walks you through the configuration process. Specifically, you can configure an agent to do the following:

■ Have an extensive description and keyword listing to help you find it later

■ Monitor for page changes, new links, or both

■ Perform the check under manual instruction or automatically at the time interval you choose (see fig. 7.19)

FIG. 7.19
You can configure an agent to automatically check a monitored site as often as you like.

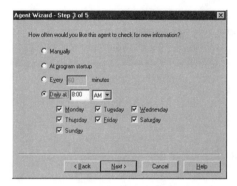

■ Save local copies of the new information it finds

Sites that are found to have changes are listed in the Agent Results folder. You can view the contents of this folder by clicking the Agent Results item at the top of the tree. Doing this modifies the Smart Bookmarks window as shown in figure 7.20. Results from the agent searches are shown on the right side of the window. Clicking one of these results shows detailed information about the change that occurred at the bottom of the window.

FIG. 7.20
Agent search results are displayed at the bottom of the Smart Book-marks window.

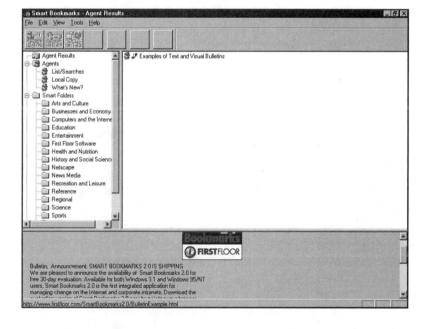

Part

II

Ch

7

Properties, Comments, and Bulletins   Each bookmark has an extensive Properties box that tells you just about everything you need to know about the bookmark. To view a bookmark's properties, follow these steps:

1. Click the desired bookmark.

2. Choose File, Properties or right-click and select Properties. The Properties dialog box appears (see fig. 7.21).

3. Select the General or Agents tab, depending on what information you want to see.

You can update bookmark information in the Properties dialog box as well, including the URL of the bookmark's address if it has changed.

Each bookmark also has a Comments and Bulletins dialog box. *Comments* are remarks that you make about a bookmarked site and *bulletins* are notices posted by Webmasters about changes to the sites they manage. Smart Bookmarks keeps a running log of all comments and bulletins posted for each bookmark. To view this log, follow these steps:

1. Click the desired bookmark.

2. Choose File, Comments and Bulletins or right-click and select Comments and Bulletins to display the Comments and Bulletins dialog box (see fig. 7.22).

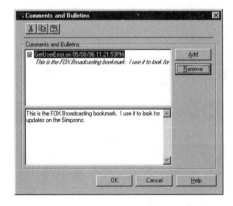

You can also add a comment to a bookmark from the Comments and Bulletins dialog box. Just click the Add button, type in the comments, and click OK when you're done. ●

## CHAPTER 8

Customizing the Microsoft Network Start Pages

When you go to the initial page of a Web site, chances are you're going to see the same thing each time. Any changes that you see in the page are put there by the Web site administrator without any input from you. Wouldn't it be nice if *you* could call the shots though? Imagine how awesome it would be to be able to specify exactly what shows up on the initial page of a site when you load it. The content of the page would be custom tailored to your information needs!

Well, imagine no more. Microsoft has made it possible for visitors to the Microsoft Network (MSN) start page (**http://www.msn.com/**) to customize what information they see when the page is loaded. This capability is handy because, unless you specify otherwise, Internet Explorer loads this page automatically at startup. So whenever you start Internet Explorer, your personalized version of the MSN start page appears. This chapter explores the ways in which you can customize the MSN start page to your own liking. ■

Fill out the online form that specifies the custom page options you want

Follow the step-by-step instructions that walk you through the customization form.

What a customized MSN start page looks like

See the results of customization for the sample page done over the course of the chapter.

How to makes changes to your customized page

Find out how to modify your customized page so it can change as your information needs do.

How "cookies" are used to create custom pages

These cookies aren't edible treats you take out of the oven—they're pieces of information that live on your computer.

Where you can find another customizable page on the Web

Excite's customizable page even keeps track of significant events like meetings, birthdays, and anniversaries!

The Microsoft Network Start Page

The default MSN start page is shown in figure 8.1. The Custom Start Page feature gets top billing on the page and the link to start the customization process is easy to find.

FIG. 8.1
The default Microsoft
Network start page is a
static page, meaning
that it looks the same
to everyone.

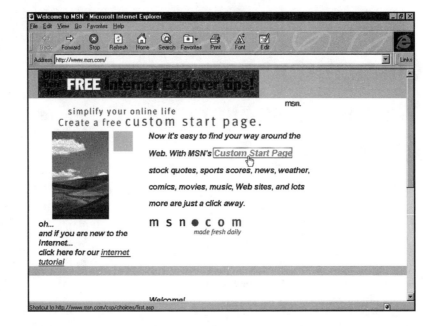

Clicking the hypertext **Custom Start Page** (shown in figure 8.1 with the mouse pointer pointing to it) takes you to the page you see in figures 8.2 and 8.3. This page details the options available to you as you design your custom page. Figure 8.2 shows the Personal Preferences and Services options; figure 8.3 shows the News & Entertainment and Internet Searches options. Once you've read the overviews, click the button below "Let's get customized!" to begin constructing your custom page.

N O T E   You can also opt to have Microsoft generate a start page for you by clicking the button
below the text "Don't have time to create a page now? Want us to create one for you?" The
generated page will be different from the default MSN start page, but not a true custom page like the
one you can build yourself. ▨

FIG. 8.2
You get an overview of the options available to you as you design your custom MSN start page before starting the customization.

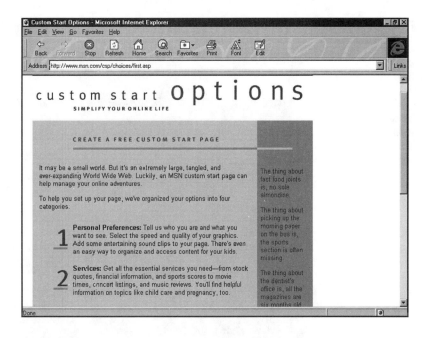

FIG. 8.3
Once you've read through the options (and the humorous remarks in the right margin), click the button under "Let's get customized!" to start.

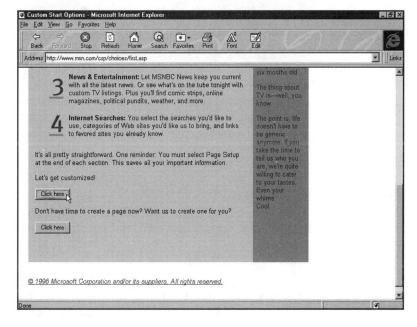

Customizing the Microsoft Network Start Page

Assuming you clicked the button under "Let's get customized!," you'll see the page shown in figure 8.4. This is the beginning of the Personal Preferences section.

FIG. 8.4

The customization begins with you specifying Personal Preferences for the page.

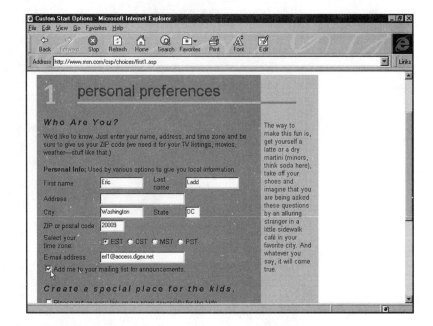

N O T E You can "customize" the MSN start page to the extent that you can select what you want from a very long list of possible page features. While Microsoft has done a great job in making many features available, you may like some that MSN does not yet support. If you have suggestions for other customization features that you would like to make to Microsoft, you can send them e-mail at **webmaster@msn.com**. ▪

Personal Preferences

The first thing you're asked for in the Personal Preferences section is your name and mailing address, followed by your time zone and e-mail address. A time zone may seem an odd thing to ask for, but it is needed to provide you with accurate TV listings, if you choose to include those on your page later on in the customization process.

How Much Personal Information Do You Need to Provide?

Some people are rightfully nervous about giving out personal information over the Internet. The form says the information is used by different options to provide you with local information. It's certainly true that you'll never get a local weather forecast without telling someone where you live, but you may still hesitate to give out your name and e-mail address.

Your first name is required only if you want to have a personalized welcome message. Otherwise, you can leave your first and last names off entirely. If you're not joining the MSN mailing list, you have no reason to provide your e-mail address either.

If you choose any options that provide local information (local weather and movie listings), you do need to fill in city, state, and ZIP code information, but it's not likely that anyone will be able to track you down based on this information alone.

Below the e-mail address box, you can check a box if you want to be included on Microsoft's announcements mailing list. Once you get to this point, you'll probably need to scroll down to see the rest of the form. Figure 8.5 shows the bottom half of the Personal Preferences form.

FIG. 8.5

But wait! There's more! The Personal Preferences options continue to include links for kids and background music.

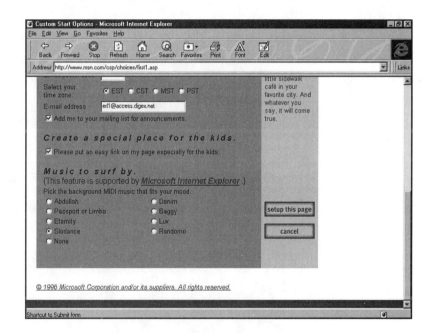

On the bottom half of the form, you can opt to include a link "for the kids." If you check this box, you'll get a link to MSN Kids on your custom page.

Finally, you can select a type of music to play in the background while your custom page is loaded. This feature harnesses Internet Explorer's ability to play MIDI files as instructed in the source code of a Web document. If your computer can't play MIDI files or if you don't want any music, you should click the button labeled None.

▶ **See** "Microsoft Extensions to HTML," **p. 487**

N O T E Internet Explorer has to download the sound file from the MSN server. If your Internet connection is slow, you may want to forgo having a music clip. ■

> **CAUTION**
>
> If you choose to have a music clip, be prepared to hear it for as long as you're on the start page. Internet Explorer loops the clip infinitely; so much like the "It's a Small World After All" ride at Disney World, you hear the same music again and again.

When you're done with the Personal Preferences form, you need to click the Setup This Page button in the right margin in figure 8.5. If you don't do this, all of the customization information data you've entered will be lost.

Services

Assuming you clicked the Setup This Page button, you'll move on to the screen you see in figure 8.6. This is the beginning of the Services portion of the customization.

FIG. 8.6
The second phase of your MSN start page customization permits you to place a number of links to information services on your page.

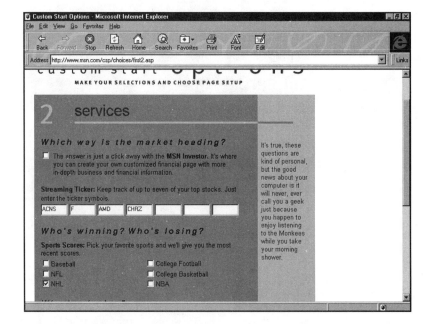

At the top of the form, you'll see some items that would be of interest to those who track the stock market. Clicking the box for MSN Investor sets up a link on your custom page to the MSN Investor site—a storehouse of valuable business and financial information. You can even make your own custom page on the MSN Investor site once you're done with your MSN custom page!

Below the MSN Investor box, you see seven fields into which you can enter the ticker symbols of specific stocks you want to track. The stocks, their current price, and amount of increase or decrease will appear on a "streaming ticker" on your page. The streaming ticker is created using Internet Explorer's support for on-screen marquees.

▶ **See** "Microsoft Extensions to HTML," **p. 487**

T I P If you're interested in a certain company's stock but don't know its ticker symbol, check out CNNfn's directory of company Web sites and ticker symbols at **http://www.cnnfn.com/resources/links/ corp.html**.

Near the bottom of the first half of the Services form, you'll find checkboxes for setting up links to the latest scores in several different sports. You can choose up to six from Major League Baseball, the NFL, the NHL, the NBA, college football, and college hoops. Once you make your sports score picks, you'll need to scroll to the bottom half of the form (see fig. 8.7).

FIG. 8.7
Entertainment and family information are available to you from the lower half of the Services form.

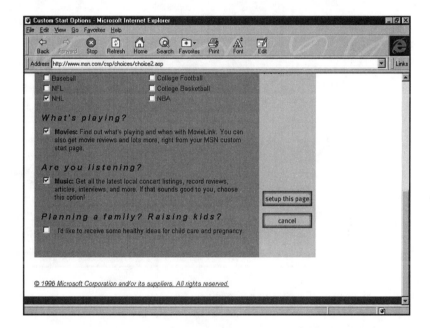

Clicking the Movies box places a link to MovieLink on your custom page. The link uses the address information you provided in the Personal Preferences section to look up what films are playing in your area. Similarly, clicking the Music box generates a list of links to local concert information, record reviews, and other entertainment articles and interviews.

Parents and parents-to-be will want to check the box at the very bottom of the Services form to set up links to sites that offer advice on family planning, pregnancy, and child care.

> **CAUTION**
>
> When you're done with the bottom half of the Services form, be sure to click the Setup This Page button so that your customization parameters aren't lost.

News & Entertainment

With the completion of the Services part of the form, you're halfway there. The next step is to move on to the News and Entertainment form (see fig. 8.8).

FIG. 8.8

Phase three of the customization lets you choose different news and entertainment links to go on your page.

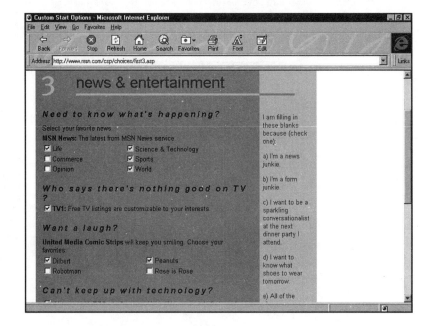

You can configure your personalized MSN start page with up to six types of news items from the MSNBC news service. Each choice sets up a link on your start page to stories from the areas you select.

Suppose you know that "Friends" is on tonight, but you're not sure whether it's a rerun. If you check the TV1 box, then you have instant access to customizable TV listings that can tell you whether a new episode is on. Checking the TV1 box puts a clickable button on your MSN start page that fetches the current night's TV listings.

Everyone seems to love Dilbert these days, and now you can link him to your MSN start page. Figure 8.8 shows the different United Media comics you can incorporate into your custom page. For each comic you check, you get a link on your MSN start page to the appropriate directory on United Media's Web server. With your comics selected, you can move on to the second half of the News and Entertainment form (see fig. 8.9).

FIG. 8.9
News and Entertainment continues with selections for technology news, election reports, and the weather forecast.

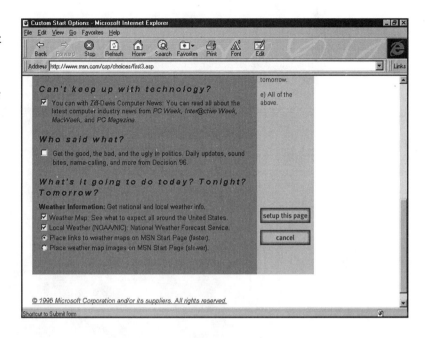

Checking the Ziff-Davis Computer News box creates a set of links on your start page pointing headlines and stories drawn from Ziff-Davis's collection of computer industry magazines. These titles include *PC Week*, *Inter@ctive Week*, *Mac Week*, and *PC Magazine*.

If you're into mudslinging, be sure to check the box that links you to updates on the race for the White House this fall. Decision '96 is sure to be newsworthy *and* entertaining.

Wondering what the weather will be like for the family picnic tomorrow? Or maybe you want to know if you should take your umbrella on that business trip to New York. You can put national and local weather information on your customized MSN start page in two ways.

The first two Weather Information boxes you see in figure 8.9 let you choose a national weather map, a local forecast, or both. The two ways to display this information are reflected in the radio buttons below. The button that is preselected places links to the requested weather information on your customized MSN page. Choosing the other button places the weather map images right on your page.

CAUTION
If your Internet connection is relatively slow, you should place links to weather information on your page. Placing the images directly on your page requires them to be downloaded from another server and increases the total time you have to wait for your page to load.

With the weather selections made, you're ready to move on to the last part of the customization. But don't forget to click the Setup This Page button first to register your News and Entertainment selections!

Internet Searches

The last step in setting up your custom MSN start page involves the selection of Internet search engines and Web sites that you want to have links for on your page. Figure 8.10 shows the top half of the Internet searches form.

FIG. 8.10

You can put as many as eight forms that let you search different Web indexes on your custom MSN start page.

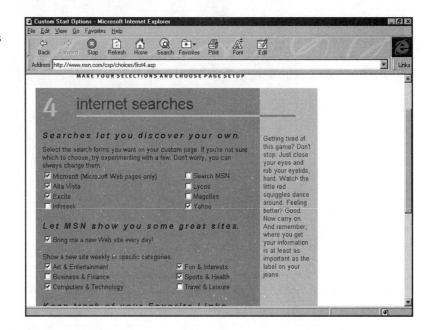

The Web is so vast that using one of the many Web indexes is almost a necessity at some point. You can place up to eight search forms on your customized MSN start page by choosing from the Search Forms list.

For each index you select, you find an input field on the Start Page prompting you for the search criteria. Internet Explorer places a button next to each search criteria input field that you can click to execute the search.

N O T E The Microsoft search explores only Microsoft's site, not the entire Web. Searches using one of the other services are limited to the Web documents that the service has indexed. ▪

The folks at Microsoft are always trying to stay on top of what's new and interesting on the Web, and you can tap into their expertise by checking the boxes that interest you under the Web picks section of the MSN start page customization form. Web surfers who can't get enough will want to check the first box to have a link to a new site each day. If you don't crave a new site quite so frequently, or if you want to know about sites pertaining to a specific area of interest, you may want to check one or more of the six boxes that give you a new site in a particular category each week. In either case, links to the chosen daily and weekly sites are placed on your MSN start page for each box that you check. With your Web picks selected, you're ready to scroll to the last half of the form to complete your customized page setup (see fig. 8.11).

FIG. 8.11

Last but not least, you can choose some favorite Web sites to link to your custom MSN start page.

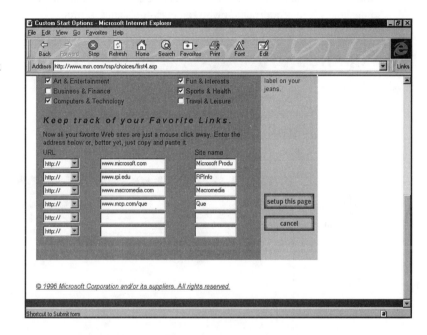

You can specify up to six favorite links to appear on your customized MSN start page. The links you choose should be the ones that you use most frequently and would want easy access to.

The form presents you with six rows of input fields for entering favorite links. Each row contains three fields that collect information about the URL of a favorite link and a plain-language name for the link. The first field you see is a drop-down menu field that lets you specify the protocol used in the link's URL. Most Web page URLs start with **http://**, and it is automatically selected for you. If you click the down arrow, you get to choose from all of the protocols on Internet Explorer—including the **wais://** and **file://** protocols.

In the middle field, you enter the rest of the URL, including the server name and the path to the file that you're linking to. For example, if you are linking to **http://www.toyota.com/ cars/camry.html**, you simply enter **www.toyota.com/cars/camry.html** in the middle field.

The last field lets you give the link a plain-language name. The text you enter here becomes hypertext on the customized version of the page. Be sure to use a name that is descriptive enough to help you remember exactly what the link points to.

You're Done!

Customizing the start page took some effort, but now you're finished. To generate your customized MSN start page, you need to once more click the button labeled Set Up Page. If you need to redo your information, you can click the Cancel button.

The Finished Product

After the MSN server processes the data you submitted on the form, it returns your customized MSN start page to Internet Explorer for display on your screen. The resulting page from the previous customization steps is shown over the course of figures 8.12, 8.13, 8.14, 8.15, and 8.16. Note as you look at these figures how the information you provided was used to construct your custom page.

FIG. 8.12

The very top of your custom page uses your name in two places and provides a link to MSN Kids, if you requested one.

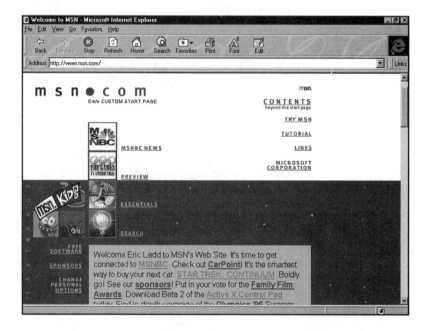

If you want to change any customization parameters for the Essentials, News, or Search sections, look for the link along the left margin just below the title of the section. Clicking one of these links reloads the corresponding customization form with your old data preloaded. To change your options, simply type over whatever you want to change and click the Setup This Page button to register the changes.

To make changes to your Personal Preferences, you need to scroll to the bottom of your custom page and find the **Change Personal Options** link. Following this link will bring you to the Personal Preferences form preloaded with your old configuration. Again, you need only type over what you want to change and click the Setup This Page button.

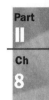

FIG. 8.13

The Essentials section of your custom page includes a streaming stock ticker and links to sports, movie, and music information.

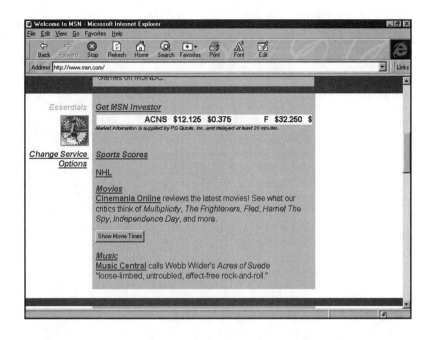

FIG. 8.14

News from MSNBC, weather forecasts, and TV listings are the highlights of the News section of your custom start page.

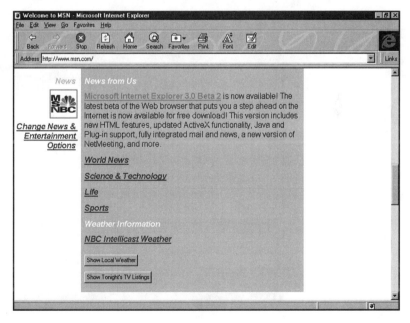

FIG. 8.15

The Search section of your custom page begins with search fields for your chosen search engines and your favorite links.

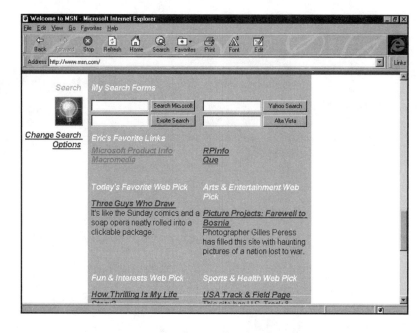

FIG. 8.16

The Search section finishes the Microsoft's daily and weekly Web picks.

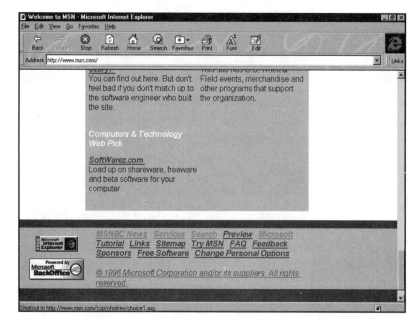

How Customization Works

Now that you've created your own MSN start page, you may be wondering what the inner workings of the customization are. After all, you don't have to fill out the customization form each time you hit the MSN site. How does MSN remember your custom options?

The answer is that customization data is stored on your computer and passed to the MSN server each time you load the URL **http://www.msn.com/**. The technology that makes this possible is called *cookie technology*. By passing the custom page options as *cookies*, the MSN server knows how to create the start page according to your specifications.

> **N O T E** If you load your custom MSN start page, then go to another site, and then come back within 30 minutes, your MSN start page is not automatically updated to reflect new information. If you come back after 30 minutes, Internet Explorer passes your cookies to the MSN server again, and you get an updated version of your custom page. ▪

TROUBLESHOOTING

I filled out the customization form, but my custom options are showing up as garbled or are not being saved until my next session. If you're not an MSN customer, your Internet service provider may be using a proxy server that cannot accommodate the large header files that need to be sent to the MSN server to produce a custom page. Microsoft is working to correct this problem so that everyone can customize MSN start pages.

Other Customizable Pages

As more and more browsers embrace cookie technology, you will see more instances of customizable Web pages. Yet even today the MSN start page is not the only customizable page on the Internet. For another example, visit the Excite Web site at **http://www.excite.com/home/** (see fig. 8.17). The form at this address lets you customize the Excite home page to include many of the same information items that go into a customized MSN start page, plus additional items like special event reminders and columns from selected publications.

FIG. 8.17

You can customize the Excite home page by filling out a form similar to the one used to customize the MSN start page.

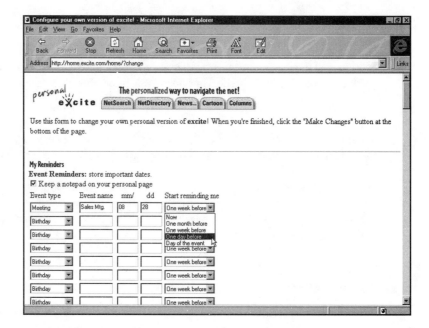

Interactive Pages and Secure Online Transactions

You hear a lot these days about interactivity on the Web being fueled by Java—the "programming language of the next decade." But Web interactivity existed before Java. It was first introduced by the use of Web forms—pages that gave users fields for typing in information and checkboxes and buttons for choosing among many options. After submitting a form, you typically get a customized reply that's generated for you by the Web server.

Even though they're not new, forms continue to occupy an important role in Web interactivity. In particular, they are essential to online commerce which raises, because there's money changing hands, a whole set of issues about Web security. After all, you can put the most attractive products in the world on the Web and charge almost nothing for them, but it won't generate any sales if customers don't feel comfortable giving their credit card numbers out over the Internet.

This chapter examines some of the roles of Web forms and some of the challenges involved in keeping Web transactions secure. ■

How forms can be used

Online commerce is just one of many different applications of World Wide Web forms.

What graphical interface controls are found on Web forms

Windows and Macintosh users will find Web form controls to be very similar to those used in their operating systems.

How to fill out a form

Learn the nuances about each form input field, checkbox, clickable button, and pull-down menu.

What happens to the form data after you submit it

The data you enter into a form take a very interesting journey once it leaves your computer.

Different approaches to electronic commerce

Not everyone agrees on how best to keep Web business transactions secure. The result is that there are several approaches to securing transactions.

What the future holds

Netscape set the stage with its Secure Sockets Layer (SSL) protocols, but now other secure protocols are emerging to compete with SSL.

What Are Forms Good For?

Forms are the Web's standard method for letting you submit information to a World Wide Web server. They are used for at least five major functions, as follows:

- Searching for information in an online database
- Requesting a user-customized action, such as the creation of a custom map or table
- Conducting online surveys
- Registering for a service or group
- Online shopping

In each of these cases, forms give you the means to send specific information to the server you're connected to, so that you can receive a customized response in return.

In contrast, normal page links allow you only to click a link from a list to retrieve a "canned" response from the server. The canned response is what's often called a *static* HTML page—one that does not change unless edited by an HTML author. Forms let Web page creators send you information and services that are tailored to your specific needs, rather than broad, generic responses built for an audience constrained by "least common denominator" considerations. Such tailored responses are called *dynamically generated* HTML pages. Dynamically generated pages are created by the programs on the server that analyze the data you submit when filling out a form.

The next five sections take a look at real-world examples from the Web, one for each of these common uses of forms.

Searching

Most popular sites today have a search capability built in. You can usually find some type of search criteria entry field prominently located on the site—perhaps even on the home page itself.

Most folks who use the Web are probably familiar with Yahoo's search facility. Rather than click a sequence of links that take you down an ever-narrower path toward the information you want, you can get a custom-generated index of links that go right to pages that contain the desired information. You do this by filling out and submitting the simple one-line form near the top of the page (see fig. 9.1). You just click in the data entry field and type a list of keywords, then click the Search button. Yahoo then searches its database of Web site information and builds a custom index composed only of the entries that contain your keywords. This takes just a few seconds. Yahoo builds and transmits a custom Web page that contains a set of links to pages that match your search criteria.

FIG. 9.1
A single form entry field allows you to search Yahoo's entire list of Web sites.

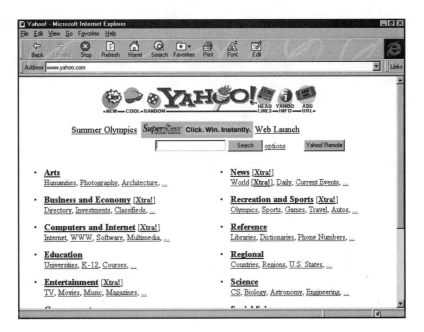

There are literally thousands of sites like Yahoo on the Web that let you use forms to search online databases and retrieve custom pages containing information on a myriad of topics. Just about every kind of information you can imagine is available on the Web somewhere in a forms-searchable database. The following are a few good examples:

- Search UseNet postings with DejaNews at **http://www.dejanews.com/**.

- Look up drugs on the Pharmaceutical Information Network at **http://pharminfo.com/ search_pin.html**.

- Find out who else was born on your birthday at **http://www.eb.com/calendar/ calendar.html**.

- Do a keyword search for jobs at **http://www.occ.com/occ/SearchAllJobs.html**.

Requesting

Forms can also be used to ask a server to run a program to perform a specific task for you. Figure 9.2 shows a form you can use to custom design your own garden (**http:// www.garden.com/**).

Because a Web server is a computer just like any other, it can run any program that any other computer can run. So the types of actions you can request of a Web server are limited only by the types of programs that can run on the server. The following is a quick list of a few of the actions you can request on the Web by submitting a form to the right site:

FIG. 9.2

Design your own custom garden layout with this form from Garden Escape.

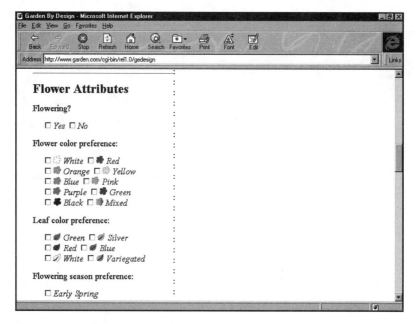

- Display an up-to-the-minute satellite view of the earth's cloud cover from a user-definable viewpoint, using the Earth Viewer at **http://www.fourmilab.ch/earthview/vplanet.html**.

- Ask a question of the cast of the TV show "Friends" at **http://inp.cie.rpi.edu/cgi-bin/friends**.

- Operate a model train at the University of Ulm in Germany at **http://rr-vs.informatik.uni-ulm.de/rrbin/ui/RRPage.html**.

- Generate custom tables of 1990 census data at **http://www.census.gov/cdrom/lookup**.

While some of these activities are definitely more useful than others, they serve to illustrate what it is possible to do over the Web if the server you are connected to provides the right forms and support programs.

Surveys

Web surveys have been used for informal data-gathering, such as collecting user feedback about a Web site, to more formal purposes, such as trying to develop a demographic profile of Internet users. Figure 9.3 shows a screen from the fourth WWW User Entry Survey developed by the Graphics, Visualization, and Usability (GVU) Center at Georgia Tech. The GVU has been working to gather Web demographics since its first survey in January 1994.

FIG. 9.3

This shows an excerpt from the Georgia Tech GVU Center's fourth Web survey.

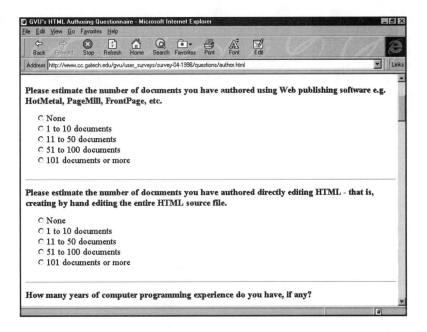

The GVU also has the results from their previous four surveys online. You can check them out at **http://www.cc.gatech.edu/gvu/user_surveys/User_Survey_Home.html**. The following list points you to some other interesting surveys and/or survey results on the Web:

- Learn about why women go online at **http://www.netcreations.com/ipa/women.htm**.
- Sound off about those pesky telemarketers at **http://www.primenet.com/~g1moore/**.
- Tell about how you used a favorite childhood toy at **http://www.winternet.com/fibblesnork/lego/survey/**.
- The Cola War comes to the Web at **http://www.csam.montclair.edu/~keene/cgi-bin/soda.cgi**.

Registering

You can use online forms to sign up for just about anything on the Web. You can enter contests and sweepstakes, join organizations, apply for credit cards, subscribe to e-mail lists on hundreds of different topics, and even sign a guest book at some of the sites you visit. Figure 9.4 shows the online application you can fill out to receive Yahoo's *Internet Life* magazine.

Most online registration forms ask you for the same information you'd supply on a paper registration form: name, address, phone, and—since this is the Internet —e-mail address. Many places also require user registration before they allow you into the deeper, and hopefully most interesting, regions of their Web site. Some may charge you for this privilege, others may not.

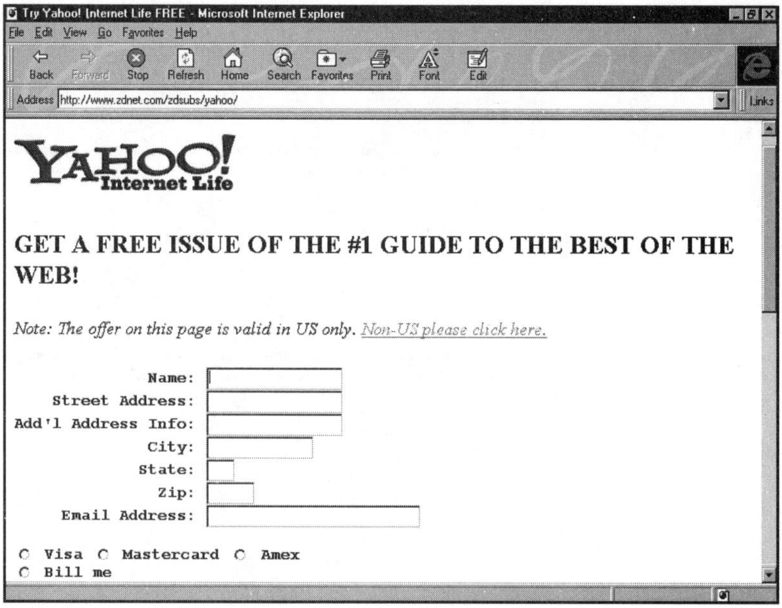

FIG. 9.4
Who needs those little
subscription cards that
fall out of magazines
when you can request
your subscription
online?

Some of the places on the Web that ask you to fill out a registration form are the following:

- Fill out a mortgage application with Mortgage One at **http://www.ibike.com/sis/mortgage/appform.htm**.
- Apply for admission to George Mason University at **http://www.admissions.gmu.edu/**.
- Apply for an AT&T Universal Card credit/phone card at **http://www.att.com/ucs/app/app_intr.html**.
- Enter the most recent contest sponsored by Gateway 2000 at **http://www.gw2k.com/cool/contest/conhub.htm**.

Shopping

You can shop 'til you drop without ever leaving home by cruising the electronic storefronts on the World Wide Web (see fig. 9.5).

Web shopping generally involves filling out an order form (or registering as a shopper) with your name, address, and credit card information. Many sites now even include an electronic "shopping cart." This allows you to browse a site, reading product descriptions and price information; when you find something you like, you just click the checkbox next to the item you want, and it is added to your cart. When you get ready to leave the online store, you go through a "checkout" where your items are totaled and you are presented with a bill, which you can then pay with your credit card or with "electronic cash."

FIG. 9.5
Forget to call the florist?
Check out the 1-800-
FLOWERS online store.

By "shopping," we really mean the process of requesting goods, "hard-copy" information like catalogs or brochures, or services that require either the action of human beings or the transfer of physical objects through delivery services. Though this certainly can involve buying things, it also includes many other services. The following is a list of some more-or-less random examples. (Please note that we are not endorsing or recommending any of these products or services. Use at your own risk!):

- The All-Internet Shopping Directory is a great place to begin your shopping trip at **http://www.webcom.com/~tbrown/**.

- Order free and low-cost government pamphlets from the Consumer Information Center at **http://www.pueblo.gsa.gov/**.

- Click checkboxes to receive hundreds of free catalogs from the Mall of Catalogs at **http://www.csn.net/marketeers/mallofcatalogs/**.

- Shop at the Quinault Country Store located in Washington state at **http://quinault.countrystore.com/**.

Form Formats

Web forms are created using the HTML form tags. With just a handful of HTML instructions, Web forms designers can create a wide range of popular form controls. Online forms can include data entry fields, checkboxes, scrolling lists, and radio buttons (sets of "pushable" buttons).

▶ **See** "Creating HTML Forms" to learn how to author HTML forms, **p. 514**

You'll run into a wide variety of form formats on the Web. Among them are inline forms, full-page forms, multiple forms on a single page, and even hidden forms.

Inline Forms

If the Web page you're visiting needs only a single item of information from you, it's likely to present you with a simplified form called an inline form.

The Microsoft Network's interface to the Magellan search engine is a good example of an inline form (see fig. 9.6). There is only one field to fill in and a single button to push when you're done. In fact, most forms that have only a single field don't even require that you push a button to submit the information you've filled in; if you just hit the Enter key when you're done, the information is sent to the server automatically.

FIG. 9.6
An inline form occurs on a single line with just an input field and a submit button.

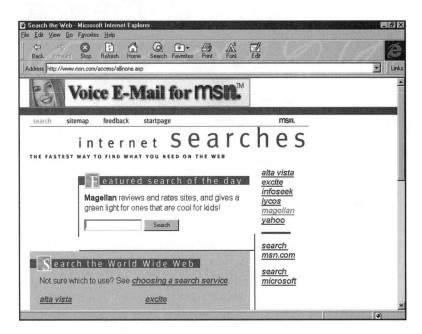

Full-Page Forms

You'll find many examples of full-page forms on the Web. These ask for more than one line of information, and may make use of all the available form elements (push buttons, checkboxes, fields, scrolling menus, and so on). However, they probably also incorporate many other HTML design elements, such as style tags, formatted text, inline images, hypertext links, links to objects that launch helper applications, and even links to other sites.

Figure 9.7, which shows an excerpt from Edahn Golan's The Quiz! Site, is a good example of a full-page form with a variety of input field types.

FIG. 9.7
A full-page form uses a variety of controls to request much more than one line of information.

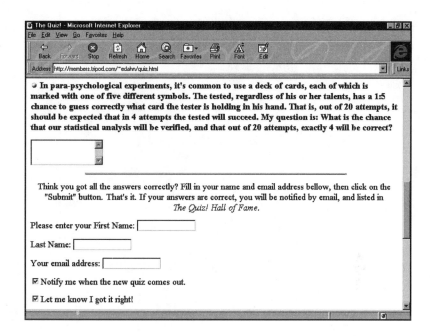

Multiple Forms

You can also put several separate forms on a single Web page. If there are multiple forms on one page, they are independent, each with its own Submit button.

Each individual form has its own associated program or script that is invoked when its Submit button is pressed. Only the data from the associated form is passed to the server. Figure 9.8 shows an example of a Web page with multiple forms.

> **CAUTION**
> If you put more than one form on a Web page, make sure you don't nest one form construct within another. Forms cannot be nested within forms.

Hidden Forms

You may have used forms without even knowing it. Sometimes forms are completely hidden. Forms can consist of nothing but hidden fields that send predefined data when an associated button, image, or link is clicked. The server can still make use of this data, just as if you had entered it yourself.

▶ **See** "Hidden Fields" to learn how to embed hidden data in your HTML forms, **p. 520**

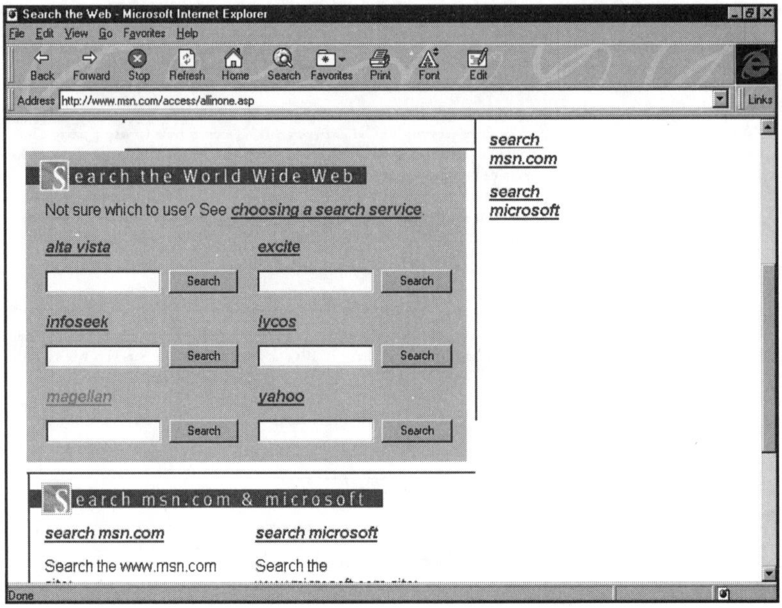

FIG. 9.8
The Microsoft Network Search page gives you several simple forms that you can use to search popular Web indexes.

Filling Out a Form

While most form input controls are fairly intuitive to the user, it doesn't hurt to take a moment to review how to properly fill out each type of form field you might encounter. Within a form, most of the controls you see are defined by just three HTML tags: <INPUT>, <SELECT>, and <TEXTAREA>. These tags are discussed from a programmer's point of view in Chapter 26, "Internet Explorer Forms and CGI Scripts." In this chapter, the focus is on what they look like on the Web page, and how to fill them in.

Our sample form as displayed in figure 9.9 is defined in the short HTML script shown in Listing 9.1.

Listing 9.1   09LST01.HTM   HTML Source for a Sample Form

```
<HTML>
<HEAD>
<TITLE>Forms Test Page</TITLE>
</HEAD>
<BODY>
<H1>Forms Test Page</H1>
<FORM ACTION="http://www.test.com/cgi-bin/binfile" METHOD=POST>
Type text in this field:
<INPUT NAME="FieldName" TYPE="TEXT" SIZE="15" MAXLENGTH="30">
Enter Password:
<INPUT NAME="pw" TYPE="PASSWORD" SIZE="5" MAXLENGTH="10"><BR>
Check all that apply:
```

```
<INPUT NAME="checkb1" TYPE="CHECKBOX" VALUE="author" CHECKED>Web author
<INPUT NAME="checkb2" TYPE="CHECKBOX" VALUE="programmer">Web programmer
<INPUT NAME="checkb3" TYPE="CHECKBOX" VALUE="master">Webmaster<BR>
I love my World Wide Web job:
<INPUT NAME="rad" TYPE="radio" VALUE="yes" CHECKED>Yes
<INPUT NAME="rad" TYPE="radio" VALUE="no">No
<INPUT NAME="rad" TYPE="radio" VALUE="maybe">Maybe<br>
<!— [Here's a HIDDEN field...] —>
<INPUT NAME="hidd" TYPE="hidden" VALUE="secret!">
<INPUT TYPE="submit" VALUE="Click Here to SUBMIT the form">
<INPUT TYPE="reset" VALUE="Click Here to RESET the Form"><P>
What's your name?
<SELECT NAME="Name" MULTIPLE>
<OPTION> Mary
<OPTION> Pete
<OPTION> Pamela
<OPTION> John
<OPTION SELECTED> Other
</SELECT>
Enter comments:
<TEXTAREA NAME="address" ROWS=5 COLS=40>
This is the comment box.  Please enter
your comments by deleting this text and
typing in what you have to say.
</TEXTAREA>
</FORM>
</BODY>
</HTML>
```

Part

II

Ch

9

FIG. 9.9

A sample form for reviewing how to fill out a form.

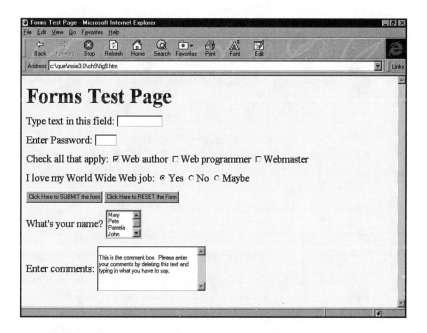

The *<INPUT>* Tag

The <INPUT> HTML tag is what is used to define most of the input areas of a Web page form. It has eight commonly used TYPE options, each of which looks and acts differently on-screen.

The TEXT type is used for entering a single line of text. The SIZE attribute specifies the visible width of a text field, while the MAXLENGTH attribute specifies the actual maximum number of characters that can be typed. (Though our example doesn't show it, you can also define a default value for input text that appears automatically in the text field by assigning VALUE="default text" in the INPUT tag line.) The following is an example:

```
<INPUT NAME="FieldName" TYPE="TEXT" SIZE="15" MAXLENGTH="30">
```

To fill in a TEXT field, point and click in the field, then type. To move from one TEXT field to the next, use the Tab key.

 Placing an <INPUT> tag in an HTML file will produce only the input field. It does not produce the prompting text to instruct the user what should be entered into the field. When coding forms, a good HTML author remembers to include appropriate prompting text for each input field.

A PASSWORD field is essentially the same as a TEXT field, but for security purposes the screen doesn't display what you type. Instead, you see a string of asterisks (*). The following is an example:

```
<INPUT NAME="pw" TYPE="PASSWORD" SIZE="5" MAXLENGTH="10">
```

You fill in a password field the same way you fill in a text field.

> **CAUTION**
>
> A password field protects your password from someone looking over your shoulder, but not from someone who might intercept your password as it moves along the Internet. Protecting data while it is in transit is discussed later in this chapter.

The CHECKBOX type is used to present a list of several options; the user can select any or all of them. When a box is checked, the value of its VALUE attribute is assigned to the variable specified in its NAME attribute. If present, the CHECKED attribute indicates that the checkbox is checked by default. An example follows:

```
<INPUT NAME="checkb1" TYPE="CHECKBOX" VALUE="author" CHECKED>
<INPUT NAME="checkb2" TYPE="CHECKBOX" VALUE="programmer">
<INPUT NAME="checkb3" TYPE="CHECKBOX" VALUE="master">
```

You check a checkbox by clicking it; you uncheck a checked checkbox by clicking it again.

The RADIO input type produces radio buttons. Radio buttons present users with a list of options; they may choose only one. This is done by giving several (at least two) radio buttons the same NAME attribute with different VALUEs. Selecting one of the buttons causes any previously selected button in the group to be deselected, and assigns the VALUE to the NAMEd variable. The

CHECKED attribute indicates which radio button is checked by default. The following is an example:

```
<INPUT NAME="rad" TYPE="radio" VALUE="yes" CHECKED>
<INPUT NAME="rad" TYPE="radio" VALUE="no">
<INPUT NAME="rad" TYPE="radio" VALUE="maybe">
```

You select a radio button by clicking it. If the radio button you click has the same variable NAME as a radio button that has already been selected, the previous button will automatically be unselected when you select the new one.

An input field of the HIDDEN type does not appear anywhere on a form, but the VALUE specified is transmitted along with the other values when the form is submitted. HIDDEN fields are not usually used on predefined Web page forms. They usually appear only on customized forms that are created "on-the-fly" by the Web server you're connected to. They are used to keep track of information specific to your request. For example, if you request information from a server and it sends back a form asking for additional details, that form might include a hidden field type that defines a request number. When you submit the second form, the server is then able to tell which request number your second form referred to. Following is a simple example from our test page, which returns just the value secret in the variable named hidd:

```
<INPUT NAME="hidd" TYPE="hidden" VALUE="secret">
```

You don't (and can't) fill out a HIDDEN field. Its value is predefined. In fact, you probably won't even know it's there.

The SUBMIT input type creates a push button which, when selected, activates the ACTION specified in the FORM definition. In most cases, this means it sends to the server the data from all of the form fields. The VALUE attribute of the SUBMIT type is actually the label that appears on the button. An example follows:

```
<INPUT TYPE="submit" VALUE="Click Here to SUBMIT the form">
```

When you are done filling out a form, click the Submit button to finish.

RESET also manifests itself as a push button, but selecting it resets all of a form's fields to their initial values. Like the Submit button, the VALUE attribute defines the button label text. An example follows:

```
<INPUT TYPE="reset" VALUE="Click Here to RESET the Form">
```

If you've totally mucked up filling out a form, click the Reset button to reset all the fields to their default values. Then you can start over.

N O T E There are other types for <INPUT> that are less often used or that are proposed for future versions, but the types just covered account for 95 percent of what you'll run into on the Web. ▨

There are two other common HTML tags besides <INPUT> that are used to create online forms: <SELECT> and <TEXTAREA>.

The <*SELECT*> Tag

<INPUT> fields of type RADIO and CHECKBOX can be used to create multiple choice forms. The <SELECT> tag, together with its companion closing tag </SELECT>, can be used to produce a multiple-choice field in the form of a pull-down list. If more than one choice is valid, the MUL-TIPLE attribute enables the selection of more than one option. Each choice is specified in a separate <OPTION> element, which can be preselected using the SELECTED attribute. An example is as follows:

```
<SELECT NAME="Name" MULTIPLE>
<OPTION> Mary
<OPTION> Pete
<OPTION> Pamela
<OPTION> John
<OPTION SELECTED> Other
</SELECT>
```

To choose a <SELECT> option, click it. To select more than one option in a MULTIPLE-enabled list, click one option and drag to select more. To select noncontiguous options, hold the Ctrl key when you click additional items. Selected items are highlighted; if you can highlight only one option, then the MULTIPLE attribute isn't enabled.

> **N O T E**   A <SELECT> menu with the MULTIPLE attribute is essentially the same as a group of checkboxes. Without MULTIPLE, a <SELECT> menu acts just like a set of radio buttons. ▓

The <*TEXTAREA*> Tag

The <TEXTAREA> and </TEXTAREA> tag pair lets you type multiple lines of text in a scrolling text box. As usual, the NAME attribute defines the variable. The ROWS and COLS attributes specify the width and height of the text area in characters. Default text (if any) is entered line by line between the <TEXTAREA> and </TEXTAREA> tags. An example follows:

```
<TEXTAREA NAME="address" ROWS=6 COLS=60>
This is the comment box. Please enter
your comments by deleting this text and
typing in what you have to say.
</TEXTAREA>
```

To fill in a <TEXTAREA> field, just click it and type. You can use all of the standard editing keys (arrows, Delete, Page Up/Down, and so on.) to move around and edit in the <TEXTAREA> box.

What Happens to the Data You Enter

Every <FORM> tag has an associated ACTION attribute that tells the browser where the program that processes the form data lives. Additionally, you can specify a METHOD attribute, which tells the browser how to send the data to the server. The two METHODs you can choose from are GET and POST.

GET

The GET method is no longer recommended, but you still see it used in some forms. It's functionally identical to the POST action described in the next section, but it sends form data appended to the URL rather than as a separate HTTP transaction. In the following example:

```
<FORM ACTION="http://www.server.com/cgi-bin/doit" METHOD=GET>
```

the form actually asks the server for a URL called **http://www.server.com/cgi-bin/doit&data&moredata&etc.**, where the items separated by ampersands at the end of the URL address are the various data fields you filled in on the form.

 Most browsers use the GET method by default, so if you like, you can skip saying METHOD=GET in your <FORM> tags.

The problem with GET is that there is a 1Kb limit on the size of a URL. If you append a lot of form data onto the ACTION URL, you run the risk of losing some of the data, since anything beyond 1Kb is ignored. The POST method was developed to work around this constraint.

POST

The form POST action sends form data back to a Web separate from the ACTION URL. This way, there's much less risk of creating a URL that's too long. The following is an example:

```
<FORM ACTION="http://www.server.com/cgi-bin/doit" METHOD=POST>
```

When submitted, this form launches a program called doit on the server, which processes your form data and performs the requested action(s).

 Even though GET is the default METHOD, more and more forms are using POST. If you code any HTML forms yourself, you should use POST whenever possible.

Data Encoding

Data sent to the server by either METHOD undergoes a process called *URL encoding*. URL encoding is not for security purposes; in fact, it's easily read by human eyes, even though it is a bit strange-looking. URL encoding is just a way for the server to identify form data and receive it reliably.

URL encoding simply runs all the form data together as a single string. It then replaces spaces with "+" characters; replaces nonalphanumeric characters with their ASCII hexadecimal equivalent, preceded by a percent (%) sign; includes NAME= in front of every field; and puts an ampersand (&) between fields.

Here's an example. Let's say the form you are submitting asks you for values for variables named YOURNAME, YOURCITY, and CHOICE. You fill it out with the following data:

Bill Clinton

Washington DC

Yes!

When you press the Submit button, the data is transmitted back to the server as follows:

`YOURNAME=Bill+Clinton&YOURCITY=Washington+DC&CHOICE=Yes%21`

The %21 in the line above is the conversion of the exclamation point. The exclamation point has an ASCII value of 33, which is equal to 21 in hexadecimal.

Fortunately, all of this is totally invisible to you. You don't have to worry about how it works at all, because the process is fully automatic.

POST and *MAILTO*

The form POST action can also simply mail form data to a specified address through the MAILTO command. The following is an example:

`<FORM ACTION="mailto:me@myserver.com" METHOD=POST>`

Rather than launching a program on the server, the MAILTO command mails the same URL-encoded data string to the specified Internet mail address. Though not all browsers support the MAILTO command, Internet Explorer does, and you'll find it used quite often on the Web.

The Form Submission Process Flowchart

So what really happens when you submit a form? The following is the step-by-step process that occurs when you submit a form:

1. While filling out the form, you can move around and edit, and even press the Reset button to clear the form back to its default settings.
2. When you are satisfied with the data you've entered, pressing the Submit button sends the form data to the server specified in the ACTION attribute of the <FORM> tag.
3. The server receives the data and executes the program specified by the ACTION attribute.
4. The program processes the data and composes a response based on the data it receives.
5. The server then sends the response back to you. If the action was successfully completed, you get a confirmation message or custom page, depending on the actions defined in the processing program. If unsuccessful, you are sent an error message.

TROUBLESHOOTING

I pressed the Submit button, but all I got back was some weird error message that I couldn't interpret. What gives? Several things can happen when you press the Submit button to result in your receiving an error message. The following are just a few:

- Between the time you received the form and the time you submitted it, the server you were connected to may have gone down.
- The server you're connected to may submit its form data to another server for processing, and that server may be down.
- The processing program may be buggy, and may have choked on your particular data.
- The processing program may be telling you that you filled out the form incompletely or incorrectly. Read the error message carefully to see if it's specific about the problem.

The fix is often no more complicated than pressing the Back button on the Internet Explorer toolbar and filling out the form correctly. If you continue to get errors, your only solution may be to e-mail the Webmaster of the site where you're experiencing the problems. There's usually an address or link on most home pages for this purpose.

Forms and Security

The first time you click the Submit button to order something using an online form, you may wonder if you should be afraid to use your credit card on the Web. But you might also wonder why no one seems to care about how much "insecurity" there is in more traditional uses of credit cards in stores, by mail order, and over the phone. It's really much more likely that someone will pull a receipt out of the trash at a store and steal your credit card number than it is that some hacker will intercept it on the Web.

The real issue is this: How trustworthy is the party you're dealing with? Your major worry should probably be the chance of running into a dishonest employee or a bogus company—online or not—that wants to steal your number outright.

That being said, it should also be noted that there really are a few dishonest hackers out there who revel in gathering information through any means possible. Some of them even go on to use it for personal gain. When this happens, it doesn't matter that the percentages are low if it's your credit card number they're playing with! And, as commerce increases on the Web, it's likely to draw larger numbers of out-and-out professional thieves, too.

Business and government are extremely concerned about security, and they won't trust their transactions to the Web until they're convinced that no one else can illegally tap in and see what's going on.

Clearly, the security of online transactions is not an issue that can be ignored.

Enter public key encryption. Encryption uses a "key" number to change readable text into unreadable code that can be sent and decrypted back into a legible message at the receiving end. A public key system uses two keys: a public key number and a private key number. Messages encrypted with the public key can be decrypted only with the associated private key, and messages encrypted with the private key can be decrypted only with the public key. You keep the private key private and make the public key as public as you want, and you've guaranteed that all of your communications will be secure.

TIP Point your Internet Explorer newsreader to the **comp.security** newsgroups for the latest discussions about security on the Web.

The following are some of the other issues involved in making sure your online communications are really secure:

- Is your computer (the client in the transaction) set up in a secure manner?
- Is the server you're connected to secure?
- Is the connection between the two systems secure?
- Is there some way you can be sure your transaction is secure?

All four of these concerns are addressed in the next few sections.

Client Security

Client security is the only area in which you have much say. Your computer is yours, and you can choose how to set it up. The chain being only as strong as its weakest link, you want to make sure that your link in the security chain is not the one that's going to snap first.

There are three areas where you have can have some major effect on the security process: how you configure helper applications and other programs, how you set up proxy servers, and how carefully you keep your passwords.

Helper Applications and Other Programs   You can get into some real security problems if you configure helper applications without first thinking about security issues (see fig. 9.10).

▶ **See** "Configuring a Helper Application" for detailed information on using the File Types dialog box to set up helper applications, **p. 243**

For example, if you configure Microsoft Excel as a helper application to view files with the extension .XLS, what happens if a spreadsheet file you view while you're browsing the Web has an autoexecute macro that runs some hidden (and sinister) procedures? At that point, your system has been breached.

You expose your PC to a great many security risks if you configure helper applications that aren't simply passive viewers or players, unless you are certain that downloaded files can never contain any malicious content.

Be careful about helper applications. Don't configure fancy helper applications that can be programmed to run sinister macros via the Web.

FIG. 9.10
You configure Internet Explorer helper applications in the File Types dialog box.

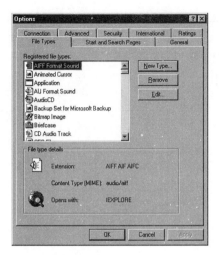

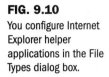

N O T E   Concern about sinister macros is very real. Recently, Microsoft addressed the issue of what it called a "prank macro" that was being distributed via a MS Word document on the Web. Though all this macro did was display a "playful" message, it could easily have done something much more harmful.

Microsoft immediately issued a prank-macro-swatter program that would kill the macro and scan all Word documents for it, to eliminate it from your system completely.

If nothing else, this real-world example illustrates how seriously Microsoft takes this issue.

Other items that support interactive content can be a threat to your system as well. CGI scripts, VBScript or JavaScript code, Java applets, and ActiveX Controls can all potentially contain ill-intentioned instructions. For this reason, Internet Explorer allows you to choose if you want any of these to be stored or run on your machine. This gives you complete control over active content applications and provides a level of safety unmatched by other browsers.

One other item that Internet Explorer provides security for is cookies. *Cookies* refer to information stored on your computer by your browser at the instruction of the Web server. You may recall from Chapter 8, "Customizing the Microsoft Network Start Pages," that cookies are a critical component in creating a custom Start Page on the Microsoft Network. In that case, a cookie file stores your customization parameters and they are sent to the MSN server when you request the MSN main page. The server uses the cookie information to construct the HTML code that produces your page and sends it back to the browser.

The security issue in this situation is that another computer (the Web server) is providing content to be written on *your* hard drive. While most sites that use cookies do so in a responsible way, it is still conceivable that there are servers in the world that are configured to dispense "bad cookies" that could damage your system. Internet Explorer gives you control over what cookies get written to your hard drive by prompting you when it receives instructions to write a cookie and by giving you the option to accept or reject the cookie.

Proxy Servers *Proxy servers*—also called *application gateways* or *forwarders*—are programs that handle communications between a protected network and the Internet. Most proxy programs log accesses and authenticate users.

If you run Internet Explorer from a machine on a network that is protected with a firewall (see "Firewalls" later in this chapter), you'll need to set up a different proxy server for each Internet application you want to use in conjunction with Internet Explorer—for example, one for FTP, one for Telnet, one for UseNet news, and so on.

Your major responsibility in this area is to make sure the proxies you use are secure and a good match to your network's firewall. In short, you should never use a proxy application that hasn't been approved by your system administrator.

N O T E If you connect to the Web via a commercial dial-up service such as America Online or CompuServe, you don't need proxies as these services already have adequate security measures in place. ▪

Passwords If you ever want to rob a bank, just walk in at noon and check around the computer terminals of people who are out to lunch. The odds are very, very good that you'll find at least one person who has left their system password on a sticky note in public view.

Of course, you'll never have to worry about anyone stealing your password, because you know the Five Basic Rules of Password Security, which are as follows:

- ▪ Choose a password that isn't obvious.
- ▪ Commit your password to memory.
- ▪ Never write down your password anywhere that's accessible by anyone but you.
- ▪ Change your password often.
- ▪ Don't ever share your password with anyone.

If you're on a network, you already have a password for network access. Odds are, you'll register for additional access passwords on many Web sites, as well.

N O T E Users on a Windows NT server network can take advantage of NT's challenge/response authentication feature. This permits increased password protection while still maintaining interoperability with other Internet servers. ▪

Server Security and Firewalls

A poorly managed Web server can be the source of many security compromises. For example, a poorly written CGI script can accidentally allow malicious intrusions into a system. The Web server administrator is responsible for managing the server in such a way as to prevent such security compromises.

It's also important that the Web server software installed on the server machine be capable of handling secure transactions over the Internet. For example, the Microsoft Internet

Information Server (Microsoft's server software package) incorporates Secure Sockets Layer (SSL) security, with support for acquiring a server certificate and communicating securely with SSL-capable browsers.

But perhaps the most important security concern regarding servers is the installation of a good firewall. A better name for the firewall might be traffic cop, because the main function of the group of programs that comprise a firewall system is to block some Internet traffic while allowing the rest to flow. There are several ways that this can be implemented on a server system, but all firewalls perform similar functions.

Some allow only e-mail traffic, which limits security concerns to "mail bombs" and other e-mail-based attacks. Others allow a full range of Internet access. In any event, a firewall performs two major functions: user authentication and access logging. The first keeps out intruders; the second provides an accurate record of what happened in case one does get through. Since all firewalls provide a single access point between the Internet and a network, they make it relatively easy to monitor communications should there be any suspected breaches of security.

Without some kind of firewall installed, a network system hooked up to the Internet is open to all kinds of security attacks.

> **N O T E**   Hummingbird Communications, Ltd. has developed the SOCKS protocol for the secure traversal of firewalls. Internet Explorer is compatible with firewalls that employ the SOCKS protocol. ■

> **T I P**   For more information on firewalls, point Internet Explorer to **ftp://ftp.greatcircle.com/pub/firewalls**, which contains the Firewalls mailing list archives.

Connection Security

Between point A (your computer) and point B (the Web server you're connected to on the Internet), there may be dozens of other computers handling the communications link. Obviously, the more computers in the chain, the more chances for some unknown someone to break into your transmission and steal your data.

Unfortunately, you don't have much control over your Internet connection. That's even more reason to make sure you do as much as you can to make the things you do have some control over as solid and secure as possible.

Transaction Security

Transaction security is the area that most people think of when they think of security on the Web. Maybe it's because it's the area that encompasses the most high-tech and romantic aspect of computer security: cryptography.

There is, of course, much more to transaction security than just data encryption. Message verification and server identification are at least as important, if not even more so. After all, what difference does it make if a message is securely encoded if its source is someone impersonating you who is trying to use your credit card or steal your data, or if a message that you legitimately sent has been intercepted and altered in transit?

A Note to Parents

What if your major concern is not making sure that data is transmitted securely, but making sure that it doesn't get transmitted at all? Many parents are concerned about (admittedly overblown) media reports about pornography and other objectionable materials that are available on the World Wide Web. They don't want their children to be able to access such data.

Parental lock-out systems can work in much the same way as the security measures employed in ensuring secure transactions. For example, a Web browser might have different accounts set up with different passwords and different encryption keys for parents' and kids' accounts. The parents' account might allow unlimited access, while the kids' account wouldn't properly decode transmissions from restricted sites. Such sites could be defined by looking for specific "ratings" tags sent by the Web server, or by setting up a list of forbidden sites. Internet Explorer has the capability of filtering out objectionable content according to a rating system.

There are many ways that parental lock-out could work. Microsoft and two other leading Internet software companies (Netscape and Progressive Networks) have formed the Information Highway Parental Empowerment Group to work on the problem.

Internet Explorer Security

Microsoft knows that security is a critical issue on the Internet, so it has incorporated support for the two major security protocols in use today: Secure Sockets Layer and Private Communication Technology.

Secure Sockets Layer (SSL)

The Secure Sockets Layer (SSL) protocol was developed by Netscape in response to the need for transmission security over the World Wide Web. SSL is application protocol-independent and provides *encryption*, which creates a secured channel to prevent others from tapping into the network; *authentication*, which uses certificates and digital signatures to verify the identity of parties in information exchanges and transactions; and *message integrity*, which ensures that messages cannot be altered en route.

SSL is layered beneath application protocols such as HTTP, Telnet, FTP, Gopher, and NNTP, and layered above the connection protocol TCP/IP. This strategy allows SSL to operate independently of the Internet application protocols. With SSL implemented on both the client and server, your Internet communications are transmitted in encrypted form, ensuring privacy.

SSL uses authentication and public-key encryption technology developed by RSA Data Security, Inc. Server authentication uses RSA public key cryptography in conjunction with ISO X.509 digital certificates. Internet Explorer delivers server authentication using signed digital certificates issued by trusted third parties known as certificate authorities. A digital certificate verifies the connection between a server's public key and the server's identification (just as a driver's license verifies the connection between your photograph and your personal identification). Cryptographic checks using digital signatures ensure that information within a certificate can be trusted.

Part
II
Ch
9

RSA Public Key Cryptography

RSA (Rivest-Shamir-Adleman) public key cryptographic technology is at the heart of most Web security schemes, including Netscape's Secure Sockets Layer protocol. The following is how it works, in a nutshell.

Encoding and decoding of messages is accomplished by using two large random numbers. One is called the public key, and is made public. The other is the private key, and is kept secret. Messages encoded with the public key can only be decoded using the private key, and vice versa. So messages sent to you can only be decoded by you, and messages you send can be verified as coming from you, since only your public key decodes them.

RSA, Inc. also makes a stand-alone security product for Windows called RSA Secure. RSA Secure integrates into the Windows File Manager to provide RSA encryption for the Windows file system. The company offers a trial version for 30-day evaluation, and checking it out is a good way to learn more about RSA encryption. For more information on RSA, Inc., or to download the free evaluation version of RSA Secure, go to their secure WWW server at **https://www.rsa.com/**.

Public key cryptography has been around only a couple of years longer than the World Wide Web. Pretty Good Privacy (PGP) is a stand-alone public-key encryption program from MIT for multiple platforms that lets you play around with and learn about public key cryptography. You can also use it for serious purposes, like encrypting mail and files on your hard disk. The latest version of PGP for Windows can be downloaded from **ftp://net-dist.mit.edu/pub/PGP**.

To learn more about PGP and public-key cryptography, point Internet Explorer to **http://bs.mit.edu:8001/pgp-form.html**.

The security of SSL comes from the fact that the numbers used in the encryption scheme are very large. Though they can be discovered by factoring, the amount of computer time required to do so is highly impractical, often running into hundreds of years. One case that took less time was the scheme used in the international version of the Netscape Navigator. This scheme was cracked in just a matter of days (see the sidebar entitled "The Cracking of SSL").

The Cracking of SSL

You may have read about it in the papers. Two University of California-Berkeley students and a researcher in France almost simultaneously posted messages to the Internet detailing their success in decoding a message that had been posted as a "Netscape security challenge." They discovered how Netscape 1.2 generates session encryption keys, enabling them to replicate the keys for that specific message with a moderate amount of computing power and, within a few days, they had deciphered it.

continues

continued

What was the problem? In a nutshell, Netscape was using a relatively small set of pseudo-random data (the number of processes running on the client computer, process ID numbers, the current time in microseconds, and so on) to generate a relatively large random number encoding key. This meant that the hackers didn't have to try every possible random 40-bit number to find the key.

The researcher in France used 120 workstations and two parallel supercomputers at three major research centers for eight days—approximately $10,000 worth of computing power. While this seems like a lot of effort to put into decoding just one simple little one-page message (and it is), it did serve to show that Netscape's security was crackable. If the same techniques had been applied to a security-critical message (for example, a hostile takeover bid for a major corporation), the consequences could be substantial.

The 40-bit key used in the "challenge" message is the international encryption mode used in export versions of Netscape Navigator. The 128-bit key encryption used in the U.S. version is export-restricted under government security regulations. It is much more robust; it would have taken many years to break the challenge message if the same amount of computing power had been used with the encoded U.S. version.

While no actual thefts of real-world information have ever been reported to Netscape Corporation, they worked quickly to provide updated software for free downloading from their home page on the Web. The new version 1.22 security patch increased the amount of random information used to generate keys from 30 bits to approximately 300 bits. With ten times as much pseudo-random data to start with, keys in the latest versions of Netscape Navigator are now effectively immune from similar "brute-force" attacks.

Internet Explorer supports both SSL 2.0 and SSL 3.0. SSL 2.0 creates a secure, encrypted channel and authenticates servers so that you know you're getting information from a genuine source. SSL 3.0 adds the ability to authenticate a server or a client and lets either one request authentication of the other. When authentication of your client is requested, Internet Explorer presents your digital identification to the server. If you have more than one digital ID, Internet Explorer gives you control over which should be presented when a server requests authentication.

Private Communication Technology

Internet Explorer also supports the Private Communication Technology (PCT) 1.0 security standard developed by Microsoft. Like SSL, PCT is layered between application protocols like HTTP and the TCP/IP connection protocol. PCT encrypts messages, authenticates servers to ensure that you are in contact with your intended party, and allows servers to request client authentication just like SSL 3.0 does. However, Microsoft boasts that PCT 1.0 is superior to SSL 3.0, particularly in the handshaking step during which client and server negotiate the secure connection. Internet Explorer supports all aspects of PCT, including the presentation of certificates during client authentication.

N O T E To read the Internet Draft for Mircosoft's PCT protocol, direct Internet Explorer to **http://www.microsoft.com/intdev/security/pct.htm.**

Business Transactions

First there was television which, from the very beginning, included commercials. Then there were those late-night infomercials. Finally, with the advent of cable TV, there was the Home Shopping Network (and its many clones).

Though the Internet began life as an infrastructure for the exchange of scholarly information, it didn't take long for someone to figure out how to turn a quick buck online with mass postings and mailings. And it took even less time for those annoying all-text "spam" messages to give way to a plethora of Web-based online shopping malls.

Not that there's anything wrong with that (though some old-timers may lament the commercialization of the Web). Let's face it—people like to buy things. And buying things on the Web is no worse than buying them from a television program or in the street. It's just different.

One of the toughest things to work out is how to pay for something you've ordered electronically. Cash and checks can't be sent by fiber-optic cable, and most people are leery about posting their credit card numbers where they might be grabbed by unscrupulous hackers.

But enterprising Web entrepreneurs have already figured out how to receive electronically the electronic equivalents of credit cards and money.

There are differences between using credit cards and using electronic cash, but the range of services available blurs the lines of distinction between the various methods of conducting financial transactions electronically on the Internet. Some schemes deal directly with banks, while some use second-tier arrangements, bonding houses, and/or third-party secure-server services.

Digital Money

Digital money is a totally new concept. Even more radical in concept than the once-preposterous idea that paper bills could represent real gold, in its most basic form digital money involves transmitting an encoded electronic packet of information that is as secure and difficult to counterfeit as a dollar bill.

Digital money is based on the same security encoding schemes as other secure transactions on the Web—encryption and authentication. But some of the proposed schemes go a step beyond.

For example, the two companies examined next have very different ideas of how digital money should work.

CyberCash   CyberCash has set up both debit and credit systems, but we're mostly interested here in the debit, or "cash" system.

In the CyberCash scheme, participating banks let customers open accounts that amount to "electronic purses." Using the company's software, a customer moves money from the checking account into the electronic purse. As with an automatic teller machine, the customer then withdraws digital tokens from the purse and uses them to make purchases on the Net. Upon receipt, the seller queries the CyberCash computer to verify that the token is valid and instructs CyberCash where to deposit the money.

To use the CyberCash system, you must install the client version of CyberCash software to work with your browser. It also requires that the Web server handling the transaction form use the CyberCash system to decrypt order information.

N O T E   For more on CyberCash, visit the company's Web site at **http://www.cybercash.com/**. ▣

DigiCash   DigiCash operates a debit system that is similar to an electronic checking account. To set up a DigiCash account, you deposit money in a bank that supports the DigiCash system, and you are issued Ecash that can be used to purchase things through the Web.

But DigiCash has a philosophy that is very different from CyberCash's. While CyberCash believes that consumers want transaction records so that they can account for their purchases, DigiCash sees records as a threat to privacy and has developed a method to create completely untraceable, anonymous, digital cash. Without anonymity, they say, electronic transactions leave a detailed trail of activity that could enable governments, personal enemies, or commercial marketers easily to trace an individual's activities, preferences, and beliefs.

DigiCash, based in the Netherlands, has created electronic tokens that can be trusted as valid money regardless of who is spending them. An ingenious double-blind encryption method makes it impossible to trace transactions unless there is mathematical proof that fraud has occurred.

But the idea of total anonymity has scared off most bankers and has government officials worried as well. Total anonymity, they fear, could provide a haven for money launderers, arms dealers, and kidnappers.

N O T E   For more information on DigiCash, check out the company on the Web at **http://digicash.support.nl/**. ▣

 T I P   For more information on digital money and the companies making it happen, check out the Yahoo index on the topic at **http://www.yahoo.com/Business_and_Economy/Electronic_Commerce/Digital_Money/**.

Credit Card Transactions

If you're concerned about security risks when using your credit card over the Web, then you should also be concerned about giving out any personal information through a Web page.

Using your credit card anywhere poses risks. Those risks are certainly more complex in the realm of Internet servers, browsers, and complex multifunctional systems. Secure communications do not eliminate all of an Internet user's concerns. The situation is analogous to telling someone your credit card number over the telephone. You may be secure in knowing that no one has overheard your conversation (privacy) and that the person on the line works for the company you wish to buy from (authentication), but you must also be willing to trust the person and the company.

That being said, let's look at a few of the schemes that are surfacing on the Web that claim to make using your credit card online as secure as, or even more secure than, using it at your local supermarket.

Netscape's Secure Courier   Netscape's Secure Courier protocol builds on its existing Secure Sockets Layer (SSL) protocol. Secure Courier observes the MasterCard and Visa security specification for bank card purchases on open networks.

While SSL encrypts data passing along the network between a client system and a server, Secure Courier keeps a transaction encrypted in a secure digital envelope when it arrives at a merchant's server or at other intermediate points on the Net. This means that the data remains wrapped, or protected, at any site at which it stops.

N O T E   To find out more about the Secure Courier protocol, connect to Netscape's Web site at the page **http://home.netscape.com/newsref/std/credit.html**. ▨

First Virtual   First Virtual Corporation is an online transaction handling company that operates a system designed for selling downloadable products, such as executable software files and information in text files. To get an account, call the company and submit your credit card information; you will be issued a First Virtual account number.

Whenever your First Virtual account number is used to purchase something online, you are notified by e-mail, and you must confirm the transaction before your credit card is charged. Once you verify, your card is charged for the purchase, and the money is deposited in the vendor's First Virtual checking account.

The First Virtual method needs no software or hardware on either end of the transaction. It's designed to be simple, fast, and efficient.

N O T E   For more detailed information on First Virtual, go to **http://www.fv.com/** on the Web. ▨

VeriSign   VeriSign, a spin-off of RSA, Inc., is collaborating with Microsoft and Netscape to provide Digital IDs (digital certificates) for direct online transactions using one company's browser or the other. The following four classes of ID are available:

- ▪ **Class 1**—Provides a low level of assurance, to be used for secure e-mail and casual browsing. Noncommercial and evaluation versions are offered for free, with a VeriSign-supported commercial version for $6 per year.

Part
II

Ch
9

- **Class 2**—Provides a higher degree of trust and security. Used for access to advanced Web sites, it costs $12 per year.

- **Class 3**—Provides a higher level of assurance for valued purchases and intercompany communications, at $24 per year.

- **Class 4**—Said to provide "a maximum level of identity assurance" for high-end financial transactions and trades. Pricing is by quote.

The Digital ID system from VeriSign is being marketed as "The Driver's License for the Internet." RSA has the good fortune to own the patents on the encryption schemes used by SSL and Secure HTTP (S-HTTP), so this gives the VeriSign system a boost.

N O T E For more information on VeriSign's approach, see **http://www.verisign.com/**.

Open Market Open Market acts as its own credit card company in a scheme that relies on its own Open-MarketPlace Server. It is unique in that it depends on the end user having a browser that supports the S-HTTP protocol, not Netscape's SSL protocol. Open Market will be worth watching, if just to see whether a company other than Netscape can help set security standards on the Web.

N O T E You can check out Open Market's Web site at **http://www.openmarket.com/**.

 For lots of links relating to credit cards, point Internet Explorer to the Credit Card Network Home Page at **http://ccn-home.html**.

For an excellent detailed discussion of how credit card transactions work on the Web, check out **http://www.netscape.com/newsref/std/credit.html**.

The Future of WWW Security

With a topic as hot as security, it's not easy to get an agreement on the question of what's secure. Though Netscape Corporation is in a powerful position, it's not powerful enough simply to dictate security standards for the World Wide Web. There are a lot of people out there—powerful, influential, and monied people in banking and credit and the government—who simply aren't convinced that Netscape's SSL protocol can protect their important transactions over the Internet.

That's why there are dozens of alternate proposals for security protocols for Web transactions. Because of Netscape's position in the Web community, it's likely that SSL will be with us well into the future, but you're still likely to start running into some sites that want you to use another protocol. The following pages offer an overview of some of the most likely contenders for real-world implementation as Web security protocols in the months and years to come.

TIP For a lengthy discussion of current Web security issues, check out **http://www-genome.wi.mit.edu/ WWW/faqs/www-security-faq.html**.

S-HTTP

S-HTTP (Secure HTTP) has emerged as the major competitor to Netscape's SSL security protocol. In fact, it has gained such a following that most commerce on the Web will be supporting both protocols—including Netscape Navigator!

Developed by EIT, CommerceNet, OpenMarket, and others, S-HTTP extends the Web's standard HTTP data transfer protocol by adding encryption and decryption using paired public key encryption, support for digital signatures, and message authentication.

Several cryptographic message format standards can be incorporated into S-HTTP clients and servers, including PKCS-7, PEM, and PGP. S-HTTP clients can also communicate with nonsecure standard HTTP servers, though without security.

S-HTTP doesn't require (though it does support) client-side public key certificates or public keys, which means that you can initiate spontaneous transactions without first having an established public key.

S-HTTP also provides for simple challenge-response freshness authentication—that is, an "are you really you" and "yes, I'm really me" secure message exchange—to make sure no one is intercepting and changing transmitted messages. It can even consider HTTP's DATE header when determining freshness.

N O T E For more information on S-HTTP, visit the following sites: **http://www.eit.com/**, **http:// www.openmarket.com/**, or **http://www.commerce.net/**. ▪

Shen

CERN (the organization in Switzerland that created the World Wide Web) is developing a new, high-level, secure protocol called Shen. It approaches security by providing for weak authentication with low maintenance and no patent or export restrictions, or strong authentication using public key encryption. Since it comes from CERN, which has the ear of the whole Web, Shen is bound to become a standard itself, or at least will influence the development of other security standards.

N O T E For more information on Shen, point Internet Explorer to **http://www.w3.org/hypertext/ WWW/Shen/ref/shen.html**. ▪

Fortezza

One of Netscape's latest security additions is integrated support for the Fortezza security card, which is based on U.S. government standard cryptography. Developed by the National Security

Agency, Fortezza is a cryptographic system delivered in a PCMCIA card format, and is now mandatory for use in many government agencies. Fortezza cards are already being used by the Department of Defense and the U.S. intelligence community.

Support for Fortezza has been added to Netscape's Secure Sockets Layer (SSL) open protocol, and Netscape will be upgrading its products to support the use of Fortezza cards.

T I P   Security is a hot topic on the Web. A good place to find out more about security online is the Virtual Library Subject Catalogue entry on the topic, at **http://www.w3.org/hypertext/DataSources/ bySubject/Overview.html**.

## CHAPTER 10

E-Mail with Internet Explorer and Microsoft's Internet Mail Client

Microsoft's first answer for an e-mail solution for their Internet Explorer Web browser, Microsoft Exchange, was overkill for many applications. While an excellent program for the heavy, corporate user, as a purely Internet e-mail client, Exchange was too big, too slow, and too hard to run.

With Internet Explorer 3, Microsoft has introduced an integrated Internet Mail Client designed to work with the Web browser to meet all of your Internet e-mail needs. The program is simple, easy to configure and use, and has many of the features you have come to expect from an e-mail program, such as encoded file attachment support, customizable folders for organizing e-mail, and an address book for frequently used e-mail addresses. ■

What is Microsoft's new Internet Mail Client?

In this chapter, you'll learn about the new Internet Mail Client Microsoft has released as a part of Internet Explorer 3.

How do I install and configure the Internet Mail Client?

Find out how to install and configure the program to work with your Internet service provider for incoming and outgoing e-mail.

How do I send and receive e-mail?

Learn how to compose and send e-mail, and read, reply to, and forward incoming e-mail.

Can I organize my incoming and outgoing e-mail?

Discover the Internet Mail Client's customizable folder structure and how you can use it to organize and archive both your incoming and outgoing e-mail.

How do I set up an Address Book?

Internet Mail Client has a system of organizing frequently used e-mail addresses.

Microsoft's New Internet Mail Client

Because Microsoft Exchange is not well suited to the average home user's Internet e-mail needs, Microsoft's Internet group—when they developed Internet Explorer 3—also created a new Internet e-mail client. Known as the Internet Mail Client, it is especially designed to interface with Internet Explorer 3 and to service all of your Internet e-mail needs. The new e-mail client provides most of the functionality that veteran Net users have come to expect from their software.

You can use the Microsoft Internet Mail Client for all of your Internet e-mail needs. Of course, you can use it to write and send messages—you can also reply to, forward, and carbon copy messages, just as users of third-party mail packages can. Message management is a snap because you have the ability to transfer your traffic to a set of custom, user-defined mail folders. Within those folders, you can sort your mail by subject, sender, or date. You can also keep and maintain a list of your most frequently used addresses.

If you're a casual e-mail user, you'll likely find that Internet Explorer 3's new mail capabilities, available through the Internet Mail Client, are all you need.

But if you're accustomed to using other mail packages—programs like Eudora and cc:Mail—you may find that Microsoft's package isn't quite complete. Power users will miss high-end features like automatic message filtering.

All in all, if you're happy with your current mail program, you'll have to make the call as to whether you want to switch to the Internet Explorer Mail Client just yet. You'd be well-advised, however, to watch carefully as it evolves in the future. It's quite clear that Microsoft is serious about making a complete set of products for accessing the Internet and the World Wide Web.

But if you're a new mail user, or if you haven't found a package quite to your liking just yet, you'll probably want to give Microsoft's Internet Mail Client a try. You may find that it meets your needs completely.

Installing the Internet Mail Client

Microsoft's Internet Mail and News Clients come bundled together in a self-extracting, self-installing file called `Mailnews95.exe`. To install either or both of these clients, follow these steps:

1. Execute `Mailnews95.exe`. The program will then self-extract the necessary files and automatically start the installation process. You will be shown an alert box giving you the option to start the installation, and asked to agree to the licensing agreement, after which the Internet Mail and News Setup Wizard will be started.

2. Fill in your name and organization and choose <u>N</u>ext. The next dialog box that appears will ask you to confirm the name and organization.

3. You can elect to install either the Internet Mail or News clients, or both. Make your choice and choose <u>N</u>ext.

4. That's it! The Internet Mail and/or News clients are now installed. The final step necessary to complete the installation process is to choose OK from the final dialog box to restart your computer.

   ▶ **See** "Reading UseNet Newsgroups with Internet Explorer," to find out how to use the Internet News Client to access UseNet news, **p. 201**

After you have restarted your computer, you will be ready to run the Internet Mail Client. You can access the Internet Mail Client by clicking the Mail & News icon located on the toolbar (see fig. 10.1).

FIG. 10.1
Internet Explorer 3 provides easy access to your Internet Mail Client.

Mail & News icon—

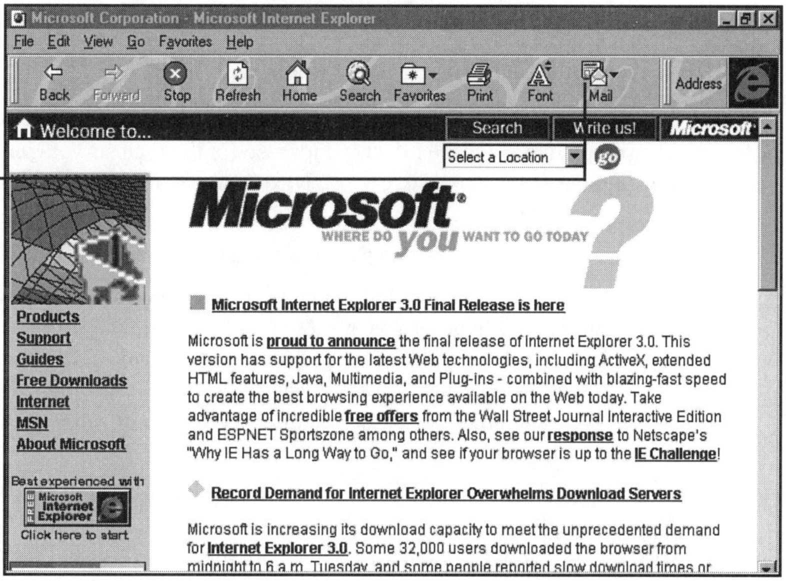

Setting Mail Preferences

The first time you run the Internet Mail Client, you will be asked to provide some basic information about yourself, your Internet provider, and your computer. The program will automatically ask you for this basic information, the minimum it needs in order to operate.

Initial Configuration

When you first run the Internet Mail Client, you will be greeted with the Internet Mail Configuration Wizard (see fig. 10.2). The purpose of this is to find out from you the minimum information needed to interface with your Internet service provider (ISP) to provide incoming and outgoing e-mail services.

N O T E   Most of the information requested in this initial configuration process should have been provided to you by your ISP, so make sure you have everything from them in front of you when you begin. If you have any problems or questions with the configuration, they're probably your best source for help. ■

Part
II

Ch
10

FIG. 10.2

The Internet Mail Configuration Wizard guides you through the process of the minimum configuration needed to send and receive Internet e-mail.

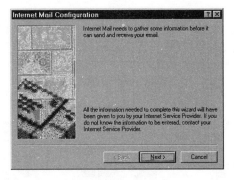

To run the initial configuration, follow these steps:

1. In the Internet Mail Configuration Wizard initial dialog box, press Next. You will then be prompted to enter the Internet addresses of the mail servers for incoming (POP3) and outgoing (SMTP) e-mail. Choose Next after you have done so.

2. Next, in order to access your e-mail account, you will be asked to enter your mail account ID and password—these are usually the same as your account ID and password.

   By default, the Internet Mail Client will remember your password and use it to connect automatically whenever you ask it to check your e-mail. However, if you consider this a security risk, you can leave the password entry blank. Then, whenever the Internet Mail Client checks for your e-mail, you will be asked to enter your password. As long as you leave the Remember Password box unchecked when entering your password, it will not be stored.

3. Next, you will be able to enter the information that the Internet Mail Client uses to "sign" your outgoing e-mail, your name and e-mail address. Normally, the e-mail address is the same as that used to send the e-mail, but there's no reason that you can't use a different one if you prefer to receive your e-mail in an account other than the one from which it is sent.

4. The final step in the initial configuration process gives you the opportunity to set the Internet Mail Client to be the default program to be used to send e-mail from your Web browser.

Configuration Options

To access all of the configuration options for the Internet Mail Client, you can select Mail, Options. Various options can be set under each of the tabs in the Options dialog box that appears.

The Read Tab   The options on this tab, shown in figure 10.3, affect the way the Microsoft Internet Mail Client checks for your e-mail, and how it informs you when you have some. You can set up the Internet Mail Client to periodically check for your e-mail whenever it is running.

FIG. 10.3

The Read tab of the Options dialog controls how the Internet Mail Client reads and reacts to incoming e-mail.

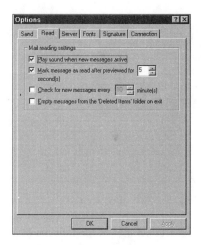

The Send Tab   The Send tab controls various aspects of the configuration for outgoing e-mail (see fig. 10. 4). The options here are pretty self-explanatory, and you should feel free to experiment with them. If you press the HTML Settings or Plain Text Settings button on this tab, you are greeted with the Settings dialog box (see fig. 10.5). Here you can control the type of encoding used for file attachments, as well as control a few other options.

> **TIP**   You'll probably want to queue your messages on disk if you do most of your work offline as a dial-in Internet user by not checking the Send messages immediately box. Send them by clicking the Send and Receive button or typing Ctrl+M.

FIG. 10.4

Send options give you control over outgoing e-mail.

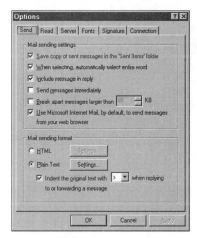

FIG. 10.5

The Settings of the Send options allow you to pick an encoding format for file attachments, and gives you more options.

 TIP For greatest compatibility, you will normally want to use Mime format, and Encode Text Using either Quoted Printable or Base 64.

The Server Tab This tab is probably the most important of the tabs on the Options dialog box. On this tab, seen in figure 10.6, you tell the Internet Mail Client how to get and send your mail. This information is necessary for correct operation of the Internet Mail Client, and so was read in when you performed the initial configuration.

FIG. 10.6

The Servers options are the heart and soul of the Internet Mail Client, as these are what allows you to send and receive Internet e-mail.

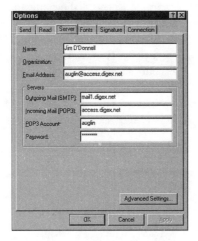

If there is anything out of the ordinary about the mail servers provided to you by your Internet service provider, you can configure your copy of the Internet Mail Client by pressing the Advanced Settings button. This causes the Mail Server Advanced Settings dialog box to appear (see fig. 10.7).

FIG. 10.7

The Mail Server Advanced Settings dialog box allows you to configure the Internet Mail Client for out-of-the-ordinary mail servers, and gives you further control over its behavior.

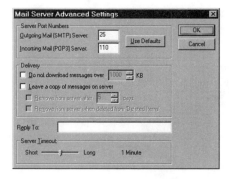

The Fonts Tab   The Fonts tab allows you to choose what fonts are used for the display of e-mail messages in the Internet Mail Client (see fig. 10. 8). You can pick the font to be used to display all e-mail, the color for outgoing e-mail, and the language encoding to use.

Part
II
Ch
10

FIG. 10.8

The Fonts tab allows you to set the display fonts for incoming and outgoing e-mail.

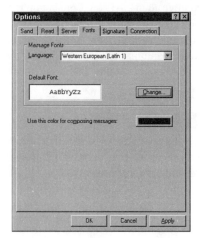

 E-Mail messages are often formatted with monospaced fonts in mind, such as Courier, so you should probably pick a monospaced display font. (I like Lucida Console.)

The Signature Tab   The Signature tab, shown in figure 10.9, allows you to select whether or not you want to include a signature text block at the end of each of your outgoing e-mail messages. If you want to, you can either specify the text directly in the area shown, or specify a file, called a *sigfile*, with the information in it.

FIG. 10.9

You can set up your signature block information using this tab.

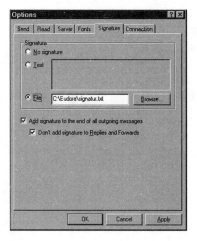

The Connection Tab   The final configuration tab is the Connection tab. This allows you to tell the Internet Mail Client how you connect to the Internet. In addition, if you use a dial-up connection, you can specify which Windows 95 Dial-Up Networking connection to use. This information will allow the Mail Client to automatically establish an Internet connection to periodically check your mail, and then to disconnect immediately afterwards.

Using the Mail Package

Now that you have your Internet Explorer 3 Internet Mail Client installed and configured, you're ready to use it to send and receive your Internet e-mail. It has many features that you can use to effectively send, receive, and organize your e-mail.

Understanding the Screen

When you run the Internet Mail Client, the window that you get is divided into several different areas. In addition to the familiar title, menu, and toolbars, there are other distinct areas. The default window setup is shown in figure 10.10.

There are many different parts to this screen. Let's get oriented with the following parts:

- At the top of the screen, just underneath the menu bar, is the Mail Client toolbar. The buttons on this toolbar perform the normal Windows 95 cut/copy/paste operations, as well as print and delete messages, check for new mail, and search mail messages.

- Underneath the toolbar is the icon bar which gives a list of Mail Client actions that you can perform.

- Also near the top of the mail screen is a drop-down menu giving you access to a list of the mail folders, currently showing the Inbox of incoming e-mail. At minimum, this listing contains your Inbox, Outbox, Deleted Items, and Sent Items—it will also contain any new folders that you create. This is also known as the status bar.

Icon bar   Toolbar   Mail folders drop-down menu

FIG. 10.10
Microsoft's Internet Mail Client's clean mail layout provides easy access to your message traffic and your personal mail folders.

Read message indicator

Unread message indicator

Preview pane

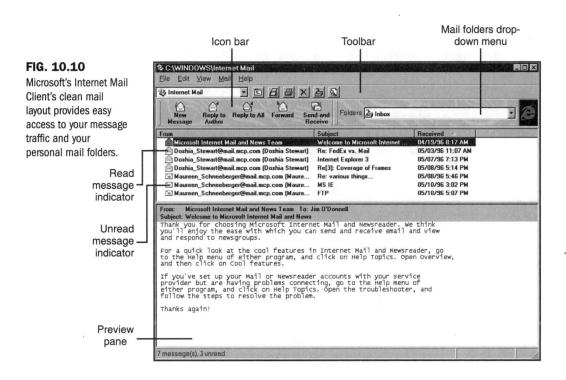

 T I P   You can adjust the amount of space taken up by these three items be grabbing them with the mouse and moving them around or dragging them up and down to conceal their text descriptions. Also, the toolbar, icon bar, and status bar can all be individually turned off or on under the View menu.

■ Underneath the mail folders drop-down menu is a scrollable list of message headers for every piece of mail in the folder you're looking at. The Inbox opens by default when you first open the Internet Mail Client. The icon shown to the left of each message header indicates whether the message has been read or not.

■ On the bottom of the screen, you see the text of the open message, along with headers indicating the message's subject, sender, and recipient. This is the Internet Mail Client's preview pane—if you want, you can view a given message in a full screen of its own by double-clicking its header in the message header pane.

N O T E   You may notice at low screen resolutions that the Internet Mail Client's mail display is a bit cramped. You can adjust the sizes of the various panes by clicking and dragging their frames. You'll find that the only real way to see what you're doing, video card permitting, is to use a higher screen resolution. Open Control Panel's Display Properties, click the Settings tab, and set the Desktop Area slider to at least 800×600 pixels for a better look. ■

Part
II

Ch
10

Checking for Mail

Whenever the Internet Mail Client is running and your Internet connection is up, the mail client will check for incoming e-mail messages in a couple of different circumstances. If you click the Send and Receive button, choose Mail, Send and Receive Mail, or press Ctrl+M, (or at fixed intervals, if you set up the Internet Mail Client to periodically check for your e-mail under the Read tab of the Mail, Options dialog), the alert box shown in figure 10.11 will be displayed. The Internet Mail Client will then contact your mail server to check for your e-mail. If you have any outgoing e-mail queued, it will also be sent at this time. Any new messages will have their headers displayed in your Inbox, and you will be able to read them.

FIG. 10.11

The Internet Mail Client is querying your POP3 mail server to see if you have any new e-mail.

Composing and Sending Mail

Microsoft's Internet Mail and News Clients use a similar front end for message composition. In the case of the Mail Client, you begin a new message either by clicking the New Message button on the icon bar; by selecting Mail, New Message; or by pressing Ctrl+N. A message form like the one shown in figure 10.12 opens.

FIG. 10.12

Internet Mail Client uses a standard form for outgoing e-mail and UseNet article. Here's an e-mail message ready to go.

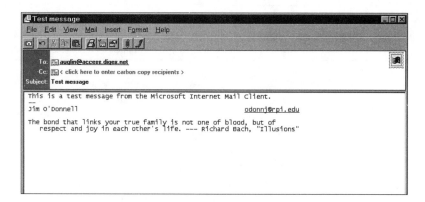

Fill out the message by following these steps:

1. Type the address of the person or organization you're writing to in the To field.

2. Type a short phrase in the Subject field describing the content of your message.

3. If you want to send copies of your message to third parties, add one or more e-mail addresses in the Cc field.

Once you have entered e-mail addresses into the To and Cc fields, you can ask the Mail Client to check them by clicking the Check Names button on the toolbar, selecting Mail, Check Names, or pressing Ctrl+K. If you do this, the Mail Client will see if the name is one from your Address Book, or verify that it is a well-formed Internet e-mail address (i.e., of the form **username@host.domain.**)

Once you have checked the names and the Mail Client has verified that they all seem to be proper, they will be underlined, as shown in figure 10.13. (For more information about the Mail Client's Address Book, see "Using the Address Book" later in this chapter.)

FIG. 10.13
Once you have asked the Internet Mail Client to check the names and e-mail addresses in the To and Cc fields, they will be displayed underlined.

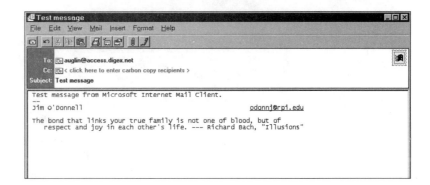

4. Click once in the main text box to set the cursor at the beginning of your message, and begin writing your text. Standard Windows 95 Cut, Copy, and Paste commands are available on the Edit menu.

5. When finished, click the Send button on the far left side of the Composition window's toolbar. Unless you have chosen the send messages immediately, this will queue the message to be sent the next time the Internet Mail Client connects to your mail server to send and receive e-mail.

Attaching Files to Mail

Most e-mail packages provide the capability to transmit binary files over the Internet by attaching ASCII-coded copies of them to your message traffic. Microsoft's Internet Mail Client is no exception. In fact, its file attachment facility is one of the most versatile around.

You can attach files to a message any time before sending it. Click the Insert File toolbar button to open the Insert Attachment dialog box (see fig. 10.14). You may also do this by selecting Insert, File Attachment.

Once the Insert Attachment dialog opens, you may add files to your message by selecting the file and choosing the Attach button. Once a file has been attached, it will appear in the message composition screen as shown in figure 10.15.

FIG. 10.14

The Insert Attachment dialog box looks and works like any other Windows 95 file-handling dialog box.

FIG. 10.15

File attachments to Internet Mail Client's outgoing messages are denoted by icons in the bottom pane on the composition screen.

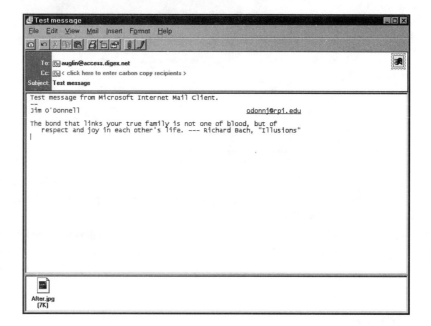

Receiving and Replying to Mail

As explained earlier, the Internet Mail Client will try to log on and retrieve messages from your mail server whenever you ask it to, or at fixed intervals.

TROUBLESHOOTING

When the Internet Mail Client tries to deliver my mail, it responds with a message that it's unable to locate the server. What's wrong? There could be one of four things wrong—three of which you can do something about. The first thing you want to do is note the name of the server the Internet Mail Client is trying to access. It'll be listed in the error message. It should be the name of your ISP's mail server. If it isn't, choose Mail, Options to open the Options dialog box. Click the Servers tab and correct the entry in the Mail (SMTP) Server field.

If the Internet Mail Client has the right mail server address but can't get through, you may be working offline or you may have another program open that's got the mail server tied up. Get online by dialing in or logging on. Close any other program that uses SMTP or POP service before you try to use the Internet Mail Client.

The remaining possibility is that your Internet provider's mail server is down. If that's the case, you can do little but wait. If your provider has a help desk, you may want to call to let them know there's a problem.

The Internet Mail Client dumps all new mail into the Inbox, unless you have configured its Inbox Assistant. This is available under the Mail, Inbox Assistant menu option, and allows you to look for words in any of the To, Cc, From, or Subject fields. If there is a match, the incoming message can be automatically routed to one of your mail folders (including the Deleted Items folder, if its from someone you really don't want to hear from).

Like most e-mail packages, the Internet Mail Client lets you respond directly to a message without having to address a new one from scratch. You do this by using the Reply to Author, Reply to All, and Forward buttons on the mail screen's icon bar.

By clicking either Reply to Author or Reply to All, you can tell the Internet Mail Client to create a pre-addressed message. The text of the message you received will be included if you checked the Include message in reply checkbox in the Send tab of the Options dialog box (see fig. 10.16). Trim the length of the included text to only what is necessary using standard editing cut, copy, and paste commands.

FIG. 10.16

By using the Reply command, you can draft understandable answers to your e-mail quickly and easily.

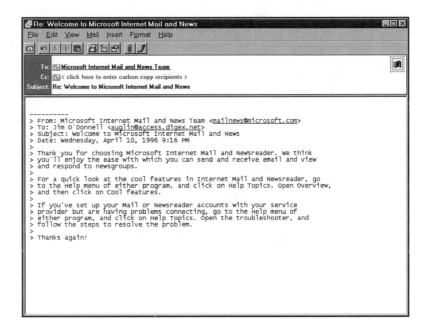

The Forward button works a bit differently. As with Reply to Author and Reply to All, clicking it creates a new message. This time, however, you supply the address of your intended recipient.

Organizing Your Mail

Fortunately, Microsoft doesn't make mail sorting hard with its Internet Mail Client. You can add and name an unlimited number of folders and shift messages between them at your discretion.

Create a folder by selecting File, Folder, Create. The Create New Folder dialog box appears (see fig. 10.17). An Internet Mail Client mail folder is nothing more than a Windows 95 file, so you can give it a name up to 255 characters long. You may want to keep your names shorter than that, though. As it displays your folders, the Internet Mail Client truncates the names of any that are too long to fit in the available window.

FIG. 10.17
User-created message
folders simplify the task
of organizing your
e-mail.

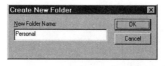

> **N O T E**   Unlike many full-featured e-mail packages, the Internet Mail Client does not offer any
> method of nesting folders within folders. High-volume mail users may find this a serious
> limitation that argues for keeping their current software. Low-volume users should be able to get along
> fine, but they may find it advisable to keep their filing system short and understandable.   ■

Conversely, you can kill an unused folder by choosing File, Folder, Delete, and selecting the name of the folder you want to delete.

The commands for shifting mail between folders—Move to and Copy to—are under the Mail menu (see fig. 10.18). Highlight either, and you'll find a list of your folders nested beneath them.

FIG. 10.18
The commands to move
and copy messages into
folders take only a
single click. Highlight
the folder you want to
send the message to,
and release the mouse
button.

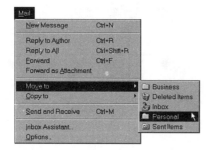

The Move and Copy commands work the same way:

1. Highlight the message(s) you want to move or copy in the Message headers pane by clicking them.
2. Click the Mail menu and select Move to or Copy to.
3. A list of your folders will pop up next to the Mail menu. Select the folder you want the message transferred to.

Choosing Move to places the selected message into the destination folder and deletes it from the source. Copy to puts a copy in the destination folder while leaving the contents of the source folder unchanged.

Within folders, the Internet Mail Client gives users several options for sorting messages. All are accessible by clicking the View menu and highlighting Sort By. The three options—Sort By From, Subject, and Received—are largely self-explanatory. Toggling the Ascending command tells the Internet Mail Client to arrange messages in ascending or descending order.

 You can send any highlighted message to the Deleted Items folder by clicking the Delete button on the toolbar; by selecting File, Delete; pressing Ctrl+D; or by transferring it there using the Message menu's Move to command. Deleted Items stay on your disk, however, until you delete the item from the Deleted Items folder, unless you have selected the Empty messages from the Deleted Items folder on exit option under the Read tab of the Mail, Options menu. This is done by deleting the item from the Deleted Items folder using any of the methods given at the beginning of this paragraph.

 In addition to deleting unwanted messages, you can further reduce the disk space needs of the Internet Mail Client by compacting mail folders by choosing File, Folder, Compact, and selecting the desired folder (see fig. 10.19).

FIG. 10.19
You can ask the Internet Mail Client to compact some or all of your mail folders—this slows down retrieval of these messages a little, but saves space on your hard drive.

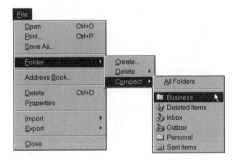

Using the Address Book

Because typing in the full e-mail address for someone every time you want to send them a message can get pretty tiresome, almost all e-mail programs include some way to assign names, nicknames, or aliases to frequently used e-mail addresses. Microsoft's Internet Mail Client is no exception.

The Internet Mail Client maintains an Address Book that you can use to store names and e-mail addresses for your correspondents. The Address Book is accessed by choosing File, Address Book—it looks like figure 10.20.

FIG. 10.20

The Mail Client's Address Book gives you an easy way to keep track of frequently used e-mail addresses, and the names of the folks they belong to.

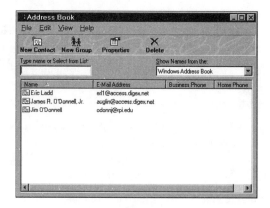

You can add someone to your Address Book—or edit the name or e-mail address of someone already in it—by clicking the New Entry or Properties buttons, respectively. In either case, you will get the Properties dialog box which will allow you to add information about the person you want to put in your Address Book under its Personal, Home, Business, and Notes tabs (see fig. 10.21).

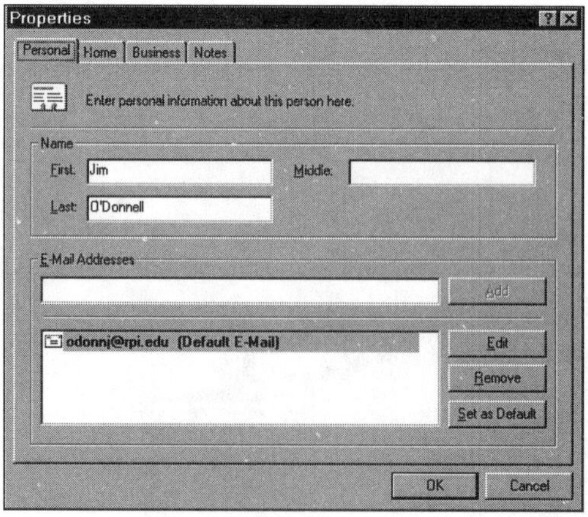

FIG. 10.21

Entries in the Address Book, consisting of a name and e-mail address, make it easier to send e-mail.

Another way to add addresses to your Address Book is right from the mail composition screen. Once you have entered an e-mail address into the To or Cc field and had the Internet Mail Client check it for validity (so that it is underlined), you can right-click it, and select Add To Address Book (see fig. 10.22). Selecting Properties from this pop-up menu also allows you to enter a name into the Address Book for the e-mail address.

FIG. 10.22

You can also add entries to your Address Book directly from a message window.

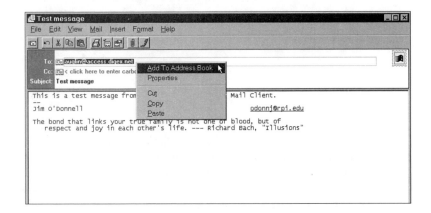

Once you have defined names in your Address Book, it is easy to include them in the To or Cc fields of messages that you are composing. You can do this by choosing Mail, Choose Recipients from the message composition window, or by clicking the small icon immediately to the right of the words To or Cc. The Select Recipients dialog appears (see fig. 10.23). You can select names from the window at left, and click the To or Cc buttons, and this adds the appropriate names to the recipients lists of your e-mail message (see fig. 10.24).

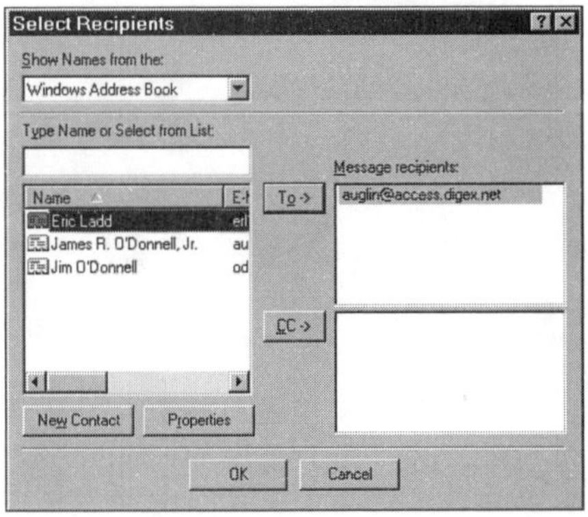

FIG. 10.23

The Select Recipients dialog box gives you an easy way to send messages to people in your Address Book.

FIG. 10.24

Mail recipients identified in your Address Book by name are listed by name in your mail messages.

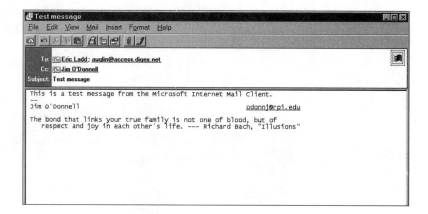

Another option you can use under the Mail Client Address Book is to set up group names. This is done by clicking the New Group button from the Address Book icon bar (or by selecting an existing group and clicking the Properties button). You can then specify a group name and a list of people in that group. Once a group has been established, you can then use that group name in the To or Cc field of an outgoing message—that message will then go to all members of that group. ●

Reading UseNet Newsgroups with Internet Explorer

With Internet Explorer 2, Microsoft added the capability to access UseNet newsgroups through its Web browser. However, this capability was rudimentary at best and a far cry from the newsgroup support available in many freeware and shareware newsreaders, such as News Xpress and Free Agent.

With Internet Explorer 3, however, Microsoft has added an Internet News Client that brings its news reading capabilities a long way. While still not possessing all of the capabilities of dedicated news readers, the Internet News Client has more than enough functionality for most of your UseNet news needs. ■

What is UseNet?

Get a brief primer on UseNet, which is necessary if this is the first time you'll be connecting up to it.

What is Microsoft's new Internet News Client?

In this chapter, you'll learn about the new Internet News Client Microsoft has released as a part of Internet Explorer 3.

How do I install and configure the Internet News Client?

Find out how to install and configure the program to work with your Internet service provider for accessing and responding to UseNet news.

How do I read and respond to UseNet news?

Learn how to browse through and access UseNet newsgroups, read articles, reply to them, and post original articles of your own.

How do I send and receive binary files?

Discover Internet News Client's capabilities to automatically encode and decode file attachments to UseNet news articles.

A UseNet Primer

Newsgroups are a bit more complicated than forums, BBSes, and cork boards. Not in a technical sense, but in a cultural sense. Newsgroups don't have official rules that are enforced by anyone in particular. They have unofficial rules that newsgroup peers enforce. Newsgroups concentrate cultures, from all over the world, in one place—a source of a lot of conflict as you can imagine.

So, take a few moments to study this section before you dive into newsgroups head first. Make sure that you understand how newsgroups and the UseNet culture works. Then, you'll learn how to use Microsoft's Internet News Client to access one of the most dynamic parts of the Internet, newsgroups, later in this chapter.

> **CAUTION**
>
> If you're particularly sensitive or easily offended, newsgroups may not be right for you. Unlike the forums and BBSes on commercial online systems, no one is watching over the content on newsgroups. The material is often very offensive to some folks. You'll find plenty of nasty language and abusive remarks in some newsgroups, just like you'd expect to find in some pubs.

The Basics of Using Newsgroups

If you've ever used a forum or BBS on a commercial online service, you're already familiar with the concept of a newsgroup. Readers post messages, or articles, to newsgroups for other people to read. They can also reply to articles that they read on a newsgroup. It's one way for people like yourself to communicate with millions of people around the world.

Newsgroups are a bit looser, however. A newsgroup doesn't necessarily have a watchdog—other than the readers themselves. As a result, the organization is a bit looser, and the content of the messages is often way out of focus. The seemingly chaotic nature of newsgroups, however, produces some of the most interesting information you'll find anywhere.

Newsgroup Variety Is Good The variety of content is exactly what makes newsgroups so appealing. There are newsgroups for expressing opinions—no matter how benign or how radical. There are other newsgroups for asking questions or getting help. And, best of all, there are newsgroups for those seeking companionship—whether they're looking for a soul mate or longing to find someone with a similar interest in whittling. The following is a sample of the types of newsgroups you'll find:

- **alt.tv.simpsons** contains a lot of mindless chatter about the Simpsons.
- **comp.os.ms-windows.advocacy** is one of the hottest Window's newsgroups around. You'll find heated discussions about both Windows 3.1 and Windows 95.
- **rec.games.trading-cards.marketplace** is the place to be if you're into collecting and trading cards.
- **rec.humor.funny** is where to go to lighten up your day. You'll find a wide variety of humor, including contemporary jokes, old standards, and bogus news flashes.

Alternative and Regional Newsgroups   Not all the newsgroups available are true UseNet newsgroups. Some newsgroups are created to serve a particular region or are so obscure that they wouldn't make it through the rigorous UseNet approval process. If something looks like a newsgroup and acts like a newsgroup, however, it can find its way onto your news server.

Here are some examples:

- Regional—Many localities, such as Dallas or San Francisco, have their own newsgroups where people exchange dining tips, consumer advice, and other regional bits of information.

- Alternative—The alternative newsgroups are responsible for most of the variety on UseNet. Some of these groups have a reputation for being downright nasty (for example, pornography), but also have groups dedicated to your favorite TV shows, books, or politicians.

N O T E   If you have a child who will be using newsgroups, you might consider finding a service provider that makes the pornographic newsgroups, such as **alt.sex.pictures** and **alt.binaries.pictures.erotica**, unavailable. ■

Moderated Newsgroups   Moderated newsgroups are a bit more civil, and the articles are typically more focused than unmoderated newsgroups. Moderators look at every article posted to their newsgroup before making it available for everyone to read. If they judge it to be inappropriate, they nuke it.

Part
II

Ch
11

So what are the advantages of a moderated newsgroup? You don't have to wade through ten pounds of garbage to find one ounce of treasure. Check out some of the alternative newsgroups and you'll get the picture. Most of the alternative newsgroups are unmoderated. As such, they can be a free-for-all of profanity, abusiveness, and childish bickering. The value and quality of the information that you'll find in moderated newsgroups is much higher than their unmoderated cousins.

The disadvantages, on the other hand, are just as clear. Some people believe that moderating a newsgroup is the equivalent of censorship. Instead of the group as a whole determining the content of a newsgroups, the judgment of a single individual determines the content of the newsgroups. Another significant disadvantage is timeliness. Articles posted to moderated newsgroups can be delayed days or weeks.

Participating in a Newsgroup   Every Internet resource that you want to use requires a client program on your computer. Newsgroups are no exception. The program that you use to read newsgroups is called a *newsreader*.

A newsreader lets you browse the newsgroups that are available, reading and posting articles along the way. Most newsreaders also have more advanced features that make using newsgroups a bit more productive. Later in this chapter, you'll learn how to use Microsoft's Internet News Client to access the news. You'll also find other ways to read the newsgroups without using a newsreader.

So How Do Newsgroups Work, Anyway?

NNTP (Network News Transport Protocol) is used to move the news from one server to another. It's very similar to e-mail in a lot of respects. Instead of all the messages sitting on your machine, however, they are stored on an NNTP news server that many other people can access. Therefore, the news only has to be sent to the server, instead of each user. Each user is then responsible for retrieving the articles he or she is interested in.

UseNet news makes its way to your news server using a process called *flooding*. That is, all the news servers are networked together. A particular news server may be fed by one news server, while it feeds three other news servers in turn. Periodically, it's flooded with news from the news server that's feeding it, and it floods all of its news to the news servers that it feeds.

Wading Through UseNet

Sometimes, you'll feel like you're knee deep in newsgroups. There are over 10,000 newsgroups available. Wading through them all to find what you want can be a daunting task. What's a new user to do?

It's all right there in front of you. There's a lot of logic to the way newsgroups are named. Once you learn it, you'll be able to pluck out a newsgroup just by how it's named. You'll also find tools to help you locate just the right newsgroup, as well as a few newsgroups that provide helpful advice and pointers to new users.

Newsgroup Organization   Newsgroups are organized into a hierarchy of categories and sub-categories. Take a look at the **alt.tv.simpsons** newsgroup discussed earlier. The top-level category is **alt**. The subcategory is **tv**. The subcategory under that is **simpsons**. The name goes from general to specific, left to right. You'll also find other newsgroups under **alt.tv**, such as **alt.tv.friends** and **alt.tv.home-imprvment**.

 alt.tv.* is a notational convention that means all the newsgroups available under the **alt.tv** category.

There are many different top-level categories available. Table 11.1 shows some that you probably have available on your news server.

Table 11.1   Internet Top-Level Newsgroup Categories

Category	Description
alt	Alternative newsgroups
bit	BitNet LISTSERV mailing lists
biz	Advertisements for businesses

Category	Description
clarinet	News clipping service by subscription only
comp	Computer-related topics like hardware and software
k12	Educational, kindergarten through grade 12
misc	Topics that don't fit the other categories
news	News and information about UseNet
rec	Recreational, sports, hobbies, music, and games
sci	Applied sciences
soc	Social and cultural topics
talk	Discussion of more controversial topics

These categories help you nail down exactly which newsgroup you're looking for. A bit of practice helps as well. If you're looking for information about Windows 95, for example, start looking at the **comp** top-level category. You'll find an **os** category, which probably represents operating systems. Under that category, you'll find an **ms-windows** category.

Part

II

Ch

11

N O T E Exactly which newsgroups are available on your news server is largely under the control of the administrator. Some administrators filter out regional newsgroups that don't apply to your area. Some also filter out the alternative newsgroups because of their potentially offensive content. ■

Searching for Newsgroups on the Web Scouring the categories for a particular newsgroup may not be the most efficient way to find what you want. Here are a couple of tools that help you find newsgroups based upon keywords that you type:

- Point Internet Explorer 3 to **http://www.cen.uiuc.edu/cgi-bin/find-news**. This tool searches all the newsgroup names and newsgroup descriptions for a single keyword that you specify.

- Another very similar tool is at **http://www.nova.edu/Inter-Links/cgi-bin/news.pl**. This tool allows you to give more than one keyword, however.

Newsgroups for New Users Whenever you go someplace new, you usually try to locate a source of information about it. Likewise, the first few places that you need to visit when you get to UseNet are all the newsgroups that are there to welcome you. It's not just a warm and fuzzy welcome, either. They provide useful information about what to do, what not to do, and how to get the most out of the newsgroups. Table 11.2 shows you the newsgroups that you might want to check out.

Table 11.2 Newsgroups for the Newbie

Newsgroup	Description
alt.answers	A good source of FAQs and information about alt newsgroups
alt.internet.services	This is the place to ask about Internet programs and resources
news.announce.newsgroups	Announcements about new newsgroups are made here
news.announce.newusers	Articles and FAQs for the new newsgroups user
news.newusers.questions	This is the place to ask your questions about using newsgroups

N O T E Don't post test articles to these newsgroups. Don't post articles asking for someone to send you an e-mail, either. This is a terrible waste of newsgroups that are intended to help new users learn the ropes. See the section "Practice Posting in the Right Place" later in this chapter to learn about a better place to post test articles. ■

news.announce.newusers

The **news.announce.newusers** newsgroup contains a lot of great articles for new newsgroup users. In particular, look for the articles with the following subject lines:

- What is UseNet?
- What is UseNet? A second opinion
- Rules for posting to UseNet
- Hints on writing style for UseNet
- A Primer on How to Work with the UseNet Community
- Emily Postnews Answers Your Questions on Netiquette
- How to find the right place to post (FAQ)
- Answers to Frequently Asked Questions about UseNet

Getting Real News on UseNet

UseNet is good for a lot more than just blathering and downloading questionable art. There's a lot of news and great information coming from a variety of sources. You'll find "real" news, current Internet events, organizational newsgroups, and regional newsgroups as well—all of which make newsgroups worth every bit of trouble.

ClariNet You can be the first kid on the block with the current news. ClariNet is a news service that clips articles from sources such as the AP and Reuters news wires. They post these services to the **clari.*** newsgroups. These newsgroups aren't free, though. They sell these newsgroups on a subscription basis. You wouldn't want to pay for them, either, because they can be expensive. Many independent service providers do subscribe, however, as a part of their service.

ClariNet has more than 300 newsgroups from which to choose. My favorite ClariNet newsgroups are shown in Table 11.3. You'll come up with your own favorites in short order. One ClariNet newsgroup that you definitely need to check out is **clari.net.newusers**. It's a good introduction to all the newsgroups that ClariNet offers.

Table 11.3 Popular Clarinet Newsgroups

Newsgroup	Description
clari.biz.briefs	Regular business updates
clari.local.*state***	Your own local news (insert your state in place of ***state***)
clari.nb.online	News about the online community
clari.nb.windows	News about Windows products and issues
clari.living.columns.miss_manners	How can you live without it?
clari.news.briefs	Regular national and world news updates

For your convenience, Table 11.4 describes each ClariNet news category. You'll find individual newsgroups under each category. Under the **clari.living** category, for example, you'll find arts, books, music, and movies.

Table 11.4 ClariNet News Categories at a Glance

Category	Description
clari.news	General and national news
clari.biz	Business and financial news
clari.sports	Sports and athletic news
clari.living	Lifestyle and human interest stories
clari.world	News about other countries
clari.local	States and local areas
clari.feature	Special syndicated features
clari.tw	Technical and scientific news
clari.matrix_news	A networking newsletter

continues

Part

II

Ch

11

Table 11.4 Continued

Category	Description
clari.nb	Newsbytes, computer industry news
clari.sfbay	San Francisco Bay Area news
clari.net	Information about ClariNet
clari.apbl	Special groups for the AP BulletinLine

Net Happenings If it seems that the Internet is moving too fast to keep up with, you're right—without help, anyway. The **comp.internet.net-happenings** newsgroup helps you keep track of new events on the Internet, including the World Wide Web, mailing lists, UseNet, and so on.

The subject line of each article tells you a lot about the announcement. Take, for example, the following announcement:

WWW>Free Internet service for first 100 visitors

The first part tells you that the announcement is about a World Wide Web site. You'll find many other categories such as FAQ, EMAG, LISTS, and MISC. The second part is a brief description about the announcement. Most of the time, the description is enough to tell you whether you want to see more information by opening the article. The article itself is a few paragraphs about the announcement, with the address or subscription information near the top.

Regional Newsgroups Is your geographical region represented on UseNet? A lot are. The Dallas/Fort Worth area has a couple of newsgroups, such as **dfw.eats**, **dfw.forsale**, and **dfw.personals**. Virtually every state has similar newsgroups. Other states might have special needs. For example, California users might be interested in the **ca.environment.earthquakes** newsgroup.

Using the Microsoft Internet News Client to Read the News

All that news is out there, just sloshing around on the news server, and you need a program to get at it. There are a lot of newsreaders out there, but you already have Microsoft's Internet News Client along with the Internet Explorer 3 Web browser. It's one of the cleanest and easiest to use newsreaders available.

Installing the Internet News Client

Microsoft's Internet Mail and News Clients come bundled together in a self-extracting, self-installing file called `Mailnews95.exe`. To install either or both of these clients, follow these steps:

1. Execute `Mailnews95.exe`. The program will then self-extract the necessary files and automatically start the installation process. You will be shown an alert box giving you the option to start the installation, and asked to agree to the licensing agreement, after which the Internet Mail and News Setup Wizard appears.

2. Fill in your Na̲me and O̲rganization and choose N̲ext. The next dialog box will ask you to confirm the name and organization.

3. You can elect to install either the Internet Mail or News clients, or both. Make your choice and choose N̲ext.

   ▶ **See** "E-Mail with Internet Explorer and Microsoft's Internet Mail Client," **p. 183**

4. That's it! The Internet Mail and/or News clients are now installed. The final step necessary to complete the installation process is to choose OK from the last dialog to restart your computer.

After you have restarted your computer, you will be ready to run the Internet News Client. You can access the Internet News Client by clicking the Mail & News icon located on the toolbar (see fig.11.1).

FIG. 11.1
Internet Explorer 3 provides easy access to your Internet News Client.

Mail & News icon

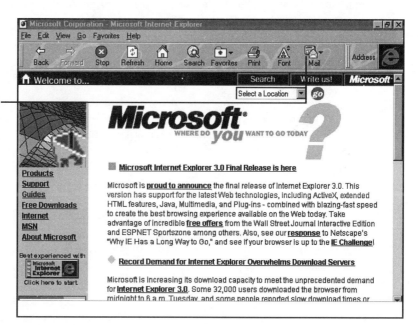

Part
II

Ch
11

Initial Configuration of the Internet News Client

When you first run the Internet News Client, you will be greeted with the Internet News Configuration Wizard (see fig. 11.2). The purpose of this is to find out from you the minimum information needed to interface with your Internet service provider (ISP) to provide access to UseNet news.

FIG. 11.2

The Internet News Configuration Wizard will guide you through the process of the minimum configuration needed to use it to access UseNet news.

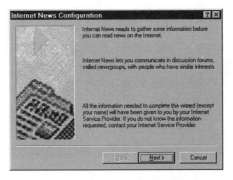

N O T E Most of the information requested in this initial configuration process should have been provided to you by your ISP, so make sure you have everything from them in front of you when you begin. If you have any problems of questions with the configuration, they're probably your best source for help. ▨

To perform the initial configuration process, follow these steps:

1. In the Internet News Configuration Wizard, press Next. The most important information needed is the News Server to be used to access UseNet news. Enter this into this dialog box. If the news server provided by your ISP requires you to log on (most do not require a separate news server logon), enter the logon information as well. When you are done, choose Next.

N O T E The Internet News Client is able to access more than one news server. You will find out how to do this later in the chapter, when you connect to Microsoft's news server and access its newsgroups. ▨

2. Next, enter your Name and E-mail Address, which is the information that the Internet News Client uses to "sign" your outgoing news article.

3. The final step in the initial configuration process gives you the opportunity to set the Internet News Client to be the default program to be used to read news from your Web browser.

TROUBLESHOOTING

Why do I get an error message that says the Internet News Client couldn't find the news server? First, make sure that you have a connection to your service provider. If you're definitely connected, make sure that you correctly configured your NNTP news server. Don't remember the exact address your provider gave you? Try this: If your domain name is **provider.net**, then add news to the front of it like this: **news.provider.net**.

Can I use the Internet News Client to access UseNet through CompuServe? Yes. The CompuServe news server is **news.compuserve.com** and the SMTP mail server is **mail.compuserve.com**.

Making the Initial Connection

Once you have configured the Internet News Client through the Internet News Configuration Wizard, it will start up. At this point, you're just about ready to access UseNet news.

Finding Newsgroups of Interest

After you've configured the Microsoft Internet News Client for your service provider and made your first connection, it will download a complete list of the newsgroups and group descriptions available on your news server (see fig. 11.3). The Internet News Client displays a dialog box warning you that this process can take a few minutes on a slow connection.

FIG. 11.3
Upon its initial connection to a news server, the Internet News Client downloads the list of news groups available on the server.

Before you can read articles in a newsgroup, you need to find newsgroups that you are interested in. After the initial download of newsgroup names and descriptions, the Internet News Client automatically pops up the Newsgroups dialog box, shown in figure 11.4 (this dialog box is also available by selecting News, Newsgroups or pressing Ctrl+W).

FIG. 11.4
The Newsgroups dialog box allows you to browse through the newsgroups available on a news server.

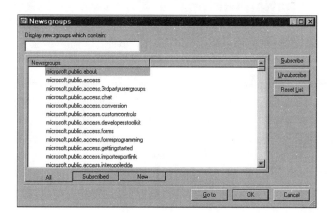

It would still be kind of difficult to find newsgroups of interest in this list if the Internet News Client didn't give you some means of narrowing down your search. And it does. By typing text into the Display Newsgroups Which Contain text area, you narrow the displayed list of newsgroups to only those that contain that text, as shown in figure 11.5.

FIG. 11.5

The Internet News Client allows you to narrow your search for newsgroups of interest, and can also include the group's description, as well as its name, in the search criteria.

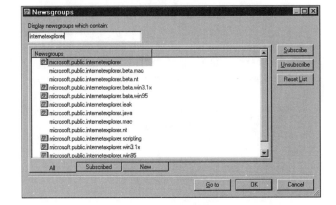

Once you have found newsgroups of interest, you can start browsing through them for articles that you'd like to read. Unlike many other news readers, the Internet News Client doesn't require you to subscribe to a newsgroup in order to read articles from it. It does allow you to subscribe to a group, which makes it easier to access. You'll learn how to do that a little later in the chapter.

Further Configuration Options

To access all of the configuration options for the Internet News Client, you can select News, Options which brings up the Options dialog box. Various options can be set under each of the tabs in this dialog box.

The Read Tab   The options on the Read tab affect the way the Microsoft Internet News Client checks for news articles (see fig. 11.6). You can set up the Internet News Client to periodically check for new articles whenever it is running.

The Send Tab   The Send tab controls various aspects of the configuration for outgoing news articles (see fig. 11.7). The options here are pretty self-explanatory, and you should feel free to experiment with them. If you select the HTML or Plain Text radio buttons on this tab, you are greeted with the Settings dialog box (see fig. 11.8). Here you can control the type of encoding used for file attachments, as well as control a few other options.

 TIP   While MIME encoding is the up-and-coming standard, UseNet has historically used UUEncode for binary file attachments.

FIG. 11.6

The Read tab controls how the Internet News Client reads and reacts to new news articles.

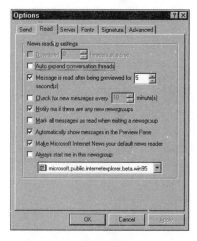

FIG. 11.7

Send options give you control over outgoing e-mail.

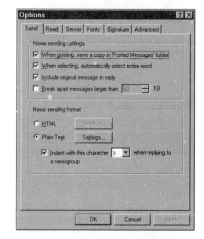

Part
II

Ch
11

FIG. 11.8

The Plain Text Settings dialog box allows you to pick an encoding format for file attachments and give you a few more options.

The Server Tab   This tab is probably the most important of the five on the Options dialog box. On the Server tab, seen in figure 11.9, you tell the Internet News Client where to get your news. This information is necessary for correct operation of the Internet News Client, and so was read in when you performed the initial configuration.

FIG. 11.9
The Server options are the heart and soul of the Internet Mail Client, as these are what allow you to send and receive Internet e-mail.

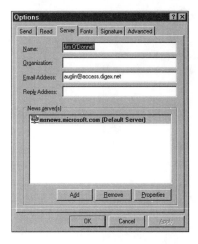

The important thing to note about this tab is that you can use more than one news server. Normally, your Internet service provider will supply you with a news server that should meet most of your needs. You may, however, find a need to connect to another server, either to get access to regular UseNet newsgroups that your provider's news server doesn't carry or to get access to a provider's news server. For instance, if you want to access Microsoft's many products, click the Add button in the Server tab. The News Server Properties dialog box appears, enabling you to enter the information to connect to a new server (see fig. 11.10).

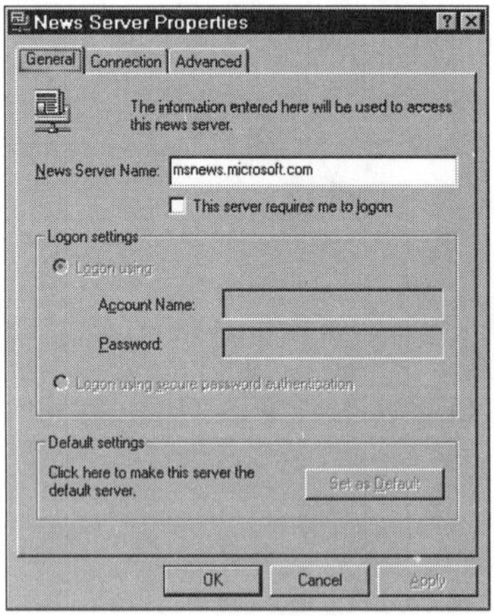

FIG. 11.10
Use the News Server Properties dialog box to connect to more than one news server.

The Fonts Tab   The Fonts tab allows you to choose what fonts are used for the display of news articles in the Internet News Client (see fig. 11.11). You can individually pick the font, the color for outgoing articles, and the language encoding to be used.

FIG. 11.11

The Internet News Client allows you to select which fonts you would like it to display.

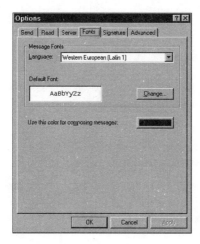

 TIP   UseNet articles are often formatted with monospaced fonts in mind, such as Courier, so you should probably pick a monospaced display font.

Signature Tab   This Options tab, shown in figure 11.12, allows you to select whether or not you want to include a signature text block at the end of each of your outgoing news articles. If you want to, you can either specify the text directly in the area shown or specify a file, called a *sigfile*, with the information in it.

FIG. 11.12

You can set up your signature block information using this Options tab.

N O T E   If you've read Chapter 10, "E-Mail with Internet Explorer and Microsoft's Internet Mail
Client," you may notice that the configuration menus are very similar. As it turns out, they're
more than just similar, some of them are shared between the two.

Similar settings in the Options dialog box's Send, Fonts, and Signature tabs in either the Internet Mail
or News Client also appear in the other. ▣

A Note about Signatures

You can easily personalize your postings with a signature. Save about three lines that say something
about yourself, such as your address and hobbies, into a text file. Here's an example of a signature
file:

```
Jim O'Donnell                   ¦              odonnj@rpi.edu
                                ¦               800-555-1212
                                ¦         Buy SE Using HTML, Now!
```

Your signature can communicate anything about yourself including your name, mailing address,
phone number, address, or a particular phrase that reflects your outlook on life. It is considered good
form, however, to limit your signatures to three or four lines.

Browsing and Reading Articles

Now that you've configured your copy of the Internet News Client and added the Microsoft
news server, let's take a look at some of the newsgroups it has to offer. You'll find out how to
subscribe to newsgroups, what it means to do that, and how to browse through and read
UseNet news articles.

Subscribing to Newsgroups

Select News, Newsgroups or press Ctrl+W to get the Newsgroups dialog box (see fig. 11.13).
This dialog box looks a little different than the one first shown in figure 11.5. This is because
there is now more than one news server configured.

FIG. 11.13
The Newsgroups dialog
box changes to
accommodate multiple
mail servers.

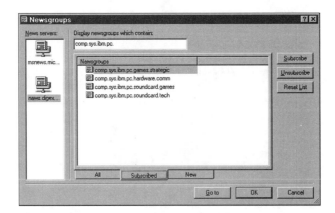

If you were interested in those Microsoft newsgroups that discussed the Internet, you would type **internet** into the Display Newsgroups Which Contain text area. To subscribe to newsgroups, either click them and then click the Subscribe button, or just double-click them. By clicking the Subscribed tab, only the current subscribed newsgroups for that news server are listed. Clicking the New tab results in a list of those newsgroups on the current news server that are new since the last time you were on. Once you have finished subscribing to newsgroups, choose OK to save your selections.

The News Client Screen

If you have used Microsoft's Internet Mail Client, you will immediately notice that its Internet News Client window is set up very similarly (see fig. 11.14). The common interface between the two makes going back and forth between them very easy.

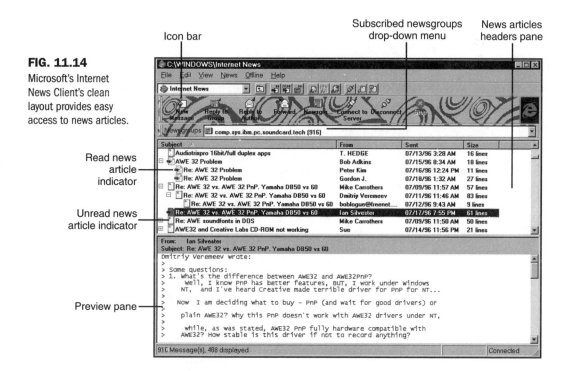

FIG. 11.14
Microsoft's Internet News Client's clean layout provides easy access to news articles.

Icon bar

Subscribed newsgroups drop-down menu

News articles headers pane

Read news article indicator

Unread news article indicator

Preview pane

Part
II

Ch
11

There are many different parts to this screen. Let's get oriented with the following parts:

■ At the top of the window is the icon bar, which gives a list of actions that you can perform. You can use the mouse to grab this icon bar and change its size.

 T I P If you think the icon bar takes up too much of the screen, you can turn it off by deselecting View, Icon Bar. This will remove the icon bar and replace the icon with much smaller buttons on the toolbar (as long as it is enabled).

- Underneath the icon bar is a drop-down menu giving you access to a list of your subscribed newsgroups for the current news server, as well as a list of news servers.

- Underneath the subscribed newsgroups drop-down menu is a scrollable list of message headers for every news article in the newsgroup you're looking at. The icon shown to the left of each news article header indicates whether the message has been read or not.

- On the bottom of the screen, you see the text of the open news article, along with headers indicating the article's subject and sender. This is the Internet Mail Client's preview pane—if you want, you can view a given message in a full screen of its own by double-clicking its header in the message header pane.

Notice that some of the articles are indented under other articles. These are replies to the articles under which they are indented. All the messages indented under an article, including the original message, are called a *thread*. The Internet News Client indents articles this way so you can visually follow the thread.

TROUBLESHOOTING

What happened to the articles that were here a few days ago? It's not practical to keep every article posted to every newsgroup indefinitely. Your service provider deletes the older articles to make room for the newer articles. Another way of saying this is that a message scrolled off. The length of time that an article hangs around varies from provider to provider, but is usually between three days and a week.

Downloading Files from Newsgroups   Posting and downloading files from a newsgroup is a bit more complicated than your experience with online services. Binary files can't be posted directly to UseNet. Many methods have evolved, however, to encode files into text so that they can be sent. The Internet News Client has the ability to automatically download and decode files that are attached to UseNet news articles. Sometimes, however, the files are encoded and attached in a way that the News Client doesn't recognize.

The downloading process works as follows:

1. A file is encoded, using UUEncode, to a newsgroup as one or more articles.

2. While you're browsing a newsgroup, you may notice a few articles with subject lines that look like this (headings are provided for your convenience):

Lines	Filename	Part	Description
5	HOMER.GIF	[00/02]	Portrait of Homer Simpson
800	HOMER.GIF	[01/02]	Portrait of Homer Simpson
540	HOMER.GIF	[02/02]	Portrait of Homer Simpson

These articles are three parts of the same file. The first article is probably a description of the file because it is part zero, and because there are only five lines in it. The next two articles are the actual file.

3. To download a file from a newsgroup, you retrieve all the articles belonging to that file. Then, you UUDecode the articles back into a binary file. See Chapter 19, "Using Compressed/Encoded Files," to learn how.

▶ **See** "Getting Your Encoded Files Decoded," **p. 361**

Replying to an Article You'll eventually want to post a reply to an article you read in a newsgroup. You might want to be helpful and answer someone's question. You're just as likely to find an interesting discussion to which you want to contribute. Either way, the following are two different ways you can reply to an article you have read:

■ **Follow up**—If you want your reply to be read by everyone who frequents the newsgroup, post a follow-up article. Your reply is added to the thread. To reply to an article, click the Reply to Group icon on the icon bar. Fill in the window shown in figure 11.15, and click the Post Message toolbar button.

FIG. 11.15

The text that starts with the greater-than sign (>) is the original article. Delete everything you don't need to remind the reader of what was posted.

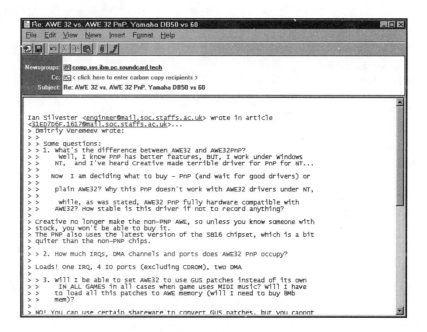

■ **E-mail**—If your reply would benefit only the person to whom you're replying, respond with an e-mail message instead. That person gets the message faster, and the other newsgroup readers aren't annoyed. To reply by e-mail, click the Reply to Author icon on the icon bar. Fill out the window shown in figure 11.16, and click the Send button.

Stay out of Trouble; Follow the Rules

Etiquette, as Miss Manners will tell you, was created so that everyone would get along better. Etiquette rules are not official rules, however; they're community standards for how everyone should behave. Likewise, *netiquette* is a community standard for how to behave on the Internet. It's important for two reasons. First, it helps keep the frustration level down. Second, it helps prevent the terrible waste of Internet resources by limiting the amount of noise. For good netiquette, follow these simple rules:

- Post your articles in the right place. Don't post questions about Windows 95, for example, to the **alt.tv.simpsons** newsgroup.

- NEWSGROUP READERS REALLY HATE IT WHEN YOU SHOUT BY USING ALL CAPS. It doesn't make your message seem any more important.

- Don't test, and don't beg for e-mail. There are a few places where that is appropriate, but this behavior generally gets you flamed (a flame is a mean or abusive message).

- Don't spam. Spamming is posting an advertisement to several, if not hundreds, of newsgroups. Don't do it. It's a waste of Internet resources.

- Don't cross-post your article to too many newsgroups. This is a waste of Internet resources, and readers quickly tire of seeing the same article posted to many newsgroups.

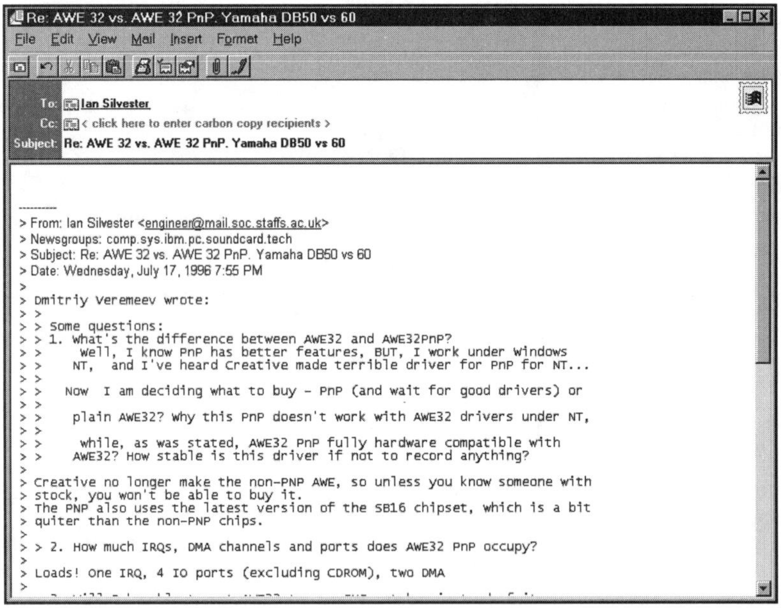

FIG. 11.16
Look carefully—the only difference between this window and the window in figure 11.15 is this window has the To: field and the previous one has the Newsgroups: field.

Posting a New Article

It's no fun being a spectator. You'll eventually want to start a discussion of your own. To post a new article, click the New Message icon on the icon bar. Fill in your message and click the Send button.

N O T E Lurk before you leap. Lurking is when you just hang out, reading the articles and learning the ropes without posting an article. You'll avoid making a fool of yourself by learning what's acceptable and what's not before it's too late. ■

Practice Posting in the Right Place You'll find a special newsgroup, called alt.test, that exists just for test posting. You can post a test article to that newsgroup all day long and no one will care.

In fact, you should go ahead and post a test article just to make sure that everything works. You'll get a good idea of how long it takes your article to show up, and you'll also learn the mechanics of posting and replying to articles.

 TIP Test your file uploads in the **alt.test** newsgroup, too, instead of testing them in productive newsgroups.

Posting a File The Internet News Client makes posting a file easy. Post a new article as described in the section, "Posting a New Article." Before you click the Send button, however, follow these instructions:

1. Click the Insert File toolbar button or select Insert, File Attachment. The Internet News Client displays the Insert Attachment dialog box.

2. Find the desired file, click it, and then click Attach.

3. Repeat steps 1 and 2 for each file you want to attach to your article (see fig. 11.17).

FIG. 11.17

Attached files are indicated by the icons in the bottom pane of the news article composition window.

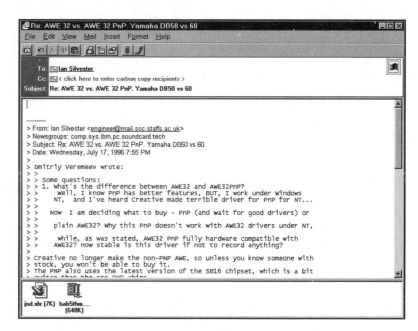

Part

II

Ch

11

After you've selected the files you want to attach to your posting, you can continue editing it normally. Click the Send button when you're finished.

Other Ways to Read the News

If browsing newsgroups with a newsreader seems like too much trouble, the tools described in this section might be just what you need. You'll learn to use Deja News Research Service, which lets you search UseNet for specific articles. You'll also learn how to use SIFT, a tool that filters all the newsgroup postings and saves them for you to read later.

Searching UseNet with Deja News

Deja News is a Web tool that searches all the newsgroup articles, past and present, for terms that you specify. Point your Web browser to **http://www.dejanews.com/**. Finding information using the Deja News service is discussed in Chapter 6, "Finding Information on the Web."

▶ **See** "Deja News Research Service" for information on using Deja News, **p. 112**

Filtering UseNet with SIFT

SIFT is a tool provided by Stanford that filters all the articles posted to UseNet. As an added bonus, it filters a lot of public mailing lists and new Web pages, too. You tell SIFT the keywords in which you're interested, and it keeps track of all the new documents on the Internet that match those keywords. Like Deja News, this is a Web tool, so point your browser at **http://sift.stanford.edu**.

The first time you access SIFT, it asks you for an e-mail address and password. You don't have one, yet. That's OK. Type your e-mail address and make up a password. You'll need to use the same password the next time that you access SIFT. Click Enter to go to the search form.

The most effective way to use SIFT is as follows:

1. Make sure the SIFT search form is open. Select the Search radio button, and type the topics for which you're looking in the Topic box. If you want to make sure that some topics are not included, type them in the Avoid box.

2. Click Submit. SIFT displays a page, containing all of today's new articles that match your keywords, on each line. The most relevant line is at the top; the least relevant is at the bottom. Read some of the articles, Web pages, and mailing list messages by clicking them.

3. If you're happy with these test results, click Subscribe at the bottom of the Web page. Then, click Submit. The next time you log on to SIFT, you'll see additional lines at the bottom of the Web page that let you delete subscriptions or review the current day's hits.

4. If you're not happy with the results, click Search at the bottom of the Web page. Then, adjust the keywords in Topic and Avoid, and click Submit. SIFT displays a similar Web page using your new search keywords.

## CHAPTER 12

Accessing Other Internet Services with Microsoft's Explorer

A common misconception about the World Wide Web and the Internet is that they are one and the same. The Web is just one part of the Internet, albeit a very popular part. Since its founding in 1991, the Web has become the second highest source of traffic on the Internet. E-mail still holds the top spot for traffic volume.

While Internet Explorer is a Web browser first and foremost, it can act as a client program for other Internet services as well. In the preceding two chapters, you learned how to use Internet Explorer for sending e-mail and reading UseNet newsgroups. This chapter extends the range of services you can access with Internet Explorer to include File Transfer Protocol (FTP), Gopher, and Telnet. ■

Download files from FTP sites

FTP sites are a goldmine where you can find everything from recipes to shareware programs.

Browse information on a Gopher server

Information on a Gopher server is organized into folders, making it easy to navigate and find what you need.

Search for information on FTP and Gopher sites

There are thousands of FTP and Gopher servers, so it's helpful to know how to search them for the information you're looking for.

Conduct a Telnet session

Away from work or home and need to log in? Telnet lets you establish a connection to a remote computer.

A Short History Lesson

Most people don't realize it, but the Internet began back in the late 1960s as a Defense Advanced Research Projects Agency (DARPA) project. The military had posed the problem of how to maintain contact among all bases in the event of a disaster or nuclear attack. In response, the Rand Corporation advised the construction of a decentralized network—one in which any computer could communicate with any other without having to rely on a central hub. The first such network was constructed in the early 1970s. It linked four computers—three in California and one in Utah—and was the beginning of what is still referred to today as *DARPANet*. The intent of this first decentralized network was to allow simple text messages to be passed back and forth between the computers on the network. Essentially, it was meant for sending electronic mail.

As computer technology advanced, people began using files that were more than just simple text. A Microsoft Word file, for example, contains much more information than just the text of the document. It also contains font characteristics, formatting instructions, and document-specific information (author's name, last updated date, and so on). Such a file is called a *binary file*. When users tried to send binary files using the e-mail protocols designed to handle simple text, they found that the files often became garbled and, hence, unusable when they reached their destination. To address this issues, Internet engineers developed the *File Transfer Protocol* (*FTP*) for the sending of binary files. FTP breaks a binary file up into smaller chunks called *packets* and sends these packets, along with reassembly instructions, to a destination computer.

The movement toward a point-and-click interface began with the founding of *Gopher*, named for the sports mascot at the University of Minnesota, where it was developed. Gopher sites are repositories of text and binary files that are organized into a hierarchy similar to the folder structure you see in Windows Explorer for Windows 95. This structure makes navigation on a Gopher server much more intuitive. Gopher is generally thought to be a precursor to the Web because of its generalized design and its hyperlink support.

Telnet arose from users' need of being able to log in to a remote computer on the Internet. When you run a Telnet client, your computer becomes a "dumb terminal" that is connected to another machine. Many people use Telnet to telecommute. They can fire up their SLIP or PPP accounts from home and use Telnet to connect to a computer at work.

All three of these applications played an important role in the early days of the Internet. FTP and Telnet are still very much with us today, but Gopher sites have taken something of a backseat to the World Wide Web, owing to the Web's appealing graphical nature.

Downloading Files Using FTP

FTP lets you examine the directories of remote systems on the Internet and lets you transfer files to and from your computer and other computers. Almost as old as the Internet itself, FTP was designed to work with the systems of the time. If you're familiar with MS-DOS, you can think of FTP as being very much like using the `cd` and `dir` commands to move from one directory to another, and to see what's in that directory only when you get there. FTP lets you transfer both text files and binary files.

Internet Explorer is programmed to understand FTP protocols and to act as an FTP client. It displays FTP information as a single column of links, each link being either a file or a directory link. An FTP directory viewed with Internet Explorer looks very similar to the directory listing in MS-DOS (see fig. 12.1). Each line of the FTP listing shows the date and time the file was added, the size of the file or <DIR> if it's a directory, and the file or directory name.

FIG. 12.1

Internet Explorer's listing of files on an FTP server resembles a directory listing in MS-DOS.

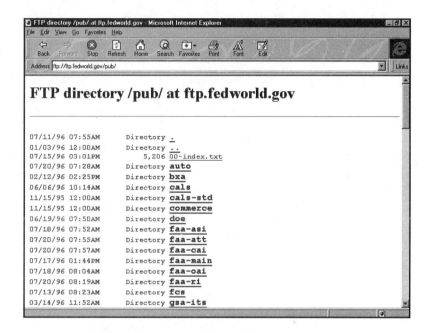

To access an FTP server using Internet Explorer, simply type the URL of the FTP server into the Address bar and press Enter. If a link to an FTP server is on a Web page, you just select that link to jump to that FTP server. Internet Explorer reduces the effort needed to access an FTP site if the hostname starts with **ftp**. For example, typing the hostname **ftp.fedworld.gov** into the location field (without **ftp://** before it) takes you to the URL **ftp://ftp.fedworld.gov/**.

 Many FTP sites store the files available for public download under the /PUB/ directory. You should also look for a README or an INDEX text file, which describes the contents of the directory or the policies of FTP access for that site.

FTP directories and subdirectories almost always have a link named Up to Higher Level Directory at the top of the page. Clicking this link takes you one step higher in that FTP site's directory hierarchy—not back one Web page as the Back button in Internet Explorer does.

If, for whatever reason, a Web site you are trying to reach has named its Web server as **ftp.whatever.com/**, you can avoid the new default by specifying the protocol identifier. So typing the URL as **ftp.whatever.com/** or as **ftp://ftp.whatever.com/** starts an FTP session with the FTP server **ftp.whatever.com/**, but typing the URL as **http://ftp.whatever.com/**

attempts to retrieve a Web page from the Web server. When you find the file you want, downloading from an FTP archive with Internet Explorer is as simple as selecting the appropriate link, and the file is transferred to your local system.

FTP server administrators couldn't possibly provide a login ID and password for each person who wants to download something from his or her site. To get around this problem, most FTP servers are set up to allow anonymous access—meaning that you do not need a login and password account set up specifically for that server. Typically, an anonymous FTP server accepts "anonymous" as the login, and your e-mail address as your password.

N O T E An FTP server administrator is not likely to do anything with your e-mail address, but the administrator's knowing it is good in case you have a problem with your download attempt. By knowing your e-mail address, the administrator can contact you and help you to complete the download. ▧

Using Internet Explorer for FTP presents some drawbacks. First, it can require substantial amounts of RAM and system resources, especially if you have a large cache or several helper applications configured. If you have a lower-end system, you may encounter problems such as running short of available RAM. Second, Internet Explorer does not allow you to send files via FTP, anonymously or not. If you use FTP extensively, you may want to consider a separate FTP application. A stand-alone FTP application, such as WS_FTP, uses less memory than Internet Explorer, lets you send FTP files as well as receive, and can be configured to retain the password for non-anonymous FTP sessions. (It is also available on the CD-ROM included with this book.)

Finding Information on Gopher Servers

Gopher servers store text and binary files in a hierarchical directory structure that's easy to navigate. Internet Explorer presents files and subdirectories of a given Gopher server in a menu format. *Gopherspace* is a common way to refer to the interlinked set of Gopher menus. Gopherspace, with its individually designed menus and no unifying taxonomy, but with frequent links from one Gopher menu to others, is generally considered to be the predecessor of the World Wide Web.

Gopherspace lacks many of the features that make the Web so popular. First, Gopher is text-based only, so it has no cool pictures, no odd little images usable as buttons or dividing rules on pages, and no large images used as menus. Second, Gopher servers don't know how to accept anything back from the Gopher client program you are running on your computer, so transactions in Gopherspace are one-way only. With no Common Gateway Interface (CGI) support, no interactive forms for shopping or surveys are available in Gopherspace. With no e-mail capability, you get no hypertext links for sending e-mail with a single click. If you want to interact with someone or some site in Gopherspace, you need to send e-mail or use the telephone.

Gopherspace, however, has some strong points. The World Wide Web didn't exist five years ago, so anybody who wanted to set up a Web-like access before 1991 that didn't require the user to have a thorough understanding of UNIX had to use Gopher.

Just as it does for FTP, Internet Explorer understands Gopher protocols and is able to function as a Gopher client. A Gopher page in the Internet Explorer window appears to be a rather ordinary looking Web page (see fig. 12.2). Indeed, if you choose View, Source, you see that Internet Explorer actually generates an HTML document containing the Gopher menu information (see fig. 12.3).

N O T E   Internet Explorer lets you leave off the **gopher://** portion of the Gopher site URL if the site's name starts with **gopher**. ■

Internet Explorer displays a Gopher page as a single column of text links. Each entry in a Gopher menu consists of a bracketed word indicating the type of the file and a description of the file. One major distinction between FTP directories and Gopher menus is that Gopher descriptions are typically in plain text, whereas FTP directories look like a directory listing from an operating system.

Some of the common Gopher link types you might see are the following:

- **Menu**—This link takes you to another Gopher menu or directory.
- **Text**—This link takes you to a text file.
- **Binary**—This link takes you an application.
- **Telnet**—This link starts a Telnet session.
- **Search**—This link starts a simple Gopher search.

FIG. 12.2
Internet Explorer displays Gopher menu pages as plain-looking Web pages.

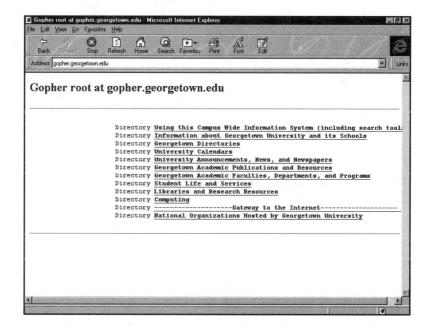

Part
II

Ch
12

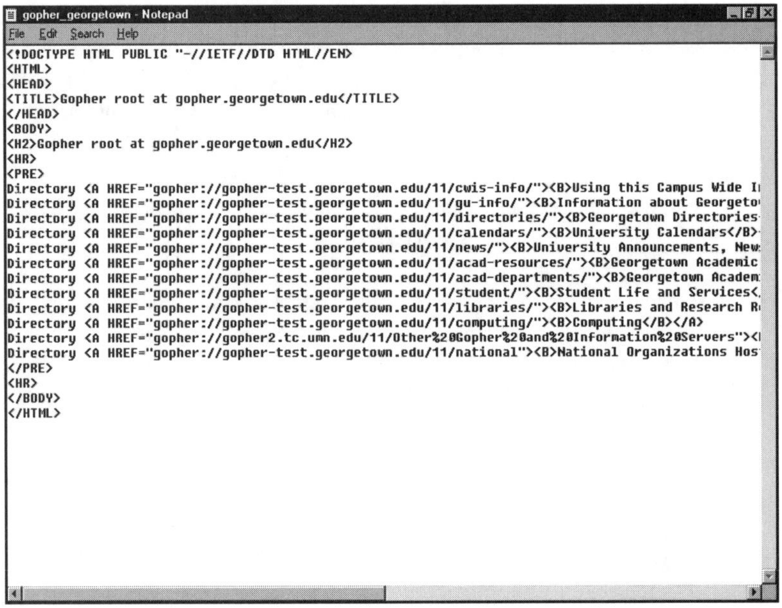

FIG. 12.3

When Internet Explorer reads in the contents of a Gopher menu, it reformats the information into an HTML document.

```
gopher_georgetown - Notepad                                              _ |5| X
File  Edit  Search  Help
<!DOCTYPE HTML PUBLIC "-//IETF//DTD HTML//EN>
<HTML>
<HEAD>
<TITLE>Gopher root at gopher.georgetown.edu</TITLE>
</HEAD>
<BODY>
<H2>Gopher root at gopher.georgetown.edu</H2>
<HR>
<PRE>
Directory <A HREF="gopher://gopher-test.georgetown.edu/11/cwis-info/"><B>Using this Campus Wide I
Directory <A HREF="gopher://gopher-test.georgetown.edu/11/gu-info/"><B>Information about Georgeto
Directory <A HREF="gopher://gopher-test.georgetown.edu/11/directories/"><B>Georgetown Directories
Directory <A HREF="gopher://gopher-test.georgetown.edu/11/calendars/"><B>University Calendars</B>
Directory <A HREF="gopher://gopher-test.georgetown.edu/11/news/"><B>University Announcements, New
Directory <A HREF="gopher://gopher-test.georgetown.edu/11/acad-resources/"><B>Georgetown Academic
Directory <A HREF="gopher://gopher-test.georgetown.edu/11/acad-departments/"><B>Georgetown Academ
Directory <A HREF="gopher://gopher-test.georgetown.edu/11/student/"><B>Student Life and Services<
Directory <A HREF="gopher://gopher-test.georgetown.edu/11/libraries/"><B>Libraries and Research R
Directory <A HREF="gopher://gopher-test.georgetown.edu/11/computing/"><B>Computing</B></A>
Directory <A HREF="gopher://gopher2.tc.umn.edu/11/Other%20Gopher%20and%20Information%20Servers"><
Directory <A HREF="gopher://gopher-test.georgetown.edu/11/national"><B>National Organizations Hos
</PRE>
<HR>
</BODY>
</HTML>
```

A Trip to Riverdale High: Search Tools for FTP and Gopher

If you're a fan of Archie comics, you may have wondered why you see so many familiar names floating around the Internet—names like Jughead, Veronica, and even Archie himself. Has Riverdale High hooked up to the Internet and turned its students loose?

The answer, of course, is no, but one unifying idea runs through all the uses of names from Archie comics. Each one is a search application to help you find items on various Internet sites. Archie is a search tool for FTP servers, and Veronica and Jughead are used to search Gopher sites.

Searching FTP Sites with Archie

The original problem with FTP was that, while FTP lets you transfer a file from a remote computer system, you had to go to that remote directory with FTP first and find what you wanted. If the person administering the FTP server had not included an index text file describing the files in the directory, you had to guess if the filename you were reading was the one you wanted.

Archie was designed to create a centralized, indexed list of files available on anonymous FTP sites. The Archie database, which as of this writing indexes over 1,000 anonymous servers and an aggregate of 2.4 million files, is mirrored at several locations around the world to reduce the load on individual systems. Over 50,000 queries are made to Archie databases every day. Many of the Archie servers now support inquiries using the World Wide Web form capability. Archie is accessible in three ways:

- A graphical and forms-capable browser like Internet Explorer
- Archie-specific client software
- Telnet

On the CD

Archie clients are available for almost every platform, and may be found with the Web interfaces to the Archie database. The Archie client WSARCHIE can be found on the CD-ROM that comes with this book. The Telnet protocol is discussed later in this chapter.

To use Internet Explorer to conduct Archie searches, you can simply use one of the many form-based Web pages that act as front ends to Archie databases. A list of such pages appears in Table 12.1. The NCSA Archie search request form is shown in figure 12.4.

Table 12.1 URLs for Web-Based Archie Searches

Sponsor	URL
NCSA	http://hoohoo.ncsa.uiuc.edu/archie.html
Rutgers	http://www-ns.rutgers.edu/htbin/archie
Spiretech	http://www.spiretech.com/archie_form.html
The Group	http://www.thegroup.net/AA.html

N O T E Whenever you are presented with a choice of multiple sites to search, trying the one closest to you first is best. International connections are often heavily loaded, and you may get a faster response from a host computer on the same continent where you live. If closer hosts don't respond, then try the other, more distant hosts from the menu. ■

Part
II

Ch
12

You can choose many ways to customize your Archie search. The default setting for matching your entry is a case-insensitive substring match, but you can choose other options from the drop-down list box. The results of your search may be given to you sorted by host or by date of the files. You can also set the "niceness" of your Archie search, from Nicest to Not Nice at All. Niceness is a priority tag that determines how fast your Archie query is processed. If you are just about to leave for your lunch break, be considerate of other people and set your query as lower priority than normal (Nice), because you don't need your query answered immediately.

To speed up your reply, you can reduce the number of answers. This capability is helpful if you have a good idea of what you're looking for. For example, if you know the exact name of the file you want, you probably don't need to receive the location of more than the first ten or so files matching that exact filename.

FIG. 12.4

You can use Internet Explorer to conduct Archie database searches.

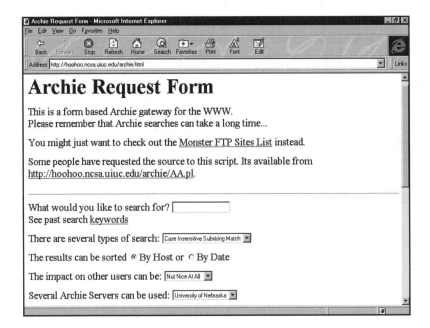

Searching Gopherspace with Veronica

Gopherspace is too large to search randomly. In addition to the fact that Gopher has been around for several years longer than the World Wide Web, every Gopher menu was organized by the individual who created it, and no particular standards exist for organizing menus. Tunneling through Gopherspace may be almost as much fun as surfing the Web, but finding what you're looking for is likely to take longer if you don't take advantage of some additional tools.

Remember how Archie searches directories and filenames available on anonymous FTP servers? Veronica is like Archie, but Veronica searches Gopher servers. While Archie is a good search tool to use if you know the exact filename you are looking for, Veronica can find items where Archie can't. Veronica's success derives from the fact that, while FTP shows just the file and directory names, Gopher menus use more descriptive names. For example, entering the words **Warner Brothers cartoons** in a Veronica search may find you a GIF of Pinky and the Brain. On the other hand, Archie doesn't find the same picture of Pinky and the Brain unless you ask Archie to search for P&TB.GIF. If you don't know exactly what you're looking for but have a good idea of what kind of thing you're looking for, Veronica is probably better than Archie.

Veronica: Stretching Things a Bit?

The name Veronica is a fine example of Silly Acronym Syndrome (SAS). Just as the UNIX variant GNU means "GNU's Not UNIX," and the name of the e-mail reader PINE is an acronym meaning "Pine Is Not Elm," Veronica's creators were inspired to create a somehow-meaningful acronym around the name of one of Archie's cartoon girlfriends. Officially, Veronica means "Very Easy Rodent-Oriented Net-wide Index to Computerized Archives."

You be the judge of whether you believe the words, or the acronym, came first.

Using Veronica is fairly simple. You can connect to a Veronica server from any Gopher server. After you establish the connection, you can enter keywords to search for. Veronica searches its index of Gopherspace looking for matches to your keywords. When Veronica's done, you receive a Gopher menu consisting of all the matches to your search.

The following steps demonstrate a search from the home Gopher site at the University of Minnesota:

1. Once you have your Internet connection up and Internet Explorer is running, enter the URL **gopher.micro.umn.edu** to jump to the University of Minnesota's Gopher server (see fig. 12.5).

2. Select the Other Gopher and Information Servers item, and the Gopher menu appears (see fig. 12.6).

3. Select the Search Titles in Gopherspace Using Veronica item to see the Gopher menu shown in figure 12.7.

Notice the two text file items in the middle of figure 12.7. The Frequently Asked Questions (FAQ) about Veronica and How to Compose Veronica Queries text files can provide additional information on this search tool.

FIG. 12.5

The University of Minnesota's Gopher server is a good starting point for a Veronica search.

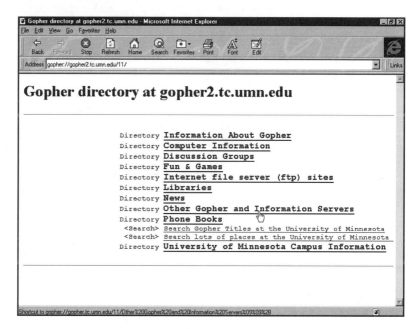

Part
II

Ch
12

4. Select the Search Gopherspace by Title words (via PSINet) item to retrieve an index search interface page (see fig. 12.8).

5. Place the cursor in the text entry field, and type anything you like. If you get a `Too many connections, please try again` soon message or some variation, try another Veronica server, or just try again in a minute or two. Servers are busy at different times of the day or week.

FIG. 12.6
Other Gopher and Information Servers is a common option on the main menus of most Gopher sites.

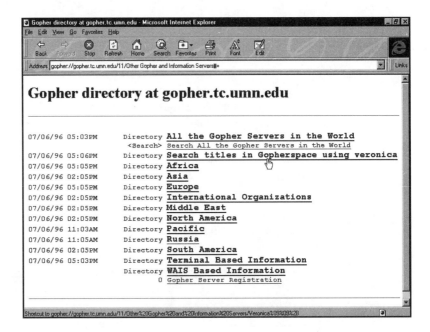

Like any tool, Veronica can be used correctly or incorrectly. Because Veronica servers are always busy, getting search results back can take time. If your search criteria are too narrow or just not quite right, you can eliminate the material you are looking for. If your search criteria are too broad, and you don't limit the number of results returned, you can get a huge result (huge searches take even longer) that is not much better than tunneling through Gopherspace until you find the right file yourself. Here are some tips on how to provide Veronica with appropriate search criteria.

Remember that Gopher servers are set up individually—sometimes very individually. You can be creative in your search keywords as long as you are creative in the way others might have been creative before. You can use multiple words to quickly narrow your search. Veronica supports the Boolean operators NOT, AND, and OR. For example, entering the search **TELEVISION AND DRAMA NOT DAYTIME** gives you Gopher items for evening drama television shows, but **TELEVISION AND DRAMA** increases the size of the search result to include all Gopher items relating to daytime soap operas.

FIG. 12.7
Most Gopher sites
include a link to several
Veronica searches.

Veronica searches ———

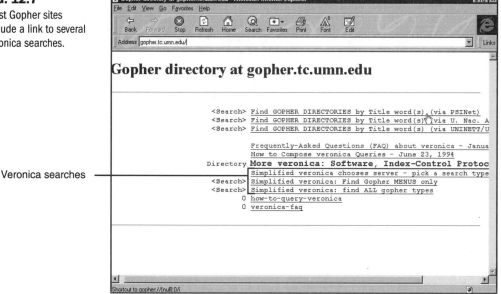

FIG. 12.8
PSINet furnishes the
Internet community with
a Veronica search page.

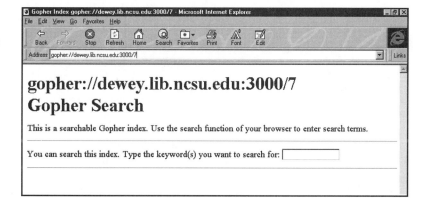

Part
II

Ch
12

You can use an asterisk (*) as a wildcard at the ends of words. A Veronica search for the keyword *director** returns Gopher items for *director*, *directory*, *directories*, *directorate*, and so on.

A useful way to narrow your search is by file type. To narrow your search to return only results of a specific file type, add **-t#** to your Veronica search keywords, where the number sign (#) is a character representing a Gopher file type. The official Gopher document types and their signifying characters are presented in Table 12.2.

Table 12.2   Official Gopher Document Types

Type Value	Description
0	Text file
1	Directory
2	CSO name server—read as text or HTML
3	An error of some sort
4	.HQX (also called BinHex, a Macintosh compression format)
5	PC binary (an uncompressed application)
6	UUEncoded file (a UNIX compression format)
7	Full text index (a Gopher menu)
8	Telnet session
9	Binary file
s	Sound (an audio file)
I	Image (any format that's not GIF)
T	TN3270 session—TN3270 is a fancy version of Telnet
g	GIF image
;	MPEG (a video file)
h	HTML (HyperText Mark-Up Language)—a Web URL (Uniform Resource Locator)
H	HTML URL Capitalized
i	Information (text) that is not selectable (like a comment line in a program)
w	A World Wide Web address
e	Event
m or M	Unspecified MIME (multi-part or mixed message)

For example, if you want to find audio clips of Paul Simon music, you could enter the Veronica search string **MUSIC AND PAUL SIMON -ts**.

Searching Gopherspace with Jughead

Another Gopherspace search tool is Jughead, which was written by Rhett "Jonzy" Jones at the University of Utah. In keeping with the Archie comics motif for Internet search engine names, the acronym came first, and the name Jughead was justified as "Jonzy's Universal Gopher Hierarchy Excavation And Display."

Like Veronica, Jughead is a Gopherspace search engine. However, Veronica searches widely, over all of Gopherspace. Jughead is most commonly configured to search only the one Gopher server it is installed on, but Jughead can search that one Gopher server very thoroughly.

N O T E System administrators rarely bother to install Jughead on a Gopher server with a small file collection. If you find a Jughead search engine on a specific Gopher server, it's because someone thought it was better to install Jughead than to do without it. ■

For an example of how Jughead works, go to North Carolina State University's library Gopher server at **gopher://dewey.lib.ncsu.edu:3000/7**. The Jughead search index of NCSU's library is shown in figure 12.9. Because the server's host name does not start with **gopher**, you have to type the **gopher://** portion of the URL.

FIG. 12.9

Jughead searches look just like Veronica searches but are limited to just one Gopher server.

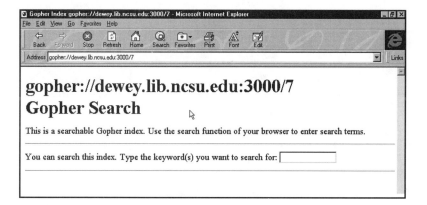

Entering search text into the field and pressing the Enter key gives you a Gopher menu made up of all matching items in the site that the Jughead server indexes.

Jughead accepts the same kind of Boolean search requests Veronica does, but Jughead has some special commands. The generic form for these commands is a question mark followed by the command (no spaces between the question mark and the command), followed by the string of characters to search for. Jughead's special commands are summarized in Table 12.3.

Table 12.3   Jughead Special Commands

Command	Result
?all string	Returns all matches to the string
?help string	Returns the Jughead help document, as well as any matches for the string
?limit=x string	Returns up to x matches for the string
?range=x1-x2 string	Returns the matches between x1 and x2

Part

II

Ch

12

The `?range` command is useful if the string matches a very large number of Gopher files.

> **N O T E** You can use only one special command per query. However, limiting your Jughead queries
> can improve response time. It's also the polite thing to do. Other people may want to use
> that server, and asking Jughead for all matches to *IBM* may be a waste of processor time if the item
> you want turns out to be the third one returned. ■

Jughead also restricts special characters for its own use. Almost all the standard special characters are treated as a space. These special characters are as follows:

```
!"#$%&'()+,-.?/\[@]{^}'~
```

This entire line is read as 24 spaces. Jughead treats a space as a Boolean AND, so it's probably best to use letters and numerals only in your search string.

Telnet Sessions

Telnet is a time-honored way to log in to other computers on the Internet. Telnet, like the World Wide Web, works because all the computers of the Internet are on and connected all the time, barring system crashes, backhoes accidentally cutting the T1 cable, and other things system administrators don't really like to think about.

> **N O T E** When people speak of the Internet, they are generally referring to those computers that are
> on and connected to the Internet all the time. If you have a SLIP or PPP dial-up connection,
> your computer has an *IP* (Internet Protocol) address and is "part of the Internet." However, this lasts
> only as long as the connection. Generally, you need to have at least a leased-line connection before
> you can consider your local system as part of the Internet. ■

You can think of Telnet as making your computer a dumb terminal for the system you are connecting to. Originally, dumb terminals were called such because they had only a keyboard and screen, directly wired into the host computer, and no processor inside. Terminals were manufactured by standard designs so they would be compatible with many different computers. A common type of terminal was the VT series manufactured by Digital Equipment Corporation. VT terminals came in several models (VT100, VT102, VT220, and so on). Your personal computer is enormously more powerful than a VT100 terminal, so a Telnet terminal emulator acts like a terminal in order to let your computer communicate with computers that are set up to connect to VT100 terminals. In other words, every time you run Telnet, you are reducing your high-end, state-of-the-art personal computer to the level of a keyboard and screen.

What you get for lobotomizing your great workstation is the ability to connect to many computer systems that, in some cases, don't have any other connectivity available. Also, because Telnet is the lowest common denominator of computer power, almost everyone can participate. Windows 95 and Windows NT include Telnet applications in the Windows folder.

You can configure Internet Explorer to launch a Telnet application as a supporting application. Both Windows 95 and Windows NT come with Telnet client programs. The QVTNet suite of client programs, included on the CD-ROM that comes with this book, includes an easy-to-use Telnet client program as well.

▶ **See** "Configuring a Helper Application," **p. 244**

N O T E If you have Windows 95 or Windows NT installed on your machine, you already have a Telnet application installed in the C:\WINDOWS\ folder as TELNET.EXE. ▪

Because Telnet and Gopher are both early Internet tools, many public Telnet sites are most easily found through Gopher menus. For example, when you use Internet Explorer to view the Gopher menu at URL **gopher://gopher.micro.umn.edu**, as you did previously in this chapter, the Gopher menu shown in figure 12.5 is displayed. As you did earlier, choose the Other Gopher and Information Servers item, and the Gopher menu displayed in figure 12.10 appears. Note the Terminal Based Information at the bottom of the Gopher menu.

When you choose the Terminal Based Information item, a Gopher menu appear (see fig. 12.11).

Select the Telnet connection for MIT TechInfo. If you have Internet Explorer configured correctly, your Telnet supporting application launches, and the TechInfo Main Menu comes up in your Telnet window. Figure 12.12 shows the Main Menu using the QVTNet Telnet client.

FIG. 12.10
Gopher menus often contain a Terminal Based Information option for accessing Telnet sites.

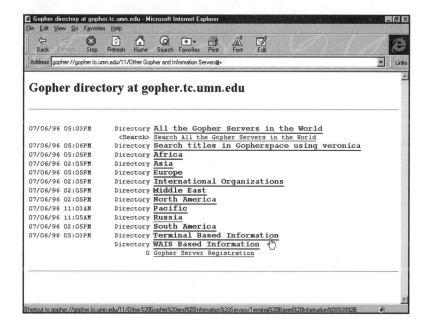

Part
II

Ch
12

FIG. 12.11

A Gopher menu of Telnet sessions is one way to get started with Telnet.

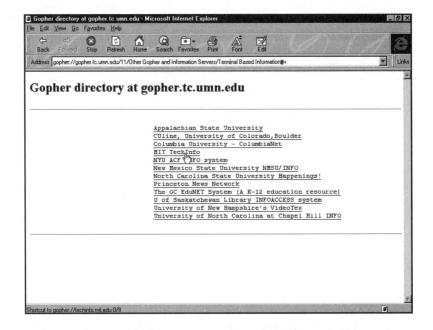

FIG. 12.12

A Telnet session to MIT's TechInfo gives you access to news and events on the Cambridge, Mass. campus.

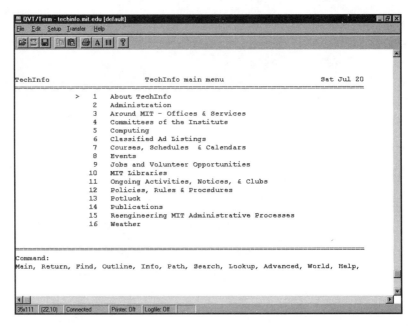

Troubleshooting Connection Problems

Sometimes you do not get where you want to go on the Internet. A site may be down, or a connection may be supporting too much activity to connect. A Web page you looked at yesterday may be deleted or moved today. This last section of the chapter offers some advice to improve your ability to get where you want to go.

Any address embedded in a link may be entered directly into the Internet Explorer Address bar. If the Web link is not the full link text, you can always see the link by moving your cursor over the link and not clicking the link. The full link description can be seen in the status bar at the bottom of the Internet Explorer window.

Normally, if the full URL has a slash at the end indicating the last part of the URL is a directory, Internet Explorer adds the slash for you as it loads the default page there. If you get a Not Found error, your first action should be to select the Refresh command either from the View menu or by clicking the Refresh button on the Internet Explorer toolbar.

T I P You can also press F5 to instruct Internet Explorer to refresh a page.

N O T E An immediate refresh is not just an impatient, "Why won't this thing do what I want?" behavior; it's often the solution. Small errors happen all the time, and refreshing may work more often than you think. Reloading is an especially good idea if images on a page are downloading badly and Internet Explorer displays a small red X where an image should have been.

Refreshing is also the right answer if you get a Too busy, try again later message when attempting to start an FTP or Gopher session. Gopher and FTP servers are often busy, and trying again is the same as redialing a telephone after you get a busy signal. ■

Your second troubleshooting option (if you are using a link from another page) is to look at the destination link displayed in the Address bar and see what it looks like. Leaving the closing </A> tag off an anchor causes the rest of the page—from the beginning of the anchor, including the text label (if it has one), the image (if you used an image as the visible part of the link), and everything else to the end of the page—to become part of the destination address. If the location looks like a URL followed by words or filenames, select the part of the address that doesn't look like a URL, and delete it. Then try to load the part of the URL you retained.

▶ **See** "Setting Up Anchors," **p. 384**

Similarly, if you are typing in the address yourself, proofread the destination address. Fix any problems you see such as spaces accidentally inserted into the middle of the URL or capitalization errors, and then select the Refresh command. If a refresh of the page doesn't work, or if you see no problems with the URL, retype the URL, and try again. If you got the URL electronically from e-mail or an article you have, try to copy the URL from where it is, and paste it into the Address bar to minimize the risk of typing errors. ●

Part

II

Ch

12

Using Helper Applications

## CHAPTER 13

Configuring Helper Applications

Which file types require helper applications, and which don't

Discover how Internet Explorer 3 uses certain file types with helper applications.

Where to get helper applications

In this chapter, learn where to get the applications that work best with Internet Explorer.

How to configure helper applications to work with Internet Explorer

There are many helper apps that allow you to utilize Internet Explorer to the best of its ability.

We can't always manage single-handedly everything that comes our way—sometimes we need a little help from our friends. Internet Explorer 3 is no different. It can't handle every single file type that it encounters on the World Wide Web. Sometimes it needs a little help from other programs and applications, which are known as *helper applications*.

Fortunately, because of the way Internet Explorer 3 is integrated into the Windows 95 operating system, configuring helper applications for it is not only pretty easy; for many, many file types, it's already done! For those file types that don't have existing applications configured for them, the hard part becomes figuring out which ones you need and where to get them. This chapter should help with the former; the enclosed CD-ROM should help you with the latter. ■

What Are Helper Applications?

Though Internet Explorer is a very versatile Web browser, you'll still run into files on the Web that it can't display: video files, audio files, odd graphics files, strange document formats, and even compressed files. One way to display or play these files is to set up helper applications.

A helper application is simply a name for a program that can be set up to interpret files that Internet Explorer can't handle itself. Almost any program can be configured to act as a helper application; the trick is figuring out which ones will be the most useful to you.

All Web browsers need helper applications. There are simply too many different file types on the Web for a browser to be able to handle them all internally.

Think about this. On a daily basis, you probably use a dozen or more different programs for word processing, spreadsheets, database management, electronic mail, graphics, and many other different applications. Each of these programs produces a different kind of data file, yet only a few of your applications are able to import even a limited number of different file types from other applications. And we're only talking about one person's files on a single computer! It's just not possible for Internet Explorer to handle all the thousands of different file types it might encounter on the Web all by itself.

N O T E ActiveX Controls (also known as *add-ins*) are Microsoft's new approach to handling animation, interactive multimedia, and much more within Internet Explorer. In a nutshell, ActiveX Controls are inline modules that add new capabilities to Internet Explorer or add support for "live objects," which appear right on the Internet Explorer screen alongside the text and inline graphics that Explorer can already display. With the proper ActiveX Controls installed, Internet Explorer can handle almost any file type inline without spawning an external helper application. While this doesn't mean the end of helper applications, it is an exciting capability of Internet Explorer 3. ■

▶ **See** "Plug-Ins, Add-Ins, and ActiveX Controls" for more information about ActiveX Controls, **p. 735**

Configuring a Helper Application

No matter what helper applications you choose to add, they all configure the same way. It takes only a few simple steps to set one up. It's made even easier by the fact that, because of the way that Internet Explorer is integrated into the Windows 95 operating system, many helper applications are already configured.

CAUTION
It looks like Microsoft might be changing the way Internet Explorer chooses the helper applications it uses. Up until this point, Internet Explorer used the program configured through the Windows 95 file types (accessed, for instance, through the File Types tab of the Options dialog box of the Windows 95 Explorer View, Options menu choice). Now, however, Microsoft has included a Viewers section under the Program tab of its own View, Options menu that might work alongside, or in place of, the Windows 95 configured file type.

At the time of this writing, however, this configuration option is grayed out. The following discussion will focus on the use of the Windows 95 file types, but take a look at the View, Options menu in the release version of Internet Explorer 3 to see what Microsoft has come up with.

If you select View, Options from the Windows 95 Explorer menu and select the File Types tab from the Options dialog box that appears, you will be greeted with the File Types configuration box (see fig. 13.1). The file types configured through this menu—or through any program that uses this database in the Windows 95 Registry—are available through all of them. So, any file type that you've configured through the Windows 95 Explorer or any that have been configured automatically through the installation process of an application are automatically configured as helper applications for Internet Explorer 3.

FIG. 13.1
The Windows 95 Explorer File Types configuration information determines what helper applications are used for different file types.

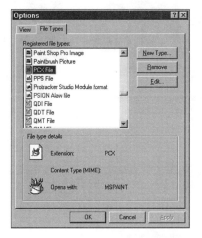

For instance, consider graphics files of .BMP and .PCX formats, which cannot be viewed directly in Internet Explorer 3. In my File Types configuration, they are configured as Microsoft Imager 1.0 Picture files. So, if I click a link to a .BMP file, Microsoft Imager 1.0 will be run and the image displayed, as shown in figure 13.2.

The steps to add a helper application, or edit an existing one, are the same as for any Windows 95 file type configuration. For instance, if you decide you want to use Paint Shop Pro—an excellent shareware graphics application that you will learn more about in Chapter 15, "Configuring Internet Explorer for Graphics"—as the helper application for .BMP and .PCX graphics files, follow these steps:

▶ **See** "Graphics Helper Applications for Internet Explorer" for information on programs that make good helper applications for graphics, **p. 282**

Part
III

Ch
13

FIG. 13.2
If Microsoft Imager 1.0 is the configured application for a .BMP file, then clicking a link to such a file in Internet Explorer 3 will run MS Imager and download and view it.

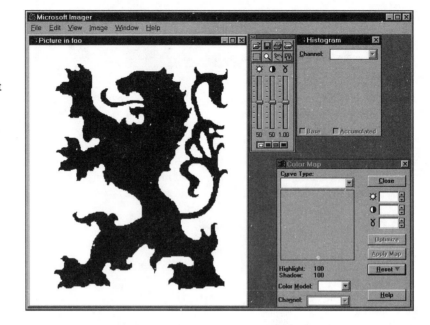

1. In the Windows 95 Explorer, choose View, Options. The Options dialog box appears.

2. Click the File Types tab.

3. Scroll down the list of file types until you see the entry for Microsoft Imager 1.0 Picture. Click it to highlight it. The extension "bmp" should appear in the Extension field.

4. Click the Edit button. The Edit File Type dialog box appears, as shown in figure 13.3.

FIG. 13.3
Each file type can be assigned one or more actions through this dialog box—the default action is the one that will be used by Internet Explorer 3.

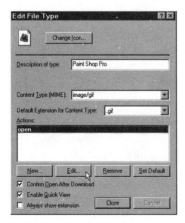

5. To change these file types to use Paint Shop Pro, change the Description of Type to Paint Shop Pro. Click the open entry in the Actions box and click Edit. The Editing Action For Type dialog box appears (see fig. 13.4).

6. Click Browse, find Paint Shop Pro, and click OK.

FIG. 13.4

Each action has an associated application used to perform the action.

7. Click OK in the Edit File Type dialog box and in the Options dialog box, and Internet Explorer 3 (and Windows 95) is now configured to use Paint Shop Pro for .BMP and .PCX image files, as well as a few other image formats.

That's it! Paint Shop Pro is officially an Internet Explorer helper application, as well as the Windows 95 default application for files of that type. The next time Internet Explorer encounters a .PCX or .BMP image, it will automatically launch Paint Shop Pro to view it (see fig. 13.5).

FIG. 13.5

Paint Shop Pro allows a more "hands-on" approach to down-loaded images. Later in this chapter, you learn the different approaches to helper applications.

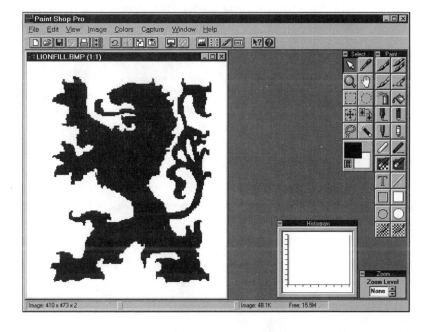

N O T E As you might have figured out for yourself by now, there are advantages and disadvantages to the way Microsoft has decided to implement helper applications for Internet Explorer 3. Because it is so tightly integrated with the Windows 95 default application mechanism, Internet Explorer helper applications will always be the same as the Windows 95 default applications for that file type. This is an advantage because it means Internet Explorer is configured by default for many different file types.

It can also be a disadvantage, though. For instance, Microsoft Word is the default application in Windows 95 for .DOC files, so if you link to one of these from Internet Explorer, Microsoft Word will be launched. However, Microsoft Word is a huge application, and when Web browsing you might prefer to view a .DOC file with something smaller like WordPad or the Microsoft Word Viewer. There's no way to use one of these as the helper application for Internet Explorer, however, without also making it the default application in Windows 95. It is possible that the new way of configuring viewers in Internet Explorer mentioned in the previous Caution is Microsoft's way of dealing with this situation. Only time, and the final release of Internet Explorer, will tell. ▪

What Kinds of Files Are on the Web?

Just about every type of file you can imagine exists somewhere on the World Wide Web. But this doesn't mean you'll run into them all.

Web pages themselves are usually composed of two elements: HTML formatted text and inline graphics. Pages meant for Internet Explorer may also make use of its built-in support for inline animations and background sounds. All Web browsers can handle the first two, and Web browsers other than Internet Explorer 3 will ignore inline animations and background sounds; you don't need to worry about configuring helper applications just to be able to read Web pages. The problem comes when you try to access an external file by clicking a link to something other than a Web page.

Even then, the problem does not loom as large as you might fear, because the Web is mostly a compendium of hypermedia documents. That is, the hyperlinks on most Web pages jump to files with some sort of multimedia content: text, audio, graphics, or video. Even if these are in formats that Internet Explorer doesn't speak natively, once you've configured helper applications for the half dozen or so most common multimedia file types, you may be able to go for months without encountering anything your configuration can't handle. (For some great online information about multimedia file types, follow the link in figure 13.6.)

FIG. 13.6
An excellent reference to the kinds of files you'll run into on the World Wide Web is Allison Zhang's online book "Multimedia File Formats on the Internet" at **http://ac.dal.ca/ ˜dong/contents.html**.

However, even if you do your best to avoid exotic file types, the day will come when you'll find a site that provides a link to some must-have file that exists only in some weird format that you've never heard of before. This happens commonly from your Windows 95 machine when you need to access files or data that is meant for a Macintosh or UNIX system. Never fear. By configuring the proper Internet Explorer helper application on the spot, you'll be able to play or display it properly. That's the beauty of helper applications. They make Internet Explorer infinitely open-ended, extensible, and expandable.

Internet Explorer's Built-In Capabilities

Before we get into the topic of the helper applications you need, let's take a moment to find out which ones you don't need. Internet Explorer already includes the built-in ability to display the three most-used graphics file formats on the Web, can display inline AVI animations, and has built-in support for the most popular Internet audio format, as well.

Built-in GIF and JPEG Image Display

You don't have to configure helper applications for GIF and JPEG images. Internet Explorer 3 displays both of these graphic file formats just fine all by itself. There are good reasons for having graphics support built right into Internet Explorer, though (see fig. 13.7). Web pages are more aesthetically pleasing if they combine text with inline graphics. But you'd be stuck with separate windows for text and graphics if Internet Explorer had to launch a helper application every time it displayed an image. All Web browsers have to be able to display at least one graphic image format internally if text and graphics are to stay together on the page.

FIG. 13.7
Internet Explorer 3
doesn't need a helper
application to display
inline GIF and JPEG
images.

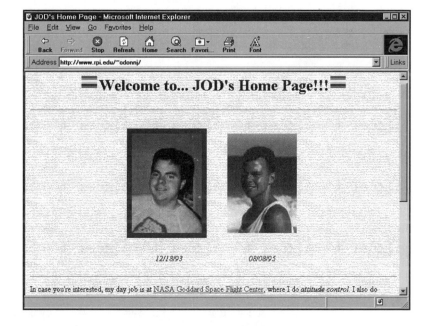

Part
III

Ch
13

Have you ever wished that Internet Explorer could grab an inline graphic from a Web page? It can! Right-click the image and you'll see a menu of options. Select <u>S</u>ave Picture As to save the image to disk, Set As <u>W</u>allpaper to make the image your Windows 95 wallpaper, or <u>C</u>opy to copy the URL of the image to the Windows 95 Clipboard.

Most of the inline graphics on Web pages are GIF (Graphics Interchange Format) images, because that's all early Web browsers could display. Like all Web browsers, Internet Explorer has built-in support for GIFs. But while compression of GIFs is good for simple line art images, it is relatively poor by today's image compression standards for photographic images. And when you're talking about a time-intensive medium like the Web, smaller is better.

JPEG images are much smaller than GIFs for photographic images—in fact, a 16-million color JPEG graphic can be as little as 1/4 the size of the same GIF image in only 256 colors! That's why Internet Explorer has JPEG image display capability. Many Web sites now include inline JPEGs on their pages, which results in faster page downloads and much better-looking Web sites.

 Look for sites with JPEG images in the new Progressive JPEG format supported by Internet Explorer. They load up to three times faster than GIFs, and preview faster, too!

GIFs and JPEGs currently account for the vast majority of the inline graphic images on Web pages. With built-in support for both, Internet Explorer 3 faithfully displays most of the images you encounter on the Web without requiring you to configure a single external helper application.

> **CAUTION**
>
> If you are designing your own Web pages, don't entirely abandon GIFs for JPEGs! There are still some people out there using older browsers that can't read JPEGs. And for small, simple images with few colors, GIFs can often be even smaller than JPEGs. Not only that, but GIFs support background transparency, which can improve the look of your pages—JPEG doesn't (at least not yet). For more information on how to implement graphics on your own Web pages, go to Chapter 23, "Advanced Graphics."

▶ **See** "Design Tips for Graphical Web Pages" for hints on effectively using graphics in your Web pages, **p. 449**

Inline Animation Support

One exciting capability of Internet Explorer 3 is the ability to play inline AVI animations, in addition to its inline graphics support. This allows a Web author to include an animation in a Web page. The HTML extensions that support this also give the Web author the ability to control the number of times the animation repeats as well as the ability to specify an alternate GIF for Web browsers that don't support inline AVIs. These animations can also include audio playing in time with the animation. Microsoft has some great examples of this at their Internet Explorer 3 Showcase site at **http://www.microsoft.com/ie/showcase/howto_3/ catalog.htm** (see fig. 13.8).

FIG. 13.8
Keep an eye and an ear out for the coffee pot and volcano at this site!

Internet Explorer Sound Support

Multimedia just isn't multimedia without sound. Text, graphics, and animation only stimulate the eyes, but sound brings a whole different sense into play. By combining graphics with sound, you activate more of the brain and get your audience more involved. (Not convinced? Try watching TV with the sound muted!)

Internet Explorer 3 has built-in support for sound in the following forms:

- Built-in support for playing links to digitized audio in Sun/NeXT (.AU or .SND) and Mac/ SGI (.AIF or .AIFF) format (see fig. 13.9). Some of these sound types are also supported by Microsoft's ActiveMovie add-in module.

FIG. 13.9
When a link to a supported sound file is clicked, the sound is downloaded and played by Internet Explorer.

- Background sound support to automatically load and play .WAV, .AU, and .MID sounds when a page is loaded.

- Automatic sound support through the use of inline animations in the Audio Video Interleave (AVI) format.

Part
III

Ch
13

Unfortunately, you'll run into more than just two sound file types on the Web. A lot more. The most obvious omission is that Internet Explorer can't play Microsoft's own .WAV sound type when loaded from a hypertext link—though it can play them automatically as background sounds. You probably have lots of .WAV files on your system right now (in your Windows directory, if nowhere else). There are also .MOD files, .MID files, and many others. (Chapter 14, "Configuring Internet Explorer for Sound," covers how to configure helper applications for all of these audio file types.)

▶ **See** "Sound Helper Applications for Internet Explorer" for examples of good helper applications for sound, **p. 267**

How Does Internet Explorer Know When it Needs a Helper Application?

Before Internet Explorer can tell if it can handle a file internally or whether it has to launch a helper application, it has to determine what kind of data it's dealing with.

If you've been using a PC for very long, you can probably identify many file types by their filename extensions. You know that a file named FOO.EXE is an executable program because the filename ends in .EXE, and that one named BOO.DOC is usually a Microsoft Word document because it ends in .DOC.

N O T E By default, Windows 95's file-handling dialog boxes hide filename extensions. For example, a file named PICTURE.GIF is listed as "picture." File types are identified by icons. To tell Windows 95 to display filename extensions in all its file dialog boxes, follow these steps:

1. Run Windows Explorer.

2. Select the View, Options menu.

3. Choose the View tab.

4. Uncheck the Hide MS-DOS File Extensions For Files That are Registered box. ■

> **CAUTION**
>
> Not every file type can be correctly identified by its filename extension. Some different file formats share the same extension, and there are also many files on the Web that have arbitrary or misleading filenames. Be sure to check for "context clues" that will help you identify a file's real file type. For example, if a file has the filename extension .EXE but the text identifies it as an archive file, the odds are good that it's not an executable program, but a self-extracting archive.

Internet Explorer can identify files on the Web by their filenames, too. But that is only its backup method of determining what kind of files it's dealing with. Its primary method is by referencing a file's MIME type.

A Brief Course in MIME Types

MIME is an acronym for *Multipurpose Internet Mail Extensions*, but this is a little misleading. MIME type definitions are not just for Internet mail; they are used to identify any file that can be transmitted over the Internet.

A MIME type definition consists of two parts, such as `type/subtype`. A real-world example would be `image/jpeg`. It's pretty easy to see that this MIME type definition describes an image file in JPEG format.

Before a Web server sends a file to Internet Explorer, it sends the MIME type definition for that file. Internet Explorer reads this definition and looks it up to see if it can handle the file internally, or if there is a helper application defined for it. In the case of the example above, Internet Explorer knows that the file it is about to receive is an image in JPEG format, which, of course, it can interpret internally; it won't try to launch a helper application.

If the server doesn't send a MIME type along before transmitting the file, Internet Explorer uses the filename extension to identify the file type.

TROUBLESHOOTING

I thought I clicked a link to a graphic, but Internet Explorer 3 displayed a screen of unreadable text instead. If Internet Explorer has to identify a file by its filename extension rather than its MIME type, it can make the same kind of misidentification that a human would make with a misnamed or ambiguously named file. If Internet Explorer tries to display a misidentified file type in its own display or in the wrong helper application, all you see is a garbled mess.

If this happens to you, hover over the file link with the hand pointer and read the filename in the status bar at the bottom of the Internet Explorer window. If the filename extension looks wrong for the type of file you're trying to view, that's probably your problem.

You can also see filenames by selecting View, Source from the Internet Explorer menu and looking for the filename in the HTML code.

If you can't figure out why a link isn't working right, you can always save the suspect file by holding down the Shift key and clicking the link. Then you can work with it later.

You can see a complete list of the MIME types that Internet Explorer recognizes by choosing View, Options from the Windows 95 Explorer, and then selecting the File Types tab from the Options dialog box and scrolling through the list. Notice that not all of the file types that Internet Explorer (and Windows 95) recognizes have MIME types associated with them— some are recognized only by their extensions. Some of the MIME types that your copy of Internet Explorer might recognize are shown in Table 13.1.

Part

III

Ch

13

Table 13.1 MIME Types That Internet Explorer Recognizes

Type/Subtype	Extensions	Description
application/x-gzip	.GZ	GNU Zip Compressed Data
application/x-compress	.Z	Compressed Data
application/x-mocha	.MOCHA, .MOC	Mocha Script
application/x-tcl	.TCL	TCL Program
application/x-sh	.SH	Bourne Shell Program
application/x-csh	.CSH	C Shell Program
application/postscript	.AI, .EPS, .PS	PostScript Program
application/octet-stream	.EXE, .BIN	Binary Executable
application/x-cpio	.CPIO	UNIX CPIO Archive
application/x-gtar	.GTAR	GNU Tape Archive
application/x-tar	.TAR	UNIX Tape Archive
application/x-shar	.SHAR	UNIX Shell Archive
application/x-zip-compressed	.ZIP	ZIP Compressed Data
application/x-stuffit	.SIT	Macintosh Archive
application/mac-binhex40	.HQX	Macintosh BinHex Archive
video/x-msvideo	.AVI	Microsoft Video
video/quicktime	.QT, .MOV	QuickTime Video
video/mpeg	.MPEG, .MPG, .MPE	MPEG Video
audio/x-wav	.WAV	WAV Audio
audio/x-aiff	.AIF, .AIFF, .AIFC	AIFF Audio
audio/basic	.AU, .SND	ULAW Audio Data
application/fractals	.FIF	Fractal Image Format
image/x-MS-bmp	.BMP	Windows Bitmap
image/x-rgb	.RGB	RGB Image
image/x-portable-pixmap	.PPM	PPM Image
image/x-portable-graymap	.PGM	PGM Image
image/x-portable-bitmap	.PBM	PBM Image
image/x-portable-anymap	.PNM	PBM Image

Type/Subtype	Extensions	Description
image/x-xwindowdump	.XWD	X Window Dump Image
image/x-xpixmap	.XPM	X Pixmap
image/x-xbitmap	.XBM	X Bitmap
image/x-cmu-raster	.RAS	CMU Raster Image
image/tiff	.TIFF, .TIF	TIFF Image
image/jpeg	.JPEG, .JPG, .JPE	JPEG Image
image/gif	.GIF	CompuServe Image Format
application/x-texinfo	.TEXI, .TEXINFO	GNU TeXinfo Document
application/x-dvi	.DVI	TeX DVI Data
application/x-latex	.LATEX	LaTeX Document
application/x-tex	.TEX	TeX Document
application/rtf	.RTF	Rich Text Format
text/html	.HTML, .HTM	Hypertext Markup Language
text/plain	.TXT, .TEXT	Plain Text

This certainly looks like a lot of different file types. Fortunately, you probably won't run into most of them if all you're doing is cruising the Web. Many are for specialized applications such as scientific document page layout, fractal image generation, or UNIX shell scripts.

Types and Subtypes   There are only seven sanctioned MIME types: text, audio, image, video, multipart, message, and application. If somebody comes up with some hot new program or data file type, they have to fit it into one of these seven MIME types if a MIME-enabled application is going to recognize it.

However, there are both "official" and "unofficial" MIME subtypes. Official subtypes appear on the list without an "x-" prefix. An "x-" prefix is the standard way to label an unofficial MIME subtype. That a MIME subtype is "unofficial" in no way makes it a second-class citizen, however. It just means that the Internet Working Group, the organization that oversees the MIME standard, hasn't defined an official subtype for it yet.

Missing MIME Types   Because Internet Explorer only has built-in support for a relatively small number of file types—mainly those specifically for HTML files and text, and a few of the most common types of graphics, sound, and animation—there are many types of files that it does not handle internally. Many of these, such as Microsoft Word .DOC files, for instance, are already set up with helper applications for Internet Explorer because of the way it integrates

Part

III

Ch

13

with Windows 95. Many of the other important file types that didn't make Internet Explorer's internal list, and are less likely to have default applications set up for them through Windows 95, will be discussed by topic in subsequent chapters in this section.

▶ **See** "How Internet Explorer Works with Video," for a discussion of helper applications for video, **p. 295**

▶ **See** "Using Compressed/Encoded Files," to find out how to deal with .ZIP and other file archive types, **p. 351**

You can create your own definitions for MIME subtypes that aren't on Internet Explorer's list by using the File Types tab of the Options dialog box, discussed earlier in this chapter. If you do, be sure to include the "x-" in the subtype name to indicate that it's unofficial, and don't duplicate a name that's already on the list.

Of course, the rest of the world won't know about MIME types that you define, so Web browsers you connect to won't send file IDs that match your MIME types. Internet Explorer will have to identify the file by its filename extension, which, in most cases, will work fine.

If Internet Explorer encounters a file with an unknown MIME type and a file extension that is not on its internal list, it will generally download the file into your cache, but not attempt to display it or give you an error message to tell you that it isn't configured to handle it. By right-clicking a link to such a file, you can elect to save it to disk and try to figure out how to view it on your own.

N O T E You can find out more about MIME types by obtaining the Internet Working Group's RFC document on the topic. It can be downloaded by pointing Internet Explorer to **ftp://ftp.isi.edu** or **ftp://ds.internic.net**. Look for the directory rfc/ and the filename RFC1521.TXT.

You can also enter into discussions about MIME on UseNet. Just point Internet Explorer's newsreader to the group **comp.mail.mime**. ▪

TROUBLESHOOTING

I configured a helper application for type/subtype, but Internet Explorer doesn't always seem to use it. And I sometimes get the message Warning: unrecognized encoding message. What's going on? If this problem is only occasional, it's probably not Internet Explorer or your helper application configuration that's at fault. The problem may be with the way the Web site you're connected to is sending MIME type information. Internet Explorer may be receiving a self-contradictory or confusing MIME type identification, and it's trying to interpret the file without really knowing what it is. If you regularly run into this problem on a particular site, e-mail the Webmaster (usually **webmaster@site**) and inform him or her of the problem.

Separating the Wheat from the Chaff

So which file types do you actually need to worry about?

You can safely ignore the ones that Internet Explorer handles internally. Though you can configure external helper applications to display the graphics files that Internet Explorer normally handles, you generally don't want to do so; it disrupts the look and feel of Internet Explorer's page display because helper applications don't appear inline. (However, this advice does not necessarily extend to the audio files that Internet Explorer handles internally. Because audio isn't visual, you can't ruin the way a page looks by configuring a different audio player.)

Of the other file types in Table 13.1, you'll probably want to configure helpers for many of the audio, graphics, and video file types listed. Subsequent chapters in this section help you decide which ones you're most likely to encounter.

Three Approaches to Helper Application Selection

There are three very different approaches to the process of selecting Internet Explorer 3 helper applications. One camp likes to configure a single monster, do-it-all helper application to juggle as many different file types as possible. Others like to use powerful stand-alone applications as helper applications so they can really manipulate the files they access. The last group prefers small, quick applications that display just one type of file. Let's look at this approach first.

The Minimal Approach

This approach makes use of small helper applications that have very few features, and do just one thing. The advantage to this approach is that your helper applications load and play quickly. They don't eat up much memory, so they're perfect for systems with slower processors and less RAM.

The disadvantage is that you may have to install and configure lots of helper applications to handle all the different file types you might run into on the Web.

The minimalist approach is best if you're running Internet Explorer on a computer with limited resources or if your needs are utilitarian: catching up on news, doing mostly text-based research, and so on.

The Hands-On Approach

If you like to work on-the-fly, you might prefer to use more powerful programs as helpers. For example, say you're involved in a project where you are downloading and converting hundreds of public domain graphics files to .BMP format. You could save yourself a lot of file manipulation time later if the helper application you have configured as your graphics viewer could convert and save them for you as you browse the Web.

Part
III

Ch
13

As you've seen, Paint Shop Pro is a good example of a powerhouse program that also makes a good Internet Explorer helper application. It can read and convert three dozen different file types and manipulate graphics in scores of different ways, but it's easy to use and is compact enough to load relatively quickly. (Paint Shop Pro is discussed in depth in Chapter 15, "Configuring Internet Explorer for Graphics.")

▶ **See** "Graphics Helper Applications for Internet Explorer" for tips on good graphics helper applications, **p. 282**

> **N O T E** You won't want to spend a lot of time manipulating and converting files while you're online if you are using a dial-up connection that charges you for connect time. Instead, save the files you want to keep and work with them offline later. ■

You can save even more time if you don't view files while you're online. Just download them directly to disk. Instead of left-clicking a file's link to display it, right-click it and select <u>S</u>ave Picture As. The file will be saved to disk without being displayed.

You never really even have to save a file you've viewed recently—it's already stored in Internet Explorer's cache directory. HTML pages, graphics, sounds, and other files that Internet Explorer loads are stored by name in its cache directory; so if your cache in enabled, you can easily find the file there and copy it into a more permanent directory.

The All-In-One Approach

The advantage of having one helper application that handles everything is that configuration is quick and easy—you install one program, go through the configuration process once, and you're done. The disadvantage is that do-it-all helper applications have a tendency to load slowly and hog system resources.

And, of course, there are no programs that will handle absolutely everything you might encounter on the Web. But you can come surprisingly close. Take VuePrint, for example. VuePrint is a program that is a veritable Swiss Army knife for audio, graphics, and video. It comes in versions for Windows 3.1 and Windows 95, and can play or display all of the following file types:

- Image files (.GIF, .BMP, .DIB, .RLE, .PCX, .TGA, .JPG, .TIF)
- Sound files (.MID, .WAV, .MCI)
- Movie files (.AVI, .MPG, .MMM, .MOV, .FLI, .FLC)
- Slide show files (.SLI)
- UUEncoded files (.UUE, .UU1, .01, .MSG)
- Zip files (.ZIP)

With a program like VuePrint installed on your system, you don't have to worry about running into files that Internet Explorer can't handle. (VuePrint's capabilities are discussed at length in Chapter 15, "Configuring Internet Explorer for Graphics.")

▶ **See** "VuePrint Pro" to find out more about VuePrint, **p. 287**

Your Personal Setup

You'll most likely want to take an approach that's a compromise among these three extremes. Like most Internet Explorer users, you'll end up configuring a handful of useful helper applications that expand Internet Explorer's native capabilities without doing too much or too little.

What Kinds of Programs Can You Use as Helper Applications?

Almost any program can be configured as a helper application for Internet Explorer. But that doesn't mean you should go ahead and configure every program you own. Keep in mind effectiveness, efficiency, and utility.

Should You Use DOS, Windows 3.1, or Windows 95 Helpers?

Stick with Windows 95 helper applications as much as you can, and only use Windows 3.1 helper applications when no version exists for Windows 95. There really isn't any reason to ever use a DOS program as an Internet Explorer 3 helper application, though you may discover a couple in the following chapters that are useful as offline file conversion utilities. DOS applications don't integrate terribly well with Windows 95. They don't make good use of system resources and don't multitask well with Windows applications like Internet Explorer.

Windows 3.1 applications don't handle long filenames, don't multitask efficiently, don't run as fast under Windows 95 as native 32-bit applications, and don't use the standard Windows 95 file dialog box. However, there may be some cases where there are not comparable Windows 95 applications, since Windows 3.1 has been around a lot longer.

Both you and Internet Explorer will be happier in the long run if you use the most advanced, up-to-date programs your system can run as helper apps. But don't forget that you want your helper applications to be quick and resource-friendly, too.

Part
III

Ch
13

Programs You Already Own

The first place you should look for helper applications is in the treasure trove of programs you already own. Both Windows 3.1 and Windows 95 come with a handful of small, efficient bundled applications that make excellent Internet Explorer helper applications.

Windows 95 and Windows 3.1 both include a program that plays .WAV audio files: Sound Recorder. It lives in your Windows directory and is probably already the program associated with .WAV files on your system. The combination of Internet Explorer's built-in audio capabilities and Sound Recorder handle the most popular digitized sound file types on the Web.

Earlier in this chapter, we discussed how to set up Paint Shop Pro, another program that is included with both versions of Windows, as a helper application for viewing .PCX and .BMP image files, as well as several other graphics formats. But, we shouldn't forget about Microsoft's Paint program, included with Windows 95. It only handles .PCX and .BMP files, and has nowhere near the functionality of Paint Shop Pro. But it's free, and you probably already have it on your machine. With Internet Explorer's native support for GIFs and JPEGs, the addition of Paint instantly sets you up for viewing the Web's four most popular graphics image file types.

And you don't want to overlook Media Player, which is bundled with Windows 95 as a player for MIDI music files (.MID) and Video-for-Windows videos (.AVI). (It plays .WAV audio files, too.) By themselves, these three "free" Microsoft programs handle most of the multimedia files you'll encounter on the Web.

All these programs are discussed in more detail in the appropriate chapters in this section. The point is, you may not have to look any further than your own system for the Internet Explorer helper applications you need.

Freeware and Shareware Solutions

You should also be prepared to mine the Web itself for helper applications. There are literally thousands of freeware and shareware programs out there, free for the downloading. The chapters in this section discuss dozens of freeware and shareware programs that you can use as Internet Explorer helper applications.

N O T E So what's the difference between freeware and shareware? Freeware is just that: free. You can download it and use it forever without ever paying anyone a dime. Shareware, on the other hand, is software you can try for free, but if you continue to use it, you're expected to pay the author for the privilege. If you use it past the trial period stated in the program's license agreement, you are effectively stealing the program, just as if you had shoplifted it from a store shelf. Fortunately, most shareware license fees are so reasonable that they won't put much of a strain on your pocketbook. ◼

So where do you go to get freely distributed helper applications?

First of all, check out the CD included with this book. It includes most of the helper applications discussed in this section. The odds are good that you won't have to go any further to get all the helper applications you need.

Here are some other software archive sites to try on the World Wide Web:

- ◼ The Virtual Software Library
  http://vsl.cnet.com
- ◼ Randy Burgess's Windows 95 Resource Center
  http://www.cris.com/~randybrg/win95.html
- ◼ PC World Online
  http://www.pcworld.com/win95/shareware

- Unofficial Windows 95 Software Archive
  http://www.netex.net/w95/windows95
- The Windows95.com 32-bit Shareware Web Site
  http://www.windows95.com/apps/
- Stroud's Consummate Winsock Applications
  http://www.cwsapps.com
- CSUSM Software Archive
  http://www.csusm.edu/cwis/winworld/winworld.html

For additional information on how to download files from the Web, see Chapter 5, "Moving Around the Web." For more about finding files, see Chapter 6, "Finding Information on the Web."

▶ **See** "How to Move Around the Web" for tips on surfing the Web, **p. 82**

▶ **See** "Finding Information on the Web" for help with how to find software and information on the Web, **p.93**

Many of the files you download from the Web will be compressed. To find out how to decompress the files you download, see Chapter 19, "Using Compressed/Encoded Files."

▶ **See** "What are File Compression and Archiving and How Is It Done?" for information on compressing files, **p. 352**

▶ **See** "The Hows and Whys of File Encoding and Decoding" for information on binary file encoding, **p. 360**

> **CAUTION**
>
> Watch out for files you download that have an .EXE filename extension. Most are self-extracting archives, not usable executable files!

Commercial Programs

Part
III

Ch
13

Of course, you could actually spend some money and buy programs to use as helper applications. If you're a real control freak, you might be considering using PhotoShop, PhotoStyler, PhotoFinish, or some other "name brand" commercial graphics, sound, or video program as an Internet Explorer helper application.

But you should be aware that most of the programs you can buy for multimedia use are huge and eat up a lot of system resources. For most people, it would certainly be overkill to buy anything like the programs mentioned above just to use as Internet Explorer helper applications.

But if you can find a small, elegant commercial program that you really like, there is certainly no reason why you can't buy it and configure it as an Internet Explorer helper. If you're inclined to go this way, I advise you to read the reviews in popular computer magazines for guidance on which ones might be right for you. But try to steer clear of the huge "professional" packages. Odds are that they would just get in the way of browsing the Web.

Configure Now or Later, or Not at All

If you want, you can try to anticipate your needs and find and configure helper applications for all the file types you think you're likely to encounter in the future. Or you can just wait for Internet Explorer to let you know that you need a helper application.

If you try to display a file that you haven't configured a helper application for and that doesn't have a Windows 95 default application based on file extension, Internet Explorer won't do anything with the file. In order to download this file, right-click its link and choose the Save Target As or Save Picture As options. Once the file is on your hard drive, you can figure out how to deal with it at your leisure.

Checking Your Work: The WWW Viewer Test Page

How can you make sure your helper applications are configured properly? Test 'em out!

The easiest way to test an Internet Explorer helper application is to open a local file of that type. If Internet Explorer launches the right helper application and the file is displayed properly, you're in business.

If you don't have a file of the type you want to check, or if you simply prefer to test your helper application "under fire" on the Web, go to the Lawrence Livermore Labs Web Browser Test Page at **http://www-dsed.llnl.gov/documents/WWWtest.html**. This page presents a menu of buttons that send you dozens of different files to exercise just about any helper application you can think of. ●

Configuring Internet Explorer for Sound

Internet Explorer 3 has built-in capabilities for playing sounds in several different formats. It can play background sounds—sounds that are automatically downloaded and played along with a Web page—in .WAV, .AU, and .MID formats. Links to .AU and .AIFF sounds are supported internally, and Internet Explorer 3 can also play sounds through its support of inline AVI animations. However, by setting Internet Explorer up with the right helper applications, you can expand its sound capabilities immeasurably.

Of course, you not only need the right sound software—you also need the right hardware. Then you'll be ready to find some noisy places to visit on the Web. Fortunately, these are in ample supply. ▪

How does Internet Explorer work with sound?

In this chapter, learn how Internet Explorer can use other applications on your system to play sound files that you download from the Internet and the World Wide Web.

What audio file formats are on the World Wide Web?

There are many different formats for audio files that you can find on the Web. This chapter will discuss the most popular ones.

Which programs make good Internet Explorer sound helper applications?

Many applications exist that can play and manipulate audio files for each of the many formats. Learn what some of the best are and how to use them.

How do you translate sounds for Internet Explorer?

Learn how to take sounds in other audio formats and convert them into formats that you can use.

What sound formats are supported by Internet Explorer and Microsoft's ActiveMovie?

Find out what sound formats are supported directly by Internet Explorer and by Microsoft's ActiveMovie control.

Hardware Requirements for Internet Explorer Sound

Back in the "old days" of personal computing—when "PC" was always followed by "XT," processor numbers were only four digits long, and software ran directly off floppy disks—every PC shipped with a little AM-radio quality speaker that beeped shrilly any time you did something wrong. Some folks managed to write a few programs that played digitized sounds on that little speaker. But these first attempts at digitized audio and music are a far cry from what is available today.

Now that we're in the high-tech age of multimedia computers—complete with 24-bit true color animations, 16-bit stereo music soundtracks, and digitized CD-ROM voice-overs by the likes of Patrick Stewart—all PCs still ship with that same tinny little speaker.

Microsoft has a Windows driver that plays music and audio using only the internal PC speaker, but it chews up a lot of system resouces, and everything still sounds like it's being fed through a weather-beaten drive-in movie speaker with a shorted connection.

To get real audio out of your PC, you need a sound card. If you bought your computer recently, or if you've spent a few bucks upgrading, the odds are good you already have a sound card. But if you don't, you can pick one up for anywhere between $30 and $800, depending on what you want it to do.

A good 16-bit stereo Sound Blaster Pro (or compatible) sound card does just about everything the average person needs done audio-wise, and does it for under $100. If you haven't invested in a sound card yet, drop this book right now, scan a few computer magazine reviews and ads, run to your local computer store, buy a sound card, and plug it in. You'll be glad you did.

How Computer Audio Works

Most of the sounds you hear coming from your PC are digitized. That is, the sound waves that make up the sound have been converted into a stream of digital bits and bytes by feeding them through some kind of analog-to-digital converter. You can do this yourself using the software that came with your sound board on any audio source, such as a microphone or tape player. Once digitized, the sound data is saved as a file on disk.

Digitized sound files vary in at least three important ways:

- **The sampling rate, or the number of times each second the audio wave form is sampled as it is converted to digital data.** PC sound file sampling rates generally range from 8,000 to 44,100 samples per second. (More samples equal the potential for higher quality sound.)
- **The way the data is organized in the file.** For example, a digitized sound file may or may not include header information which describes the file, may interleave the data from multiple sound tracks (i.e., two tracks for stereo), or may be comprised of a library of different instrument sound samples followed by a "play list" for using them to play a song.

- **The way data in a sound file may be compressed to save disk space and transfer time.** For example, MPEG audio files are compressed at a 6:1 ratio.

There are a dozen or more relatively popular sound file types, each of which varies in the way it stores sound data. Most programs only play one or two kinds of sound files. Fortunately, Internet Explorer supports a couple of formats internally, and if you have helper applications configured to play the three or four most popular types, you won't run into many audio problems cruising the Net. You don't have to worry about the rest unless you're a real sound freak or have some specialized application.

N O T E You can find out more about audio file formats by checking out the Audio FAQ (Frequently Asked Questions) list on UseNet. You can retrieve the latest version by pointing Internet Explorer to **ftp://ftp.cwi.nl/pub/audio**. Look for the files **AudioFormats.part1** and **AudioFormats.part2**.

More information can also be obtained by reading the UseNet newsgroup **alt.binaries.sounds**. ■

How Internet Explorer Works with Sounds

In the past, Web pages didn't generally include audio files inline because Web browsers couldn't play them without launching a helper application. Most Web pages that have an audio component make sounds optional; they ask you to click a link to load an external sound file.

This is beginning to change with some of Internet Explorer's built-in capabilities. With Internet Explorer, Web authors can add background sounds that are loaded and played automatically along with their Web page. Also, through its support of inline Audio Video Interleave (AVI) animations, Internet Explorer has another form of inline audio support.

Additionally, Internet Explorer 3 has internal support for two digitized audio file formats: Sun/ NeXT (`.AU`, `.SND`) and Mac/SGI (`.AIF`, `.AIFF`) (see fig. 14.1). To cope with other sound file types, you need to configure additional audio helper applications. And because Internet Explorer's built-in support is so limited in what it can do, you may even want to configure a different player for `.AU` and `.AIF` sounds, as well.

FIG. 14.1
Internet Explorer
includes built-in
support for a few
audio formats.

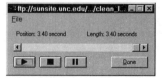

Sound File Formats

Internet Explorer recognizes audio files the same way it identifies all the files it accesses on the Web: by MIME type first, and then (if it doesn't receive a valid MIME type from the Web server it's connected to) by filename extension. (For more about MIME types, see Chapter 13, "Configuring Helper Applications.")

▶ **See** "A Brief Course in MIME Types" for information on what MIME is, **p. 253**

The audio file MIME types and filename extensions that Internet Explorer knows about are listed in Table 14.1.

Table 14.1 Three Audio File Types Recognized by Internet Explorer

Type/Subtype	Extensions	Description
audio/basic	.AU, .SND	ULAW Audio Data
audio/aiff	.AIF, .AIFF, .AIFC	AIFF Audio
video/avi	.AVI	Audio Video Interleave

Note that while, technically, AVI is of MIME type `video`, AVI files include audio, and so are one of the "audio" file types that Internet Explorer recognizes.

This is certainly not a very extensive list. There are over a dozen other sound file types out there on the Web. Table 14.2 lists some of the other audio formats you're likely to encounter while browsing the Web.

Table 14.2 Other Audio File Types You'll Find on the World Wide Web

Type/Subtype	Extensions	Description
audio/x-fssd	.SND, .FSSD	Mac, PC
audio/x-iff	.IFF	Amiga
audio/x-midi*	.MID, .MIDI, .RMI	MIDI music
audio/x-mod	.MOD, .NST	Amiga, Atari ST
audio/x-sf	.SF	IRCAM
audio/x-ul	.UL	US telephony
audio/x-voc	.VOC	Sound Blaster
audio/x-wav*	.WAV	Windows RIFF

You'll probably want to configure helper applications for these file types right away.

The two you'll probably want to configure helper applications for right away are MIDI music files (`.MID`) and WAV (`.WAV`) format digitized sound files. As discussed in Chapter 13, however, because of the way Internet Explorer is currently integrated into Windows 95, the standard File Types configuration determines what its helper applications are. Because of this, it is possible that your system already has helper applications configured for these two types of sound files, and maybe some of the others. Typically, Windows 95, and therefore Internet Explorer, might be set up so that .WAV files use the Sound Recorder program that comes with Windows 95, while .MID files call the Media Player.

WAV Files

The WAV format is Window's own standard file format. All Window's warning beeps, whistles, and clangs live in your Windows directory as files with .WAV extensions. Because it is such a standard fixture on Windows computers, thousands upon thousands of WAV files have made their way onto the World Wide Web.

As mentioned previously, it's possible that the Windows program Sound Recorder may already be set up to act as a helper application for .WAV files. You can test this by using the Windows 95 Explorer to find a .WAV file and double-click it to see what happens. The file that gets loaded to play that sound is both the Windows 95 default application for files with that file type, and the Internet Explorer helper application for files of MIME type audio/wav and files with the extension .WAV.

Most of the programs described in this chapter can play .WAV format files.

MIDI Music Files

MIDI music files (.MID, .MIDI) are completely different than other sound file formats. Originally developed to control electronic musical instruments, the MIDI file format has become extremely popular on PCs since the advent of MIDI-capable sound cards.

MIDI files combine sound definitions called instruments with MIDI sequence control commands that tell a MIDI device (like your PC's sound board) which instruments to play when, for how long, and with what settings. In a way, a MIDI file is more like a printed sheet-music score than a digitized sound file. In fact, MIDI files don't contain digitized sounds at all, unless the file uses custom instrument definitions.

 TIP You guessed it! Microsoft has supplied you with a program that plays MIDI files, too. Also located in the Windows directory in both Windows 3.1 and Windows 95, Media Player will typically be the default application—and Internet Explorer helper application—for playing .MID files. It also plays Video-for-Windows (.AVI) movies and, like Sound Recorder, WAV (.WAV) audio files. Use the MIME types audio/x-mid and video/avi. Add audio/wav if you want it to play WAV files, too.

Sound Helper Applications for Internet Explorer

N O T E For information on where to find helper applications and how to configure them once you've found them, see Chapter 13, "Configuring Helper Applications." ■

Now that we've finished the appetizers, we can get down to the meat-and-potatoes. Just what are the best audio helper applications for Internet Explorer 3?

There are dozens of programs that fit the bill, but we'll discuss a few of the very best, or most useful, in our discussion here. The rest of the chapter will focus on a collection of excellent freeware and shareware audio programs that should satisfy the most discerning Internet Explorer user, whether you are mainly interested in just *hearing* what is available, or are a real audio afficionado looking for ways to download and *work* with Internet and Web audio.

Windows 95 Sound Programs

As a Windows 95 user, you should try to stick to Windows 95 helper applications for Internet Explorer. Not only do they understand long filenames and have the unmistakable Windows 95 look and feel, they multitask better than Windows 3.1 programs and run faster because they're 32-bit applications.

Though Windows 95 is relatively new, there are already some good freeware and shareware audio applications out there. The following are some of the best.

MIDI JukeBox 2   Pocket-Sized Software's MIDI JukeBox 2 is a simple little Windows 95 shareware program, and its main purpose is to act as a MIDI jukebox that plays background music as you work (see fig. 14.2). But it also makes a nifty helper application for Internet Explorer. It can be configured as a helper application for playing both WAV(.WAV) and MIDI (.MID, .MIDI, .RMI) sound files.

FIG. 14.2
MIDI JukeBox 2 can play WAV and MIDI audio files for Internet Explorer, and it's a great background music program, too.

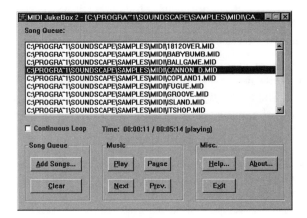

The program is small (only 42 KB) and offers a minimum of features: you can pause sounds or replay them. That's it. It's a perfect example of a helper application for the devout minimalist.

But if you like working to background music and have access to an extensive collection of music files, MIDI JukeBox 2's background music capability is a nice plus. It lets you load and play a list of MIDI and WAV files from your hard drive or network, and you can jive all day while using very little in the way of system resources.

Because it was written for Windows 95, the program is fast and efficient and multitasks well. Best of all, the shareware fee is only $10.

If you're looking for a single, simple Windows 95 application to augment Internet Explorer's .AU and .AIF sound-playing capabilities in order to play links to WAV and MIDI files, look no further than MIDI JukeBox 2.

TrueSpeech Internet Player Any sound can be digitized, including speech. But sounds digitized in the proprietary TrueSpeech format by DSP Group, Inc., can be compressed and still retain excellent quality. DSP says that its technology can compress one minute of digitized speech to a file only 64 KB in size. It licenses this technology to developers (for a fee) but provides the freeware TrueSpeech Internet Player—the filename of the executable is TSPLAY32.EXE—to users who want to play audio files in the TrueSpeech format (see fig. 14.3).

FIG. 14.3
The TrueSpeech Internet Player plays WAV files and is optimized for playing digitized speech.

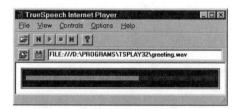

TSPlay32 is a Windows 95 program (there's also a Windows 3.1 version) that plays TrueSpeech files and regular WAV files to boot. This program can easily be configured as an Internet Explorer helper application for playing all the waves that come its way.

One of its best features is that it can play sound files in real-time, as they are downloading; you don't have to wait for a file to download first. If you don't like what you hear, you'll know right away and can cancel the transfer in midstream. This can save you lots of expensive connect time if you're previewing many sound files, but keeping only a few. Of course, nothing is perfect—TrueSpeech sometimes gets ahead of a download and has to pause and wait for it to catch up, but you can always hit the Play button to start the file playing over again from the beginning.

TrueSpeech is unique in that it is on the forefront of a new World Wide Web technology: programs that can access the Web independently of a browser. You can run TSPlay32 all by itself and choose to load and play a file from your disk or network, of course; but you can also tell it to load a URL and it will connect to the Web and play a file directly from the site where it is stored, all without the aid of Internet Explorer or any other browser. This kind of independent program is going to open up the Web and make it seem like more of a wide-area network than a communications service. Look for more programs like TSPlay32 in the near future.

In the meantime, TSPlay32 also makes a good helper application for Internet Explorer. Though at 275 KB, it's not exactly compact; but it's not a monster, either. And you'll have fun playing sounds right off the Web when Internet Explorer's not even running.

Sound Gadget Pro If you like to play with the sounds you download, just listening to sounds is never enough for you. You want to dissect them, tear them apart, and put them back together again in new and different ways.

Part
III

Ch
14

If this is you, then Sound Gadget Pro (270 KB) will be your favorite sound helper application for Internet Explorer (see fig. 14.4). Not only can it load and play .AU and .SND files, it also handles .WAV and .VOC (Sound Blaster) sound formats, as well as raw sound files.

FIG. 14.4

Sound Gadget Pro lets you do much more than just listen to sound files. It lets you view and edit them, too.

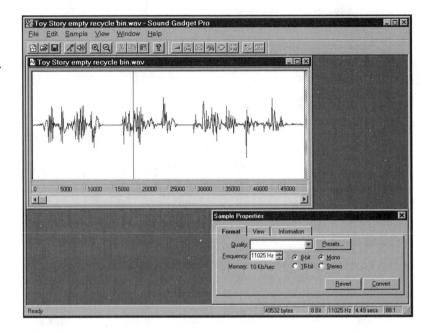

Even though shareware author Nigel Magnay has chosen to inconvenience you a bit when this program is launched (you have to hit three randomly selected buttons before it will run), and even though files don't play automatically (you have to hit the Play button first), this program is such a nice sound editor you won't mind these minor inconveniences. Heck, you'll probably even figure out how much £10 is in American money and send Nigel his shareware fee.

Sound Gadget Pro (SGPro) lets you view a sound's waveform and manipulate it in many different ways. You can reverse it, convert it to another format, change it from eight to 16 bits or vice versa, and likewise from mono to stereo. You can fade, cross-fade, cut, paste, and even apply a dynamic envelope. You'll be turning staid voice-overs into Hollywood-style sound effect extravaganzas after only a few minutes of playing around with SGPro's highly intuitive Windows 95 interface.

If you're concerned about connect time, you might want to configure something simpler as your Internet Explorer audio helper application and just use SGPro on files you've saved offline.

RealAudio Player Like the TrueSpeech player for Windows 95, RealAudio plays sound files off the Web in real-time, and can do so all by itself, without the assistance of a Web browser (see fig. 14.5). It only plays its own proprietary (.RA, .RAM) files. The RealAudio format was designed to be able to deliver high-quality, real-time audio content over the Internet.

FIG. 14.5

The RealAudio Player only plays the RealAudio format developed by Progressive Networks.

 A good place to find .RA files is the Internet Radio Network at **http://town.hall.org/radio/**. They have over 200 hours of files online, and regularly broadcast the proceedings of Congress over the Web in real-time. (The files are available in .WAV format, too.)

If you're interested in real-time audio on the Web, check this program out. For more information, and for a list of sites that have RealAudio content, take a look at Progressive Networks' home page at **http://www.realaudio.com**.

Windows 3.1 Sound Programs

There are still some excellent freely distributed sound programs on the Web (and on this book's CD, as well) that are only available as Windows 3.1 programs. Even under Windows 95, some of these Windows 3.1 programs can nicely fill the gap until Windows 95 specific programs are available that have similar features. They are as follows:

- **Windows Play Any File**—This ideal helper application, usually called WPLANY.EXE, has no user interface at all. It launches to play a sound file, in .AU/.SND, .VOC, .WAV, and/or .IFF formats, and then closes down afterwards.

- **Waveform Hold and Modify**—WHAM.EXE is another good helper application for sound, supporting .AU/.SND, .VOC, .WAV, .IFF, and/or raw sound files. WHAM also allows you to edit sound files, as well. WHAM can be configured to launch its window and play an incoming sound file, or, like WPLANY.EXE, to launch, play a sound file, and quit without ever popping up a window.

- **StreamWorks Player**—This player allows you to play MPEG-compressed audio on the Web. While MPEG is usually thought of as a video format, it can also be used to produce very compact, high-quality audio.

- **MidiGate**—MidiGate is a small helper application for playing MIDI format files. It can be configured to run with its window visible, or minimized.

Microsoft ActiveMovie

ActiveMovie, from Microsoft, is a system for playing many audio and video formats over the World Wide Web. An ActiveMovie Player is available as an add-in module for Internet Explorer 3 through the Internet Explorer Web site at **http://www.microsoft.com/ie/** (see fig. 14.6).

Part
III

Ch
14

FIG. 14.6
ActiveMovie's progressive playback feature allows you to start listening to incoming sounds before they are fully downloaded.

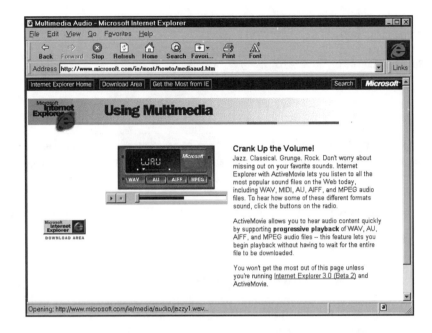

Through ActiveMovie, Internet Explorer 3 adds sophisticated support for .WAV, .AU, .AIFF, MIDI, and MPEG encoded sounds. As shown in figure 14.6, because it is an add-in module, the controls for it can be embedded directly in the Web page.

▶ **See** "Plug-Ins, Add-Ins, and ActiveX Controls" for more information about the Internet Explorer's add-in capabilities, **p.735**

Translating Sounds for Internet Explorer

The following are a couple of good reasons why you might find yourself interested in translating sound files from one format to another:

■ If you find an absolutely must-have sound online in some strange format and you don't have anything on hand that will play it

■ If you are creating your own Web pages and need to translate a lot of odd sound files that you have lying around to some more popular format (like .AU or .WAV)

Either way, you have to find a program that can read the original and write the target sound file format. Many of the programs mentioned in this chapter can do that to some degree. For example, if you want to convert a dozen .AU files to .WAV format, you can do it with WHAM or Sound Gadget Pro.

But what if the formats you need to be able to read and/or write are real oddballs? Well, the good news is, there's a solution. The bad news is, you're going to have to run it from DOS.

That's because one of the most versatile tools for converting among various audio formats is a multi-platform application called SOX (Sound Exchange). It doesn't exist in Windows 3.1 or Windows 95 formats, but the DOS version is a very versatile tool.

SOX can read and write over a dozen different audio file formats. They are listed in Table 14.3.

Table 14.3 Audio File Types That SOX Can Read and Write

Extension	Type
.AIFF	Apple/SGI
.AU	SUN
.AUTO	Guess the Type
.CDR	CD Audio
.DAT	Text Data
.HCOM	Macintosh HCOM
.RAW, .UB, .SB, .UW, .SW, .UL	Raw
.SF	IRCAM
.SMP	SampleVision
.VOC	Sound Blaster
.WAV	Windows RIFF

In its simplest usage, SOX merely converts from one format to another. For example, to convert a file called BLOOP.AU to one called BLOOP.WAV, you would type the following:

```
sox bloop.au bloop.wav
```

DOS programs don't get much easier than that.

If you want to add special effects like tweaking the volume, changing the sampling rate, or converting from stereo to mono, SOX does all that, too. But we're not going to get into all the subtle details of SOX here. If you want to perform such esoteric tasks, check out the SOX documentation. ●

Part

III

Ch

14

## CHAPTER 15

Configuring Internet Explorer for Graphics

Graphics, graphics, graphics! Everybody loves 'em, and they're what makes life on the Web so interesting. Without inline graphics, Web pages would boil down to interlinked pages of plain text—not much more than a fancy version of Gopher.

Most Web graphics are stored in one of two formats, and Internet Explorer knows how to display both kinds. Sometimes though, Internet Explorer encounters a file format that it doesn't know how to process. At this point, helper applications come in. If Internet Explorer encounters an image format that has a specific viewer configured, it launches the viewer application and allows you to see the image. This process isn't quite as elegant as displaying the image right in the Internet Explorer window, but it's better than not showing the image at all.

This chapter examines some of the specifics surrounding Web graphics and what programs are available to act as helper applications for viewing images that Internet Explorer can't handle on its own. ■

The minimum hardware requirements for viewing Web graphics

To fully appreciate Web graphics, you'll want to have equipment at least as good as what's described in this chapter.

The basics of how computer graphics are stored

Images can be bitmapped, stored in vector format, or as a combination of the two.

What graphics file formats are used most often on the Web

Learn about GIF and JPEG—the two biggest Web graphics formats.

What Windows 95 and Windows 3.1 programs make good Internet Explorer helper applications for viewing graphics

Internet Explorer can't display every one of the scores of graphics formats, so you'll need a helper application or two to view some images on the Web.

What programs you can use to handle more exotic image conversions

Some of the handiest utility programs are those that convert files from one graphics format to another. Find out about a few of them here.

Hardware Requirements for Internet Explorer Graphics

Many older desktop PCs and notebook computers are limited in their graphics capabilities. If your machine can't display any more than 16 colors, this chapter probably isn't for you.

The minimum for surfing the Web these days is a 640×480 screen capable of displaying 256 colors. If your computer can do at least this well, you'll be able to view about 85 percent of the graphics you find on the Web with no problem.

Of course, the real cutting-edge sites out there have pages that look good only on an 800×600 (or larger) screen, with 16-bit (65,536) or 24-bit (16,777,216) color palettes. While pretty, these sites are murder if you're dialing in on a 14.4 Kbps connection because they take so long to download.

 Trying to view a big page on a small screen? No problem! Just use the scroll bar at the bottom of the Internet Explorer window to move horizontally. Most people don't pay any attention to it on "normal" size screens, so they forget it's there when viewing pages that are a little wider than normal.

Still, some of those images are well worth waiting for. And once you've got them, you've got to have some way to display them. As you read in Chapter 13, "Configuring Helper Applications," Internet Explorer can display many types of graphics *inline*, meaning it doesn't need help from an outside program. Other images that Internet Explorer can't display inline have to be viewed with a helper application.

You should check the manual for your PC's display card and see what it's capable of. If your display card is more than a couple of years old, you may want to upgrade so you can handle those big, beautiful images. If your pocketbook says "no," don't despair. You can still look at them if you're willing to compromise a bit.

 Read your display card manual carefully! Even if your display isn't what you'd like it to be, you may be able to plug in more video RAM and bring it up to speed. This solution is much cheaper than buying a whole new graphics card.

How Computer Graphics Work

Computer graphics are bitmapped images; that is, they consist of a grid of dots called *pixels* that are mapped to a color palette. For example, the minimum Windows 95 display screen is 640 pixels wide by 480 pixels high (640×480), with a palette of 16 colors.

Many of the graphics images you'll encounter on the Web come in one of four "standard" sizes, which happen to match the screen sizes of common computer displays: 320×200, 640×480, 800×600, and 1,024×768. However, you can find bitmaps on the Web in sizes ranging from tiny thumbnails with dimensions of only a few pixels to images so huge your computer can't even load them, much less display them.

The number of colors in an image is dependent on how many bits are used to define the color for each pixel (see fig. 15.1). Table 15.1 shows how many bits are required for the five most common color palette depths.

Table 15.1   The Number of Bits Needed To Define Different Image Color Palettes

Number of Bits	Colors in Palette
1	2
4	16
8	256
16	65,536
24	16,777,216

 TIP A two-color image (1-bit) is always monochrome (black and white). But 4- and 8-bit images are sometimes grayscale images, with each pixel's value indicating brightness, rather than color.

An image's color palette is generally defined in one of two ways. For images with 16,256 or 65,536 colors, the number that defines each pixel's color is usually a pointer into a table of predefined or user-definable colors. For example, a bit with the color 233 points to the 233rd color defined in the color palette table. A color palette table defines colors using more bits than are used to indicate the color for each pixel. In this way, you can have images that, for example, use 256 colors out of a possible 24-bit color palette of more than 16 million.

But images with 24-bit color definitions usually indicate color values directly. This is done on a pixel-by-pixel basis using the same scheme that defines color palettes for entire low-color images—by splitting the number of bits for each color value into RGB (red, green, blue) values. (This happens because a video monitor builds up an image from red, green, and blue dots.) For example, a 24-bit image splits the palette into eight bits each for red, green, and blue values. That is, each color is made up of 256 different shades, each of the three colors, for a total of 16,777,216 possible colors in a single image.

FIG. 15.1
The same photo in one, four, and eight bits per pixel.

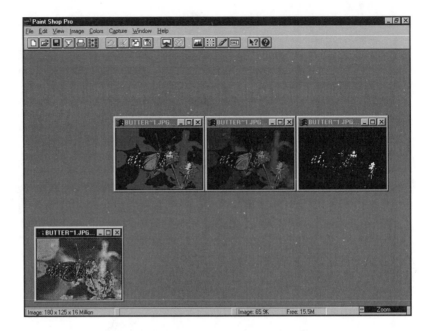

How Internet Explorer Works with Graphics

Most computer graphics images do not share the same set of colors. This can result in color "thrashing" if, for example, your computer tries to display two 256-color images with different color palettes on the same 256-color screen. You can also run into problems trying to display an image with more colors than your display can handle, like a 16-million color JPEG on a 256-color screen. Fortunately, Internet Explorer is very clever about how it displays inline graphics. It handles these problems by using a process called *dithering*.

Dithering uses a pattern of available colors to create a visual illusion of displaying more. For example, if the Internet Explorer screen palette had no orange available to it, it might try to "fake" orange by displaying a grid of yellow and red pixels. Your eye interprets the area as orange-ish, if you don't look at it too closely.

Graphics File Formats

Most computer graphics file formats store image information as bitmaps. After all, that's how a computer displays them. Both image types that Internet Explorer can display—GIFs and JPEGs—are bitmapped images.

Well, Not Really...

Saying that GIFs and JPEGs are bitmapped image files is not precisely true; they're compressed bitmapped image files.

GIFs are 256-color (or fewer) images that are compressed using LZW compression, a technique similar to the file compression algorithms used in various archive file formats.

A JPEG image begins life as a 24-bit bitmapped image; then a very sophisticated image compression algorithm takes over. This algorithm analyzes the picture and compresses it to a very high ratio. JPEG compression is actually *lossy*—that is, it usually doesn't care if it throws away some picture detail in order to make the image a whole lot smaller.

When it comes to graphics image file formats, many extremely different ways to store an image are available.

Vector image files take a different approach—they actually describe how an image is drawn. When a computer displays a vector image file, it follows the instructions in the file to redraw the image. While it sounds tedious, vector images are much easier to rescale to different sizes because the image doesn't have a hard-and-fast correlation between its definition in the file and the pixel-by-pixel image on the screen.

Metafiles use a combination of bitmapped and vector image definition. Windows Metafile (.WMF) format images are used quite often under Windows for clipart images that frequently need to be resized.

N O T E You can find out more about graphics file formats by checking out the four-part Graphics FAQ list on UseNet. You can retrieve the latest version by pointing Internet Explorer to **ftp:/ /rtfm.mit.edu/pub/usenet/news.answers/graphics/fileformats-faq** or **http:// www.smartpages.com/faqs/graphics/fileformats-faq/part[1-4]/faq.html**. This FAQ is also distributed monthly on the UseNet newsgroups **comp.graphics**, **comp.answers**, and **news.answers** as four separate files.

You can also obtain more information on graphics files by reading the UseNet newsgroup **comp.graphics.misc**. ■

TROUBLESHOOTING

I downloaded an image that looks just fine in [*insert the name of your favorite generic graphics display program here*], but the program I have configured as my Internet Explorer helper application doesn't display it properly. You're probably running into an older (or newer) version of that particular image file format. Though most image-display and manipulation programs can handle older versions of various file formats just fine, some "choke" on unknown variations. And standards groups are always updating file format definitions, sometimes coming up with variations that "break" older viewers. Because of the real-time nature of the Internet, these changes often show up first on the Web. Make sure your Internet Explorer graphics helper applications can always handle the latest versions of a graphics file format.

Internet Explorer recognizes graphics files the same way it identifies all the files it accesses on the Web: by MIME type first and then (if it doesn't receive a valid MIME type from the Web server it's connected to) by filename extension.

> **CAUTION**
>
> Several very different image file formats share the file extensions .PIC ("picture") and .IMG ("image"). The only way to properly identify what kinds of images they really are is by MIME type or to use a program that actually reads and interprets the file's header information. Don't assume that either of these (or any other) file extensions can be used to identify an image's real file type accurately.

Internet Explorer can display inline GIF and JPEG images. These two formats account for a large percentage of the inline images on the Web. But external images are another matter. If you click a link and it leads to a file in a format that Internet Explorer can't handle, you have to configure a helper application for it.

▶ **See** "Configuring a Helper Application" for information on how to configure a helper application, **p. 244**

The graphics file MIME types and filename extensions that Internet Explorer knows about are listed in Table 15.2.

Table 15.2   The Graphics File Types Recognized by Internet Explorer

MIMEType/Subtype	Extensions	Description
image/x-MS-bmp**	.BMP	Windows Bitmap
image/x-portable-pixmap	.PPM	PPM Image
image/x-portable-graymap	.PGM	PGM Image
image/x-portable-bitmap	.PBM	PBM Image
image/x-portable-anymap	.PNM	PBM Image
image/x-cmu-raster	.RAS	CMU Raster Image
image/tiff	.TIFF, .TIF	TIFF Image
image/jpeg*	.JPEG, .JPG, .JPE	JPEG Image
image/gif*	.GIF	CompuServe Image Format

Images that Internet Explorer can display internally are marked with an asterisk (*). The file type you'll probably want to configure a helper application for right away is indicated with two asterisks (**).

Of course, dozens more graphics image file formats are in use on the World Wide Web. Table 15.3 lists some of them, though it is by no means an exhaustive list.

Table 15.3   Other Graphics File Types You Find on the World Wide Web

Extension	Description
.CGM	Computer Graphics Metafile
.DEM	Digital Elevation Model
.DXF	Autodesk Drawing Exchange Format
.IFF	Interchange File Format
.NAPLPS	North American Presentation Layer Protocol Syntax
.PCX*	ZSoft Paint
.PIC	Pegasus Imaging Corporation Format
.PNG	Portable Network Graphics
.PSD	Adobe Photoshop
.RIFF	Microsoft Resource Interchange File Format
.SGI	Silicon Graphics Image File Format
.SPIFF	Still Picture Interchange File Format
.TGA	Truevision (Targa) File Format
.WMF	Windows Meta File
.WPG	WordPerfect Graphics Metafile

The one you may want to configure a helper application for right away is indicated with an asterisk (*).

N O T E   The hottest new graphics file type on the World Wide Web is the Portable Network Graphics (.PNG) format, which was created mostly as a response to the Unisys/CompuServe GIF graphics copyright controversy (see **http://www.xmission.com/~mgm/gif/**). According to the first drafts of the PNG specification, "The PNG format is intended to provide a portable, legally unencumbered, simple, lossless, streaming-capable, well-compressed, well-specified standard for bitmapped image files which gives new features to the end user at minimal cost to the developer." Look for PNG graphics to carve a major niche for themselves on the Web in the months to come. ▪

Note that in each of these tables we've indicated a file type for which you'll probably want to configure an Internet Explorer helper application right away. The two we've targeted are Windows Bitmap (.BMP) and ZSoft Paint (.PCX) files. Though the GIFs and JPEGs that Internet Explorer can handle internally are much more popular on the Web, you'll run into enough BMPs and PCXs to make configuring helper applications for these two file formats worthwhile.

Windows Bitmaps

Because BMPs are the native graphics file format of Microsoft Windows, you'll find quite a few of them on the Web. (And if not on the Web itself, on the rest of the Internet, at the very least.)

Most of the programs described in this chapter can display .BMP format image files.

 TIP Windows 3.1 and Windows 95 users both have access to a program called Paintbrush that displays both .PCX and .BMP images. For a step-by-step guide to setting up Paintbrush to work with Internet Explorer, see Chapter 13, "Configuring Helper Applications."

ZSoft Paint Files

.PCX (ZSoft Paint) format files were really popular on the PC when all it could run was MS-DOS. Even with the onset of graphical interfaces such as Microsoft Windows, .PCX files have persevered to this day.

Fortunately, many of the programs discussed in this chapter can display .PCX files, too.

Graphics Helper Applications for Internet Explorer

With GIF and JPEG support built into Internet Explorer, you already have direct access to the most popular graphics file types on the Web. But by adding helper applications for a few more, you'll be assured of being able to see an even greater percentage of Web graphics without a fuss. The rest of this chapter discusses some programs that make excellent graphics helper applications for Internet Explorer, whether it's running under Windows 3.1 or Windows 95.

NOTE For up-to-date information about the latest versions of these and other graphics programs for Windows 3.1 and Windows 95, check out Brian Stark's excellent Graphic Utilities site on the World Wide Web at **http://www.public.iastate.edu/~stark/gutil_sv.html** (see fig. 15.2).

Windows 95 Graphics Programs

Windows 95 helper applications are your best choice if you're running Internet Explorer under Windows 95. They understand long filenames, have the Windows 95 user interface, multitask better than Windows 3.1 programs, and run faster because they're 32-bit applications.

Some good freeware and shareware graphics applications are available for Windows 95. In the following sections, we introduce you to some of the best.

 LView Pro Good news for Windows 95 users: LView Pro is now available in a 32-bit version (see fig. 15.3). A longtime favorite among Windows 3.1 users, LView Pro can view, manipulate, and convert among seven popular graphics image file formats: JPEG, BMP, TIFF, TGA, GIF, PCX, and PBM.

FIG. 15.2
Learn about the most recent graphics utility programs from Brian Stark's Graphic Utilities site.

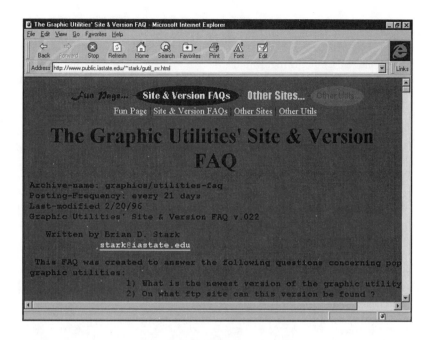

FIG. 15.3
LView Pro can manipulate all kinds of images and act as an Internet Explorer helper application as well.

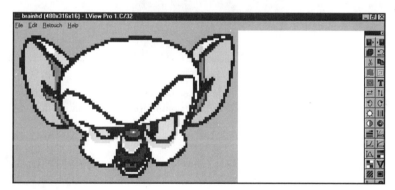

LView Pro is a time-honored tool of Web page creators because of its ability to write transparent background color information in the GIF89a format. This is the means used to create Web graphics that let a Web browser's background color or image show through the background color of inline images. Without this special feature of the GIF89a format, Web pages worldwide would be stuck showing nothing but rectangular graphics. Unfortunately, most graphics programs don't seem to support GIF background transparency. That's reason enough for Web artists to keep a copy of LView Pro on hand.

LView Pro can also save JPEG images as progressive JPEGs. Progressive JPEGs are analogous to interlaced GIFs in that they "fade on" to your screen over several passes. This way, users get a sense of what the entire image will look like on just a few passes, rather than making them wait until the entire image is loaded from top to bottom.

▶ **See** "Converting Images to Progressive JPEGs," **p. 443**

Add in its ability to view and convert other popular file formats, and you have a very useful tool, indeed. Combine that with the dozens of ways LView Pro can tweak images and that it can serve as an Internet Explorer helper application, and you've got a program you just can't live without.

LView Pro is, quite simply, a must-have and, in fact, you already *do* have it. You can find a copy of LView Pro on the CD-ROM that comes with this book. MMedia Research requests a $30 shareware registration fee if you use LView Pro past the trial period. Given the quality of this software package, the expense is well worth it.

Paint Shop Pro   Previously available only in a 16-bit version, Paint Shop Pro has a 32-bit version (version 3.12) that runs native on Windows 95 (see fig. 15.4). PSP is a favorite among Web graphics people because of its ability to work with many file formats, to edit images, and even to do screen captures.

FIG. 15.4

Paint Shop Pro is a high-end image editor and viewer, as well as a paint and screen-capture program.

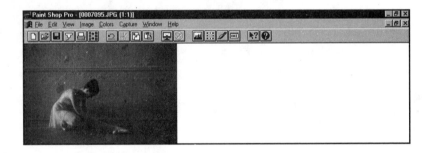

PSP directly supports 35 file formats and can handle more through the use of external filters, including the ones shipped with Microsoft Office. PSP's native file types are listed in Table 15.4.

Table 15.4   File Types Supported by Paint Shop Pro

File Extension	File Type
.BMP	RGB encoded Microsoft Windows
.BMP	RGB encoded OS/2
.BMP	RLE encoded Microsoft Windows
.CDR	CorelDRAW!
.CGM	Computer Graphics Metafile
.CLP	Bitmap Windows Clipboard
.CLP	Device Independent Bitmap Windows Clipboard
.CUT	Dr. Halo

File Extension	File Type
.DIB	RGB encoded Microsoft Windows
.DIB	RGB encoded OS/2
.DIB	RLE encoded Microsoft Windows
.DRW	Micrografx Draw
.DXF	Autodesk
.GEM	Ventura/GEM
.GIF	Version 87a (interlaced) CompuServe
.GIF	Version 87a (noninterlaced) CompuServe
.GIF	Version 89a (interlaced) CompuServe
.GIF	Version 89a (noninterlaced) CompuServe
.HPGL	Hewlett Packard Graphics Language
.IFF	Compressed Electronic Arts
.IFF	Uncompressed Electronic Arts
.IMG	New Style GEM Paint
.IMG	Old Style GEM Paint
.JIF	Huffman compressed Joint Photo. Expert Group
.JPG	Huffman compressed Joint Photo. Expert Group
.LBM	Compressed Deluxe Paint
.LBM	Uncompressed Deluxe Paint
.MAC	With header MacPaint
.MAC	Without header MacPaint
.MSP	New version Microsoft Paint
.MSP	Old version Microsoft Paint
.PBM	Portable Bitmap UNIX
.PCD	Kodak Photo CD
.PCX	Version 0 ZSoft Paintbrush
.PCX	Version 2 (with palette information) ZSoft Paintbrush
.PCX	Version 3 (without palette information) ZSoft Paintbrush
.PCX	Version 5 ZSoft Paintbrush
.PGM	Portable Graymap UNIX

continues

Table 15.4   Continued

File Extension	File Type
.PIC	Lotus Development Corp.
.PIC	Pictor/PC Paint
.PNG	Portable Network Graphics
.PPM	Portable Pixelmap UNIX
.PSD	RGB or indexed Photoshop
.RAS	Type 1 (Modern Style) Sun Microsystems
.RAW	Unencoded pixel data
.RLE	CompuServe
.RLE	Microsoft Windows
.TGA	Compressed Truevision
.TGA	No compression Truevision
.TIFF	Fax Group 3 compressed Aldus Corporation
.TIFF	Fax Group 4 compressed Aldus Corporation
.TIFF	Huffman compressed Aldus Corporation
.TIFF	LZW compressed Aldus Corporation
.TIFF	No compression Aldus Corporation
.TIFF	Pack bits compressed Aldus Corporation
.WMF	Microsoft Windows Metafile
.WPG	Version 5.0 WordPerfect
.WPG	Version 5.1 WordPerfect
.WPG	Version 6.0 WordPerfect

PSP can convert among all these formats. It can also manipulate graphics images in a plethora of useful ways, with features such as edge detection, histogram functions, gamma correction, deformations, and even user-defined transformations. You can use it as a versatile image-capture program, and its file browser acts as a handy thumbnail graphics cataloger. PSP also includes built-in scanner support and a full set of paint tools.

Paint Shop Pro is a big program at 844 KB. A program this size takes longer to launch as an Internet Explorer helper application, so you may want to think twice about configuring it as such. Still, PSP is such a handy all-around graphics tool that you'll want to keep it on hand for offline graphics work, if nothing else.

PolyView   PolyBytes's PolyView displays and converts BMP, GIF, JPEG, Photo-CD, PNG, and TIFF images (see fig. 15.5). You can use it to adjust the brightness and contrast of images, and it displays a pretty nice slideshow. For a shareware fee of only $20, you couldn't ask for much more.

Its Photo-CD and PNG support are worth noting. If these formats are important to you, setting up PolyView makes good sense. Though this application is not small (662 KB), if all you're looking for is a simple Internet Explorer helper application for these file types, PolyView can do the job.

FIG. 15.5
PolyView's support for Photo-CD and PNG formats makes it a handy graphics utility.

VuePrint Pro   If you're beginning to tire of all this talk about Internet Explorer helper applications, and you're starting to wonder if you'll ever get helper applications configured for all the file types we've talked about, have we got a deal for you!

VuePrint Pro is an all-in-one solution for displaying multimedia files (see fig. 15.6). You can configure it as an Internet Explorer helper application for all 23 of the sound, graphics, video, and compressed file formats listed in Table 15.5.

Table 15.5 Multimedia and Compressed File Types That VuePrint Pro Can Display or Play

Source	Filename Extensions
Images	`.GIF, .BMP, .DIB, .RLE, .PCX, .TGA, .JPG, .TIF`
Sounds	`.MID, .WAV, .MCI`
Movies	`.AVI, .MPG, .MMM, .MOV, .FLI, .FLC`
Slide Show	`.SLI`
UUEncoded files	`.UUE, .UU1, .01, .MSG`
Zip files	`.ZIP`

FIG. 15.6
VuePrint Pro is an all-purpose multimedia player and viewer.

Not only can VuePrint Pro display all the file types listed in Table 15.5, but it also can convert among them, print them, and tweak them in lots of different ways. It can also install screen savers, display slide shows, and load multiple files at once. In short, VuePrint Pro can do just about everything you need to do with multimedia files.

With all VuePrint Pro's capabilities, you would expect it to be a huge program, and it is, though not as large as many programs that do much less: 672 KB. Configured as an Internet Explorer helper application, it takes a while to load. That's a good reason to consider configuring several smaller Internet Explorer helper applications instead, saving VuePrint Pro for use as a stand-alone multimedia viewer/editor.

Drag And View   Drag And View is a versatile viewer program for Windows 95 (see fig. 15.7). Basically an expansion on Microsoft's own Quick View, Drag And View attaches itself to the drop-down menu you access by clicking the right mouse button and lets you view a variety of common file types including the following:

- ASCII
- Hexadecimal
- Microsoft Word and Word for Windows, including version 7
- Microsoft Works and Works for Windows, including version 3
- Windows Write
- WordPerfect and WordPerfect for Windows, including version 6
- Word Pro
- Q&A Write
- dBASE
- FoxPro
- Clipper
- Excel, including version 6
- Lotus 1-2-3
- Symphony
- Quattro, Quattro Pro, and Quattro Pro for Windows
- `.WMF`, `.BMP`, `.ICO`, `.PCX`, `.GIF`, `.TIF`, `.JPEG`, and `.TGA` images
- `.ZIP` and `.LZH` archives
- `.TTF` TrueType Fonts

FIG. 15.7
Drag And View is a simple viewing program that can handle dozens of file formats.

Support for even more file formats is added in the registered version ($35). With it, you get the following:

- CorelDRAW! version 3 (`.CDR`)
- AutoCad (`.DXF`)

- Micrografx Designer (.DRW)
- Microsoft PowerPoint (.PPT)
- Encapsulated PostScript/Adobe Illustrator (.EPS/.AI)
- Hewlett Packard Graphics Language (.HPGL)
- Lotus (.PIC)
- Computer Graphics Metafile (.CGM/.CTM)
- WordPerfect Graphics (.WPG)
- Adobe Acrobat (.PDF)

Pretty amazing! And you get all of it in a program that's only 108 KB in size. Drag And View makes a great bare-bones Internet Explorer helper application for all of the listed file types.

Windows 3.1 Graphics Programs

Windows 3.1 has been in existence long enough to serve as the operating platform for some of the best graphics programs around. Whether you're running Internet Explorer under Windows 3.1 or are a Windows 95 user looking to augment your collection of 32-bit graphics programs, the following sections direct you to some useful image-display and processing applications.

ACDSee   All ACDSee does is display images (see fig. 15.8). That's it. But sometimes, that's all you want. It's a medium-sized (449 KB), quick image viewer for Windows 3.1 that displays .BMP, .GIF, .JPEG, .PCX, Photo-CD, .PNG, .TGA, and .TIFF files. ACDSee has online help, and it works as both a slideshow program and an Internet Explorer helper application. The shareware fee requested by ACDSee is $15.

FIG. 15.8
If you're just interested in viewing images, give ACDSee a try.

WinJPEG   Despite its deceptively small size (375 KB), WinJPEG has a real graphics wallop (see fig. 15.9). It can display and convert among eight popular graphics file formats: `.BMP`, `.GIF`, `.IFF`, `.JFIF`, `.PCX`, `.PPM`, `.TGA`, and `.TIF`. It also packs a nice set of photo image-processing features, such as edge detection, gamma correction, bit slicing, and color adjustment. PVS asks a $25 registration fee for WinJPEG.

FIG. 15.9

WinJPEG is a small yet powerful image viewer, editor, and converter that handles eight popular file formats.

Translating Graphics for Internet Explorer

Chances are, you may never need much more than LView Pro and Paint Shop Pro to handle the bulk of your image viewing, manipulating, and converting needs. On a rare occasion though, you may need an application that is better able to handle some more exotic conversions. For those times, we present the following list of programs that, in spite of being Windows 3.1- or DOS-based, are quite good at what they do:

- **JASC Media Center**—The folks who brought you Paint Shop Pro are back with this program—a full-fledged multimedia cataloger, converter, and player system. JASC Media Center scans your directories and creates thumbnail catalogs of 37 different multimedia file formats. Like Paint Shop Pro, it can support additional types through the use of external filters. Unfortunately, it can load files only from its thumbnail albums, so it can't be configured as an Internet Explorer helper application. But it you can use it as an extremely flexible file type converter. You can order JASC Media Center from JASC by calling 1-800-622-2793.

- **Graphics Workshop**—Though it doesn't work as an Internet Explorer helper application, Alchemy Mindworks' Graphics Workshop could be just the program you need if you're looking for a good all-around graphics tool for Windows. You can use it to create thumbnail catalogs of your graphics files, and then manipulate and convert them in dozens of ways. For information, check out Alchemy Mindworks' Web site at **http://www.mindworkshop.com/alchemy/alchemy.html**.

- **Graphics Display System**—Though it's a DOS program, the Graphics Display System has a mouse-and-menu system that makes for pretty comfortable use for Windows users. GDS is a powerful graphics-conversion program that can read and write over 30 different file formats. GDS can also create catalogs of your images, and it makes a nice slideshow program, as well. Find out about the latest release of GDS from the Photodex Corporation's Web site at **http://www.photodex.com/**.

- **DISPLAY**—DISPLAY is tough to set up, but at least it has a DOS user interface that's a few steps above the command-line level. And if you're serious about manhandling graphics image files, DISPLAY handles more kinds than any other program. It can read, write, and preview dozens of formats. You can download your copy of DISPLAY from **ftp://ftp.uoknor.edu/SimTel/msdos/graphics/disp188a.zip**.

## CHAPTER 16

Configuring Internet Explorer for Video

Since most people love Web graphics, it stands to reason that they'll be euphoric if you put the graphics in motion. In fact, Web users aren't very far from that state of happiness. Many video clips are currently available on the Web. The main problem with them right now is that the files are so large that users with slower connections don't have the patience to wait for them to download.

You can use Internet Explorer to view video on the Web, and in most cases without a helper application to pull it off. While it won't replace the television quite yet, video on the Web is still in its formative stages and promises many exciting possibilities in the future. This chapter focuses on how you can use Internet Explorer to view video files. ■

What hardware you need to view video on the Web

There are certain minimum hardware and software requirements you need to fulfill before trying to view Web video.

Video file formats

Audio/Video Interleave (AVI), QuickTime, MPEG, and Autodesk Animation are the video formats you'll encounter most frequently on the Web.

How Internet Explorer works with video files

Microsoft's new ActiveMovie technology allows Internet Explorer to display AVI, QuickTime, and MPEG video with the use of a helper application.

What helper applications are available for each format

Find out which file formats each program handles, and how much (if anything) each one will cost.

How to convert between formats

In the event that you need to convert a video file from one format to another, these conversion utilities will help you through it.

Hardware Requirements for Internet Explorer Video

Video combines audio and graphics, so the hardware requirements for Internet Explorer video are basically a combination of those spelled out in the previous two chapters (a 16-bit stereo sound card, plus a display card capable of displaying at least 640×480 pixel resolution in 256 colors).

However, because video files play sound and display graphics simultaneously, and because the images in video files move, you also need a fast processor and lots of RAM to keep things running at a smooth pace in real-time. You'll want a big hard drive, too, if you're planning to keep many video files on hand—it's not unusual for a computer movie file to run to 1 MB or more.

Since you'll most likely be downloading video files from the Web, you may also wish to invest in a 28.8 modem so that you don't spend a lot of time waiting for these large files to transfer. To exploit the capabilities of a 28.8 modem, you'll need an appropriately fast Internet connection as well. The luckiest Net video fans are those who can use their high-speed leased line connections at work or school.

 With videos more than with any other multimedia element, it's extremely easy to overrun your hard drive with downloaded files. At a megabyte or more apiece for the typical `.MPEG`, `.AVI`, or `.MOV` file, it doesn't take long for your drive to fill up. If you regularly save video files to disk, make sure you also regularly purge unused files.

 If you're looking for a good place to start your search for video on the Internet, direct Internet Explorer to **http://www.netvideo.com/**. You'll find many sample clips and links to other video-related sites. One clip on the site is an MPEG promo clip for Television Associates that runs for 15 minutes and 28 seconds. The MPEG file containing the clip is 161.5 MB. On a 28.8 connection, it would take you over 12 hours just to download the file!

Though the minimum requirements for PC video are often stated to be something along the lines of a 386SX20 with 4 MB of RAM and a 40 MB hard drive, if your system doesn't have at least a 486DX33 processor, 8 MB of RAM, and a 540 MB hard drive, playing video files may prove to be more of an exercise in frustration than an enjoyable experience.

MPEG, a popular video format covered later in this chapter, has special requirements. It incorporates file compression technology that works best with a dedicated MPEG decoder board. If you get serious about video on your PC, you may want to look into buying an MPEG board or a video card with MPEG built in.

How Computer Video Works

Video playback under Windows 3.1 and Windows 95 is usually handled though MCI (Media Control Interface) software drivers in your C:\WINDOWS\SYSTEM directory, which can be called by any application. This means that you need to install a driver for a particular video format only once, and it can be called by any number of different viewer programs.

N O T E You can find out more about PC video by checking out the video newsgroups on UseNet. These include: **comp.multimedia**, **comp.graphics.animation**, **comp.os.ms-windows.video**, **rec.video.desktop**, and **comp.publish.cdrom.multimedia**.

There are also many excellent multimedia resources on the Web. One good example is the University of Geneva's multimedia documentation directory at **http://tecfa.unige.ch:80/pub/documentation/multimedia/**. On this site, you'll find a load of informative files, FAQs, and demos. ■

How Internet Explorer Works with Video

Except for `Autodesk Animation` files, Internet Explorer uses Microsoft's ActiveMovie technology to display video right in the browser window. You can download and install ActiveMovie by completing the following steps:

1. Direct Internet Explorer to **http://www.microsoft.com/ie/download/**.
2. In the drop-down menu you see, select the Additional Features & Components option and click the Next button.
3. On the next page you see, select ActiveMovie for Windows 95 and NT 4.0 in the drop-down box and click the Next button.
4. The Microsoft server will respond with a set of download links. Click the link that corresponds to the location nearest you.
5. Save the downloaded file to a temporary directory on your hard drive.
6. Run the downloaded executable file to install ActiveMovie.

Once it's loaded, you have instant, inline support for AVI, QuickTime, and MPEG files right in Internet Explorer. No separate viewers are necessary!

ActiveMovie: More Than Just Video

You've already read that Microsoft's new ActiveMovie technology enables Internet Explorer to render AVI, QuickTime, and MPEG video right in the browser window. In addition to that, ActiveMovie can handle several different types of audio file formats as well. These include WAV, AU (Real Audio), MIDI, and AIFF.

As ActiveMovie evolves, developers will be able to use it to create and present synchronized audio and video on multiple platforms. Even in its earliest release, ActiveMovie replaces most digital video APIs found in the Windows Software Developers Kit. Microsoft boasts ActiveMovie's architecture as "future-proof," saying it is flexible enough to permit the integration of new technologies and enhancements over time.

Eventually, ActiveMovie will come bundled with Internet Explorer; so when you download your copy of the browser, check to see if ActiveMovie is already built-in.

While ActiveMovie is great for handling three of the four major video formats, there's still the issue of the Autodesk Animation format. Additionally, Windows 3.1 users cannot harness the capabilities of ActiveMovie because it only runs on 32-bit platforms. If you plan to view

Autodesk Animations or if you use Windows 3.1, you're still going to need to configure video helper applications. To set up Internet Explorer to launch a helper application, perform the following steps:

▶ **See** "Configuring a Helper Application" for more information on configuring helper applications for Internet Explorer, **p. 244**

▶ **See** "AVI Video Clips" to learn how to set up inline AVI clips, **p. 492**

1. Select View, Options from the Internet Explorer menu bar. The Options dialog box appears.
2. Click the Programs tab and then click the File Type button.
3. Click the New Type button to call up the Add New File Type dialog box (see fig. 16.1).

FIG. 16.1

You can configure Internet Explorer to launch a video viewer for MPEG and Quicktime movies in the Add New File Type dialog box.

4. Fill in the dialog box fields for whichever video format you want the helper application for, instructing Internet Explorer to open the program you choose.
5. Click OK.

N O T E   Even if you don't download ActiveMovie, Internet Explorer is preconfigured to launch the Windows Media Player for AVI video clips (see fig. 16.2).

Additionally, Internet Explorer can play AVI clips *inline* (without a helper application) when the clip is read in with an <IMG> tag that uses the DYNSRC attribute. ■

T I P   Internet Explorer's disk cache (which is usually located in the C:\PROGRAM FILES\PLUS!\ MICROSOFT INTERNET\ cache subdirectory) contains all the files you've viewed recently on the Web. By looking in this subdirectory with the Windows Explorer and sorting the files there by type, you can zero in on any video clips that might still be in the cache.

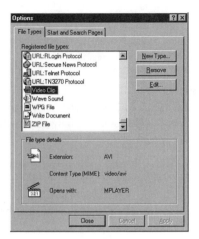

FIG 16.2
Internet Explorer automatically launches the Windows Media Player for video clips stored in the AVI format.

Video File Formats

Internet Explorer recognizes video files in the same way it identifies all the files it accesses on the Web: by MIME type first, then (if the Web server it's connected to doesn't send one) by filename extension. (See Chapter 13, "Configuring Helper Applications," for more on MIME.)

The most popular video file MIME types and filename extensions are listed in Table 16.1. If you plan to watch movies on the Web, you'll want to have either ActiveMovie or a set of appropriate helper applications configured for all four of these file types.

Table 16.1 Video MIME Types

Type/Subtype	Extensions	Description
video/x-msvideo	.AVI	Microsoft Video
video/quicktime	.QT, .MOV	QuickTime Video
video/mpeg	.MPEG, .MPG, .MPE	MPEG Video
video/x-fli	.FLI, .FLC	Autodesk Animation

The last type, Autodesk Animation, is used frequently for animation and CAD/engineering applications.

MPEG Files

MPEG (MIME: video/mpeg; extensions: .MPEG, .MPG, .MPE) is an acronym for Moving Pictures Expert Group, the body in charge of the MPEG standard. Though it sounds like JPEG, the only thing they really have in common is that their standards groups are part of the same ISO (International Standards Organization) subcommittee, and the committees meet in the same place at the same time.

You can pick up lots of useful information like this from Frank Gadegast's useful and entertaining MPEG FAQ (Frequently Asked Questions) list on UseNet. The latest version can be read online by pointing Internet Explorer to **http://www.cs.tu-berlin.de/mpegfaq/**.

MPEG exists because video files are big. The MPEG format compresses video files to a more reasonable size. Unfortunately, MPEG compression at its best requires a dedicated hardware decoder board. However, there are some MPEG software-only players that work pretty well on a fast processor.

There is no standard MCI driver for MPEG, though some players install their own, and Microsoft has promised to provide one eventually. Many MPEG movie viewers choose to do their own internal decoding. Fortunately, you don't have to sort this out yourself; if a driver is needed for an MPEG viewer program, it's always included in the distribution file.

Video for Windows Files

Video for Windows (MIME: `video/x-msvideo`; extension: `.AVI`) is Microsoft's own native video format for Windows and Win95. The AVI in the file extension stands for Audio Video Interleave.

The most recent versions of the Video for Windows (including Windows 95) drivers incorporate several advanced *codec* (compression/decompression) algorithms for both audio and video. The latest are Intel's Indeo codec and Supermac's Cinepak codec, which allow for playback of color video images of up to 320×240 pixels at up to 30 fps (frames per second).

N O T E A codec (compression/decompression) algorithm actually does most of the work in a video driver. Most video formats incorporate several different codecs, and different video files in the same format can use different codecs, depending on whether quality, speed, or some other factor is most important. Some codecs that you may see references to in various video file format specifications are the following:

- Animation
- Cinepak
- Component Video
- Graphics
- Intel Indeo
- Intel-RAW
- None (no codec used)
- Photo-JPEG
- TrueMotion
- Video

In general, you don't have to worry about which codec a video file uses. Your driver will sort it all out and use the decompression scheme that matches the file's compression scheme without human intervention. ▪

There are also hooks in Video for Windows that allow programmers to capture video sequences; add custom user interfaces; integrate text, music, and still graphics with videos; and so on. While this might not mean much to you directly, it does mean that it's relatively painless for programmers to create really nice video playback programs for the rest of us.

Video for Windows started out as Microsoft's answer to Apple's QuickTime, but it has become so popular on the Net that there are now Mac players for Video for Windows, too.

The Video for Windows Driver   If you're running Windows 95, a 32-bit version of Video for Windows has already been automatically installed on your system. If you're a Windows 3.1 user and you haven't played videos before, you may have to install the right driver first. To check, open the Drivers icon in the Control Panel and check the list. If the [MCI] Microsoft Video for Windows driver isn't there, refer to your Windows manual for details on how to install it from your Windows 3.1 installation disks.

If for some reason you don't have the Video for Windows driver available on your Windows 3.1 system and can't find it on your installation disks, it can be downloaded from Microsoft's FTP site. Point Internet Explorer to **ftp://ftp.microsoft.com/kb/softlib/mslfiles** and download the file WV1160.EXE. This is version 1.1 of the Video for Windows driver—if there is a more recent version in the Microsoft library, grab that instead. Follow the instructions in the file for installation.

Once the Video for Windows driver is correctly installed, you can go ahead and find a suitable viewer to use as a Video for Windows helper application.

Media Player: The Windows Player for Video for Windows   Microsoft includes a program with Windows and Windows 95 called Media Player, which plays .WAV digitized sounds, .MID MIDI music, and .AVI Video for Windows movies (see fig. 16.3). Media Player is preconfigured as Internet Explorer's helper application for .AVI video clips.

FIG. 16.3
The Windows Media Player plays video clips stored in Video for Windows format (.AVI) as well as .WAV and .MID sound files.

You can set Media Player's Options to make a video file repeat or rewind automatically at the end of the file, and you can optionally dither the image to a set of VGA standard colors. You can also scale the image size from 1/16 to full-screen size, with specific selections for standard and double-size playback.

QuickTime Files

Apple's QuickTime video format (MIME: `video/quicktime`; extensions: `.QT`, `.MOV`) was originally developed for the Macintosh, but quickly migrated to the PC platform. As the original
microcomputer video format, QuickTime is very popular among creative types (who tend to
prefer the Mac anyway) and it is the format of preference for many of the most experienced
videographers on the Web. This means that many of the best movies out there are in
QuickTime format.

TROUBLESHOOTING

**I clicked the link for a QuickTime movie, and it seemed to download and launch my viewer, but all
I got was an error message. I've played QuickTime movies successfully before. What's going on?**
Not all QuickTime movies are viewable under Windows. In order for a QuickTime file to be viewable on
anything but a Macintosh, it has to be flattened; that is, it must be run through a converter program on
the Mac that builds a cross-platform-compatible file. (Unfortunately, there is currently no such
converter for Windows or UNIX.) While most QuickTime videos you'll run into on the Web have been
converted, you may run into one occasionally that has not. If you find a QuickTime movie that won't
play for you, this may be your problem.

Like Video for Windows, QuickTime also includes the Indeo and Cinepak codecs (among
others), and can mix audio, still images, and text with video. The latest QT driver can even
handle integrated MIDI music and—with a hardware card—MPEG compression.

The QuickTime for Windows Driver   The QuickTime for Windows video driver is not freely
distributed. However, it has been licensed for distribution with many products, so you may
already own a copy without knowing it. Check video collections on CD-ROM, CD-ROM magazines, or Windows graphics and animation programs. One of these may have already secretly
installed the QT driver on your machine. (Look for the file `MCIQTW.DRV` in your `Windows/System`
directory.)

QuickTime can also be purchased online directly from Apple Computer at **http://
quicktime.apple.com/**. The current price is $10 for personal use. Upgrades are available on
Apple's FTP site at **ftp://ftp.support.apple.com/**.

Apple also occasionally makes QuickTime available free to download. Check the Web site to
see if this is one of those times.

The QuickTime Viewers   If you get Apple's QuickTime video driver from the archive file mentioned earlier, you'll find that when you decompress the archive you also get two stand-alone
viewer programs, one for still images and one for QuickTime videos.

The Picture Viewer displays Macintosh PICT (`.PIC`) and JPEG (`.JPG`) still images (see fig.
16.4). Though it can display more than one image at a time in scaleable, zoomable windows, its
lack of support for more than two file formats makes it a dubious choice as your image viewer
of choice. You might consider using it as a helper application, though, if you regularly need to
view Macintosh format images.

FIG. 16.4

The Picture Viewer that comes with Apple's QuickTime video driver displays multiple PICT and JPEG still images.

The Movie Player plays QuickTime and MPEG movies (see fig. 16.5). The menus give you some control over image size and looping, and you can bring up a window that tells you some information about the movie you're playing. It can even handle multiple videos at once.

FIG. 16.5

The Movie Player bundled with the QuickTime video driver is a handy utility that gives you lots of control over playback.

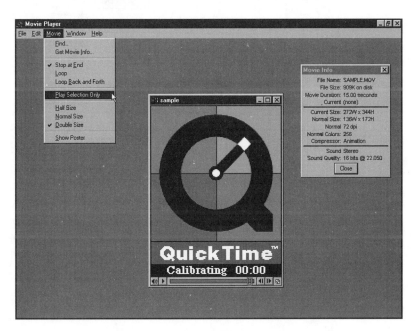

Autodesk *.FLI* Animation Files

AutoCAD is the most popular Computer Aided Design program for the PC. Unlike traditional CAD programs, AutoCAD is not limited to producing flat, monochrome, two-dimensional images. It can also generate them in 3D color, with realistic lighting and shading. Not only that, but with the assistance of a couple of different AutoCAD add-on programs, you can create 3D animations from AutoCAD drawings.

Needless to say, engineers have had a lot of fun with the 3D animation capabilities of the AutoCAD system. This means that there are more than a few animations available on the World Wide Web in the native AutoCAD .FLI file format (MIME: video/x-fli; extensions: .FLI, .FLC).

If you're into CAD, engineering, or animation, you may find that you want to set up an Internet Explorer helper application to view .FLI animations. To do so, you need the Autodesk Animator add-on driver and AAPlay player/script editor in the file AAWIN.ZIP, which is available from many online FTP file download sites, including **ftp://ftp.netnet.net/pub/mirrors/truespace/utils** and **http://hyperreal.com:70/tools/pc/graphics/video** (see fig. 16.6).

FIG. 16.6

AAPlay is useful for playing back AutoCAD animations and for developing scripts to direct playback.

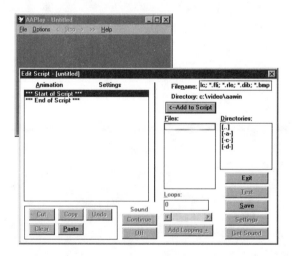

.FLI animations allow a surprising number of options, including associating sound files, using scripts to tie together strings of animations, looping, color cycling, and much more. You can even preload an animation into memory for smoother playback, and hide the animation until it begins playing. There's an option for setting the number of times the animation loops, and you can specify a transition at the beginning and end of play. Sound tracks can be from CD or video-disc audio, .WAV files, or MIDI sequences. In short, you get a lot of options.

The only downside to all of this is that the Autodesk software for creating .FLI animations is in the "professional" price category. But at least we can play them back for free.

Video Helper Applications for Internet Explorer

Assuming you've found and installed the video drivers you need, you now need to find just the right video viewer programs. Fortunately, they're not hard to come by in the multimedia-crazy computing community.

You'll run into the same options over and over when previewing Windows video players. The following are the most popular:

- **Looping**—This option determines whether a video stops at the end of play, or loops back and replays forever. Some viewers allow a specified number of loops or add the option simply to rewind at the end of play.

- **Color**—Many players let you choose to play videos back in monochrome, grayscale, colors dithered to a set palette, or full original color.

- **Scaling**—Most videos are created to play back at a resolution of approximately 1/4 the size of a "standard" 640×480 computer screen size, or about 320×200 pixels. Most viewers let you choose other playback sizes, from 1/16 to full-screen.

- **Information**—You can usually pick a menu option to view information about the file you're playing, such as resolution, number of colors, and so on.

- **Playback Controls**—Most viewers have a Play button. Some have a Pause button, though this may be the same as the Play button. Others may include Fast Forward, Rewind, and Step by Frame Forward and/or Backward buttons. There may be a slider to select the current frame. If the player can play back sound, you may find a volume control as well.

- **File Options**—All the viewers mentioned here let you load and save videos to disk. If you have a viewer you have configured as a helper application that automatically exits when the video is done playing, you may have to be fast with the mouse on the Pause button to stop the player, so that you have time to pick Save from the File menu.

- **Additional Options**—Look for the ability to save individual frames, print a frame to the printer, and so on. Some players offer a surprising number of additional options.

For information on where to find helper applications and how to configure them once you've found them, see Chapter 13, "Configuring Helper Applications."

 Don't forget to look at Chapter 15, "Configuring Internet Explorer for Graphics," for graphics viewers and converters that can also display video formats. Specifically, see the listings for VuePrint Pro, Graphics Workshop, and JASC Media Center. And remember that they need to have video drivers installed before they can play movies.

Windows 95 and Windows NT

When Microsoft designed Windows 95, it had multimedia very much in mind. Every aspect of Windows 95 is optimized for fast video, graphics, and audio throughput. Microsoft knows the future of computing is closely tied to multimedia and the company is eager for Windows to be the platform of choice for multimedia-hungry users well into the future. The release of ActiveMovie for Windows 95 and NT is Microsoft's first big step in that direction.

If you choose not to download ActiveMovie to work with Internet Explorer on your 32-bit platform, you can still make use of one or more of the video viewers discussed next.

MPEGPlay   Michael Simmons's Windows 95/NT shareware program MPEGPlay is a port of the Berkeley MPEG player for UNIX, a sort of standard in the computing community (see fig. 16.7). The MPEGPlay distribution file includes two versions of the viewer, one of which includes support for the Microsoft WinG gaming library, which is also installed automatically when you install MPEGPlay.

FIG. 16.7

MPEGPlay is a 32-bit Windows version of Berkeley's MPEG player for UNIX that supports two types of frame encoding and four display modes.

This player can play standard MPEG files that include P and B frame encoding, as well as large 354×288 movie files. It has several user-selectable display modes, including monochrome, grayscale, color dither, and full color. (8 MB of RAM is recommended for playing large-image MPEG files.)

MPEGPlay offers several versatile color and scaling options, as listed in Table 16.2.

Table 16.2   MPEGPlay Color and Scaling Options

Option	Description
Mono Threshold	Monochrome, white/black decision at 50 percent luminance
Mono	Dithered monochrome
Gray	Luminance is mapped to 256 grays
Gray 2×2	256 grays, scaled up by two, interpolates extra pixels
Ordered	Dithers to 128 fixed color palette
2×2	As above, but scaled up by two
Full Color	Luminance and chrominance are converted to 24-bit

Option	Description
Fs2fast	Fast error diffusion of two error values
Fs2	Error diffusion of two error values
Fs4	Error diffusion of four error values
Hybrid	Ordered dither for luminance, error diffusion for both chrominance channels
Image Scaling	Actual size or stretched to fit scaled window
Bitmap Color	Use palette colors or use palette indices defined in player

Part

III

Ch

16

P and B Frame Encoding

What's all this about P and B frames? MPEG movies save file space by not including all the data from each separate frame in a movie file. There are actually three different video frame types in an MPEG file. I, or intra, frames are complete computer bitmap images (compressed, of course). P, or predicted, frames are predicted from the most recently reconstructed I or P frame; they don't contain complete image data, just different information. B, or bidirectional, frames are predicted from the closest two I or P frames, one in the past and one in the future. The sequence of decoded frames usually runs: IBBPBBPBBPBB... (repeat). There are only 12 frames from I frame to I frame, because you need a fresh starting point 2.5 times per second. The interleave of P and B frames was arrived at mostly by experimentation.

MPEGPlay makes a great Internet Explorer MPEG helper application. The unregistered version displays an About box at startup to remind you to pay the $25 shareware fee, and it will not handle MPEG movies larger than 1 MB.

XingMPEG Player and Encoder   Xing Technology Corporation now offers 32-bit versions of its MPEG Player and Encoder for Windows 95. The player comes bundled with drivers and a screensaver feature that will play an MPEG movie in place of using one of the normal Windows 95 screen savers. The XingMPEG Player costs $29.95 and is currently available only over CompuServe (type **GO XING**). Xing expects to have other distribution channels for MPEG Player in the future.

The XingMPEG Encoder can produce fully compliant MPEG-1 system streams from both audio and video source files, and can directly compress files from video capture cards and video editing software. It also comes bundled with the XingMPEG Player, so you can view your work as you create it. The XingMPEG Encoder will set you back $89.95, and is also available only over CompuServe.

N O T E   Be sure to check Xing's Web site at **http://www.xingtech.com/products/xingmpeg/** to see if any new distribution channels have been set up for the XingMPEG Player and Encoder. ▨

Ladybug   If you're looking for a small, neat, Windows 95-specific MPEG player, Ladybug should work well for you. It has no menu bar; user options are all on a drop-down menu accessed by the right mouse button (see fig. 16.8). It does little more than play MPEGs, but if that's all you need, this program will do it. Best of all, it's free! You can download your copy from **http://www.mathematik.uni-marburg.de/~dippel/software/win32/graphics/ladybug2.zip**.

FIG. 16.8
Ladybug is a great choice if you just need a simple freeware viewer that plays MPEGs.

Windows 3.1

ActiveMovie only works on 32-bit platforms, so if you're using Windows 3.1, you're definitely going to need some helper applications to view Web video. The next few sections look at several of these programs.

VMPEG   VMPEG is the freely distributed MPEG viewer written by Stefan Eckart (see fig. 16.9). It can handle MPEG-1 audio in stereo as well as MPEG video/wave audio file pairs.

FIG. 16.9
VMPEG is a freeware MPEG player for Windows 3.1 that comes with its own MCI driver.

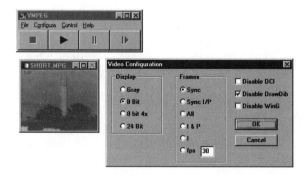

On a Pentium 90, VMPEG says it can display a 352×240 video sequence at up to 33 frames per second. It supports the following four display modes:

- 4×4 ordered dither normal size (8-bit)
- 4×4 ordered dither double size (8-bit)

- grayscale (8-bit)
- True Color (24-bit)

VMPEG also allows arbitrary scaling of the video output, and supports DCI-enabled graphics cards for displaying full-screen, 24-bit, real-time movies.

Unlike MPEGPlay, which incorporates an integral MPEG decompressor, VMPEG installs an MCI (Media Control Interface) driver. This means that other programs—like Microsoft's Media Player, for example—can hook into VMPEG's driver and use it to display MPEG movies, too. In other words, you can install VMPEG, delete the player, keep the driver, and use Media Player to play MPEG movies. You can download a copy of VMPEG from **ftp://ftp.netcom.com/pub/cf/cfogg/vmpeg/vmpeg17.exe**.

NET TOOB If you want one program that will display all three of the major movie file formats—Video for Windows (.AVI), QuickTime (.MOV), and MPEG, you should take a look at NET TOOB (see fig. 16.10). It'll even display Autodesk Animations (.FLI) if you install a driver for them.

FIG. 16.10
NET TOOB plays video clips in all three major file formats: MPEG, QuickTime, and Video for Windows and gives you good playback control that even includes a screen saver.

 Duplexx's FTP site at **ftp://cove.com/pub/duplexx/** has downloadable drivers for .AVI, .MOV, and .FLI files. Even if you decide to use another video viewer, you should check out this FTP site for one-stop shopping for drivers.

NET TOOB plays MPEG-2 audio files, allows you to play videos in 1/8, 1/4, or full-screen-sized windows, and supports interleaved, synched audio. Duplexx also promises real-time playback of MPEG audio and video in a future release. NET TOOB can even act as a video screensaver, if you want.

To download NET TOOB, direct Internet Explorer to **http://www.duplexx.com/**. If you decide to register NET TOOB, the fee is $14.95; if you decide not to, the software "cripples" itself after two weeks so that it can't play MPEG files at all, and it won't play other video files over 1 MB in size.

Part
III

Ch
16

Translating Video

QuickTime is the video format of choice among Mac users; Windows users prefer Video for Windows. MPEG video is becoming more popular. It definitely represents the future of video on the Web.

If you're going to provide video content on your Web pages, the day will come when you'll want that video to be in MPEG format—and that day may come sooner than you think.

But be forewarned—the conversion process is not easy.

SmartVid

Converting between QuickTime and Video for Windows is much easier than converting to MPEG—you just need a copy of Intel's freely distributable SmartVid program, which comes in both DOS and Windows versions (see fig. 16.11). All you do is load a file of one format, select Convert from the menu, and type in a filename for the target file. That's it. If all goes well, you get a .MOV file from an .AVI file, or vice versa.

FIG. 16.11

SmartVid converts QuickTime movies into Video for Windows format and vice versa.

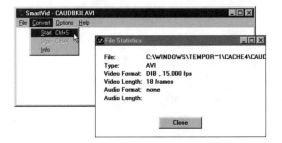

If you need to convert a QuickTime movie to MPEG, you have to use both sets of utilities: SmartVid to change the .MOV to .AVI format, and then the CONVMPEG3 tools to turn the .AVI into an .MPEG.

CONVMPEG3

Mike Negus' CONVMPEG3.ZIP is an archive file that contains a toolkit full of DOS programs for converting .AVI files back and forth between .AVI and .MPEG format. However, this is not a point-and-click operation. In fact, there are five separate tools in this archive, one for each step of the process. This procedure is not for those who are inexperienced with convoluted DOS file conversion processes. Still, if you must convert (bidirectionally) between .MPEG and .AVI formats, this is a set of tools that will get you there. You will also need a copy of Microsoft's VidEdit utility.

The Future of Video on the Web

The major limitation to viewing killer video on the World Wide Web is bandwidth. Data compression, cable television network connections, ISDN lines, and new technologies such as Novell's NEST (Novell Embedded Systems Technology)—which promises to make computer networks available to a billion users by the year 2000—could make bandwidth a dead issue. Until it does, viewing video on the Internet is at best an exercise in patience.

 TIP For more on NEST—Novell's billion-user network that promises to interconnect everything from Coke machines to automobile factories to babies' crib monitors by the year 2000—check out Novell's NEST site at **http://nest.novell.com/**.

But there are always exciting new developments that foreshadow what video on the Web might be like in the near future.

Multimedia Add-Ons

Add-ons are an innovative new way that Internet Explorer can expand its multimedia capabilities. Plug-ins are basically add-on viewers that allow Internet Explorer to display multimedia content inline in real-time. This means that sound, video, and even interactive multimedia can be added to Web pages, and Internet Explorer won't have to launch external viewers to display them; they can all appear together on one page. ActiveMovie is a good example of such an add-on as it enables Internet Explorer to handle three major video formats without assistance from another program.

Video Conferencing

Video conferencing involves two or more participants who transmit live video and audio to each other simultaneously. Most of the video conferences held today are between business people who use dedicated software and secure links.

However, that may end soon. Though there are still bandwidth problems with Internet video conferencing, some brave pioneers are testing the waters. One of the first "open-air" video conferencing experiments is Cornell University's CU-SeeMe Project (see fig. 16.12). With free software for PCs and Macs, CU-SeeMe can link two to eight participants at a time for black-and-white push-to-talk video conferencing through Internet "reflector sites" that take care of all the routing and trafficking problems. Hardware costs for hooking up can be as low as $100 for a cheap black-and-white CCD video camera with built-in interface, and view-only kibitzing is free.

While it's far from a mature discipline, expect video conferencing to become a major player in the future of Internet communications.

For more information, point Internet Explorer to Cornell's CU-SeeMe site at **http://CU-SeeMe.cornell.edu/**. Or you can check out White Pine Software's site for information on the commercial version of CU-SeeMe at **http://www.cu-seeme.com/**.

FIG. 16.12

Cornell University has pioneered Internet video conferencing with its CU-SeeMe software, now distributed by White Pine Software.

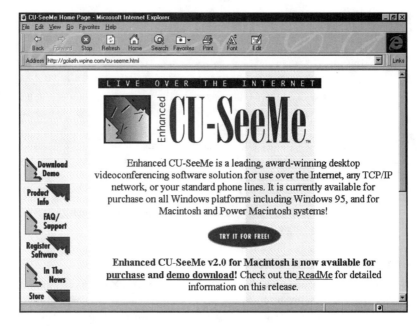

MBONE Live WWW Video Broadcasts

The MBONE (Multicast Backbone) is a network of computers on the Internet that form a backbone network for the transmission of live video and audio broadcasts. So far, it has been used for experimental broadcasts of events as disparate as scholarly meetings and a portion of a Rolling Stones concert. It is also capable of supporting live multipoint real-time audio and video conferencing.

The MBONE is a "virtual network" that is layered on top of the physical Internet. It packages real-time multimedia in such a way that normal networks (like Ethernet) pass it along without noticing that anything is other than normal. The MBONE network is composed of a string of network routers at different locations on the Internet, all running the MBONE software. These "islands" are linked by virtual point-to-point links called tunnels, through which pass the video and audio data packets of a live MBONE multicast.

N O T E   The MBONE is a more-or-less permanent arrangement, and requires a commitment at the network administration level. If you want your workstation-based LAN to become part of the MBONE, the IP multicast software is available by anonymous FTP. To find out how to download and set up the MBONE software, get the document MBONE-CONNECT from **ftp://genome-ftp.stanford.edu/ pub/mbone/**. But first, read the MBONE FAQ (Frequently Asked Questions) list at **http:// www.best.com/~prince/techinfo/** for more details about how MBONE works. ■

Though setting up an MBONE connection requires a real commitment of time and resources, and though there is not much live broadcast traffic on MBONE yet, it certainly shows that there is a lot of potential for video to grow and become a more important part of the World Wide Web. Look for MBONE (or a technology very like it) to make a real impact on the Web in a couple more years.

StreamWorks

StreamWorks, developed by Xing Technology, is a new commercial product for delivering live and on-demand video and audio (see fig. 16.13). The National Broadcasting Company (NBC) and Reuters news service are already using this technology for broadcast delivery of financial news programming to subscribers in the U.S. and Europe. New applications are being developed with StreamWorks for distance learning, corporate communications, news delivery, and computer-based training in corporate, educational, government, and health care markets. Xing says that it can even allow Internet providers to effectively get into the cable-TV-via-the-Web business.

FIG. 16.13

Xing Technology Corporation's StreamWorks can deliver real-time audio and video over the Internet and other networks.

StreamWorks can deliver live or on-demand multimedia content to multiple simultaneous users over local and wide-area networks such as the Web. Xing's approach is built around international standards such as UNIX and Windows NT servers, TCP/IP connections, MPEG video and audio compression, and HTTP/HTML client/server communication.

Expect many, many more players to get into the video-via-the-Web market in the coming months. There's a lot of money to be made in Web video, and there's no leader yet.

For more information on StreamWorks, point Internet Explorer to **http:// www.xingtech.com/streams/index.html**. ●

## CHAPTER 17

Internet Collaboration with Microsoft NetMeeting

With the release of NetMeeting, Microsoft has made freely available a communications client to allow two or more people to exchange information over the Internet. More than a chat or Internet phone client, however, NetMeeting allows collaboration via audio, chat, whiteboard, and file sharing. Perhaps most exciting, it also allows any Windows-based application to be shared over the Internet. This could allow two or more people, spread out over your office or over the globe, to collaboratively work on the same Microsoft Word or Excel document. ■

What is Microsoft NetMeeting?

In this chapter, learn about Microsoft NetMeeting, an application for conferencing and collaboration over the Internet.

How can NetMeeting be used to facilitate Internet collaboration?

Learn about how to use NetMeeting to set up multi-user data- and application-sharing, to allow multiple people to collaboratively work on a project in real-time.

How do I obtain and install NetMeeting?

Find out how to get the latest release of NetMeeting from the Microsoft NetMeeting Web site, and how to install and configure it for use.

What are NetMeeting's capabilities?

Learn about NetMeeting's different capabilities for communicating and sharing data with multiple people via the Internet.

Microsoft NetMeeting

Microsoft NetMeeting is a freely-available, real-time communications client that provides support for multi-user conferencing anf application sharing over the Internet. It does this using international communications standards, and makes the sharing of voice, data, files, and applications with two or more people over the Internet as easy Web browsing is with Internet Explorer.

NetMeeting's application-sharing capabilities allow two or more people to simultaneously share virtually any existing Windows-based application across any Internet or intranet, or over the phone via phone. Any conference member can view and control a shared application, allowing such things as presentations to be made from remote sites or telecommuting via NetMeeting. NetMeeting also offers whiteboard, chat, audio, and file transfer capabilities to allow information interchange among groups of people in many different fashions.

With NetMeeting, Microsoft is staking a position in support of compatibility and international standards. It is the first application available over the Web that supports International Telecommunications Union (ITU) and Internet Engineering Task Force (IETF) standards for multi-user data conferencing, file transfer, and real-time communications. The support for these standards allows conference participants to be separated by countries and continents. It also allows NetMeeting to be compatible with planned or currently shipping conferencing products from more than 20 other companies.

N O T E At the time of this writing, Microsoft NetMeeting is a work-in-progress. When using the program, you may find certain menu items or configuration options greyed out and disabled. An example of this is the ability to add people to your favorites list, similar to what you can do with Web sites in Internet Explorer. These disabled options represent features that will probably be included in future releases of the program. ▪

Downloading and Installing NetMeeting

As mentioned previously, Microsoft's NetMeeting application is freely available through the World Wide Web. For just the cost of the download time, you can obtain the software. Once you have it, installing and configuring it is very straightforward.

Obtaining NetMeeting from the Microsoft Web Site

NetMeeting can be obtained directly from Microsoft's NetMeeting Web site—the latest version of the NetMeeting software can be obtained from **http://www.microsoft.com/ie/conf/**.

Installing NetMeeting

Once you have downloaded the NetMeeting software, you should have the self-extracting, self-installing file MSNETMTG.EXE in a temporary directory on your hard drive. To install NetMeeting, simply execute the file—the installation process is completely automatic.

Configuring NetMeeting

NetMeeting can be used to communicate and collaborate with other people over the Internet, a company LAN or intranet, or with one other person with a direct connection via the telephone lines and a modem. Before you start using NetMeeting, and then whenever the way you use it changes, you will need to configure some of its options.

Initial Startup   The first time you run Microsoft NetMeeting, you will be run through the initial configuration process. The steps in this process are as follows:

1. NetMeeting will ask you to enter your name. This is the name by which you will be listed when you are in conference, or when your name is listed on a User Location Server.

2. Decide whether or not you want to be listed in a User Location Server when you are running NetMeeting. If you want to be listed, you can also select the name of the server upon which you'd like to be listed (see fig. 17.1).

FIG. 17.1

Microsoft's User Location Server keeps track of who is currently using NetMeeting. You can use such a server to establish connections, or make yourself available.

A User Location Server lists the people who are currently using NetMeeting. Microsoft runs a User Location Server at **uls.microsoft.com**, which is the default location.

N O T E   When you are first learning how to use NetMeeting, the folks listed in Microsoft's User Location Server are a great resource! Many of them, like yourself, are hoping to experiment with the capabilities of Microsoft NetMeeting. (In fact, I did the examples in this chapter with the help of Michael Hyldsgaard, a kind gentleman from Denmark who called me, based on my listing in the User Location Service.) ▪

3. The final steps in the initial configuration process concern NetMeeting's Audio Tuning Wizard. To best use the audio capabilities of NetMeeting, the Audio Tuning Wizard attempts to pick the best settings. First, as shown in figure 17.2, it identifies your audio hardware and allows you to choose Full or Half Duplex (if your sound card is only capable of half duplex, you will not have an option).

Part
III

Ch
17

FIG. 17.2
The Audio Tuning Wizard configures NetMeeting for the best audio it can get given your audio hardware and Internet connection speed.

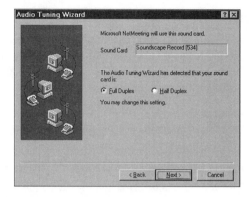

4. Next, the Audio Tuning Wizard asks you to specify your connect speed. It uses this information to determine how much to compress your audio.

5. In the last step in the audio tuning process, NetMeeting asks you to read a passage for eight seconds while it uses your voice to set the volume level of your microphone.

Configuring NetMeeting Options   Once you have completed the initial configuration, NetMeeting is ready to use. It does have other configuration options that you are able to set, available under the Tools, Options menu item. This menu item offers a series of tabs for configuring different aspects of the way NetMeeting works (see fig. 17.3).

FIG. 17.3
NetMeeting's Option menus allow you to configure the way it operates with other people in conference.

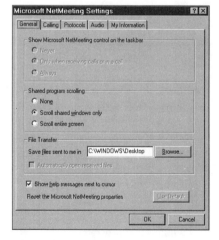

1. The General options tab gives access to some basic NetMeeting options. These concern the behavior of shared applications, file sharing, and the programs help system.

2. The Calling options tab controls the way NetMeeting makes connections (see fig. 17.4). You can configure it to automatically accept incoming calls, and determine how it makes its connections—generally either via Internet or modem and telephone lines.

FIG. 17.4

The Calling Options tab controls how NetMeeting responds to incoming calls, and allows you to set your communications parameters.

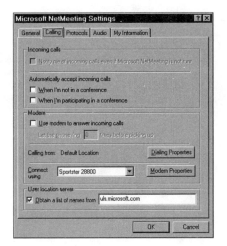

3. The Protocols options tab allows you to set which Internet communications protocol NetMeeting will use, if your computer is connected to the Internet.

4. If you are dissatisfied with the settings that NetMeeting set with the Audio Tuning Wizard in the initial configuration, or if you change your hardware, you can change these settings by selecting the Audio options tab.

5. Finally, you can change the way you are listed in the User Location Server, or on someone's screen when you are in conference with them, through the My Information options tab.

Using NetMeeting

When you start up NetMeeting, you will see the main NetMeeting screen shown in figure 17.5. From here, you can initiate or receive a conference, and when in a conference you can access NetMeeting's different tools.

Initiating a Conference

When you first start using NetMeeting, particularly when you are exploring its capabilities, you'll probably want to make use of the directory offered by Microsoft's User Location Server. Many of the people on this directory are, like yourself, interested in experimenting with NetMeeting. You can call up the Directory window by selecting Call, Directory; pressing Ctrl+D; or clicking the Directory toolbar button (see fig. 17.6).

FIG. 17.5

The NetMeeting main window gives you access to all of its tools, shows who you are in conference with, and allows you to initiate connections.

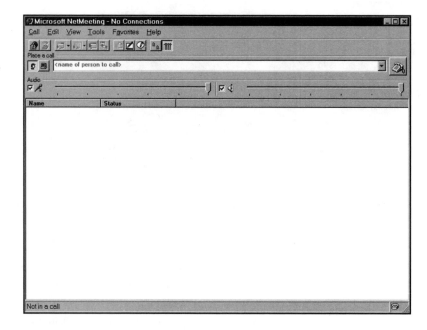

FIG. 17.6

The directory maintained by the User Location Server maintains a list of people currently using NetMeeting.

From the Directory window, you can initiate a call by selecting a name and clicking the Call button, or by simply double-clicking a name. This initiates a call with the other person. The possible outcomes are the following:

- The other person is not currently in conference, and they will be given the option of beginning a conference with you. You will be informed of their decision.

- If the other person is in conference, you will get the alert box shown in figure 17.7. This gives you the option of asking to join the conference. Again, the initiator of the conference will have the option of accepting or ignoring your request.

FIG. 17.7
NetMeeting allows more than two people to collaborate at once, so it is possible to join existing conferences.

Of course, another way to become part of a conference is if someone places a call to you. Unless you have configured NetMeeting to automatically accept incoming calls, whenever someone attempts to call you, your terminal will ring and you will see an alert box similar to the one shown in figure 17.8. At this point, you can either Accept or Ignore the request. If you accept it, the conference will be started, and the NetMeeting main window will reflect this (see fig. 17.9).

Audio Capabilities

One of the ways you can communicate with NetMeeting, if you and the other members of your conference have a sound card and microphone, is via audio. Once the call has been established, you can exchange voice messages simply by speaking into your microphone and listening to your speakers. If your sound card is only capable of half-duplex audio, you will not be able to do these activities at the same time.

FIG. 17.8
NetMeeting allows you to accept or ignore incoming connection requests, unless you configure it to automatically accept them.

CAUTION
Make sure your microphone isn't too close to your speakers when exchanging voice messages with NetMeeting. At best, this will result in an annoying echo effect for the other members of your conference, as their incoming voice messages get sent back to them through your microphone. At worst, it could set up a screeching audio feedback loop.

FIG. 17.9
Once a connection is established, NetMeeting's main window is updated to reflect the connection status.

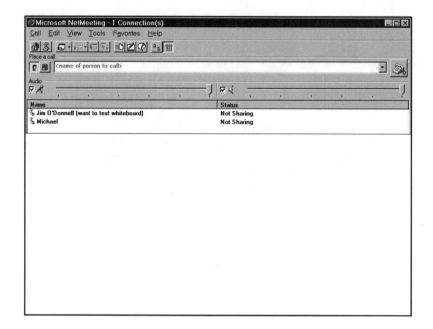

The NetMeeting Whiteboard

The NetMeeting Whiteboard—called up by selecting Tools, Whiteboard; pressing Ctrl+W; or clicking the Whiteboard toolbar button—is a lot like the Microsoft Paint screen, with the difference that everyone in the conference can draw on it simultaneously. The Whiteboard, shown in figure 17.10, allows the quick exchange of graphical and textual information. The drawing tools are not very sophisticated, but you can also cut-and-paste information from other sources directly into the Whiteboard.

When using the Whiteboard, unlike the application sharing capabilities described below where only one person at a time can work in the application, each member of the conference can work on the Whiteboard at the same time. In essence, it is not the application that is being shared, but the pixels of the Whiteboard itself. The tools that are included allow freeform drawing, along with some basic graphics elements and text. Additionally, more complicated graphics, text, or anything that can be displayed on your screen can be added to the Whiteboard using its cut and paste capabilities.

Chat with NetMeeting

NetMeeting has a very straightforward Chat capability. To employ it, select Tools, Chat; press Ctrl+T; or click the Chat toolbar button. You will see a window similar to the one shown in figure 17.11. Any messages that you enter into the bottom window are sent to all of the members of the conference when you press Return, or click the Send button.

FIG. 17.10
NetMeeting's Whiteboard gives the conference members a common scratchpad to write on and exchange ideas.

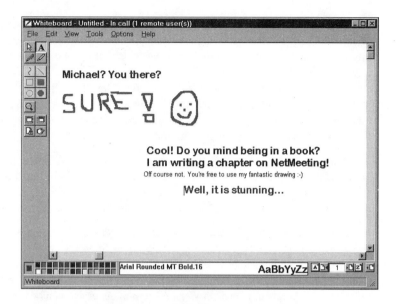

FIG. 17.11
The Chat window allows conference members to exchange real-time text messages.

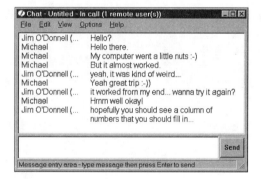

File Sharing

Once in conference, NetMeeting gives you an easy way to send files back and forth to other members of the conference. This is done by selecting Tools, Send File; pressing Ctrl+F; or clicking the Send File toolbar button. You can then send any file from your local system to other members of the conference. You can select Tools, Cancel Send or Tools, Cancel Receive to interrupt a file transfer.

Sharing Applications via Microsoft NetMeeting

One of the most fascinating capabilities of Microsoft NetMeeting is the ability to share just about any Windows-based application. This allows multiple people to truly collaborate on a project, each editing in turn a Microsoft Word document or Excel spreadsheet.

Sharing of an application is initiated by first starting the application in question—for instance, Microsoft Excel. To enable sharing of that application, you select Tools, Share Program or click the Share Program toolbar button, and select Microsoft Excel from the resulting list. When first initiated, you are in control of the application. Any member of your conference can take control of the application by selecting Tools, Take Control, or clicking the Take Control toolbar button. When someone else is in control of your application, the mouse pointer appears with their name beside it, and you can follow their movements around as they work in that application, entering data into the spreadsheet, for instance.

To retake control of applications that you have shared, you simply need to click the mouse button. If you want to continue sharing the application, but disable anyone else in the conference from taking control of it, select Tools, Work Alone, or click the Work Alone toolbar button. In this case, they can still watch you work in the application, but will not be able to take control.

Figure 17.12 shows an example of my collaboration with Michael Hyldsgaard on an Excel spreadsheet. I formatted our separate contributions differently after the fact, so that you could see which information had been entered by each of us. Obviously, this is a very simple example, but you can easily imagine collaborations where co-authors separated by thousands of miles can collaborate in Microsoft Word on an outline, or any of a host of other uses.

FIG. 17.12

NetMeeting allows conference members to collaboratively operate on data and information by sharing applications across the Internet.

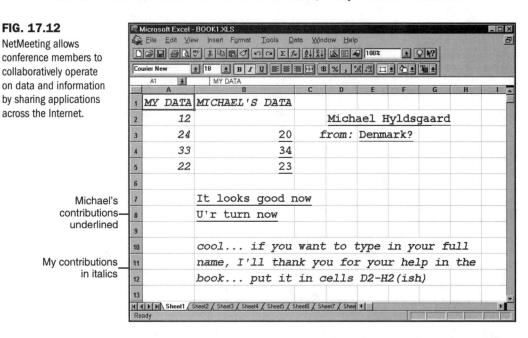

Michael's contributions— underlined

My contributions— in italics

CAUTION

Be careful what applications you share, and with whom! If you share the Windows 95 Explorer, for instance, whoever has control of it can use it to do anything on your machine that you could do with it, including delete files.

NetMeeting and Internet Explorer

In its current incarnation, NetMeeting is a helper application for Internet Explorer. While it can certainly be used stand-alone, it also is integrated with Internet Explorer. Microsoft's User Location Server Web site maintains a list of all of the NetMeeting users that are currently connected to the server. If you click any of these links, NetMeeting is launched and the users are called (see fig. 17.13).

Part

III

Ch

17

FIG. 17.13

Once NetMeeting is installed, you can place calls through Internet Explorer and Microsoft's User Location Server Web site.

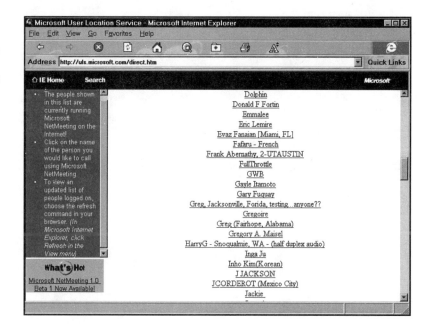

## CHAPTER 18

Using VRML and ActiveVRML

The advent of the World Wide Web (WWW), the Hypertext Markup Language (HTML), and Web browsers capable of viewing HTML documents including text, graphics, and sound revolutionized the Internet. Previously, the most common way of exchanging information was through e-mail and UseNet discussion groups. Because these methods could only handle text, the only way to exchange graphics, sound, or other binary information was for the sender to encode it and the receiver to decode it. HTML and the WWW changed this by making it possible to create true multimedia information sites on the Internet, offering real-time display and exchange of text, graphics, sound, and other information.

The next big step beyond HTML for information distribution on the Internet may be the Virtual Reality Modeling Language (VRML). HTML's hypertext links, and the Web browsers that make use of them, create an essentially two-dimensional interface to Internet information. VRML expands this by allowing the creation of three-dimensional worlds on the WWW, offering a much more natural way of presenting information. This chapter covers the basics of VRML and Microsoft's ActiveVRML, a second-generation VRML standard. ■

What is the Virtual Reality Modeling Language?

In this chapter, you learn about the Virtual Reality Modeling Language (VRML), a standard for creating 3D content on the Web, allowing the creation of three-dimensional worlds containing the full variety of text, graphics, and other multimedia content available through HTML.

What is required for VRML programming?

You'll read about some of the basic notions of creating VRML worlds, and how it compares to HTML authoring.

What VRML browsers and authoring tools are available?

You'll get to take a look at the authoring tools you can use with Internet Explorer 3.

What non-VRML virtual reality standards are there?

Offerings by Chaco Communications, Worlds, Inc., and Apple show other takes on virtual reality on the Web.

What is Microsoft's ActiveVRML standard?

Find out a little about the status of ActiveVRML, Microsoft's ill-fated proposed for the VRML 2.0 standard.

What is VRML?

The Virtual Reality Modeling Language (VRML) is a language intended for the design and use of three-dimensional, multi-person, distributed interactive simulations. To put it in simpler language, VRML's designers intend it to become the building block of cyberspace.

The explosion of the World Wide Web was caused by its ease of use: anything reachable on the Web is reachable by its own unique address, its URL (Universal Resource Locator). This ability to immediately jump from any point on the Web to any other has the effect of making the Web very much like a single, enormous hard disk. The Web's advantages can be seen in its rapid growth as people convert their Internet resources to HTML format and in the enormous popularity of Web browsers such as Internet Explorer as tools to access the Web.

The World Wide Web is based on HTML (HyperText Markup Language), which was developed from the SGML (Standard General Markup Language) standard. SGML and HTML are fundamentally designed as two-dimensional text formatting toolsets. Mark D. Pesce, Peter Kennard, and Anthony S. Parisi presented a paper called "Cyberspace" at the First International Conference on the Web in May 1994 in which they argue that, because humans are superb visualizers and we live and work in three dimensions, extending the Web with a third dimension would allow for better organization of the masses of data already on the Web. They called this idea Virtual Reality Markup Language. The concept was welcomed, and the participants immediately began searching for a format to use as a data standard. A mailing list was started by Brian Behlendorf at *Wired* magazine, with Mark Pesce as the list moderator. About this time, the *M* in VRML was changed from *Markup* to *Modeling* to accentuate the difference between the text-based nature of the Web and VRML.

N O T E The paper "Cyberspace" is available over the Web at **http://www.hyperreal.com/~mpesce/www.html**. ▪

After intense discussion, Silicon Graphics' Open Inventor was settled on as the basis for creating the VRML standard. Open Inventor is an object-oriented (C++) developer's toolkit used for rapid development of three-dimensional graphic environments. Open Inventor has provided the basis for a number of standards, including the Keystone Interchange Format used in the entertainment industry and the ANSI/ISO's X3H3 3D Metafile specification.

The current VRML 1.0 specification was written by three people: Gavin Bell of Silicon Graphics (known as one of the two principal designers of Open Inventor), Anthony Parisi of Intervista Software, and Mark Pesce, moderator of the VRML mailing list.

VRML's design specifications were guided by the following three goals:

- Platform independence
- Extendibility
- The ability to work over low-bandwidth connections

All three of these are characteristics, already possessed by HTML and the Web, which the designers of VRML felt would be required if their standard was to have any popular acceptance. VRML 1.0 is not the cyberspace of pop culture and science fiction: it defines the parameters for defining three-dimensional models (called *worlds*) and hyperlinking them by using the Web.

N O T E   The official VRML 1.0 specification can be found on the Web at **http://vrml.wired.com/ vrml.tech/vrml10-3.html**.

Instructions on how to join any of the several mailing lists on the Web that affect the decisions for the next version of the VRML standard are also on the Web at **http://vrml.wired.com/**.

The VRML FAQ can be found at **http://www.oki.com/vrml/VRML_FAQ.html**. ∎

Meanwhile, the VRML technology continues to move fast and furious. Though VRML 1.0 is still in relative infancy, the competition to set the standard for the next version of VRML has already come and gone. Microsoft's proposal for VRML 2.0 is known as ActiveVRML. (While a competing proposal from a consortium led by Netscape and Silicon Graphics, known as Moving Worlds, has been selected as the VRML 2.0 standard, the fate of Microsoft's ActiveVRML is still up in the air.) In this chapter, you'll concentrate on the basics of VRML, in order to learn the basic concepts and applications, that can then be expanded upon.

Example VRML World

To get a feeling of what navigating around a VRML world is like and how it is different than regular HTML, we'll take a look at a very simple VRML world. First, though, we'll need to install a VRML browser.

VR Scout   VR Scout is a VRML browser produced by Chaco Communications, Inc. It is available through their Web site at **http://www.chaco.com/.**

VR Scout comes in several versions—the one you will want to download is the stand-alone version that can be used as a helper application for Internet Explorer. To download and install VR Scout, follow these steps:

1. Use your Web browser to connect to the Chaco Communications, Inc. Web site at the URL shown previously, and download the stand-alone, helper application version of VR Scout. Put this file, which will be called something like SCOUT122.EXE, into a temporary directory. Note that this file is over 3 MB, so the download may take a little while.

2. This file is a self-extracting ZIP file. Run it, and it will create a bunch of files organized into three subdirectories, named disk1, disk2, and disk3.

3. Move to the disk1 subdirectory and run the program SETUP.EXE to install VR Scout.

4. The setup process is very straightforward. The only thing you need to enter is the directory to which you'd like VR Scout to be installed—that is, if you don't like the default choice of C:\Program Files\VRScout.

Part

III

Ch

18

CAUTION

Make sure that you aren't running any Web browsers while you are installing VR Scout. Because the stand-alone version of VR Scout attempts to install itself as a helper application for VRML, trying to do this while running a Web browser may cause the installation to fail.

5. That's it! VR Scout is now installed and ready to run. You can go ahead and delete all of the files in your temporary directory, as well.

Loading a VRML World   The sample VRML world you will use in this example is created by a VRML author named David Fox and known as road.wrl. This VRML world is available at **http://found.cs.nyu.edu/dfox/road.wrl.**

Once VR Scout has been installed and is running, you can load this world by pressing the Open button on the toolbar—or by selecting File, Open Location—and entering the URL shown above. The VRML world is now loaded. At this point, this looks much like an HTML imagemap. The pointer even turns into a hand pointer when placed on one of the hypertext links embedded in the world. However, this is a three-dimensional world that you can navigate around in (see fig. 18.1).

Navigating through VRML Worlds

VR Scout gives you three modes for navigating through and/or examining VRML worlds. You can walk through, fly through, or examine the world. Figure 18.2 shows the toolbar buttons you can select for each of these three modes.

FIG. 18.1

When you enter this sample VRML world, you'll see this gateway to "David Fox's Home."

Open button ⎯⎯⎯⎯

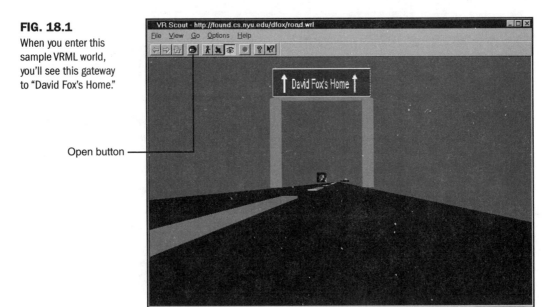

FIG. 18.2
You can select your
method of navigating
through the VRML world
with these toolbar
buttons.

Examine button
Fly button
Walk button

The quickest way to show the three-dimensional nature of the VRML world at this point is to click the Fly button, and press and hold the down arrow key, which is used in "fly" mode to thrust backward. You quickly see the gateway and road recede into the distance (see fig. 18.3).

Once you have gotten some distance away, you can reverse course and approach it by pressing the up arrow key to thrust forward. By using this key, you can retrace your steps from where you began to thrust backwards—you can also keep going through the gateway and down the road (see fig. 18.4).

FIG. 18.3
By pressing the down
arrow to thrust
backwards, you can
move away from the
road shown in this
VRML world.

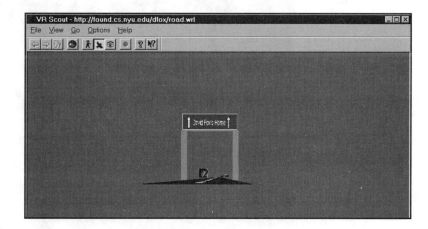

VRML Hypertext Links

Just as with an HTML document, it is possible to link together VRML worlds by using hypertext links. It is even possible to interchangeably link VRML worlds and HTML documents. Most VRML browsers offer this capability, whether they are Web browser plug-ins, helper applications, or stand-alone applications. For instance, in the previous sample world, when the pointer is placed on the house, the pointer turns into the hand pointer indicating the presence of a hypertext link. As shown in figure 18.5, the hand pointer and a label for the hypertext link, which appears in the status bar, indicates where the link takes you. In the case of this world, clicking it takes you to David Fox's HTML home page.

FIG. 18.4
By pressing the up arrow to thrust forwards, you can move forward, through the gateway, and down the road on this VRML world.

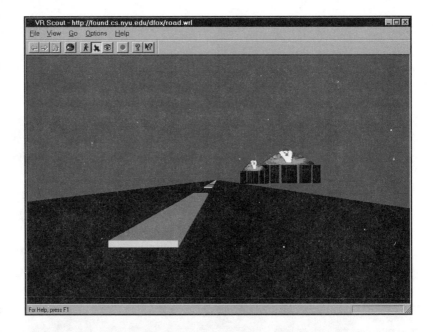

FIG. 18.5
When you move the pointer over an object that is a hypertext link, like an HTML anchor, it turns into the hand pointer and an URL label for the link is displayed in the status bar.

Hand pointer ————

URL label ————

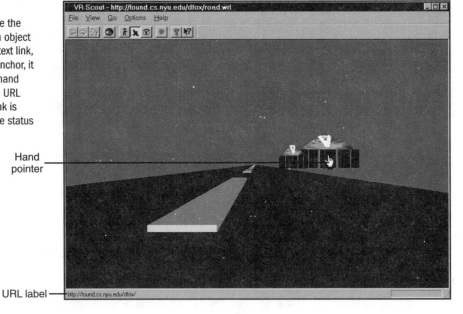

VRML Basics

VRML is both similar to, and very different than, HTML. They are similar in that they are both languages that can be used to present information content in a variety of forms, and that, through the use of hypertext links, can link this information throughout the Internet and the World Wide Web. At first glance, you might be tempted to say that VRML is simply an extension of HTML into three dimensions. HTML documents are two-dimensional while VRML worlds are three-dimensional. An HTML document is like a bulletin board, where text and graphics can be displayed, and each also can represent a hypertext link to another place in the document, or another document entirely. On the other hand, a VRML world is more like a room filled with three-dimensional objects. Because of the three-dimensional nature of the VRML world, you can navigate around and see objects from all sides. Like HTML, each of these objects can also be a hypertext link.

But other than the similarities of multimedia and hypertext content, VRML and HTML are very different. It's important to remember that the *M* in VRML stands for *Modeling*, while it stands for *Markup* in HTML. HTML is a markup language, meant to use tags to mark up text documents through the addition of formatting and multimedia content. You can look at an HTML document's source and have a good chance of determining most of its content. In VRML, on the other hand, source documents are models of three-dimensional objects. As we will see, the process for creating VRML worlds is very different than creating HTML documents.

Browsing VRML and HTML

With a VRML-compatible Web browser, you can navigate back and forth between HTML documents and VRML worlds. You can get a VRML-compatible Web browser either by using a plug-in or an add-in module to a Web browser, by setting up a VRML browser as a helper application for a Web browser, or by using a stand-alone VRML browser that also supports HTML. Inside an HTML document, if there is a hypertext link to a VRML world, it is loaded and the Web browser placed into a VRML browsing mode. Conversely, HTML links from a VRML world lead back to conventional Web page viewing.

Programming in VRML

Just as with HTML documents, VRML worlds are defined by VRML source code. However, as you might imagine from the fact that VRML worlds are models of three-dimensional objects, the source code is much more complex. Because of this, the VRML language is very different than HTML.

There are many tools being written to enable HTML authors to more easily create Web pages and documents—it is, however, possible to create fairly sophisticated Web pages programming directly in HTML. This is not the case with VRML. The source code to describe even a relatively straightforward three-dimensional world, one containing only a handful of objects, is much too involved to program manually. You can see this for yourself from VR Scout by selecting View, Show Source to see the VRML source. Even a relatively simple object is described by a long series of coordinates. It would be very difficult to program this directly.

It is necessary to use a VRML authoring tool for the creation of VRML 3D objects and building them into a world. Libraries of VRML objects are also available on the Internet.

VRML Tools

A variety of tools for viewing and creating VRML worlds has begun to appear in various formats: freeware, shareware, and commercial. Because of the relative infancy of the VRML standards, most of these products are still in the beta test stage, and are available for at least trial use through the Internet. VRML tools are primarily being developed for two platforms—Windows (3.1, for Workgroups, 95, and NT) and UNIX (primarily SGI and Sun) machines. Access to many of the VRML tools is available through the VRML Repository at **http://rosebud.sdsc.edu/vrml/**.

VRML Browsers

Some of the VRML browsers currently available are described in the following list, along with the platform for which they are made. The individual URLs for each program are listed here, but they, and several others, can be accessed through the browsers section of the VRML Repository at **http://rosebud.sdsc.edu/SDSC/Partners/vrml/software/browsers.html**:

- **Microsoft VRML Add-In for Microsoft Internet Explorer**—This is a recent addition to the VRML browser field, and is Microsoft's VRML browser for Internet Explorer 3.0 and Windows 95. It is available through Microsoft's Internet Explorer Web pages at **http://www.microsoft.com/ie/**.

- **ActiveVRML**—ActiveVRML is the Microsoft proposal for the VRML 2.0 standard. With the selection of the competing Moving Worlds VRML standard for VRML 2.0, the fate of ActiveVRML is, at the time of this writing, unknown.

- **VR Scout**—This is a stand-alone and Netscape Navigator plug-in VRML browser that runs under Windows 3.1 and Windows 95, available from Chaco Communications, Inc. Its VR Scout Web page is at **http://www.chaco.com/vrscout/**.

- **Cosmo Player**—This is part of SGI's VRML WebSpace suite of programs, and runs under SGI, Sun, and IBM UNIX systems, as well as Windows 95 and NT platforms. It can be obtained from **http://webspace.sgi.com/WebSpace/**.

- **WorldView**—This was the first Windows VRML browser. It can act as a stand-alone program or as a helper application, and works under any flavor of Windows. The Microsoft VRML Add-In for Internet Explorer 2.0 was based on the WorldView browser. WorldView is available at **http://www.webmaster.com/vrml**.

- **TerraForm**—This VRML browser was developed by Brilliance Labs, Inc. and allows direct manipulation of individual objects within the virtual world. Support for Microsoft's ActiveVRML is planned. TerraForm operates under Windows 95 and NT and is available at **http://www.brlabs.com/**.

- **Sony Cyber Passage**—This is a VRML 1.0 compatible browser with extensions to support behaviors using TCL scripts. A beta version for Windows 95 is available from

http://vs.sony.co.jp/VS-E/vstop.html or from Sony's U.S. mirror site at **http://sonypic.com/vs/index.html**.

■ **Live3D**—Live3D is Netscape's plug-in VRML browser that supports its Moving World's VRML standard. With Internet Explorer's support of Netscape Navigator plug-ins, this plug-in can also be used.

▶ **See** "Netscape Navigator Plug-Ins" for a description of Internet Explorer's support of Netscape plug-ins, **p. 754**

VRML Authoring Tools

VRML worlds can be considerably more complex than HTML documents, which makes sense considering that they are three-dimensional models. A full discussion of creating VRML worlds would require a book in itself, but we'll go over the types of tools you are liable to require. Later in the chapter, in the "Authoring VRML Worlds Using Pioneer" section, you'll learn about a very simple example of creating a VRML world using Pioneer by Caligari Software. Like most of the software listed in this chapter, access to these tools is available through the VRML Repository, this time through the modelers section at **http://www.sdsc.edu/SDSC/Partners/vrml/software/modelers.html**.

Some of the actual modeling tools that can be accessed through this Web site include the following:

■ **ClayWorks**—This is a 3D modeler that can export VRML files, among other formats. It has an extensive range of intuitive drawing tools. This tool is available as a free beta; in order to save directly in VRML, however, the commercial version is required. ClayWorks runs under any flavor of Windows, and the beta can be downloaded from **http://cent1.lancs.ac.uk/tim/clay.html**.

■ **Pioneer/Caligari worldSpace**—This is an integrated VRML authoring and browsing tool that lets anyone browse and build VRML home worlds. It supports hypertext links, inlining, and levels of detail, and has a wide array of creation tools. It runs under any flavor of Windows and can be downloaded through the Caligari Web site at **http://www.caligari.com/**.

■ **Virtual Home Space Builder**—This is an easy-to-use and inexpensive 3D program that provides rich content, an easy-to-use creative interface, and a fast rendering engine for even middle- to low-end machines. A downloadable, "light" version is available for all Windows platforms from **http://www.us.paragraph.com/whatsnew/homespce.htm**.

In addition to the preceding authoring tools, there are other VRML resources available that will help you to create VRML worlds. These include the following:

■ **Object editors**—To create a three-dimensional world, it only makes sense that you need dimensional objects. There are several ways that this can be done; one is to create your own with a VRML object editor, which enables you to create a 3D VRML object to be used in one or more VRML worlds.

Part
III

Ch
18

- **Object libraries**—It's likely that many of the 3D objects you will need—cubes, spheres, trees, and so forth—have already been created by someone else. There are VRML object libraries available on the Internet from which you can get these objects. For example, Mesh Mart maintains an objects library through its Web site at **http://cedar.cic.net/ ~rtilmann/mm/vrml.htm**.

- **Conversion utilities**—Another way to produce 3D VRML objects is to convert them from other programs and other formats. Utilities that do this for several different kinds of 3D objects exist, and many of them can be accessed through the VRML Repository Geometry Translators Web page at **http://www.sdsc.edu/SDSC/Partners/vrml/ software/geom_trans.html**.

For more information on VRML world authoring, a good resource is Que's *Special Edition Using VRML*.

Using VR Scout, a VRML Browser

You got a small taste of VR Scout by installing it and looking at a sample world. In this section, you'll learn how to use the program in more detail, including configuring it and navigating through a VRML world.

Virtual World Navigation Using VR Scout

VR Scout offers three different modes for navigating around and examining a three-dimensional VRML world: walk, fly, and examine. Other VRML browsers may have different means of navigation—the VRML source file defines the layout of the world, but the browser dictates how you travel through it.

All movement in VR Scout is executed either by left-clicking and dragging the mouse pointer or by pressing one of the four arrow keys. Whenever the left mouse button is clicked, a cross hair appears on the screen—the direction of movement then depends on where the mouse cursor is dragged from the center of the crosshair. Depending on the mode, and whether the shift or control key is pressed, these actions produce different results.

Movement in walk, fly, and examine modes work as shown in Tables 18.1, 18.2, and 18.3. Note that Shift means to change your position without changing your viewpoint. So, to turn left would be like standing in place and turning to the left. Shifting left, on the other hand, would be like walking sideways to the left while continuing to face in the same direction.

Table 18.1   VR Scout Navigation Controls in Walk Mode

Direction of Mouse Drag or Arrow Key	No Modifier Key Pressed	Shift Key Pressed	Control Key Pressed
Left	Turn left	Shift left	
Right	Turn right	Shift right	
Up	Walk forward	Shift up	Look up
Down	Walk backward	Shift down	Look down

Table 18.2   VR Scout Navigation Controls in Fly Mode

Direction of Mouse Drag or Arrow Key	No Modifier Key Pressed	Shift Key Pressed	Control Key Pressed
Left	Turn left	Shift left	Tilt left
Right	Turn right	Shift right	Tilt right
Up	Fly forward	Shift up	Look up
Down	Fly backward	Shift down	Look down

Table 18.3   VR Scout Navigation Controls in Examine Mode

Direction of Mouse Drag	Rotation of World About Point Where Mouse Button was Pressed		
Left	Rotate left		
Right	Rotate right		
Up	Rotate up		
Down	Rotate down		

Arrow Key Pressed	No Modifier Key Pressed	Shift Key Pressed	Control Key Pressed
Left	Turn left	Shift left	Roll left
Right	Turn right	Shift right	Roll right
Up	Move forward	Shift up	Roll up
Down	Move backward	Shift down	Roll down

Part

III

Ch

18

Configuring VR Scout

VR Scout enables you to customize its behavior in several different ways. This customization is achieved through the Options, Preferences menu. When this is selected, the Preferences dialog box appears (see fig. 18.6).

FIG. 18.6

You can configure aspects of VR Scout's behavior using this dialog box.

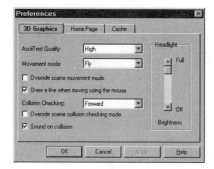

The configuration options available on the different tabs on this dialog box are as follows:

- **3D Graphics**—In this tab, shown in figure 18.6, you can change the quality of displayed ASCII text, the movement mode, the state of collision checking, and the brightness of the headlight—a light source that shines forward from your viewpoint.

- **Home Page**—From this tab, you can set the VRML world home page that VR Scout loads upon startup (see fig. 18.7).

FIG. 18.7

VR Scout allows you to specify a VRML world, either on the Web or a local file, to be loaded at startup.

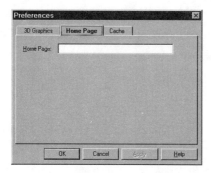

- **Cache**—Figure 18.8 shows the Cache tab. This allows you to control how big the VR Scout cache is, where it is located on your computer, and how often VR Scout uses it.

FIG. 18.8
The VR Scout caching options are similar to those in most Web browsers.

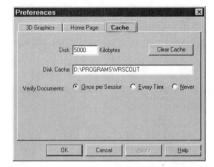

Example VRML World on the World Wide Web

Here is an example VRML world that you can find at **http://www.tristero.com/coffee/ vrcoffee/coffee.wrl**.

By loading this VRML world into VR Scout, you can see the options you have for navigating through it. If you start up VR Scout and load the above URL, you'll see the scene shown in figure 18.9.

FIG. 18.9
When you load the Coffee Gallery VRML world, this is the initial scene you see.

Part
III

Ch

18

To take a look around, you can put VR Scout in either walk or fly mode and move around a bit. After negotiating your way around the tables (or after turning collision checking off and walking right through them!), you can make your way to the cash register and see something like what is shown in figure 18.10.

FIG. 18.10

Walk around a bit, and you can see different parts of the room.

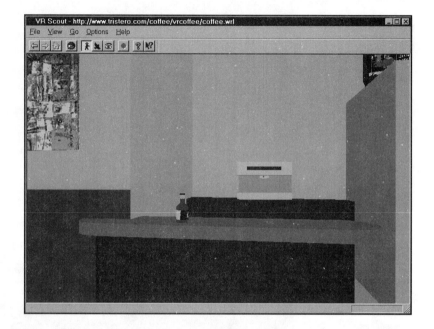

As you learned earlier, VRML worlds and HTML documents can call one another interchangeably. The Coffee Gallery uses this capability to not only convey the three-dimensional layout of the room, but also to connect to different Web sites. Consider figure 18.11; if you place the cursor on the large screen shown in the upper right, you'll see a hypertext link, indicated by the presence of the hand cursor and the URL label in the status bar. By clicking this link, your default Web browser is loaded and the corresponding HTML Web page is loaded into it (see fig. 18.12).

Because the VRML world is a three-dimensional model, you can look at it from any angle, including from below (which isn't very helpful), from above, and even from outside the defined room, as shown in figure 18.13.

FIG. 18.11
By placing the pointer on a hypertext link to the Coffee Gallery HTML home page and clicking it...

Hand pointer—

URL label—

FIG. 18.12
...you can load that Web page and read the information it contains about the Coffee Gallery.

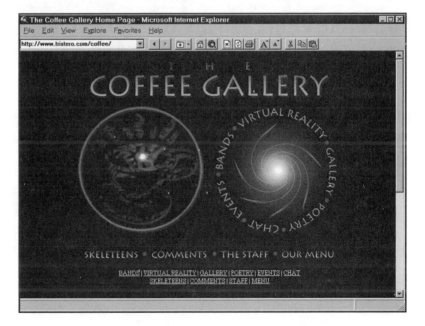

FIG. 18.13
You can even move completely away from the defined objects in the VRML world and see them from the outside.

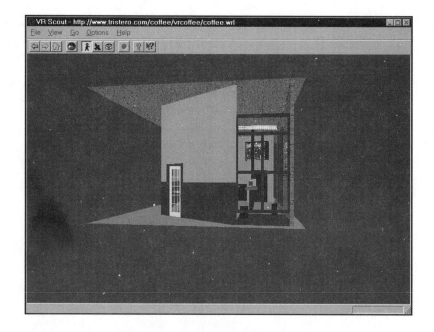

Authoring VRML Worlds Using Pioneer

It would take an entire book to fully discuss VRML authoring, and if you'd like to look at a good one, check out *Special Edition Using VRML* by Que; but for now, you can take a quick look at Caligari Software's Pioneer.

Installing Pioneer

On the CD

Pioneer (formerly known as Fountain) by Caligari is on the CD, and can also be obtained through Caligari's Web site at **http://www.caligari.com/**.

Installing Pioneer is a very straightforward process; just follow these steps:

1. Copy the file cp09b8.exe (or similar) from the CD or the Caligari Web site into a temporary directory on your hard drive.

2. Run the program you downloaded in step 1. This puts a set of files into the temporary directory.

3. Run SETUP.EXE. The installation process is fairly straightforward; you can accept the default responses, unless you want to install the Pioneer software in a different location.

4. You should get a message indicating a successful installation. Pioneer is now installed on your computer. To use it, choose Start, Programs, Caligari Pioneer, and run Pioneer.

VRML Authoring Example Using Pioneer

You'll now go through an example of creating a very simple VRML world using Pioneer; just follow these steps:

1. Start Pioneer and choose File, Scene, New to create a new VRML world. You're going to need the Primitives Panel, so click the Primitives Panel button on the toolbar. You then see a screen similar to that shown in figure 18.14.

FIG. 18.14
When you start Pioneer and begin a new document, you see a screen similar to this.

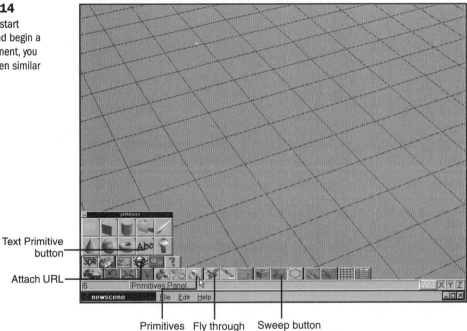

Text Primitive button

Attach URL

Primitives   Fly through   Sweep button

Part
III

Ch
18

2. Select the Text Primitive button and type some text. In my example, I have typed my initials, JOD. After you are done typing the text, click the Sweep button to extrude the letters to make them three dimensional. By grabbing an edge of the text and dragging the cursor, you can extrude the object further (see fig. 18.15).

3. Select the Attach URL Link button to get to the Attach URL Link dialog box where you can add a hypertext link to the selected object. In figure 18.16, I am adding a link to my home page.

FIG. 18.15

After selecting the Text Primitive button, you can type the desired text and extrude it to get a 3D object.

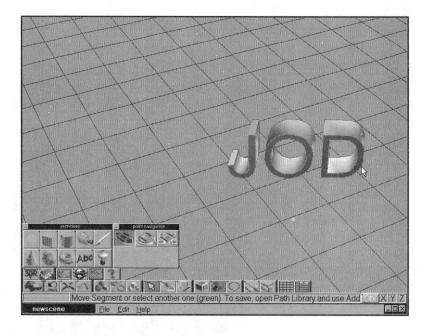

FIG. 18.16

An URL link can be attached to any VRML object. This link can point to an HTML document.

At this point, you save the document by choosing File, Scene, Save, using the filename `jod.wrl`. To see if you were successful, try to load this file with VR Scout. This gives you the screen shown in figure 18.17. You can see that the hypertext link is there—when the cursor is moved over the text object, it turns into a hand pointer and the URL label appears in the status bar. Since this is a three-dimensional model, you can navigate around, getting closer or farther away from the objects there, changing your viewpoint (see fig. 18.18).

FIG. 18.17
If I click the JOD text object, the hypertext link takes me to my HTML home page.

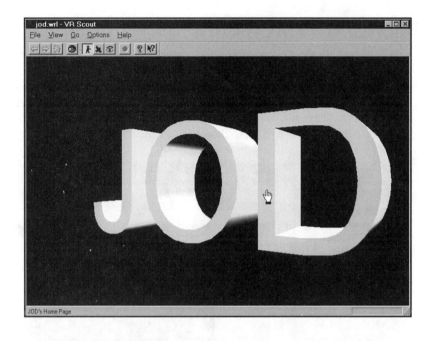

FIG. 18.18
Because this is a three-dimensional world, you can move in and around the world's objects.

Part

III

Ch

18

Microsoft VRML Add-In

Microsoft recently introduced VRML 1.0 support for Internet Explorer 3, in the form of an add-in module. This module is available through the Microsoft Internet Explorer Web site at **http://www.microsoft.com/ie/** and is in the self-extracting file vrmlocx.exe. The file can be downloaded to your hard drive and installed simply by executing it. After it is installed, hypertext links to VRML worlds, either by themselves or embedded in HTML documents, will load the VRML add-in and be displayed (see fig. 18.19).

FIG. 18.19
Microsoft's VRML add-in supports embedding VRML worlds within HTML documents.

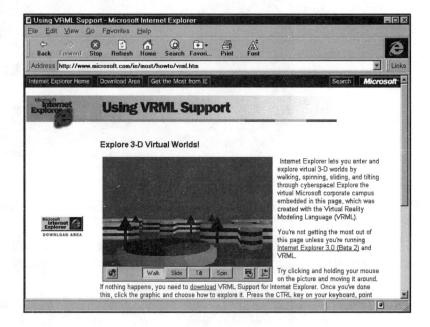

The movement, navigation, and viewing options in the VRML add-in are very similar to those in VR Scout. The different modes and commands are accessible through the button at the bottom of the viewer, or through a pop-up menu accessible by right-clicking the mouse within the VRML scene.

Note that the Microsoft VRML add-in supports the VRML 1.0 standard. At this time, it is not compatible with either the Moving Worlds/VRML 2.0 standards, or ActiveVRML.

ActiveVRML

ActiveVRML was Microsoft's proposal for the next version of the Virtual Reality Modeling Language (VRML) standard. ActiveVRML, along with other proposed standards, increases the functionality of VRML 1.0 and adds animation and greater interactivity. ActiveVRML was designed to allow for the creation of interactive animations in as natural a way as possible—using both continuous and discrete events. For instance, a bouncing ball is a combination of continuous trajectories with discrete collisions. It becomes a series of events, with each collision resulting in a new trajectory.

Using ActiveVRML, simple or complex animations can be created without conventional programming. While many cels of animation may be needed to show even a few seconds of continuous motion, for the aforementioned bouncing ball, for instance, it can be created in ActiveVRML by creating two objects—the ball and the floor—and modeling the interactions between them.

With the selection of the Netscape/SGI Moving Worlds VRML standard to form the basis for VRML 2.0, the fate of ActiveVRML is uncertain. At the time of this writing, Microsoft's ActiveVRML Web site at **http://www.microsoft.com/intdev/avr/** indicates that Microsoft is working on the next release of ActiveVRML, though it is not currently available. Microsoft has stated that they will support the VRML 2.0 standard, if it catches on. If you are interested in keeping up with Microsoft's efforts with ActiveVRML, you should keep an eye on this ActiveVRML Web site.

Live3D

With Internet Explorer's support of Netscape Navigator plug-ins—not yet perfect, but likely to continually improve over time—a whole new realm of VRML viewers is open to users of Internet Explorer. In fact, Live3D, Netscape's own flagship VRML browser, works pretty well under Internet Explorer. Figure 18.20 shows the unlikely sight of Internet Explorer viewing Netscape's Live3D Web site, with the Live3D plug-in showing the spinning, rotating, "Netscape cubes" within the browser window.

Part
III

Ch
18

FIG. 18.20
The Live3D plug-in for Netscape Navigator can also be used to display VRML scenes within Microsoft Internet Explorer.

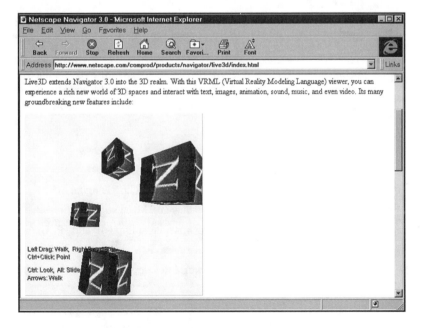

Non-VRML 1.0 Standards

Much in the same way that Microsoft and Netscape are extending the HTML standard by adding new enhancements, some of the VRML development initiatives are not waiting for VRML 2.0 to be defined and come into wide use before they release their own implementations of portions of the standard. Two of these are Chaco Software's IVRML (the I is for Interactive), used in its Pueblo software, and Worlds Inc. VRML+. Also, with its QuickTime VR technology, Apple offers yet another new take on virtual reality.

Chaco's Pueblo—Adding VRML to MUDs

Chaco Communications, Inc. released a beta version of its Pueblo Internet game client in August of 1895. Pueblo helps role-playing game authors add multimedia features to current or new MUDs.

N O T E   MUDs (*Multi-User Dimensions*) have been popular on the Internet for years. A MUD is client/server-based software that has many clients operating on various computers, and a server that acts as the central point of communication between the many clients. Typically, a MUD server is connected to the Internet, and the clients Telnet to the server to participate in the play. The participants interact by typing messages to each other. Besides a decent typing speed, the ability to think quickly is important, as there are people waiting for you to read their message to you and for you to compose and type your reply. MUD players interact in real-time, unlike the participants in a UseNet newsgroup. A simple analogy of a MUD is a text-based telephone party line. There are currently a few hundred MUDs of various types, most of which are active on a constant basis. ■

Chaco's built-in 3D graphics system IVRML (Interactive Virtual Reality Modeling Language) is based on VRML. As Mark Pesce, one of the originators of VRML, stated in a Pueblo press release, "This is what I had in mind when I started VRML."

Pueblo is a MUD client that works with text MUDs or hypermedia MUDs. On startup, you can see a hierarchy of existing MUDs. If you select a Pueblo-enabled world, the screen changes from a text-based terminal window to show a hypertext window, a command window, and a graphics window.

Pueblo includes the following capabilities:

- IHTML (Interactive Hypertext Markup Language)
- IVRML (Interactive Virtual Reality Modeling Language)
- Sound and music (waveform files and MIDI support)
- Flat images in a variety of formats, including GIF and JPEG
- Support for compressed transmissions
- A toolkit of C++ classes for world development

The freeware beta release of Pueblo runs on Windows 95 and Windows NT. A non-3D version is available for Windows 3.1. Pueblo is designed for Internet connection speeds of 14.4 kilobits/second and greater. The Pueblo client is being distributed free from Chaco's Web server at **http://www.chaco.com/pueblo/**.

Worlds Chat—Adding VRML to IRC

Worlds Chat is basically a three-dimensional version of the Internet's IRC (Internet Relay Chat) service. IRC was initially developed as an improvement to the UNIX talk program, allowing many people to communicate in real-time by typing. To communicate on IRC, you must have an IRC client, connect to an IRC server, and choose a channel. All users' input scroll up your screen, and you can join in as appropriate. Mostly, IRC is used as a recreational communications service.

The Worlds VRML+ incorporates the following three features absent in the VRML 1.0 standard:

- *Avatar* definitions (of yourself, visible to others, and vice versa)
- Motion (of others, visible to you)
- Text communication (between yourself and others)

N O T E *Avatar* is originally a term from mythology, and meant the embodiment of a god come down to Earth. Neal Stephenson used the word in his 1993 novel *Snow Crash* to describe the visual representations of the characters as they interacted in a three-dimensional, worldwide, decentralized visual environment called the *Metaverse*. Stephenson's definition of avatar has already been adopted by many of those involved with VRML creation. ▦

Avatars are described using VRML. Each client sends a message to the Worlds multi-user server that contains the description for that client's avatar. Due to packet size limitations, the avatar description message size is relatively small. One way to work around this packet size limitation is for the client to send an avatar description message that consists of a WWWInline node pointing to a file containing a more fully detailed image of the avatar. This could eventually be extended so the avatar file includes sound, animation, and so on.

Motion data contains information about the most recent positions of avatars in the three-dimensional space visible to the client, regardless of the physical location of the other clients. Motion has to be time-sensitive or it is meaningless information.

Simple text-based communication similar to the "chat" mode on many networks is the third major distinction between VRML+ and VRML 1.0. The capability to broadcast a message to multiple users, or just some of the multiple users within a range, may be added later.

More information on Worlds Inc. and its products can be found via the Web at **http://www.worlds.net/**.

DOOM Conquers the World?

One enterprising project is a parser that converts a WAD file (a map file from Id Software's incredibly popular first-person marine-kills-demons game) to an IV (Open Inventor) file. So, to those of you who played DOOM and DOOM II on DOS, UNIX, and Macintoshes until carpal-tunnel syndrome set in, in a short time, you might be surfing a 3D shopping mall and thinking to yourselves, "This floor plan looks familiar, there's a pig-demon around the corner here! Don't go in!" To those of you who spent days designing fascinating layouts for others, don't wipe those .WAD files—they might be your VRML architecture portfolio.

Information on the wadtoiv project (and the source code) can be found at **http://wwwwhite.media.mit.edu/~kbrussel/wadtoiv.html**.

QuickTime VR: A Different Look at Three Dimensions

Besides VRML, there are other standards for the display of three-dimensional scenes and information on the Internet and the World Wide Web. One of these is Apple's QuickTime VR. QuickTime is Apple's standard for showing video on the computer, similar to Microsoft's AVI standard, and is available for Windows as well as the Macintosh. An add-on to QuickTime, called QuickTime VR, enables you to move around inside a video.

Installing QuickTime and QuickTime VR

The QuickTime and QuickTime VR software for Windows is available through Apple's QuickTime VR home page at **http://qtvr.quicktime.apple.com/**.

The two files you need are the files QTINSTAL.EXE, which contains the necessary files for Apple QuickTime, and QTVRWINS.EXE, the QuickTime VR add-on.

Installing QuickTime and QuickTime VR is a very simple process. To install QuickTime, place the file QTINSTAL.EXE in a temporary directory and run it. It extracts the files from itself and automatically launches its setup program. The install program is fairly straightforward, and should install in no time.

After QuickTime is installed, the QuickTime VR add-on is added very easily by following these steps:

1. Run QTVRWINS.EXE. This extracts the single file, QTVRW.QTC.
2. Move the file QTVRW.QTC to C:\Windows.
3. In Internet Explorer 3, set up the QuickTime Player as a helper application for video/QuickTime documents.

That's it! You're ready to view QuickTime VR sites.

▶ **See** "QuickTime Files" for more information about using Apple's QuickTime format with Internet Explorer 3, **p. 300**

Using QuickTime VR

Whereas VRML enables authors to create a VRML world that people can download and navigate in—including hypertext links to other VRML worlds, HTML documents, and other Web resources—QuickTime VR enables creators to put their viewers inside a video. Once the QuickTime VR file is downloaded, viewers can, depending on the video, navigate around the video, changing their viewpoint, panning, and zooming in and out.

When a QuickTime VR link is used, the QuickTime Player application starts and the information downloads. This example is a QuickTime VR site showing parts of Berlin's downtown, which is available from **http://qtvr.quicktime.apple.com/cityscope/cityscope.html** (see fig. 18.21).

FIG. 18.21
After the QuickTime movie is downloaded, the player launches and QuickTime VR puts you in the movie.

Part
III

Ch
18

In this particular site, it is possible to zoom in and out and pan right, left, up, and down from a fixed viewpoint (see figs. 18.22 and 18.23). Other QuickTime VR sites offer views of a single object from a moving viewpoint or views of a variety of scenes as the viewpoint moves through them.

FIG. 18.22
By using QuickTime VR, you can zoom in and out of any viewpoint.

FIG. 18.23
QuickTime VR enables you to pan around the QuickTime movie scenes as well.

VRML Resources on the Internet

Once you have your system set up to view VRML documents, you'll want to start cruising the Internet and the World Wide Web to see what VRML resources and worlds are there. The list is growing every day. The following are a few of the bigger sites that will direct you to many other VRML resources—browsers, authoring tools, worlds, and object libraries:

- Microsoft's ActiveVRML Web pages can be reached through **http://www.microsoft.com/INTDEV/avr/**.

- Netscape maintains a directory of many VRML worlds located at **http://www.netscape.com/comprod/products/navigator/live3d/cool_worlds.html**.

- A group called Mesh Mart also maintains a Web site of many VRML resources, including browsing and authoring tools and VRML worlds at **http://cedar.cic.net/~rtilmann/mm/vrml.htm**.

- NCSA, the authors of NCSA Mosaic, have a VRML Web page at **http://www.ncsa.uiuc.edu/General/VRML/VRMLHome.html**.

- A repository of VRML information is maintained at http://rosebud.sdsc.edu/vrml/.

- *Wired* has a VRML forum at **http://vrml.wired.com/**.

- Silicon Graphics is very active in VRML development. A site with information about their WebSpace products is located at **http://webspace.sgi.com/**.

T I P If you don't find what you're looking for in one of these sites, call up your search engine and look for VRML!

## CHAPTER 19

Using Compressed/ Encoded Files

File compression and encoding are two things that go on all the time throughout the Internet and the World Wide Web, but most people don't even think about it. Both are file conversion operations you'll likely perform sooner or later, but often you do them without thinking too hard about it (when popping a zip archive into WinZip) or without even realizing it (when Microsoft Exchange or Eudora encodes a file attachment to a mail message).

You might be able to avoid worrying about binary file encoding on your own if you don't frequent UseNet newsgroups, but you'll find it nearly impossible to escape using compressed files, especially considering the number of examples of .ZIP archive files that are used just in this book. ■

How does Internet Explorer work with compressed and encoded files?

In this chapter, learn how to deal with compressed and/or encoded files you may find while surfing the Web with Internet Explorer.

What types of compressed files are you likely to encounter on the Internet?

Learn about the variety of file compression methods used and that are likely to be found on the Internet.

How do you convert compressed and encoded files?

Find out how to use the most popular Windows 95 and DOS tools for decompressing and decoding files.

Where do you find the Internet Explorer helper applications you need?

Find out about the best resources for finding tools and utilities that work with all of the compressed and encoded file types that you will run into.

What are File Compression and Archiving and How Is It Done?

Explaining file compression and archiving is relatively easy. Simply stated, it is a method of reducing the size of one or more files so the files can either be stored in a smaller space, or transmitted in a shorter time and later returned to their "normal" size. A file archive is when more than one file is stored into another, single file, preferably with all directory information intact. The .ZIP files that are most common in Windows 95 are compressed archives, usually made up of multiple compressed files. As a way of contrast, on UNIX systems these two processes are usually done by separate programs—a group of files will be archived by the program tar into a single file named something like archive_file.tar. This file archive will then be compressed using compress or gzip into archive_file.tar.Z or archive_file.tar.gz.

TIP   Compressed and gzipped UNIX archives are often named something like archive.taz and archive.tgz to make them compatible with DOS/Windows 3.x filename constraints.

File compression works by examining a file for repeating characters (or bytes) or repeating sequences of characters, removing those repeating characters, and replacing them with a symbol representing how many characters were in the original sequence.

Here is a highly simplified example of how basic file compression works. For example, suppose a compression program examined a file and found the following sequence of characters:

```
XmmP XmmP XmmP AAAA AAAA XmmP XmmP XmmP AAAA AAAA AAAA
```

This sequence of characters could be replaced with the following representation:

```
3(Xmmp) 2(AAAA) 3(Xmmp) 3(AAAA)
```

Or, it could be replaced with this representation:

```
2(3(Xmmp) 2(AAAA)) 4(A)
```

In this example, the original character sequence is 55 characters (bytes) long (counting the trailing space). The first representation is only 32 characters long, and 58 percent as large as the original sequence. The second representation is only 24 characters long, and 43.6 percent as large as the original sequence.

Either of these "compressed" representations of the original character sequence can be used to re-create the original.

This is a highly simplified description of what is correctly referred to as a substitutional compression scheme. To paraphrase from several FAQs (specifically, Frequently Asked Questions 1/3, 2/3, 3/3) in the newsgroup **comp.compression**: The basic idea behind a substitutional compression scheme is to replace an occurrence of a byte sequence in a piece of data, with a reference to a previous occurrence of that sequence. There are two main classes of these schemes, named after Abraham Lempel and Jacob Ziv, who first proposed these schemes in 1977 and 1978.

The Lempel-Ziv 77 and 78 compression schemes have been the basis from which the following other compression schemes have been derived:

- LZ77 with hashing
- LZ77 using a tree data structure
- LZ77 with a history buffer
- LZRW1
- LZRW3-A
- LZFG

The original LZ77 scheme is the foundation on which many of the well known PC compression programs are built (for example, `.ARJ`, `.LHZ`, `.ZIP`).

Another popular compression algorithm that has spawned numerous derivations is called *Huffman coding*. The following is a reasonably accurate description of the Huffman coding scheme also paraphrased from several FAQs in the newsgroup **comp.compression**:

> Huffman coding is a statistical data compression technique that reduces the average code length used to represent the symbols of an alphabet. Huffman coding is an example of a compression scheme that is optimal in the case where all symbol probabilities are integral powers of 1/2.

While all of the compression algorithms and their derivatives mentioned in this chapter perform the same basic function, they differ in how they sample the data they are compressing, and record exactly what data has been substituted and compressed.

What's important to remember is that you don't have to understand how compression schemes work their magic in order to use compression utilities. If, however, you have a greater interest in file compression and want more detailed information, check out the FAQs in the newsgroup **comp.compression** (for more information on reading FAQs in newsgroups, see Chapter 11, "Reading UseNet Newsgroups with Internet Explorer"). Finally, Allison Zhang has online information about file compression techniques at **http://ac.dal.ca/~dong/compress.htm** (see fig. 19.1).

FIG. 19.1

This Web page is a good online source of information about understanding and using different file compression techniques.

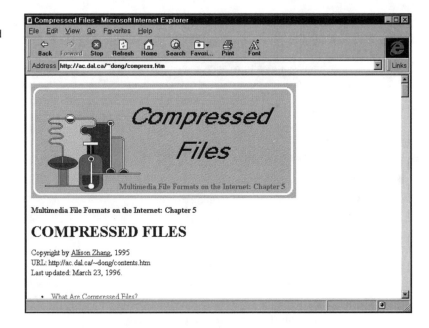

Compression Applications

Now that we've gotten past the theoretical, it's time to get down to the practical side of file compression, which is basically deciding what works best and getting that up and running. Since Internet Explorer 3 does not have any built-in capability to work with compressed archive files, you need another program to decompress archive files you download from FTP sites.

There are numerous programs you can set up that will work in Windows 95 to work with Internet Explorer. Probably the best known is WinZip, a Windows application that was originally designed as a graphical user interface to the popular PKZIP file compression utility.

WinZip

WinZip, by Nico Mak Computing, is a shareware product patterned after the highly successful and ubiquitous DOS-based file compression utility PKZIP. Without a doubt, you will find WinZip to be a highly useful and versatile Windows-based application for many of the following reasons:

- The vast majority of compressed files you are likely to download from FTP sites are in a .ZIP archive format.
- WinZip supports the native .ZIP format without the need for PKZIP or PKUNZIP, and also supports the .ARJ, .LZH, and .ARC file compression formats in the PC environment.
- WinZip is a Windows application and easily integrates into your Windows environment.

- WinZip 6.1 is a 32-bit application designed to work in the Windows 95 32-bit environment and supports numerous Windows 95 features, including long filenames. WinZip 6.1 also includes the WinZip Wizard which uses the Windows 95 Wizard interface to guide novice users through the zip/unzip process.

- WinZip also supports other popular Internet compression and archiving formats such as TAR, gzip, and UNIX compress.

You can find WinZip on the WinZip page at **http://www.winzip.com/** (see fig. 19.2).

FIG. 19.2
The WinZip Home Page is where to find the latest information and versions of the WinZip program.

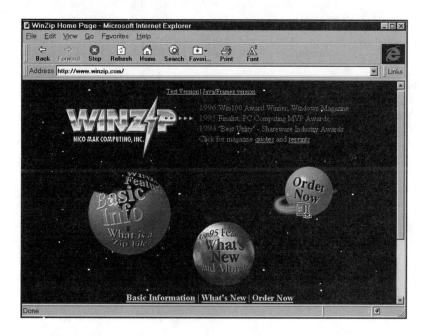

Installing WinZip   Because WinZip is a Windows-based program, you install and use it the same as most other Windows programs. To install the Windows 95 version of WinZip 6.1, follow these steps:

1. Copy the self-extracting archive file WINZIP95.EXE into a temporary folder and run the file to extract the installation files and automatically begin the installation process.

2. WinZip uses a Windows 95 Installation Wizard to install itself. Using this Wizard, it is an extremely straightforward process to install WinZip. Unless you have special needs, select Express Setup when prompted, and WinZip will install in its default location.

3. If you are a beginner using WinZip, select the WinZip Wizard interface—this interface will give you a gentle introduction to zipping and unzipping files. If you have used WinZip before, select the WinZip Classic interface.

Once the Installation Wizard has completed, WinZip is installed and ready to run!

Using WinZip   Using WinZip to compress files into an archive is fairly simple. Follow these steps:

1. Start WinZip and select File, New Archive; press Ctrl+N; or select the New icon.
2. Give the archive a name and select the folder (or directory) where you want the archive file stored.
3. Select the files you want to compress and place them in the archive. Select OK.

As part of the installation process of WinZip, it will make itself the default application for most of the compressed file types, making it a helper application for Internet Explorer. From the Windows 95 Explorer, choose View, Options and the Options dialog box appears with the File Types tab selected indicating the file extensions that WinZip is set up for (see fig. 19.3).

FIG. 19.3

WinZip installs itself as the default application and Internet Explorer 3 helper application for a collection of compressed file types.

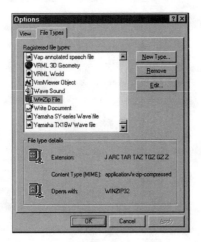

N O T E   Even though WinZip performs basic archiving operations without outside help, some advanced archiving features do require PKZIP and PKUNZIP from PKware, Inc., LHA.EXE from Haruyasu Yoshizaki, or the Shareware ARJ product from Robert Jung. Mainly these advanced archiving features center around creating archives rather than decompressing or extracting files from archives. ▆

You can also create what are called *self-extracting archive files* using the WinZip Self-Extractor utility. A self-extracting archive file decompresses the files stored in its archive without the need for WinZip. This is becoming a popular method for distributing software. Many companies now distribute their software products over the Internet in self-extracting archive files.

Self-extracting archive files have an .EXE extension instead of the .ZIP extension and are "run" the same as you would any other executable program to decompress the files stored in its archive. The WinZip Self-Extractor utility can also be downloaded from the WinZip home page at **http://www.winzip.com/**.

Other Compression Utilities

Quite frankly, once you have WinZip installed and set up, you may never need another file compression and archiving utility. WinZip can decompress and dearchive just about every format in common use today.

However, that being said, there are some things that WinZip cannot do, and then you may need to look into obtaining some of the more specialized utilities for dealing with the different formats. For the most part, these are DOS programs and they have special features that you may need that WinZip doesn't have, particularly when dealing with the creation of file archives.

If such a situation comes up, you should probably head straight to **http://www.mcad.edu/ Guests/EricB/xplat.comp.html**, which is a good source for utilities needed when moving a file archive from one platform to another, and **http://simtel.coast.net/Simtel/msdos/ archiver.html** which maintains a pretty complete collection of archiving software. In general, the extension of a file archive will tell you what program you need to deal with it—for instance, if you need some help with a file called ARCHIVE.ARJ, you should probably look for an UNARJ utility (see figs. 19.4 and 19.5).

FIG. 19.4

The Cross-Platform Page is an especially good source for when you need to take a file archive from one platform to another.

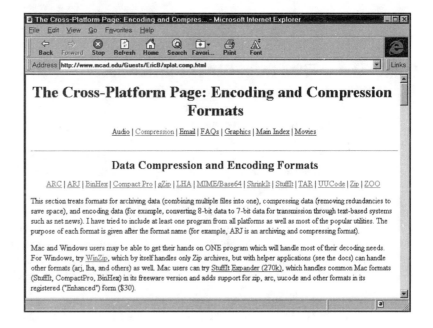

Part
III

Ch
19

FIG. 19.5

The SimTel archive has a wide variety of DOS and Windows software. This section of it houses a wide variety of file compression and archiving software.

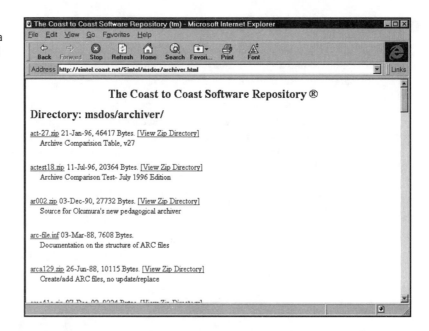

The Coast to Coast Software Repository (tm) - Microsoft Internet Explorer

File   Edit   View   Go   Favorites   Help

Back   Forward   Stop   Refresh   Home   Search   Favori...   Print   Font

Address http://simtel.coast.net/Simtel/msdos/archiver.html

The Coast to Coast Software Repository ®

Directory: msdos/archiver/

act-27.zip 21-Jan-96, 46417 Bytes. [View Zip Directory]
   Archive Comparision Table, v27

actest18.zip 11-Jul-96, 20364 Bytes. [View Zip Directory]
   Archive Comparison Test- July 1996 Edition

ar002.zip 03-Dec-90, 27732 Bytes. [View Zip Directory]
   Source for Okumura's new pedagogical archiver

arc-file.inf 03-Mar-88, 7608 Bytes.
   Documentation on the structure of ARC files

arca129.zip 26-Jun-88, 10115 Bytes. [View Zip Directory]
   Create/add ARC files, no update/replace

Compressed Files from Other Platforms

A relatively uncommon occurrence for most people, but one likely to be quite frustrating, is getting a file meant for one platform that needs to be used on another. Now obviously, there's very little reason for you to be moving UNIX or Macintosh executables over to your Windows 95 machine, but you may sometimes find the need to access binary data, images, or sounds that originated on those platforms. If you are getting these files off the Internet or through the Web, they will very often be archived and compressed. But, since these are not Windows 95 machines, the formats may present more of a problem.

UNIX Archive Formats   For getting files from UNIX systems, you are in luck. By far the most popular way to archive files on UNIX machines is using tar, a UNIX mnemonic for Tape ARchive. tar originated, and is still often used, as a program for spooling backups to tape. The most common ways to compress files are using UNIX's compress or the GNU gzip commands. If you need to access files in these formats, you are fortunate because WinZip 6.0a has built-in support for all of them.

Macintosh Formats   Macintosh files, on the other hand, present a bit more of a problem. The most common compressed archive format on the Macintosh—as ubiquitous on the Mac as ZIP is on the PC—is the StuffIt format. Unfortunately, WinZip does not handle this format's files.

Fortunately, there is a great freeware utility called StuffIt Expander for Windows put out by Aladdin Systems, the company that developed StuffIt, that allows StuffIt archives to be decompressed and dearchived under Windows. As shown in figure 19.6, when the self-extracting archive containing StuffIt Expander (called SITEX10) is run, it starts an installation process to install it on your hard drive.

FIG. 19.6
The StuffIt Expander installation process allows you to control where the utility is stored and what file types to associate it with.

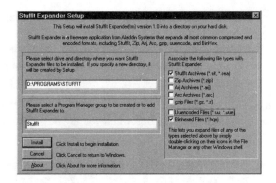

Of special note is the part of the configuration to the right that allows you to associate StuffIt Expander with file types of various different extensions. You will see that there is some overlap between what StuffIt Expander supports and what, for instance, WinZip supports, so you might want to deselect those options that are not Mac specific. By associating StuffIt Expander with .SIT, .SEA, and .HQX files, you are also setting it up to be your Internet Explorer helper application for those files.

Once StuffIt Expander is installed, you can run it and it gives the small window shown in figure 19.7. Notice that, in addition to the menus and toolbar button, you can simply drag a file of the appropriate type into the StuffIt Expander window, and it will be processed appropriately.

FIG. 19.7
StuffIt Expander is a Windows 3.1 application, but it is very useful for dealing with Macintosh format files.

NOTE The .SIT and .SEA file extensions are for Macintosh StuffIt format archives and self-extracting archives, respectively. An .HQX file is a Macintosh BinHex format encoded file. File encoding will be discussed in the next section. ▪

Automatic ZIP Format Support

One important technique to note that is becoming more common is built-in support for ZIP archives within programs. This is true especially of Windows 95 Explorer replacements like Norton Navigator. There are also Windows 95 Shell enhancements that allow similar functionality inside the Windows 95 Explorer.

What these applications and extensions allow you to do is to keep file archives zipped, and to deal with them and treat them as file folders. For instance, if you opened a .ZIP file archive that was visible in Norton Navigator or an enhanced Explorer, rather than launching WinZip to open the archive, it would behave exactly as if the archive was a file folder. It would be opened and the contents of it displayed. Files could be moved into and out of the archive transparently, as easily as moving them in and out of a folder, with the compression and decompression done automatically.

If you are running an application like this, it is important to remember that you may still need to set up an application to preform this function when you are downloading compressed file archives via Internet Explorer 3.

The Hows and Whys of File Encoding and Decoding

While file compression can be viewed as a convenience (you really don't have to save time and space), file encoding and decoding are a necessity. File encoding grew out of the need to be able to post binary files on UseNet newsgroups.

The first UseNet was created in 1979 between Duke and the University of North Carolina using UUCP (UNIX-to-UNIX Communications Protocol, also called UNIX-to-UNIX CoPy). Then as now, UseNet was only set up to copy 7-bit ASCII files, since originally only text files (messages) were intended to be posted and sent between UseNet systems. Posting binary files presented a problem. Binary files, such as programs, graphic files, and even compressed archive files, require eight bits. So in order to post binary files to newsgroups, either you change news-groups to work with 8-bit files, or you need a means of converting 8-bit binary files to 7-bit ASCII files. The solution is what has been termed UUEncoding—encoding 8-bit binary files to a 7-bit ASCII text file format (and *UUDecoding* to convert the ASCII files back into their original binary format). Figure 19.18 shows what an encoded binary looks like.

FIG. 19.8

A binary file
UUEncoded into
7-bit ASCII.

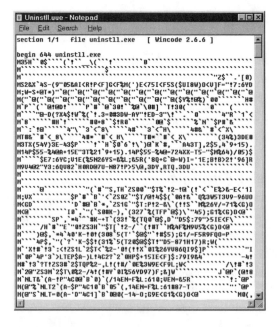

TIP As you might guess, whenever you encode a binary file to ASCII, the result is a larger file since it often takes several "text" characters to represent binary information. For this reason, it is a common practice to compress binary files before encoding them.

Another limitation of UseNet carried over from its earlier days is a 32 KB limit on file and message size because some early computers could only handle files up to this size. This file and message size limitation is why you often see long messages and large files broken into two or more parts.

N O T E Even though many newsgroup users still adhere to the 32 KB limit on file and message size, many newer systems are not restricted by this limitation, so you still see files and messages exceeding 32 KB. ▦

Initially (back in the olden days of UNIX shell accounts), separate utility programs were used for encoding (UUEncode) binary to ASCII, and decoding (UUDecode) ASCII back to binary. This also meant that if you received the encoded file in several pieces, you had to edit the text file pieces back into one file before you could decode the ASCII file back into a binary format. You were lucky if the encoding program you were using had enough smarts to be able to put the pieces back together. Fortunately, now many newsreaders, including Microsoft's Internet News Client, have built-in UUEncode/UUDecode functionality, allowing you to download/view or upload/attach binary files on-the-fly (and put the pieces back together).

▶ **See** "Downloading Files from Newsgroups" to find out how Microsoft's Internet News Client handles attached binary files, **p. 218**

Getting Your Encoded Files Decoded

In order to encode and decode binary files that you get through UseNet or otherwise, there are a number of applications that you can use. There are a few you can find on FTP sites, but the one that you will find the most helpful is the Windows program WinCode.

WinCode

WinCode is one of two Windows-based encoding/decoding programs explained in this chapter, which you can use to manually encode or decode binary files (see fig. 19.9). WinCode is distributed as freeware, but the author charges $5 if you want the Help file.

FIG. 19.9
WinCode is a simple Windows encoding/decoding application.

Start WinCode to open its main operating screen. From WinCode's main operating screen, you perform all basic encoding and decoding operations as well as set options for both. WinCode creates a status report after each file coding operation you perform so you can see if there were any problems.

WinCode can also use PKZIP to archive large binary files prior to encoding. Select Zip/Unzip on the Options menu.

Macintosh BinHex Files

Macintosh systems have their own way of encoding and decoding files, known as *BinHex*. Files of this type are very common on Macintosh newsgroups. As mentioned previously, the freeware program StuffIt Expander for Windows can decode binary files that have been BinHex-ed. ●

IV

Building World-Class Web Pages for Internet Explorer

## CHAPTER 20

Basic HTML

After seeing enough World Wide Web pages, you get to the point where you want to create your own pages with content that is either about you or important to you. When you reach that point, you need to learn Hypertext Markup Language, or HTML. HTML is a page description language that allows you to take plain-text content and format it into paragraphs, headings, lists, and other structures. Additionally, HTML lets you set up links between related pages making it easy for your audience to jump from one document to another.

In spite of all it can do, HTML is remarkably simple to learn and use. It is a text-based language in which formatting instructions called tags are embedded in the informational text of your document. These tags instruct browsers like Internet Explorer 3 how to format and present information on-screen. ■

Use the HTML document structure tags

Each HTML document done in good style has a very specific structure that you need to set up with a few key tags.

Format text into paragraphs, lists, and headings

For your content to make the most sense, you have to be able to organize it into digestible chunks that readers can understand.

Apply physical and logical styles to text

Physical styles refer to type attributes like bold or strikethrough. Logical styles refer to the meaning of text in the context of the document.

Set up links to other documents

Linking related documents is a key feature of the World Wide Web. HTML lets you link to documents with a given Web site or to documents on a completely different site.

Comment your HTML documents

Just as commenting your code in computer programming is important, commenting your HTML code is a good practice as well—especially if other people will be working on the same files.

Preliminaries

Before diving right in, it is helpful to review some introductory remarks on HTML so you can have a sense of what it is, where it came from, and where it is heading.

History

HTML is based on the Standard Generalized Markup Language (SGML). Specifically, HTML is a *document type definition* (*DTD*) of SGML, meaning that it is a specific application of the rules of SGML.

The first version of HTML—HTML 0—was developed at CERN in 1990 and is largely out of use today. HTML 1.0 incorporated inline images and text styles (highlighting) and was the version of HTML used by most of the initial Web browsers. HTML 2.0 is the current standard. In May 1996, the World Wide Web Consortium (W3C) released HTML 3.2—a new version of HTML with tags to support tables, Java applets, client-side imagemaps, and new types of text formatting. W3C plans to continue to work with members of industry and academe to expand HTML to support mathematical characters, style sheets, and embedded multimedia objects.

HTML is a Text-Based Language

It was noted in the introduction to this chapter that you create an HTML document by placing HTML tags in the document's plain-text informational content. HTML tags are character sequences that begin with a less-than sign (<) and end with a greater-than sign (>). Tags can be used to, among other things, apply a style to text, insert a line break, or place an image in the document. The idea is similar to older word processors and page layout systems that require insertion of formatting tags to specify bold, underlined, or italicized type. Newer word processors use the same premise, but usually hide these tags from the user. In WordPerfect, however, you can use the Reveal Codes menu option to have the formatting tags displayed.

For a look at some HTML, first consult figure 20.1 which shows how Internet Explorer 3 renders the Webwise site (**http://webwise.walcoff.com/**). Choosing View, Source in Internet Explorer 3 calls up a window with the HTML source loaded. The HTML source corresponding to figure 20.1 is shown in figure 20.2. Note that the source code is just plain text. It is up to the browser to interpret the tags it finds and present the information accordingly.

N O T E   Viewing the source code of a document is a great way to learn HTML, but you should be aware that not all browsers have this feature. ▮

FIG. 20.1
Webwise is a useful guide to the Web for beginners.

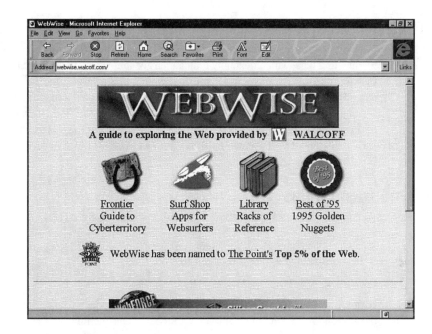

FIG. 20.2
The View, Source option is a useful way to learn HTML.

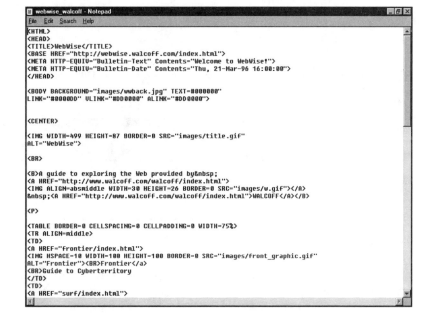

Part
IV

Ch
20

Platform Independent

Most of HTML's formatting features specify logical rather than physical styles. For example, the heading tags, which normally indicate larger font sizes, do not specify which size to use. Instead, a browser chooses a size for the heading that is larger than its default text size. This approach allows for platform independence, meaning that a document you authored on a Macintosh can be served by a UNIX box and viewed with a Windows-based browser. The disadvantage to this approach is that it is impossible to control the exact formatting of any HTML document because users can configure the fonts and physical styles to go with each HTML logical style.

Three Basic Rules

Web browsers consistently follow three rules when parsing HTML:

- White space is ignored.
- Formatting tags are not case-sensitive.
- Most formatting tags occur in pairs.

White Space is Ignored   The fact that browsers ignore white space is often a source of frustration for the beginning HTML author. Consider the following HTML code:

```
<TITLE>A Simple Rhyme</TITLE>
Rain, rain
go away.
Come again
another day.
```

The address looks fine on the page, but look at how Internet Explorer 3 renders it in figure 20.3.

FIG. 20.3
Spacing in HTML source does not translate into the same spacing on a browser screen.

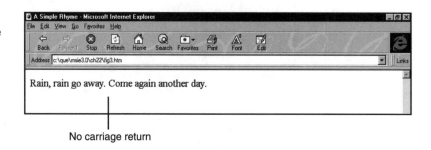

No carriage return

Internet Explorer displays the rhyme all on one line! The carriage returns in the file, which make the poem look fine in an editor or on a printout, are ignored by the browser. The same is true of other white space characters like tabs and extra spaces.

Formatting Tags are not Case Sensitive   You can write all HTML formatting tags in upper-, lower-, or mixed case. For example, browsers interpret <BODY>, <body>, and <Body> the same way. The one exception to this rule is that text placed in double quotes is interpreted literally.

For example, the HTML tags `<A HREF="index.html">` and `<A HREF="Index.html">` would not be equivalent.

 T I P Many HTML authors find it easier to edit their documents if they make the text inside their HTML tags uppercase. This makes the tags stand out better.

Most Formatting Tags Occur in Pairs With only a few exceptions, HTML formatting tags occur in pairs in which the beginning tag activates an effect and the ending tag turns off the effect. Tag pairs are often called *container tags*, since the effects they turn on and off are what is applied to the text they contain. For example, to specify that a line of text appear in bold, you write the following:

`<B>This text will appear in bold.</B>`

The text inside the ending tag in the pair is always preceded by a slash. Among the basic HTML tags, the exceptions to this rule are the `<BASE>` (base information), `<BR>` (line break), `<HR>` (horizontal rule), and `<IMG>` (image) tags, which occur by themselves.

Uniform Resource Locators (URLs)

While not directly related to HTML, Uniform Resource Locators (URLs) are an important part of HTML documents used in many different tags. For this reason, a quick refresher on URLs is in order.

A URL is basically the address of a document on the World Wide Web. The URL scheme is a way of compactly identifying any document on any type of Web-compatible server anywhere in the world. The URL consists of four parts: a protocol, server name, port, and filename. With the exception of the News protocol, the general format for a URL is ***protocol:// server_name:port/filename***.

The ***protocol*** used to serve most Web documents is **http** which stands for *HyperText Transfer Protocol*. The ***server_name*** is the English-language name or the *Internet Protocol* (*IP*) address of the computer that houses the document. Specifying a ***port*** is usually not required, since most servers use port 80 for serving Web pages. Some servers may not use port 80 though, and URLs for these servers would have to include the port number that the server is configured to use. The ***filename*** includes both the directory path to the file and the name of the file itself.

N O T E You may have seen some URLs, like **http://www.yahoo.com/**, that appear to lack a file name specified. Yet, if you visit this URL, the browser is able to find a file and load it. This is because servers are generally configured to serve the file `index.html` when no other filename is specified. ■

A URL that specifies a protocol, Internet address, and filename is said to be *absolute*, or *fully qualified*. In some cases, it is also possible to specify one URL relative to a base URL, resulting in a *relative*, or *partially qualified* URL. For example, suppose your base URL is **http://**

www.sports.com/team_sports/hockey/penalties.html and you need to specify the URL of the file `scoring.html` located in the `football` directory (one directory level up from `hockey`). You could do this with the absolute URL **http://www.sports.com/team_sports/football/ scoring.html**, but it may also be appropriate to give the URL relative to the base URL. In this case, the relative URL would be **../football/scoring.html**. The two dots followed by a forward slash (**../**) are an indicator to move up one directory level. If you needed to specify the URL of the file `capitals.html` in the `teams` directory, a subdirectory of the `hockey` directory, you could use the relative URL **teams/capitals.html**.

The HTML Document Structure Tags

The HTML document structure tags define the beginning and end of different parts of a document. Although many browsers can properly interpret an HTML document without them, it is considered good style to include them. If you're just learning HTML now, you should make an effort to include these tags in each document you author.

 Many HTML authoring programs available today come with template files that have these tags built in. Others insert these tags for you whenever you start a new document. If you're using an authoring program, check to see if it has either of these features.

The HTML Declaration: *<HTML>...</HTML>*

The `<HTML>` and `</HTML>` tag pair encloses all other tags and informational content of the document. The `<HTML>` tag should be the first line in the file and the `</HTML>` tag should be the last line in the file. Including these tags declares everything between them to be HTML code.

The Document Head

The head of an HTML document contains information about the document itself. The document head should come immediately after the `<HTML>` tag and is defined by the `<HEAD>` and `</HEAD>` container tags. Thus, your basic HTML document so far looks like the following:

```
<HTML>
<HEAD>
...
</HEAD>
...
</HTML>
```

While there are many pieces of information you can put into the head of your documents, there are two items you should always specify: the document's title and base URL.

The Document Title You can give your document a title by placing the text of the title between the `<TITLE>` and `</TITLE>` tags. A document's title shows up at the top of the Internet Explorer 3 window (refer to fig. 20.1) and also appears in the History and Favorites drop-down lists.

When you choose a title, you should make it detailed enough to describe the content of the document, but not so long that it exceeds the space available along the top of the browser window. A good rule of thumb is to make your titles 40 characters or less.

You extend a courtesy to those who view your pages by including titles on your documents. In the absence of a specified title, the document's URL is displayed at the top of the browser window and in the History and Favorites lists. URLs aren't as descriptive as titles are, so it's more difficult to look at History and Favorites listings and try to remember what documents contained from their URLs than it is from their titles.

The Base URL   You specify the base URL of a document in the `<BASE HREF="base_url">` tag. The base URL is set equal to the document's absolute URL. Once you set a base URL, all other URLs can be specified relative to it. This can save you an immense amount of typing when absolute URLs start to become large. For example, if a document's base URL is **http://www.microsoft.com/products/office/word/datasheet.html** and you wanted to specify the URL of the file `features.html` in the `/products/office/excel` directory on the same server, you could do so by using **../excel/features.html** rather than typing out **http://www.microsoft.com/products/office/excel/features.html**.

Another good reason to specify a base URL is to enchance the portability of documents. Suppose you have to move an entire Web site to a different server. Imagine the effort it would take to go through and change every URL in every HTML document to reflect the change! You can greatly reduce this effort by having a base URL in each document. In this case, you could just change the server name in the base URL and, assuming the directory structure and filenames haven't changed, all of your links will work fine!

The Document Body

The body of your HTML document contains all of the informational text plus all of the HTML tags used to format the text. The body comes immediately after the document head and is contained in the `<BODY>` and `</BODY>` tags. Thus, the basic structural shell of an HTML document would look like this:

```
<HTML>
<HEAD>
<TITLE>Insert document title here</HTML>
<BASE HREF="base_url">
</HEAD>
<BODY>
...
</BODY>
</HTML>
```

What remains is to investigate what tags you can use between the `<BODY>` and the `</BODY>` tags. You will do this over the course of the rest of this chapter and the five chapters that follow. The balance of this chapter focuses on the most basic HTML tags: those used to format text and those used to set up links between and within documents.

Part
IV

Ch
20

Formatting Text

This section focuses on the markup part of Hypertext Markup Language. Marking up plain text with HTML tags allows you to organize it into logical, digestible chunks or apply a specific format to it. In particular, the tags you'll learn about in this section allow you to specify the following:

- Paragraphs and line breaks
- Heading styles
- Physical styles
- Logical styles
- Lists
- Special characters

Paragraphs and Line Breaks

The `<P>` tag is used to indicate the start of a new paragraph. Ending a paragraph with the `</P>` tag is a good idea since under HTML 3.2, the `<P>` tag supports an `ALIGN` attribute that can be used to change the alignment of the text in the paragraph. For example, you can now write HTML like the following:

```
<P ALIGN=CENTER>
This text is centered!
</P>
```

Since the browser will need to know when to stop using the prescribed alignment, the use of the `</P>` tag becomes essential.

Paragraphs are separated by a blank line. To start a new paragraph without the extra line of separation or to just move to the next line, you can use the `<BR>` tag (line break). Line breaks were what we needed back in figure 20.3 to render our poem properly. The following HTML code uses both paragraphs and line breaks:

```
<B>A Simple Rhyme Revisited</B>
<P>
You can tell it's Spring with all of the rain we're getting.
It makes me want to recite the rhyme:
</P>
<P>
Rain, rain<BR>
go away.<BR>
Come again<BR>
another day.
</P>
```

Figure 20.4 shows the difference between the paragraphs and line breaks in the above code.

FIG. 20.4
Paragraphs and line
breaks help to offset
sections of a docu-
ment.

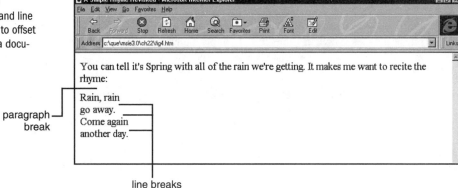

paragraph
break

line breaks

Heading Styles

HTML supports six heading styles, which are used to make text stand out by varying degrees.
The styles are numbered one through six, with 1 being the largest in size. To format text in a
heading style, enclose it in the <H*n*> and </H*n*> tags, where *n* is the number of the heading
style you want to apply. The corresponding HTML is as follows:

```
<H1>Heading Style 1</H1>
<H2>Heading Style 2</H2>
<H3>Heading Style 3</H3>
<H4>Heading Style 4</H4>
<H5>Heading Style 5</H5>
<H6>Heading Style 6</H6>
```

Figure 20.5 shows how the six heading styles are rendered in Internet Explorer 3 by default.

FIG. 20.5
Headings are used to
name and separate
sections of a docu-
ment.

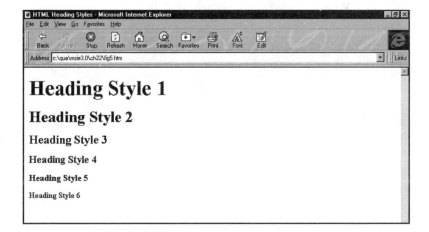

Part
IV

Ch
20

N O T E In addition to changing the size of the text and making it boldface, applying a heading style
adds some white space above and below the line containing the heading. ■

Physical Styles

Physical styles are actual attributes of a font, such as bold or italics. HTML supports the four physical styles shown in Table 20.1. To apply a physical style, simply place the text to be formatted between the appropriate tag pair in the table.

Table 20.1 Physical Styles in HTML	
Style	**Tag**
Bold	`<B>...</B>`
Italics	`<I>...</I>`
Underline	`<U>...</U>`
Typewriter (fixed-width)	`<TT>...</TT>`

Do not assume that any given style is available in all browsers. In many browsers, for example, the underline style is reserved for displaying hyperlinks and the `<U>` and `</U>` tag pair is ignored. Microsoft Internet Explorer 3 does support the underline physical style, as illustrated in figure 20.6.

FIG. 20.6
Internet Explorer 3 does not ignore the `<U>` and `</U>` tags like some browsers do.

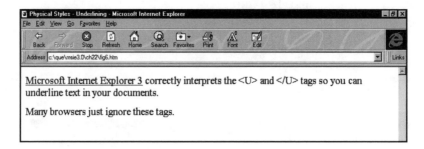

N O T E The HTML specification allows nesting of physical text styles though not all browsers support this. Internet Explorer 3 does permit nested styles. ■

Logical Styles

Logical styles indicate the meaning of the text they mark in the context of the document. Since they are not related to font attributes, logical styles can be rendered differently on different browsers. Table 20.2 lists the common logical styles and their meanings and typical renderings. Closing tags are required for all logical styles, but have been omitted in the table to save space. To create a closing tag, just add a slash before the tag name, like </ADDRESS>.

Table 20.2   Logical Styles in HTML

Style Name	Tag	Typical Rendering
Address	<ADDRESS>	Italics
Block quote	<BLOCKQUOTE>	Left and right indent
Citation	<CITE>	Italics
Code	<CODE>	Fixed-width font
Definition	<DFN>	Bold or bold italics
Emphasis	<EM>	Italics
Keyboard	<KBD>	Fixed-width font
Sample	<SAMP>	Fixed-width font
Strong	<STRONG>	Bold
Variable	<VAR>	Italics

For example, look at how the following HTML uses many of the logical styles:

```
<H1>Logical Styles</H1>
According to <CITE>The Handbook of Federal Telecommunications Regulations</
CITE>:<BR>
<BLOCKQUOTE>
All access providers <STRONG>must</STRONG> furnish their clients with prompt
and accurate invoices. Charges on invoices <STRONG>must</STRONG> show date of
the charge, duration of connect time, and the rate charged per minute.
</BLOCKQUOTE>
Failure to comply with this statute may result in <EM>large fines</EM>.
<P>
For more information, send e-mail to <ADDRESS>info@telcom.net</ADDRESS>.
```

Figure 20.7 shows how Internet Explorer 3 renders the logical styles in the HTML code.

N O T E While some browsers allow it, nesting logical styles often does not make sense. For example, why would you put a block quote inside an address? ■

Part
IV

Ch
20

FIG. 20.7
The logical styles
indicate the meaning
of marked up text in
the context of the
document.

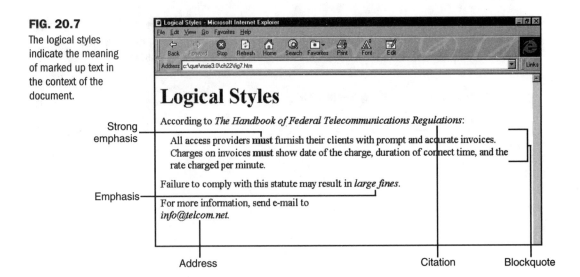

Strong
emphasis

Emphasis

Address

Citation

Blockquote

Preformatted Text

Text tagged with the `<PRE>` and `</PRE>` tags is treated as *preformatted text* and rendered in a fixed-width font. Since each character in a fixed-width font has the same width, it is easy to line text up into columns and produce a table. The following HTML produces the table you see in figure 20.8:

```
<H1>Preformatted Text</H1>
<PRE>
Course          Credits        Grade
— — —           — — —          — —
Composition      3              B-
Calculus 2       3              B+
Genetics         3              A
Basketweaving    1              C+
</PRE>
```

N O T E Extra spaces, tabs, and carriage returns inside the `<PRE>` and `</PRE>` tags are *not* ignored. Also, a `<PRE>` tag introduces a paragraph break. ■

 T I P Before you go making all of your tables with preformatted text, you should look into the table tags accepted as part of HTML 3.2. Many browsers, such as Internet Explorer, already support these tags.

▶ **See** "Tables," **p. 394**

FIG. 20.8
Preformatted text is rendered in a fixed-width font and includes extra white space characters, making it easy to create tables.

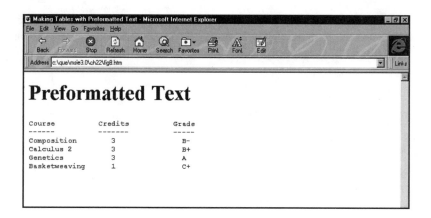

Lists

HTML lists provide an easy and attractive way to present information in your documents. All lists require a pair of tags indicating the type of list and a tag beginning each list item. Table 20.3 lists the five types of formatted lists.

Table 20.3   HTML Lists

Type	List Tag	Item Tag(s)
Ordered	<OL>...</OL>	<LI>...</LI>
Unordered	<UL>...</UL>	<LI>...</LI>
Description	<DL>...</DL>	<DD>...</DD><DT>...</DT>
Menu	<MENU>...</MENU>	<LI>...</LI>
Directory	<DIR>...</DIR>	<LI>...</LI>

Items in an ordered list are automatically numbered by the browser, starting with the number one. The automatic numbering is convenient, because it spares you from having to do it if you rearrange list items. Unordered list items are bulleted rather than numbered. Description lists allow you to present a term, followed by a description below and indented from the term. Not all browsers support menu and directory lists which are similar to unordered lists, but are generally taken to have short list items.

N O T E   Description lists are sometimes called *definition lists* since they are useful in presenting the term/definition structure of a glossary. ■

Part
IV
Ch
20

List items in all five list types are indented from the left margin, making it easy to distinguish them from the rest of the body text. Figure 20.9 shows examples of unordered, ordered, and description lists as produced by the following HTML:

```
<H2>Unordered Lists</H2>
<UL>
<LI>Bulleted list items</LI>
<LI>List items are indented</LI>
</UL>
<H2>Ordered Lists</H2>
<OL>
<LI>Numbered list items</LI>
<LI>List items are indented</LI>
</OL>
<H2>Description Lists</H2>
<DL>
<DT>First term</DT>
<DD>Description of first term</DD>
<DT>Second term</DT>
<DD>Description of second term</DD>
</DL>
```

FIG. 20.9

Unordered, ordered, and description lists provide an easy way to break out information.

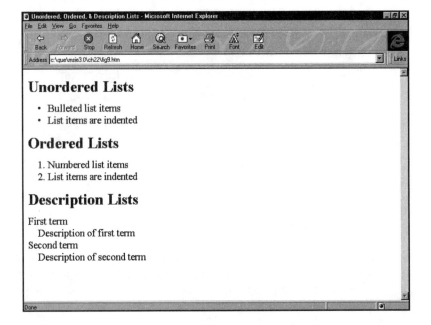

CAUTION

Many browsers will "forgive" you if you leave off the `</LI>` tag at the end of a list item. The next `<LI>` tag is enough to tell the browser to end the current list item and start a new one. However, browsers *won't* forgive you if you leave off a `</DT>` or a `</DD>` tag, so don't forget them.

You can nest lists inside of other lists, as in the following HTML:

```
<H1>Nested Lists</H1>
<UL>
<LI>Web Browsers</LI>
<OL>
<LI>Microsoft Internet Explorer 3</LI>
<LI>Netscape Navigator 2</LI>
<LI>NCSA Mosaic</LI>
</OL>
<LI>HTML Authoring Tools</LI>
<OL>
<LI>HTMLEd Pro</LI>
<LI>HotDog Pro</LI>
<LI>HoTMetaL</LI>
</OL>
</UL>
```

Figure 20.10 illustrates how this appears in a browser.

FIG. 20.10

Nesting ordered lists inside an unordered list lets you create an outline structure.

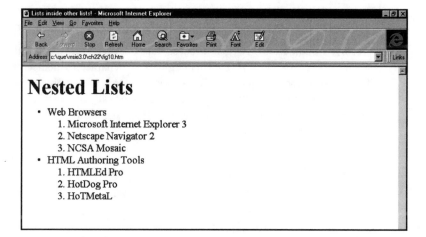

If you prefer a little white space between your list items, you can put a <P> tag after each </LI> tag. Technically, this is not an appropriate use of the <P> tag, but it produces the desired result. Since you're only using the <P> tag for spacing properties, a </P> is not needed. For example, the following HTML produces the list you see in figure 20.11:

```
<H1>Chocoholic's Wish List</H1>
<OL>
<LI>Godiva Truffles</LI><P>
<LI>Hershey Kisses</LI><P>
<LI>Toblerone Bars</LI><P>
</OL>
```

Part

IV

Ch

20

FIG. 20.11

You can put additional space between list items with the <P> tag.

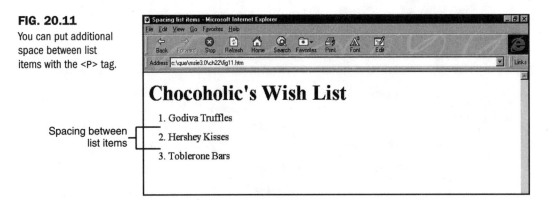

Spacing between list items

If you're writing HTML code to produce HTML code on a browser screen, you will use the sequences in Table 20.4 frequently. As an example, consider the following HTML:

Special Characters

Because many characters have special meanings in HTML, it is necessary to use special character sequences when you intend for special characters to show up as themselves. You can also use special character sequences to produce foreign language characters and symbols.

Reserved Characters   Because the less-than (<), greater-than (>), and quotation mark (") characters are used in HTML formatting tags, the characters themselves must be represented by special character sequences. The ampersand (&) is used in these special sequences, so it also must be represented differently. Table 20.4 lists all the special character sequences HTML reserved characters. The semicolon is necessary to indicate where the character description ends and normal text resumes.

Table 20.4   Special Character Sequences for HTML Reserved Characters

Sequence	Appearance	Meaning
<	<	Less than
>	>	Greater than
&	&	Ampersand
"	"	Quotation mark

If you're writing HTML code to produce HTML code on a browser screen, you will use the sequences in Table 20.4 frequently. As an example, consider the following HTML:

```
<H1>HTML to Produce HTML</H1>
The HTML:
<P>
&lt;B&gt;Warning!&lt;/B&gt; Be sure to back up your hard drive first!
<P>
produces the line:
<B>Warning!</B> Be sure to back up your hard drive first!
```

The <B> and </B> character sequences produce the <B> and </B> tags that appear on-screen. The result is shown in figure 20.12.

FIG. 20.12
Writing HTML to produce on-screen HTML requires the use of special character sequences.

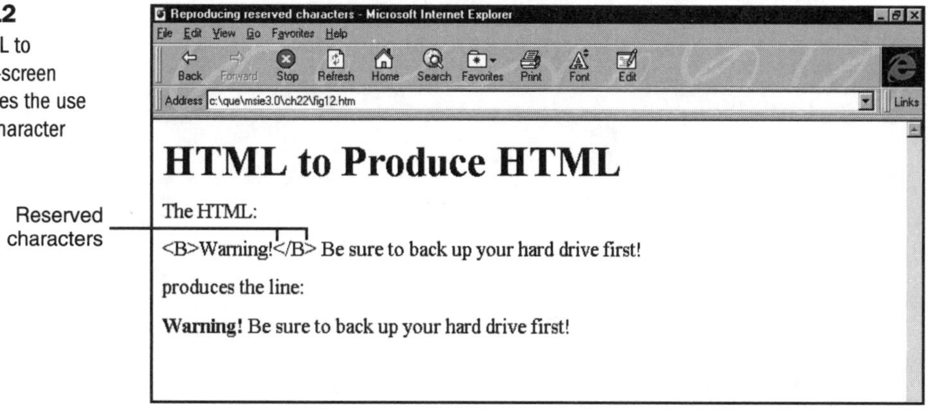

Reserved characters

HTML to Produce HTML

The HTML:

<B>Warning!</B> Be sure to back up your hard drive first!

produces the line:

Warning! Be sure to back up your hard drive first!

Foreign Language Characters   HTML uses the ISO-Latin1 character set, which includes foreign language characters for all Latin-based languages. Since these characters are not on most keyboards, you need to use special character sequences to place them in your documents. Like the other special character sequences in HTML, these sequences begin with an ampersand (&) followed by a written-out description of the character and a semicolon (;). Table 20.5 lists all the foreign-language sequences available.

Table 20.5   Foreign Language Characters in HTML

Character	Sequence
Æ, æ	&Aelig;, æ
Á, á	Á, á
Â, â	Â, â
À, à	À, à
Å,å	Å, å
Ã,ã	Ã, ã
Ä,ä	Ä, ä
Ç, ç	Ç, ç
Ð, ð	Ð, ð
É, é	É, é
Ê, ê	Ê, ê

Part
IV

Ch
20

continues

Table 22.5 Continued

Character	Sequence
È, è	È, è
Ë, ë	Ë, ë
Í, í	Í, í
Î, î	Î, î
Ì, ì	Ì, ì
Ï, ï	Ï, ï
Ñ, ñ	Ñ, ñ
Ó, ó	Ó, ó
Ô, ô	Ô, ô
Ò, ò	Ò, ò
Ø, ø	Ø, ø
Õ, õ	Õ, õ
Ö, ö	Ö, ö
ß	ß
Þ, þ	Þ, þ
Ú, ú	Ú, ú
Û, û	Û, û
Ù, ù	Ù, ù
Ü, ü	Ü, ü
Ý, ý	Ý, ý
ÿ	ÿ

 TIP Many HTML authoring programs have toolbars or palettes that make it easy to insert foreign language characters into your documents.

Characters by ASCII Number You can reference any ASCII character in an HTML document by including the ampersand (&) and pound sign (#) followed by the character number in decimal and a semicolon (;). For example, to include the copyright symbol (©) in an HTML document, you write:

```
Copyright &#169;, 1996
```

Windows users can use the Character Map program that comes with Windows to see the codes for all ASCII characters.

Comments It is possible to include comment lines in HTML that do not show up in browsers. You should consider placing comments in documents that you and others will be working on together. Many stand-alone HTML editors provide templates that include a comment area for information like the author's name and the date the document was last changed. The format for a comment is as follows:

```
<!-- Everything in here is part of the comment. -->
```

N O T E Server-side include commands embedded in HTML use the same character sequence as comments. This is so that the server-side include commands do not show up even when a server does not support server-side includes. Documents utilizing server-side includes must have the extension SHTML; this distinguishes them from documents containing normal comments. ■

Non-breaking Space You can prevent a browser from breaking a line between two words by inserting a non-breaking space between the words. Non-breaking spaces are represented by the special character sequence .

 Non-breaking space characters can also be used to put in extra white space where you need it. A browser ignores the last two spaces in a sequence of three space characters, but it does print three spaces if you use   .

Hypertext

With the markup portion of HTML covered, you can now turn to the hypertext component. *Hypertext* is text linked to another document that is somehow related to the text. By setting up hypertext links among your documents, you create a "non-linear" structure in which a user can move through your pages in almost any order, rather than going through each one in a pre-scribed sequence. Hypertext is also what lets you start a Web surfing session at a corporate site looking at available job openings and, 15 minutes later, end up at a site that lets you punch-out Rush Limbaugh!

A hypertext link consists of two parts: an anchor and a URL. The *anchor* is the text that the user clicks to go somewhere. The *URL* points to the document that the browser will load when the user clicks on the anchor. Text anchors usually appear underlined and in a different color than normal text on graphical browsers and in bold on text-only browsers such as Lynx.

Part

IV

Ch

20

Setting Up Anchors

Any text can be a hypertext anchor in HTML, regardless of size or formatting. An anchor can consist of a few letters, words, or even lines of text. The format for an anchor address pair is simple:

```
<A HREF="URL">text of the anchor</A>
```

The letter A in the `<A HREF="URL">` tag stands for "anchor," and HREF stands for "hypertext reference." Everything between the `<A HREF="URL">` and `</A>` tags is the text of the anchor, which appears underlined or bold, depending on the browser.

Other formatting codes can be used in conjunction with hypertext anchors. For example, to create a text anchor to appear in italics, you write the following:

```
<A HREF="URL"><I>Click here to go on.</I></A>
```

The order of nesting formatting codes is not important. It's also possible to write:

```
<I><A HREF="URL">Click here to go on.</A></I>.
```

 If a hypertext anchor doesn't seem to be working right, check to see that the URL in the `<A...>` tag is completely enclosed in quotes. Omitting the final quotation mark is a fairly common mistake.

Setting Up Named Anchors

When you click a piece of hypertext, Internet Explorer 3 will load the document the hypertext points to, starting from the top of the linked document. This is fine, unless the document is long and the information you really want displayed isn't near the top. In this case, users have to scroll through the document to find the information you wanted them to see. An alternative to inflicting this on your users is to set up *named anchors* in longer documents and then having your hyperlink references to point directly to the named anchors.

As an example, suppose you have a ten-part document stored in the single file `longdoc.html` and that each section has its own heading. You can set up named anchors on each of the headings using the `<A NAME="anchor_name">` and `</A>` tags as follows:

```
<A NAME="one"><H1>Part One</H1></A>
```

With all of the anchors established, you can instruct a browser to link to a specific anchor by including a pound sign (#) and the anchor's name at the end of the long document's URL, as in the following example:

```
View <A HREF="longdoc.html#seven">Part Seven</A>.
```

When users click the hypertext Part Seven, they are taken directly to part seven in the document, rather than to the top of the document where they would be made to scroll all the way down to part seven.

Named anchors can also be useful within a given document. You can use named anchors to set up a miniature table of contents at the top of a long document with links pointing to the different sections. Users appreciate this courtesy as it spares them from excessive scrolling and searching through the document.

## CHAPTER 21

Adding Graphics and Tables

In the last chapter, you learned just enough HTML to be dangerous. With the tags you've seen so far, you could certainly post any amount of text-based information in an attractive, logical way. The downside is that your documents would be all text. Text-intensive documents tend to lose their audiences very quickly unless there is something to break up the monotony of large blocks of words.

Thankfully, HTML supports the inclusion of page constructs that you can use to make your documents more readable. Chief among these are graphics. It is unlikely that the World Wide Web would have the broad appeal that it does without colorful logos and pictures on Web pages. Another helpful page construct is the table, which allows you to organize data into rows and columns. The structure of a table typically makes it easier for a reader to understand the meaning of the data the table contains. ▪

The GIF and JPEG graphic storage formats

GIF and JPEG are the two most popular image formats on the Web and each has its own advantages and drawbacks.

How to place images in a document using the <IMG> tag

The <IMG> tag and its many attributes not only place an image on a page, but control how other page items are layed out around the image.

How to hyperlink an image

Linking an image to another document creates the button-like effect that is so popular on Web pages.

The logical structure of HTML tables

HTML tables tend to be confusing at first. Once you master a few simple rules of structure though, they become easy to compose.

The fundamental table tags

The basic table tags place content into table cells and control how the content is aligned.

Some examples of clever uses of tables

Creative HTML authors don't just use tables to present columns of data. Because tables give you very fine control over alignment, they're ideal for creating attractive page layouts.

Graphics

Graphic elements go a long way toward breaking up the text on a Web page. Web graphics can range from a simple line to an elaborate image that took hours to create in Adobe Photoshop. What's important about Web graphics is not their simplicity or complexity, but how effective they are in helping you communicate your message.

Horizontal Rule

Horizontal lines are an easy way to split up large sections of text or to offset part of a document. Placing a horizontal line is easy: just put an <HR> ("horizontal rule") tag in where you want the line to go. No closing </HR> tag is required. For example, Listing 21.1 shows a horizontal line used to offset a document footer.

Listing 21.1   Horizontal Rule to Offset a Footer

```
<H1>CompuCorp</H1>
Assisting you with all of your Internet needs, including:
<UL>
<LI>Connectivity</LI><P>
<LI>Web server setup</LI><P>
<LI>Web site design</LI>
</UL>
<P>
<HR>
<P>
For more information, e-mail <ADDRESS>info@compucorp.com.</ADDRESS><BR>
<I>Last updated 31 March 1996</I>
```

Figure 21.1 shows how this appears in a browser.

 TIP Placing a <P> tag before and after an <HR> tag puts some additional white space above and below the horizontal line. This is often more attractive than just the horizontal line alone.

Graphic Images

If you've done much work with computer graphics, you probably know that there are several formats in which graphic data are stored. When you shift your focus to the World Wide Web, the field narrows to just two formats: GIF and JPEG.

▶ **See** "Image File Formats," **p. 436**

GIF   The GIF (Graphics Interchange Format) format was originally developed for users of CompuServe as a standard for storing image files. The GIF standards have undergone a couple of revisions since their inception. The current standard is GIF89a.

FIG. 21.1
Horizontal lines can be used to break up blocks of text or to offset different parts of a document.

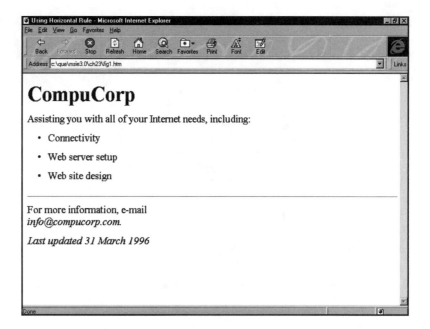

Graphics stored in the GIF format are limited to 256 colors. Thus, you probably won't store full-color photos as GIFs. GIF is best used with line art, logos, and icons. If you do store a full-color photo as a GIF, it will be reduced to just 256 colors and not look as good on your Web page.

The GIF89a standard supports the following three desirable Web page effects:

- **Interlacing**—With this effect, non-adjacent parts of the image are stored together. As a browser reads in an interlaced GIF, the image appears to "fade in" over several passes. This is useful because the user can get a sense of what the entire image looks like without having to wait for the whole thing to load.

  ▶ **See** "Using Interlaced GIFs," **p. 439**

- **Transparency**—In a transparent GIF, one of the colors is designated as transparent, allowing the background of the document to show through. Figure 21.2 illustrates a transparent and non-transparent GIF. Note in the non-transparent GIF that the bounding box around the oval is visible. By specifying the color of the bounding box to be transparent, the background color shows through and the oval appears to just be sitting on the background.

Part
IV

Ch
21

FIG. 21.2

In a transparent GIF, one color is designated as transparent so that the background can show through.

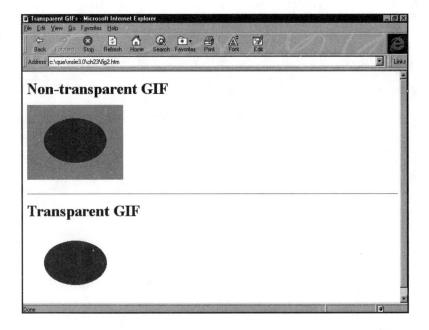

Transparent GIFs are very popular and many of the graphics programs available today support the creation of transparent GIFs. On the PC, LView Pro is one program that can create transparent GIFs. PhotoGIF is a plug-in to Photoshop that allows you to create both transparent and interlaced GIFs. Both UNIX and Windows users can use a program called Giftrans to create transparent GIFs from existing images.

▶ **See** "Using Transparent GIFs," **p. 440**

■ **Animation**—Animated GIFs are created by storing the sequence of images used to produce the animation in one file. A browser that fully supports the GIF89a standard will know to present the images in the file one after the other to produce the animation. The programs that let you store the multiple images in the GIF file also let you specify how much delay should occur before beginning the animation and how many times the animation should repeat.

▶ **See** "Using Animated GIFs," **p. 443**

JPEG   JPEG (an acronym for Joint Picture Experts Group) refers to a set of formats that supports full-color images and stores them in a compressed form. Most popular graphical browsers, including Internet Explorer 3, are able to display JPEG images, though previously these images had to be viewed in a separate program. The *progressive JPEG* (p-JPEG) format has recently emerged and gives the effect of an image fading in just as an interlaced GIF would. Transparency is not possible with JPEG images because the compression tends to make small changes to the image data. If a pixel originally colored with the transparent color is given another color, or if a non-transparent pixel is assigned the transparency color, the on-screen results would be very unattractive.

While JPEG is the format of choice for full-color photos, it is not well-suited to images where there are very sharp changes in color. This is because the rapid color change won't survive the mathematical manipulations involved in the compression process. If you have an image with sharp color changes, you should consider storing it in the GIF format.

The <IMG> Tag

You must save images as separate files even though they are referenced and displayed inside an HTML document. To place an image on a page, you use the <IMG> tag. In its most basic form, the <IMG> tag has the syntax <IMG SRC="*URL*"> where *URL* is the URL of the file that contains the image data.

The SRC attribute is mandatory and specifies the URL of the image file. Because URLs can point anywhere, you can reference images on remote servers as well as your local server. Browsers can load images from a server running any protocol supported by the browser, including FTP and Gopher. You can modify the <IMG> tag by several other attributes as well (see Table 21.1).

CAUTION

Because browsers can load images from any server on the Internet, browsers establish separate server connections for each image in a document, even if all images are on the same server. For small images, it takes more time to establish the connection than to transfer the image data. Therefore, you should avoid numerous small images. Reusing the same small images is not as bad, since Internet Explorer can retrieve them from its cache rather than reloading them.

Table 21.1 <IMG> Tag Attributes

Attribute	Description
ALIGN="*location*"	Location of text next to image (can be TOP, MIDDLE, or BOTTOM)
ALT="*text*"	Text to show instead of image
ISMAP	Used to make imagemaps

Part

IV

Ch

21

N O T E Two other attributes to the <IMG> tag that bear an early introduction are WIDTH and
HEIGHT. These attributes are set equal to the width and height of the image in pixels. The
advantage of doing this is that it allows the browser to leave an appropriately-sized space for the
image as it lays out the page. Thus, page layout is finished quickly, without having to wait for the image
to load completely so that the browser can determine its size. Internet Explorer 3 is able to correctly
parse WIDTH and HEIGHT attributes in an <IMG> tag. ■

The *ALIGN* Attribute   The ALIGN attribute controls the location of text that follows the image,
not how the image is aligned on the page (images are automatically placed flush left on the
page). By default, text appears at the bottom of an inline image. Listing 21.2 shows how you can
use the ALIGN attribute to change the text to be aligned with the middle or top of the image.
Specifically, ALIGN=MIDDLE aligns the baseline of the text with the middle of the image and
ALIGN=TOP aligns the top of the text with the top of the image (see fig. 21.3).

Listing 21.2   Aligning Text Adjacent to Images

```
<H2>ALIGN=TOP</H2>
<IMG SRC="/images/books.gif" ALIGN="TOP">Visit our Library!
<P><HR><P>
<H2>ALIGN=MIDDLE</H2>
<IMG SRC="/images/books.gif" ALIGN="MIDDLE">Visit our Library!
<P><HR><P>
<H2>ALIGN=BOTTOM (default)</H2>
<IMG SRC="/images/books.gif">Visit our Library!
```

FIG. 21.3

The ALIGN attribute lets
you align text with the
middle and top of an
image.

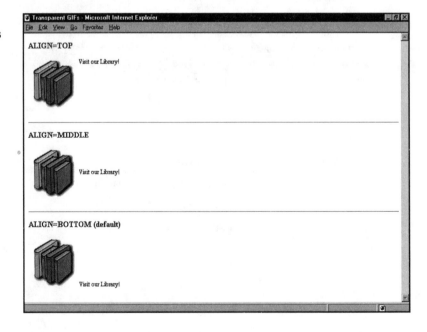

The *ALT* Attribute   The ALT attribute specifies alternate text to be shown in place of an image in text-only browsers. Including the ALT attribute tag is a courtesy to users with this type of browser; don't overlook this courtesy. For example, to include text-only support in the previous example, the line would look like this:

```
<IMG SRC="/images/books.gif" ALIGN="TOP" ALT="BOOKS"> Visit our Library!
```

In a text-only browser like Lynx, this line would appear as the following:

```
[BOOKS] Visit our Library!
```

Because of connection troubles, graphical browsers are sometimes unable to load an image file. When this happens, the browser will display the alternate text in place of the image.

The *ISMAP* Attribute   ISMAP is a stand-alone attribute that signifies that the image is to be used as a server-side imagemap.

▶ **See** "Setting Up a Server-Side Imagemap," **p. 466**

Creating Hypergraphics

You can hyperlink graphics to create button-like effects and provide a nice alternative to clicking plain text. The format for a graphic anchor is the same as a text anchor. However, instead of putting text between the <A HREF="*URL*"> and </A> tags, you put an <IMG> tag between them, as in the following example:

```
<A HREF="http://www.ice.eecs.uic.edu/~rsteven/">
<IMG SRC="images/drew.jpg"></A>
Drew says "Check out the Boxer Home Page!"
```

Figure 21.4 shows the hyperlinked image produced by the HTML.

FIG. 21.4

You can click a hyperlinked image just as you can click hyperlinked text.

Linked image has a border

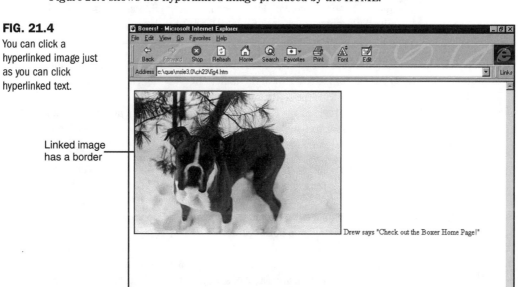

Part
IV

Ch
21

In this example, when the user clicks Drew's picture, the browser jumps to the Boxer Home Page.

Tables

Until now, the only means at your disposal for creating tables has been to use preformatted text. HTML 3.2 calls for several table tags that make it possible to build tables on Web pages without having to convert everything to a fixed-width font. Many browsers implemented these tags well before they were accepted into the 3.2 standard.

The remainder of this chapter is devoted to introducing you to the HTML table tags so that you can use them to not only format tabular data into an easy-to-read form, but also to format entire Web pages.

HTML Table Structure

To understand the table tags better, it helps to take a moment to consider how HTML tables are structured. The fundamental building blocks of an HTML table are *cells*, which can contain a data element of the table or a heading for a column of data. Related cells are logically grouped together in a *row* of the table. The rows, in turn, combine to make up the entire table. If you can keep this breakdown in mind as you read the next few sections, the syntax of the table tags will make much more sense to you.

The Basic Table Tags

To start a table, you need to use the <TABLE> tag. <TABLE> has a companion closing tag, </TABLE>, and together these tags contain all of the tags that go into creating a table. The <TABLE> tag can take the BORDER=*n* attribute, which places a border of *n* pixels around the table. By default, a table has no borders.

Since tables are built out of rows, you need to know how to define a row. The <TR> and </TR> tags contain the tags that comprise a row of the table. The <TR> tag can take the ALIGN and VALIGN attributes. ALIGN controls the horizontal alignment of cell contents in the row and can be set to LEFT, RIGHT, or CENTER. VALIGN controls the vertical alignment and can be set to TOP, BOTTOM, or MIDDLE. Values of ALIGN or VALIGN given in a <TR> tag apply to each cell in the row and will override all default alignments.

With a row defined, you're ready to put in the cells that make up the row. If a cell contains a table data element, you create the cell with the <TD> and </TD> tag pair. The text between <TD> and </TD> is what appears in the cell. Similarly, you use <TH> and </TH> to create a header. Header cells are exactly like data cells, except that header cell contents are automatically rendered in boldface type and are aligned in the center.

N O T E Text isn't the only thing you can put in a table data cell. You can make a blank cell by putting a non-breaking space in the cell (<TD> </TD>) or by just using <TD> and </TD>. You can also place an image in a table cell by putting an <IMG> tag between the <TD> and </TD> tags.

If you really want to give yourself a headache, you can even put another table inside of a single table cell! Nested tables are tough to think about, so it helps to draw out a sketch of what you want before attempting to code it. ■

There are default horizontal and vertical alignments associated with each type of cell. Both types of cell have a default vertical alignment of MIDDLE. Data cells have a default horizontal alignment of LEFT, while header cells have the aforementioned CENTER alignment. You can override any of these defaults *and* any alignments specified in a <TR> tag by including the desired ALIGN or VALIGN attribute in a <TD> or <TH> tag, as Listing 21.3 shows.

Listing 21.3 Table of Ice Cream Flavors

```
<H1>Ice Cream Flavors</H1>
<TABLE BORDER=1>
     <TR>
            <TH></TH>
            <TH>Vanilla</TH>
            <TH>Chocolate</TH>
            <TH>Rocky Road</TH>
     </TR>
     <TR ALIGN=RIGHT VALIGN=TOP>
            <TD><H2>Prices</H2></TD>
            <TD ALIGN=LEFT VALIGN=BOTTOM>$1.99</TD>
            <TD>$1.99</TD>
            <TD ALIGN=LEFT VALIGN=MIDDLE>$2.49</TD>
     </TR>
</TABLE>
```

Figure 21.5 shows how Internet Explorer 3 renders this simple table.

 TIP Using indents when writing HTML to produce a table helps you keep better track of what you're doing.

The $1.99 price for Vanilla is horizontally aligned along the left edge of the cell (ALIGN=LEFT overrides the ALIGN=RIGHT in the <TR> tag) and vertically aligned along the bottom of the cell (VALIGN=BOTTOM overrides the VALIGN=TOP in the <TR> tag). In the second cell, the $1.99 price for Chocolate is aligned according to the alignments given in the <TR> tag, since there are no alignments specified in the second <TD> tag. Finally, the $2.49 price for Rocky Road is horizontally aligned left (again, ALIGN=LEFT overrides the ALIGN=RIGHT in the <TR> tag) and vertically aligned in the middle (VALIGN=MIDDLE overrides VALIGN=BOTTOM in the <TR> tag). Note that Rocky Road's price alignment is the same as the default alignment for any data cell, but we had to undo the alignments set forth in the <TR> tag to get back to the defaults.

Aligning data elements and headers in your tables may seem a bit confusing, but if you keep the following hierarchy in mind, you can master table alignment quickly:

■ Alignments specified in <TD> or <TH> tags override all other alignments, but apply only to the cell being defined.

■ Alignments specified in a <TR> tag override default alignments and apply to all cells in a row, unless overridden by an alignment specification in a <TD> or <TH> tag.

■ In the absence of alignment specifications in <TR>, <TD>, or <TH> tags, default alignments are used.

FIG. 21.5

A simple table with varying alignments.

ALIGN=LEFT;
VALIGN=BOTTOM

ALIGN=RIGHT;
VALIGN=TOP

ALIGN=LEFT;
VALIGN=MIDDLE

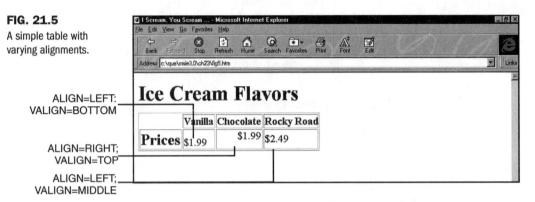

With what you've read so far, you can construct the following table template. This template is a good starting point for building any HTML table:

```
<TABLE BORDER=1>
    <TR>                        <!— Row 1 ->
        <TD>...</TD>
        <TD>...</TD>
        ...
        <TD>...</TD>
    </TR>
    <TR>                        <!— Row 2 ->
        <TD>...</TD>
        <TD>...</TD>
        ...
        <TD>...</TD>
    </TR>
    ...
    <TR>                        <!— Row m ->
        <TD>...</TD>
        <TD>...</TD>
        ...
        <TD>...</TD>
    </TR>
</TABLE>
```

The template above gives you a skeleton for a table with m rows that has no borders. You can adjust this structure however you like by adding or deleting the appropriate tags and attributes.

Adding Captions

To put a caption on your table, enclose the caption text between the <CAPTION> and </CAPTION> tags. Captions appear centered over the table and the text may be broken to match the table's width. You can also use physical style tags to mark up your caption text. If you prefer your caption below the table, you can include the ALIGN=BOTTOM attribute in the <CAPTION> tag.

 TIP Put your caption immediately after the <TABLE> tag or immediately before the </TABLE> tag to prevent your caption from unintentionally being made part of a table row or cell.

Cells That Span More Than One Row or Column

By default, a cell spans (takes up) one row and one column of a table. You can alter this default by using the ROWSPAN and COLSPAN attributes in a <TD> or <TH> tag. ROWSPAN and COLSPAN are set equal to the number of rows and columns, respectively, a cell is to span. If you try to extend the contents of a cell into rows that don't exist on the table, the contents of the cell are truncated to fit the number of rows available.

Sample Tables

To illustrate the utility of HTML tables, this section presents some examples of how to use them. The primary intent of the table tags is to give you a means of presenting tabular data without having to resort to preformatted text. Most tables that do this can be constructed from the template previously given. For example, the table in figure 21.6 was produced by the HTML in Listing 21.4.

Listing 21.4 A Sample Phone Directory

```
<TABLE BORDER=1>
    <CAPTION ALIGN=BOTTOM>Employee Directory</CAPTION>
    <TR>                <!— Row 1 ->
        <TH>Name</TH>
        <TH>Office</TH>
        <TH>Extension</TH>
        <TH>E-mail</TH>
    </TR>
    <TR>                <!— Row 2 ->
        <TD>Patrick Shaughnessy</TD>
        <TD ALIGN=CENTER>5-123</TD>
        <TD ALIGN=CENTER>x549</TD>
        <TD ALIGN=CENTER>pshaughnessy@compucorp.com</TD>
    </TR>
    <TR>                <!— Row 3 ->
        <TD>Jane Sorenson</TD>
        <TD ALIGN=CENTER>3-024</TD>
        <TD ALIGN=CENTER>x770</TD>
        <TD ALIGN=CENTER>jsorenson@compucorp.com</TD>
    </TR>

    <TR>                <!— Row 4 ->
        <TD>Brenda Thomas</TD>
        <TD ALIGN=CENTER>1-228</TD>
        <TD ALIGN=CENTER>x250</TD>
```

Part
IV
Ch
21

continues

Listing 21.4   Continued

```
            <TD ALIGN=CENTER>brendat@compucorp.com</TD>
        </TR>
</TABLE>
```

FIG. 21.6
The HTML table tags
make it easy to produce
tables without using
preformatted text.

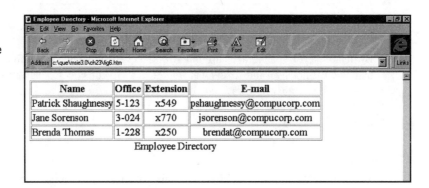

Note that in the table in figure 21.6 all office, extension, and e-mail information is centered
below the respective column headings. This is accomplished by the ALIGN=CENTER attribute in
each of the <TD> tags that creates a cell containing directory information. The ALIGN=BOTTOM in
the <CAPTION> tag places the caption below the table instead of above it.

As noted earlier, table cells can contain much more than just plain text. Listing 21.5 creates a
one row table with an image in the first and a heading in the second cell (it is illustrated in
figure 21.7). Note also that the text in the second cell is formatted as a level 2 heading.

Listing 21.5   Formatted Items Inside a Table Cell

```
<TABLE BORDER=1>
    <TR>
        <TD><IMG SRC="images/books.gif" ALT="BOOKS"></TD>
        <TD ALIGN=CENTER><H2>Visit our Library!</H2></TD>
    </TR>
</TABLE>
```

FIG. 21.7
Table cells may contain
inline images in
addition to text.

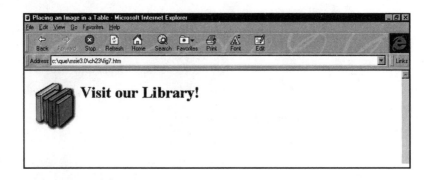

Examples of Intelligent Use of Tables

Tables certainly have their use as a way to present large sets of data in a readable format. However, clever HTML authors have come up with ways to use tables as a design tool. Thanks to all of the alignment control you get with the table tags, it becomes easy to produce a page that is much more cleanly formatted than if done without tables.

Aligning Custom Bullet Graphics   Some people get tired of the plain-old bullet point that is used in rendering an unordered list. Instead, they choose to develop their own graphics to use as bullets. Not so long ago, you probably saw colored spheres used as bullets. These publicly-available graphics quickly became overused and are not as prominent on the Web today.

Whether your bullet graphic is overdone or custom-created to match the graphic theme of your site, you may find that you have trouble aligning it with the text adjacent to it. As a first attempt, you would probably try something like Listing 21.6, which produces the table you see in figure 21.8.

Listing 21.6   A Bulleted List with Custom Bullets

```
<H2>Microsoft Products Shopping List</H2>
<IMG SRC="images/mybullet.gif" ALT="*">Microsoft Word<BR>
<IMG SRC="images/mybullet.gif" ALT="*">Microsoft Excel<BR>
<IMG SRC="images/mybullet.gif" ALT="*">Microsoft PowerPoint<BR>
<IMG SRC="images/mybullet.gif" ALT="*">Microsoft Front Page<BR>
<IMG SRC="images/mybullet.gif" ALT="*">Microsoft Internet Studio (was due out
for MSN, but is now being retooled to Internet standards)
```

N O T E   The alternate text for the `<IMG>` tag that places the custom bullet is an asterisk so that there is a "bullet-like" character in place of the image on text-only browsers. ▪

FIG. 21.8
Using custom bullet graphics can create all sorts of alignment problems.

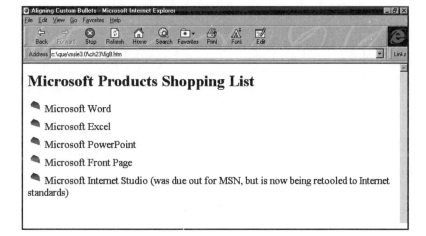

There are several problems to note. First, the list item text is much closer to the bullet than it is in a normal unordered list. Next, the center of the bullet graphic is not aligned with the center of the line of text. Finally, if the list item text runs long and breaks onto the next line, it is not indented to line up under the first word in the list item. Instead it wraps to a point just below the bullet.

Redoing this list as a table can solve all of these layout problems (see Listing 21.7).

Listing 21.7 Custom Bullet Graphics in a Table

```
<H2>Microsoft Products Shopping List</H2>
<TABLE>
     <TR>
            <TD><IMG SRC="images/mybullet.gif" ALT="*"></TD>
            <TD>Microsoft Word</TD>
     </TR>
     <TR>
            <TD><IMG SRC="images/mybullet.gif" ALT="*"></TD>
            <TD>Microsoft Excel</TD>
     </TR>
     <TR>
            <TD><IMG SRC="images/mybullet.gif" ALT="*"></TD>
            <TD>Microsoft PowerPoint</TD>
     </TR>
     <TR>
            <TD><IMG SRC="images/mybullet.gif" ALT="*"></TD>
            <TD>Microsoft Front Page</TD>
     </TR>
     <TR>
            <TD><IMG SRC="images/mybullet.gif" ALT="*"></TD>
            <TD>Microsoft Internet Studio (was due out for MSN, but is
                now being retooled to Internet standards</TD>
     </TR>
</TABLE>
```

When rendered on Internet Explorer 3, Listing 21.7 produces the screen you see in figure 21.9. Notice that all of our issues are gone! The spacing that normally occurs between cells of a table adds more space between the bullet graphics and the list item text. Since items in table cells have a default vertical alignment of MIDDLE, the center lines of both the bullet graphic and the list item text come into alignment. And if list item text breaks to a new line, it does so within its cell and does not end up under the bullet graphic.

If your bullet text runs longer than two lines, your bullet graphic may look strange because it is vertically aligned in the middle of the cell by default. To avoid this, set VALIGN=TOP in the <TD> tag that creates the cell containing the bullet graphic.

FIG. 21.9
Placing custom bullet graphics in a table alleviates many of the alignment troubles.

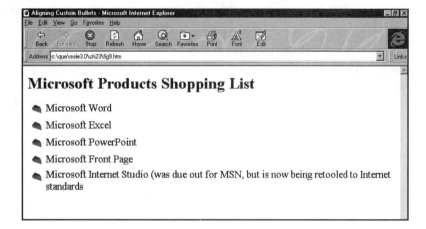

Pull Quotes   Pull quotes are excerpts from a manuscript that are replicated prominently on a page. Pull quotes are usually a restatement of some key point made in the document. You can make pull quotes in your HTML documents by using HTML tables. Consider Listing 21.8 with a table embedded in the middle of it.

Listing 21.8   Using Tables to Produce Pull Quotes

```
<H2>The Preamble</H2>
<TABLE ALIGN=LEFT>
<TR>
<TD ALIGN=CENTER><HR><B>...form a more perfect union...<HR></TD>
</TR>
</TABLE>
"We, the People, in order to form a more perfect union, establish justice,
ensure domestic tranquillity, provide for the common defense, promote the
general welfare and secure the blessings of liberty, for ourselves and our
posterity, do ordain and establish this Constitution for the United States of
America." That's how our Founding Fathers began the Constitution back in the
summer of 1787.
```

 T I P   To put a little bit of white space around your pull quote text, place the text between the `<BLOCKQUOTE>` and `</BLOCKQUOTE>` tags. This will indent the text from the edges of the cells.

Figure 21.10 shows how Internet Explorer 3 rendered this HTML code. The table contains the pull quote ...to form a more perfect union... between two pieces of horizontal rule. The text of the Preamble itself is to the right of the table and eventually wraps around it once it gets long enough.

Part
IV

Ch
21

FIG. 21.10

Pull quotes highlight key phrases from a manuscript and are easy to make with HTML tables.

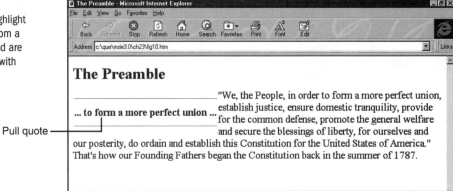

Pull quote ——

In a sense, it's a bit unfair to spring this example on you because you need to understand how the ALIGN attribute of the <TABLE> tag is needed to make the pull quote work. Normally a table is left-justified, so you may be asking yourself why ALIGN=LEFT appears in Listing 21.8 at all. The reason is so that the text following the table will wrap around it, rather than starting below it. If you remove the ALIGN=LEFT from the <TABLE> tag above, you get the screen seen in figure 21.11. Note how the effect of the pull quote is lost when the text starts below the table.

FIG. 21.11

This is the same page without ALIGN=LEFT. Note how the text no longer wraps around the table.

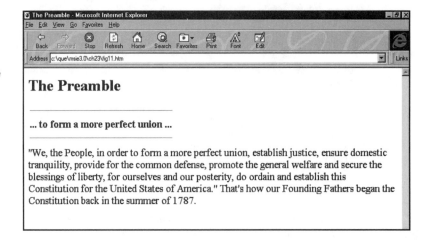

As you'll see in Chapter 25, "HTML 3.2 and Microsoft Extensions to HTML," you can set ALIGN equal to LEFT or RIGHT in an <IMG> tag or a <TABLE> tag to cause the image or table to "float" in the left or right margin. Floating images and tables are different from non-floating images and tables in that text can appear in the empty space next to them and eventually wrap around them. The values LEFT and RIGHT are called *extensions* of the ALIGN attribute. Such extensions are not understood by all browsers. Those browsers that do interpret them correctly will be able to properly render pull quotes for you.

Aligning Form Data Fields   One other handy application of tables also requires a little fore-shadowing. HTML forms are used to collect information from people who visit Web sites. You can use a form to request a visitor's name and e-mail address or to administer an entire marketing survey. Data collected from HTML forms are sent back to your Web server for processing and storage.

Forms are easy to make because there are only a few HTML tags you need to know to create form input fields. The most useful of these tags is the <INPUT> tag, which can be used to create something as simple as a text entry field, to something as intricate as a set of radio buttons. The <INPUT> tag only creates the field though. It's up to you to put some descriptive text next to the field so the user knows what to enter there. This is where problems arise, because if you use descriptive text of varying lengths, the forms fields won't line up properly. From a technical standpoint, this isn't a big deal. The form will still work. From a design standpoint, however, a form is much more attractive if all of its inputs fields are nicely aligned. You want your forms to be attractive and inviting since you are asking the user to make the effort to fill them out.

▶ **See** "Creating HTML Forms," **p. 514**

Tables are particularly handy for lining up input fields on an HTML form. Figure 21.12 shows a form that asks for the user's name and address. None of the fields are neatly aligned with each other because the words that precede them are of varying lengths.

FIG. 21.12

Form input fields are typically not aligned because of size differences in the text that precede them.

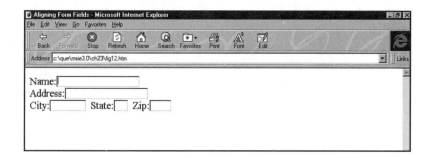

By putting the prompting text and the fields into their own table cells, the fields will automatically be aligned. Listing 21.9 creates the same form but with tables. By using COLSPAN in the first two rows, you're even able to get the City, State, and Zip fields to fit across the same width as the fields above them.

Listing 21.9   Using Tables to Align Form Fields

```
<TABLE>
    <TR>
        <TD>Name:</TD>
        <TD COLSPAN=5><INPUT NAME="name" TYPE="text" SIZE=30></TD>
    </TR>
    <TR>
        <TD>Address:</TD>
        <TD COLSPAN=5><INPUT NAME="address" TYPE="text" SIZE=30></TD>
    </TR>
    <TR>
```

Part
IV

Ch
21

continues

Listing 21.9   Continued

```
            <TD>City:</TD>
            <TD><INPUT NAME="city" TYPE="text" SIZE=11></TD>
              <TD>State:</TD>
            <TD><INPUT NAME="state" TYPE="text" SIZE=2></TD>
            <TD>Zip:</TD>
            <TD><INPUT NAME="zip" TYPE="text" SIZE=5></TD>
        </TR>
    </TABLE>
```

Figure 21.13 illustrates how this table might appear in a browser.

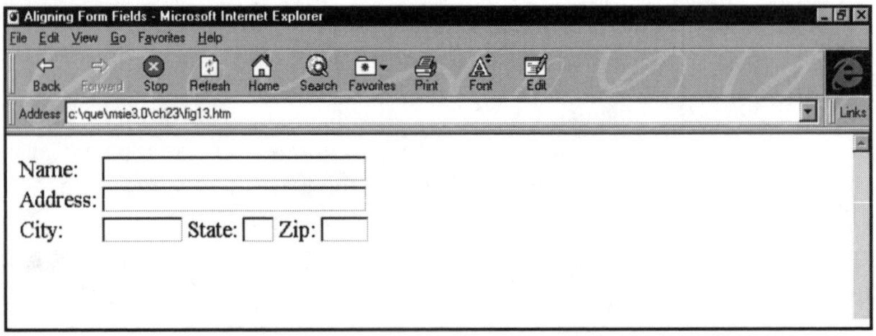

FIG. 21.13

Placing form input fields in table cells is an easy way to get them to align properly.

Using Microsoft Internet Assistants and HTML

Now that you've spent a few chapters learning the basics of HTML, you're ready to take a moment to investigate the many software tools written to help HTML authors compose documents. Microsoft has developed several tools called Internet Assistants that are meant to work together with key programs in the Microsoft Office suite. Other software development groups have created add-ons to existing word processing programs or completely separate programs to support Web authors.

This chapter surveys the Microsoft Internet Assistants and some of the word processor add-ons and stand-alone programs that can help you author and edit HTML. ■

Microsoft Internet Assistant for Word

An add-on for Microsoft Word that stores many HTML formatting tags as Word styles and that converts Word into a fully functional Web browser.

Microsoft Internet Assistant for Excel

A useful utility for converting all or part of a spreadsheet in an HTML table.

Microsoft Internet Assistant for PowerPoint

Internet Assistant for PowerPoint allows you to convert your presentation slides into graphical and text-only Web pages easily.

GT_HTML and WebAuthor plug-ins for Microsoft Word

Two Word plug-ins that expand Word's menus and toolbars to include special functionality for HTML editing.

HoTMetaL, HTMLed, and HotDog stand-alone editors

Three programs with high-powered support for virtually all HTML authoring tasks.

Using Microsoft Internet Assistant for Word

On the CD

There are a large number of HTML authoring add-ons for Microsoft Word, so it's no surprise that Microsoft itself has produced one. Internet Assistant for Word is a no-cost add-on that includes styles, toolbars, and tools for editing HTML and turns Word into a Web browser.

N O T E   The information in this section is based on the beta release 4 of Internet Assistant version 2.0z. This beta was written to work with Word 7.0 in Windows 95 or with Word 6.0 in Windows NT. For the latest release and links to the downloadable file, direct your browser to **http://www.microsoft.com/msoffice/freestuf/msword/download/ia/default.htm**. Microsoft will also ship a copy on floppy disk to registered owners of Word for a shipping and handling charge of $5. Call 1-800-426-9400. ■

After downloading the file, the installation of Internet Assistant is fairly easy. If you have installed a Microsoft program yourself, this process should be familiar. During the installation, you are given the option to make Internet Assistant your default HTML browser. If you choose to do this, the Internet Assistant add-on will be placed in your Word Startup directory. This causes Internet Assistant's functionality to be loaded each time you start Word.

CAUTION

Be sure to close all open Windows applications, especially Word, before you install Internet Assistant. This minimizes the risk of crashing your computer.

The Internet Assistant Web Browser

When you start Word with Internet Assistant installed, the only difference you'll notice at first is the addition of the button labeled with a pair of glasses (see fig. 22.1). This is the Switch to Web Browse View button. Clicking this button takes you to the browser side of Word that Internet Assistant creates. As you can see in figure 22.2, the Word browser has most of the usual features found in other popular browsers, including forward and backward navigation buttons, reload and stop buttons, and the ability to store the URLs of your favorite sites (Favorites). To return to the Word editing window, you can click on the Switch to Edit View button.

Loading and Editing Documents

When you start a new document, you will find that you have access to a new template called HTML.DOT. This template provides an extensive set of HTML styles and additional menu options and toolbars to support HTML authoring. Figure 22.3 illustrates the modified toolbars. If you want to edit an existing HTML document, Word will automatically open the HTML template when you select a document with an .HTM extension.

N O T E   In the figure, both the Standard and Formatting toolbars are open. Keep in mind that you can customize these toolbars, like all of the toolbars in Word. You can add buttons and rearrange their order; your toolbars may look different, therefore, from those shown in figure 22.3. ■

FIG. 22.1
The Switch to Web Browse View button activates the Web browser features included as part of Internet Assistant.

The Switch to Web Browse View button

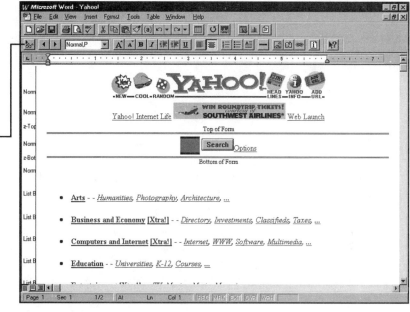

FIG. 22.2
The Word Web browser supports most popular browser features for navigation and bookmarking.

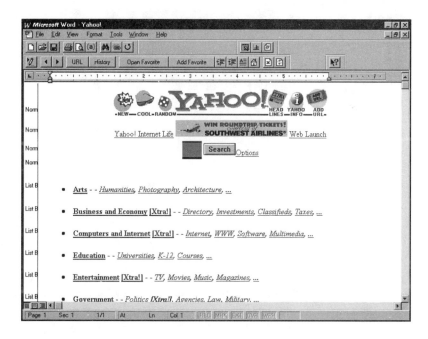

FIG. 22.3

Starting a new document with Internet Assistant's HTML template modifies Word's Standard and Formatting toolbars.

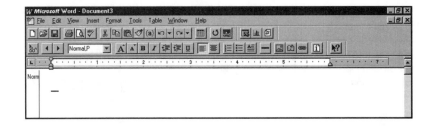

As you type in the text of your Web page, you can mark it for specific text effects, such as bold or italic, using the standard Word tools. Word automatically translates those effects into HTML tags. You can also format text in HTML modes, such as Strong or Preformatted, by using the styles available under the HTML template. You can select a style using the Styles tool in the Formatting toolbar, or you can open the Format menu and choose either Style or Style Gallery.

Internet Assistant also provides a way to place special codes such as diacritical marks, copyright and trademark symbols, or other special punctuation. To access these special characters, open the Insert menu and choose the Symbol option. A Symbol dialog box with listings of special characters appears (see fig. 22.4). Double-clicking a specific character places it in the text where the I-beam cursor is located.

FIG. 22.4

You can place HTML entities in your document by selecting the desired character from this dialog box.

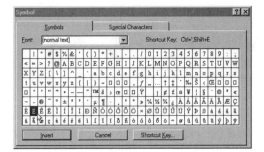

Handling HTML Codes not Supported by Internet Assistant

There are also several HTML tags and effects that Internet Assistant does not accommodate through styles or tools. To enter these additional tags (or any extra HTML code), open the Insert Menu and choose HTML Markup. A dialog box with a large window for entering direct HTML code appears (see fig. 22.5). The entered text is handled and displayed as HTML code without ever being translated into Word format. This feature is nice because it lets you include newly introduced HTML tags in your document, although you do have to type the tags out yourself.

FIG. 22.5

Internet Assistant's
Insert HTML Markup
dialog box lets you
enter unsupported
HTML tags.

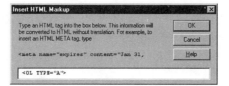

Creating Forms Using Internet Assistant

Internet Assistant has some fairly extensive features for creating HTML forms. You can begin a form by opening the Insert menu and choosing the Form Field option. This causes Internet Assistant to enter the HTML tags that surround a form. The Form Field dialog box and Forms floating tool palette are shown in figure 22.6.

▶ **See** "Creating HTML Forms" to learn about the tags used to produce HTML forms, **p.514**

FIG. 22.6

The Form Field dialog
box and a floating tool
palette make compos-
ing HTML forms easy.

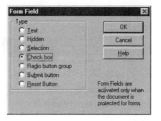

If you've created forms in Microsoft Access, you may recognize the look of some of these form tools. The Forms tool palette gives you point-and-click access to creating checkboxes, pull-down list boxes, radio buttons, and textboxes. This palette also provides standard Submit and Reset buttons. When you place a field in the form area, additional dialog boxes open to help you create the necessary choices for a drop-down list box or other controls to help make the form work.

Saving Documents in HTML Format

Internet Assistant for Word saves documents in HTML format by default. The resulting document is then ready to be used on your Web server. This is a contrast to many of the third-party templates discussed in this chapter, which require a special File menu option to save your document in ASCII format.

Using Microsoft Internet Assistant for Excel

Spreadsheets are a great way to convey information, and Microsoft Excel is one of the most popular spreadsheet programs around. By using Internet Assistant for Excel, you get an easy way to convert portions of your Excel spreadsheets into HTML tables without having to code all of those table tags yourself!

Downloading and Installing Internet Assistant for Excel

To download Internet Assistant for Excel, just follow these steps:

1. Direct Internet Explorer to the URL **http://www.microsoft.com/msexcel/internet/ ia/html.xla**.

2. Save the file HTML.XLA to the C:\MSOFFICE\EXCEL\LIBRARY directory.

3. Start up Excel and select Tools, Add-Ins.

4. Check the box next to Internet Assistant Wizard (see fig. 22.7).

FIG. 22.7

Selecting the Internet Assistant Wizard option installs Internet Assistant for Excel.

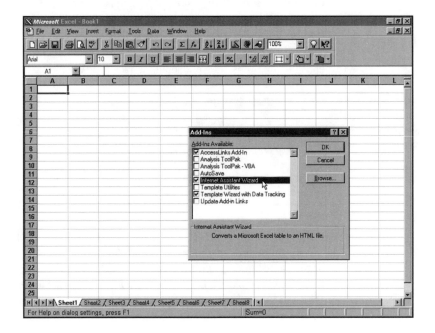

5. Click OK.

Excel will then load the file and add the Internet Assistant Wizard option to the bottom of the Tools menu (see fig. 22.8).

FIG. 22.8

Once installed, Internet Assistant for Excel is available through the Internet Assistant Wizard option under the Tools menu.

How To Use Internet Assistant for Excel

Using Internet Assistant for Excel is almost as easy as installing it. Figure 22.9 shows an Excel spreadsheet to be converted to an HTML table. To perform this conversion, all you need to do is activate the Internet Assistant Wizard, and it will lead you through each of the conversion steps.

FIG. 22.9
An Excel spreadsheet to convert into an HTML table.

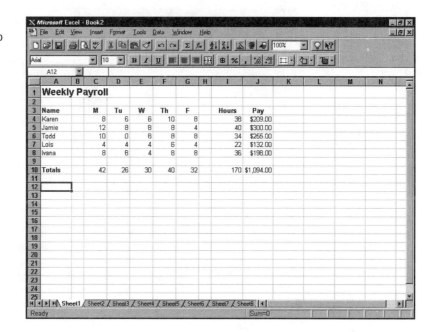

Once you start the Internet Assistant Wizard by choosing Tools, Internet Assistant Wizard, you'll be prompted for the following information:

1. What is the range of cells to convert (see fig. 22.10)?

FIG. 22.10
Enter the range of cells to convert to HTML at the bottom of this dialog box.

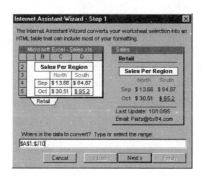

2. Do you want the HTML table to appear in an existing HTML document or a new, separate one? If you want it to appear in an existing document, you need to place the text "##Table##" at the point in the file where you want the table inserted. If you want it stored in a new file, you'll be prompted for title, header, and other document-related information (see fig. 22.11).

FIG. 22.11

If you're saving the converted spreadsheet to a new HTML file, you also need to supply title, header, and other document-related information.

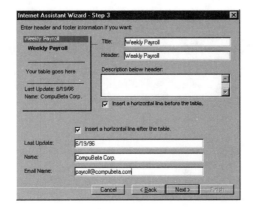

3. Do you want Excel formatting (bold, italics, right aligned, etc.) preserved?
4. What is the directory path to the existing file or to where the new file should be created?

Once you've entered the directory path, click Finish to execute the conversion. The range of cells you've specified is converted to HTML and placed in either a new or an existing file, according to your instructions. It's that simple!

Using Microsoft Internet Assistant for PowerPoint

PowerPoint is a standard tool for creating corporate presentations. By placing text and graphics on PowerPoint slides, you can author a professional-looking presentation easily. Now Internet Assistant for PowerPoint lets you make your PowerPoint presentations Web-ready in a snap. Internet Assistant for PowerPoint will automatically do the following:

- Retain the design and layout of your slides.
- Create two versions of each slide—one graphical and the other text-only.
- Hyperlink all of the files that contain the individual slides in the presentation.
- Create imagemaps for PowerPoint objects that are linked to slides.
- Set up links from slides to other resources accessible by one of the common Internet protocols such as HTTP and FTP.

Downloading and Installing Internet Assistant for PowerPoint

To download Internet Assistant for PowerPoint, perform the following steps:

1. Direct Internet Explorer to **http://www.microsoft.com/kb/softlib/mslfiles/ pptia.exe**. When Internet Explorer asks where you want to save the file, instruct it to do so in the C:\MSOFFICE\POWERPNT directory.

2. The file PPTIA.EXE is a self-extracting archive. Run this file to unarchive the installation program (IA4PPT95.EXE) and the installation instructions in both Word and HTML format.

3. Run the file IA4PPT95.EXE to install Internet Explorer for PowerPoint.

Once installed, Internet Assistant for PowerPoint adds the Export as HTML option to the File menu, as shown in figure 22.12.

FIG. 22.12
Internet Assistant for PowerPoint adds an Export as HTML option to the PowerPoint File menu.

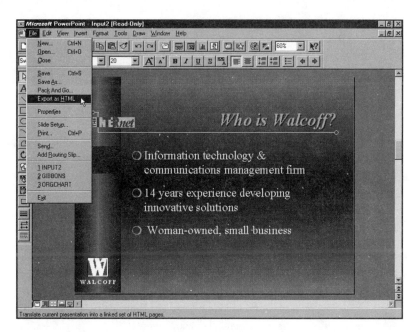

How To Use Internet Assistant for PowerPoint

Once you have identified a presentation you want to place on the Web, load it into PowerPoint and choose File, Export as HTML to open the HTML Export Options dialog box you see in figure 22.13. Fields in the dialog box prompt you to choose between grayscale and color graphics, GIF or JPEG graphic storage formats, and how much compression to use if storing your slides as JPEGs. If you choose a high level of compression, you'll get smaller files, but the image quality will be reduced. Finally, you need to specify where to save the converted presentation.

▶ **See** "Image File Formats" to learn more about the GIF and JPEG formats, **p. 436**

FIG. 22.13

Before converting your presentation, Internet Assistant for PowerPoint prompts you for color or grayscale images, and GIF or JPEG file formats.

> **CAUTION**
>
> Before clicking OK, make certain that there are no tools or dialog boxes visible near the upper left portion of the PowerPoint window. These items can be inadvertently built into your converted presentation if left open.

Once you've specified all of the information the dialog box requires and have closed up all extraneous tools and dialog boxes, click OK to begin the conversion. During conversion, you will see a "slide show" occurring in the PowerPoint window as Internet Assistant converts each slide.

> **CAUTION**
>
> Be careful not to move your mouse pointer over the slide show during the conversion. This could inadvertently cause the slide show Popup menu to appear and be incorporated into the HTML version of your presentation.

When the conversion is finished, you'll find the following three items in the folder you specified for saving the presentation:

- A file INDEX.HTM which contains a header for your presentation and a set of hyperlinks to each of the slides in the presentation.

- A set of files named SLDXXX.HTM which contain the graphical versions of your presentation slides. XXX corresponds to where the slide occurs in the presentation. 001 is the first slide, 002 is the second slide, and so on.

- A set of files named TSLDXXX.HTM which contain the text-only versions of your slides. The numbering scheme is the same as it is for the graphical versions.

Buttons giving you the option to go forward or backward one slide in the presentation are automatically built into each file. Additionally, any PowerPoint objects defined as buttons that link to another slide will be hyperlinked to the appropriate HTML file, and any objects with an associated Run command set equal to an Internet URL will be linked to that URL.

 You can link a PowerPoint object or associate a Run command with a PowerPoint object by using the Interactive Settings option under the Tools menu.

To run through your converted presentation, load the file INDEX.HTM into Internet Explorer and click the hyperlink to the first slide in the presentation. From there, you can use the arrow buttons at the bottom of each slide to navigate through the presentation.

Tips on Using Internet Assistant for PowerPoint

Using Internet Assistant for PowerPoint requires a little more initial planning than do the other Microsoft Internet Assistants to produce the best results. Some tips for getting the most out of Internet Assistant for PowerPoint follow:

- **Hidden slides**—PowerPoint lets you designate slides as hidden so that they don't appear in your presentation. Internet Assistant for PowerPoint does not ignore hidden slides. It will go right ahead and convert hidden slides just like any other. If you want to convert a presentation without the hidden slides, make a copy of the presentation and remove the hidden slides from the copy. Save the modified copy and perform the conversion on that.

- **Grouped text**—Internet Assistant for PowerPoint can't convert text that is grouped together with other graphical elements. To make sure that the maximum amount of information is available for conversion, ungroup any objects that contain text. This is particularly important for the text-only versions of your slides.

- **Template files**—Internet Assistant for PowerPoint uses two template files—IMAGE.TPL and TEXT.TPL—to generate the graphical and text-only versions of your slides. These files are just shells of HTML documents that the Assistant plugs things into. You can modify either of these templates in a simple text editor such as Notepad to reflect any specific content or formatting you'd like. For example, you might include an <IMG > tag that places the company logo on each page in the IMAGE.TPL template. This way, any graphical version of a slide will always include the logo.

Other HTML Authoring and Editing Tools

The Internet Assistants from Microsoft are a fine way to convert documents you've created with other Microsoft software products. However, there are many other general-purpose software programs to help you with your HTML authoring tasks. These come in two basic flavors, as follows:

- **Word processor plug-in**—A set of macro commands that work together with an existing word processing package to give the user enhanced abilities to compose and edit HTML documents

- **Stand-alone editing programs**—Software packages developed specifically for the tasks that go into HTML authoring

The next few sections examine some of the available programs under each kind.

Plug-ins for MS Word

Most of the HTML plug-in packages have been developed for Microsoft Word. The advantage of plug-ins is that users get increased functionality for handling HTML editing while not having to leave an editing environment that they're familiar with. This section looks at two plug-ins for Word: GT_HTML, a free package from Georgia Tech, and WebAuthor, a commercial package from Quarterdeck.

GT_HTML   GT_HTML is template add-on for Word developed at Georgia Tech. It is easy to install and supports a surprising number of editing features.

> **N O T E**   The following section is based on GT_HTML, version 6.0d. You can download GT_HTML by pointing your browser to **http://www.gatech.edu/word_html/**. Look for the download link to the file `GT_HTML.ZIP`. ■

Installation of GT_HTML is simple; just copy the template file `GT_HTML.DOT` into your templates subdirectory for Word. If you activate the template when you open a new document in Word, you have the ability to add the two new toolbars shown in figure 22.14. To activate the toolbars, open the Yiew menu and choose Toolbars. In the Toolbars dialog box, select the Toolbar 1 (Gt_html) and Toolbar 2 (Gt_html) checkboxes.

FIG. 22.14

When you install GT_HTML, you have the option of turning on two toolbars to help you edit HTML.

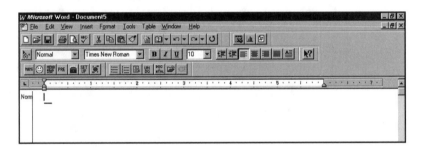

In addition to the two toolbars, GT_HTML adds HTML-related options to most of Word's pull-down menus. The new options appear at the bottom of each pull-down menu, and start with the word HTML. Since GT_HTML doesn't load a lot of additional styles into Word, most of your special formatting will be done using the new menu options.

One of the more helpful menu options is the HTML Browser option under the File menu. Selecting this option opens the browser you want to work with GT_HTML. Having quick access to a browser while you edit makes it easier to test your documents as you develop them.

Another helpful menu option is the HTML Toolbox under the Tools menu. You can quickly insert tags for rules, titles, comments, centering and blinking text, and line breaks using selections from the Toolbox. The Toolbox also gives you a way to launch GT_HTML's handy HTML Form Creator and HTML Table Converter. The Forms Creator launches a second dialog box in which you can configure your form input fields, while the Table Converter will convert a simple Word table (no cell in the table spans more than one row or one column) to HTML format. Toolbox items are shown in fig. 22.15.

▶ **See** "Creating HTML Forms" to learn about the HTML tags used to create forms, **p. 514**

FIG. 22.15
GT_HTML's HTML
Toolbox makes it easy
to insert many types of
HTML tags.

The Format menu includes options for formatting highlighted text as a heading, preformatted text, or a numbered or bulleted list. To apply bold, italic, and underline styles, you can use Word's normal formatting toolbar. GT_HTML converts these formats to HTML tags when it saves the HTML version of your document.

Quarterdeck WebAuthor 2.0   Quarterdeck has recently released version 2.0 of its HTML editing plug-in for Word 6.0 called WebAuthor. WebAuthor 2.0 offers a number of enhancements over earlier versions, including new toolbars for text and paragraph formatting, support for HTML 3.0 and Microsoft extensions, and faster importing and exporting of documents.

N O T E   The information in this section is based on the trialware version of WebAuthor 2.0. You can download the self-extracting archive containing the trialware files from Quarterdeck's Web site at **http://www.qdeck.com/**. You may evaluate the trialware version of WebAuthor 2.0 for 30 days, after which time the features that convert and save files to HTML will disable. If you choose to purchase the full WebAuthor package after the evaluation period, you will also get WebImage, a useful image editor and converter, and the Quarterdeck Mosaic browser. For current pricing information, consult Quarterdeck's Web site or contact the sales department at 1-800-354-3222. ▨

N O T E   Windows 95 and NT users should note that the current release of WebAuthor works only with Word 6.0 (a 16-bit application). Quarterdeck anticipates releasing a 32-bit version of WebAuthor 2.0 during 1996. Consult the Quarterdeck Web site at **http://www.qdeck.com/** for the status of this release. ▨

It's easy to install WebAuthor once you've downloaded the archive file. A standard install program will walk you through the installation steps and set up a Windows program group. Once WebAuthor is installed, you'll find an extra option under the Microsoft Word Tools menu, as shown in figure 22.16.

N O T E   WebAuthor places GIF images in your Windows document by converting the images to the Windows BMP format. When you access WebAuthor through the Tools menu, it checks to see if this converter has been installed. If you get a warning message telling you that your GIF graphics converter has not been installed, you'll need to run your Word Setup program to install it. The filter you want to install is the CompuServe GIF filter. ▨

FIG. 22.16

Installing WebAuthor 2.0 adds a WebAuthor option to the Word Tools menu.

You activate WebAuthor's capabilities by selecting this new menu option under the Tools menu. When you do, you're presented with a dialog box that gives you four options on how to proceed (see fig. 22.17). You can use the Create a New HTML Document option if you have yet to write any, or use the Open/Import Existing Documents for Editing option. Additionally, you can choose either the Convert Existing Documents to HTML option or the Set/Change Options for Document Conversion to HTML option.

FIG. 22.17

WebAuthor gives you four different options when you activate it from the Word Tools menu.

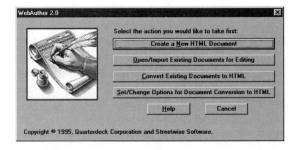

If you choose to start a new document, WebAuthor immediately presents you with a dialog box where you can enter the document's title and other HTML tags found in the document head. Once you specify a title and other document head information, you'll see a screen like the one in figure 22.18. Note that WebAuthor adds an extra toolbar to your Word window. Buttons on this toolbar let you create new documents (Word and HTML), open files (with or without converting), save files (in Word and HTML formats), toggle to the Edit view where you can make changes to your document, format characters and lists, or activate one of WebAuthor's special function managers. The three buttons on the end of the toolbar, labeled "Char," "Para," and "Form," toggle additional toolbars on and off. Figure 22.18 shows the new toolbar with the additional three toolbars turned on.

The document view you see in figure 22.18 is called the Edit view. While in this view, you can make additions or changes to your document. The Toggle Document View button in the main WebAuthor toolbar switches you to a near-WYSIWYG (what you see is what you get) view that gives you a sense of how your document might look on a browser screen. You can't make edits while you're in the near-WYSIWYG view, so be sure to toggle back to the Edit view to make changes.

FIG. 22.18
WebAuthor gives you an extra toolbar that you can use to activate as many as three other toolbars.

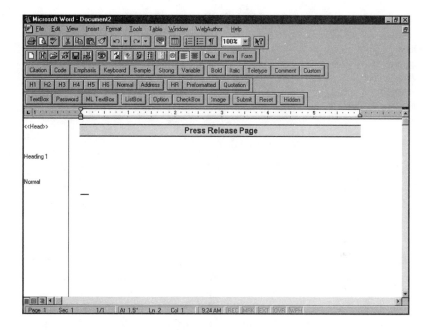

If you choose to open or import an exiting HTML file, WebAuthor will look for documents that have the .DOC, .HTM, or .RTF (Rich Text Format) extensions. Find the document you want and click OK to load it.

 After you load a document, you may find that WebAuthor has placed a blank toolbar in your toolbar area. The blank toolbar has no real useful purpose. To delete it, find the Hide Blank Toolbar button at the left edge of the empty space and click it to recapture the space for your editing window.

The other two choices you get when activating WebAuthor deal with converting existing documents to HTML format. If you choose to convert an existing document, WebAuthor lets you select a Word (.DOC) or Rich Text Format (.RTF). Once you select the file, WebAuthor loads it into Word and then performs the conversion to HTML according to a set of customizable conversion options.

If you choose to set conversion options, you'll activate the Options File Editor. Selections under the Options menu in this program let you specify conversion parameters for logical and heading styles (Styles), physical styles (Direct Formatting), document head information (Document Information), hyperlinks (File Links), and tables (Tables). The Options File Editor with the File Links dialog box active is shown in figure 22.19.

Once you have started a new document or have loaded a new one, it's fairly easy to make edits using WebAuthor's many editing features. The extra Char and Para toolbars make it very easy to apply logical, physical, and heading styles to highlighted text. Buttons on the Form toolbar can be used to drop form elements wherever your cursor is positioned.

FIG. 22.19

The Options File Editor utility program lets you specify how WebAuthor should perform conversions to HTML from Word or RTF formats.

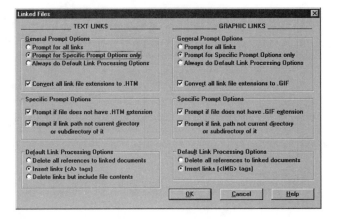

WebAuthor also gives you three different "managers" to assist you with placement of more complicated items. The Anchor Manager lets you specify an internal or external anchor to which a hypertext link can point. The Image Manager dialog box, shown in figure 22.20, prompts you for a GIF or JPEG file, the size of the image, how it should be aligned, and what alternative text should be used if the image is unavailable. The Form Manager walks you through a set of dialog boxes in which you indicate what input fields should be used to build the form, as well as the URL of the processing script, and how the form data should be sent to the script. Each of WebAuthor's special managers is accessible by a button on the main WebAuthor toolbar.

FIG. 22.20

WebAuthor's Image Manager prompts you for the basic informa- tion needed to place an inline image into your document.

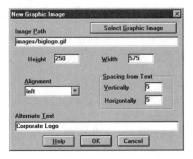

The List button on the main WebAuthor toolbar lets you create any one of the five types of HTML list. The Insert Symbol button gives you a dialog box full of special characters such as copyright and trademark symbols, and characters with diacritical marks.

To save a document in HTML format, choose Save to HTML under the File menu, or click the Save to HTML button on the main WebAuthor toolbar. If you save using an option rather than these two, your document will be saved in Word format and it will not be suitable for transfer to your server.

Stand-alone HTML Editors

The other type of HTML authoring tool is the stand-alone editing program. These packages are developed around the tasks involved in HTML authoring and tend to offer very powerful support. This section considers three such programs: HoTMetaL FREE, HTMLed Pro, and Hot-Dog Pro.

HoTMetaL FREE   If your objective is to write nearly perfect HTML on the first try, you should look into HoTMetaL 2.0 from SoftQuad. There are two versions of HoTMetaL 2.0 available. HoTMetaL FREE 2.0 is intended for use in academic settings and for internal business purposes. Commercial users are required to purchase HoTMetaL PRO 2.0. When you pay for a license, you also get technical support and some features that are not active in the freeware version, including a spellchecker, thesaurus, and user-defined macro capability.

N O T E   This review of HoTMetaL 2.0 is based on HoTMetaL FREE 2.0, which you can download by visiting **http://www.sq.com/products/hotmetal/hm-feat.htm**. The features discussed here are also available in the PRO version, along with the added functionality noted above. ■

When you open a new document in HoTMetaL, you see the window shown in figure 22.21. The figure shows HoTMetaL's standard document template, which is stored in the file TUTOR.HTM. Notice that the tags in the template are easy to pick out, with starting and ending tags both pointing inward toward the text they contain. Also notice that the template is very complete. All of the tags that are technically required are present, including <HTML>, <HEAD>, <TITLE>, <BODY>, and their corresponding closing tags.

FIG. 22.21
HoTMetaL's standard document template is in proper HTML form and encourages you to title your document immediately.

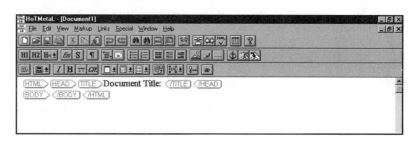

The completeness of HoTMetaL's default template points to one of the program's strengths: it forces you to use good HTML. HoTMetaL's Rules Checking feature makes it almost impossible to insert an inappropriate tag into your document. When Rules Checking is on, the tag insert features of HoTMetaL are context-sensitive, and you are limited to inserting only those tags that are legal at the current cursor position. For example, if you were inside the <DL> and </DL> tags, you could insert only <DT> and </DT> tags or <DD> and </DD> tags. HoTMetaL prevents you from inserting other tags by graying them out or by just not presenting them.

T I P   Rules Checking can be annoying if you're a seasoned pro who has developed a particular authoring style. You can turn Rules Checking off or on by pressing Ctrl+K.

In addition to Rules Checking, HoTMetaL also comes with an SGML validator that tests your document for conformance to the rules of proper HTML. These features make HoTMetaL a great choice for the HTML beginner, since they encourage good authoring habits right from the start.

HoTMetaL provides three toolbars to assist with typical editing tasks. The Standard toolbar is at the top and provides buttons for frequently used file (New, Open, Save) and editing (Cut, Copy, Paste) operations. Other buttons support searching the document (Find, Find Next); showing, hiding, inserting, and removing HTML tags; and activating the SGML validator. In the freeware version of HoTMetaL, the buttons to activate the spell checker and thesaurus are grayed out.

The Common HTML toolbar is below the Standard toolbar and lets you quickly tag markup text with heading styles, frequently used logical styles (Emphasis, Strong, Block Quote, Address), and list tags. Buttons toward the end of the toolbar are not style-related; they let you place images, horizontal rules, line breaks, and hyperlinks.

At the bottom, you'll find the Other toolbar. The Other toolbar is something of a concession on HoTMetaL's part, because it allows for the use of the extensions to standard HTML. This becomes significant when you consider that earlier versions of HoTMetaL refused to recognize these tags and wouldn't even *open* documents that contained them. The HTML extensions are accessible on a pull-down menu that you see when clicking and holding the HTML Extensions button. Other such pull-down menus give you quick access to tags for the document head, computer-related logical styles (Code, Keyboard, Variable, Sample), compact list tags, and form tags. You can also mark up text with physical styles using buttons in the Other toolbar. Pressing the Special Characters button produces the floating palette you see in figure 22.22. This palette is handy when coding multilingual pages, as it lets you place special characters by pointing to and clicking them, rather than having to remember the escape sequence of the character. To close the special characters palette, just double-click the button at the upper left corner of the palette.

NOTE You can suppress the display of any of the HoTMetaL toolbars by choosing the View, Toolbars option. ▉

FIG. 22.22
The floating Special Characters palette makes placing foreign language characters as easy as pointing and clicking.

Figure 22.23 shows part of an HTML document open in the HoTMetaL window. Note how *all* tags—even tags such as <HR> and <BR>, which ordinarily occur by themselves—have a closing tag. You can also get a sense of HoTMetaL's tolerance for non-standard HTML tags—note that it let us load a document that contained <FONT SIZE=-2> and </FONT> tags.

FIG. 22.23

Unlike its predecessors, HoTMetaL 2.0 lets you load documents with non-standard HTML tags.

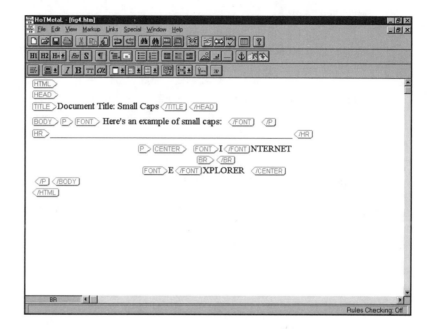

As you edit the document, you'll notice that HoTMetaL treats tag pairs as a single unit. If you delete one tag in the pair, its companion tag and all of the text between them is deleted as well. This is helpful in that it saves you some keystrokes and provides an almost iron-clad guarantee that there will be no stray tags floating around in your document.

> **CAUTION**
>
> When you delete a tag pair, you also delete all text that appears between the two tags. Make sure you cut and paste this text to another position in your document if you don't want to lose it.

When it's time to insert a tag, choose Markup, Insert Element. You can then choose the tag you want to insert from the dialog box that appears. Remember that if Rules Checking is on, you'll be restricted to inserting only those tags that are legal at that point in the document.

The Publish option under the Links menu is handy if you've developed the pages for a site with all hyperlinks pointing to files on your local hard drive, and you need to change those URLs once you place the documents on your server. Once you've validated and saved your documents, you can use the Publish option to prepare your documents for life on the Web server. The Publish dialog box lets you do a search for all URLs that start with the **file:** protocol, and replace them with URLs that start with **http:**.

HTMLed Pro Many of the good stand-alone HTML editors come from outside the United States. HTMLed Pro, developed by Internet Software Technologies in Canada, is an example of such an editor. Featuring extensive toolbar support and a highly customizable editing environment, HTMLed Pro is a very useful tool for both beginning and expert HTML authors.

N O T E The information about HTMLed Pro presented here is based on the demo copy of version 1.1b. You can download the most recent version from Internet Software Technologies by visiting **http://www.ist.ca/**. If you choose to buy HTMLed Pro, the license costs $99.95 (US) plus $10 (US) for shipping and handling. ■

When you first start HTMLed Pro, the editing window is empty. To actually work on an HTML file, you need to start a new one or open an existing one. If you start a new file by choosing File, New, you'll first see a dialog box asking for document structure tags to include in the new file and what comments (author, creation date, and so on) you want included in the file. After you make your selections and click OK, HTMLed Pro creates a new file with the specified tags and comments already inserted (see fig. 22.24).

FIG. 22.24

A newly created document in HTMLed has all of the necessary document structure tags already in place.

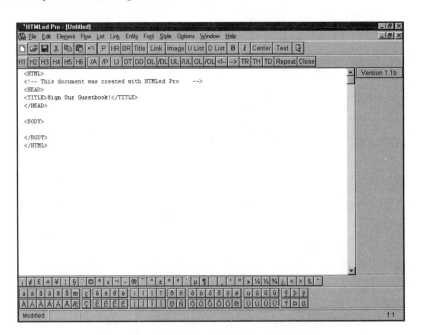

You can also start a new file using an existing document template by choosing File, New with Document Template. Selecting this option opens a dialog box from which you can choose the template you want to use. HTMLed Pro templates end with the .HTT extension.

You have even more options when you go to open an existing file. By choosing File, Open, you open an HTML file on a local drive. More interestingly, there are two ways that you can open files on remote machines. File, Open Remote opens a file on a remote machine using the FTP protocol, and File, Open URL downloads a copy of the HTML file at the URL you specify and opens the copy in the HTMLed Pro window. If you have any files stored in Rich Text Format (RTF), you can choose File, Import RTF option to read it into HTMLed Pro and convert it to HTML.

When you looked at figure 22.24, you probably noticed the abundance of toolbars HTMLed Pro provides. In HTMLed Pro vernacular, toolbars are called "speedbars," referring to the fact that they give you single-click access to many of the program's best functions.

The topmost speedbar in figure 22.24 is called the Standard speedbar. Buttons on the Standard speedbar let you perform common file (New, Open, Save) and editing (Cut, Copy, Paste, Undo) functions, and give you access to the HTML tags used to produce frequently used document features such as paragraph and line breaks, horizontal rules, titles, hyperlinks, images, bulleted lists, definition lists, and bold and italic formatting. The Test button lets you view your work-in-progress by launching a browser program of your choice and loading your file into the browser.

 TIP If you're unsure about what a speedbar button does, place your mouse pointer over the button and look at the status bar at the bottom of the HTMLed Pro window. You'll see a short description of the button's function.

NOTE Many of HTMLed Pro's speedbar keys are labeled with only the contents of HTML tags. For example, the paragraph break button is labeled with a P. This means that if you don't have a decent working knowledge of the basic HTML tags, you may want to use an editor with more descriptive button labels. ■

Just below the Standard speedbar is the Common Tags speedbar, which, as the name suggests, gives you buttons that let you place the most commonly used HTML tags. Specifically, you can insert tags for all six heading styles, closing tags for hyperlinks and paragraphs, tags to create bulleted, numbered, and definition lists, comment tags, and table tags using buttons on this speedbar.

Near the bottom of the screen in figure 22.24, you'll see three other speedbars. The uppermost of the three is called the Extended Characters speedbar. HTML supports all characters in the ISO-Latin character set, but only part of this set is available from your keyboard. By clicking a button on the Extended Characters speedbar, you can insert the appropriate escape sequence to produce the character on the face of the button.

The two speedbars below the Extended Characters speedbar make up the Special Characters speedbar. These two speedbars contain the upper- and lowercase versions of characters that are frequently found in words of languages other than English. If you're coding HTML pages with multilingual content, the Special Characters speedbar will be invaluable.

HTMLed Pro supports one other speedbar that is not visible at program startup. The Custom speedbar can contain up to ten buttons that perform functions you can specify. For example, if you use bold and italics together frequently, you could store both the <B> and <I> tags together on a button on the Custom speedbar. To do this, right-click your mouse on the empty region near the right side of the editing window. This produces the pop-up menu you see in figure 22.25. Choose the New Button option to place on the Custom speedbar a new button entitled "Button 1."

FIG. 22.25
Right-click your mouse in the empty region near the right side of the screen to insert a new button on the Custom speedbar.

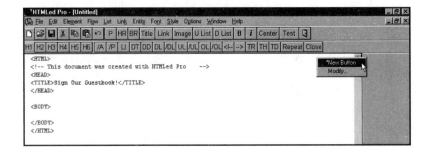

With the button placed, you now need to specify its function. To do this, right-click the Custom speedbar again and choose Modify. This opens a dialog box containing a list of the buttons on the speedbar. Select Button 1 and click Edit to produce the dialog box you see in figure 22.26. In this dialog box, you can give the button its own descriptive name and specify what tags it should place in your document when you click it.

FIG. 22.26
You can specify the name and function of each Custom speedbar button.

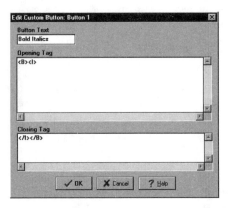

One of HTMLed Pro's best features is its extensive support of tags adopted in HTML 3.2, as well as tags that are Microsoft and Netscape extensions to HTML. If you need to insert such a tag into your document, chances are good that you'll find it under one of HTMLed Pro's menus.

CAUTION
While many HTML editing programs such as HTMLed Pro support HTML 3.2 and Microsoft and Netscape extension tags, several browsers do not. As more of these tags become part of the HTML standard, they should be more widely supported by browsers.

Under the Element menu, you'll find options to launch both the Form and Table Designers. The designers let you compose a form or table right inside the dialog box, and write the HTML to reproduce the file on your Web document once you're done. The Form Designer dialog box, shown in figure 22.27, is particularly easy to use. You just click the form element you want from the menu on the left, and then drag and drop it on the blank region on the right.

FIG. 22.27
HTMLed Pro's Forms Designer makes composing a form as easy as drag-and-drop.

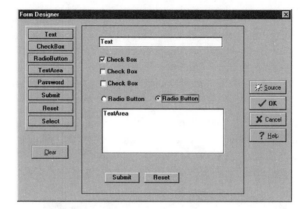

The HTML Page Builder, found under the Options menu, walks you through the creation of your own web page. By asking you questions in a series of dialog boxes, the HTML Page Builder collects information about you and uses it to produce a personal home page.

Another nice feature of HTMLed Pro is that it is highly customizable. In addition to the Custom speedbar, you can also configure up to 26 QuickKeys in which you can store frequently typed text. To configure a QuickKey, choose Options, Preferences to open the HTMLed Pro Setup dialog box. Select the QuickKeys tab in this box to view a list of the QuickKeys and how each is currently defined. HTMLed Pro lets you customize many other aspects of the editing environment as well, including color and typeface of the font used in the editing window, and what elements are available on right-click menus.

When you've finished with a document and are ready to save it, you should first spellcheck it by pressing F7. Once this is done, you have several saving options. You can save the file to a local drive in either DOS or UNIX (no carriage returns) format. You can also choose to Save As Remote to save the file on a remote machine by FTP. Finally, the Save without HTML Tags option strips out all HTML tags from a document, and leaves you with a plain-text file with the document's informational content.

HotDog Pro   Another popular editor from outside the U.S. is HotDog Pro, produced by Sausage Software in Australia. HotDog Pro has become immensely popular with Web authors, owing to its extensive support of HTML 3.2 tags and Netscape and Internet Explorer extensions, its advanced features, and its humorously irreverent interface.

N O T E The following information on HotDog Pro is based on the fully functional, 32-bit demo that you can download from Sausage Software's Web site at **http://www.sausage.com/**. You have 30 days to review the demo. After that, you can pay $99.95 (US) to license HotDog Pro, or let the demo expire. If you choose to pay for a license, Sausage Software will send you a registration number by e-mail, saving you shipping and handling charges. ▪

To download HotDog Pro, direct your browser to **http://www.sausage.com**. Follow the links to the download page and transfer the file HD32.EXE to your machine. Running this executable installs several support files that HotDog needs to run properly. Then download the file HD32INST.EXE (32-bit version for Windows 95) to its own directory on your hard drive and run it. The program unarchives the necessary program files, installs them in the C:\PROGRAM FILES\HOTDOG32 folder, and creates a HotDog item on your Start button.

The first time you run HotDog Pro, you'll see the screen shown in figure 22.28. The most striking feature is the large "toolbone" at the top of the window that gives you single-click access to HotDog Pro's most useful features. You also get a standard document template loaded in your editing window that includes HTML declaration, head, body, and title tags.

FIG. 22.28
HotDog Pro loads a
standard document
template and three
toolbars at start-up.

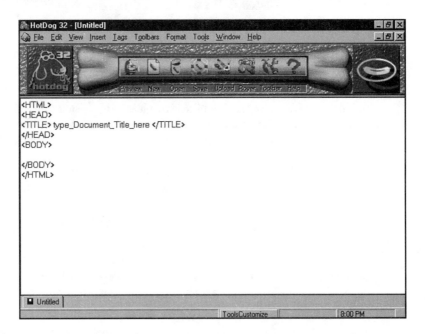

Note the bar just below the horizontal scroll bar in figure 22.28. This is the Documents bar, and it contains a tab for each HTML document you have open. It gives you a quick way to switch between the different files you're working on. You can store several related files together as a *project*.

Immediately below the Documents bar is the Status bar. In addition to the time, the Status bar displays messages that tell you what HotDog Pro is doing at any point.

The project feature of HotDog Pro resides under the File menu. You can open an existing project or use the Project Manager to create a new project. You can also publish your documents from the File menu. Publishing prepares the document for transfer to a Web server on the Internet. You can specify the publishing parameters (like changing all backward slashes (\) to forward slashes (/) in directory path names) under the Publishing tab of the Options dialog box.

The Edit menu supplies the customary editing functions plus a Tag Information option that lets you change the tag associated with a certain type of markup or create your own customized tags. You can also choose to color your HTML tags on-screen from the Edit menu.

The View menu contains just four options:

- The Toolbone option enables you to turn the toolbone at the top of the screen on or off.
- The Tags and Special Characters options launch floating palettes from which you can choose different markup (see fig. 22.29).

FIG. 22.29
The Tags and Special Characters palettes are activated by options under the View menu.

- The Tags palette is extensive and gives you quick access to just about every HTML tag and attribute.
- The Special Characters palette makes it easy to insert reserved and other-than-English language characters.

From the View menu, you can also launch the HotDog File Manager, which is handy for dragging and dropping files into your documents as local hyperlinks, images, or preformatted text.

The Insert menu provides several options for inserting items into your document. You can place Images, Embedded OLE items, Marquees (a Microsoft extension to HTML), Form Elements, Hypertext Targets, Tables, Lists, Horizontal Lines, and Text Files. A Special option lets you insert system-related information like date and time, what version of HotDog Pro you're running, and your name. A special section of the menu is dedicated to inserting hyperlinks of all sorts—to internal anchors, to local files (**file:**), to remote files (**http:**) and to URLs that use other Internet protocols like **ftp:, gopher:,** and **mailto:**.

The Tags menu launches palettes containing sets of related tags. If you're doing lots of image placing, you might want to call up the set of graphics-related tags. Tag groupings include Document, Body, Content, Headings, Attributes, Graphics, Font, Lists, Forms, Tables, and Miscellaneous. You can also customize your own palette with the Custom option.

The Toolbars menu options let you toggle toolbars on and off. The four toolbars listed initially—16-Bit Elements, File and Edit, Text 'n' Stuff, and Tools—are the toolbars that come preconfigured. As you read, you'll discover that you can customize each toolbar to meet your own editing needs.

You can apply different font, document, and alignment formats from the Format menu. You can also apply Bold, Italics, Underline, Center, and Blinking formats to highlighted text. The Big First Letter option gives you an easy way to make the first letter of a word larger than the rest of the letters in the word.

The Tools menu offers several ways to customize the HotDog Pro environment. Choosing Options lets you set parameters on eight different tabs. You can define your own Shortcut Keys and Customize Toolbars from this menu as well (see fig. 22.30). HotDog Pro's HTML syntax checking and spell-checking features are invoked from the Tools menu, as is the Real Time Output Viewer (ROVER), which opens a nearly-WYSIWYG window beneath your editing window.

> **CAUTION**
>
> If you define a shortcut key that is typically assigned to another function, your definition will override the default. However, menu options whose shortcut keys were appropriated will still show the original shortcut key next to them.

> **N O T E**   Because the ROVER window isn't quite true WYSIWYG, you should also check your documents in a separate browser. You can do this by choosing File, Preview Document. ◼

If nothing else, HotDog Pro is easily customized. The Options dialog box alone (choose Tools, Options) lets you specify more than 50 attributes of the editing environment. You can also tailor the toolbars and floating tag insertion palettes to your needs. If you don't like the way something is configured in HotDog Pro, odds are you can find a way to change it.

FIG. 22.30

You can customize each HotDog toolbar button by choosing Tools, Customize Toolbars.

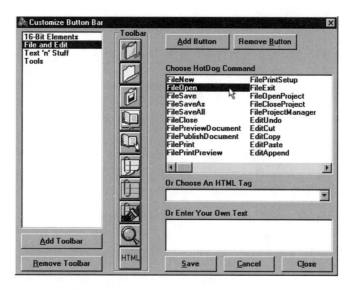

The Project Manager feature of HotDog Pro is a welcome one. A complete Web site is comprised of several documents, not just a few isolated ones. Storing all the documents as a project keeps them grouped together, enabling you to open, close, and save them all at once. Another handy feature is the Project Manager report that checks the whole project for what image files and links are used. You can use the report to make sure that all of your image files get uploaded to your Web server and that all of your links are still valid.

HotDog Pro has many other attractive components as well. Single-click publishing makes it simple to convert your documents for transfer to a UNIX system. The drag-and-drop capabilities of the HotDog Pro File Manager mean easy setup of local links, easy image placement, and insertion of preformatted text. The HTML syntax-check, spell-check, and ROVER features are also helpful tools. ●

## CHAPTER 23

Advanced Graphics

World Wide Web pages benefit from the use of graphic elements, yet sophisticated graphics can significantly slow down the transfer of a site. Developing an attractive and yet responsive site is the focus of this chapter.

You saw in Chapter 21 that Web graphics come in two flavors: GIF (for Graphics Interchange Format), a format developed by CompuServe, and JPEG (for Joint Picture Experts Group). Each format has its merits and drawbacks, and you'll want to choose one or the other based on how you're using images on your pages. Information in this chapter will help you make that choice. Additionally, you will also read about some extensions to standard HTML that give you control over backgrounds and color schemes in your documents. ■

Which file formats are best for your Web site

Many factors go into the choice between GIF and JPEG. Read about them here and make the most informed decisions you can about your Web graphics.

Guidelines to optimize image download time

Users don't like to wait long for images to load. This chapter shares some tips and tricks you can use to minimize image download time.

How to develop and use thumbnail images

Thumbnails are smaller versions of a larger image. Because they are small, the size of the files containing them is small and it doesn't take much time to load them.

How to modify backgrounds and text colors

Very few Web sites make use of the gray background that Internet Explorer uses by default. Instead, they create new backgrounds with colors and images.

How to align images and wrap text

HTML 3.2 permits images that "float" in the left or the right margins so that text may wrap around them.

Developing Graphics for the Web

Developing graphics for use on the World Wide Web is significantly different from designing for the printed page. A closer analogy can be drawn between multimedia and the Web, as visitors to a Web page do not merely read information, but interact with the medium. In order to facilitate this interaction, care must be taken to develop an interface for a Web site that is useful and attractive. The ability to mix graphic elements with text and other media is much more limited in HTML than in other types of multimedia authoring. Often Web pages are limited to the constraints of HTML, which was developed solely as a page description language. Web page designers are also limited by differences in the user's connection to the Internet and choice of browser. Browsers such as Internet Explorer 3 and Netscape Navigator 2 are popular because they support extensions to standard HTML that give Web authors more freedom in page design.

HTML: Page Description Language or Design Tool?

If you've read any of the UseNet newsgroups about HTML authoring, you've probably seen a skirmish or two in the battle to determine if HTML is a page description language or a design tool. A typical exchange might begin with someone asking a question about how he or she might use HTML to accomplish a certain design objective. Those who embrace HTML as a design tool will do their best to answer the person's question, but those who see HTML as a page description language will get up on their soapboxes and decry such an effort. Amid all of this bickering, you might be wondering who is right or, at least, who occupies the moral high ground.

Remember that standard HTML is a document type definition of SGML. Thus, standard HTML is *intended* to be a page description language. In the early days of the Web, HTML was used in a way consistent with this intent. As the Web became more popular, creative Web authors began to develop ways to use HTML that strayed from the original intent. It was at this point that HTML started to become more of a design tool.

The Microsoft and Netscape extensions to standard HTML have fueled the tendency toward design uses. These extensions allow Web authors to create very dynamic and attractive pages. As users became accustomed to seeing these extensions used on Web pages, there was no turning back. Thus, while standard HTML was still intended to be a page description language, *extended HTML* became the key tool in developing creative and engaging Web documents.

So, which is right? The answer is neither. It's up to you to consider the merits of both philosophies and adopt the one that's right for you. If you see HTML as a page description language, that's fine as long as you're able to cope with all of the design-related HTML extensions springing up all around you. If you use HTML as a design tool, that's fine, too, and you won't have to worry about being hauled away by the "HTML Police" or some such fanatical group.

Options for Developing Your Own Images

There are a number of excellent software products on the market for developing graphics. While shopping for these, pay particular attention to those designed specifically for working with graphics for the screen. As mentioned previously, developing images for print and for screen involves two separate issues.

Graphics programs are usually designed to produce either vector or raster image files. *Vector files* contain mathematical equations describing the makeup of the image. These equations describe the relationship between objects in the image. For this reason, vector graphics are frequently used for Computer Aided Design (CAD) and images that contain distinct geometric shapes. Vector graphics were developed to print cleanly, much like the PostScript fonts. *Raster files*, also known as bitmapped graphics, store information about the individual placement and color of pixels in the image. Bitmapped graphics are primarily developed to be viewed on the computer screen. Printing bitmapped graphics is similar to printing bitmapped fonts—they appear more jagged around the edges than their vector counterparts.

The image files currently supported by Internet Explorer 3 are all bitmapped graphics files. For this reason, it is recommended that you purchase a graphics program that is capable of developing bitmapped images. The most popular graphics program for the World Wide Web is Adobe Photoshop. This piece of software has been the leading graphics design package for years due to its ability to produce original bitmapped images and also touch up existing images. Additionally, there are many plug-in programs and filters that work with Photoshop to produce specialized effects. This power comes with a price though, as a single-user license for Photoshop can set you back as much as $1,000.

Options for Using Existing Images

Often you will want to use on your site graphics and images that have already been developed. For example, you may want to include a professionally designed logo on your company home page, or maybe a photo of your dog on a personal profile Web page. These images may have to be converted to a digital format and possibly retouched in an image processing program before they can be used on the Web. There are a number of options available to help you with this process.

Desktop Scanners   A growing number of relatively inexpensive (under $600) scanners on the market can capture photographs, line art, transparencies, slides, prints, and other two-dimensional images. Once captured, these images can be enhanced and resized in an image processing program such as Photoshop or Paintshop Pro, and saved in a format that can be used with graphical browsers.

Service Bureaus   A graphics service bureau or color separation house can scan images with a much higher degree of precision than is possible with desktop scanners. Some of these agencies may also convert your existing files to formats used on the World Wide Web. The use of a service bureau is generally the most expensive option for converting images to digital formats. Prices vary considerably for individual services and between different locations in the country. You should explore the other possibilities first; if there is a particular need to have a high-resolution image scanned for your site, contact a number of service bureaus for price quotes.

Kodak PhotoCD   If the images you want to use are photographs, slides, or negatives, and you do not have access to a desktop scanner, consider having them placed on a PhotoCD. This method does require that you have an extended architecture CD-ROM drive and software capable of reading this type of compact disc; most dual-speed, multisession CD-ROM drives are compatible with this standard. Check the documentation of your graphics software to see if it can read the image format used for this process. PhotoCDs are capable of holding up to a hundred photographs on each CD-ROM. The photos are scanned and saved on the CD in five different resolutions, ranging from 128×192 pixels to 2048×3072 pixels. PhotoCDs can be ordered just about anywhere you can have prints made. The compact disc itself costs between $10 and $20, and each photo added to the CD costs between $1 and $2.

Digital Cameras   A number of cameras have appeared on the market in recent years that record images directly to disk in a digital format. These cameras are still relatively expensive, averaging around $700, and the images produced are generally of lower quality than photographs converted by one of the previous scanning methods. The advantage to using digital cameras is the fact that they store the photographs directly in a digital format, and the photos can be used immediately.

Stock Photo and Clipart CDs   This option allows you to work with images that are already in a digital format. As a last resort, stock photo and clipart collections allow you to include some graphical elements into your Web pages where there would otherwise be none. There are a number of sites on the Web where you can download individual images or libraries of clipart in file formats ready to use for your own site. For instance, Barry's Clip Art Server at **http:// ns2.clever.net/~graphics/clip_art/clipart.html** archives a number clipart collections. When using clipart from the World Wide Web or from CD-ROM, always read the copyright notice; although most can be used royalty-free, some require payment or simple acknowledgment.

Image File Formats

World Wide Web browsers support a limited number of file formats for inline images, and not all browsers are capable of displaying every type of image format within the same window as the HTML document. The two most popular formats supported by Internet Explorer 3 and most other graphical browsers are GIF and JPEG.

GIF Images

The GIF format was originally developed by CompuServe as a standard for storing and transmitting images. GIF is an 8-bit format, meaning that GIF images are limited to 256 (2^8) colors. The current GIF specification is GIF89a, released by CompuServe in 1990.

How GIF Works   Image data in GIF format is organized into related blocks and subblocks that can be used to reproduce the graphic. When transmitting a GIF, a program called an *encoder* is used to produce a GIF data stream of control and data blocks that are sent along to the destination machine. There, a program called a *decoder* parses the data stream and assembles the image.

GIF employs a compression scheme called *LZW compression* to reduce the amount of data it needs to send to describe the image completely. LZW compression works best on simple images such as line drawings or graphics with only few distinct colors. For more color-rich images, LZW is less efficient, producing compression ratios of around 2:1 or less.

When To Use GIF Images   GIF is the most popular format for inline images because it is supported by all graphical browsers. It is also the only format that supports transparent backgrounds, interlaced display, and animation. The GIF format is best suited for the following types of images:

- Black-and-white line art and text
- Images with a limited number of distinct colors
- Graphics that have sharp or distinct edges (most menus, buttons, and graphs fit this category)
- Graphics that are overlaid with text

The images you see on the Web page in figure 23.1 are all GIFs.

JPEG Images

The JPEG (Joint Picture Experts Group) format refers to a set of standards for compressing full-color or grayscale still images. JPEG's ability to work with full-color images (24 bits per pixel, 16.7 million colors) makes it preferable to the GIF format (8 bits per pixel, 256 colors) for working with photographs, especially nature-related art, where the entire color spectrum is in play.

How JPEG Works   JPEG can handle so many colors in a relatively small file because it *compresses* the image data. You can control how big or small the image file ultimately is by adjusting the parameters of the compression. A highly compressed file can be very small, but the quality of the image on-screen will suffer for it.

FIG. 23.1

Logos, line art, and buttons are best stored as GIFs.

When you decompress a JPEG image, there is always some amount of *loss,* meaning the image will not look exactly the way it did originally. Fortunately, JPEG's compression/decompression scheme is such that the lost image data is in the higher color frequencies, where it is harder for the human eye to detect the differences. In spite of this loss, you can still use JPEG to achieve compression levels of about 10:1 or 20:1 without appreciable change in the image. This means you've changed from storing 24 bits per pixel to 1 or 2 bits per pixel—very impressive savings! As noted previously, you can take the compression ratios even higher, but as you do, the loss becomes more and more detectable.

When To Use JPEG Images The JPEG format is best suited for the following types of images:

- Scanned photographs and ray-traced renderings
- Images that contain a complex mixture of colors
- Any image that requires more than a 256-color palette

CAUTION

Because the compression computations work better with a continuum of color, JPEGs are not well suited to images that have very sharp color changes.

The photograph you see in figure 23.2 is stored as a JPEG image.

For more information on GIF, JPEG, and other image formats, consult the World Wide Web FAQ at **http://www.boutell.com/faq/**.

FIG. 23.2
JPEG's support of full color makes it desirable for storing photographs.

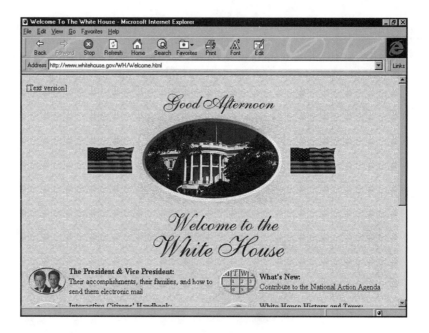

Desirable Effects for Web Graphics

Beyond the way they store image data, both GIF and JPEG support different effects that are desirable on Web pages. *Interlaced GIFs* and *progressive JPEGs* (p-JPEGs) both behave in pretty much the same way—both types of image "fade in" to the page, allowing the viewer to get a sense of what the entire image is without having to wait for all of the image data to load. In a *transparent GIF*, one color is specified as transparent so that the background can show through. An *animated GIF* file stores several images that the browser presents in sequence to render an animation on the screen. The next few sections discuss how you can create each of these effects with your image file.

Using Interlaced GIFs   During download, a GIF file that is saved without the interlaced option appears in the Internet Explorer window starting with the top of the image and filling down as it is received and decoded. Internet Explorer 3 has been enhanced to take advantage of interlaced GIFs. An interlaced GIF stores the image in a sequence of nonadjacent sets, or what you might think of as layers. Internet Explorer begins to process and display the image as it is received, which results in a gradual emergence of the image. Because the whole image appears on the screen in sections, rather than gradually filling in from the top down, viewers can see much of the image before the download is complete.

Part
IV

Ch
23

You can convert images to interlaced GIFs by using a number of commercial and shareware programs. The shareware program LView Pro, developed by Leonardo Loureiro, includes the option to open a number of common file formats and save them as interlaced GIFs. The file formats that can be converted to and from GIFs and JPEGs using LView Pro include JPEG, Windows bitmap, OS/2 bitmap, GIF, TARGA, PCX, PPM, and TIFF. To convert images to interlaced GIFs in LView Pro, perform the following steps:

1. Open LView Pro by double-clicking its icon.

2. Choose File, Open; in the Open Image dialog box, highlight the image file you want to convert. Click OK.

3. Once the image is open, choose File, Properties, select the GIF tab, and check the box titled Save Interlaced (see fig. 23.3).

FIG. 23.3
LView Pro makes it easy to save an image as an interlaced GIF.

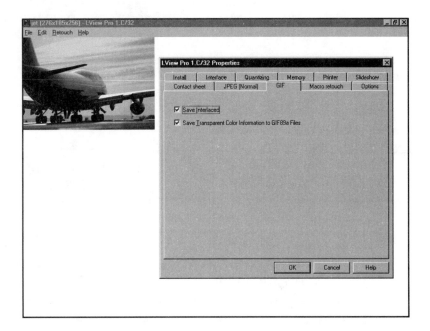

4. Save the image as an interlaced GIF by selecting File, Save As. In the Save Image As dialog box, rename your image with the .GIF extension and select the GIF89a file type. Then click the Save button.

The image is now saved as an interlaced GIF.

Using Transparent GIFs You were introduced to transparent GIFs back in Chapter 22 when you looked at figure 21.2. That screen is replicated here in figure 23.4. In the nontransparent image, the bounding box around the oval shows up against the white background. The transparent version of the same image designated the color of the bounding box to be transparent, allowing the white background to show through. This gives the oval the appearance of floating on the background.

FIG. 23.4

Nontransparent and transparent versions of the same image.

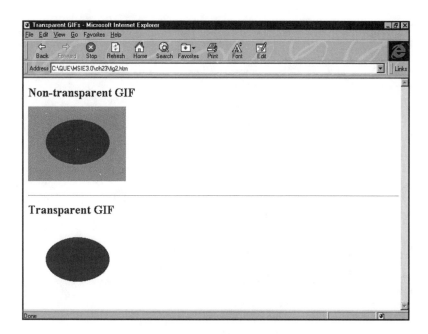

As with interlaced GIFs, there is a number of shareware utilities that convert images to transparent GIFs. To do so using LView Pro, follow these steps:

1. Open LView Pro by double-clicking its icon.

2. Choose File, Open; in the Open Image dialog box, highlight the image file you want to convert, and then click OK.

3. Select Retouch, Color Depth. To save as a GIF, your image must be a palette image. Converting from True Color to Palette Image in LView changes the color depth of your image to a maximum of 256 colors. In the Color Depth dialog box, select the Palette Image radio button (see fig. 23.5). Next you see options for palette creation and quantizing. Select 256 colors, uncheck the Dithering option, and click OK.

N O T E A GIF image can contain up to 256 different colors specified in its color lookup table. In order to convert images with more than 256 colors in LView Pro, you must first select the Palette image option to create a 256-color lookup table for the image. It is best to use the 256 colors (including Windows Palette) option when creating the palette unless you are sure that your image will look acceptable in 16 colors or in black and white.

Often in the process of creating a 256-color palette for an image, some colors in the original do not find a perfect match. The Enable Floyd-Steinberg Dithering option instructs LView Pro to recolor an image using a technique that creates the look of more colors than the image actually has. Dithering should be avoided if possible, because more complex images take longer to download. ▪

FIG. 23.5

You need to convert
your image to a palette
image before saving it
as a transparent GIF.

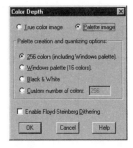

4. Now you're ready to identify the transparent color. Select Retouch, Background Color, and you'll see the Select Color Palette Entry dialog box. This window provides you with the color palette used by the image (see fig. 23.6).

FIG. 23.6

The Select Color Palette
Entry dialog box shows
you all of the colors
used in the image.

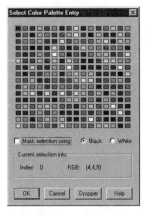

5. If you can identify the color you want to make transparent, click that color once in the Select Color Palette Entry dialog box, and check the Mask selection box with either the White or the Black option. This masks your selection with either black or White, which enables you to see if the correct color for transparency was chosen. Don't be alarmed, the mask does not change the color of your image—it's just a helpful way of showing you the transparent selection.

6. If you have trouble seeing the exact color you want to make transparent, click the Dropper button in the Select Color Palette Entry dialog box. The dropper, shown in figure 23.7, allows you to click the image directly to indicate where you want the color to be transparent. Be careful: When the dropper is clicked, it disappears from the screen. However, the color that you clicked will be highlighted in the Select Color Palette Entry dialog box. You can test it by masking the selected color with black or white. If this is the correct color, choose OK; otherwise select the Dropper button again and click the desired color.

7. To save the image as a transparent GIF, select File, Save As; in the Save Image As dialog box, select the GIF89a file type. Click Save to save the file.

FIG. 23.7
The Dropper lets you sample pixels in the image to help you determine which color should be designated as the transparent color.

Dropper

More information about transparent and interlaced GIFs can be found on the Transparent/Interlaced GIF Resource Page, at **http://dragon.jpl.nasa.gov/~adam/transparent.html**.

> **CAUTION**
> When creating images to be used as transparent GIFs, be sure that the desired transparent color is used only in those areas you want to be transparent.

Using Animated GIFs   You can create simple animations using GIF files as well. The GIF89a standard allows you to store all the images that make up the animation in the same file. When a decoder detects a file with multiple images, it decodes and presents them in sequence to produce the animation.

In addition to storing the individual frames of the animation, the GIF file can also contain information on how to present the frames. You can specify parameters such as the following:

- How much delay there should be between frames
- Waiting for user input before starting the animation
- Whether or not you want the last frame of the animation to stay on the screen

More and more programs are becoming available to help you prepare your GIF animations. You can check out **http://www.mindworkshop.com/alchemy/alchemy.html** to learn more about Alchemy Mindworks GIF Construction Set for Windows. The program is easy to use and will cost you only about $10 to register. For general information about animated GIFs, as well as links to other software tools, visit **http://members.aol.com/royalef/gifanim.htm**.

N O T E   A browser must be fully compliant with the GIF89a standard to decode an animated GIF properly. ■

Converting Images to Progressive JPEGs   Internet Explorer 3 includes support for a recent implementation of JPEG compression called the *progressive JPEG*. Not too long ago, use of inline JPEG images was limited to simple, or baseline, JPEGs. Baseline JPEGs store the image information as a top-to-bottom scan of the image. Baseline JPEGs appear in the Internet Explorer window beginning at the top of the image and fill downward as image data is received. The progressive JPEG is similar to the interlaced GIF, in that the image is stored as a series of scans. The first scan, or layer, of a progressive JPEG appears in the Internet Explorer window as soon as the download begins.

The advantage of using progressive JPEG images in your Web site is that viewers of your page will begin to see the full image in rough detail as soon as the download begins. Existing baseline JPEGs must, however, be converted to the progressive format to take advantage of its features. To save images with progressive JPEG compression in LView Pro, follow these simple steps:

1. Open LView Pro by double-clicking its icon.

2. Choose File, Open; in the Open Image dialog box, highlight the image file you want to convert, and then click OK.

3. When the image is open, choose File, Properties, JPEG (Normal), and check the Progressive compression box, as shown in figure 23.8.

FIG. 23.8
Choose the Progressive Compression option on the JPEG tab of the LView Properties dialog box to save a file as a p-JPEG.

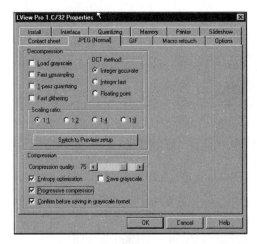

4. To save the image as a progressive JPEG, select File, Save As; in the Save Image As dialog box, select the JPEG file type.

For more information on JPEG, consult the JPEG image compression FAQ, at **http://www.cis.ohio-state.edu/hypertext/faq/usenet/jpeg-faq/top.html**.

Bandwidth Considerations for Image Use

When designing images for use on the Web, it's important to think about who the end user is and what type of setup he or she will use for viewing your pages. Basic information relating to who is accessing your site can usually be found in the HTTP log maintained by your server software. This log file records data about each visitor to your site. Log file statistics are generally no more than the date and time of access and the user's IP address. More sophisticated log programs can track what browser users are using to view your site. Unfortunately, no log program can capture information about the user's Internet connection, computer system, or monitor size and settings, all of which are important to consider when developing the graphics for your site.

A number of demographic reports and surveys have been published to present a better understanding of the typical Web surfer. These findings reveal the following:

- Over 90 percent are using graphical browsers.
- There is a fairly even distribution of Windows, Macintosh, and UNIX users.
- Most users have a 14-inch monitor with a 256-color palette.

Guidelines for Image Sizes

Because the majority of users are set up to view Web pages on a 14-inch monitor capable of displaying a 256-color palette, you should consider that to be the standard for designing graphics for your site. The typical screen size of a 14-inch monitor is 640 pixels wide by 480 pixels high. When developing images to fit within this size, you should first consider that the user's browser will take up part of that viewing area. Depending on how it is configured, a browser may leave as little as 600×400 pixels as the viewing area. As a general rule, any image on your site should fit within these dimensions. Images larger than this will not fit on most users' screens. They will also take longer to transfer.

Using the Image Tag with *HEIGHT* and *WIDTH* Attributes

One way to reduce the amount of time someone waits for your inline graphics to load is to tell the browser the size of the image in advance. Internet Explorer uses this information when determining the page layout; when it receives an HTML document, it spends a bit of time figuring out where to place the different elements on the screen. By knowing the exact dimensions of an incoming graphic element, Internet Explorer can immediately lay out the text areas relative to where the graphic will eventually be.

In Chapter 21, you learned that the <IMG> tag can take the extended attributes WIDTH and HEIGHT. The height and width of an image are measured in pixels. The <IMG> tag that places an image with a height of 250 pixels and a width of 332 pixels would be written as follows:

```
<IMG SRC="URL" WIDTH=332 HEIGHT=250>
```

It doesn't matter whether the HEIGHT or WIDTH attribute comes first, but they should both be included to expedite the layout of the page.

You can use any number of software programs to determine the dimensions of an inline image. Most professional paint and draw programs provide information about the dimensions of an open document. You may, however, have to change the preferences in a specific program to show the dimensional units in pixels rather than inches or centimeters. Check the user manual for the specific paint program you are using to determine a document's height and width information.

LView Pro can be used to determine the height and width of an image in pixel coordinates in the following way:

1. Open LView Pro by double-clicking its icon.

2. Choose File, Open; in the Open Image dialog box, highlight the image you want to measure.

3. When the image is open, choose Edit, Resize (Ctrl+R). You will see the Resize Image dialog box shown in figure 23.9. The size of the open image is reported in pixels at the top of this dialog box. The image width is the first number, followed by the height.

FIG. 23.9
It's easy to determine the width and height in pixels of an image using LView Pro.

 When you have determined the size of an image, write it down on a scrap of paper or add it to your HTML document immediately. Don't just write down something like 137×281; you'll risk forgetting which number is the height and which is the width. Getting these numbers reversed will change the shape of your image on the Internet Explorer screen.

N O T E   Text is transferred much more quickly than images are. If width and height information is included for images, Internet Explorer will begin to layout text as soon as it is received. You should always include the width and height of an inline image in the HTML of the page so the reader can read the text while the image is loading. Paying attention to download time will increase the satisfaction of those who visit your Web site. ■

Using and Developing Thumbnail Images

Thumbnail images on a Web page are small representations of larger graphics (see fig. 23.10). They are particularly useful on index pages as graphical links to the full-sized image. Because of the reduced size, thumbnails transfer to a user's browser more quickly than the full-sized graphics.

FIG. 23.10

Thumbnails are smaller versions of a large image that take less time to load and less room on the screen.

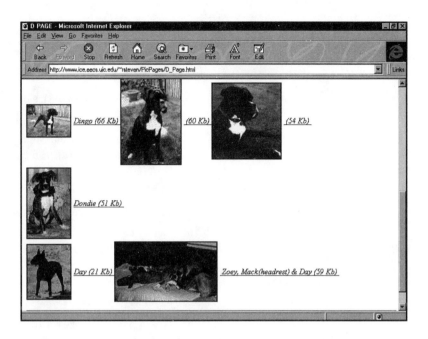

The easiest way to create a thumbnail is to reduce the size of the original image in a paint or image processing program. Photoshop and other image processing packages do an excellent job of proportionately reducing the size of an image. Many of the lower-end paint programs have options to scale images; however the result will most likely not produce a professional-looking image.

LView Pro does an excellent job of resizing images for use as thumbnails. To produce a thumbnail image in LView Pro, follow these steps:

1. Open LView Pro by double-clicking its icon.

2. Choose File, Open; in the Open Image dialog box, highlight the image from which you will create a thumbnail.

3. When the image is open, choose Edit, Resize (Ctrl+R). You will see the Resize Image Window shown in figure 23.9. The size of the original image is reported in pixels at the top of this dialog box. The image width is the first number, followed by the height. To change the height or width of the image, simply type the height or width of the desired thumbnail image or use the slider bars below New Size/Current Size Ratio to adjust the percent of scaling. Be careful to check the Preserve Aspect Ratio option if you want the image to be reduced in size proportionally.

4. Save the thumbnail image as either a GIF or JPEG by choosing File, Save as, and rename the image.

TIP

If the images you want to make thumbnails of are photographs, consider having them put on a Kodak PhotoCD. This process not only scans the images into digital files, but also provides you with duplicates of the images in a number of sizes.

Internet Explorer 3 lets you adjust the size of an image simply by changing the HEIGHT and WIDTH attributes in the <IMG> tag. Although this could be used to decrease the size of an image on the screen, the entire graphic must still be transferred to the user's browser. If your goal is to decrease the frustration time of potential viewers, this method will not help.

The image HEIGHT and WIDTH attributes can be used to alter the size of an image in the following ways:

- To reduce the size of an inline image, make its height and width proportionately smaller. For instance, an image 200 pixels high by 200 pixels wide can be displayed at half this size in the following way:

  <IMG SRC="*URL*" HEIGHT=100 WIDTH=100>

  This image will appear on a viewer's Internet Explorer screen at half its original size.

- To increase the size of an inline image, make its height and width proportionately larger. For instance, the same 200 by 200 image can be displayed at twice this size in the following way:

  <IMG SRC="*URL*" HEIGHT=400 WIDTH=400>

  The image will appear on a viewer's Internet Explorer screen at twice its original size.

- It is also possible to increase or decrease an image size relative to the viewer's Internet Explorer window. In this case, the percent of increase or decrease is provided for either the HEIGHT or the WIDTH or for both. For instance, an image can be displayed at half of Internet Explorer's window height in the following way:

  <IMG SRC="*URL*" HEIGHT=50%>

  The image in this case will occupy 50 percent of the height of the window. The width will remain proportional to the height of the image, not to the window size. Similarly, the following will occupy 50 percent of the width of the window:

  <IMG SRC="*URL*" WIDTH=50%>

  The height will remain proportional to the width of the image, not to the window size. Finally, the following will occupy 50 percent of the height and 50 percent of the width of the Internet Explorer window:

  <IMG SRC="*URL*" HEIGHT=50% WIDTH=50%>

CAUTION

Changing the aspect of an image with both a WIDTH and a HEIGHT percent will most likely distort your image.

Making Use of Cached Images

The Internet Explorer cache allows repeated images to appear more quickly than they did when they were first loaded. The browser's ability to store recent items can be used to decrease download time for graphics by using the same images on each page of your site for things such as title bars, menus, buttons, and bullets.

As you develop graphics for your Web site, consider taking advantage of the browser's cache. When Internet Explorer downloads an image during a session, it keeps a copy of that image in its cache. Subsequent requests for that image result in a faster display, because the image is now stored in the cache and doesn't have to be transferred from the server.

Images that appear on multiple pages on your site should be developed to take advantage of the viewer's cache. Designing shared navigation items such as menu buttons and image maps common to all pages not only increases the ease of use, but also decreases the amount of time a viewer will spend waiting for images to load.

Part
IV
Ch
23

 To best keep track of images used on your Web site, it is best to keep them all in a common images directory. This practice can help eliminate multiple copies of the same image that can slow down your site by not taking advantage of the user's cache to store images.

Design Tips for Graphical Web Pages

When developing graphical Web pages for Internet Explorer, you can take advantage of extensions to HTML that affect the background and text of your page. Table 23.1 lists the extensions to the <BODY> tag that include the use of background images and colors, as well as the designation of text and link colors. HTML extensions such as these make it easier to design pages that have visual impact. Chapter 28, "Creating a World-Class Web Site for Internet Explorer," further explores the use of background images and techniques that are used in first-rate Web sites.

Table 23.1 Extensions to the *<BODY>* Tag

Attribute	Result
BACKGROUND	Loads an image to use as a background
BGCOLOR	Specifies the browser's background color
BGPROPERTIES	Allows background to be fixed (nonscrolling)
TEXT	Specifies the text color
LINK	Specifies the link color
ALINK	Specifies the active link color
VLINK	Specifies the visited link color

Using Backgrounds and Text Colors

A welcome set of improvements to assist graphical development is the development of extensions to the <BODY> tag. With Internet Explorer, it is possible for the designer of a Web page to distinguish the color and appearance of a page in the end user's window, as well as specify the document's text and link colors. Most of the <BODY> attributes make use of the viewer's browser to change the page's appearance, thereby costing no more download time for viewing. The BACKGROUND attribute is an exception to the rule; it requires the use of an image to display as a background.

The *BACKGROUND* Attribute   Internet Explorer and a growing number of graphical World Wide Web browsers support the BACKGROUND attribute of the <BODY> tag. As mentioned previously, this extension instructs the browser to use an image as a background for a page. A GIF or JPEG image is specified in the tag in the following way:

```
<BODY BACKGROUND="URL">
...
</BODY>
```

In this, *URL* is the URL of the background image file.

An image used as the background is tiled across and down the viewer's window. Because they are tiled in this fashion, background images must be created to appear in the browser's window without visible connection points—their edges must appear seamless. Textured graphics can be made seamless with the help of image processing software such as Photoshop. There are also a growing number of Web sites dedicated to background images, and many of the better ones include high-quality seamless images you can download and use on your own site. Figure 23.11 shows Netscape's background image page, at **http://home.netscape.com/assist/ net_sites/bg/backgrounds.html**.

N O T E   Background images need to be downloaded before the rest of the page is displayed. To minimize download time, always use the smallest image possible for backgrounds. A 100×100 pixel image should be the largest background image used. ■

T I P   Background images—such as an inline image—are stored in Internet Explorer's cache. You can increase access time to your site by using a common background image for all pages.

The *BGCOLOR* Attribute   The BGCOLOR attribute of the <BODY> tag is also understood by Internet Explorer. It differs from the BACKGROUND attribute in that the BGCOLOR changes the background color of a viewer's browser window. This attribute does not require Internet Explorer to download and tile an image. For this reason, use of the BGCOLOR changes the window's background color immediately upon receiving the HTML tag, and doesn't delay layout of the document.

You use the BGCOLOR in the <BODY> tag in the following way:

```
<BODY BGCOLOR="#RRGGBB">
...
</BODY>
```

"#RRGGBB" refers to the hexadecimal color triplet that described the color you want the background to be. The contribution of red to the desired color occupies the first two digits, followed by two for green and two for blue. Each of these two-color components must consist of one of

16 characters—numbers 0 through 9 followed by A through F—where 0 is the lowest value and F is the highest.

FIG. 23.11
Several background images are publicly available from Netscape's Web site.

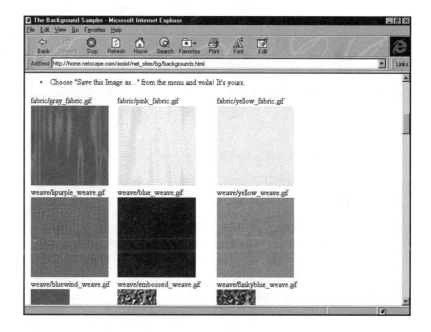

Table 23.2 outlines eight basic color combinations in hexadecimal code.

Table 23.2   Hexadecimal RGB Triplets

Color	Code
White	#FFFFFF
Red	#FF0000
Green	#00FF00
Blue	#0000FF
Cyan	#00FFFF
Magenta	#FF00FF
Yellow	#FFFF00
Black	#000000

Using *BGCOLOR* **and** *BACKGROUND* **Together**   If you use both BGCOLOR and BACKGROUND together, Internet Explorer will immediately render the background with the color specified by BGCOLOR. Later, when the BACKGROUND file has been loaded, Internet Explorer tiles the file and replaces the BGCOLOR. Knowing that the BGCOLOR will be displayed first, many Web authors choose to use a BGCOLOR that is similar to the dominant color in the BACKGROUND image file. This way, the BGCOLOR is displayed immediately and creates a smoother transition to the BACKGROUND image, since the two are alike. Without BGCOLOR, the default gray background would appear first, followed by the BACKGROUND image—a transition that can be harsh to the user's eyes. Also, if the BACKGROUND image fails to load, then the BGCOLOR will be present, giving an approximation of the color you wanted.

Text and Link Attributes   In addition to controlling the background color of a user's browser, it is possible to change the text and link colors. These extensions to the <BODY> tag use the same hexadecimal triplet scheme as BGCOLOR to describe colors. The attribute for changing the color of a document's text is TEXT followed by a specific color code. For example, to change a document's body text to green, the <BODY> tag would read as follows:

```
<BODY TEXT="#00FF00">
...
</BODY>
```

Similarly, colors can be assigned to hyperlinks—both hypertext and the border that surrounds a hyperlinked image. LINK specifies the color to be used for links that have not been visited. The ALINK attribute is the color a link momentarily flashes as it is clicked, or activated. VLINK is a link that has previously been visited.

An example of the <BODY> tag with all attributes designated—BGCOLOR set to black, TEXT set to white, LINK set to yellow, ALINK set to magenta, and VLINK set to green—is written as follows:

```
<BODY BGCOLOR="#000000" TEXT="#FFFFFF" LINK="#FFFF00" ALINK="#FF00FF"
VLINK="#00FF00">
...
</BODY>
```

There are many excellent resources on the World Wide Web for previewing colors in hexadecimal code. Consult the following references on the World Wide Web for more information on background colors and images:

- Controlling Document Backgrounds, at **http://home.netscape.com/assist/ net_sites/bg/index.html**
- Yahoo's Index on Backgrounds, at **http://www.yahoo.com/ Computers_and_Internet/Internet/World_Wide_Web/Programming/ Backgrounds/**
- Background Color Index, at **http://www.infi.net/wwwimages/colorindex.html**

Image Alignment and Wrapping Text Around Images

Internet Explorer recognizes extended values of the ALIGN attribute of the <IMG> tag that allow you to create very sophisticated pages. Specifically, the LEFT and RIGHT values of ALIGN produce *floating images* and make it easy to wrap text around an image. Figure 23.12 shows an image floated in the left and right margins with text centered in the open margin next to the image.

FIG. 23.12

The LEFT and RIGHT values of ALIGN let you float images in the margins and wrap text around them.

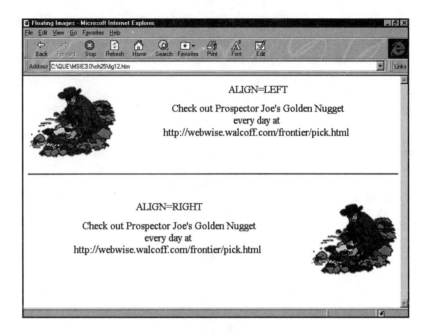

Part
IV

Ch
23

N O T E Only one value of the ALIGN attribute can be used with each image. If two or more are included with the IMG tag, only the first one in the line will be used. ■

The ability to float images and wrap text around them is important to developing both an attractive and useful site, as the World Wide Web was not initially developed with screen layout in mind. Prior to these attributes, using inline images with text resulted in a linear-looking page. Now it is possible to dictate the position of images with respect to text elements.

To wrap text around an image on a Web page it is necessary to use one of the ALIGN attributes with the <IMG> tag. The desired text should then be included immediately after the <IMG> tag. The result will vary with the attributes, as follows:

- ■ ALIGN=LEFT causes the image to align with the left margin of Internet Explorer's window; text following this tag wraps to the right of the floating image.

- ■ ALIGN=RIGHT causes the image to align with the right margin of Internet Explorer's window; text following this tag wraps to the left of the floating image.

To get good results with floating images with text requires practice with extensions to the <BR> tag. The basic <BR> tag employed with text following an ALIGN attribute will merely break the line without stopping the effect of the floating image. In order to break the line and clear the margin to the right or left of the floating image, you must use one of the extensions to the <BR> tag. These attributes are outlined in Table 23.3. The <BR> tag with a CLEAR attribute is used at the point where you want to clear the right or left margin of a floating image. For example, if you aligned an image on the left with text wrapped to the right, it would be necessary to clear the left margin before another element could be placed there (see figs. 23.13 and 23.14). The HTML to produce figure 23.13 is:

```
<IMG SRC="http://webwise.walcoff.com/images/joepanning.gif" ALIGN=LEFT>
<CENTER>
<H2>Prospector Joe</H2>
</CENTER>
<BR CLEAR=LEFT>
<P>
<IMG SRC="http://webwise.walcoff.com/images/joehorse.gif">
```

Figure 23.14 is produced by the same code without the `<BR CLEAR=LEFT>` tag.

FIG. 23.13

The `CLEAR` attribute of the `<BR>` tag moves to the first clear left or right margin before continuing to lay out page elements.

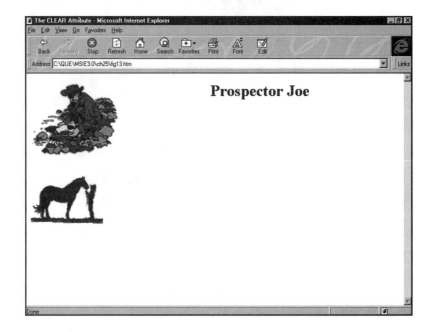

When in doubt as to which `CLEAR` attribute to use, begin with `CLEAR=ALL`. This clears both margins and allows you safely to add new elements to the page.

**Table 23.3   Extensions to the _
_ Tag**

Attribute	Result
CLEAR=RIGHT	Breaks the line and clears the right margin
CLEAR=LEFT	Breaks the line and clears the left margin
CLEAR=ALL	Breaks the line and clears both margins

CAUTION

Aligning two images on the same margin without the appropriate `<BR>` attribute in between will cause one image to appear on top of the other.

FIG. 23.14

With the CLEAR attribute, the next page element is placed alongside the floating image.

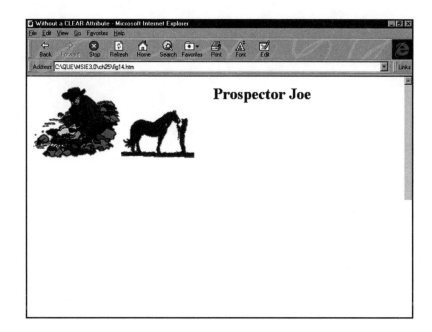

## CHAPTER 24

Using Imagemaps

In Chapter 23, you learned how to make a *hypergraphic*—an image you could click to jump to a different URL. If you've visited many Web sites though, you've probably encountered hypergraphics that seem to take the "clickable image" concept a step further. Specifically, this type of image sends you to one of many different URLs depending on where you click. This type of multiple-linked image is called an *imagemap*.

When imagemaps were introduced, only one kind was available: the server-side imagemap. Depending on what server software your server was running, you may have had to make slight modifications in how you set up the imagemap, but an interaction with the server was always necessary to make the map work. Today, two kinds of imagemap are available: server-side and client-side. Client-side imagemaps are now officially part of the HTML standard, even though people have been making use of them with browsers such as Internet Explorer 3 that can correctly process them.

This chapter focuses on how you can develop imagemaps for your own Web pages and what tools are available to help you. ■

The advantages and disadvantages of using imagemaps

While imagemaps are immensely popular with most Web users, not everyone has a browser that lets them fully appreciate an imagemap.

How to choose an appropriate imagemap graphic

Learn some tips on creating an imagemap that's functional and intuitive.

How to implement server-side imagemaps

Server-side imagemaps are the "original" type of Web imagemap.

How to implement client-side imagemaps

Two types of client-side imagemap were proposed for HTML 3.0 and one was adopted as part of HTML 3.2. You can read about each of them here.

How to use imagemap utility programs to create and test map files

Imagemap utilities take much of the tedium out of preparing an imagemap.

What Are Imagemaps?

Imagemaps allow for a friendly way for users to go to Web pages by pointing and clicking in a picture. One of the big advantages of the Web over other Internet-related stores of information is that it's graphically oriented, which makes it more approachable and intuitive. Instead of bland text menus, such as with Gopher clients, with imagemaps users can see what they want to get information on (see fig. 24.1).

FIG. 24.1

Imagemaps give users a graphical representation of what they're able to link to.

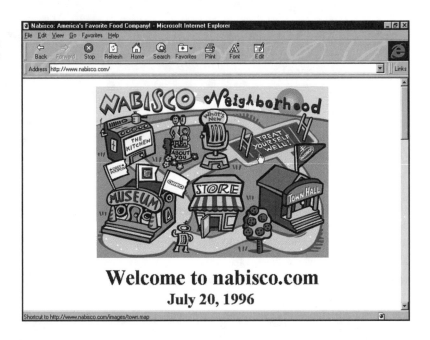

Imagemaps are simply pictures with areas called *hot regions* that users can click to go to different Web pages. The image can indicate clickable areas in a lot of different ways. Usually, a border or some text in the picture indicates where users should click to go someplace else.

When the user clicks the imagemap, the coordinates of the click are used to determine which hot region he or she clicked. Once the hot region is known, the user is sent to the URL associated with the region.

Advantages and Disadvantages of Imagemaps

Using imagemaps presents some good and bad points. Most are aesthetic points, but a few are technical. Understanding the advantages and disadvantages of imagemaps is important to making the decision whether you want to include imagemaps on your pages.

Advantages to Using Imagemaps

Imagemaps are most useful in the following situations:

- Imagemaps represent spatial links, such as geographical coordinates, which would be difficult to layout using single image buttons or text links (see fig. 24.2).

FIG. 24.2
Imagemaps are useful for representing spatially related links.

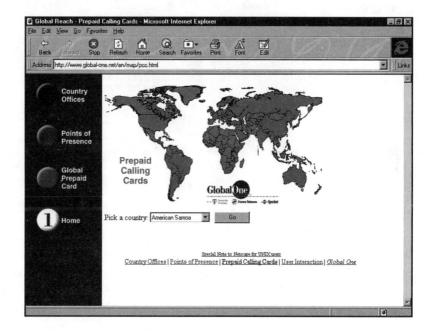

- Imagemaps are useful as a top level menu bar that appears on each page in your Web site. The use of imagemap menus offers users the option of going anywhere in your site at any time. With the advent of frames, many sites feature such a menu bar in small horizontal frames on their pages.

  ▶ **See** "Frames," **p. 495**

- Creating the common menu bar graphic for your site saves time in developing HTML documents because this graphic refers to the same imagemap information. Consistent menus also present a consistent look to a site, which eases user navigation. Instead of having to go into each page and put in links to other parts of your site, you can just refer to the common menu bar graphic (see fig. 24.3).

Part
IV

Ch
24

FIG. 24.3

A common navigational imagemap on each page gives the users a consistent set of options for moving around your site.

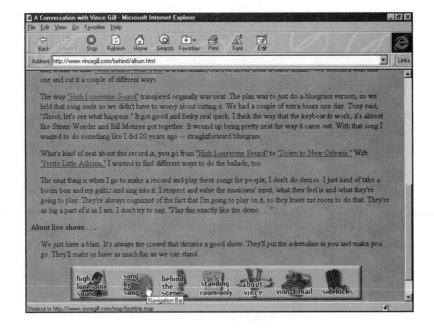

Disadvantages of Using Imagemaps

Imagemaps aren't the end-all feature of Web pages; otherwise, everyone would use them. Remember, after all, that some folks visiting Web sites are using text-only browsers. Imagemaps would be pointless for users with these capabilities.

In certain situations, you shouldn't use imagemaps. You also should consider some technical issues before using them. Imagemaps have a number of inherent drawbacks, including the following:

- Not all imagemaps can be used when running your site locally off a hard drive. This is only true for server-side imagemaps that require a program on the server to process them.

- Unless you provide an alternative text menu, users who cannot load graphics or have turned graphics loading off have no means of navigation (see fig. 24.4).

- Imagemaps tend to be larger than single-image buttons and, therefore, take longer to download.

- Use of a single imagemap menu for your site offers users the option of clicking the reference to the page they are presently viewing. This can cause confusion in navigation.

Depending on which imagemap approach you use, you also need to consider other issues. The next two sections discuss the approaches available to Web authors today: server-side imagemaps and client-side imagemaps.

FIG. 24.4
Providing alternative text links is an important courtesy to users who have text-only browsers or who have turned image loading off.

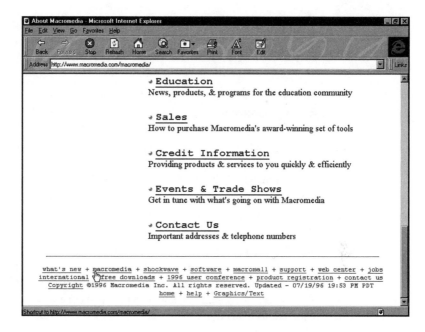

Server-Side Imagemaps

The first imagemaps were server-side imagemaps implemented by engineers at CERN in Switzerland. Shortly afterward, developers at the University of Illinois' National Center for Supercomputing Applications (NCSA) came up with a slightly different way to implement imagemaps. In writing HTML to support imagemaps, the only difference between the CERN and NCSA approaches you need to be concerned with is how the data that defines the hot regions is specified.

NOTE Before you set up a server-side imagemap, it is imperative that you talk to the administrator of your Web server to find out what type of software is running on your machine. Knowing this information makes a difference in how you set up both your map files and your links to the imagemap processing script. ■

The Basic Idea

When a user clicks one of the hot regions of a server-side imagemap graphic, the mouse pointer's position on the *image* relative to the upper left corner is sent to the Web server. A *program* on the server uses these coordinates and a *map file* that contains the definitions of the hot regions to figure out which hot region the user clicked. Thus, the three key ingredients you need to create a server-side imagemap are an image, an imagemap processing program, and a map file. Each of these elements is discussed in the sections that follow.

The Image   In Chapter 23, you learned about guidelines for developing graphics for use in World Wide Web sites. Many of these ideas are also useful when deciding on the graphics to use for an imagemap. Let's review some of the more important issues with respect to inline images:

- Inline images should be saved in the GIF file format whenever possible because it is the only format supported by all graphical World Wide Web browsers.

- You should save or convert images to be Interlaced GIFs. This format allows the graphic to be displayed in "layers" as it is transmitted from the server. That is to say the image is presented in ever-increasing detail as it's being received by Internet Explorer. Users will begin to see the image without waiting for the entire file to download.

- You should develop graphics to be no more than 500 pixels wide and 200 pixels high. Most users will be viewing your site on a 14-inch monitor. Graphics that exceed this size cannot be easily viewed without scrolling.

- Graphics download faster if they are created with a limited number of colors. Scanned images should be retouched to eliminate dithering. *Dithering* is the process in which an image has more colors than can be displayed. When you're retouching a scanned image, simply change as many similar colors to a common color as you can. For example, if you have a picture with three shades of red and they look similar, then just change them all to be just one color.

N O T E   Transparent GIFs used as imagemaps can present a problem. Recall that transparent GIFs are images in which the browser background color shows through in certain spots. Having a transparent background can make the image appear to have no border and "float" on the Web page. If you use a transparent GIF as an imagemap, some of the active graphic will not be apparent to the user. These imagemaps should contain some form of feedback or help as the default URL setting. ∎

In addition to these issues, you also want your imagemap graphic to be intuitive enough that users will know what regions to click and have an idea of what they'll see when they get to the page linked to the region they selected.

Figure 24.5 shows an image we use as an example throughout the chapter. Note how it is clear where you'll end up if you click the different regions of the image.

The Imagemap Processing Program   NCSA, CERN, and Windows HTTP Web server programs feature imagemap support, although they do have some differences. NCSA requires two files for imagemap support. The first is a script called *imagemap*, which must be compiled for your machine and placed in the CGI-BIN directory. CERN servers require a similar file. With Windows HTTP servers, the imagemap script is pre-installed and ready to go.

FIG. 24.5

The image for this chapter's example imagemap calls for links to Yahoo, Webcrawler, and Lycos.

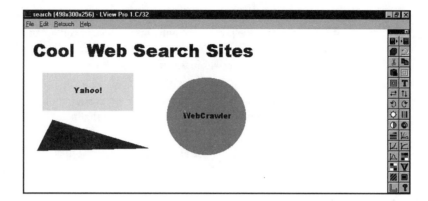

Second, for NCSA and CERN, you need write permission to the file IMAGEMAP.CONF in the server's CONF directory. This file maps image names, which you create independent of the name of the file containing the image, to their associated map files. You or the site administrator have to add a line to this file for each new imagemap you create. The format of the IMAGEMAP.CONF file is simple:

```
image_name : physical_path
```

The path to the map file is not a URL; it's the physical path on your system. A sample IMAGEMAP.CONF is as follows:

```
homepage : /maps/homepage.map
buttonbar : /maps/buttons.map
usmap : /maps/countries/us.map
```

Windows HTTP servers do not require an IMAGEMAP.CONF file.

The Map File   The map file is a text file that contains information about the hot regions of a specific imagemap graphic. For this reason, a separate map file is necessary for each imagemap graphic you want to use. The definition specifies the type of region located in the graphic as either a rectangle, circle, polygon, or point.

These regions, as their names suggest, refer to the geometric shape of the active region. Their defining coordinates are determined as pixel points relative to the upper left corner of the imagemap graphic, which is taken to have coordinates 0,0. The following list identifies basic imagemap shapes and their required coordinates:

- **rect**—This shape indicates that the region is a rectangle. The coordinates required for this type of shape are the upper left and lower right pixels in the rectangle. The active region is the area within the rectangle.

- **circle**—This shape indicates that the region is a circle. Coordinates required for using a circle are the center-point pixel and one edge-point pixel (a pixel on the circle itself). The active region is calculated as the area within the circle.

- **poly**—This shape indicates that the region is a polygon. Coordinates are required as a list of vertices for the polygon. A polygon region can contain up to 100 vertices. This permits some very strangely shaped polygons. Some are even in the form of letters! The active region is the area within the polygon.

- **point**—This shape indicates that the region is a point on the image. A point coordinate is one specific pixel measured from the upper left corner of the imagemap graphic. A point is considered active if the click occurs closest to that point on the graphic yet not within another active region.

- **default**—This shape indicates all the area of an imagemap graphic not specified by any other active region.

 An imagemap definition file should, whenever possible, be configured with a default HTML link. The default link takes the user to an area that isn't designated as being an active link. This URL should provide the user with feedback or helpful information about using that particular imagemap.

CAUTION

An imagemap definition file should never contain both a point and a default region. If point regions are defined, and a user does not click a hot region, the server sends the user to the URL associated with the closest point region, and the default URL will never be used.

Following each type of region in the imagemap definition file is the URL that is returned to the user when a click within that area is recorded. Active regions in the definition file are read from the first line down. If two regions overlap in their coordinates, only the one referenced first is activated by the imagemap program.

CAUTION

URLs in map files should always be *absolute* or *fully qualified* URLs—that is, the URL should specify a protocol, server name, and filename (including the directory path to the file).

N O T E You can use the pound sign (#) to comment a line in the imagemap definition file. Any line with a pound sign at the beginning is ignored by the imagemap program. Comments are useful for adding information such as the date of creation, the physical path to the imagemap graphic, or specific comments about the server configuration. ■

Two primary types of map file configurations exist: one for CERN and one for NCSA. Both use the same types of hot region and the same coordinates to define each type. However, the formatting of this information in each map file is different. For this reason, you should check with the system administrator about the particular imagemap setup of the server you are using.

The CERN Map File Format   Lines in a CERN-style map file have the following form:

```
region_type coordinates URL
```

The coordinates must be in parentheses, and the x and y coordinates must be separated by a comma. The CERN format also doesn't allow for comments about hot regions. A sample CERN-style hot region definition might look like the following:

```
rect (56,47) (357,265) http://www.rectangle.com/
```

The NCSA Map File Format   NCSA developed a slightly different format from CERN's for the map file information. Their format is as follows:

```
region_type URL coordinates
```

The coordinates don't have to be in parentheses, but they do have to be separated by commas. The equivalent of the map data line presented previously in NCSA format is as follows:

```
rect http://www.rectangle.com/ 56,47 357,265
```

Table 24.1 shows the coordinates of the hot regions in the example image from figure 24.5 and the URLs associated with each of these hot regions. All of this information is necessary for setting up the map file. For now, you should take these coordinates as given. When you read about imagemap utility programs, you'll find out how to determine these coordinates yourself.

Table 24.1   Hot Region Coordinates and URLs

Shape	Coordinates	URL
Rectangle	(41,90),(228,165)	**http://www.yahoo.com/**
Circle	(296,97),(457,252)	**http://www.webcrawler.com/**
Polygon	(30,246),(61,182),(257,240)	**http://www.lycos.com/**

With the information in Table 24.1, you can set up the map file for the example in CERN format, as follows:

```
rect (41,90) (228,165) http://www.yahoo.com/
circle (296,97) (457,252) http://www.webcrawler.com/
poly (30,246) (61,182) (257,240) http://www.lycos.com/
```

Or you can set it up in NCSA format, as follows:

```
rect http://www.yahoo.com/ 41,90 228,165
circle http://www.webcrawler.com/ 296,97 457,252
poly http://www.lycos.com/ 30,246 61,182, 257,240
```

Setting Up a Server-Side Imagemap

Now that you know the basic ingredients of server-side imagemaps, you need to know the recipe for combining them into a functional product. Because of the differences in imagemap processing programs on different servers, you can use two techniques for setting up imagemaps.

NCSA and CERN Servers   After you create a map file for an image, you must make it an anchor to include it in an HTML file, like this:

```
<A HREF="/cgi-bin/imagemap/searchsites">
<IMG SRC="images/searchsites.gif" ISMAP></A>
```

The hypertext reference must contain the URL to the imagemap script followed by a slash (/) and the name of the map defined in the IMAGEMAP.CONF file. The actual picture is then included with the <IMG> tag. The <IMG> tag also includes the ISMAP attribute, indicating that the image placed by the tag is to be an imagemap.

For this example to work, the IMAGEMAP.CONF file must also include a line pointing to a map file for the imagemap searchsites. That line might look like the following:

```
searchsites : /maps/searchsites.map
```

N O T E   The CERN server includes a slightly different version of the imagemap script called htimage that eliminates the need for the IMAGEMAP.CONF file. Instead, htimage allows you to specify a URL to the map file directly. Using htimage instead of imagemap in the preceding example, you would write the following:

```
<A HREF="/cgi-bin/htimage/maps/searchsites.map">
<IMG SRC="images/searchsites.gif" ISMAP></A>
```

TIP   You can use CERN's htimage script even if you run the NCSA server.

Windows HTTP Servers   Linking to the imagemap script on the server is somewhat easier under Windows HTTP. For this program, you just use the following line with an NCSA-style map file:

```
<A HREF="/maps/searchsites.map">
<IMG SRC="images/searchsites.gif" ISMAP></A>
```

These servers don't require the IMAGEMAP.CONF file, so you can "eliminate the middle man" and point directly to the map file.

Client-Side Imagemaps

The other type of imagemap is the client-side imagemap. Client-side imagemaps were recently made part of HTML 3.2, but some browers (including Internet Explorer) have been able to implement them for a while. Initially, two proposals were presented to the World Wide Web Consortium (W3C) on how to build clent-side imagemap functionality into HTML. This section introduces you to both approaches, but with a greater emphasis on the approach chosen for HTML 3.2.

The Basic Idea

Having the server do the work to find out where the user clicked and where to send the user based on the click involves a lot of wasted resources. The client has to open another HTTP connection to the server to pass the coordinates and get the response back regarding what URL to load next. The computations the server has to do to find out what hot region the user clicked are straightforward, and there's no reason they couldn't be done by the client. Slow transmission times between client and server mean that users may have to wait quite awhile from the time they click the mouse to the time the new URL is loaded.

Until recently, the compelling reason for having the server do the imagemap computations was that the map file data resided on the server. If there was a way to get this information to the client, then the client could do the computations, and the imagemap process would become much more efficient. This is the spirit behind client-side imagemaps.

Part

IV

Ch

24

Client-side imagemaps involve sending the map data to the client as part of the HTML file rather than having the client contact the server each time the map data is needed. This process may add to the time its takes to transfer the HTML file, but the increased efficiency is well worth it.

Two Proposals

As noted previously, there were initially two proposals for implementing client-side imagemaps exist. Both provide a way to get the map file data to the client, but specifics of each approach are different. One proposal suggested the use of the `<FIG>` and `</FIG>` tag pair with map file data contained in `<A>` tags between them. The other, which is the one adopted in HTML 3.2, proposed a new tag pair—`<MAP>` and `</MAP>`—with `<AREA>` tags between them to contain the map file data.

Client-Side Imagemaps with the `<FIG>` Tag The key to using the `<FIG>` and `</FIG>` tags for a client-side imagemap is that these tags can contain text that acts as an alternative to the image being placed by them. Thus, any text between the `<FIG>` and `</FIG>` tags is much like text assigned to the `ALT` attribute of the `<IMG>` tag. For example, the following two HTML code fragments do the same thing:

```
<IMG SRC="stopsign.gif" ALT="STOP!" WIDTH=50 HEIGHT=50>

<FIG SRC="stopsign.gif" WIDTH=50 HEIGHT=50>
STOP!
</FIG>
```

To implement the example map as a client-side imagemap with the `<FIG>` and `</FIG>` tags, you need to place the information previously found in the map file between these tags. You do so using the `<A>` tag as follows:

```
<FIG SRC="images/searchsites.gif" WIDTH=498 HEIGHT=300>
<B>Select a search site :</B>
<UL>
```

```
<LI><A HREF="http://www.yahoo.com/" SHAPE="rect 41,90,228,165">Yahoo!</A>
</LI>
<LI><A HREF="http://www.webcrawler.com/" SHAPE="circle 296,97,457,252">
WebCrawler</A></LI>
<LI><A HREF="http://www.lycos.com/" SHAPE="polygon 30,246,61,182,257,240">
Lycos</A></LI>
</UL>
</FIG>
```

The HREF attribute in each <A> tag contains the URL to load when the user clicks a hot region, and the SHAPE attribute contains the information needed to define each hot region. SHAPE is assigned to the shape of the hot region, followed by a space, and then followed by the coordinates that specify the region. Each number in the coordinate list is separated by a comma.

SHAPE also has a secondary function in this setting. If the image file specified in the SRC attribute of the <FIG> tag is placed on the page, then the browser ignores any HTML between the <FIG> and </FIG> tags unless it is an <A> tag with a SHAPE attribute specified.

On the other hand, if the image is not placed, then the browser renders the HTML between the two tags. The result for the preceding HTML is a bulleted list of links that can act as a text alternative for your imagemap. This important feature of client-side imagemaps is done with the <FIG> and </FIG> tags: they degrade into a text alternative for nongraphical browsers, for browsers with image loading turned off, for browsers that don't support the <FIG> and </FIG> tags, or when the desired image file cannot be loaded.

N O T E To read the full proposal on using the <FIG> and </FIG> tag pair proposed for HTML 3.0, visit **http://www.w3.org/pub/WWW/MarkUp/html3/figures.html**. ■

Client-Side Imagemaps with the *<MAP>* Tag While working on a version of Mosaic that could read from CD-ROM, the folks at Spyglass had an immediate need for client-side imagemaps. Since the browser was reading from the CD-ROM drive on the same machine, no server was involved to contact for map information. The developers needed to come up with some way to store the map data on the CD and program Mosaic to interpret it properly.

Their solution was to introduce a <MAP> and </MAP> tag pair to contain the hot region information previously found in map files. Each map defined by these tags is given a unique name so that it can be referenced from the <IMG> tag used to place the graphic for the imagemap.

Using the <MAP> and </MAP> tags for client-side imagemaps is the approach that has been the early favorite among Web browsers that support client-side imagemaps. It is also the approach recently adopted by the W3C. If you're creating a client-side imagemap for that is HTML 3.2 compiant, you'll need to use this approach.

To define a map for the preceding example map, you use the following HTML:

```
<MAP NAME="searchsites">
<AREA SHAPE="RECT" COORDS="41,90,228,165" HREF="http://www.yahoo.com/">
<AREA SHAPE="CIRCLE" COORDS="296,97,457,252"
HREF="http://www.webcrawler.com/">
```

```
<AREA SHAPE="POLYGON" COORDS="30,246,61,182,257,240"
HREF="http://www.lycos.com/">
</MAP>
```

The NAME attribute of the <MAP> tag gives the map information a unique identifier. The <AREA> tags between the <MAP> and </MAP> tags are used to define the hot regions and the URLs they link to. You can have as many <AREA> tags as you like. If the hot regions defined by two <AREA> tags overlap, the <AREA> tag that is listed first gets precedence.

> **N O T E**   A well-planned imagemap shouldn't have any overlapping hot regions. ■

The <AREA> tag can also take a NOHREF attribute, which tells the browser to do nothing if the user clicks the hot region. Any part of the image that is not defined as a hot region is taken to be a NOHREF region, so if users click outside a hot region, they don't go anywhere by default. This approach saves you from setting up an <AREA SHAPE="DEFAULT" NOHREF> tag for all your maps.

The HTML used to define a map region can reside in the same file in which the <IMG> tag for the graphic lives or in an entirely different file. If the map definition is in the same file, you reference the map as follows:

```
<IMG SRC="images/searchsites.gif" WIDTH=498 HEIGHT=300 USEMAP="#searchsites">
```

The USEMAP attribute in the <IMG> tag tells the browser it's dealing with a client-side imagemap and what the name of the map is. If you store all your map information in a separate HTML file, the tag to link to the map would be as follows:

```
<IMG SRC="images/searchsites.gif" WIDTH=498 HEIGHT=300
USEMAP="maps.html#searchsites">
```

USEMAP can be set equal to a fully qualified URL, if needed.

Storing all your maps in a single file is a good idea if you're placing the same imagemap on several pages. This is frequently the case with navigational button bars.

> **N O T E**   To read the Spyglass proposal for client-side imagemaps, visit **http://www.ics.uci.edu/ pub/ietf/html/draft-seidman-clientsideimagemap-01.txt**. ■

Using Server-Side and Client-Side Imagemaps Together

Client-side imagemaps are a great idea since they permit faster imagemap processing and enhance the portability of your HTML documents. Unfortunately, not all browsers support even one of the client-side imagemap approaches just described. If you're trying to write HTML that is as friendly to as many browsers as possible, you should consider combining server-side and client-side imagemaps whenever possible.

To combine a server-side imagemap with the `<FIG>` and `</FIG>` tag approach to client-side imagemaps, you can modify the earlier example as follows:

```
<FIG SRC="images/searchsites.gif" WIDTH=498 HEIGHT=300>
<A HREF="maps/searchsites.map"><IMG SRC="images/searchsites.gif"
WIDTH=498 HEIGHT=300 ISMAP></A>
<B>Select a search site :</B>
<UL>
<LI><A HREF="http://www.yahoo.com/" SHAPE="rect 41,90,228,165">Yahoo!</A></LI>
<LI><A HREF="http://www.webcrawler.com/" SHAPE="circle 296,97,457,252">
WebCrawler</A></LI>
<LI><A HREF="http://www.lycos.com/" SHAPE="polygon 30,246,61,182,257,240">
Lycos</A></LI>
</UL>
</FIG>
```

The second line in the preceding HTML code is new. It places the same map graphic on the page and links it to the map file SEARCHSITES.MAP on the server. If the browser recognizes the `<FIG>` tag and places the image it specifies, the additional line of HTML is ignored.

To combine a server-side imagemap with the `<MAP>` and `</MAP>` tag approach, you can modify the earlier HTML as follows:

```
<A HREF="maps/searchsites.map">
<IMG SRC="images/searchsites.gif" WIDTH=498 HEIGHT=300
USEMAP="#searchsites" ISMAP>
</A>
```

Flanking the `<IMG>` tag with `<A>` and `</A>` tags makes it point to the `searchsites.map` map file on the server. You need to include the ISMAP attribute in the `<IMG>` tag to let the browser know that the image is linked as a server-side imagemap as well.

N O T E You can link NCSA- and CERN-style server-side imagemaps to client-side imagemaps by having the HREF in the `<A>` tag point to the imagemap script, instead of pointing directly to the map file. ■

Providing an Alternative

While having imagemaps is great, you must also consider your entire audience. A significant number of people browsing the Web are using text-based browsers. You should provide for some means of letting them navigate around your home page. You can put in a separate section with a description of the links and the corresponding URLs. You can also have a link that takes the users to a text-only menu that has the same links as the imagemap. Whichever approach you take, be sure to put in an alternative for text-only users.

N O T E For a good tutorial on imagemaps, consult **http://fpg.uwaterloo.ca/Courses/ IM-FM/TOC.html**. ■

Tools to Create and Test Imagemaps

Whether you're creating a server-side or client-side imagemap, determining and typing in all the coordinates of the points you need to define hot regions can be cumbersome. Luckily, programs are available to help you through this process. They let you load your imagemap image, trace out the hot regions right on the screen, and then write the appropriate map file or HTML file to implement the imagemap. The following sections describe two of these programs: Mapedit and Map This!.

Mapedit

On the CD

Mapedit 2.1 is a shareware imagemap tool produced by Boutell.Com, Inc. This version of Mapedit supports client-side images and images in the JPEG format. It also cleans up a number of small bugs in the 2.0 release.

Using Mapedit is easy. From the File menu, choose Open/Create to begin. In the dialog box that appears, you need to specify whether you are doing a server-side or client-side imagemap. If you choose server-side, you then need to select either NCSA or CERN formats and specify a name for the map file. If you choose client-side, you need to tell Mapedit the name of the file to which it should write the HTML code. Finally, you tell Mapedit the file containing the image for the imagemap. When you click OK, the image file is loaded into the Mapedit window, and you're ready to start defining hot regions.

You can choose Rectangle, Circle, or Polygon tools from the MapEdit Tools menu. Each tool lets you trace out a hot region shaped like the name of the tool. To use the Rectangle tool, point your mouse to the upper left corner of the rectangular hot region, and click the left mouse button. Then move your mouse pointer to the lower right corner of the region. As you do, a black rectangular outline is dragged along with the pointer, eventually opening up to enclose your hot region (see fig. 24.6).

FIG. 24.6
Mapedit lets you trace out hot regions using your mouse.

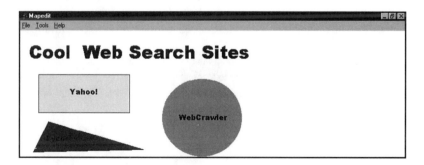

With the mouse pointer pointing at the lower right corner, left-click the mouse again. When you do, you see a dialog box like the one shown in figure 24.7. Type the URL that is associated with the hot region you're defining into the dialog box, along with any comments you want to include, and click OK. Mapedit puts this information into the file it's building and is then ready to define another hot region or to save the file and exit.

Part

IV

Ch

24

FIG. 24.7
Once a hot region is defined, Mapedit prompts you for the associated URL and any comments.

Mapedit's C̲ircle and P̲olygon tools work similarly. With the C̲ircle tool, you place your mouse pointer at the center of the circular region (which is sometimes difficult to estimate!) and left-click. Then move the pointer to a point on the circle, and left-click again to define the region and call up the dialog box. To use the P̲olygon tool, simply left-click the vertices of the polygon in sequence. When you hit the last unique vertex (that is, the next vertex in the sequence is the first one you clicked), right-click instead to define the region and reveal the dialog box.

 T I P   If you're unhappy with how your trace is coming out, just press the Esc key to erase your trace and start over.

Other Mapedit T̲ool menu options let you move an entire hot region (M̲ove), add (A̲dd Points) or remove points (R̲emove Points) from a polygon, and test the imagemap file as it currently stands. The E̲dit Default URL option under the F̲ile menu lets you specify a default URL to go to if a user clicks somewhere other than a hot region. Mapedit's test mode (choose T̲ools, T̲est+Edit) presents the imagemap graphic to you and lets you click it. If you click a hot region, the URL dialog box opens and displays the URL associated with the region you clicked.

> **N O T E**   Mapedit is available from the CD-ROM that comes with this book. After a 30-day evaluation period, you must license Mapedit at a cost of $25. Site licenses are also available. Educational and nonprofit users do not have to pay for a license but should register their copies of Mapedit. ■

Map This!

On the CD

Map This! is a freeware imagemap tool written by Todd C. Wilson. It runs on 32-bit Windows platforms only, but that's about the extent of its limitations. Map This! can help you with server-side and client-side imagemaps and can load images in both the GIF and JPEG formats. Figure 24.8 shows the Map This! main window with the search sites graphic loaded.

FIG. 24.8

Map This! is a freeware imagemap tool that supports server-side and client-side imagemaps on graphics in both GIF and JPEG format.

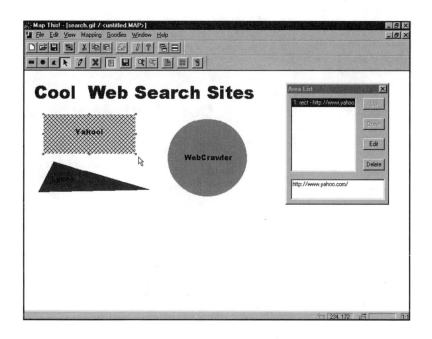

Most of Map This!'s features are accessible through buttons in the main window. The rectangle, circle, and polygon tools occupy the first three buttons in the second row. The circle tool is particularly nice because you drag out the circle from one point on the circle to the point that is diametrically opposite it instead of trying to start on the exact center of the circle. As you use one of the tools, you get instructions on what to do next in a box at the bottom left of the window. You can enable the shading feature to make the hot regions you define easier to see.

The Area List shown in figure 24.8 is a floating box that you can activate to show the regions you've defined and what URLs they're linked to. You can also turn on a grid pattern to help you measure hot regions with greater accuracy.

The Map This! testing mode opens up a completely separate window, as shown in figure 24.9. As you move your mouse pointer over a hot region, its corresponding URL shows up in the box at the bottom left.

Map This! lets you work on multiple images, and you have the choice of cascading or tiling the windows that contain the images. When you're ready to save your work, you can save in CERN or NCSA format for server-side imagemap map files or in HTML format for client-side imagemaps. Other useful features of Map This! include the following:

- The ability to add points to or delete points from polygons
- Color support, all the way up to 24-bit color
- The ability to zoom in and out
- A Preferences window where you can set the map type and color choices for outlining and shading hot regions

FIG. 24.9
As you move your
mouse over a hot
region in the Map This!
test window, the URL
you jump to shows up
at the bottom left.

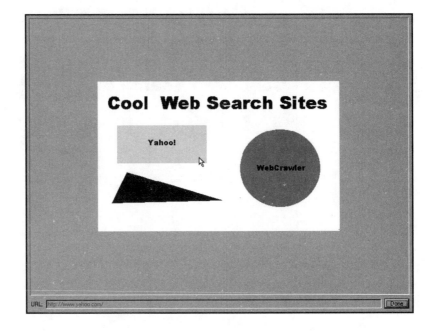

- A Mapfile Information window where you can specify a default URL, the map title, your name, and other descriptive comments
- Context-sensitive menus accessible by right-clicking the mouse

N O T E   If no imagemap utility programs with a testing feature are available to you, you have to put your map or HTML files on a server and test them with a browser. You can make small changes to these files using a simple text editor, if needed. If you're testing a client-side imagemap with a browser, make sure that the browser understands the <MAP> tag. ■

## CHAPTER 25

HTML 3.2 and Microsoft Extensions to HTML

The HTML you learned back in Chapter 20, "Basic HTML," and Chapter 21, "Adding Graphics and Tables," is fairly standard HTML in the sense that most graphical browsers support the tags discussed in those chapters. HTML is constantly evolving, though, and what is standard next year may include many more tags than those you've seen so far. Indeed, there are many proposals within the Web community for new and interesting additions to HTML.

Another driving force in the evolution of HTML are browser software companies. In an effort to enhance their product, these companies extend their browsers' ability to support tags that are not part of standard HTML. Such tags are called *HTML extensions,* and are usually associated with the name of the company that introduced them. This chapter takes a look at some of the directions in which HTML is evolving. ■

The tags accepted as part of HTML 3.2

HTML 3.2 was adopted in May 1996 and incorporates many tags that were once proposed as HTML extensions. Not all the proposals were accepted though and the World Wide Web Consortium will continue to weigh the merits of these proposals.

The HTML extensions that Internet Explorer is able to render

Internet Explorer is able to understand many of the extensions to HTML, including tags that were introduced by Microsoft and tags that were proposed for HTML 3.2, but have yet to be accepted.

The HTML extensions that internet Explorer is not able to render

There is also a handful of tags that Internet Explorer cannot parse. You need to be aware of these tags as your design Web sites with Internet Explorer in mind.

HTML 3.2

The currently accepted HTML standard is known as HTML 2.0. Last year, the HTML 2.0 specification was compiled and released as a Request for Comment (RFC) by the World Wide Web Consortium (W3C). The 2.0 spec sought to summarize the de facto HTML standard and describe how people should be using the HTML in existence. Since then, the W3C and the Internet Engineering Task Force (IETF) have been considering proposals for HTML 3.0. While proposals were under consideration, many were implemented by Internet Explorer and other browsers in anticipation of their acceptance. In May 1996, the W3C released the official specification for HTML 3.2—a markup language that incorporates many of the features proposed for HTML 3.0. The tags that comprise HTML 3.2 and others still under consideration are discussed over the next several sections.

N O T E To learn more about the HTML 3.2 spec, direct Internet Explorer to **http://www.w3.org/pub/WWW/MarkUp/Wilbur**. ■

What Happened to HTML 3.0?

HTML 3.0 got a lot of attention for a very long time, due in part to the fact that it was a large departure from HTML 2.0. The W3C felt that implementing HTML 3.0 as proposed would create difficulties because of the vast number of changes that would have to be made. As a compromise, HTML 3.2 was drafted and adopted so that HTML could continue to evolve, though at a more gradual pace. This smaller evolutionary step also makes backward compatibility with HTML 2.0 much easier.

The HTML 3.2 spec is largely rooted in HTML 2.0. New HTML 3.2 tags were drawn from many of the proposals made for HTML 3.0 as well as those made for HTML+.

The *<RANGE>* Tag for the Document Head

The <RANGE> tag was proposed for HTML 3.0, but was not made part of the HTML 3.2 spec. According to the proposal, placing a <RANGE> tag in the document head allows you to set up a range in the document for searching. <RANGE> takes the CLASS attribute, which is set equal to SEARCH to set up a search range, and the FROM and UNTIL attributes, which designate the beginning and end of the search range. A sample <RANGE> tag might look like the following:

```
<RANGE CLASS=SEARCH FROM="startspot" UNTIL="endspot">
```

The "startspot" and "endspot" markers are set up in the body of the document using the <SPOT ID="startspot"> and <SPOT ID="endspot"> tags at the points where you want the search range to begin and end, respectively.

Tags in the Document Body

Most of the proposals for HTML 3.0 relate to tags that go in the body of an HTML document. Many of these tagss were accepted as part of the HTML 3.2 spec. The highlights of these proposals include the following:

- Several new physical and logical styles for formatting text
- New tags and attributes to give you finer control over page layout
- A <FIG> tag with several useful attributes to support wrapping of text around figures and placement of captions and overlays
- A <DIV> tag for creating named divisions of a document
- A <NOTE> tag for producing on-screen warnings and admonishments
- New tags and entities for rendering mathematical characters

Formatting Text   Several new physical styles have been accepted as part of HTML 3.2. Table 25.1 summarizes these additions. Closing tags are left out of the tables in the interest of space.

Table 25.1 New Physical Styles Adopted in HTML 3.2

Style Name	Tag	Rendering
Strikethrough	<STRIKE>	Text is struck through with a slash (/)
Big	<BIG>	Makes text bigger than its current size
Small	<SMALL>	Makes text smaller than its current size
Subscript	<SUB>	Makes text a subscript
Superscript	<SUP>	Makes text a superscript

While there are no new logical styles in HTML 3.2, several of them were proposed as part of HTML 3.0. The styles are shown in Table 25.2. Since many of these proposals are still under consideration, it's still possible that you'll see any or all of these tags used in the future.

Table 25.2 New Logical Styles Proposed in HTML 3.0

Style Name	Tag
Abbreviation	<ABBREV>
Acronym	<ACRONYM>
Author's name	<AU>
Deleted text	<DEL>
Inserted text	<INS>
Language context	<LANG>
Person's name	<PERSON>
Short quotation	<Q>

Part
IV

Ch
25

N O T E   Recall that logical styles are often rendered differently on different browsers. How you see a
logical style rendered in Internet Explorer may differ from how the style is rendered by
another browser. ■

Most of the new physical and logical styles are self-explanatory. Text marked with the <Q> style
will appear in quotation marks appropriate to the document's language context. The <INS> and
<DEL> styles are expected to be useful in the context of legal documents. The <PERSON> style
marks a person's name for easier extraction by indexing programs.

Finer Layout Control   A number of HTML 3.0 proposals give authors greater control over
page layout. One interesting proposal that was not made part of HTML 3.2 calls for the addition
of a <TAB> tag, which would allow you to set up your own tab stops in a document. To use a tab
stop, you need first to define it using the ID attribute:

```
My first tab stop is <TAB ID="first">here, followed by some other text.
```

The HTML above would set up the first tab stop in front of the letter "h" in the word "here." To
use the tab stop, you use the <TAB> tag with the TO attribute:

```
<TAB TO="first">This sentence starts below the word "here."
```

On the browser screen, the "T" in the word "This" will be aligned directly below the "h" in the
word "here."

Other enhancements to layout control come in the form of new attributes to existing tags. For
example, under HTML 3.2, you can center, or right-justify, headings and paragraphs using the
ALIGN=CENTER or ALIGN=RIGHT attributes in your <H1>–<H6> and <P> tags. Additionally, the
CLEAR attribute will be available on many tags, giving you the ability to clear one or both margins or to leave a specific amount of space between page items.

N O T E   When specifying a quantity of spacing, the units of the CLEAR attribute can be in pixels, en
spaces, or em spaces; for example, CLEAR="5 en" or CLEAR="40 pixels." ■

Placing Graphics   The <FIG> tag was proposed as an alternative to the <IMG> tag for larger
graphics, though it was not included in the HTML 3.2 spec. As you might expect, <FIG> requires the SRC attribute to specify the URL of the image file to be loaded. <FIG> can also take
the attributes shown in Table 25.3. The BLEEDLEFT and BLEEDRIGHT values of the ALIGN attribute
align the figure all the way to the left and right edges of the browser window, respectively.

Table 25.3   Attributes of the <FIG> Tag

Attribute	Purpose
SRC="url"	Gives the URL of the image file to load
NOFLOW	Disables the flow of text around the figure
ALIGN=LEFT¦RIGHT¦ CENTER¦JUSTIFY¦ BLEEDLEFT¦BLEEDRIGHT	Specifies an alignment for the figure

Attribute	Purpose
UNITS=*unit_of_measure*	Specifies a unit of measure for the WIDTH and HEIGHT attributes (default is pixels)
WIDTH=*width*	Specifies the width of the image in units designated by the UNITS attribute
HEIGHT=*height*	Specifies the height of the image in units designated by the UNITS attribute
IMAGEMAP	Denotes the figure as an imagemap

The <FIG> tag is different from the <IMG> tag in that it has a companion </FIG> tag. Together, <FIG> and </FIG> can contain text, including captions and photo credits, which should be rendered with the figure. Captions are enclosed with the <CAPTION> and </CAPTION> tags, and photo credits are enclosed with the <CREDIT> and </CREDIT> tags. Regular text found between the <FIG> and </FIG> tags will wrap around the figure unless the NOWRAP attribute is specified.

Figure 25.1 shows an example of a photo with a caption, photo credit, and surrounding text. To accomplish the layout you see in the figure, the HTML author had to use a two-column table and a floating image. Once the <FIG> tag is fully implemented, layouts with figure captions, credits, and wrapping text should be much easier to create.

Part

IV

Ch

25

FIG. 25.1

Once adopted as standard HTML, the <FIG> tag will be used to produce captions, credits, and text around images.

Another feature proposed for the <FIG> and </FIG> tag pair is the ability to overlay two images. This is accomplished with the <OVERLAY> tag, which specifies a second image to overlay the image given in the <FIG> tag. HTML to produce an overlay might look like the following:

```
<FIG SRC="main_image.gif" WIDTH=250 HEIGHT=186 ALIGN=LEFT>
    <OVERLAY SRC="overlay.gif">
    <P>The image to the left is actually two images,
    one on top of the other.
</FIG>
```

The <FIG> tag also plays a role in the one of the HTML 3.0 proposals for the implementation of client-side imagemaps. This proposal was passed over in HTML 3.2 for the <MAP> tag approach to client-side imagemaps.

▶ **See** "Client-side Imagemaps" to learn about the proposal for client-side imagemaps with the <FIG> and <MAP> tags, **p. 466**

Document Divisions   The <DIV> and </DIV> tags work similarly to the <P> and </P> tags, except that <DIV> and </DIV> denote a special division of the document. As proposed for HTML 3.0, the <DIV> tag takes the CLASS attribute, which describes the type of division being defined. Division types include abstracts, chapters, sections, and appendixes. According to the proposal, the <DIV> tag can also take the attributes shown in Table 25.4, allowing greater control over how that division is formatted. A sample <DIV> . . . </DIV> container pair might look like the following:

```
<DIV CLASS=CHAPTER ALIGN=JUSTIFY CLEAR=ALL>
... the text of the chapter goes here ...
</DIV>
```

The above HTML produces a chapter that starts with clear left and right margins and that has justified text throughout.

Table 25.4   Attributes of the <*DIV*> Tag

Attribute	Purpose
CLASS	Specifies the type of document division being marked
ALIGN=LEFT¦RIGHT¦ CENTER¦JUSTIFY	Sets the alignment for the entire division
NOWRAP	Turns off autowrapping of text. Text lines are broken explicitly with tags.
CLEAR=LEFT¦RIGHT¦ALL	Starts the division clear of left, right, or both margins

The <DIV> tag was adopted as an HTML 3.2 tag, but the early documentation suggested that it will initially only take the ALIGN attribute.

N O T E You also can use the CLEAR attribute to specify spacing between the division and any page items around it. For example, CLEAR="2 em" leaves two em spaces between the division and the item it wraps around. ▪

Admonishments   The <NOTE> tag proposed for HTML 3.0 lets you set up admonishments such as notes, warnings, and cautions on your pages. The text of the admonishment appears between the <NOTE> and </NOTE> tags. Additionally, you can include an image with your admonishment using the SRC attribute of the <NOTE> tag. SRC and other attributes of <NOTE> are summarized in Table 25.5.

Table 25.5   Attributes of the <NOTE> Tag

Attribute	Purpose
CLASS=NOTE¦ CAUTION¦WARNING	Specifies the type of admonishment
SRC="url"	Provides the URL of an image to precede the admonishment text
CLEAR=LEFT¦RIGHT¦ALL	Starts the admonishment clear of left, right, or both margins

As with the <DIV> tag, you can also use the CLEAR attribute to compel browsers to leave a certain amount of space between the admonishment and surrounding page items. A sample admonishment might look like:

```
<NOTE CLASS=WARNING SRC="images/stopsign.gif" CLEAR=ALL>WARNING! You are
about to provide your credit card number to a non-secure server!</NOTE>
```

As compelling as it may be to have admonishments on your Web pages, the <NOTE> tag was not made part of the HTML 3.2 standard.

Mathematical Symbols   If you've ever tried to prepare a document with mathematical content for the Web, you've probably ended up with a substantial headache. Prior to the HTML 3.0 draft, mathematical symbols such as Greek letters, integral signs, and vector notations had to be read in and placed *as separate images* in the document. Just imagine the number of <IMG> tags required, to say nothing about the effort it would take to align them properly! The proposed HTML 3.0 spec called for tags and entities to make the preparation of mathematical documents much less agonizing.

Under the proposal, all mathematical tags and entities need to be contained inside the and tags. Greek letters are to be drawn from the Symbol font, and are incorporated into documents with their entity names. For example, γ would produce a lowercase gamma (γ) and Γ would produce an uppercase gamma (Γ). Other variables, notations, and operator symbols are built in through a large number of special tags and entities. For a complete run down on the proposals for these new tags and entities, direct Internet Explorer to **http://www.hp.co.uk/people/dsr/html3/maths.html**.

Part IV

Ch 25

Unfortunately for those who have to markup mathematical content for the Web, the <MATH> tag and related math entities were not made part of HTML 3.2. W3C offered assurances though that it would continue to work with industry and academic partners to develop extensions for mathematical characters.

TIP If you are familiar with the LaTeX language for mathematical typesetting, you should have little trouble with HTML math formatting; the two use very similar approaches. If you don't have experience with LaTeX and you will be preparing documents with mathematical content for the Web, you can get a jump on things by reading up on LaTeX before the HTML math tags and entities become widely supported.

Centering   Though it was hotly debated when it was first introduced, the <CENTER> tag survived its review by the W3C and is now part of HTML 3.2. Anything on a page—be it text, a list, an image, or a table—will be centered if it is found between the <CENTER> and </CENTER> tags. Early HTML 3.2 documentation points out that the <CENTER> tag will center items on a page, but that the <DIV ALIGN=CENTER> and </DIV> tag pair is "a more general solution."

English-language Color Names   If you've ever modified a text, link, or background color, you probably know the anguish of having to convert your chosen color to its equivalent RGB hexadecimal triplet. A new feature of HTML 3.2—English-language color names—promises to spare you this anguish for at least 16 colors. According to the HTML 3.2 spec, you can use the following color names whenever you would use an RGB triplet:

- AQUA
- BLACK
- BLUE
- FUSCHIA
- GRAY
- GREEN
- LIME
- MAROON
- NAVY
- OLIVE
- PURPLE
- RED
- SILVER
- TEAL
- WHITE
- YELLOW

This means you can now have <BODY> tags like the following to set your background, text and link colors:

```
<BODY BGCOLOR="WHITE" TEXT="RED" LINK="BLUE" VLINK="TEAL" ALINK="FUSCHIA">
```

A very welcome relief!

Java Applets and Scripting   Two other new HTML 3.2 tags are meant for handling Java applets and applications written in a scripting language like JavaScript. The <SCRIPT> and </SCRIPT> container tags have been reserved under HTML 3.2 for "future use with scripting languages." While the exact sytax of this pair is not yet clear, you should expect to find these tags only in the document head (between the <HEAD> and </HEAD> tags).

The <APPLET> tag and its companion closing tag </APPLET> are used to embed Java applets in HTML documents. <APPLET> takes the attributes shown in Table 25.6. The content between the two tags is used if the applet can't load.

Table 25.6   Attributes of the <APPLET> Tag

Attribute	Purpose
ALT	Supplies a text alternative for text-only browsers
ALIGN=LEFT¦CENTER¦RIGHT	Indicates the horizontal alignment of the applet on the page
CODE	Provides the name of the class or program that accepts the parameters and runs the applet
CODEBASE	Says where the class is (directory path to the class)
HEIGHT=*pixels*	Indicates the height of the space on the page occupied by the applet
HSPACE=*pixels*	Indicates how many pixels of white space to leave to the left and right of the applet
NAME="*name*"	Gives the applet a name so it may be called by other applications (e.g., a JavaScript program)
VSPACE=*pixels*	Indicates how many pixels of white space to leave above and below the applet
WIDTH=*pixels*	Indicates the width of the space of the page occupied by the applet

Part
IV
Ch
25

HTML 3.2 also supports a <PARAM> tag that you can use to pass parameters to the applet. <PARAM> takes the NAME and VALUE attributes where NAME is set equal to the name of the parameter and VALUE is set to the parameter's value.

Style Sheets

HTML 3.2 calls for the <STYLE> and </STYLE> tags to be reserved for use in defining HTML style sheets. A *style sheet* is much like a style in Microsoft Word—it is a set of font, character, and paragraph characteristics stored together and applied to a portion of a document. Using style sheets will help eliminate the need to keep adding new formatting tags to HTML, since any new formatting instructions can be placed in the style sheet and not in the HTML file. Style sheets also promise to make updating pages much easier, since formatting will be divorced from content.

Even though the exact syntax of style sheets has yet to be finalized, Internet Explorer is already able to make use of them. In fact, Internet Explorer will support styles in each of the following different ways:

- ■ **Embedded styles**—Style information is defined in the document head using the `<STYLE>` and `</STYLE>` tags.

- ■ **Linked styles**—Style information read in from a separate file specified in the `<LINK>` tag.

- ■ **Inline styles**—Style information is placed inside an HTML tag and applies to all content between that tag and its companion closing tag.

Embedded Style Sheets   Figure 25.2 shows the Microsoft corporate page, which makes use of an embedded style sheet. The style information is stored in the document head as shown in the HTML source listing in figure 25.3. The structure of the style information always take the form of an HTML tag name, followed by braces containing the style characteristics. For example, regular text in the document body is 9-point Arial, colored according to the hexadecimal triple 336699; whereas links are in 10-point bold Arial and colored with 003366 or 0099cc depending on whether they have been visited or not.

FIG. 25.2

Microsoft is leading the way when it comes to implementing Web style sheets.

The style information you see in figure 25.3 is enclosed in comment tags (`<!—` and `—>`) so that browsers that don't understand style sheets will ignore the style information, rather than presenting it on-screen. Another way you can give style sheet-challenged browsers a heads-up is by including the `TYPE=text/css` attribute in the `<STYLE>` tag. "css" stands for "cascading style sheet" and refers to the set of rules and precedences a browser will use when resolving conflicts between multiple styles. For example, the style assigned to body text in the style sheet above is overridden by any of the other styles defined in the embedded style sheet.

FIG. 27.3

Embedded style sheet information is stored in the document head between the <STYLE> and </STYLE> tags.

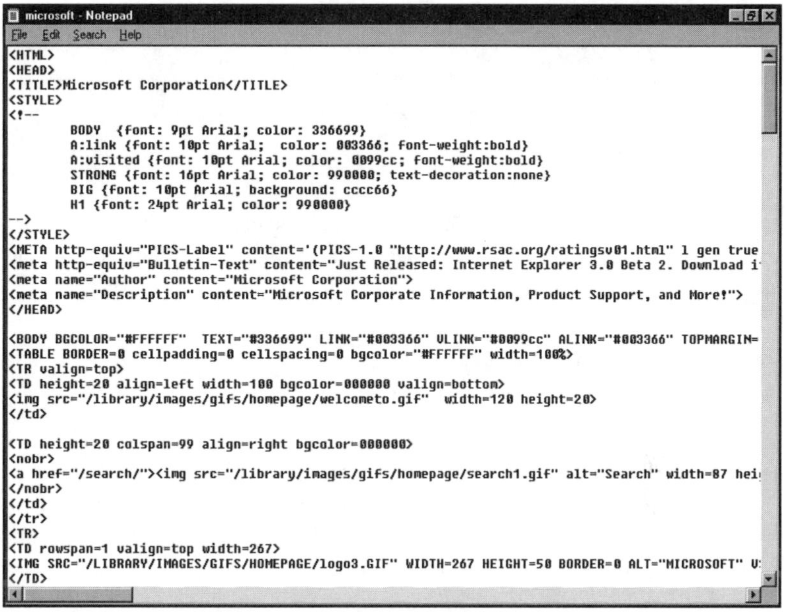

```
微 microsoft - Notepad                                                _ 8 X
File   Edit   Search   Help
<HTML>
<HEAD>
<TITLE>Microsoft Corporation</TITLE>
<STYLE>
<!--
        BODY    {font: 9pt Arial; color: 336699}
        A:link {font: 10pt Arial;  color: 003366; font-weight:bold}
        A:visited {font: 10pt Arial; color: 0099cc; font-weight:bold}
        STRONG {font: 16pt Arial; color: 990000; text-decoration:none}
        BIG {font: 10pt Arial; background: cccc66}
        H1 {font: 24pt Arial; color: 990000}
-->
</STYLE>
<META http-equiv="PICS-Label" content='(PICS-1.0 "http://www.rsac.org/ratingsv01.html" 1 gen true
<meta http-equiv="Bulletin-Text" content="Just Released: Internet Explorer 3.0 Beta 2. Download i
<meta name="Author" content="Microsoft Corporation">
<meta name="Description" content="Microsoft Corporate Information, Product Support, and More!">
</HEAD>

<BODY BGCOLOR="#FFFFFF"  TEXT="#336699" LINK="#003366" VLINK="#0099cc" ALINK="#003366" TOPMARGIN=
<TABLE BORDER=0 cellpadding=0 cellspacing=0 bgcolor="#FFFFFF" width=100%>
<TR valign=top>
<TD height=20 align=left width=100 bgcolor=000000 valign=bottom>
<img src="/library/images/gifs/homepage/welcometo.gif"  width=120 height=20>
</td>

<TD height=20 colspan=99 align=right bgcolor=000000>
<nobr>
<a href="/search/"><img src="/library/images/gifs/homepage/search1.gif" alt="Search" width=87 hei
</nobr>
</td>
</tr>
<TR>
<TD rowspan=1 valign=top width=267>
<IMG SRC="/LIBRARY/IMAGES/GIFS/HOMEPAGE/logo3.GIF" WIDTH=267 HEIGHT=50 BORDER=0 ALT="MICROSOFT" V
</TD>
```

Part

IV

Ch

25

Linked Stylesheets   You don't have to store your style sheet information inside each of your HTML documents. In fact, if you anticipate applying the same styles across several HTML pages, it is much more efficient for you to store the style information in one place and have each HTML document link to it. This makes it *much* easier to change the formatting of all your pages—you just change the style sheet instead of changing every page!

To set up a linked style sheet, you need to first create the style sheet file. This takes the form of a plain-text file with style information entries like the ones you saw in figure 25.3. For example, your style sheet might look like:

```
BODY {font: 10 pt Palatino; color: red; margin-left: 0.5in}
H1 {font 18 pt Palatino; color: blue}
H2 {font 16 pt Palatino; color: AA4D60}
```

Once you've created your style sheet file, save it with a .css extension and place it on your server. Then you can reference it using the <LINK> tag in the head of each of your HTML documents as follows:

```
<HEAD>
<TITLE>A Document that Uses Style Sheets</TITLE>
<LINK REL=STYLESHEET HREF="styles/sitestyles.css">
</HEAD>
```

The REL attribute describes the relationship of the linked file to the current file—namely that the linked file is a stylesheet. HREF specifies the URL of the style sheet file.

CAUTION

Style sheet files are of MIME type `text/css` though not all servers and browsers register this automatically. If you're setting up a site that uses style sheets, be sure to configure your server to handle the `text/css` MIME type.

Inline Style Sheets   Inline styles can be specified right inside an HTML tag. The style information given applies to the document content up until the defining tag's companion closing tag is encountered. Thus, with the following HTML:

```
<P STYLE="text-align: center; color: yellow">
Yellow, centered text
</P>
<P>
Back to normal
</P>
```

The text `Yellow, centered text` will be centered on the page and colored yellow. This styling applies up until the `</P>` tag, at which point the browser reverts back to whatever styles it was using before the inline style.

Style Sheet Characteristics   In the preceding examples, you've seen some of the font and paragraph characteristics you can specify in a style sheet. Table 25.7 provides a complete list of such characteristics, along with their possible values. Remember that the syntax for specifying a characteristic has the following form:

```
characteristic: value
```

Multiple characteristic/value pairs should be separated by semicolons (;).

CAUTION

There is a great temptation when you first start to work with style sheet to use the syntax `characteristic=value`. Make sure you use the syntax noted above!

Table 25.7   Font and Paragraph Characteristics Allowable in HTML Style Sheets

Characteristic	Possible Values
`font-family`	Any typeface available to Windows
`font-size`	Any size in points (pt), inches (in), centimeters (cm), or pixels (px)
`font-weight`	Normal, bold
`font-style`	Italics
`text-decoration`	None, underline, italic, line-through

Characteristic	Possible Values
color	Any RGB hexadecimal triplet or HTML 3.2 English-language color name
text-align	Left, center, right
text-indent	Any number of points (pt), inches (in), centimeters (cm), or pixels (px)
margin-left	Any number of points (pt), inches (in), centimeters (cm), or pixels (px)
margin-right	Any number of points (pt), inches (in), centimeters (cm), or pixels (px)
line-height	Any number of points (pt), inches (in), centimeters (cm), or pixels (px)
background	Any image URL, RGB hexadecimal triplet, or HTML 3.2 English-language color name

N O T E line-height in Table 25.7 refers to the leading or space between lines that the browser uses. ▪

Part
IV

Ch
25

Microsoft Extensions to HTML

Like many browsers, Microsoft has "extended" HTML by programming Internet Explorer to understand some tags that are not part of standard HTML. These HTML extensions are often design-oriented, and allow Web authors to create pages that are much more attractive than standard HTML would allow. The next several sections examine the HTML extensions supported by Internet Explorer.

CAUTION

When you use an extension to HTML, you are automatically precluding users with browsers that can't parse the extension from seeing what you want them to see. Unless you're sure that your audience has a browser that's able to render the extended tag, you should keep the use of extensions to a minimum.

Aren't They Called Netscape Extensions?

If you've been around HTML much, you've probably seen some of the tags in this section described as Netscape extensions to HTML. The tags have that label because they were introduced by Netscape, and at first were understood only by Netscape's browser. Over time, other browsers such as Internet Explorer were also able to parse these tags correctly.

All of the extensions discussed in the sections that follow will be called Microsoft extensions to HTML. You should take this to mean only that Microsoft Internet Explorer is able to render properly the effects these tags create. While some of them are Microsoft extensions in the truest sense (tags originally introduced to the Web community by Microsoft), most were developed and introduced by the folks at Netscape.

Tags in the Document Head

Internet Explorer extends the <META> tag in the document head to include a value of "Refresh" for the HTTP-EQUIV attribute. Refresh instructs the browser to reload the same document or a different document after a specified number of seconds. The time delay and the URL of the next document, if applicable, are stored in the CONTENT attribute. The syntax for the <META> tag in this situation is:

```
<META HTTP-EQUIV="Refresh" CONTENT="n; url">
```

where *n* is the number of seconds to wait and *url* is the URL of the next document to load. If you want to reload the same document, just use CONTENT="*n*" with no URL specified.

> **CAUTION**
> URLs in the CONTENT attribute should be fully qualified.

This dynamic reloading of documents is called *client pull*. The name is appropriate because the client automatically pulls in the next document with no prompting from the user.

▶ **See** "Creating Dynamic Documents" to learn about some practical applications of client pull, **p. 572**

Another extended tag in the document head is the <ISINDEX> tag. The <ISINDEX> tag designates a document as searchable and gives the user an input field into which search criteria is entered. The default prompting text in front of this search field is "You can search this index. Type the keyword(s) you want to search for:." The PROMPT attribute is a Microsoft extension of the <ISINDEX> tag that lets you change the default prompting text to whatever you like. For example, the following HTML produces the search field shown in figure 25.4:

```
<HEAD>
<TITLE>An Application of the PROMPT Attribute</TITLE>
<ISINDEX PROMPT="Staff Directory - Enter the name to search on:">
</HEAD>
```

▶ **See** "An Exception to the Rule: <ISINDEX>" to learn how to use <ISINDEX> to create a searchable document, **p. 525**

Tags in the Document Body

As with HTML 3.2, most HTML extension tags are meant to go in the body of a document. Microsoft extensions that are permissible in the document body include tags that perform the following functions:

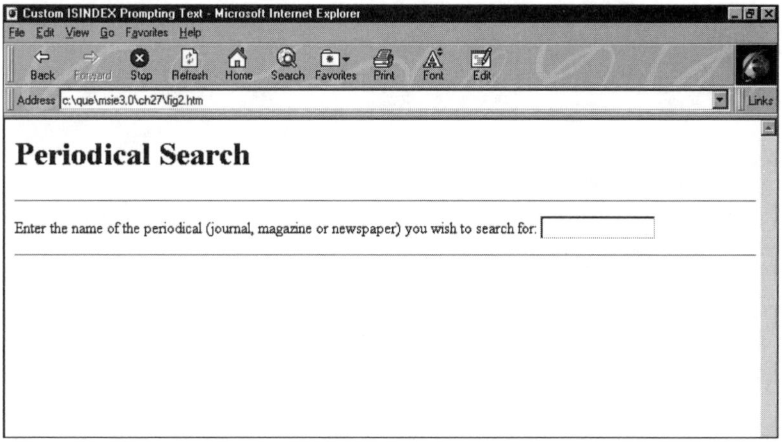

FIG. 27.4
The PROMPT attribute
of the <ISINDEX> tag
gives you control over
the search field
prompting text.

- Specify background sounds
- Control top and left margins of a page
- Create a watermark (nonscrolling background)
- Specify a size, typeface, and color for text
- Support the playing of video clips in the AVI format
- Permit control of the background colors in the individual cells of a table
- Create scrolling text messages
- Divide up the screen into multiple regions called frames
- Support very fine control of image placement and space of page elements around an image
- Modify the presentation of items in ordered lists
- Create different effects with horizontal rules

Background Sound   You can have a background sound play while your Web pages are open by using the <BGSOUND> tag in your document. <BGSOUND> takes the SRC attribute, which is set equal to the URL of a file containing the sound. The file can be in .WAV, .AU, or .MID (MIDI) format.

<BGSOUND> also takes the LOOP attribute, which lets you specify how many times to play the sound. LOOP can be set to a number of times to repeat the sound or to INFINITE to play the sound as long as the page is open. For example,

```
<BGSOUND SRC="hello.wav" LOOP=3>
```

prompts Internet Explorer to say hello three times when the page is opened. The following HTML:

```
<BGSOUND SRC="hello.wav" LOOP=INFINITE>
```

causes Internet Explorer to say hello for as long as the page is open.

Part
IV

Ch
25

CAUTION

Keep your sound files small. Large sound files can take a long time to download—users may be off your page before the sound has finished downloading.

Controlling Page Margins   Internet Explorer supports LEFTMARGIN and TOPMARGIN attributes of the <BODY> tag. You can set either one to the number of pixels of white space you want Internet Explorer to leave along the left and top edges of the browser window.

N O T E   You can set both LEFTMARGIN and TOPMARGIN to 0 to bring both margins right to the edge of the Internet Explorer window. ■

Creating a Watermark   You can use an image as the background of your documents by using the BACKGROUND attribute of the <BODY> tag. BACKGROUND is set equal to the URL of the image to be used. If the image is not big enough to fit the entire screen, it will be tiled (both horizontally and vertically) to fill the available space. Figure 25.5 shows a page from a site that uses a background image.

FIG. 25.5

You can use an image as a background for your pages with the BACKGROUND attribute of the <BODY> tag.

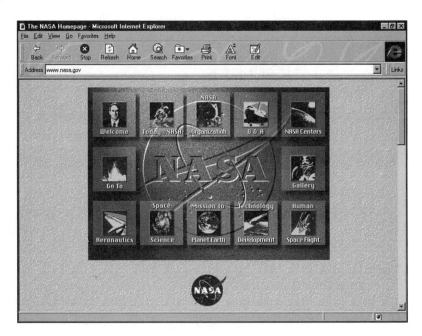

If you use the BACKGROUND attribute of the <BODY> tag to tile a graphic as your document background, the background scrolls as you scroll through the document. Internet Explorer gives you greater control over scrolling by supporting a BGPROPERTIES attribute. If you set BGPROPERTIES to FIXED, the background image will not scroll as you move through the document, creating a "watermark" effect.

Text Effects   The `<FONT>` and `</FONT>` container tags give you control over the size, color, and typeface of the text they contain. To modify the size of the text, you use the `SIZE` attribute in the `<FONT>` tag. `SIZE` can be set to any number between 1 and 7. The default text size is 3. You can also specify `SIZE` relative to the base font size by indicating how many sizes above (+) or below (-) the base font size you want the text to be. Thus, with a base font size of 3, the following two lines of HTML do the same thing:

```
<FONT SIZE=5>This text is big!</FONT>
<FONT SIZE=+2>This text is big!</FONT>
```

Similarly, to go two sizes below 3, you could use either of the following:

```
<FONT SIZE=1>This text is small!</FONT>
<FONT SIZE=-2>This text is small!</FONT>
```

The base font size is always 3, unless you change it with the `<BASEFONT SIZE=n>` tag. *n* can be any number between 1 and 7.

A popular effect you can create with the `SIZE` attribute is "small caps." With small caps, each letter in a word is in uppercase, but the first letter of each word is bigger than the others. Figure 25.6 shows some text in small caps as produced by the following HTML:

```
<FONT SIZE=+2>I</FONT>NTERNET <FONT SIZE=+2>E</FONT>XPLORER
```

FIG. 25.6
You can create text in small caps using the `SIZE` attribute of the `<FONT>` tag.

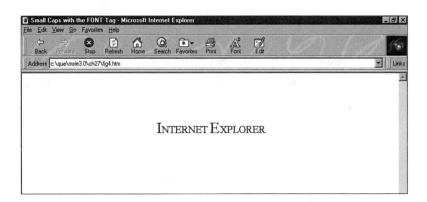

You can also change the color of text between `<FONT>` and `</FONT>` by using the `COLOR` attribute of the `<FONT>` tag. `COLOR` is set equal to the `RGB` (Red/Green/Blue) hexadecimal triplet of the color you want. Thus, the following HTML:

```
Here is some <FONT COLOR="#00FF00">green text.</FONT>
```

instructs Internet Explorer to render the words green text. in green.

> **TIP** See Table 28.1 for an extensive list of colors and their respective RGB triplets.

If dealing with hexadecimal numbers is unappealing to you, you'll be happy to know that Internet Explorer can also recognize the 16 English-language color names adopted in HTML 3.2.

Recall that these colors include BLACK, WHITE, GREEN, MAROON, OLIVE, NAVY, PURPLE, GRAY, RED, YELLOW, BLUE, TEAL, LIME, AQUA, FUSCHIA, and SILVER. Thus, the following HTML does the same thing as the HTML in the example you saw earlier:

```
Here is some <FONT COLOR="GREEN">green text.</FONT>
```

You can use the FACE attribute of the <FONT> tag to specify a typeface that Internet Explorer should use when rendering text. You can even set FACE to a list of typefaces, giving the browser other options if the most desirable face is not available. For example, the following HTML:

```
<FONT FACE="Palatino,Times,Helvetica">Custom Typefaces!</FONT>
```

would instruct Internet Explorer to render the text Custom Typefaces! in Palatino if that type-face were available. If Palatino weren't available, Internet Explorer would then try to use Times, followed by Helvetica.

N O T E The <FONT> tag, along with the SIZE and COLOR attributes, was adopted as part of HTML 3.2. ■

AVI Video Clips   Microsoft has greatly extended the <IMG> tag to provide exceptional support of inline video clips and VRML worlds stored in the Audio Video Interleave (AVI) format. The extended attributes are shown in Table 25.8.

Table 25.8   Internet Explorer Extensions to the <IMG> Tag

Attribute	Purpose
DYNSRC="url"	Specifies the URL of the AVI file containing the video clip
CONTROLS	Places a control panel in the browser window so the user can control the playing of the clip
START=FILEOPEN¦ MOUSEOVER	Specifies when to start the video clip
LOOP=n¦INFINITE	Controls how many times the clip is repeated
LOOPDELAY=n	Specifies how many milliseconds to wait before repeating the clip

For example, the following HTML tag:

```
<IMG DYNSRC="commercial.avi" CONTROLS START=FILEOPEN LOOP=2>
```

instructs Internet Explorer to play the clip stored in COMMERCIAL.AVI two times when the file is opened. A control panel will be present while the clip is playing, so that the user may stop, rewind, or fast-forward (see fig. 25.7).

 You can set START to both FILEOPEN and MOUSEOVER together (START=FILEOPEN,MOUSEOVER). This configuration will play the clip once when the file is opened and then once each time the mouse is moved over the clip window.

FIG. 25.7
Internet Explorer supports a control panel for playing AVI video clips.

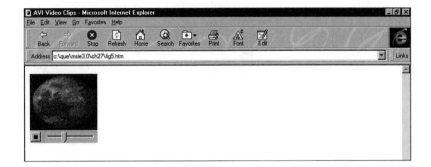

Tables In the <TABLE> tag, you can specify the BORDERCOLOR attribute to control what color Internet Explorer uses when rendering table borders. BORDERCOLOR should be set equal to the hexadecimal RGB triplet or an English-language color name that describes the desired color.

You can also use the BGCOLOR attribute in a <TD> tag to change the background color of a table cell. BGCOLOR is also set equal to a hexadecimal RGB triplet or an English-language color name.

> **CAUTION**
> Be careful about coloring each of your table cells with different colors. This can be very harsh on a reader's eyes.

Part
IV
Ch
25

Marquees The <MARQUEE> and </MARQUEE> tag pair places a scrolling text marquee on your Web page. The text that scrolls is the text found between the two tags.

The <MARQUEE> tag can take a number of attributes that give you very fine control over the appearance and behavior of the marquee. These attributes are summarized in Table 25.9.

Table 25.9   Attributes of the <MARQUEE> Tag

Attribute	Purpose
BGCOLOR="RGB triplet"	Specifies the background color of the marquee window
BEHAVIOR=SCROLL¦ SLIDE¦ALTERNATE	Specifies how the text should move in the marquee window
DIRECTION=LEFT¦RIGHT	Controls the direction in which the marquee text moves
SCROLLAMOUNT=n	Sets the number of pixels of space between successive presentations of marquee text
SCROLLDELAY=n	Sets the number of milliseconds to wait before repeating the marquee text
HEIGHT=pixels¦percent	Specifies the height of the marquee window in either pixels or a percentage of the browser window height

continues

Table 25.9   Continued

Attribute	Purpose
WIDTH=*pixels¦percent*	Specifies the width of the marquee window in either pixels or a percentage of the browser window width
HSPACE=*n*	Specifies how many pixels to make the left and right margins of the marquee window
VSPACE=*n*	Specifies how many pixels to make the top and bottom margins of the marquee window
LOOP=*n*¦INFINITE	Controls how many times the marquee text should scroll
ALIGN=TOP¦MIDDLE ¦BOTTOM	Specifies how text outside the marquee window should be aligned with the window

While the purposes of most of these attributes are straightforward, the BEHAVIOR attribute values require some explanation. Setting BEHAVIOR to SCROLL make the marquee text scroll on and then off the marquee window in the direction specified by the DIRECTION attribute. If BE- HAVIOR equals SLIDE, the text will slide into the window and stay there. If BEHAVIOR is set to ALTERNATE, the text will bounce back and forth in the window.

Marquee text is a nice Web page effect that you can accomplish on other browsers only by using something more advanced such as Java or Shockwave. Figure 25.8 shows some marquee text sliding onto a page.

FIG. 25.8

Marquee text can scroll or slide onto a page from one of the edges of the screen.

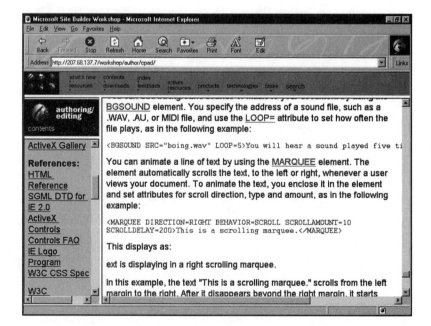

Frames Internet Explorer supports an exciting new concept called *frames*. Using the frame tags, you can break up the browser window into separate areas that can each load its own HTML document. This is a valuable feature because it lets you put static items, like tables of contents and navigation aids, in small, yet permanent windows while still leaving a considerable amount of space for changing material. Thus, users can look at different documents in the largest frame and always have the useful static items available in smaller frames.

The first step in creating a framed document is to split the Internet Explorer screen up into the frames that you want. You accomplish this with an HTML file that uses the <FRAMESET> and </FRAMESET> container tags instead of the <BODY> and </BODY> tags. <FRAMESET> and </FRAMESET> are not just container tags, though. Attributes of the <FRAMESET> tag are instrumental in defining the frame regions.

The <FRAMESET> tag can take one of two attributes: ROWS, to split the screen up into multiple rows, or COLS, to split the screen up into multiple columns. Each attribute is set equal to a list of values that tells Internet Explorer how big to make each row. The values can be a number of pixels, a percentage of a browser window dimension, or an asterisk (*), which acts as a wildcard character and tells the browser to use whatever space it has left. For example, the following HTML:

```
<FRAMESET COLS="40%,50%,10%">
...
</FRAMESET>
```

breaks the browser window into three columns. The first column has a width equal to 40 percent of the browser screen width, the second column, 50 percent, and the third column, 10 percent. Similarly, the following HTML:

```
<FRAMESET ROWS="50,125,3*,*">
...
</FRAMESET>
```

splits the window into four rows. The first row is 50 pixels deep and the second is 15 pixels deep. The remaining space is divided between the third and fourth rows, with the third row being three times as big (3*) as the fourth (*).

N O T E Internet Explorer also recognizes the FRAMESPACING attribute of the <FRAMESET> tag. You can set FRAMESPACING equal to the amount of space you want between frames. ■

To produce really interesting layouts, you can nest <FRAMESET> and </FRAMESET> tags. Suppose you want to split the browser window into four equal regions. You can first split the screen into two equal rows with the following HTML:

```
<FRAMESET ROWS="50%,50%">
...
</FRAMESET>
```

Part
IV

Ch
25

This produces the screen shown in figure 25.9.

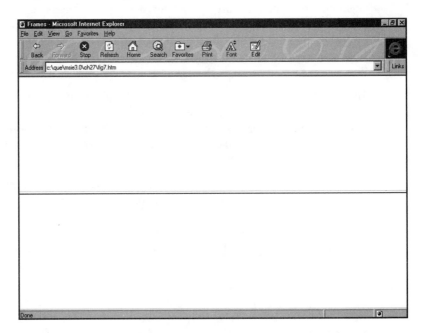

Next you need to divide each row in half. To do this, you need a `<FRAMESET>` and `</FRAMESET>` pair for each row that splits the row into two equal columns. The HTML `<FRAMESET COLS="50%,50%">` and `</FRAMESET>` will do the trick. Nesting these tags in the previous HTML produces the following:

```
<FRAMESET ROWS="25%,25%,25%,25%">
    <FRAMESET COLS="50%,50%"> <!— Split Row 1 into two columns —>
        ...
    </FRAMESET>
    <FRAMESET COLS="50%,50%"> <!— Split Row 2 into two columns —>
        ...
    </FRAMESET>
</FRAMESET>
```

This HTML completes the task of splitting the window into four equal regions. The resulting screen is shown in figure 25.10.

Not sure whether to do a `<FRAMESET>` with ROWS or COLS first? Make a pencil-and-paper sketch of what you want the browser window to look like. If you have unbroken horizontal lines that go from one edge of the window to the other, do your ROWS first. If you have unbroken vertical lines that go from the top of the window to the bottom, do your COLS first. If you have both unbroken horizontal and vertical lines, it doesn't matter which one you do first.

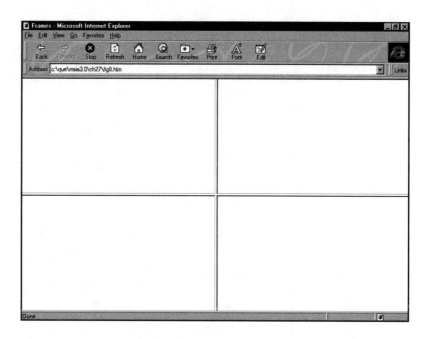

Part
IV
Ch
25

With your frames all set up, you're ready to place content in each one with the <FRAME> tag. The most important attribute of the <FRAME> tag is SRC, which tells Internet Explorer the URL of the document you want to load into the frame. The <FRAME> tag can take the attributes summarized in Table 25.10 as well. If you use the NAME attribute, the name you give the frame must begin with an alphanumeric character.

Table 25.10 Attributes of the *<FRAME>* Tag

Attribute	Purpose
MARGINHEIGHT=n	Specifies the amount of white space to be left at the top and bottom of the frame
MARGINWIDTH=n	Specifies the amount of white space to be left along the sides of the frame
NAME="name"	Gives the frame a unique name so it can be targeted by other documents
NORESIZE	Disables the user's ability to resize the frame
SCROLLING=YES¦ NO¦AUTO	Controls the appearance of horizontal and vertical scrollbars in the frame
SRC="url"	Specifies the URL of the document to load into the frame
FRAMEBORDER=n	Specifies the width to use for the border between frames (0 is an acceptable value)

To place content in each of the four equal regions you created earlier, you can use the following HTML:

```
<FRAMESET ROWS="25%,25%,25%,25%">
    <FRAMESET COLS="50%,50%"> <!— Split Row 1 into two columns —>
        <FRAME SRC="one.html">
        <FRAME SRC="two.html">
    </FRAMESET>
    <FRAMESET COLS="50%,50%"> <!— Split Row 2 into two columns —>
        <FRAME SRC="three.html">
        <FRAME SRC="four.html">
    </FRAMESET>
</FRAMESET>
```

The resulting screen appears in figure 25.11.

FIG. 25.11

The <FRAME> tag lets you place a different HTML document into each frame.

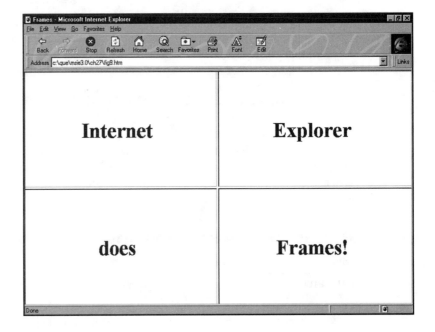

If you create a document with frames, people who are using a browser other than Internet Explorer 3 or Netscape 2.0 will not be able to see the content you want them to see because their browsers don't understand the <FRAMESET>, </FRAMESET>, and <FRAME> tags. As a courtesy to users with "frames-challenged" browsers, you can place alternative HTML code between the <NOFRAMES> and </NOFRAMES> container tags. Any HTML between these two tags will be understood and rendered by other browsers. A "frames-capable" browser, on the other hand, ignores anything between these tags and works just with the frame-related HTML.

> **CAUTION**
> The <NOFRAMES> and </NOFRAMES> tags must occur after the initial <FRAMESET> tag, but before any nested <FRAMESET> tags.

Adding Frames to Your Web Site

Now that you've mastered the frames tags, you're probably eager to make frames versions of your Web pages.

First, think about the visitors to your site. Ask yourself if they are likely to have a frames-capable browser like Internet Explorer. If most of the hits on your site are from browsers that don't support frames, you should probably rethink your efforts to create pages with frames.

Once you're convinced that frames are the way to go, spend some time designing your framed window. Most sites that make good use of frames have a fairly narrow navigation frame on the left or right side of the window and use the rest of the space of changing content. You can create such a set-up with the following HTML:

```
<FRAMESET COLS="25%,75%">
<FRAME NAME="nav" SRC="navigate.html">
<FRAME NAME="main" SRC="main.html">
</FRAMESET>
```

This creates a navigation frame in the left-most quarter of the screen and loads the document navigate.html into that frame. The remaining three-fourths of the screen is dedicated to changing content and the first document loaded into this frame is main.html. You could easily place the navigation frame on the right side of the window by setting COLS="75%,25%" in the <FRAMESET> tag and by switching the order of the two <FRAME> tags.

Once of the nice things about frames is that once you have them set up, you can continue to use existing HTML documents. In the previous example, you can have documents you've already written simply loaded into the frame named main. You can also "recycle" existing HTML documents by copying them between the <NOFRAMES> and </NOFRAMES> tags so that even users with frames-challenged browsers will be able to see the content you want them to see.

Probably the trickiest thing about frames is getting content to appear where you want it to appear. This is where naming the frames you create becomes critical. By naming the changing content frame main, you can then use the TARGET attribute in all of your <A> tags to direct all hyperlinked documents to be loaded into that frame. Thus, an example link in the file navigate.html might look like the following:

```
<A HREF="press/index.html" TARGET="main">
Press Releases
</A>
```

If all of the links in navigate.html should target the frame named main, you can use the <BASE> tag in the head of the document to set a value for TARGET that applies to all links, like the following:

```
<HEAD>
<TITLE>Site Navigation Options</TITLE>
<BASE TARGET="main">
</HEAD>
```

Images   In addition to the attributes for viewing AVI video clips, the ALIGN attribute of the <IMG> tag has been extended by Microsoft. Internet Explorer understands the values of ALIGN shown in Table 25.11.

Table 25.11   Values of the *ALIGN* Attribute of the *<IMG>* Tag

Value	Effect
TOP	Aligns text following the image with the top of the image
MIDDLE	Aligns the baseline of text following the image with the center of the image
BOTTOM	Aligns the baseline of text following the image with the bottom of the image
LEFT	Floats the image in the left margin, allowing text to wrap around the right side of the image
RIGHT	Floats the image in the right margin, allowing text to wrap around the left side of the image

What's new and interesting are the LEFT and RIGHT values of ALIGN, which produce *floating images* and make it easy to wrap text around an image. Figure 25.12 shows images floated in the left and right margins with text wrapping around them.

FIG. 25.12

Using ALIGN=LEFT or ALIGN=RIGHT lets you float images in the left or right margins.

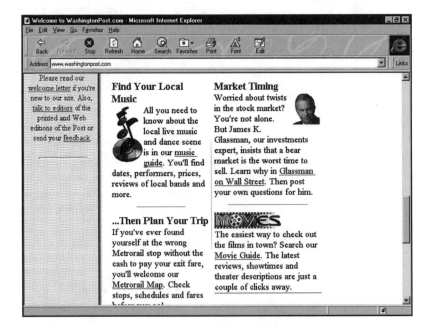

N O T E The availability of floating images also makes it necessary to be able to break to the next line that is clear of a floating image. To handle this, Internet Explorer recognizes the CLEAR attribute to the <BR> tag. CLEAR can be set to LEFT, to move to the first line whose left margin is clear of floating images; RIGHT, to move to the first line whose right margin is clear of floating images; or ALL, to move to the first line that is completely free of floating images. ▪

Beyond the new values for the ALIGN attribute, Internet Explorer also understands three other attributes of the <IMG> tag. The BORDER=*n* attribute lets you specify the thickness of the border around your images. The default value of *n* is 1, but you can change it to any value you choose, including zero. Setting BORDER to zero is useful with transparent GIFs because it eliminates the rectangular box that would otherwise surround the image.

CAUTION

Setting BORDER=0 on a hyperlinked image will remove the colored border, and users may not be able to tell that the image is linked.

Since it's possible to wrap text around a floating image, it becomes necessary to have a way to put some additional space around the image so that wrapping text doesn't bump right up against it. The HSPACE=*n* attribute lets you insert *n* pixels of white space to the left and right of the floating image. VSPACE=*n* works similarly to put white space above and below the image.

Part
IV

Ch

25

N O T E The ALIGN=LEFT, ALIGN=RIGHT, BORDER, HSPACE, and VSPACE attributes of the <IMG> tag were accepted as part of HTML 3.2. ▪

Floating Frames Microsoft introduced the concept of a *floating frame* with Internet Explorer 3. You can think of a floating frame as a smaller browser window that you can open in your main browser window—much like the "picture-in-a-picture" feature that comes with many television sets. Just as with regular frames, you can load any HTML document you want into a floating frame. The primary difference is that floating frames can be placed anywhere on a page that you would put an image. In fact, you'll find the HTML syntax for placing floating frames to be very similar to that for placing an image.

You place a floating frame on a page by using the <IFRAME> and </IFRAME> tags. Internet Explorer will ignore anything between these two tags, allowing you to place an alternative to the floating frame (most likely, text or an image) on the page as well. This way, browsers that don't know how to render floating frames can ignore the <IFRAME> and </IFRAME> tags and act on what is found between them.

The <IFRAME> tag has three required attributes: WIDTH, HEIGHT, and SRC. WIDTH and HEIGHT specify the width and height of the floating frame in pixels or as a percentage of the browser screen width and height. SRC is set equal to the URL of the HTML document you want loaded into the floating frame. Thus, your basic floating frame HTML looks like the following:

```
<IFRAME WIDTH=300 HEIGHT=200 SRC="http://www.myserver.com/floatme.html"
Text or image based alternative to the floating frame
</IFRAME>
```

Figure 25.13 shows an example of a floating frame.

FIG. 25.13

Floating frames are windows to other HTML documents that you can place on your pages with the same flexibility you have when placing images.

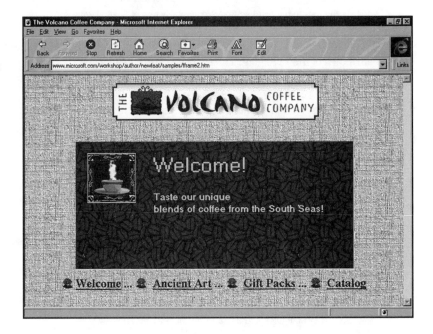

In addition to the three required attributes, the `<IFRAME>` tag takes several other attributes that give you good control over the floating frames appearance. These include the following:

- **FRAMEBORDER**—You'll notice in figure 25.13 that the floating frame has a beveled border that gives it the appearance of being recessed in the main browser window. If you prefer a more seamless look, you can use the FRAMEBORDER attribute in the `<IFRAME>` tag. Setting FRAMEBORDER=0 eliminates the beveled border.

- **SCROLLING**—Internet Explorer will put a scrollbar on the floating frame if the document in the frame exceeds the dimensions of the frame. You can suppress the scrollbars by specifying SCROLLING=NO in the `<IFRAME>` tag.

- **HSPACE and VSPACE**—If your floating frame needs some clear space around it, the HSPACE and VSPACE attributes of the `<IFRAME>` tag work the same way they do for the `<IMG>` tag: HSPACE adds clear space to the left and right of the floating frame and VSPACE adds clear space above and below.

- **ALIGN**—You can float the floating frame in the left or right margins by specifying ALIGN=LEFT or ALIGN=RIGHT. Any text following the floated frame will wrap around it to the right or left. You can use the `<BR>` tag with the appropriate CLEAR attribute to break to the first line clear of floated frames.

■ **NAME**—Naming a floating frame allows you to target it with the TARGET attribute in an <A> tag. This allows you to set up links to documents and have them appear in the floating frame.

Ordered Lists   The TYPE attribute is a useful extension to the <OL> tag that Internet Explorer understands. By default, ordered list item are numbered with consecutive integers starting with "1." By setting TYPE equal to "A," "a," "I," or "i," you can change the scheme to be upper-case letters, lowercase letters, uppercase Roman numerals, or lowercase Roman numerals, respectively. Having these five numbering schemes makes it easy to replicate the standard outline format using ordered lists. Figure 25.14 illustrates this point. The HTML to produce the figure is as following:

```
<OL TYPE="I">
    <LI>Introduction</LI>
    <OL TYPE="A">
        <LI>Problem statement</LI>
        <LI>Results of previous research</LI>
    </OL>
    <LI>Approach</LI>
    <OL TYPE="A">
        <LI>Research objectives</LI>
        <LI>Equipment</LI>
        <OL>
            <LI>Lab equipment</LI>
            <LI>Computing equipment</LI>
        </OL>
        <LI>Techniques</LI>
    </OL>
    ...
</OL>
```

FIG. 25.14
Creating outlines in HTML is simple with the TYPE attribute of the <OL> tag.

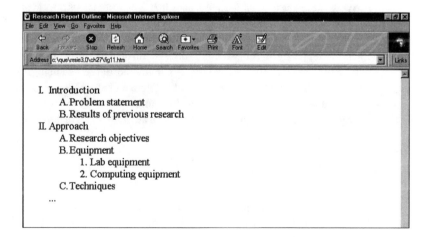

Part
IV
Ch
25

A related extension to the <OL> tag is the START attribute, which lets you change the starting value of the list item numbering. START=1 by default, but you can change it to any number you choose. If you're using a TYPE different from the default numbering scheme, you can still specify a different starting value using numbers. Internet Explorer automatically converts the new starting value to the chosen numbering scheme for you. Thus, the following HTML produces the list seen in figure 25.15:

```
<P>Users' favorite Internet applications
after e-mail and the World Wide Web were:
<OL TYPE="i" START=3>
<LI>Usenet newsgroups</LI>
<LI>FTP</LI>
<LI>Telnet</LI>
<LI>Internet Relay Chat (IRC)</LI>
</OL>
```

FIG. 25.15

The START attribute of the <OL> tag lets you begin numbering an ordered list at any value.

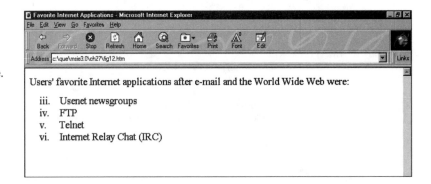

NOTE According to initial documentation, HTML 3.2 includes the START attribute of the <OL> tag, but not the TYPE attribute. ■

Finally, Internet Explorer extends list type control all the way down to the list item level by adding the TYPE attribute to the <LI> tag. In an unordered list, using TYPE in an <LI> tag lets you change the bullet character for that list item and all subsequent items. For ordered lists, a TYPE attribute in an <LI> tag changes the numbering scheme for that list item and each one after it. The <LI> tag can also take the VALUE attribute in an ordered list. VALUE lets you change the numbering count to any other number you choose.

NOTE TYPE and VALUE are valid attributes of the <LI> tag under HTML 3.2. ■

Horizontal Lines   Internet Explorer supports several attributes to the <HR> tag that give you control over the width, thickness, alignment, color, and shading characteristics of ruled lines. The new attributes are summarized in Table 25.12.

Table 25.12 Attributes of the *<HR>* Tag

Attribute	Purpose
WIDTH=pixels¦percent	Allows you to change the width of the rule to a set number of pixels or a percentage of the browser screen width
ALIGN=LEFT¦RIGHT¦CENTER	Sets the alignment of a piece of rule (default is CENTER)
SIZE=*n*	Controls the thickness of the rule (default is 1)
COLOR=RGB hexadecimal triplet¦color name	Controls the color in which the rule is rendered
NOSHADE	Disables the shading Netscape uses when rendering rule, producing a solid bar

Figure 25.16 illustrates some of the new types of rules you can produce with these extensions. The corresponding HTML is as follows:

```
<HR>
Normal rule<P>
<HR SIZE=8 WIDTH=40% ALIGN=RIGHT>
Size 8, 40% width, flush right alignment<P>
<HR SIZE=12 NOSHADE>
Size 12, no shading<P>
<HR SIZE=16 NOSHADE WIDTH=80% ALIGN=LEFT>
Size 16, no shading, 80% width, flush left alignment<P>
```

Part
IV

Ch
25

FIG. 25.16

Internet Explorer extensions to the <HR> tag let you specify width, thickness, alignment, color, and shading of your horizontal rule.

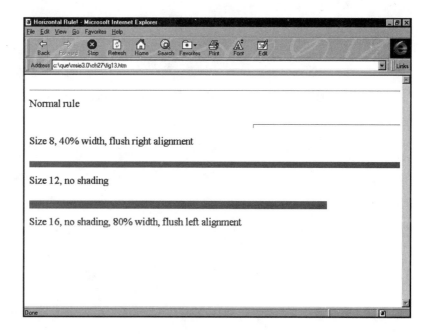

N O T E   The ALIGN, NOSHADE, SIZE, and WIDTH attributes of the \<HR\> tag are now part of the
HTML 3.2 spec.   ■

  Since you can't know how many pixels wide every user's browser screen is, you should always specify
WIDTH in terms of a percentage rather than a set number of pixels.

HTML Tags not Recognized by Internet Explorer

In spite of the many HTML "extras" that Internet Explorer supports, there is an attribute of one tag that it will not parse.

As you nest unordered lists, Internet Explorer continues to use a solid circle as the bullet character. Netscape, on the other hand, changes the bullet character to open circles and squares as you nest ordered lists. To give you control over the type of bullet character in use, Netscape introduced a TYPE attribute to the \<UL\> tag. TYPE can be set to DISC for a solid circle, CIRCLE for an open circle, or SQUARE for a square. Internet Explorer ignores this extension and continues to use solid circles for all bulleted lists. You can expect that Microsoft will implement this tag in Internet Explorer soon though, since the TYPE attribute of the \<UL\> tag is part of the newly released HTML 3.2 spec.

N O T E   Like most browsers, if Internet Explorer encounters a tag that it doesn't recognize, it simply
ignores it.   ■

## CHAPTER 26

Internet Explorer Forms and CGI Scripts

The HTML documents you've learned to write so far are unchanging in the sense that you can reload the same HTML code a hundred times and you'll always see the same thing in your Internet Explorer window. Such documents are called *static* because they never change unless changes are made to the HTML source code.

Unfortunately, we live in a world that craves fresh content. We tire of the "same old thing" very quickly. For this reason, good Web sites get a graphic makeover every three months or so. A new look every once in a while keeps users coming back.

Another way to keep users engaged is by having your pages be interactive. Saying this is easy, but you cannot do it with HTML alone. Interactive implies a two-way exchange between the user and the server. Since the server really knows only how to serve Web pages, and users want to go beyond simply requesting and receiving pages, the server software needs to be able to access other functionality on the machine where it resides. And once you grant access to other programs running on the server, you need to also furnish users with a means of supplying input to those programs.

HTML forms and Common Gateway Interface (CGI) scripts are the keys to creating interactive Web pages. ■

The basic principles of CGI

Form data follows a very specific processing path from client to server and back again.

How to write CGI scripts in the Bourne shell and Perl scripting languages

Four different examples give you a sense of what's possible with even very simple scripts.

The HTML tags used to create forms

For as powerful as forms are, you only need to know a handful of HTML tags to create them.

What happens to form data after the user enters it?

Form data is packaged in a very specific way and sent to the server by one of two methods: GET or POST.

Where you can find publicly available code to assist you in writing scripts

Many CGI programmers have written useful routines that they have released into the public domain so that the rest of us can benefit.

Interactivity on the Web

Two elements go into making interactivity on the Web possible: forms and CGI scripts. While these elements are probably two of the most misunderstood—and confusing—aspects of creating a Web site, they are also the two most powerful. With them, you can do anything from asking the user to guess a number to taking an order for a pizza to offering free searches of your comprehensive Web database, as shown in figure 26.1.

FIG. 26.1

Forms let users interact with programs on your server.

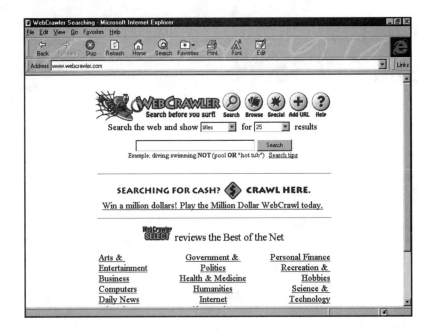

To get true interactivity on the Web, you need to understand and use both CGI scripts and forms because they are two sides of the same coin. Forms allow the users to enter data—information about themselves, their requests, their purchase orders, or anything else—into Internet Explorer and send it through the World Wide Web to your server. This side is the front-end that users see and interact with.

CGI scripts make up the back-end. They take the information sent to the server through the Web and process it—querying databases, placing orders, or simply logging accesses. This process all happens behind the scenes, but it's where the real work takes place. The results are then passed back in an HTML document generated by the script. When a script writes an HTML page, the page is said to be *dynamically generated*, or created *on-the-fly*.

Though they can seem confusing, CGI scripts and forms are worth the trouble. They can transform your site from something static and predictable to something dynamic and exciting.

The Common Gateway Interface (CGI)

The Common Gateway Interface is the full name of CGI, and it is a way for your Web server to extend its capabilities by running external programs. CGI is a "gateway" to functionality not preprogrammed into your server, and it allows you to use all your computer's capabilities, instead of just those that are already part of the server software.

To a user, a link to a CGI program looks like a link to any other URL. It can be clicked like any other link and results in new information being displayed just like any other link.

But a CGI program, under the hood, is much more than a normal Web page. When a normal URL is selected, a file is read, interpreted, and displayed in the Internet Explorer window. When a URL to a CGI program is selected, it causes a program to be run on the server system, and that program can do just about anything you want it to: scan databases, sort names, or send mail. CGI scripts allow for complex back-end processing.

CGI changes the definition of what's possible on the Web. While normal pages are static and unchanging, CGI programs allow a page to be anything you want it to be.

Scripts Versus Programs

What's the difference between a CGI script and a CGI program? Semantics, mostly. The term script is left over from the early days of the Web, when it ran exclusively on UNIX machines. A UNIX script is a list of commands run in sequence, a lot like DOS batch files. The first CGI programs were written using these scripts, so the name CGI scripts caught on. Later, true programs (written in Perl or C, usually) were used to perform the same functions. No functional difference exists between scripts and programs—neither the user nor the server software can tell them apart—and both terms are used interchangeably in this chapter.

Getting Set Up

Before you can begin to use CGI scripts, you must take care of a few preliminaries. They really have nothing to do with Internet Explorer since CGI scripts live and run on the server. Thus, we will just touch on the requirements, which are as follows:

- **You must have access to a Web server, or the ability to install and configure one.** This job can be complicated and tedious, so you should ask your company's or school's system administrator or Webmaster whether a server that you can use is already set up.

- **You should know at least some UNIX.** Though Web servers exist for many different platforms and the concepts discussed in this chapter apply to all of them, the details contained here are UNIX-specific.

- **You must know a computer language.** CGI scripts are not written in HTML like normal Web pages. Instead of static instructions to be interpreted by Internet Explorer, they are actual computer programs. As a result, they have a flexibility that normal Web pages don't have, but using scripts also increases their complexity. Before you can write CGI scripts, you must know how to program.

While you can use almost any language to write your CGI scripts, the most popular are Bourne shell (on UNIX), batch files (on Windows NT and Windows 95), Perl, and C. Each has strengths and weaknesses, and while a discussion of each is beyond the scope of this book, many excellent references are available.

For smaller CGI scripts, UNIX Bourne shell scripts or Windows NT or 95 batch files are good choices. They are easy to write, easy to test, and don't take much of a time investment. If a simple script needs to evolve into something more complex—maybe it needs the ability to search a text file—you can use the command-line tools, such as `grep`, `awk`, `sed`, or any number of others.

For medium-sized CGI scripts, Perl is a good choice. It's fast, flexible, and easy to program. You can set variables, call subroutines, and do everything a "real" language allows, without a lot of the hassle.

For large or time-critical CGI scripts, the most common choice is a true C program. While C can be difficult to use and even harder to debug, it is incredibly flexible and often the only way to get to external functionality—Microsoft's Telephony API (TAPI), for instance, can be used only from C.

■ **You must have permission to install your script correctly on the server.** For UNIX Web servers, by default, a subdirectory called `cgi-bin` is located off where the server software itself is installed. All CGI scripts go in this directory, though you need specific UNIX permissions to access it. Again, talk to your system administrator or Webmaster for details.

Sample CGI Scripts

With the preliminaries out of the way, you can now take a look at some sample scripts. The best way to see what CGI scripts can actually do is by writing a few and seeing how they perform. Following are three simple examples that demonstrate some of the power that CGI scripts give to Web pages.

Sending a Simple Message   While many CGI programs are extremely complex, they don't have to be. Probably the simplest example possible is the UNIX shell script in Listing 26.1.

Listing 26.1   A Very Simple CGI Script

```
#!/bin/sh
echo "Content-type: text/html"
echo ""
echo "<HTML>"
echo "<HEAD>"
echo"<TITLE>Listing 28.1</TITLE>"
echo"</HEAD>"
echo "<BODY>"
echo "This is a <EM>simple</EM> CGI script."
echo "</BODY>"
echo "</HTML>"
```

A lot is happening in this short CGI program, and all of it is vital for the script to work as intended.

The first line of this program (`#!/bin/sh/`) tells UNIX that this script is to run in the Bourne shell, one of the many available in UNIX. Bourne is the most common, however, and the only one that every UNIX ships with, so it is the most often used. If this program were a Windows NT or 95 batch file, you could leave off this first line.

The second line tells Internet Explorer what kind of information it is about to receive. The `Content-type:` is required for all CGI scripts, and it must correspond to a valid MIME type. Multipurpose Internet Mail Extensions (or MIME) is a method for delivering complex binary data over networks, and Web browsers like Internet Explorer use it to encode and decode that data invisibly. The two most common MIME types used by CGI scripts are `text/html` for HTML output, and `text/plain` for ASCII text.

> **CAUTION**
>
> One common error when writing CGI scripts is to have an incorrect `Content-type` for the type of data that is being sent. If your script sends HTML, as Listing 26.1 does, but the `Content-type:` is `text/plain`, none of the HTML tags are interpreted by Internet Explorer, leaving your page looking like HTML source code.

The third line is simply an empty space to tell the server that what follows is the data described by the Content-type. You must include this empty line; otherwise, nothing separates this header information from the main body of the message.

N O T E While `Content-type:` is by far the most common header sent from CGI scripts, Internet Explorer (and most other browsers) understand another one as well.

If you have a `Location:` URL line, Internet Explorer automatically ignores any following content and jumps to the new URL. This way, sites like URoulette can send you to a random URL—a CGI script picks from a database of URLs and returns a randomly generated `Location:` line. ■

The remaining lines produce the actual HTML code that is to be sent to the Internet Explorer. These lines are passed through the server and interpreted, just as the same instructions would be if they'd been read from an HTML file that looks like the following:

```
<HTML>
<HEAD>
<TITLE>Listing 26.1</TITLE>
</HEAD>
<BODY>
This is a <EM>simple</EM> CGI script.
</BODY>
</HTML>
```

TROUBLESHOOTING

I keep getting errors when I try to run my CGI program. What do they mean? And what's the best way to debug my script? The most common error is `500 Server Error`; it means that you either forgot to send the `Content-type:` line before your data, or your CGI program failed somehow part way through. Both cases mean you have some debugging to do.

If you get error `403 Forbidden`, you need to set certain permissions on your CGI script. When a Web server is installed, it is owned by a specific user on the system (usually root), and that user must be able to read and execute the CGI script itself and traverse the directories that contain it. Talk to your system administrator or Webmaster to correct this problem.

The best way to debug CGI programs is to execute them from the command line instead of through the Web server. Set any appropriate environment variables by hand—environment variables are discussed later in the chapter—and simply run your program. This way, you can see any errors your script generates instead of the generic `500 Server Error` message.

Sending a Dynamic Message   Of course, the simple CGI program in Listing 26.1 outputs only static data—no matter how many times you call it, the output doesn't change—and a user wouldn't be able to tell it from a normal Web page. You can see the real power of CGI scripts when they go beyond this stage, when they start generating dynamic data—something that's impossible for a normal page to do.

The CGI script in Listing 26.2 displays a new fortune each time you run it.

Listing 26.2   A Dynamic CGI Script

```sh
#!/bin/sh
echo "Content-type: text/html"
echo ""
echo "<HTML>"
echo "<HEAD>"
echo "<TITLE>Fortune</TITLE>"
echo "</HEAD>"
echo "<BODY>"
echo "Words of wisdom:"
echo "<PRE>"
FORTUNE=/usr/games/fortune
if [ "$FORTUNE" = "" ]; then
echo "A wise system administrator installs 'fortune' for his _users."
echo "     — Anon"
else
     echo $FORTUNE
fi
echo "</PRE>"
echo "</BODY>"
echo "</HTML>"
```

Instead of just printing out a predefined message, this script—through the UNIX `fortune` command—shows dynamic information each time it is run. If a user selects the link that runs this script twice in a row, it produces totally different results (unless `fortune` is not installed).

Just about any UNIX utility, or combination of utilities, can be used in place of the `fortune` command in the preceding example. The real power of CGI scripts is to allow the entire capability of the computer to go into generating the Web page, and this example only hints at the possibilities.

If you're feeling adventurous—and know UNIX Bourne shell scripting—try modifying this script to do something other than print a fortune. Use `finger` to show who is currently logged on, or `uptime` to show how long the server has been running, or any command that you can think of. Be creative!

Using Server-Provided Information While dynamic Web pages can be powerful, they can be even more so if they use some of the information that the server provides every CGI program. A CGI script that uses server information isn't doing anything special to get the server to provide that information, it's just taking advantage of what is always there.

When a CGI script is run by the server, several *environment variables* are set, each containing information about the server software, the browser the request came from, and the script itself. These variables can then be read by the CGI program and used in various ways.

For example, the program in Listing 26.3 greets each user with the name (or Internet address) of his or her machine and the name of the browser software he or she is using.

Listing 26.3   A CGI Program That Uses Server Information

```
#!/bin/sh
echo "Content-type: text/html"
echo ""
echo "<HTML>"
echo "<HEAD>"
echo "<TITLE>Greetings</TITLE>"
echo "</HEAD>"
if [ "${REMOTE_HOST}" == "" ]; then
    REMOTE_HOST=${REMOTE_ADDR}
fi
if [ "${HTTP_USER_AGENT" == "" ]; then
    HTTP_USER_AGENT="a browser I don't know about"
fi
echo "<BODY>"
echo "You are running ${HTTP_USER_AGENT}, on ${REMOTE_HOST}."
echo "</BODY>"
echo "</HTML>"
```

Part
IV

Ch

26

This program uses three environment variables set by the server to find out the name of the machine running the browser: `REMOTE_HOST`, `REMOTE_ADDR`, and `HTTP_USER_AGENT`. `REMOTE_HOST` normally contains the Internet host name of the browser's machine—for example, `www.server.com`. But if, for some reason, this variable is empty, `REMOTE_ADDR` always contains the IP address of the browser—123.45.67.123, for example. HTTP_USER_AGENT, if set, is a string that describes the browser software the user is running.

That's all this program does—gets this information, does a little checking on it, and returns it to the user.

Many environment variables like the ones used in Listing 28.3 do exist. Some of the most common are listed in Table 26.1.

Table 26.1   CGI Environment Variables

Variable	Contents
REMOTE_HOST	The Internet name of the machine the browser is running on; may be empty if the information is not known
REMOTE_ADDR	The IP address of the machine the browser is running on
SCRIPT_NAME	The program currently running
SERVER_NAME	The Internet name or address of the server itself
HTTP_USER_AGENT	The browser software that the user is running

A complete list of CGI environment variables is available at **http://hoohoo.ncsa.uiuc.edu/docs/cgi/env.html**.

By using these environment variables creatively, you can perform all sorts of neat tricks. For example, combining SERVER_NAME and SCRIPT_NAME can produce a URL to the currently running script, allowing it to reference itself.

Creating HTML Forms

Now that you've seen the back-end of Web interactivity, you're ready to take a look at how to create HTML forms to be the front-end. HTML's form support is simple and yet surprisingly complete. A handful of HTML tags can create the most popular elements of modern graphical interfaces, including text windows, checkboxes and radio buttons, pull-down menus, and push buttons.

Composing HTML forms might sound like a complex task, but you need to master remarkably few tags to do it. All form-related tags occur between the <FORM> and </FORM> container tags. If you have more than one form in an HTML document, the closing </FORM> tag is essential for distinguishing between the multiple forms.

TIP   Adding a </FORM> tag immediately after creating a <FORM> tag is good practice; then you can go back to fill in the contents. Following this procedure helps you avoid leaving off the closing tag once you've finished.

Each HTML form has three main components: the *form header,* one or more named *input fields,* and one or more *action buttons.*

The Form Header

The form header is really just the <FORM> tag and the attributes it contains. The first is the ACTION attribute. You set ACTION equal to the URL of the processing script so that the Internet Explorer knows where to send the form data once it is entered. ACTION is a mandatory attribute of the <FORM> tag. Without it, the browser would have no idea where the form data should go.

The ACTION URL can also contain extra path information at the end of it. The extra path information is passed on to the script so that it can correctly process the data. It is not found anywhere on the form and is therefore transparent to the user. Allowing for the possibility of extra path information, an ACTION URL has the following form:

protocol://server/path/script_file/extra_path_info

You can use the extra path information to pass an additional filename or directory information to a script. For example, on some servers the imagemap facility uses extra path information to specify the name of the map file. The name of the map file follows the path to the imagemap script. A sample URL might be **http://cgi-bin/imagemap/homepage**.

The name of the script is imagemap, and homepage is the name of the map file used by imagemap.

The second attribute found in the <FORM> tag is the METHOD attribute. METHOD specifies the HyperText Transfer Protocol (HTTP) method to use when passing the data to the script and can be set to values of GET or POST. When you're using the GET method, the browser appends the form data to the end of the URL of the processing script. The POST method sends the form data to the server in a separate HTTP transaction.

METHOD is not a mandatory attribute of the <FORM> tag. In the absence of a specified method, the browser uses the GET method.

Part
IV

Ch
26

CAUTION

Some servers may have operating environment limitations that prevent them from processing a URL that exceeds a certain number of characters—typically 1 kilobyte of data. This limitation can be a problem when you're using the GET method to pass a large amount of form data. Since the GET method appends the data to the end of the processing script URL, you run a greater risk of passing a URL that's too big for the server to handle. If URL size limitations are a concern on your server, you should use the POST method to pass form data.

In summary, a form header follows this syntax:

```
<FORM ACTION="URL" METHOD={GET¦POST}>
```

Named Input Fields

The named input fields typically comprise the bulk of a form. The fields appear as standard GUI controls such as text boxes, checkboxes, radio buttons, and menus. You assign each field a unique name that eventually becomes the variable name used in the processing script.

 TIP If you are not coding your own processing scripts, be sure to sit down with your programmer to agree on variable names. The names used in the form should exactly match those used in coding the script.

You can use several different GUI controls to enter information into forms. The controls for named input fields appear in Table 26.2.

Table 26.2   Types of Named Input Fields

Field Type	HTML Tag
Text Box	`<INPUT TYPE="TEXT">`
Password Box	`<INPUT TYPE="PASSWORD">`
Checkbox	`<INPUT TYPE="CHECKBOX">`
Radio Button	`<INPUT TYPE="RADIO">`
Hidden Field	`<INPUT TYPE="HIDDEN">`
File	`<INPUT TYPE="FILE">`
Text Window	`<TEXTAREA>…</TEXTAREA>`
Menu	`<SELECT>…<OPTION>…</SELECT>`

Text and Password Fields   Text and password fields are simple data entry fields. The only difference between them is that text typed into a password field appears on-screen as asterisks (*).

CAUTION

Using a password field may protect users' passwords from the people looking over their shoulders, but it does not protect the password as it travels over the Internet. To protect password data as it moves from browser to server, you need to use some type of encryption or similar security measure.

The most general text or password field is produced by the HTML (attributes in square brackets are optional):

```
<INPUT TYPE="{TEXT[vb]PASSWORD}" NAME="Name" [VALUE="default_text"]
[SIZE="width"] [MAXLENGTH="wmax_width"]>
```

The NAME attribute is mandatory because it provides a unique identifier for the data entered into the field.

The optional VALUE attribute allows you to place some default text in the field, rather than have it initially appear blank. This capability is useful if a majority of users will enter a certain text string into the field. In such cases, you can use VALUE to put the text into the field, thereby saving most users the effort of typing it.

The optional SIZE attribute gives you control over how many characters wide the field should be. The default SIZE is typically 20 characters, though this number can vary from browser to browser. MAXLENGTH is also optional and allows you to specify the maximum number of characters that can be entered into the field.

N O T E Previously, the SIZE attribute used to take the form SIZE="width,height", where setting a height other than 1 produced a multiline field. With the advent of the <TEXTAREA>...</TEXTAREA> tag pair for creating multiline text windows, height has become something of a vestige and is ignored by most browsers. ▪

As an example, suppose you are given the task of supporting your company's Web site, and the boss wants a form that can capture the following information about a user:

- Name
- E-mail address
- Computing platforms used
- Gender
- Any comments he or she might have about the site
- What products he or she is interested in

   Your company has three main products—widgets, gadgets, and thingamajigs—and the site has one page for each of these product lines. The boss wants this form to be available on each of the three pages.

You now have a lot of information to gather, but you can get a start on it by using an <INPUT> tag with TYPE=TEXT, as follows:

```
<FORM ACTION="http://www.server.com/cgi-bin/userinfo.cgi METHOD="POST">
Name: <INPUT TYPE="TEXT" NAME="FULLNAME" SIZE=30><BR>
E-mail: <INPUT TYPE="TEXT" NAME="EMAIL" SIZE=30><BR>
...
</FORM>
```

So far, you know that the processing script is called userinfo.cgi, and it is found under the cgi-bin directory of your server. You also have a form with the two input fields shown in figure 26.2.

N O T E The <INPUT> tag and other tags that produce named input fields just create the fields themselves. You, as the form designer, must include some descriptive text next to each field so that users know what information to enter. ▪

TIP Because browsers ignore white space, lining up the left edges of text input boxes on multiple lines is difficult because the text to the left of the boxes is of different lengths. In this instance, HTML tables are invaluable. By setting up the text labels and input fields as cells in the same row of an HTML table, you can produce a nicely formatted form. The forms you see in the figures in this chapter have been formatted with tables for better readability.

FIG. 26.2

The beginning of this form collects several pieces of data from users interested in different product offerings.

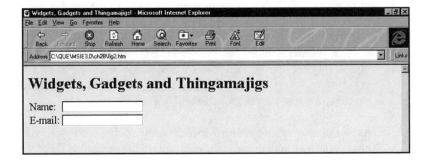

Checkboxes Checkboxes are used to provide users with several choices, from which they can select as many as they want. An <INPUT> tag to produce a checkbox option has the following syntax:

```
<INPUT TYPE="CHECKBOX" NAME="Name" VALUE="Value" [CHECKED]>
```

Each checkbox option is created by its own <INPUT> tag and must have its own unique NAME. If you give multiple checkbox options the same NAME, the script has no way to determine which choices the user actually made.

The VALUE attribute specifies what data is sent to the server if the corresponding checkbox is chosen. This information is transparent to the user. The optional CHECKED attribute preselects a commonly selected checkbox when the form is rendered on the browser screen.

You can add a checkbox to the form you're creating for work to collect information on what computing platforms your visitors use. Since people can use more than one platform, the most flexible approach is to present them with a list of checkbox options and let them select as many or as few platforms as they actually use. You can build this flexibility into the code for your form as follows:

```
<FORM ACTION="http://www.server.com/cgi-bin/userinfo.cgi METHOD="POST">
Name: <INPUT TYPE="TEXT" NAME="FULLNAME" SIZE=30><BR>
E-mail: <INPUT TYPE="TEXT" NAME="EMAIL" SIZE=30><BR>
<P><HR><P>
Please check any computing platform you regularly use:
<UL>
<INPUT TYPE="CHECKBOX" NAME="WINDOWS" VALUE="YES" CHECKED> Windows<BR>
<INPUT TYPE="CHECKBOX" NAME="MACINTOSH" VALUE="YES"> Macintosh<BR>
<INPUT TYPE="CHECKBOX" NAME="UNIX" VALUE="YES"> UNIX<BR>
</UL>
...
</FORM>
```

The updated form is shown in figure 26.3.

FIG. 26.3

Checkboxes allow users to choose many items from a list of several options.

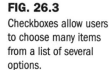

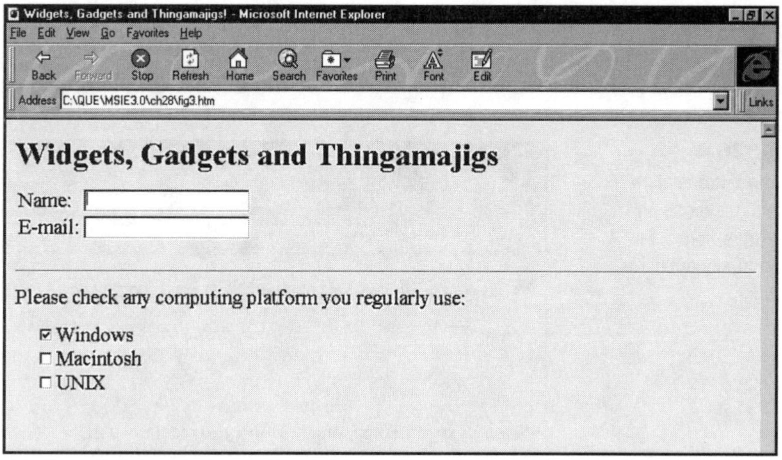

NOTE Checkboxes show up in the form data sent to the server only if they are selected. Checkboxes that are not selected do not appear. ▨

Radio Buttons   Radio buttons are used to present users with several options, from which they can select only one. When you set up options in a radio button format, you should make sure that they are mutually exclusive so that a user won't try to select more than one.

The HTML code to produce a set of three radio button options is as follows:

```
<INPUT TYPE="RADIO" NAME="Name" VALUE="VALUE1" [CHECKED]>Option 1<P>
<INPUT TYPE="RADIO" NAME="Name" VALUE="VALUE2">Option 2<P>
<INPUT TYPE="RADIO" NAME="Name" VALUE="VALUE3">Option 3<P>
```

The VALUE and CHECKED attributes work exactly the same as they do for checkboxes, though you should have only one preselected radio button option. A fundamental difference with a set of radio button options is that they all have the same NAME. This use is permissible because the user can select only one of the options.

A radio button is perfect for requesting the sex of visitors to your site since a person is either male or female. You can build this request into your growing form as follows:

```
<FORM ACTION="http://www.server.com/cgi-bin/userinfo.cgi" METHOD="POST">
Name: <INPUT TYPE="TEXT" NAME="FULLNAME" SIZE=30><BR>
E-mail: <INPUT TYPE="TEXT" NAME="EMAIL" SIZE=30><BR>
<P><HR><P>
Please check any computing platform you regularly use:
<UL>
<INPUT TYPE="CHECKBOX" NAME="WINDOWS" VALUE="YES" CHECKED> Windows<BR>
<INPUT TYPE="CHECKBOX" NAME="MACINTOSH" VALUE="YES"> Macintosh<BR>
<INPUT TYPE="CHECKBOX" NAME="UNIX" VALUE="YES"> UNIX<BR>
</UL>
<P><HR><P>
Sex: <INPUT TYPE="RADIO" NAME="SEX" VALUE="M"> Male
<INPUT TYPE="RADIO" NAME="SEX" VALUE="F"> Female
```

Part
IV

Ch

26

```
...
</FORM>
```

Figure 26.4 shows how the form looks on the Internet Explorer screen after this change.

FIG. 26.4

Radio buttons allow users to choose only one item from a list of mutually exclusive options.

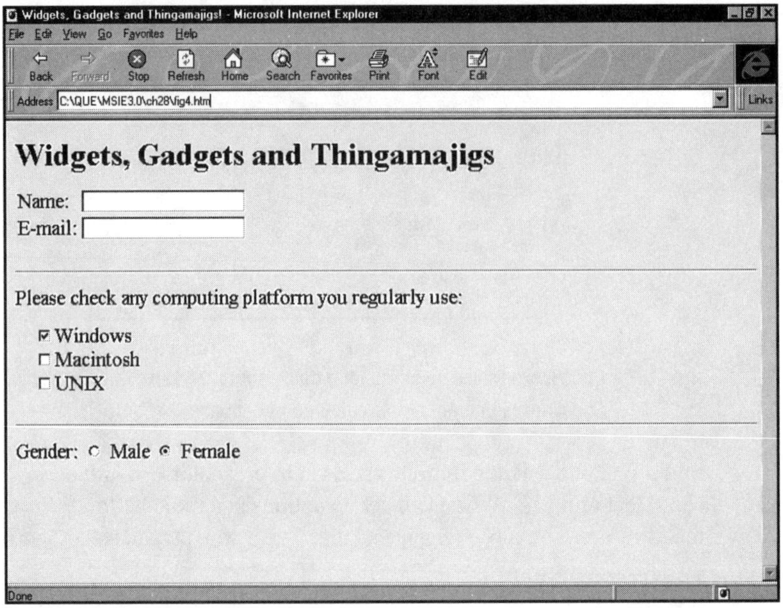

Hidden Fields Technically, hidden fields are not meant for data input. However, you can send information to the server about a form without displaying that information anywhere on the form itself. The general format for including hidden fields is as follows:

```
<INPUT TYPE="HIDDEN" NAME="name" VALUE="value">
```

One possible use of hidden fields is to allow a single general script to process data from several different forms. The script would need to know which form is sending the data, and a hidden field could provide this information without requiring anything on the part of the user.

This use of hidden fields is appropriate in this example since your boss wants to know what products visitors are interested in and a registration form appears on each product page. To meet this requirement, you could place a hidden field in the code for the form on each page. The NAME of the hidden field is the same for all three pages, but the VALUEs can be different depending on which page you're coding. For example, for the form on the widgets page, you could use the following HTML code (the second line contains the hidden field):

```
<FORM ACTION="http://www.server.com/cgi-bin/userinfo.cgi" METHOD="POST">
<INPUT TYPE="HIDDEN" NAME="PRODUCT" VALUE="WIDGETS">
Name: <INPUT TYPE="TEXT" NAME="FULLNAME" SIZE=30><BR>
E-mail: <INPUT TYPE="TEXT" NAME="EMAIL" SIZE=30><BR>
<P><HR><P>
Please check any computing platform you regularly use:
<UL>
```

```
<INPUT TYPE="CHECKBOX" NAME="WINDOWS" VALUE="YES" CHECKED> Windows<BR>
<INPUT TYPE="CHECKBOX" NAME="MACINTOSH" VALUE="YES"> Macintosh<BR>
<INPUT TYPE="CHECKBOX" NAME="UNIX" VALUE="YES"> UNIX<BR>
</UL>
<P><HR><P>
Sex: <INPUT TYPE="RADIO" NAME="SEX" VALUE="M"> Male
<INPUT TYPE="RADIO" NAME="SEX" VALUE="F"> Female
...
</FORM>
```

The hidden field is invisible to the user, so it doesn't really matter where you put it in the HTML code. It also means that if you viewed the preceding code on Internet Explorer, it would look exactly like what you see in figure 26.4.

Multiline Text Boxes   Text and password boxes are used for simple, one-line input fields. You can create multiline text windows that function in much the same way by using the <TEXTAREA> and </TEXTAREA> container tags. The HTML syntax for a text window is as follows:

```
<TEXTAREA NAME="Name" [ROWS="rows"] [COLS="columns"]>
Default_window_text
</TEXTAREA>
```

The NAME attribute gives the text window a unique identifier just as it does with the variations on the <INPUT> tag. The optional ROWS and COLS attributes allow you to specify the dimensions of the text window as it appears on the browser screen. The default number of rows and columns varies by browser. Internet Explorer uses three rows and 30 columns as defaults.

Multiline text windows are ideal for entry of long pieces of text such as feedback comments or e-mail messages. Conveniently, this data is another piece that you need to collect on your form. You can build in a comments section using the following HTML code:

```
<FORM ACTION="http://www.server.com/cgi-bin/userinfo.cgi METHOD="POST">
<INPUT TYPE="HIDDEN" NAME="PRODUCT" VALUE="WIDGETS">
Name: <INPUT TYPE="TEXT" NAME="FULLNAME" SIZE=30><BR>
E-mail: <INPUT TYPE="TEXT" NAME="EMAIL" SIZE=30><BR>
<P><HR><P>
Please check any computing platform you regularly use:
<UL>
<INPUT TYPE="CHECKBOX" NAME="WINDOWS" VALUE="YES" CHECKED> Windows<BR>
<INPUT TYPE="CHECKBOX" NAME="MACINTOSH" VALUE="YES"> Macintosh<BR>
<INPUT TYPE="CHECKBOX" NAME="UNIX" VALUE="YES"> UNIX<BR>
</UL>
<P><HR><P>
Sex: <INPUT TYPE="RADIO" NAME="SEX" VALUE="M"> Male
<INPUT TYPE="RADIO" NAME="SEX" VALUE="F"> Female
<P><HR><P>
<TEXTAREA NAME="COMMENTS" COLS=80>
Please let us know what you think of our site by entering your comments here.
</TEXTAREA>
...
</FORM>
```

Now your form looks like the one shown in figure 26.5.

Part

IV

Ch

26

FIG. 26.5

Multiline text boxes give users a way to enter large amounts of text input.

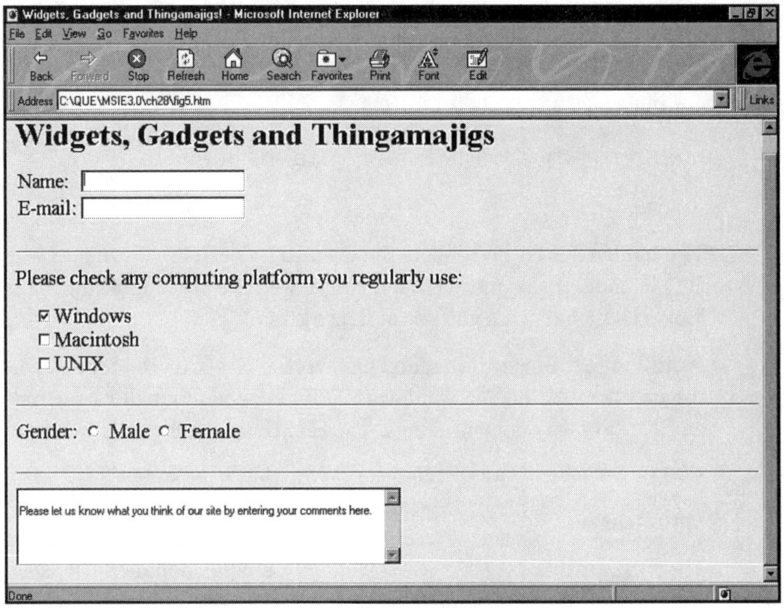

Creating Menus The final technique for creating a named input field is to use the `<SELECT>` and `</SELECT>` container tags to produce pull-down or scrollable menus of options. The HTML code used to create a general menu is as follows:

```
<SELECT NAME="Name" [SIZE="size"] [MULTIPLE]>
<OPTION [SELECTED]>Option 1
<OPTION [SELECTED]>Option 2
<OPTION [SELECTED]>Option 3
...
<OPTION [SELECTED]>Option n
</SELECT>
```

In the `<SELECT>` tag, the NAME attribute again gives the input field a unique identifier. The optional SIZE attribute lets you specify how many options should be displayed when the menu is rendered on the browser screen. If you have more options than you have space for displaying them, you can access them either by using a pull-down window or by scrolling through the window with scroll bars. The default SIZE is 1. If you want to let users choose more than one menu option, you can include the MULTIPLE attribute. When MULTIPLE is specified, users can choose multiple options by holding down the Control key and clicking the options they want using the mouse.

N O T E If you specify the MULTIPLE attribute and SIZE=1, a one-line scrollable list box is displayed instead of a drop-down list box. This box appears because you can select only one item (not multiple items) in a drop-down list box. ■

Each option in the menu is specified with its own `<OPTION>` tag. If you want an option to be preselected, you can include the SELECTED attribute in the appropriate `<OPTION>` tag.

You may have noticed that there is no VALUE attribute for the <SELECT> or <OPTION> tags. They don't have this attribute because the values passed to the server are the text items that appear after each <OPTION> tag.

Your boss is impressed at your cleverness at capturing product information using hidden fields, but she is concerned that a person filling out the form on the gadgets page may also be interested in your other products as well. A hidden field can't supply that information, so you decide to build in a menu from which people can choose the product lines that interest them. Your updated form code now looks like the following:

```
<FORM ACTION="http://www.server.com/cgi-bin/userinfo.cgi METHOD="POST">
<INPUT TYPE="HIDDEN" NAME="PRODUCT" VALUE="WIDGETS">
Name: <INPUT TYPE="TEXT" NAME="FULLNAME" SIZE=30><BR>
E-mail: <INPUT TYPE="TEXT" NAME="EMAIL" SIZE=30><BR>
<P><HR><P>
Please check any computing platform you regularly use:
<UL>
<INPUT TYPE="CHECKBOX" NAME="WINDOWS" VALUE="YES" CHECKED> Windows<BR>
<INPUT TYPE="CHECKBOX" NAME="MACINTOSH" VALUE="YES"> Macintosh<BR>
<INPUT TYPE="CHECKBOX" NAME="UNIX" VALUE="YES"> UNIX<BR>
</UL>
<P><HR><P>
Sex: <INPUT TYPE="RADIO" NAME="SEX" VALUE="M"> Male
<INPUT TYPE="RADIO" NAME="SEX" VALUE="F"> Female
<P><HR><P>
<TEXTAREA NAME="COMMENTS" COLS=80>
Please let us know what you think of our site by entering your comments here.
</TEXTAREA>
<P><HR><P>
Please select the product lines that interest you:<BR>
<SELECT NAME="PRODUCTS" SIZE=3 MULTIPLE>
<OPTION>Widgets
<OPTION>Gadgets
<OPTION>Thingamajigs
</SELECT>
...
</FORM>
```

Part
IV

Ch

26

Figure 26.6 shows the form produced by the preceding HTML code. At this point, your form collects all the information the boss requires. Before you go ask for that raise, though, you need to resolve one more issue—adding the action buttons.

 You can replace radio buttons with pull-down menus to save space on-screen. Including the MULTIPLE option in a <SELECT> tag allows you to use menus to replace checkboxes, as well.

Submit and Reset Buttons

The handy <INPUT> tag returns to provide an easy way of creating the form action buttons you see in the preceding figures. Buttons can be of two types: Submit and Reset. Clicking a Submit button instructs the browser to package the form data and send it to the server. Clicking a Reset button clears out any data entered into the form and sets all the named input fields back to their default values.

FIG. 26.6

Menus are another means of providing users with several options.

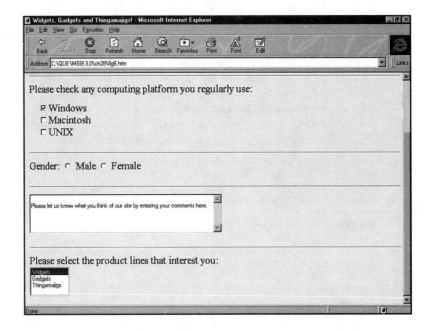

Any form you compose should have a Submit button so that users can submit the data they enter. The one exception to this rule is a form containing only one input field. For such a form, pressing Enter automatically submits the data. Reset buttons are technically not necessary but are usually provided as a user courtesy.

To create Submit or Reset buttons, you use the <INPUT> tags as follows:

```
<INPUT TYPE="SUBMIT" VALUE="Submit Data">
<INPUT TYPE="RESET" VALUE="Clear Data">
```

The VALUE attribute is used to specify the text that appears on the button. You should set VALUE to a text string that concisely describes the function of the button. If VALUE is not specified, the button text reads "Submit Query" for Submit buttons and "Reset" for Reset buttons.

To round out the form you're developing for work, you should add Submit and Reset buttons as follows:

```
<FORM ACTION="http://www.server.com/cgi-bin/userinfo.cgi METHOD="POST">
<INPUT TYPE="HIDDEN" NAME="PRODUCT" VALUE="WIDGETS">
Name: <INPUT TYPE="TEXT" NAME="FULLNAME" SIZE=30><BR>
E-mail: <INPUT TYPE="TEXT" NAME="EMAIL" SIZE=30><BR>
<P><HR><P>
Please check any computing platform you regularly use:
<UL>
<INPUT TYPE="CHECKBOX" NAME="WINDOWS" VALUE="YES" CHECKED> Windows<BR>
<INPUT TYPE="CHECKBOX" NAME="MACINTOSH" VALUE="YES"> Macintosh<BR>
<INPUT TYPE="CHECKBOX" NAME="UNIX" VALUE="YES"> UNIX<BR>
</UL>
<P><HR><P>
Sex: <INPUT TYPE="RADIO" NAME="SEX" VALUE="M"> Male
<INPUT TYPE="RADIO" NAME="SEX" VALUE="F"> Female
```

```
<P><HR><P>
<TEXTAREA NAME="COMMENTS" COLS=80>
Please let us know what you think of our site by entering your comments here.
</TEXTAREA>
<P><HR><P>
Please select the product lines that interest you:<BR>
<SELECT NAME="PRODUCTS" SIZE=3 MULTIPLE>
<OPTION>Widgets
<OPTION>Gadgets
<OPTION>Thingamajigs
</SELECT>
<P>
<INPUT TYPE="SUBMIT" VALUE="Send my info!">
<INPUT TYPE="RESET" VALUE="Clear the decks!">
</FORM>
```

The resulting form is shown in figure 26.7. Now you can go ask for that raise!

FIG. 26.7
You should place
Submit and Reset
buttons on all your
forms.

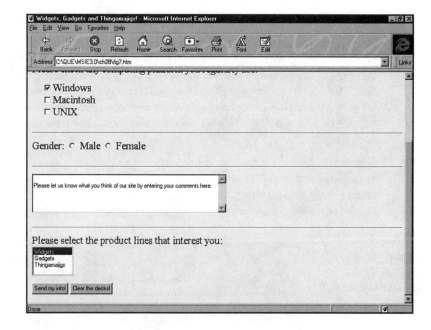

Part
IV

Ch
26

N O T E Normally, forms include only one Submit button. In some cases, however, you may want to include multiple buttons that take different actions. You can achieve this effect by naming Submit buttons with a NAME attribute so that the NAME and VALUE of the button selected show up in the query string. However, this capability is not yet part of standard HTML and is not supported by many browsers. ▩

An Exception to the Rule: *<ISINDEX>*

An exception to the rule about forms having headers, input fields, and action buttons does exist. You can use the <ISINDEX> tag to create a single field form. No other tags are required. <ISINDEX> fields are used to allow a user to enter search criteria for queries against Gopher servers or database scripts. For example, you may be maintaining a directory of employees where you work that is searchable by a person's last name. You can use an <ISINDEX> field as a front end to search the directory. Figure 26.8 shows the input field created by an <ISINDEX> tag.

FIG. 28.8

The <ISINDEX> tag creates a one-field form. No other form tags are required.

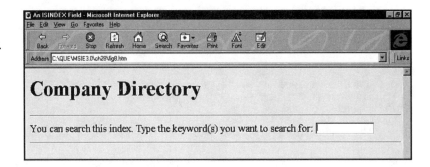

You may be wondering where the data entered into an <ISINDEX> field goes. After all, it doesn't have a <FORM> tag with an ACTION specified. How does the client know which URL to send the data to? The answer is that it sends the data to the URL of the page containing the <ISINDEX> field. This action requires one of two things: (1) that the page be created by some sort of a script, since a static HTML page could not receive and process the data, or (2) that the <ISINDEX> field be part of a Gopher document, since Gopher servers are configured to process such queries.

Note that in figure 26.8, the <ISINDEX> field is preceded by the default text You can search this index. Type the keyword(s) you want to search for:. Internet Explorer supports a PROMPT attribute of the <ISINDEX> tag, thus allowing you to alter this default and make the text in front of the field more descriptive. Figure 26.9 shows an example.

FIG. 26.9

Internet Explorer lets you customize the ISINDEX field text with the PROMPT attribute.

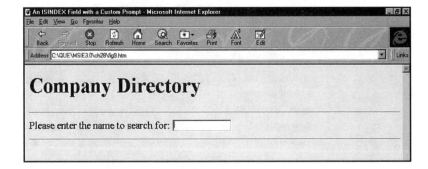

Bringing CGI and Forms Together

Now that you've got some basic background on both CGI scripts and forms, you're ready to bring them together to allow true user interaction with your Web site. The combination of CGI scripts and forms can bring a Web page to life, turning what was a static display of information into a customized and dynamic experience.

The program in Listing 26.4 is a guestbook, an electronic version of the familiar visitor log used by hotels and museums. It first displays a list of signees and then uses a form to ask the current user to add his or her signature. It is written in Perl and uses a form-input library called `cgi-bin.pl` to parse or untangle the packaged data sent by Internet Explorer.

Listing 26.4 A CGI Program To Process Form Input

```
#!/usr/local/bin/perl
print "Content-type: text/html\n\n";
# Load the library
do "cgi-bin.pl" || die "Fatal Error: Could not load cgi-bin.pl";
&ReadParse;
# Set the location of the guestbook
$guestbk = "guestbk.gbk";
# Get the sign-in's name
$name = $in{'name'};
# Only add to the log if they entered something
if (length($name) > 0) {
    open(FILE,">>$guestbk");
    print FILE "$name\n";
    close FILE;
}
# Show the current sign-ins
print "<HTML>\n<HEAD><TITLE>Guestbook</TITLE></HEAD>\n";
print "<BODY>\n<H1>Guestbook</H1>\n<H2>Current signees:</H2>\n<HR>\n<UL>\n";
open(FILE,"<$guestbk") || print "You'll be the first!\n";
while (<FILE>) {
    print "<LI>$_";
}
close FILE;
print "</UL>\n";
# Request new sign-ins
print "<HR>\n<FORM METHOD=\"GET\" ACTION=\"$ENV{'SCRIPT_NAME'}\">";
print "Your name: <INPUT TYPE=\"text\" NAME=\"name\" SIZE=\"20\">";
print"<INPUT TYPE=\"submit\" VALUE=\"Sign in!\"></FORM>\n</BODY>\n</HTML>\n";
```

Part
IV

Ch
26

N O T E The \n you see in the print commands in Listing 26.4 is an instruction to break to a new
line. ■

You should note a few things about this CGI script. The first, and probably most important, is that it is not only a CGI script; it does processing, like a normal script, but it also generates its own form. The last three lines, in the Request new sign-ins section, generate the HTML code to request more information from the user.

This neat trick, where a CGI script also generates a form, is becoming standard practice on many Web sites. It allows a single program to both process and request data. You could even expand it to generate its own error message pages, too.

Secondly, you should note that the program uses the cgi-bin.pl library to extract the information the user has typed into the form. By using this utility, the user-entered information is pulled out of the request, decrypted, and stored in a Perl table called $in, easily and conveniently. You can get the values of each named form input field by asking `$in` for it, referencing the field by its unique name. For instance, if a text input field has the NAME `address`, the following line of Perl code would return the value the user entered:

```
$addr_variable = $in{'address'};
```

Of course, before you can use `$in`, you must have loaded `cgi-bin.pl` and called the library routine that sets up the table—lines four and five in Listing 26.4.

> **CAUTION**
> When creating forms and CGI scripts, you should be aware that, normally, none of the data passed between Internet Explorer and the Web site is encrypted. This means that any private data (credit card numbers, love letters, and so on) can be "sniffed" by machines between the sender and receiver. Keep this point in mind not only when you're designing your own forms and CGI scripts but also when using others.

stdin and *stdout*

So far, we've glossed over the details of how a CGI script accepts input from and sends output to the Web server. There are a few reasons for this omission, but the main one is that you can do quite a lot without ever having to understand how the mechanism works. All the previous examples in this chapter work without your having special knowledge of how the transfer is performed. But in some rare instances, you need to know how this transfer takes place.

Every program running on UNIX has two channels, `stdin` ("standard input") and `stdout` ("standard output"). These two channels are how normal processes communicate with the world, and if the program is run from the UNIX command line, `stdin` reads from the keyboard, and `stdout` writes to the screen.

When a CGI script is executed from a Web server, it redirects these two channels away from the screen and the keyboard and takes control of them itself. This way, the server can send specific data into the script and receive answers back.

Every one of the previous examples, for instance, just echoes or prints its output. Normally, this process would just send the text to the screen, but because the script is run from the server, the output is captured and sent through the server to Internet Explorer for viewing.

Reading input is a more complicated matter. While utility libraries such as `cgi-bin.pl` automatically take care of the complexities of decoding input, you can do it yourself if you're feeling adventurous.

GET and *POST*

You have two ways to read the form data submitted to a CGI script, depending on the METHOD the form used. The type of METHOD the form used—either GET or POST—is stored in an environment variable called REQUEST_METHOD, and based on that, the data should be read in one of the following ways:

- ■ If the data is sent by the GET method, the input stream is stored in an environment variable called QUERY_STRING. As noted previously, this input stream usually is limited to about 1 kilobyte of data, which is why GET is losing popularity to the more flexible POST.

- ■ If the data is submitted by the POST method, the input string waits on stdin, with the number of bytes waiting stored in the environment variable CONTENT_LENGTH. POST can accept data of any length, up into the megabytes, though it is not very common yet.

Encoding

When a user clicks the Submit button on a form, Internet Explorer gathers all the data and strings it together in NAME=VALUE pairs, each separated by an ampersand character. This process is called *encoding*. It is done to package the data into one string that will be sent to the server.

Consider the following HTML code:

```
<FORM ACTION="http://www.server.com/cgi-bin/form.sh" METHOD="POST">
    <INPUT TYPE="TEXT" NAME="first">
    <INPUT TYPE="TEXT" NAME="last">
    <INPUT TYPE="SUBMIT">
</FORM>
```

If a user named Joe Schmoe enters his name into the form produced by the preceding HTML code, Internet Explorer creates the following data string and sends it to the CGI script's stdin:

```
first=Joe&last=Schmoe
```

If the GET method is used instead of POST, the same string is appended to the URL of the processing script, producing the following *encoded URL:*

```
http://www.server.com/cgi-bin/form.sh?first=Joe&last=Schmoe
```

A question mark (?) separates the script URL from the encoded data string.

Part
IV

Ch

26

Storing Encoded URLs

As you learned in the previous discussion of URL encoding, packaging form data into a single text string follows a few simple formatting rules. Consequently, you can "fake" a script into believing that it is receiving form data without using a form. To do so, you simply send the URL that would be constructed if a form were used. This approach may be useful if you frequently run a script with the same data set.

For example, suppose you frequently search the Web index Yahoo for new documents related to the scripting language JavaScript. If you are interested in checking for new documents several times a day, you could fill out the Yahoo search query each time. A more efficient way, however, is to store the query URL in your Internet Explorer Favorite Places. Each time you select that item from your list of Favorites, a new query is generated as if you had filled out the form. The stored URL would look like the following:

http://search.yahoo.com/bin/search?p=JavaScript

Further encoding can occur with data that is more complex than a single word. Such encoding simply replaces spaces with the plus character and translates any other possibly troublesome character (control characters, the ampersand and equal sign, some punctuation, and so on) to a percent sign followed by its hexadecimal equivalent. Thus, the following string:

```
Here I am!
```

becomes

```
Here+I+am%21
```

Parsing

When a script receives the string that contains all the NAME=VALUE pairs, the script must first break the string apart into the individual pairs. This process is called *parsing*. For your CGI script to actually use this information, it first must search for each ampersand to get each NAME=VALUE pair and then split the pair at the equal sign.

After your script has read the submitted data, parsed it into NAMEs and VALUEs, it must finally decode the data (convert plus signs back to spaces, hexadecimal values back to their ASCII equivalents, and so on) into the actual data that the user entered into the form. Then the data is ready to use.

Protecting Yourself and Your Users

While programming CGI scripts and their forms is fun, the following are several tips you should keep in mind to protect yourself and your users:

- **Elegantly handle the submission of an empty form.** If a user just clicks the Submit button without entering any information into your form, what does your CGI script do? A well-written program handles this situation gracefully, without even trying to process the submission.

  When you receive an empty request, you should either return an error telling the user what he or she did wrong or—even better—return the form that needs to be filled out. That way, as with the guestbook example, a single CGI script can both request and process the data, guaranteeing that both situations are handled. This approach is also handy for the first time the URL is jumped to, when the CGI script automatically presents the form to request data.

- **Always be careful about trusting the data sent to you.** Some people on the Web would love nothing more than to cause you trouble. Purely out of a sense of vindictiveness, they may try to make your life as hard as it can be. Your CGI scripts need to take this fact into account.

  For example, cleverly written queries can be used to gain privileges on your server that you never intended to grant. One common trick involves sending a shell command appended to some piece of requested data, so that when the CGI program uses that piece of data in an external command, the "piggy-back" command is executed as well.

  Imagine a user entering **nasty@hackers.com;rm -rf /** into a form. If you know UNIX, you recognize rm -rf / as the command that deletes everything on the computer. A badly written CGI script might simply add "finger" to the front of the request and execute it as a shell command, causing `finger nasty@hackers.com` to be executed first, followed by `rm -rf /`.

Or, even worse, an unfriendly user could enter **nasty@hackers.com;cat '+ +' > ~/ .rhosts** and give the world login access to your Web server; the `cat '+ +' > ~/.rhosts` command removes password protection from a UNIX account.

■ **Be mindful that your users might not have a secure connection, and warn them if you are requesting sensitive data.** You should be wary of requesting sensitive data—bank account numbers, passwords—and, if you must, explicitly warn the users of the possibility (no matter how remote) of the data being sniffed.

Using the Public Domain

Form and CGI programming can be frustrating in the beginning. You have to follow many rules, most of which can be obscure or complex. Even getting a simple script up and running can be a chore.

One of the best ways to get over these first few hurdles and start CGI programming is to look at existing code. By reviewing (or simply using) already-existing CGI scripts, you can not only save yourself a lot of time but also teach yourself new techniques.

Existing code almost always makes a good base from which you can expand. Instead of implementing a new script from scratch, an older program can often be expanded (or shrunk) to suit your needs. The guestbook program presented in this chapter, for example, could be modified to add the name of the computer the user is connecting from automatically, if that's what you wanted your guestbook to do.

Often rivaling the abilities of commercial offerings, many public domain CGI programs exist, free for the taking. Even if these scripts are too general for your specific needs, you can mine them for techniques and methods that you can then use in your own programs.

Also, experienced CGI programmers are almost always happy to share their code and talents with you. They've probably already solved any problem you might have and can save you hours of frustration with a word or a clue. Just ask. And be sure to return the favor when you become an expert.

You can also find many public domain CGI references and scripts on the Web itself. The following are good places to begin looking:

■ **http://www.yahoo.com/Computers_and_Internet/Internet/World_Wide_Web/ CGI___Common_Gateway_Interface/**

■ **http://hoohoo.ncsa.uiuc.edu/cgi/**

■ **news:comp.infosystems.www.authoring.cgi**

Because every CGI program that receives data from a form must go through the bothersome parsing and decoding steps to get the information the user entered, common libraries have been created to handle the trouble for you. Using this existing code is much easier than going to the trouble of writing your own decoding and parsing routines because these existing libraries come tested and are free:

- **ftp://ftp.ncsa.uiuc.edu/Web/httpd/Unix/ncsa_httpd/cgi/cgi-lib.pl.Z** (for Perl)
- **ftp://ftp.ncsa.uiuc.edu/Web/httpd/Unix/ncsa_httpd/cgi/ncsa_default.tar.Z** (for C)

If you're adventurous, you can try writing your own routines, but you really have no reason to—these routines work great. ●

## CHAPTER 27

Using Microsoft FrontPage

There's a lot more to administering a Web site than just authoring HTML pages. You need to be able to change the structure of the site to mesh new with new content. Users will look to you for interactive components such as site search engines and threaded discussion groups. And even the HTML part of site administration can be difficult. If you move just one file, you have to check the whole site for links to the file and change the URL in the tags that set up the links.

The programs you learned about in Chapter 22, "Using Microsoft Internet Assistants and HTML," are fine for authoring just a few Web pages. But if you're putting together an entire site, you need software that supports you in all facets of Web site creation and maintenance.

To address this need, Microsoft has released FrontPage—the Web site management tool of the Microsoft Office suite of programs. FrontPage's many features give you end-to-end assistance during the site creation process. ■

Learn about FrontPage Editor

FrontPage Editor is a powerful WYSIWYG Web page editor that you can use even if you don't know HTML.

What is FrontPage Explorer?

Similar to the Windows 95 Windows Explorer, the FrontPage Explorer supports you in many basic Web site management tasks.

Tell me more about FrontPage TCP/IP Test

This is a handy utility that checks your computer for Internet information used by the Personal Web Server.

Create a personal Web server

Turn your computer into a Web server that can host your own site plus sites with other domain names.

Discover the Server Administrator

The Server Administrator gives you complete control over the configuration of your server, including who has authoring access to your files.

FrontPage has server extensions to give you more control

Harness FrontPage's power on other popular Web servers with Microsoft's free server extensions.

Overview

Microsoft FrontPage is actually a collection of programs that support Web site managers in their various tasks. After you install FrontPage, you can run the following programs:

- FrontPage Editor
- FrontPage Explorer
- FrontPage TCP/IP Test
- Personal Web Server
- Server Administrator

The FrontPage Editor is a WYSIWYG Web page editor that lets you compose pages easily—even if you don't know HTML! You can get a handle on the structure of your Web site using the FrontPage Explorer. The Explorer can show you your site in both hierarchical and graphical views. The FrontPage TCP/IP Test checks your machine for a Winsock layer, IP address, and other items needed to establish a connection to the Internet. This information can be used in support of the Personal Web Server and Server Administrator—two programs you can use to turn your machine into a World Wide Web server.

FrontPage packs a lot of power, and you'll need to run it on a machine that is full-featured enough to support it. FrontPage requires the following:

- A 486 MHz or higher processor
- A 32-bit operating system such as Windows 95 or Windows NT (version 3.51 or later)
- 16 MB of RAM, though you can get away with 8 MB on a Windows 95 machine that's not running the Personal Web Server
- 15 MB of hard drive space
- A 3.5" high-density disk drive
- VGA (or higher) video adapter (Microsoft recommends SVGA with 256 colors)
- A Microsoft Mouse or other compatible pointing device

Once you have sufficient hardware power and you're ready to install FrontPage, you'll need to pay $149 for the package. Microsoft has advertised that this price is good until March 31, 1997, and that owners of Microsoft Office or one of the Office component programs will receive a $40 rebate. The FrontPage Server Extensions will be available free of charge.

N O T E   To get the most up-to-date information on FrontPage pricing and retail availability, point Internet Explorer to **http://www.microsoft.com/frontpage/**. ■

Installing FrontPage

Once you have the FrontPage setup files—presumably either by downloading a review copy or by purchasing the software outright—in a temporary directory on your hard drive, follow these simple steps to install FrontPage:

1. From the Windows Explorer, run the program SETUP.EXE.

2. Specify the directory where the Installation Wizard should install the program files. If the default of C:\PROGRAM FILES\MICROSOFT FRONTPAGE is okay, click the Next button. Otherwise, you can browse to find a directory that's acceptable to you.

3. Choose between Typical and Custom installation of the program. A Typical installation installs the files that would be of value to the "average" user. More advanced users can use the Custom option to configure the installation parameters to their specific needs.

 TIP If you're not sure which type of installation to use, choose the Typical installation.

4. Tell the Installation Wizard where to install the Personal Web Server. The default directory is C:\FRONTPAGE WEBS, but you can browse to a different one if you like.

5. Give the Windows program folder a name if you don't want to use the default of Microsoft FrontPage.

6. Confirm the installation settings you've specified so far. The Installation Wizard will show you a dialog box like the one you see in figure 27.1. If you're happy with the settings, click the Next button, and the files will be installed. Clicking the Back button will take you backward through the installation process, and allow you to edit any settings you want to change.

FIG. 27.1
The FrontPage Installation Wizard asks you to confirm the installation parameters in this dialog box.

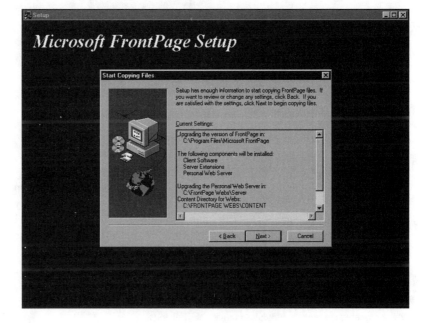

Part
IV

Ch
27

7. Enter an authoring access password in the field provided and then re-enter the password to confirm. The Server Administrator program runs automatically as part of the installation and asks you for a password to grant authoring access to Web page files.

8. If desired, run the FrontPage Explorer by clicking the Yes button in the last dialog box you see. Otherwise, click the No button to end the installation process.

With the installation complete, you'll see a Microsoft FrontPage entry in your set of program folders (see fig. 27.2). Inside the folder you'll find the five applications that comprise the FrontPage suite. Each of these applications is discussed over the next several sections.

FIG. 27.2
The Microsoft FrontPage program folder gives you quick access to the five main applications in the FrontPage suite.

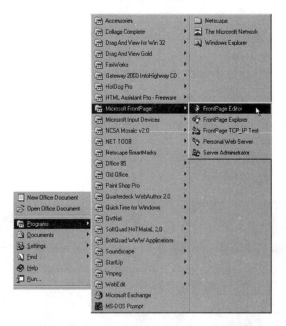

Using the FrontPage Editor

When you fire up the FrontPage Editor, you see a screen like the one in figure 27.3. The Editor gives you a WYSIWYG (what you see is what you get) environment in which you can create your Web documents—all without even typing an HTML tag. The idea is that you compose the page as you would have it look on the Internet Explorer screen, and the Editor writes the HTML file for you.

TIP   While technically you don't need to know HTML to use the FrontPage Editor, it helps to have a good working knowledge of HTML as you use it, since many of the dialog boxes in the Editor prompt you for what are essentially attributes of different HTML tags.

FIG. 27.3
Composing HTML documents is easy with the FrontPage Editor— even if you don't know HTML!

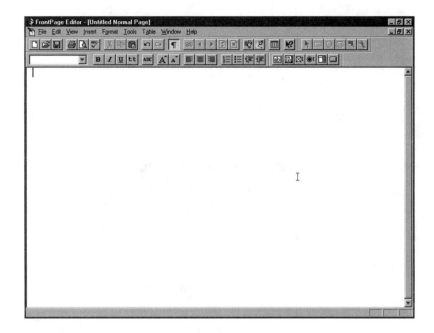

Starting a New Document

When you select File, New to start a new document, you don't just get a blank screen to work in. Rather, you are given the option to activate one of the Editor's many templates and page creation wizards. Templates give you a structured document with several informational "holes" that you can fill in with appropriate text (see fig. 27.4). Page creation wizards collect information from you through a series of dialog boxes and then uses the information you supply to author a page. Figure 27.5 shows a dialog box from the Frames Wizard—a useful feature for developing framed pages without having to worry about all of those confusing <FRAMESET> tags!

The FrontPage Editor comes with three wizards—Forms Page, Frames, and Personal Home Page—and over twenty templates, including the following:

- Bibliography
- Directory of Press Releases
- Employee Directory
- Feedback Form
- Frequently Asked Questions
- Glossary
- Guest Book

- Meeting Agenda
- Press Release
- Table of Contents
- What's New

 T I P If you want to start with a blank document, choose the Normal template.

FIG. 27.4

The Employment Opportunities template gives you a structure into which you can enter the job openings available at your company.

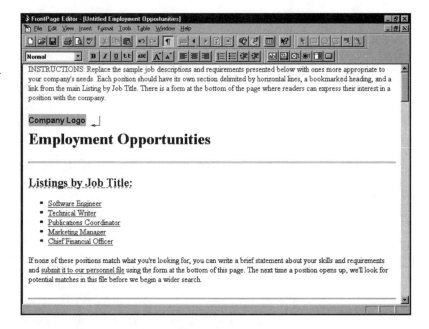

FIG. 27.5

Frames can be simple when you use the FrontPage Editor's Frames Wizard.

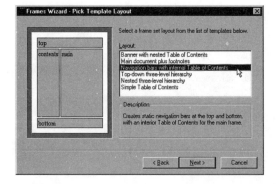

Editing Your Document

Once you have a document started or have loaded one in from an existing Web, you can make use of the Editor's many useful features to create or change the page.

> **N O T E** In FrontPage vernacular, a "Web" is a set of documents that comprise a Web site. When you load in a document from a Web, you have read in a document that is part of a site created by FrontPage. ■

The Editor Toolbars Figure 27.6 shows the Editor with all of its toolbars active. Many are just like the toolbar buttons you would see in other Microsoft Office applications.

FIG. 27.6

FrontPage's Editor supports document authoring with four different toolbars.

Of particular note are the Image toolbar and the Forms toolbar. When you select an image on the page, the Image toolbar becomes active and allows you to trace hot regions for imagemaps or to make a color in the image transparent. The Forms toolbar places form controls at the cursor's position on your page.

 If you're ever in doubt as to what a toolbar button does, just hold your mouse pointer over the button for a few seconds to reveal the Tool Tip for the button.

 You can toggle the display of any of the toolbars under the Editor View menu.

Formatting Text You can apply styles to text in many different ways. The physical styles are available to you right on the toolbar. All you need to do is highlight the text to format and click the appropriate button. The Style drop-down box works similarly and gives you access to a much greater range of styles, including heading and list styles (see fig. 27.7).

Next to the physical style toolbar buttons are the Text Color button, which lets you paint highlighted text with a different color, and the Increase/Decrease Text Size buttons.

For several formatting options at once, select Format, Characters to reveal the Character Styles dialog box you see in figure 27.8. Clicking different styles in this box applies them to highlighted text.

Part

IV

Ch

27

FIG. 27.7

To apply a style, just highlight the text and click the desired style in the Styles drop-down list.

FIG. 27.8

The Character Styles dialog box gives you lots of formatting options that correspond to different HTML formatting tags.

Inserting Images To place an image on your page, choose Insert, Image to open the Insert Image dialog box you see in figure 27.9. In the box, you get the option to load the file from a local drive or from a URL, so you can pull down any image you want from the Web.

FIG. 27.9

You can place images from local or remote sources in your FrontPage Editor document.

By default, the image is placed at the current cursor location and is left-justified. You can exercise greater control over the placement of the image in its Properties box. To reveal the image's properties, right-click the image and select the Properties option you see in the context-sensitive pop-up menu. The Properties dialog box, shown in figure 27.10, allows you to specify image alignment, border size, horizontal and vertical spacing, low-res and text alternatives for the image, and, if it is hyperlinked, what URL it is linked to.

FIG. 27.10

An image's Properties dialog box gives you finer control over image attributes.

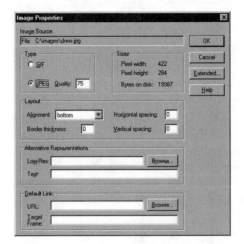

T I P If you want to use an attribute of the `<IMG>` tag that isn't available in the Properties dialog box, click the Extended button to open a dialog box where you can enter the attribute and its value manually.

Setting Up Hyperlinks To create hypertext, highlight the text to serve as the anchor and click the Create or Edit Link toolbar button. You'll then see a dialog box like the one in figure 27.11. In the box, you can choose to link to a page that is currently open in the Editor, a page that is part of the Web that you're working on, any page on the World Wide Web, or a page that you ask the Editor to create for you.

Setting up a linked image is virtually the same as setting up linked text. Simply click the image you wish to link and then click the Create or Edit Link button to open the dialog box, as shown in figure 27.11.

If you click an object that is already linked and then click the Create or Edit Link button, you'll be in an edit mode in which you can change the attributes of the link.

T I P If you're setting up an imagemap, click the image and make use of the buttons on the Image toolbar to trace rectangular, circular, and polygonal hot regions.

FIG. 27.11

The Create Link dialog box lets you link to files on your site, files out on the Web or files you have yet to create.

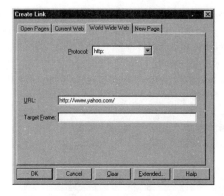

Creating Tables   To insert a table, choose Table, Insert Table or click the Insert Table toolbar button. When you do, you'll see the Insert Table dialog box like the one in figure 27.12. After entering the table size and border, alignment, padding, and spacing attributes, the Editor will place a blank table in your document (see fig. 27.13) and you can fill in the cells with text, images, form fields, and even other tables.

FIG. 27.12

Set up a table in your document by filling out the Insert Table dialog box.

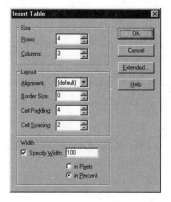

> **N O T E**   Most of the options under the Table menu are grayed out unless the cursor is in a table cell. ▪

Changing Page Properties   The FrontPage Editor will use a standard set of colors for page background, text, and links unless you tell it to use a different scheme. You do this by selecting File, Page Properties and choosing the colors you want in the Page Properties dialog box (see fig. 27.14). In addition to color preferences, you can specify a background image and a base URL and target frame (if you're using frames). You can also click the Meta button to create any <META> tags you want in your document head.

FIG. 27.13
The FrontPage editor places a blank table at the current cursor position and lets you fill in the cells with content.

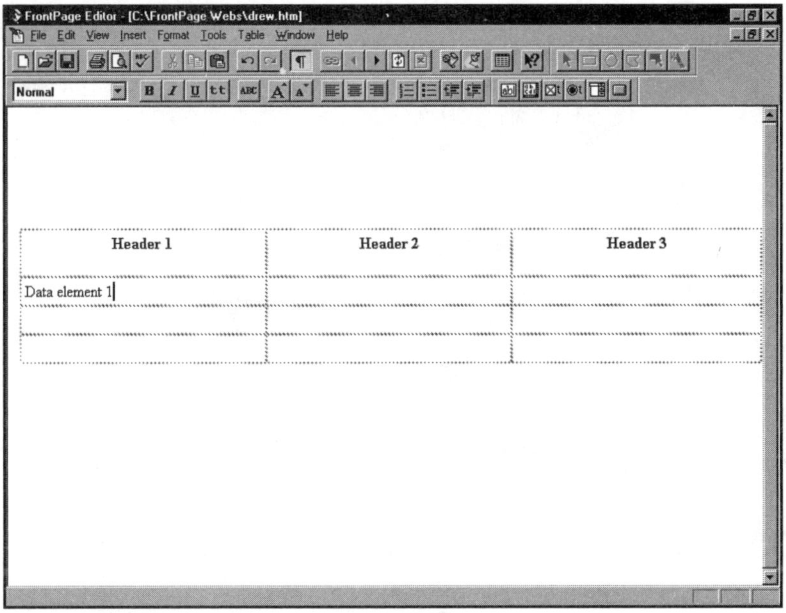

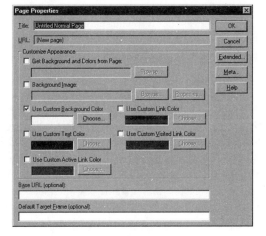

FIG. 27.14
Many of the attributes you would specify in the document head or the <BODY> tag are available from the Page Properties dialog box.

Saving Your Document

To save your document for the first time, select File, Save As to open the dialog box shown in figure 27.15. Note in the box that you can save the document as a normal file or as a document template.

> **CAUTION**
>
> Make sure your document has an appropriately descriptive title before you save it. Remember that good titles are an important reader service!

FIG. 27.15

When saving for the first time, you can make your document into a template for reuse at a later time.

If you're working on multiple files and want to save them all simultaneously, choose File, Save All.

Other Useful Editor Features

In case you hadn't noticed yet, the FrontPage Editor gives you a very comprehensive environment for creating and editing Web documents. In addition to the features previously noted, some other handy functions that the Editor provides are as follows:

■ **Spellchecker**—Spellchecking is a good quality-control measure for all of your Web documents. To use the Editor's built-in spellchecker, press F7 or choose Tools, Spelling.

■ **HTML Viewer**—As you author a page, you never see an HTML tag unless you choose View, HTML. When you do this, a pop-up window opens and shows you the HTML that corresponds to your Editor document.

■ **Special Characters**—Choosing Insert, Special Characters opens a window in which you can choose a special or reserved character. The Editor will automatically convert it into the appropriate HTML entity.

■ **Web Bots**—Web bots are preprogrammed dynamic objects that run when you save a file or when a user views your file online. The FrontPage Editor comes with several bots that you can build into your pages, including Table of Contents, Search, Timestamp, Scheduled Image, and Include bots. Microsoft expects to release a FrontPage developers' toolkit that will allow users to create and save their own bots as well. To see the list of available Web bots, choose Insert, Bot.

■ **To Do List**—Trying to keep track of all of your changes is sometimes an insurmountable task. To help you remember all you need to get done, the FrontPage Editor comes with a To Do list where you can store details of tasks that you need to accomplish. To access your To Do list for a given Web, click the To Do List toolbar button or choose Tools, Show To Do List.

Using the FrontPage Explorer

The FrontPage Explorer is the application in the FrontPage suite that manages entire Web sites (see fig. 27.16). By giving you three different ways to look at a site, you can readily see how information is organized and linked, and where bad links may exist.

FIG. 27.16
FrontPage's Explorer allows you to create and manage entire Web sites.

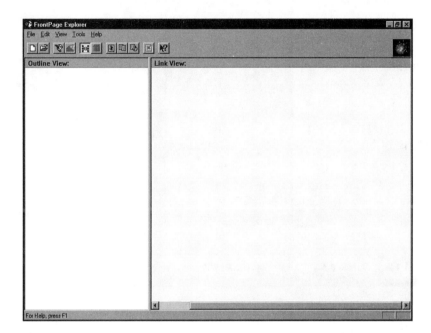

Creating a New Web

To start a new Web site (or, in FrontPage terminology, a new Web), choose File, New Web or click the New Web toolbar button. You will then see the dialog box shown in figure 27.17. From the box, you can choose one of six Web site templates or one of two Web site wizards. Figure 27.18 shows the Explorer window after selecting the Personal Web option.

Part
IV

Ch
27

FIG. 27.17
The Explorer gives you eight different options when creating a new Web.

FIG. 27.18

The Personal Web template comes preconfigured with links to co-worker and manager pages and a mailto link.

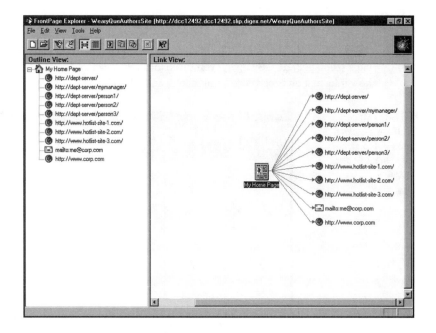

> **T I P** To build a Web from scratch, choose the Empty Web option.

> **N O T E** Choosing one of the wizards instructs the Explorer to walk you through a series of dialog boxes to gather information about the Web structure before it creates the Web. ■

Viewing a Web

Once you have started a new Web or have loaded in an existing one (File, Open Web), you can examine it in different ways: the Outline View, the Link View, and the Summary View. Each view is briefly discussed over the next three sections.

The Outline View The Outline View is always found in the left side of the Explorer window (refer to fig. 27.18). It shows a hierarchical view of your Web site, in much the same way as the left side of the Windows Explorer shows you the hierarchical folder structure on your hard drive. If you click a plus sign (+), it expands the hierarchy found below the object with the plus sign. Clicking a minus sign (–) collapses an expanded hierarchy.

The Link View The Link View is the default view on the right side of the Explorer window (refer to fig. 27.18). This view depicts your site more graphically, illustrating with arrows links to other pages within the site and off the site. The Link View makes it easy to see how your documents are linked together, and where you might be missing some critical links.

The Summary View   By clicking the Summary View toolbar button or by choosing View, Summary View, you change the right side of the Explorer window to the Summary View (see fig. 27.19). The Summary View is very much like the right side of the Windows Explorer window, as it details document-specific information such as titles, filenames and sizes, last change dates, who made the most recent edits, and the document's URL.

FIG. 27.19

The Summary View gives you all of the details on all of the component files in a Web site.

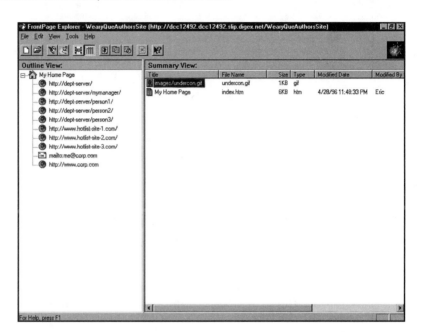

Editing Documents from the Explorer

When you use an Explorer template or wizard to set up a Web, you'll eventually need to edit the component documents in the Web to build in your own information. Or, in the case of an existing site, you'll need to update the content of the site often. Thankfully, it's easy to launch the FrontPage Editor from the Explorer so you can make these changes. To do this, simply follow these steps:

1. Click the document you want to edit (in any view).
2. Click the Show FrontPage Editor toolbar button or select Tools, Show FrontPage Editor.

Figure 27.20 shows the document "My Home Page" after it is loaded into the Editor.

TIP   Double-clicking a document in the Link or Summary View will launch the FrontPage Editor and load the selected document into the Editor.

Part

IV

Ch

27

FIG. 27.20
You can move between the Explorer and the Editor to make changes to individual pages during site management activities.

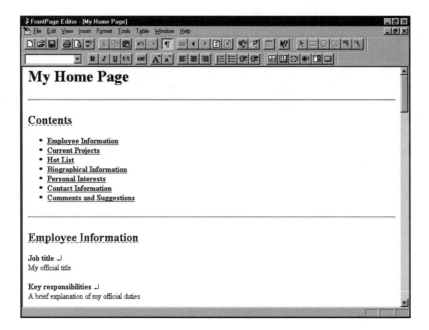

Link Tools

Visiting a Web site that has broken or outdated links can be one of a Web surfer's most frustrating experiences. It's frustrating for the site administrator, too. Keeping track of all links on a large site requires incredible attention to detail. Keeping track of links to other sites is all but impossible without checking each link individually on a regular basis. Fortunately for both parties, the FrontPage Explorer comes with some link utilities that help to alleviate these problems.

Verify Links   Choosing Tools, Verify Links instructs the Explorer to perform a check on all of the links in your Web, including links to pages that are not on your Web. The Explorer reports its findings back to you in a window like the one you see in figure 27.21. Links to pages within your site are shown with a red circle and the word "Broken" if they are broken, or are not shown at all if they're working. Links to pages not on your site are shown with a yellow circle and a question mark in front of them. This indicates that they have yet to be verified. You can verify each external link by selecting it in the window and clicking the Verify button. If an external link is verified, the Explorer places a green circle with the work "OK" in front of the link. If an external link is broken, it gets a red circle with the word "Broken."

Recalculate Links   The Recalculate Links command (choose Tools, Recalculate Links) updates the displays in each of the three views to reflect any changes made by you or other authors. Specifically, the Recalculate Links command does the following three things:

- It refreshes the Outline, Link, and Summary Views of your Web.

- It regenerates all *dependencies* in the open Web. Dependencies are items that get read into a page like Include bots.

■ It updates the index created by the Search bot.

Link recalculation actually occurs on the Personal Web Server that comes as part of the FrontPage suite. Once the server has finished recalculating, control returns back to the Explorer.

FIG. 27.21
You can generate a report on the integrity of all internal and external links by choosing Tools, Verify Links.

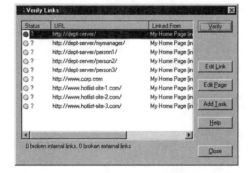

CAUTION

Be patient during recalculation. If you recalculate for a large Web, it could take several minutes to complete the operation.

Other Useful Explorer Features

The FrontPage Explorer comes with some other handy features that can make your life as a Web site administrator much easier. These include the following:

■ **View Menu Options**—The Links to Images, Repeated Links, and Links Inside Page options under the View menu toggle the display of these types of links on and off. When these options are on, it modifies the three views to show the type of link selected. You can toggle these options from the Explorer toolbar as well.

■ **Proxy Server Setup**—Choosing Tools, Proxies opens a dialog box that allows you to specify a proxy server (or firewall) for your Web server.

■ **Import/Export of Individual Documents**—You can import an existing document into the Web you're working on by selecting File, Import. Likewise, choosing File, Export Selected exports a selected document.

Part
IV

Ch

27

Using the FrontPage TCP/IP Test

The FrontPage TCP/IP Test program does a quick check for your machine's host name, IP address, and other information required for it to act as a Web server on the Internet. When you start the TCP/IP Test, you see the FrontPage TCP/ IP Test dialog box shown in figure 27.22. To start the test, click the button that says Start Test.

FIG. 27.22

The FrontPage TCP/IP
Test programs gathers
information critical to
your computer's role
as a Web server.

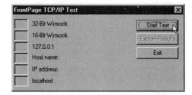

When the test has finished, the empty boxes on the left side of the dialog box fill with the words "Yes" or "No," depending on what the program was able to find. If you click the Explain Results button, you get an explanation of the test results in plain English (see fig. 27.23).

FIG. 27.23

The TCP/IP Test program
explains the test results
to you in easy-to-
understand terms.

Using the Personal Web Server

A Web server program's main responsibility is to field requests for Web pages from client programs such as Internet Explorer and send the pages to the requesting program. Since this isn't a highly visible activity, a Web server often runs "in the background" with no on-screen display of what's going on.

This is the case with FrontPage's Personal Web Server program. When it is active, it usually sits on your Task Bar. The label on the Task Bar will read "Idle" if the server isn't doing anything, and "Busy" if it is serving pages. If you click the Task Bar item for the Personal Web Server, you'll see the window shown in figure 27.24. The only two menu options are File, Exit and Help, About Web Server—both of which are pretty self-explanatory.

Even though the Personal Web Server doesn't seem to be as "high-profile" as the Editor or the Explorer, it does have some desirable features, including the following:

■ Complete support of HTTP and CGI standards

■ Supports *multi-homing* (assigning multiple domain names to the same machine)

■ Recalculation of links when requested by the Explorer

FIG. 27.24
This is the only screen you'll ever see when running the Personal Web Server.

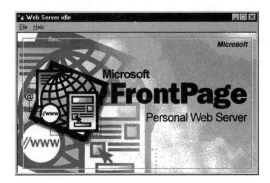

N O T E To have your computer act as a Web server, you need to connect it to the Internet. Since most of us can't afford a dedicated Internet connection, it's likely that you won't be able to have your server running all of the time. Make sure people know when you intend to have your server available. ▓

Using the Server Administrator

The more visible side of having a Web server is seen in the Server Administrator program. From the Server Administrator Window, you can perform the following admin functions (see fig. 27.25):

- ▓ Install, Upgrade, or Uninstall FrontPage server extensions (see the section entitled "Server Extensions" for more information) on the selected server.
- ▓ Check the configuration of any FrontPage server extensions on the selected server.
- ▓ Enable or disable Authoring rights on the selected server.
- ▓ Add a username and password to the list of server administrators (Security).

FIG. 27.25
The FrontPage Server Administrator allows you to modify many of your server's attributes.

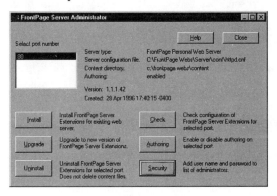

Part
IV

Ch

27

Server Extensions

When you install FrontPage, the only server it really knows how to work with is the Personal Web Server that comes bundled as part of it. To harness the full functionality of FrontPage using a different server program, you need to install FrontPage server extensions. Initially, Microsoft charged $200 for each set of server extensions, but now they are available free of charge. The server extensions currently available are shown in Table 27.1.

Table 27.1   FrontPage Server Extensions

Operating System	Web Servers
Solaris 2.4	NCSA, CERN, Apache, Netscape Communications, Open Market Web Server
SunOS 4.1.3	NCSA, CERN, Apache
IRIX 5.3	NCSA, CERN, Apache, Netscape Communications, Open Market Web Server
HP/UX 9.03	NCSA, CERN, Apache
Windows NT or 95	O'Reilly & Associates' WebSite version 1.0
Windows NT Server	Microsoft Internet Information Server

Once the appropriate set of server extensions is installed, it becomes a simple matter to copy a Web between platforms and to other servers while preserving all programming, access controls, and imagemaps.

The Future: Microsoft Internet Studio

Internet Studio, Microsoft's planned online publishing tool with the codename "Blackbird," was originally scheduled for release in early 1996. In December 1995, Microsoft announced its plans to abandon development of Internet Studio based on Microsoft Network standards and to move directly to a version based on the open standards of the Internet. In the meantime, Microsoft has shared glimpses of some of Internet Studio's anticipated functionality at conferences. These features have included the following:

- A "Visual Basic-like" system that allows you to drop controls and text onto a workspace
- Standards for layering

As of this writing, there's not much more information available about the program or its planned release date. A Microsoft statement to members of its Developers Network assures us that "Internet Studio will be a high-end offering for commercial publishers and professional developers who want to create sophisticated, interactive Web content." Keep checking Microsoft's Web site at **http://www.microsoft.com/** for more information about Internet Studio. ●

Building World-Class Web Sites and Servers for Internet Explorer

## CHAPTER 28

Creating a World-Class Web Site for Internet Explorer

Looking at all of the Web sites that are out there might compel you to think of that Clint Eastwood movie, *The Good, The Bad, and The Ugly.* There are many first-rate sites out on the Web, but as indexes like Mirsky's Worst of the Web will attest, there are some pretty awful ones, too.

You can't just slap a few HTML pages together and hope to have a good Web site. The best Web sites have hours of thoughtful planning and design put into them before the first HTML page is coded. And once you do start coding, you need to make intelligent use of the HTML tags available to produce attractive pages. This can be particularly challenging because HTML is not meant to be a design tool. You may find it hard to accomplish your design objectives just using standard HTML. This suggests the use of HTML extensions, but then you run the risk of your designs being lost on users who don't have browsers that support the extensions you used.

This chapter focuses on what makes the good sites good and what you can do to avoid making Mirsky's list. ■

What you need to start up your own Web site

To get a Web site online, you need to choose a computer, server software, an Internet connection, and people with the skills to build your site.

How to plan your site

Site planning is perhaps the most important component of creating a Web site. You need to put careful thought into how to present your information and how to let a user move around your site.

How to use advanced graphic design elements such as drop shadows and embossing

Making your images appear three-dimensional adds depth to your pages.

How to gain finer layout control with existing HTML tags

Even though HTML isn't a design language, the effects of some HTML tags can be harnessed to produce attractive layouts.

How to build interactivity into your pages

Users love interactive pages. Including interactive pages in your site is a great way to keep users coming back for more.

Running Your Own Web Site

As much fun as running a Web site might be, there are a number of technical issues to consider. You should think about all the points here before actually starting your own Web site. Most individuals really don't need to run their own Web site, while some companies should consider it. If you're sure you want to run your own Web site, you should make certain that the site does the following two things:

- It effectively communicates your message.
- It is intuitively designed so that visitors can move around it easily.

Depending on your expertise with computer graphics, you may not be able to make your site look as impressive as some, but you can still do a decent job with a few simple graphics and a thoughtful layout (see fig. 28.1).

FIG. 28.1

Deutsche Telekom, France Telecom, and Sprint used high-end graphics to create a site that conveys their message in the context of an "Under Development" theme.

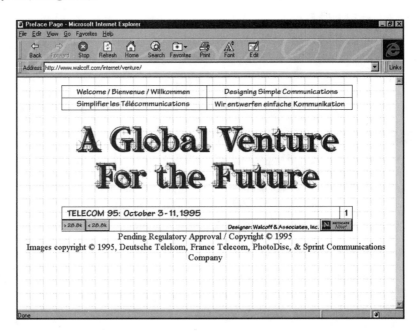

But, first things first. Before you begin to design your site, you need to have the following ingredients in place:

- **A computer**—Most Web sites are run off UNIX-based workstations because they are proven powerhouses. UNIX is more robust, reliable, and fault-tolerant than Windows 95 or Macintosh. Any of the big-name workstation makers, such as Sun, Hewlett Packard, Silicon Graphics, and Digital, are good choices. Unfortunately, these machines cost a lot more money than PCs.

On the CD

■ **Web server software**—There are a lot of Web software programs out there, both free and for sale. In fact, you have a copy of one Web server package already! Microsoft's Internet Information server is on the CD-ROM that comes with this book. Chapter 29, "The Microsoft Internet Information Server," gives you all the details on how to set up the software to run your site.

■ **A connection to the Internet through an Internet service provider (ISP)**—If your company is already on the Internet, you can skip this requirement. Otherwise, don't worry; details about costs and who to talk to are forthcoming later in this chapter.

■ **A system administrator**—Because you're going to have a computer running a Web server, you're going to need someone to manage it. If your company uses a lot of computers or is already on the Internet, you've probably got this covered already.

■ **A person knowledgeable with HTML**—Since Web pages are written in HTML, finding someone who knows HTML is essential to your Web site. If you're lucky, you might be able to find a person who can both author your Web pages and act as a system administrator.

Because there are so many factors involved in running a Web site, it's difficult to calculate the cost. The cost of the computer and Web server software vary from free to more than tens of thousands of dollars. A connection to the Internet requires two payments: one to the telephone company, and another to the ISP. The telephone company sells leased lines of various capacities for about $300 to $2,000 per month. A typical ISP charges around $500 to $1,000 a month to get Internet traffic routed to your site. Set-up costs for these are a little bit more expensive but are one-time up-front charges. The position of Webmaster could be filled from people you already have, so an extra employee might not be needed. Otherwise, you could pay a salary as high as $80,000 for a good Webmaster.

Though these costs are pretty nebulous, the fact of the matter is that running a Web site is a full-time job. It requires a computer dedicated to being on the Internet. The average yearly cost just for having such a computer starts at around $10,000 and goes up from there. If you were to buy a new computer, the Web server software, and pay for a Webmaster, the cost could easily triple. That's not to say that average people can't run Web sites; it's entirely possible to run a part-time or slower-speed Web site for much less. Also, if you're already on the Internet, you've already absorbed most of these costs, so starting a Web site could cost much less.

Planning the Web Site

In light of all the possible costs involved in running a Web site, the next thing you should think about is the purpose of it. Do you want a site that provides sales literature and generates revenue? Do you want a Web site that merely provides technical support for your existing customers? Do you want both of these? None of these? By answering these questions, you determine what type of site you want and what to put on it.

Part
V

Ch
28

The first thing you should consider is what you want your Web site to do for you. If you want just to provide sales literature and generate revenue, you probably won't be sending a lot of graphics to people. As a result, you can get by with a much slower Internet connection, which would reduce your set-up costs. For such sites, a 28,800 baud connection to the Internet should suffice. On the other hand, if you want to provide technical support for your existing users, you can't get away with a slow connection. It's not that you'll necessarily have graphics-intensive Web pages, but that you'll be sending more data across your Internet connection. It's far easier for people to go to your Web site and get the latest patch to your software than to contact your company for it. This type of Web site may require a very fast connection to the Internet and increased set-up costs. Such a connection would be a 56 KB line or above, which requires special hardware on your site's end.

The second thing you should consider before creating the Web pages for your site is your target audience. Are you looking to have your Web site accessed by everybody on the Internet, or are you aiming for a specific target group? Will your audience want to, and be able to, buy your products from your Web page? This will seriously affect which Web server software programs are available to you. Possible legal problems might also arise if a customer's credit card number is somehow compromised. You should ask yourself how the target audience is even going to know about your site. If you do the work to set up a Web site, you should also do some follow-up work to market it properly. Finally, you should consider if it's really appropriate for you to be creating a site. If you're running a sidewalk cafe, establishing a Web presence probably won't do much for your business.

Basic Design Issues Dos and Don'ts

The usability of a Web site was not much of a concern to developers in the early days of the Web. In the beginning, most folks were delighted that they could put a couple of links and a simple graphic on their Web pages. Over the past year, World Wide Web sites have become much more sophisticated. One of the most important changes taking place is that designers are beginning to address the overall look of their sites. Browser-specific HTML tags, like those introduced by Microsoft and Netscape, have been instrumental in this evolution, as it has given developers a broader range of tags with which to work. If you're fully convinced you want to start a Web site, there are a few basic design issues to be mindful of.

The interface design of your page relates to how easily a user can interact and access information in your site. The design of Web sites has become a legitimate concern as the number of sites competing for our attention has increased. Sites that are well designed are more frequently visited than those that are laid out in a sloppy or haphazard fashion. Good examples of well-designed Web sites are Yahoo (**http://www.yahoo.com/**) and Discovery Channel Online (**http://www.discovery.com/**).

Organizing Your Web Site

Before you sit down and start creating your site, you should think about how the information on it is going to be organized. Whether it's for a company or an individual, the most important thing is to decide what information you want to present. Are you going to include answers to common technical support questions? Are you going to put a directory of employees and their phone numbers? A good exercise is to write down on an index card each discrete chunk of information you plan to use. Next, figure out an organizational structure for these chunks of information by arranging the cards into logical groupings. For example, a company that sells lots of products might choose to organize its site by product lines. Build your Web site around these groupings, so that people can easily find what they want.

You can take this a step further by writing short descriptions for each category (see fig. 28.2). This makes it easier for people new to your site to find out what you have and how to get there. This also makes it very easy for you to add new information later on. Additionally, having text descriptions guarantees that visitors using text-only browsers will have something to see when they get to your main page.

FIG. 28.2
Short descriptions of each section of your site clarify what information visitors will find there.

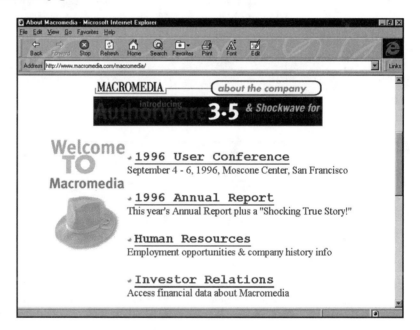

Making Sure Your Message Gets Across

A mistake that some people make with their Web sites is to make them too flashy. They figure that because they can put in lots of graphics and flashing text, they should. This is wrong. Typically, this makes the Web page very busy, and it's difficult for people to get the information they want. Don't muddle your message in a confusing background image, a bad color scheme, or an overuse of graphics. Figure 28.3 illustrates an example of a bad color scheme. The background color of this Web page is too close to the link color, so the hypertext is washed out.

One of your guiding design principles should be to focus on the information you're trying to get across and save the emphasis for later. The blinking text, cool animation, or large images impress people the first time, but become tiresome the fortieth time.

Part
V

Ch

28

FIG. 28.3
Choosing a text or link color that is too close to the background color reduces contrast and makes the content of your pages harder to read.

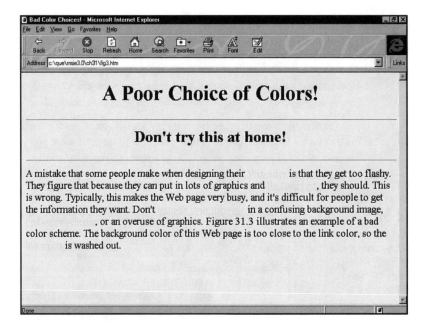

T I P Consider using a light background with darker colored text and links to avoid the problem you see in figure 28.3.

Letting Everybody See What You've Got

Many new Web page authors are putting graphics-intensive pages on the Web. Think twice before you do this. While most people use a graphics-capable browser such as Internet Explorer, not *everybody* does. Add to this the fact that not everybody has an extremely fast connection to the Internet. For these two reasons, you should be very careful about using *any* sort of graphics on your Web site. Don't make your imagemaps and inline pictures so large that it takes a long time for them to load (see fig. 28.4). The bigger the image, the longer it takes for image file to be transferred to the user's computer. Just because a 200K GIF looks good in Photoshop doesn't mean everyone has the patience to wait for it to load. Using multiple images can also take a long time, because a separate HTTP connection is opened for each one. Know the graphical limitations of your audience, and design your site around them.

N O T E This is a good time to remind you always to include a text-based alternative to your graphics. You can do this with the ALT attribute of the <IMG> tag or by placing descriptive text next to your images. ■

Site Navigation: You *Can* Get There From Here

Even the best-designed Web sites might be confusing to some. As a result, when designing pages for your site, make sure to put in navigational aids for the user. Give the user a way back to the main page, major informational sections, and important functions such as help, search engines, and feedback forms (see fig. 28.5). If possible, cross-index your Web pages to each other, so that related pages are just a click away. Try to anticipate other related categories that a person might be interested in on each page, and put links to them. If a person has selected a Web page that lists jobs in Los Angeles, put in links to job listings for other Southern California cities. A few buttons here and there or a menu bar that's always around go a long way in helping users. The more you help them out, the more likely they are to come back.

FIG. 28.4
Single large images take a long time to load and may discourage a potential visitor to your site.

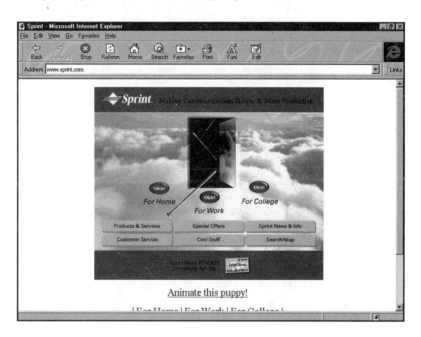

Make Everything Look the Same

Web pages usually aren't created in one sitting or by one person and, as a result, each page may have a different look and feel. By having an inconsistent look and feel to your Web site, users may get the feeling that you threw the pages together. It won't seem as professional, and it won't be a site they'll eagerly return to.

Each page of your site should make consistent use of text size, headers, navigational aids, and menus. Before designing new pages, ground yourself by looking at the existing pages already on your site.

 A good way to check whether your Web site is consistent is to have other people try it out before you put it online. Have them go through all the various links and see if the pages have a consistent look. While you have them there, get their opinions on the intuitiveness of the site's organization and use of graphical icons. Piloting your site before it "goes live" is always a good way to improve your design.

FIG. 28.5
Consistently placed navigational tools like Yahoo's let users navigate your site easily.

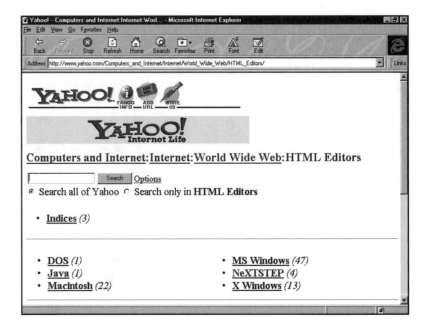

Working with Frames

As you read in Chapter 25, "HTML 3.2 and Microsoft Extensions to HTML," frames are a new Web page feature introduce by Netscape. Because frames can be used to keep key items like menus or navigation aids always on the browser screen, they're an excellent tool for your Web pages (see fig. 28.6). Because clicking in one frame can change the content of another frame, you can use them as a way of offering better search capabilities. Instead of having the user go back and forth between the search page and the results page, you can have the search frame update the results frame. This feature is also especially useful for offering all your product literature online. You can offer all your products in one frame, and when a user selects a particular product, the corresponding literature pops up in the modified frame.

 As with everything else, make sure that the frames are well planned. Make sure that each page allocates the same amount of space for the frame. Change the frame size only when absolutely needed.

Testing Your Design

As noted earlier, it's a good idea to let other folks try out your site before you unveil it. Your testers should have little to no knowledge of your design or of what information is on the site. Sending them in blind may seem a bit cruel, but you'll get better feedback as a result. As they test your site, encourage them to ask the following questions:

■ Do the pages have a consistent look?

■ Is information on the site organized in a logical way?

- Are there enough navigation options to let a user get to each major section of the site?
- If there are menu bars, are they consistently placed?
- Do the graphics and color scheme overpower the message of the site?

FIG. 28.6
Frames let you keep static page items such as tables of contents and navigation menus on screen at all times.

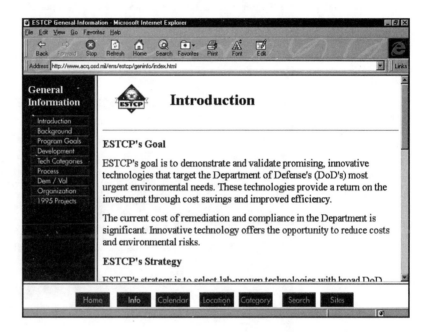

N O T E Along with your e-mail address, you should also include a phone number and postal address in key areas of your site. This allows customers to contact you for more information or to give you feedback on the site. ▓

Adding Color to Your Site

A few touches of color here and there make a site more appealing. But just like planning out your Web pages, you should plan out your color scheme. As you saw in figure 28.3, you don't want link or text colors to look too much like the background color. As long as you use it thoughtfully, color can liven up your Web pages a great deal.

Color Considerations

Before using color in your Web pages, there are a few things to think about. You might want to consider using distinctive colors for emphasis, rather than just using HTML tags like <B>, <I>, or <EM>. Also, if you're planning on running a commercial Web site, try to avoid using black as a background color. Some people might want to print out a particular page on your site, and a black background throws off some browsers. Similarly, white text may not print well either.

Appropriate Use of the *<BODY>* Tag for Backgrounds

Attributes for the <BODY> tag were introduced in Chapter 23, "Advanced Graphics." There are attributes for background colors and background images. The background color attribute, <BODY BGCOLOR="#RRGGBB">, instructs the browser to display a particular color as the background for the HTML document. These colors are represented in respect to their red, green, and blue components. The body background image attribute, <BODY BACKGROUND="URL_of_image">, loads and tiles an image across the background of the user's browser (see fig. 28.7).

FIG. 28.7
Tiled background images make a nice backdrop as long as they don't overpower information in the foreground.

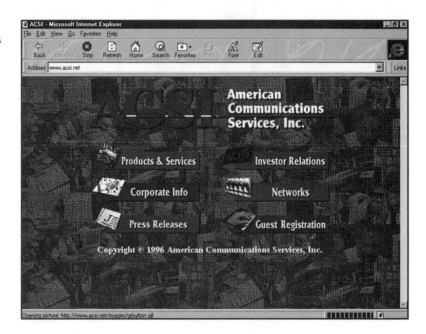

Some key design guidelines for using background colors and images are as follows:

- Text is more legible against a light background than against a dark one. Most images, however, are enhanced against a dark background.
- A white background on most computer monitors is too harsh on the eyes for pleasant reading. It is better to use a light gray or a pastel color on pages that have extended passages of text.
- Busy background images should not be used, as they will greatly reduce the readability of text and irritate your audience.

Text and Link Colors

In addition to background color and image, the <BODY> tag can specify a text color and various link colors. These attributes were introduced in Chapter 23, "Advanced Graphics," and are worth discussing here beacause they relate to the interface design of your site. You can modify the text color from its default black by using the TEXT attribute of the <BODY> tag. Unvisited, visited, and active links can be colored with the LINK, VLINK, and ALINK attributes, respectively.

Like the BGCOLOR attribute, the text and link color attributes are set equal to a triplet of hexadecimal numbers that describes the colors red, green, and blue components of the color you want. More often than not, people find the hexadecimal code confusing. If this is true for you, you may want to refer to Table 28.1, which lists the codes for several colors.

TIP The Color Manipulation Device program found on the CD-ROM with this book is an excellent way to preview background colors and images as well as text and link colors. Even better, as you select custom colors, CMD computes the hexadecimal codes for you and composes a <BODY> tag that you can copy and paste right into your HTML document.

Table 28.1 Background, Text, and Link Colors

Color	RGB Code	Color	RGB Code
Aquamarine	#70DB93	Medium Blue	#3232CD
Baker's Chocolate	#5C3317	Medium Forest Green	#6B8E23
Blue Violet	#9F5F9F	Medium Goldenrod	#EAEAAE
Brass	#B5A642	Medium Orchid	#9370DB
Bright Gold	#D9D919	Medium Sea Green	#426F42
Brown	#A62A2A	Medium Slate Blue	#7F00FF
Bronze	#8C7853	Medium Spring Green	#7FFF00
Bronze II	#A67D3D	Medium Turquoise	#70DBDB
Cadet Blue	#5F9F9F	Medium Violet Red	#DB7093
Cool Copper	#D98719	Medium Wood	#A68064
Copper	#B87333	Midnight Blue	#2F2F4F
Coral	#FF7F00	Navy Blue	#23238E
Cornflower Blue	#42426F	Neon Pink	#FF6EC7
Dark Brown	#5C4033	New Midnight Blue	#00009C
Dark Green	#2F4F2F	New Tan	#EBC79E
Dark Green Copper	#4A766E	Old Gold	#CFB53B

Part
V

Ch

28

continues

Table 28.1 Continued

Color	RGB Code	Color	RGB Code
Dark Olive Green	#4F4F2F	Orange	#FF7F00
Dark Orchid	#9932CD	Orange Red	#FF2400
Dark Purple	#871F78	Orchid	#DB70DB
Dark Slate Blue	#6B238E	Pale Green	#8FBC8F
Dark Slate Grey	#2F4F4F	Pink	#BC8F8F
Dark Tan	#97694F	Plum	#EAADEA
Dark Turquoise	#7093DB	Quartz	#D9D9F3
Dark Wood	#855E42	Rich Blue	#5959AB
Dim Grey	#545454	Salmon	#6F4242
Dusty Rose	#856363	Scarlet	#8C1717
Feldspar	#D19275	Sea Green	#238E68
Firebrick	#8E2323	Semi-Sweet Chocolate	#6B4226
Forest Green	#238E23	Sienna	#8E6B23
Gold	#CD7F32	Silver	#E6E8FA
Goldenrod	#DBDB70	Sky Blue	#3299CC
Grey	#C0C0C0	Slate Blue	#007FFF
Green Copper	#527F76	Spicy Pink	#FF1CAE
Green Yellow	#93DB70	Spring Green	#00FF7F
Hunter Green	#215E21	Steel Blue	#236B8E
Indian Red	#4E2F2F	Summer Sky	#38B0DE
Khaki	#9F9F5F	Tan	#DB9370
Light Blue	#C0D9D9	Thistle	#D8BFD8
Light Grey	#A8A8A8	Turquoise	#ADEAEA
Light Steel Blue	#8F8FBD	Very Dark Brown	#5C4033
Light Wood	#E9C2A6	Very Light Grey	#CDCDCD

Color	RGB Code	Color	RGB Code
Lime Green	#32CD32	Violet	#4F2F4F
Mandarin Orange	#E47833	Violet Red	#CC3299
Maroon	#8E236B	Wheat	#D8D8BF
Medium Aquamarine	#32CD99	Yellow Green	#99CC32

Advanced Graphic Design

Incorporating sophisticated graphics into your World Wide Web pages can make the difference between a run-of-the-mill site and one that stands out from the online crowd. The following are a few graphic design elements that add a look of sophistication to your site:

■ **Drop Shadows**—Soft-edged drop shadows on text and graphics make them appear to float above the browser's background, and add depth to the page (see fig. 28.8). The use of a dark drop shadow with a slight offset can make text more legible against a dark background. Several leading graphics packages, such as Fractal Design Painter, provide options to add drop shadows to images. Furthermore, Photoshop plug-ins, such as the Black Box filters, offer a wide range of user options for adding drop shadows to selected objects.

FIG. 28.8
Drop shadows behind text and images add depth to Web pages.

Part
V

Ch
28

■ **Emboss**—As with the use of drop shadows, images that have embossed (or beveled) edges stand out on the viewer's screen. Embossed images make good buttons and menus, as they mimic buttons found on VCRs and cassette players (see fig. 28.9). They also break up the visual monotony of browsing two-dimensional Web pages. Developing embossed images is best done in sophisticated graphics packages such as Photoshop (employing the use of plug-ins such as the Black Box filters) or Adobe Gallery Effects.

FIG. 28.9

Embossing Web page buttons make them more three-dimensional and give a feel similar to buttons on modern electronic devices.

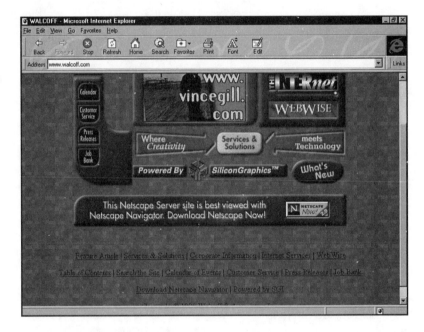

■ **Ray Tracing**—Ray-traced images provide a much more dramatic three-dimensional experience than those with embossed edges or drop shadows. Ray-traced 3D images give the appearance of floating on the viewer's screen, and can be used to show off a new product or package or can simply add impact to your page (see fig. 28.10).

N O T E   When developing graphics with drop shadows or embossed edges, decide on the angle of a common light source before you begin. Most graphics programs that create embossed images and drop-shadowed text allow you to preview the light-source configuration. Use this feature to decide on a good light-source position, and keep it consistent with other similar images. Individual light sources for each are distracting to the user. ■

The *LOWSRC* Attribute of the *<IMG>* Tag

The LOWSRC attribute of the <IMG> tag was designed to allow a low-resolution graphic to load initially on the Internet Explorer screen, replaced by a higher-resolution image during the final layout of the page. This attribute allows developers to present the general look of a page quickly to the viewer, replaced with more detailed images as the download continues.

FIG. 28.10
Ray-traced images have a much stronger three-dimensional look.

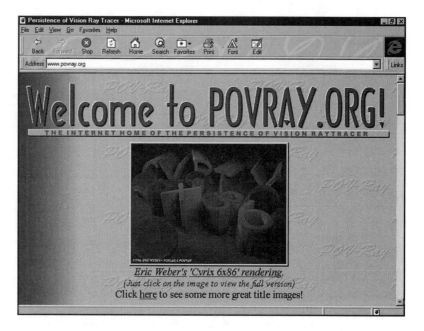

The LOWSRC attribute is built into the <IMG> tag as follows:

`<IMG SRC="URL_of_high_resolution_image" LOWSRC="URL_of_low_resolution_image">`

The LOWSRC image can further reduce download time by specifying the height and width of the final image. As discussed in Chapter 23, "Advanced Graphics," on using thumbnail images, an image can be resized on the browser's screen by specifying the HEIGHT and WIDTH attributes for the image. This can be used with LOWSRC by loading a thumbnail image as the low-resolution image with the specified HEIGHT and WIDTH attributes of the high-resolution image. For instance, with a high-resolution image of 200 pixels wide by 100 pixels high and a thumbnail image with the dimensions of 20 pixels wide by 10 pixels high, you could use the LOWSRC in the following way:

`<IMG SRC="URL_of_high_resolution_image" WIDTH=200 HEIGHT=100`
`LOWSRC="URL_of_thumbnail_image">`

In this instance, the LOWSRC image stretches to fit the final image area of 200 pixels wide by 100 pixels high on the browser window. The final image replaces the stretched thumbnail image on the final pass.

> **N O T E** Even if you don't use the LOWSRC attribute in your <IMG> tags, you should always use the WIDTH and HEIGHT attributes to speed up the layout of pages on the browser screen. ■

Developers have taken advantage of the LOWSRC attribute to incorporate the appearance of simple animation. Because the original LOWSRC image is replaced by the final image, it is possible to leave out part of the final image in the LOWSRC image, thereby giving the viewer the illusion that the image is being "filled in." This LOWSRC trick can be used, for instance, to

Part
V

Ch
28

"morph" an old logo into a new one, or initially to load a black-and-white image which is then replaced by a full-color graphic.

> **CAUTION**
>
> When doing an animation using LOWSRC, the image used as the LOWSRC must be the same size as the final image. The final image won't be loaded directly over the LOWSRC image if the sizes aren't the same. Similarly, make sure that the HEIGHT and WIDTH of the final image are the same as the LOWSRC's image.

Advanced Layout Design

While there are a lot of features in HTML, the language doesn't provide nearly as much control for the HTML author as a desktop publishing (DTP) program like Pagemaker or Quark Express. Something as simple as indenting a paragraph is impossible with standard HTML, because extra spaces before and after words are ignored. Until Microsoft introduced the LEFTMARGIN and TOPMARGIN attributes of the <BODY> tag, Web authors didn't have control over margins as they do in most DTP packages. This section presents a few tricks for acquiring greater control over your page layouts. Most of these tricks aren't widely known, because they either require a bit of work or aren't intuitive. All of them provide for improved control over the flow of the text and placement of images, which makes your page stand out more. A few of these may not be rendered properly by some browsers, but by and large, you can use them to make a dazzling page.

Aligning Text and Images with *<BLOCKQUOTE>*

The <BLOCKQUOTE> tag is used widely in the development of sophisticated Web pages. To see why, look at the text in a printed book such as this one and then look at the text on a WWW page. What are the differences? The first thing you might notice is that the book has a right and left margin, whereas, most likely, the text in the Internet Explorer window runs from edge to edge with no discernible margin. The <BLOCKQUOTE> tag allows you to pull in the text and graphics by an equal distance from the edges of the browser's window and create a margin on both the left and right sides. This makes your long passages of text more readable, as it is easier to move from one line of text to the next.

The <BLOCKQUOTE> tag is also a unique way to create the look of multiple columns when combined with floating images. As discussed in Chapter 23, "Advanced Graphics," floating images are those graphics specified with an ALIGN attribute in the <IMG> tag. Text following a floating image naturally wraps around the image based on the alignment specified. For instance:

```
<IMG SRC="URL_of_image" ALIGN=LEFT>
text passage
```

This image is aligned on the left, and the related text passage wraps around the right edge of the image.

Using <BLOCKQUOTE> before the text in the previous example creates a margin between the image and text, as well as the appearance of a two-column layout for the page. The text continues to flow down the page in this fashion until the appropriate <BR> tag is specified to clear the browser's margin:

```
<IMG SRC="url_of_image" ALIGN=LEFT>
<BLOCKQUOTE>
text passage
</BLOCKQUOTE>
<BR CLEAR=LEFT>
```

Aligning Text and Images with Tables

As more and more browsers are able to parse the HTML table tags correctly, it becomes possible to make regular use of HTML tables as layout tools. The great advantage of tables is the control you get over alignment. You can control horizontal alignment (ALIGN=LEFT¦RIGHT¦CENTER) and vertical alignment (VALIGN=TOP¦MIDDLE¦BOTTOM) in each cell of the table. This lets you place text and images almost exactly where you want them on a page.

You've already seen in Chapter 21, "Adding Graphics and Tables," how tables can be used to align custom bullet graphics, pull quote text, and form fields. Figure 28.11 shows a Web page that makes extensive use of the ALIGN and VALIGN attributes of the HTML table tags to produce a layout that would be all but impossible with standard HTML.

▶ **See** "The Basic Table Tags" for a refresher on the ALIGN and VALIGN attributes, **p. 394**

FIG. 28.11

Placing text and images in tables gives you exceptionally fine control over their alignment and page position.

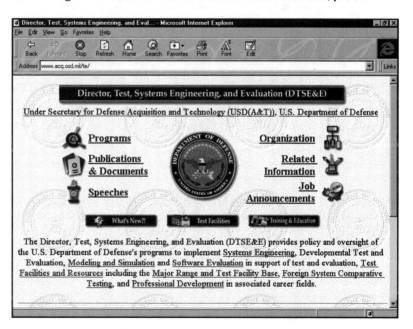

Part
V
Ch
28

Adding Interactivity

One way to get people's attention to your Web site is to provide for user interaction. This basically means that users have a certain amount of control over the Web site. It's not as frightening as it might sound, since this is always under your control. Your site can give users as much, or as little, interaction with whatever you want them to have on your system. Be it clicking a link to start an automatic slide show, playing an online game, or participating in an online forum, you ultimately control it all.

Creating Dynamic Documents

Netscape introduced the ability to create what is known as "dynamic documents" in a Web site. To understand this mechanism, it might be helpful to review the relationship between a browser and server. The World Wide Web has been based upon a static document principle, in which the browser requests a document from a server when there has been some form of user input—such as clicking a text or graphic link. When the request has been received and processed by the server, the connection to that browser is broken until another request is made. Dynamic documents, on the other hand, allow the browser and server to maintain a dynamic relationship through one of the following techniques:

- **Client Pull**—The HTML document received by Internet Explorer contains a directive that instructs the browser either to reload the current document or to fetch another document after a specified period of time.

- **Server Push**—The connection between browser and server remains open as directed by the server. This is usually done through a Common Gateway Interface (CGI) program that sends new information to update the browser's screen.

Because server pushes require writing a CGI program, they are typically not very easy to implement. Client pull, on the other hand, requires only one additional tag in the HTML document and can be incorporated quite easily into any Web page. A popular use for client pull is the development of a series of HTML documents similar to a slide presentation program. Incorporating this type of self-running presentation into your Web site provides visitors a guided tour of the most important areas of your site.

Writing client pull elements into an HTML document begins with the <META> tag, the attributes of which specify the subsequent document to be loaded by the browser and the length of time (in seconds) before the loading occurs. For instance, if we were to use client pull to move from an HTML document named SLIDE1.HTML to a document named SLIDE2.HTML after a period of 30 seconds, the HTML to produce SLIDE1.HTML would read as follows:

```
<HTML>
<HEAD>
<META HTTP-EQUIV="Refresh" CONTENT="30; URL=path_to_slide2.html">
```

Once received, the <META> tag in SLIDE1.HTML instructs the browser to fetch the document named SLIDE2.HTML after a period of 30 seconds. Using client pull with the <META> within each document of a slide show allows you to guide a visitor through the most important elements of your Web site or to set up a self-running information kiosk.

> **CAUTION**
>
> Try to avoid putting dynamic documents in your site's main page. Every time a Web page is loaded, or reloaded, the dynamic document is also loaded. This means that whenever users go to your main page, even if they've been there many times, they'll see the dynamic document. Forcing users to see documents they've already seen could upset them.

> **CAUTION**
>
> The browser receiving a client pull begins to count the seconds before reload as soon as the HTML document is received. Be sure to specify enough time for the complete download of all elements on a page before sending a user to another page. Test your client pull documents on a variety of Internet connections to ensure that visitors with even the slowest connection have sufficient time to download and comprehend each page before being sent on.

Advanced Interactive Elements

The best World Wide Web sites are those that allow visitors to interact with elements contained within the site. The simplest form of interaction is the use of text and graphic links to other documents within your site or elsewhere on the Web. More advanced forms of interaction usually require specific CGI programs to handle the user requests. Developing CGI programs is much more sophisticated than HTML; it is covered in Chapter 26, "Internet Explorer Forms and CGI Scripts." There are a number of good online references to programming CGI scripts and a number of sites that have simple programs available for downloading. Many of these programs can be used "as is" or are easily converted for use on your site. Unique CGI programs for your site can be written for a number of interesting purposes.

One type of site that uses interactive pages frequently is a Web index site like Yahoo (**http://www.yahoo.com/**) or AltaVista (**http://altavista.digital.com/**). These sites take your search criteria, check their databases for matches, and then dynamically generate a custom page just for you with the results of your search query.

User Feedback and Discussion Forums One of the primary concerns for most companies developing a presence on the Web is how to encourage repeat visitors to their sites. Incorporating user discussion areas into Web sites is an interesting way of dealing with this problem. A site can develop a community of its own by providing an online forum for visitors to ask questions about the company's products, provide answers to frequently asked questions, and allow users a means of communicating with each other. The following are some different types of discussion programs that are used on the Web:

- **Chat Areas**—Similar to the chat areas of commercial online services such as America Online and CompuServe, World Wide Web chat areas allow users to interact with the site and with areas that require immediate feedback.

Part
V

Ch
28

■ **Threaded Discussion Forums**—Threaded discussion programs on the WWW are similar to UseNet newsgroups. With this type of discussion area incorporated into their sites, companies can begin threads of discussion based upon the needs and interests of visitors.

Online Games   Incorporating games into your site is another example of how to increase visitors through interaction. Games and sweepstakes can be changed periodically to encourage users to visit your site on a regular basis. Examples of games on the World Wide Web can be found at Yahoo's index on Interactive Web Games, at **http://www.yahoo.com/Recreation/ Games/Internet_Games/Interactive_Web_Games/**. ●

## CHAPTER 29

The Microsoft Internet Information Server

The Personal Web Server that comes bundled with Microsoft FrontPage is fine for—as the name implies—personal Web sites that are made up of a dozen or so pages and that don't get a vast number of requests each day. But if you're setting up a server that you expect will be busier—a marketing site or an internal communications (intranet) site for your company, for example—you'll need a server program that can serve up documents fast. Indeed, many corporate Web servers deliver millions of pages each day. Additionally, you may want your server to work with other applications (like databases) and to provide security to keep communications between client programs and your server encrypted. The Personal Web Server can't do all of this for you, so if you want advanced server functionality, you'll have to trade up.

Enter the Microsoft Internet Information Server (IIS), Microsoft's high-end Web server solution for Windows NT. IIS has all of the advanced features you need for a busy Web server, and it adds the benefit of easy integration with the Microsoft BackOffice family of products. This chapter escorts you through Microsoft's IIS "product tour." ■

Minimum requirements for setting up IIS

At the very least, you need to be running Windows NT Server 3.51 to be able to install IIS.

How to download IIS

Just make sure you have a spare 14 megabytes on your hard drive, and follow simple steps!

IIS Security

IIS provides security at several levels, including user access restrictions, file permissions, log audits, and transaction encryption.

The IIS Internet Service Manager

Get a handle on HTTP, FTP, and Gopher services running on your server.

Performance Monitoring

IIS gives you several measures of system performance that you can use to fine-tune your server.

Other IIS features

Learn about the benefits of IIS that don't fit into the above three categories.

Minimum System Requirements

You can't install IIS on just any system. At a minimum, you need the following software in place:

- Microsoft Windows NT Server 3.51.
- NT Service Pack No. 3 appropriate to the language used on your server. You can download Service Pack No. 3 from **http://www.msn.com/InfoServ/sp3.htm**.

> **CAUTION**
>
> Don't install the English-language version of IIS on a non-English server. The software packages are not compatible.

- A signed digital certificate from a Certification Authority if you plan to use Secure Sockets Layer (SSL) security.

 TIP Visit **http://www.verisign.com/microsoft/** to learn how to get a signed digital certificate for IIS.

Once you have all of these items, you can acquire your copy of IIS. You can do this in the following four ways:

- Purchase the Windows NT Server Value Pack, which includes NT Server 3.51 and IIS, for $999.
- If you already own NT Server 3.51, you can order IIS from Microsoft on disk for $99 by calling 1-800-360-7561.
- Get a copy of IIS as part of your membership in the Microsoft Developer Network.
- Download IIS from Microsoft's Web site.

The last option is the least expensive (you pay just for connection time), so most people will likely be attracted to that one. By directing Internet Explorer to **http://www.microsoft.com/ infoserv/iisinfo.htm**, you get the first in a series of pages that walk you through the downloading process. Part of this process involves acknowledging Microsoft's software licensing agreement and filling out a short registration form and survey. Ultimately, you'll get a list of download sites, from which you should choose the one closest to you.

> **CAUTION**
>
> Read the different download options carefully to find the version of IIS that will run on your platform.

N O T E The file you download will be very big—possibly as large as 14 MB. Make sure you have enough disk space and an Internet connection that will be stable for a long period of time. ■

The file you download is a self-extracting archive. Place the file in a temporary directory and run the executable using the `-d` switch to preserve the directory structure of the archive. Once the archive is extracted, run `SETUP.EXE` to install IIS.

> **CAUTION**
>
> Don't forget to use `-d` when unarchiving! Leaving off the `-d` option when you unarchive the IIS files will be disastrous during installation, because the anticipated directory structure won't be present.

IIS Product Tour

With IIS installed on your machine, you're now ready to take a tour to learn about what IIS can do. The next several sections escort you through Microsoft's IIS product tour, pointing out the key functionality of IIS and how you can put it to work to create a first-rate Web site.

N O T E The Microsoft IIS product tour begins at **http://www.microsoft.com/InfoServ/ tourstart.htm**.

Security

Security is of enormous concern to the Web community. Site administrators don't want ill-intentioned users trying to break into their servers, and users don't want ill-intentioned hackers trying to snatch their credit card numbers and other personal information. In a time when people clamor for privacy of information, the protection of data as it moves over the Web will continue to be of paramount importance.

IIS provides several security options that protect both the server and the end user. These options are discussed in the next sections.

Windows NT Server Security   For starters, the NT Server is a very secure operating system that permits fine control over access to network files and resources. NT's security measures are designed to comply with the standards set forth in US C2 and European E3 certification. Because it is tightly integrated with the NT Server, IIS is able to avail itself of some of NT's functionality to provide a good basic level of security.

The *IUSR_servername* Account   When you first set up IIS, it creates an IUSR account for that server you're configuring. For example, the server wwweb2 would have the IUSR account `IUSR_wwweb2`. The main purpose of this account is to handle all IIS client requests—that is, all of the clients logged onto the IUSR account. Rights to the IUSR account are only granted locally, so no one outside of your system should be able to gain unauthorized access. You can instruct IIS to grant remote access by the IUSR account, in which case remote users do not need an ID and password and they have only the permissions assigned to that account.

N O T E For additional security, you can require users to log on and provide passwords to gain access to your server. Because of IIS's seamless integration with Windows NT, password authentication is easily accomplished using NT security tools. ▨

Anonymous User Access   If you use FTP to download files, you've probably logged onto an FTP server using anonymous login. What this means is that the server does not verify who you are, nor does it restrict access to certain files only. This kind of situation leaves you vulnerable to attack.

IIS supports an anonymous user login ID that provides a context for handling all anonymous requests made of the server. As the site administrator, you can grant or deny access to files for this ID (see fig. 29.1), thereby keeping users you don't know away from important documents.

FIG. 29.1

IIS supports an anonymous user ID that lets you restrict access to key files.

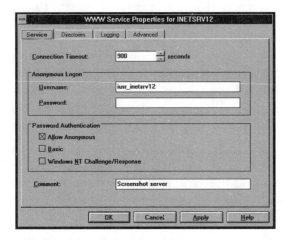

N O T E If a user tries to access a document that is not available by an anonymous account, an NT user name and password will be required to authenticate the request. This information is not encrypted, so it is possible that hackers could learn user names and passwords on your system this way.

One possible workaround is to use the NT challenge/response encrypted password transmission. This would protect user names and passwords as they travel over the Internet. The biggest drawback to this is that NT authentication is currently only supported by Internet Explorer. However, as noted in the last section of this chapter, the IIS comes bundled with a copy of Internet Explorer that network users can install. ▨

Registered User Access   Users who are known to you might include those who have registered to be on your site or, in the case of an intranet, employees in your company. IIS works with the NT server to authenticate (verify the identity of) the users before granting them access to files on the server. You can restrict access on an individual basis, or group individuals together and set access parameters for the whole group.

Document Permissions   IIS's integration with the NT Server pays off again when it comes to granting access to specific documents. You can use the NT File Manager with IIS to set document permissions for anonymous and registered users alike (see fig. 29.2).

FIG. 29.2
The Windows NT File Manager works with IIS to determine permission settings of individual documents.

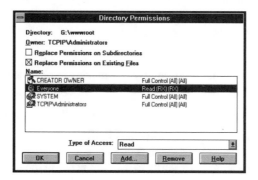

Auditing Access   Auditing refers to the tracking of who accessed what documents, and when they did it. IIS harnesses the auditing capabilities that are already present in the Windows NT Server. The Event Detail dialog box in the NT File Manager makes it easy to see who was the last person to access a file, and at what time the access occurred.

Restricting Access to Selected Hosts   You can also control right of entry by IP address, allowing only certain hosts or networks access to and from your server. This is useful for intranets, because you can lock down your server so that only IP addresses assigned to your company can access it. Conversely, on an open server, you can shut out computers whose users are being troublesome. Figure 29.3 shows the Advanced tab of the Web Service Properties dialog box, where you can specify which IP addresses do or don't have access.

FIG. 29.3
You can let only certain IP addresses have access to your server, helping you to keep out users you don't know.

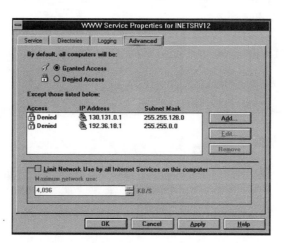

N O T E   You can also regulate the amount of network bandwidth available to your server from the Advanced tab of the Web Services Properties dialog box. ▨

Using Secure Sockets Layer (SSL)   The Secure Sockets Layer (SSL) protocol was put forward by Netscape as a means of protecting data as it moves over the Internet. SSL performs the following three main security functions:

- Data encryption
- Server authentication (is the machine you're talking to really the machine it claims to be?)
- Message integrity (is the message that arrived the one that was supposed to get there?)

SSL works as an intermediate "layer" between TCP/IP (the Internet connection protocol) and HTTP. When a client and server first connect, SSL initiates a "handshake" in which the client and server figure out what level of security to use, and perform the necessary authentications. Once the connection is established, SSL encrypts and decrypts the data as it moves between client and server.

To enable SSL for a directory, you just check the Require Secure SSL Channel box you see in figure 29.4. The SSL option is accessible under the IIS's Internet Service Manager.

N O T E   Remember that you need a signed digital certificate before you can use SSL on your site. Visit **http://www.verisign.com/microsoft/** for more details. ▨

FIG. 29.4
Just click the Require
Secure SSL Channel
box to enable SSL
for a directory.

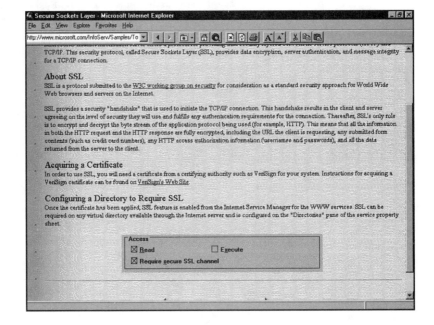

Using Microsoft Internet Service Manager (ISM)

Microsoft's Internet Service Manager (ISM) comes with IIS to make management of Internet services on your network much easier. You can use ISM to get an overarching view of all Internet Services running on your network, to monitor these services, and to start, stop, pause, or configure any of the services.

ISM with Windows NT   You can do some Internet service management right from Windows NT. The NT Control Panel has a Services option that lets you designate how and when Internet services should run. You can even specify that the service restart automatically in the event of a reboot.

The Windows NT Server Manager also permits some Internet service management by administering servers individually or as a group (see fig. 29.5).

FIG. 29.5
You gain some control over how Internet services run on your network through the NT Server Manager.

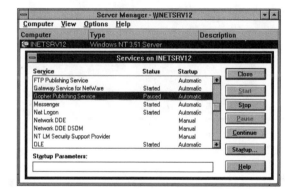

Service Views   The ISM gives you three different ways to look at the services available on your network, as follows:

- The Servers View breaks out the list of services by server.
- The Services View organizes the services by type (FTP, Gopher, HTTP).
- The Report View is less graphical than the other views, but it provides comprehensive information about each service that's running.

Once inside a view, you can filter the view further or sort the items in the view to assist you in your service management tasks.

How To Configure Logging   Each IIS service can be configured to log each transaction it's involved in. Such logging is useful for site capacity planning, content assessment, and server auditing. You can choose to log to a file or to an SQL-compatible database. IIS supports common log file formats and can automatically create new log files for you on a daily, weekly, or monthly basis (see fig. 29.6).

CAUTION

Periodically creating new log files is called *log file cycling*. Cycling your log files is a good idea because otherwise your single log file can grow to monster proportions. This can create difficulty for access statistics report generators that have to parse huge log files to produce their results.

FIG. 29.6

IIS can write logs to files or to SQL databases, and can automatically create new log files at time intervals you specify.

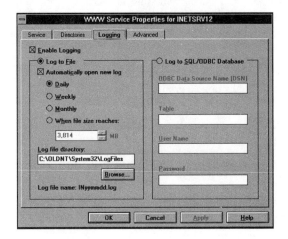

N O T E   Logging to SQL databases increases the load on the server, and requests for other Internet services may suffer as a result. Busy servers should log to files to minimize reductions in performance. ■

Virtual Directories   *Virtual directories* refer to the document tree structure that IIS lets you set up, so that you can access files across volumes of the same server or on an entirely different computer on your network. IIS utilizes Windows NT secure file-sharing to retrieve documents from other computers, so you can keep Web pages on a separate machine with very little risk of being compromised.

Bandwidth Usage Control   If service requests begin to overtax your bandwidth, you can tell IIS to begin refusing requests. Once the demand goes back down, IIS will resume request processing. If usage is close to maximum, IIS will delay some requests, so that demand can subside and no services will be refused.

Performance Monitoring

If you're running a server, you'll want to check performance statistics on a regular basis. This information can help you make decisions about allocating network resources to meet peak demand times and to avoid errors and system crashes. IIS provides two different tools to support performance monitoring—the Performance Monitor and the Simple Network Management Protocol (SNMP) agent.

The Performance Monitor tool (see fig. 29.7) is actually part of the Windows NT Server. It gives you a graphical display of server activity, logs usage statistics, generates usage reports from logged statistics, and alerts you if any performance measures fall outside specified ranges.

FIG. 29.7
The NT Server Performance Monitor gives you a visual representation of server activity.

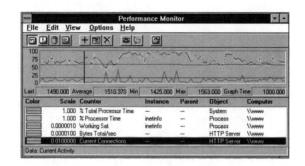

The Performance Monitor supports a standard set of *counters*—quantities that measure specific performance aspects. IIS expands on the Performance Monitor's set of counters to give you an extensive set of performance metrics you can track easily (see Tables 29.1 and 29.2).

If you use SNMP to help manage your network, IIS's SNMP agent reports performance measures to an SNMP management station. All counters available from the Performance Monitor are available from the SNMP agent as well.

Performance Monitor Counters   Table 29.1 shows the Performance Monitor counters that IIS provides for each Internet service active on your server. Table 29.2 shows counters that are specific to HTTP services. IIS supports more than 30 counters for FTP and Gopher protocols as well.

Table 29.1   Internet Information Server Performance Monitor Counters

Counter	Description
Cache Hits	Total number of times (since service start-up) a file open, directory listing, or service-specific object's request was found in the IIS cache
Cache Hits %	Ratio of cache hits to all cache requests
Cache Misses	Total number of times (since service start-up) a file open, directory listing, or service-specific object's request was not found in the cache
Cache Size	The configured maximum size of the shared HTTP, FTP, and Gopher memory cache

continues

Table 29.1 Continued

Counter	Description
Cache Used	The current number of bytes containing cached data in the shared memory cache (this includes directory listings, file handle tracking, and service-specific objects)
Cached File Handles	The current number of open file handles cached by all of the IIS services
Current Blocked Async I/O Requests	The current number of async I/O requests blocked by bandwidth throttling
Directory Listings	The current number of cached directory listings cached by all of the IIS services
Measures Async I/O Bandwidth Usage	The measured bandwidth in bytes of async I/O averaged over one minute
Objects	The current number of objects cached by all of the IIS services (includes file handle tracking objects, directory listing objects, and service-specific objects)
Total Allowed Async I/O Requests	Total (since service start-up) async I/O requests allowed by bandwidth throttling
Total Blocked Async I/O Requests	Total (since service start-up) async I/O requests blocked by bandwidth throttling
Total Rejected Async I/O Requests	Total (since service start-up) async I/O requests rejected by bandwidth throttling

Table 29.2 Internet Information Server HTTP-Specific Counters

Counter	Description
Bytes Received/sec	Rate at which data bytes are received by the HTTP server
Bytes Sent/sec	Rate at which the HTTP server sends data bytes
Bytes Total/sec	Sum of bytes sent and received
CGI Requests	The total number of CGI requests executed since service start-up
Connection Attempts	The number of connection attempts that have been made to the HTTP server

Counter	Description
Connections/sec	Rate at which HTTP requests are being handled
Current Anonymous Users	The number of anonymous users connected to the HTTP server
Current CGI Requests	The number of CGI requests simultaneously being processed
Current Connections	The total number of connections to the HTTP server (sum of anonymous and non-anonymous)
Current ISAPI Extension Requests	The number of ISAPI requests simultaneously being processed
Current Non-Anonymous Users	Number of non-anonymous users connected to the HTTP server
Files Received	Total files received by the server since service start-up
Files Sent	Total files sent by the server since service start-up
Files Total	Total files transferred by the server since service start-up
GET Requests	The number of HTTP GET requests received
HEAD Requests	The number of HTTP HEAD requests received (HEAD requests generally mean that a client is querying to see if a document needs to be refreshed)
ISAPI Extension Requests	The number of HTTP ISAPI extension requests received (ISAPI extension requests are Dynamic Link Libraries (.DLL))
Logon Attempts	The number of logon attempts made by the server
Maximum Anonymous Users	The largest number of anonymous users simultaneously connected to the server since service start-up
Maximum ISAPI Extension Requests	The largest number of ISAPI extension requests simultaneously processed by the server since service start-up

continues

Table 29.2 Continued

Counter	Description
Maximum Connections	The largest number of users simultaneously connected to the server since service start-up
Maximum Non-Anonymous Users	The largest number of non-anonymous users simultaneously connected to the server since start-up
Not Found Errors	The number of requests that could not be satisfied because the server could not find the document (HTTP error code 404)
Other Request Methods	The number of HTTP requests that are not GET, POST, or HEAD requests
Post Requests	The number of HTTP requests using the POST method
Total Anonymous Users	The total number of anonymous users that have ever connected to the server since service start-up
Total Non-Anonymous Users	The total number of non-anonymous users that have ever connected to the server since service start-up

FTP and Gopher Servers

IIS can serve more than just Web pages. It can also turn your NT server into an FTP and Gopher server as well. Once the Web server is installed and configured, setting up FTP and Gopher services takes just a few minutes more.

FTP

The File Transfer Protocol (FTP) was developed to facilitate the transfer of files of any type between any two machines (one running an FTP server, the other running an FTP client). FTP sites are typically repositories of valuable files that are made available to the Internet community at large. In the case of an intranet application, access would be granted to those IP addresses corresponding to machines on the company's network.

▶ **See** "Downloading Files Using FTP," **p. 224**

FTP has the chief advantage of being a two-way service: an FTP client program can download files from an FTP server as well as upload files to it. HTTP can only send files one way—from server to client.

Part

V

Ch

29

Files sent by FTP can be of virtually any type: simple text, binary executable, compressed archive, application-specific files (like a Word document or an Excel spreadsheet), and multimedia files (including graphics, audio, and video files). Your copy of Internet Explorer can act as an FTP client and you can configure it to launch an appropriate helper application when downloading a file. If you'd rather view the file offline, you can simply instruct Internet Explorer to save it.

Providing FTP service for your site gives users more than just the advantage of two-way file transfer. Files on an FTP service are organized for easy browsing as they are set up in a directory structure much like files in the Windows Explorer. Additionally, you pick up the following advantages:

- **Users only need an FTP client to connect to your server.** Not that Web clients are hard to get, but this makes the resources of your server available to a broader audience.

- **FTP clients are better suited to file management tasks than Web clients.** Very often, FTP clients will let you delete or rename files and create or remove directories.

- **FTP servers permit longer time-out periods.** Files downloaded by FTP can be quite large—especially in the case of executable files. Documents served by Web servers tend to be much smaller and the time-out periods on these servers are correspondingly small. A longer time-out period on an FTP server makes it more likely that a user will be able to complete a download without interruption—particularly, if his or her Internet connection is slow.

Gopher

Gopher is an Internet application that is generally thought of as a text-only predecessor of the Web. Gopher servers house documents organized into an intuitive folder structure for easy browsing. Additionally, you can find searches and links to other computers on a Gopher site. Internet Explorer understands the Gopher protocol and can act as a Gopher client program for you.

▶ **See** "Finding Information on Gopher Servers," **p. 226**

Gopher can just about match the Web as far as navigability, but it falls way short on matters of presentation. The use of Gopher has faded quickly in the face of the Web because of the Web's ability to handle graphics. While you can download graphic files from a Gopher server, Gopher clients can't display them like Web clients can. Nevertheless, Gopher provides a nice interface for information browsing and can be a handy way of making a lot of text-based content available to Internet and intranet users.

Setting Up FTP and Gopher Servers

The FTP side of IIS is easy to set up, especially if you've already set up the Web server side. You can use the User Manager to restrict login access (if you choose not to make anonymous access available), and the File Manager allows you to set up directories and make them secure.

Setting up the IIS Gopher server is equally as simple: you just copy your files to the `\Intserv\Gophroot` directory and users can browse your files easily. You can add some bells and whistles to your Gopher service by adding *tag files*—files that make it possible to link to other computers and Internet services. IIS Gopher service also supports annotation of files and directories and creation of customized menus.

Other IIS Features and Benefits

Microsoft's product tour gives a good overview of many of IIS's key features, but there are some others that deserve mention as well. These include the following:

- Copies of Internet Explorer for installation by network users.
- Scalability to higher-powered platforms. IIS is able to grow with the NT Server as you move it to more sophisticated equipment.
- Optimal and reliable performance through IIS's integration with the NT Server.
- The ability to work with all Web clients running on any platform (though IIS is optimized for Internet Explorer).
- Easy hosting of multiple Web sites on the same server by establishing virtual servers.
- Seamless integration with Microsoft's BackOffice suite.
- Support for connection to many standard databases including the Microsoft SQL Server, Microsoft Access, Oracle, Sybase, and other databases that comply with Microsoft's Open Database Connectivity (ODBC) standard.
- Support for Internet standards including Common Gateway Interface (CGI) and Perl.

Many companies are already taking advantage of IIS's power and easy integration with other Microsoft software. For example, Micrografx (**http://www.micrografx.com/**) is using IIS alongside an SQL server and the Exchange server. ●

## PART VI

Advanced Internet Explorer Customization

## CHAPTER 30

Microsoft's ActiveX Technologies

With the announcement of their corporate Internet policy and in subsequent press releases and professional developer conferences, Microsoft put forth a bold vision of full integration of all elements of its operating systems and desktop applications with the Internet. The cornerstone of Microsoft's Internet strategy lies with its ActiveX Technologies. Through this, Microsoft not only supports existing technologies, such as Sun Microsystem's Java and Netscape's JavaScript, it also establishes a model for providing both server and client support for continually evolving, "active," content and capabilities across the Internet and the World Wide Web. ■

What are Microsoft's ActiveX Technologies?

In this chapter, you'll find out about ActiveX Technologies, Microsoft's newest technologies to create interactive multimedia content to "activate the Internet."

What are some of the ActiveX components?

Learn about some of the major new technologies that Microsoft has developed and is offering through Internet Explorer, such as Java, scripting languages, ActiveVRML, and ActiveX Controls. Other components of Microsoft's ActiveX are discussed, including some of the pieces on the drawing board.

What Are ActiveX Technologies?

Microsoft's ActiveX Technologies are a series of Internet computing technologies designed to give as many software developers and designers as possible the tools to produce and provide dynamic, interactive, "active" content over the Internet and the World Wide Web. By using an open standard and open framework, intended to work on a variety of hardware and software platforms, ActiveX Technologies provide the means to access the future and the past. While being designed to allow maximum innovation and the continual evolution of capabilities and techniques, they also provide the tools to integrate data and information from existing systems and applications directly into the Web.

ActiveX Technologies are built on a series of client- and server-side systems. Because of the open standard, developers providing active content using ActiveX will be able to target multiple hardware and software (including multiple Web browser) platforms.

ActiveX Controls

From the client side, ActiveX Technologies provide a variety of ways for content providers to create and distribute interactive information over the Internet and the Web using *existing* software applications and data, such as in the following list. The key to this is the support for ActiveX Controls and active scripts, and their use to create ActiveX Documents:

- **ActiveX Controls**—Formerly called OLE Controls or OCXs, these allow a wide variety of software components and content to be embedded directly into HTML documents. They are small software components that use the existing Object Linking and Embedding (OLE) specifications developed by Microsoft to seamlessly incorporate any supported data type directly into the window of a compatible Web browser such as Internet Explorer 3.

- **Active Scripts**—These complement ActiveX Controls. While the use of ActiveX Controls give the Web designer and user *access* to a vast array of information, active scripts allow the Web browser to interact with that information. For instance, a Web browser might be able directly to view a Microsoft Excel spreadsheet using an ActiveX Control, but could also manipulate and interact with that spreadsheet data using an active script.

- **ActiveX Documents**—Through the combination of ActiveX Controls and active scripting, data managed by a wide variety of applications become accessible as Web pages, and become ActiveX Documents. This can make the entire gamut of information available within an organization—documents, spreadsheets, graphics, video, and so on—accessible via the Internet or through an intranet without requiring the different applications to be run to view each type of data, and without the expensive process of converting the data to a different format, such as HTML.

Server-Side ActiveX Applications

Another key part of ActiveX is the Server Framework to support the server end of providing, displaying, and interacting with active information content. The framework is based on Microsoft's Internet Information Server to allow developers to create sophisticated interactive applications that will operate over the Web, yet allowing them to use their existing knowledge, experience, and software development tools. The pieces of the Server Framework are as follows:

- **Server Scripting**—These are server scripts that can be written using a host of scripting languages such as Perl, JavaScript, and Visual Basic (VB) Script and that interact with Server Controls to provide server applications and interfaces to other systems.

- **Server Controls**—These controls are the essential components to providing active content over the Internet, while at the same time allowing access to existing systems, application, and data. This allows the provider to give access to a much greater range of information, without requiring it all to be put in a new form.

- **Integration**—Using the Server Controls and Scripts together opens up the full range of information and content, both old and new, to information users through the use of ActiveX Technologies.

Cross-Platform Compatibility

The development of ActiveX by Microsoft has involved input from hundreds of Internet vendors, developers, Web designers, and service providers, and the draft specifications have been freely available on the Web to developers. They will also be submitted to the World Wide Web Consortium (W3C) and the Internet Engineering Task Force (IETF) for review.

Additionally, Microsoft is working in concert with other companies to make the ActiveX Technologies available on a variety of hardware and software platforms including Windows 3.1 and Macintosh. Also, Microsoft and NCompass Labs, Inc. have developed a Netscape Navigator plug-in to allow that browser to use ActiveX Controls to view active content. This plug-in allows Web content developers and providers to target more than just one browser when creating Web pages using ActiveX.

You can get more information about ActiveX Technologies and the kinds of capabilities they can support through Microsoft's Internet developer's website, at **http://www.microsoft.com/intdev/** (see fig. 30.1).

FIG. 30.1
Microsoft's ActiveX Technologies encompass a wide variety of techniques meant to facilitate the development of Internet applications and content.

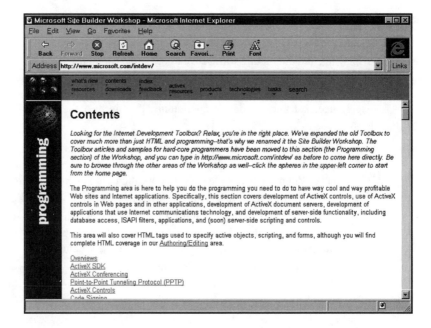

ActiveX and Java

With Internet Explorer 3, Microsoft adds support for Sun Microsystem's Java Programming Language. Java is an object-oriented programming language designed, in part, to be transmitted over the Internet and to be executed on any Java-compatible Web browser. Through the use of small applications written in Java, called *applets*, Web authors are able to add dynamic content and interactivity to Web pages and continually enhance the capabilities of a Web browser.

You may think that Java applets add similar capabilities for providing "active" content to Web pages as do Microsoft's ActiveX Technologies. And you would be right. Microsoft's support for Java comes *within* its support for ActiveX within Internet Explorer 3. This means that Java applets and ActiveX Controls can coexist and interact within the Web browser environment. As each becomes an object (or multiple objects) within that environment, both Java applets and ActiveX Controls can control and interact with one another or with the Web browser, and can in turn be controlled by the user through the browser or by scripting languages such as JavaScript and Visual Basic Script.

For more information about about Java and how it is supported in Internet Explorer 3, check out the next three chapters in this section. On the Internet, a good place to find out more is at Sun's Java Programming Web site at **http://java.sun.com**.

▶ **See** "Sun's Java and Internet Explorer" for an overview of Sun's Java language, **p. 607**

▶ **See** "Java for C++ Programmers" for information on programming in Java for the C++ programmer, **p. 627**

▶ **See** "Java Tools" for a description of some available tools for Java development, **p. 649**

Internet Scripting Languages

Along with support for Java and the general object model of the Internet Explorer 3 Web browser and the ActiveX Technologies upon which it is built, Microsoft has built support for Internet scripting languages into its Web browser. And again, rather than just electing to support the current standard for Web browser scripting, Netscape's JavaScript, Microsoft has gone one better by adding general scripting support under the Object Linking and Embedding (OLE) model.

This OLE scripting capability provides a standard way for authors of Internet applications to add specific scripting capabilities. It allows them to create, as Microsoft puts it, "pluggable" scripting engines for each application, such as Internet Explorer 3.

In this way, Internet Explorer has been built with support for both Netscape's JavaScript and Microsoft's own Visual Basic (VB) Script. Along with these scripting capabilities—which will be described in the following sections, and in much greater detail in later chapters—Microsoft has created object models of ActiveX objects, the Internet Explorer browser itself, and also for models for HTML elements. These object models give JavaScript and VBScript authors a clear interface for interacting with the Web browsing environment, allowing them to verify or set items in an HTML form, display alert and dialog boxes within the Web browser, control the operation of an ActiveX Control or Java applet, and many other things.

Part

VI

Ch

30

JavaScript

The best known Web browser scripting language is currently JavaScript, developed by Netscape and built in to Netscape Navigator 2 Web browsers. JavaScript, modeled after the Java programming language, includes a variety of statements, commands, and functions for adding dynamic content and interaction to a Web page.

As mentioned previously, Internet Explorer 3 includes full support for the JavaScript language. Figure 30.2 shows Internet Explorer 3 connecting up to the Web site at **http:// www.cris.com/~raydaly/javatell.html**.

This Web page is a simple test to see if your Web browser has JavaScript—the answer to the question will dictate what appears on the Web page. As shown in figure 30.2, the answer for Internet Explorer 3 is "yes."

Figure 30.3 shows another typical use of JavaScript, a way to use it to add interactivity to a Web page in a manner far superior to the means that used to be available. This Web site allows you to calculate your current Grade Point Average (GPA), according to the number of credits you are taking and your grade in each class. Formerly, in order to calculate this information, you would first have to enter the information, it would be submitted back to the server, a program would run on the server to calculate the results, and they would be transmitted back. Using JavaScript, this is all done locally.

FIG. 30.2
Internet Explorer's
support of Netscape's
JavaScript language
allows it to access many
"Netscape-enhanced"
Web sites.

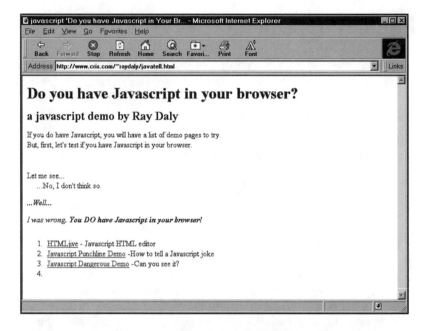

FIG. 30.3
JavaScript supports
interactive forms that
can perform calcula-
tions locally as soon
as data is entered.

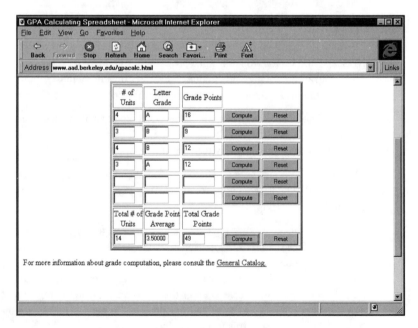

For more information on JavaScript and its use in Internet Explorer 3, see Chapter 34,
"JavaScript." You can also check out **http://home.netscape.com/comprod/products/
navigator/version_2.0/script/script_info/index.html**.

Visual Basic Script

VBScript is another scripting language supported by Internet Explorer 3. It provides much the same functionality as JavaScript, giving the Web author access to a set of statements, commands, and functions that can be used to add active content to a Web page and to interact with an object (Java applets, ActiveX Controls, the Web browser itself) within the Web browser environment.

Unlike JavaScript, which is based on Java, VBScript is a subset of Microsoft's Visual Basic and Visual Basic for Applications programming languages. The syntax of the VBScript commands is the same as that used in its parent languages, so developers who are familiar with them will find it very simple to program in VBScript.

Figure 30.4 shows the classic first example of any programming language, the "Hello, world!" example, as progammed in VBScript.

FIG. 30.4

The classic "Hello, world!" example, this time done in VBScript.

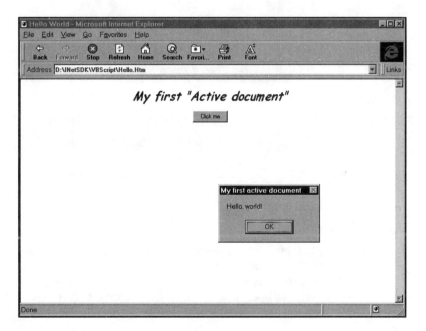

Figure 30.5 shows how VBScript can interact with HTML forms. When a selection is made from the radio boxes on the right, the checkboxes under the Toppings heading, the text description, and the price are all automatically updated. When the order is submitted by clicking the Order button, an alert box is dynamically generated by VBScript and displayed (see fig. 30.6).

For more information on VBScript and its use in Internet Explorer 3, see Chapter 35, "Visual Basic Script." You can also check out the Web page **http://www.microsoft.com/vbscript/default.htm**.

FIG. 30.5
VBScript can be used to fill in forms fields, as in this example, where the type of pizza selected checks the appropriate toppings checkboxes, the description, and the price.

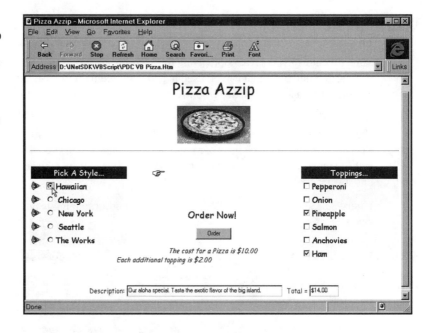

FIG. 30.6
It is possible using VBScript to create dialog and alert boxes dynamically to reflect user input.

ActiveVRML

ActiveVRML is Microsoft's proposal for the next version of the Virtual Reality Modeling Language (VRML) standard. VRML is a language for bringing virtual reality and three-dimensional models to the Web. ActiveVRML, along with other standards proposed by a consortium led by Netscape/SGI and another led by Apple, increases the functionality of VRML 1.0 and adds animation and greater interactivity.

Microsoft has an ActiveX Control to add ActiveVRML capability to Internet Explorer 3. Microsoft maintains a Web site about ActiveVRML at **http://www.microsoft.com/intdev/avr/**.

One of the capabilities that ActiveVRML adds to a Web browser is the ability to perform a variety of two-dimensional cel animations, using multiple two-dimensional images. Multiple images can be animated and switched in and out using a variety of zooming, spiral, slide, or other transition effects.

A more common type of application expected using VRML techniques and supported by ActiveVRML is one involving three dimensions and virtual reality. This extends the two-dimensional, "web" paradigm of the World Wide Web to allow the creation of three-dimensional sites that you can travel through. ActiveVRML extends the virtual reality supported by VRML 1.0, and allows you to animate and control the objects in the VRML world, either as a VRML author, or through scripting languages such as JavaScript or VBScript.

ActiveX Controls and Internet Explorer Add-Ins

Part
VI

Ch
30

A term very familiar to users of Netscape Navigator is "plug-in." Plug-ins for Netscape Navigator are software applications that add functionality to the Navigator Web browser that occurs, unlike with helper applications, within the browser itself. For instance, a VRML plug-in for Netscape Navigator would allow it, when following a link to a VRML world, to display that world directly within the browser window rather than launching a separate application to view it.

Internet Explorer 2 had a much smaller number of such applications, usually referred to as *add-ins*. Through the added capabilities of ActiveX Technologies, the possibility of increasing the functionality of Internet Explorer through "plugging," or "adding," in ActiveX Controls is greatly increased.

OLE Controls, OCXs, and ActiveX Controls

A technology originally introduced by Microsoft into its Windows operating system, Object Linking and Embedding (OLE) allowed objects from one application to be linked into and embedded in another. Then when one was changed, the other would be immediately updated. For instance, you could embed a graphic from an Excel spreadsheet into a report written in Word or a presentation produced in PowerPoint. If you changed the data in the spreadsheet, thus changing the graphic, the next time you looked at your document or presentation, it would be automatically updated.

ActiveX Controls, originally known as OLE Controls or OCXs, along with OLE scripting, allow you to add new behaviors to a Web page and to access information from other applications; in essence, this means you can *embed* documents from other applications into a Web page and interact with that information.

ActiveX Controls are not restricted to giving you access to documents and information in existing applications, however. The ActiveX Technologies framework allows you to add increased functionality to support new types of information and applications as they become available. Conceptually, an ActiveX Control, depending on how it is written, can duplicate the functionality of either a Web browser plug-in or add-in—a capability added by you to support viewing certain kinds of data with your Web browser—or something like a Java applet, which is automatically transmitted to your Web browser from a Web site and dynamically and transparently adds capability to your browser specific to that site.

And one thing that sets ActiveX Controls apart from similar technologies—plug-ins for Netscape Navigator, for instance—is that ActiveX Controls can be used by any compatible application, not just a Web browser. Microsoft's next generation of operating systems and desktop applications will have support for ActiveX Controls built right into them. In fact, the Internet Explorer browser itself is an ActiveX Control that can be used to add Internet and Web functionality to any other compatible application.

ActiveX Controls

Figure 30.7 shows a very simple example of a Web page making use of an ActiveX Control. It's a charting control that can be used to plot data from a file in a wide variety of different formats.

FIG. 30.7
This Web page uses the Chart Control to chart data included in another source file.

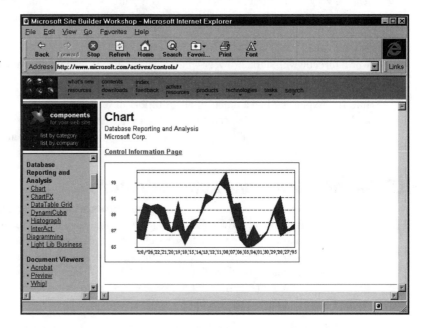

Listing 30.1 shows the HTML code needed to include the Chart Control in a Web page. A full example of how to use the Chart Control and other example ActiveX Controls, and how to download all of them, can be found through the Internet Explorer Web site at **http://www.microsoft.com/ie/**.

Listing 30.1 HTML Code to Use Chart Control

```
<OBJECT
     classid="clsid:FC25B780-75BE-11CF-8B01-444553540000"
     CODEBASE="/ie/download/activex/iechart.ocx#version=4,70,0,1086"
     id=chart1
     width=400
     height=200
     align=center
     hspace=0
     vspace=0
```

```
>
<param name="hgridStyle" value="3">
<param name="vgridStyle" value="0">
<param name="colorscheme" value="0">
<param name="DisplayLegend" value="0">
<param name="BackStyle" value="1">
<param name="BackColor" value="#ffffff">
<param name="ForeColor" value="#0000ff">
<param name="Scale" value="100">
<param name="url" value="/ie/appdev/controls/chart/chrtfiles/ms95HLCW.txt">

</OBJECT>
```

▶ **See** "Plug-Ins, Add-Ins, and ActiveX Controls" for more information on Microsoft ActiveX Controls, **p. 735**

Part

VI

Ch

30

Microsoft's Internet Control Pack

Microsoft provides a collection of ActiveX Controls meant to add greater Internet functionality within Web pages, known as the Internet Control Pack (see fig. 30.8). These Internet ActiveX Controls provide capabilities for dealing with such Internet protocols as FTP, HTML, HTTP, NNTP (news), POP, and SMTP (mail), as well as basic TCP and UDP communications protocols. While Internet Explorer 3 obviously has many of these capabilities built into its different functions, these controls provide Web authors and applications developers with greatly increased flexibility to interact with the protocols in customized fashions.

FIG. 30.8
Microsoft has provided a set of controls to enable Web authors and Internet developers to add Internet connectivity to their Web pages and applications.

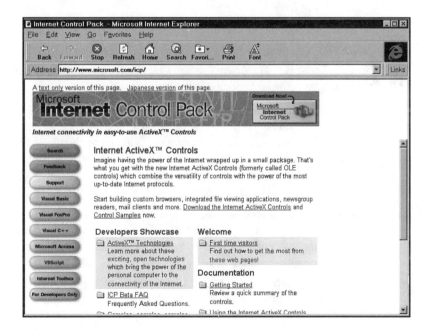

Other ActiveX Technologies

The ActiveX Framework includes or makes use of other technologies meant to increase the usability of the Internet and the World Wide Web. These technologies provide a variety of additional capabilities to users of the Web.

▶ **See** "Plug-Ins, Add-Ins, and ActiveX Controls" for more information on the Microsoft Internet Control Pack, **p. 735**

Internet and Web Security

The safety of transactions that take place over the Internet and the Web, as well as the safety of information and applications obtained in that manner, is a continual element of concern to Web users. When you buy a service through your Web browser, you want to know that your credit card information is safe. When you download a file or some software from the Internet, you want to know that it is coming from where you think, and that it is exactly what you are expecting. The ActiveX Technology framework includes a variety of standards to ensure these different things.

Downloading Safety and Trust   The components that implement this part of the ActiveX Framework provide the following capabilities:

- Verification of the safety and security of code downloaded from the Internet.
- Verification of the digital signature of a software provider to ensure that the product is authentic.
- Verification and installation of software components delievered over the Internet. Internet Explorer 3 uses this system to install ActiveX Controls and Documents.

Security Services   The ActiveX security services concern conducting safe transactions over the Internet and the Web. Some of the services provided are:

- **Private Communication Technology**—This is a protocol designed to ensure privacy in a transaction between two applications over the Internet. Typically, these will be a client and a server; this system also allows the client to authenticate the identity of the server, and the server, optionally, to do the same for the client.
- **HTTP Authentication**—This is a network service for servers under Windows NT to support secure browsing on intranets.
- **Digital Signatures of Executables**—Just as people and organizations can be given digital signatures to verify their identity, executables, the binary information transmitted over the Internet most likely to be able to damage your local computer, can also be given digital signatures used to verify and authenticate such software.
- **Cryptography**—A system to support providers of encryption services that includes information on usage and export restrictions.

ActiveMovie

Microsoft's ActiveMovie system will allow developers and content providers to create and deliver full multimedia content—video, synchronized audio, and special effects—to multiple platforms. The system, part of Microsoft's ActiveX and DirectX Internet and multimedia technologies, offers users the following:

- Full-screen, television-quality MPEG playback on typical systems
- Streaming playback over the Internet for responsive, available-on-demand delivery of all types of media
- A flexible architecture for easy extensibility to new technologies

You can find out more information on Microsoft's ActiveMovie specification at **http://www.microsoft.com/imedia/activemovie/activem.htm**.

DirectX and Direct3D

Microsoft's DirectX is a companion technology to the ActiveX system that is intended to provide some of the same sort of advantages in the Windows 95 game-playing arena that ActiveX gives to Internet functionality. Direct3D is the latest component of DirectX, and is intended to provide the tools for creating three-dimensional objects and virtual reality.

While these may seem to be two disparate technologies, they are related in how they work. With a combination of the two, it's not too hard to imagine powerful local game engines supporting games running on many different machines while linked interactively over the Internet. Also, ActiveVRML and ActiveMovie, elements of the ActiveX Technologies framework, make use of DirectX and Direct3D.

The components of DirectX and Direct3D will be discussed briefly below. To get more information about them, check out Microsoft's Interactive Media Technologies Group at **http://www.microsoft.com/imedia/default.htm**.

DirectX   The components of the DirectX interactive media technologies provide a platform upon which to develop games and other applications in a device-independent manner. This allows developers to create applications that will run on and make use of a wide array of hardware platforms. Through the DirectX Technology system, applications can make full use of whatever hardware exists in the system they're running on—developers do not have to create games and applications that are a compromise or that are programmed for the least-common-denominator system.

The following components exist for DirectX:

- **DirectDraw**—This allows games and applications to access the device-dependent features of the display hardware they're running on in a way that is transparent to the user and the developer. The developer can program what he or she wants to happen, and let DirectDraw worry about how to utilize the hardware on each target machine to run the program in the fastest manner possible.

- **DirectSound**—This is analagous to DirectDraw, but for sound instead of graphics. It was developed to provide high-fidelity sound and sound mixing capabilities, allowing realistic sounds and effects for games and applications. Again, all the developer needs to worry about is what sound or sounds should be played; DirectSound knows how to play them on the various sound hardware components that can run under Windows 95.

- **DirectPlay**—This facilitates multiplayer games and applications by providing a means for two such applications to communicate. It provides a DirectPlay object, which handles communication between the game or application and a DirectPlay server in communication with the connection hardware (see fig. 30.9).

FIG. 30.9
By using DirectPlay, programmers don't need to worry about what hardware will be used to connect the players in the game.

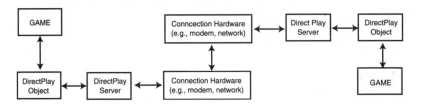

Using DirectPlay, the programmer needs to communicate only with the DirectPlay object. All communication between the two users is handled by the DirectPlay object and server. Under this scheme, the connection hardware doesn't need to be the same on each end.

- **DirectInput**—This provides a function analogous to the other DirectX components in the area of user input. DirectInput abstracts the types of user input away from the specific types available from given devices, and allows the developer to program based on those types of user input. The DirectInput object itself then translates, for each machine and type of hardware available, the user input into an appropriate action type presented to the game or application. Not only does this simplify the development effort, it also allows new input hardware to be easily incorporated into existing applications through updates to the DirectX environment, not the application itself.

Direct3D   The latest component of the DirectX system is Direct3D, designed to deliver real-time, interactive, three-dimensional content to the full gamut of applications—Internet, entertainment and games, education, and business.

Direct3D is a full set of services for real-time three-dimensional graphics. As a component in the DirectX interactive media technology group, it is meant to provide device-independent access to its capabilities. Like the other DirectX elements, programming applications using Direct3D would allow the developer to create an application independent of specific hardware that would then make full use of the performance and hardware under which it was specifically run.

Further information about Direct3D can be obtained at **http://www.microsoft.com/imedia/direct3d/direct3d.htm**.

Upcoming Technologies

Microsoft is continually developing new computing software and technologies. Now that the company has fully committed itself to integrating its products into the Internet, you can expect to see a continual stream of products from Microsoft that support Internet connectivity in some way or another.

Some of the specific technologies that Microsoft is working on for inclusion into Internet Explorer 3, ActiveX Technologies, and its overall Internet platform are as follows:

- **Platform for Internet Content Selection (PICS)**—The PICS rating system is the standard for the creation of rating systems and information and content. Microsoft will support this system as a way of keeping minors from accessing adult content on the Internet.

- **Palette Control**—This system would allow Web authors and providers of ActiveX Controls and Documents enhanced control over the presentation of information on local systems through the specification of a preferred palette.

- **Component Categories**—This system will define a way to categorize the software objects used in Web browsers, ActiveX Controls, and ActiveX Documents, to describe what their interfaces are to other components, and to describe how they may be used.

- **Asynchronous Storage**—By allowing Web authors control over the order in which different pieces of information in Web documents are downloaded, this system will allow authors to maximize the productivity of slow links to the Internet.

ActiveX Resources on the Web

For more information on the topics discussed in this chapter, see the rest of the chapters in this section, or check out some of the following Web sites:

- The Interactive Media Technologies Group, for more information on ActiveMovie, DirectX, and Direct3D:

  http://www.microsoft.com/imedia/default.htm

- The Internet Explorer Web site:

  http://www.microsoft.com/ie/

- The Internet Developer's Web site, which contains information on the ActiveX Technologies and allows you to download the ActiveX Development Kit:

  http://www.microsoft.com/intdev/

- A description of Microsoft's Visual Basic (VB) Script programming language:

  http://www.microsoft.com/vbscript/default.htm

- The ActiveVRML Web site:

  http://www.microsoft.com/intdev/avr/

- Source URL for Microsoft's Internet Control Pack, a collection of ActiveX Controls for interacting with the Internet:

  http://www.microsoft.com/icp/icpmain.htm

- Sources for more information on ActiveX (OLE) Controls:

  ftp://ftp.microsoft.com/developr/drg/OLE-info/

  http://www.ncompasslabs.com/

  http://www.r2m.com/windev/

  http://olebroker.com/

- A working document of the World Wide Web Organization's Internet multimedia object specification:

  http://www.w3.org/pub/WWW/TR/WD-object.html

- A working document of the World Wide Web Organization's specification for HTML extensions to support executable scripts, such as JavaScript and VBScript:

  http://www.w3.org/pub/WWW/TR/WD-script.html

## CHAPTER 31

Sun's Java and Internet Explorer

What is Java?

In this chapter, learn about Java, a programming language developed by Sun Microsystems that can be used to deliver and execute small applications, called applets, over the World Wide Web.

What are Java applets and what can they do?

Learn about some of the capabilities of Java applets, and what kinds of applications are possible to perform with them.

How does Java work in Internet Explorer?

Find out how Java works with Internet Explorer 3, how applets are executed, and how Internet Explorer ensures that they don't do anything improper to your system.

Where do you find Java information and examples?

Find out where to find information and sample applets for Java on the World Wide Web.

Java is a relatively new programming language, created by Sun Microsystems, that has caused a lot more excitement than new programming languages usually generate. Programmers are excited about Java because the language supports many of the useful features of C++, such as an object-oriented structure, intuitive multithreading, and built-in network support. Unlike C++, however, Java programs are not compiled into executables that can be immediately run on a given type of computer. Instead, they are semi-compiled—a Java compiler creates a file containing bytecodes that can then be executed on any computer running a compatible Java interpreter.

With the introduction of Internet Explorer 3, Microsoft has given its Web browser a built-in Java interpreter. Now, in addition to downloading text, pictures, sound, and the other media types available through the Web, Internet Explorer can also download and execute small Java programs, called *applets*, which are then run on your computer. These applets can display animations, allow you to play games, or get stock prices from a remote computer, while Internet Explorer's Java interpreter makes sure they don't do anything dangerous to your system. ∎

Why Java is Waking Up the Internet

In the spring of 1995, Sun Microsystems released a Web browser called HotJava. This Web browser was written in a new programming language called Java, a language originally intended to handle such tasks as interactive television and coordination of household appliances. The explosion of the Web in 1994 revealed the real opportunity for Java, and work on HotJava commenced.

Though HotJava was rough around the edges, it could do some things no other Web browser at that time could do. With HotJava, a user could see animation, play games, and even view a ticker tape of up-to-date stock prices. Soon after its release, Netscape decided to license the Java technology to incorporate it into its browsers, followed soon thereafter by Microsoft. Microsoft's incorporation of this technology into Internet Explorer makes it available to a much wider audience than before. This wider audience, along with the capabilities that Java provides, is revolutionizing the Web.

What is a Java Applet?

Internet Explorer can run Java applets, which are typically small programs that are downloaded from a Web server. Nothing is special about how Internet Explorer performs this task; it downloads a Java applet in precisely the same manner as it downloads any file. Just as any browser displays an image as it is received, a Java-compatible browser runs the Java applet. When the Java applet runs, it is much (but not exactly) like any other program that can run on your computer. It can take input from your keyboard, mouse, or even a remote computer. The output displays on your screen.

But you can note differences between a Java applet and the applications that sit on your desktop. You wouldn't want Internet Explorer to download a virus. At the same time, you wouldn't want to have to check every program that comes down because most programmers have no interest in harming your computer. Because of the way the Java language is structured, you don't have to worry about a Java applet harming your computer.

But having a safe structure doesn't mean that restrictions have been placed on Java applets. In fact, a Java applet knows next to nothing about your computer. It can't look or write to any file in your file system. It can use your computer's memory but not directly. These restrictions on a Java applet keep your computer safe from harm and also protect your privacy.

How a Java Applet is Different from the CGI Program

Anyone who has been around the Web for a while knows that non-Java programs can be run on the Web. One of the reasons the Web has become so popular, even before the advent of Java, is that the Web allows simple interaction across the Internet. It allows this interaction by using the *Common Gateway Interface* (*CGI*), which underlies Web browser electronic forms, imagemaps, and search engines. Basically, CGI allows you to run a program that resides on the server. The program, called a *CGI program*, outputs a Web page, and that Web page is sent back to the client (see fig. 31.1).

FIG. 31.1
CGI programs are
executed by the Web
server at the request of
a client. Their results
are then transmitted
back to the client.

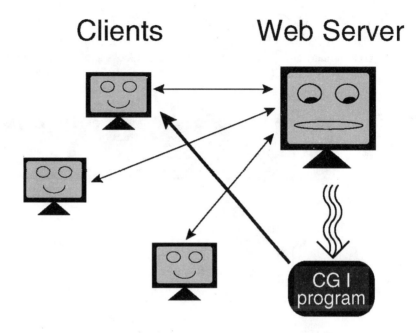

The Common Gateway Interface puts the Web a step above other information protocols such as FTP and Gopher because it allows you to tell a remote computer to do things for you. It is great for information providers who can now let you do very specific tasks without having to give you, and the rest of the world, the run of their machines.

CGI programs are great for many purposes. For instance, say that you are an officer of a club that is running a Web server. Through the use of a simple CGI program, you can give your members a way to keep their mailing addresses up to date. You can put an electronic form on your Web site, and if someone moves, he or she can just access that form and enter his or her new address. Then the CGI program takes that information and updates the database.

The differences between Java applets and CGI programs are summarized in Table 31.1.

Table 31.1   Differences Between CGI Programs and Java Applets

Property	Java Applet	CGI Program
Get information from remote computer	Yes	Yes
Computer that it runs on	Client	Server
How it handles input and output	Instantaneously	Only after transmission across the Internet

Part
VI

Ch
31

To explore what the differences shown in Table 31.1 mean in practice, consider an example. Figure 31.2 shows a tic-tac-toe game created by using a Java applet. Tic-tac-toe also has been created many times using CGI programs, and it looks a lot like this figure. The game looks the same for both the CGI implementation and the applet implementation—you simply click where you want your X to go.

FIG. 31.2

Playing tic-tac-toe with a Java applet.

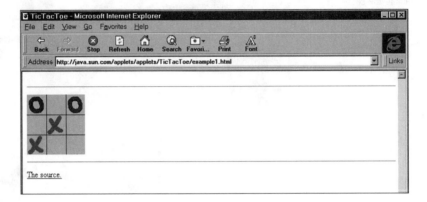

First, look at how the CGI implementation handles the input. Your Web browser takes that information and transmits it to the Web server. The Web server runs the CGI program, which figures out the best response and constucts a Web page indicating this information. That page is then transmitted back across the Internet.

When tic-tac-toe is implemented using a Java applet, the Java applet figures out the best move locally, on your computer. Because no communication takes place across the Internet, it is much faster.

Of course, for a game as simple as tic-tac-toe, you could argue that speed isn't very important. But for a game like Tetris, speed is important (see fig. 31.3). Tetris would be boring if you had to wait several seconds between each move of a piece. Because a Java applet runs on your computer, it provides real-time animation. Also, when you interact with the applet by clicking the mouse or pressing a key, the applet knows about this event immediately. A CGI program can know only after the data has been transmitted across the Internet.

Consider the many other examples of Web applications that are best created by applets. For instance, an applet can ticker the current prices of your stocks across your screen. You can download a virtual world in the form of an applet, and if you make changes in that virtual world, your view of it is immediately updated.

Java applets are faster because, while they themselves must be transmitted through the Web, they don't have to transmit input and output across as well. They are also better than CGI programs for many applications because the server doesn't have to process anything. The first attempts at animation and interactivity, developed by Netscape—called *server push* and *client pull*—both based on the Common Gateway Interface, suffered from this problem. After the page was loaded, a CGI program would hold the connection open and update the page as necessary. This way, a Web page designer could make a page dynamic and interactive.

FIG. 31.3
Playing Tetris with
a Java applet.

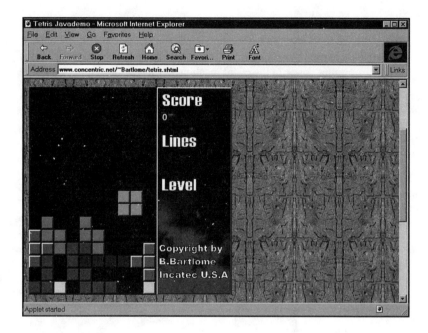

But Tetris, for example, has two distinct disadvantages as a CGI program. First, playing the game is slower because input and output still have to be transmitted across the Internet. Second, the increased load resulting from such rapid-fire contact slows down the server enough that other clients experience the delay, as you see in figure 31.4.

FIG. 31.4
Interactive programs
using CGI can often
be slow because of
transmission delays
and Web server
loading.

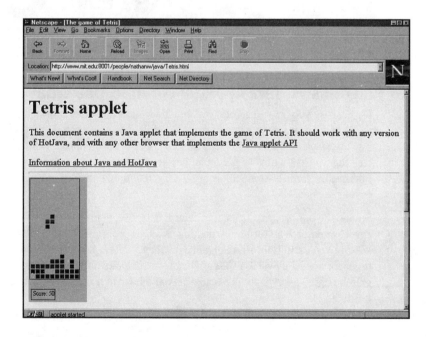

Part
VI

Ch
31

Because server push and client pull have such an ill effect on the server, many Web sites have banned their information providers from using it. This restriction is a real shame because any machine powerful enough to run a graphical Web browser could easily be a Web server. The processing power of the client machine sits idle while a busy server handles the computation.

The use of applets means that your machine can do processing that the server doesn't have to do, leaving the server to concentrate on its real purpose: serving information. Even in cases where speed might not be crucial, using Java applets for interactivity is still better. The processing is more evenly balanced, as shown in figure 31.5.

FIG. 31.5
Using Java applets can help to balance out the processing responsibilities for client and server.

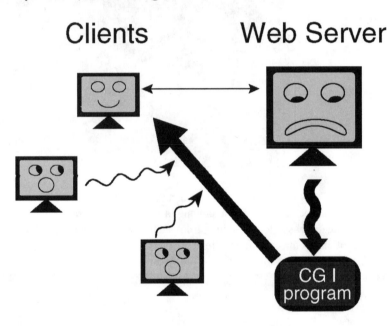

CGI Programs vs. Java Applets: When To Use What

If you are a Web page designer, you may be wondering when a Java applet is appropriate and when a CGI program is. For two reasons, applets do not completely replace the Common Gateway Interface. First, not all Web browsers are able to run applets. Unless you can be guaranteed that the users of your particular service are going to have a Java-compatible version of Internet Explorer or some other browser, you should consider providing an alternative version of your service.

Second, if your program is using a central database, you should use a CGI program. For example, a search engine should function as a CGI program. Advanced search engines, such as WAIS, Lycos, and Harvest, maintain a database of keywords. Instead of directly searching Web pages for some keyword, a CGI program simply looks in the database. An applet can't act as a search engine nearly as well because it would have to traverse the network looking for a keyword.

In the search engine example, the database is only read. Since an applet isn't allowed to write to any file system, you can't use an applet to modify a database either. If you want visitors to your Web site to fill out a survey, you would probably want to use a CGI program.

Unless you are dealing with a central store of information, you should consider using Java applets. They reduce the load on the Web server and allow more interactivity. They also make more dynamic Web pages. Also, because many Internet service providers restrict the sorts of CGI programs that can be run on their Web servers, Java applets may be your only choice.

Remember, Java applets and CGI programs are not mutually exclusive. Consider the search engine example again. You definitely don't want an applet to search the entire Web when a CGI program can just do a quick lookup in its database. But by writing an applet that communicates with the CGI program, you can provide superior interactivity. The CGI program can generate the raw results of the search, while the applet provides an advanced interface. Instead of just providing a list of pages containing a keyword, an applet can display a map for each of those pages. That map can show the pages that are directly linked from a certain page containing that keyword. Then you can focus your energies on those parts of the Web where the information you want is most centralized.

Also, an applet can easily keep track of what a user has done. Consider again the example of someone modifying a database that resides on your Web server. If you want people to be able to make several modifications, you have to assume that they are going to make some mistakes. An applet can easily keep track of what they have done and correct any mistakes with the press of a button. However, a CGI program has a hard time providing this functionality since it is responsible for answering many users. It is quite difficult for a CGI program to keep track of who has done what, and even more difficult for it to provide an intuitive interface.

Expand this example a bit. Say that many databases on different machines need to be manipulated by some user. An applet can give the appearance that all the databases are the same. When the user wants information from a certain database, the applet figures out which CGI program to connect to. This approach is more intuitive and less time consuming than forcing the user to link directly to the CGI program. Also, the applet can be used to prescan the input to the CGI program to make sure that the correct syntax is used, catching these errors without wasting transmission of Web server processing time. The applet can also maintain a record of what input the user has made locally, and allow the user to recall, repeat, or even undo past actions.

How Java Allows the Web To Evolve Itself

By using Java, Web authors are not limited to the current capabilities of Web browsers. If a Web browser doesn't have some capability, you can often write a Java applet to allow a Java-compatible Web browser to perform that function. Such possible capabilities include interactive features that you expect from your normal desktop applications and the ability to understand new protocols. When you're writing an applet, you don't have to write an entire Web browser.

This point is important because expecting the entire Internet to adapt to a new way of doing things is hard, even if it is a great idea. If a new way of compressing video data were to be invented, the inventors wouldn't have to convince everyone that the idea was great. Instead, they could just write an applet that utilizes their new method. They wouldn't have to distribute software that users would then have to install on their computers. They wouldn't have to wait for Web browser makers to adopt their technology. The applet could simply be downloaded at the same time the data is. If the developers decide to add a feature, they could just do it, and their improved software would be available instantly.

Java allows the Web to become a programming platform. Without Java, new network programs have to be developed from the ground up. Before, if you wanted to develop an Internet-wide conferencing system, you had to develop an application that would run on the users' desktops. Your users would have to acquire the software and install it themselves. With Java available on the Web, you can simply write an applet and put it on your Web site. Anyone with a Java-compatible browser, such as Internet Explorer 3, has whatever level of access to the software that you allow. Your distribution costs drop to nothing. Also, the development is easier because the Java language is designed for distributed network computing.

This functionality is what makes Java revolutionary. Given a Web server, anyone who can write a Web page can add information to the Web. With Java, any programmer can add capabilities to the Web. The Web will not grow only in terms of content, but now has the capability of evolving itself. Instead of your bank or travel agent merely having information online, the future will see you being able to do all your banking and booking an entire trip from your computer. The applets that you use will have interfaces of equal or better quality than any other application on your desktop. Plus, you won't have to download them and install them on your computer; they will be instantly downloaded when you access the particular Web site.

What Java Can Do Beyond the Web

Knowing that Java is not just a part of the Web is important. Java is a complete, object-oriented programming language designed to overcome some of the limitations of C++. Right now, applets as you know them can run only in some Web browsers. But applets aren't bound just to Web browsers. Any application that sits on your desktop can be upgraded to connect to the Web and make use of special applets.

Imagine that your spreadsheet program can deal with special applets. One of these special Java applets can talk to a server sitting on Wall Street. When the price of one of your stocks changes, the server tells the Java applet, and the Java applet updates your spreadsheet automatically. Now your formulas that deal with stock prices always deal with live data. They do so because, when you open your spreadsheet, it downloads the applet that puts the appropriate stock prices into the places they are supposed to be. No longer do you have to look up the prices and enter them into your spreadsheet. They are already there, and they are current. When you take your report to your meeting, the data is as current as when you printed it out.

Still, these changes aren't the end of what Java can do for the Internet and the programming world. You may or may not turn off your computer when you leave for home. Could you be persuaded to leave your computer on all night if it could help solve some massive problem, like finding extraterrestrial intelligence, which requires enormous computing power to analyze signals received by radio telescopes all over the world?

Consider the following scenario: a central computer checks with your computer at some appointed time, a few hours after you go home. If your computer isn't busy, the central computer sends an applet across the Internet. Your computer runs that applet all night. When you come in the next morning and press a key, your computer sends the applet back across the Internet to the central "problem server." The problem server takes the data that has been crunched and incorporates it into a database. With the help of your computer and thousands of others, the problem is eventually solved. Better yet, the research institution working on this problem didn't have to buy several supercomputers to solve it. And you were able to help solve a problem like finding extraterrestrial intelligence—that requires the processing of an enormous amount of data generated by the telescopes and astronomical antennas of the world—by simply going home.

The thrust of these examples is based on a simple fact: a lot of information and a lot of processing power exists on the millions of computers all over the world. Java allows computers to access and deal with all that information safely. You should not have to insert data manually into a program when it is available on the Internet. Your computer is capable of getting the data and inserting it. Along the same lines, there is no reason that your computer should sit idle when pressing problems need to be solved. The use of Java in software can not only make the end user's life easier, it also can bring all the computers on the Internet into a true working community.

How Java Works in Internet Explorer

Internet Explorer can run Java applets. Because of the nature of the Java interpreter built in to Internet Explorer, Java applets can find out next to nothing about your computer. Therefore, you don't have to worry about a Java applet doing damage to your computer. Now, if you just want to see and use cool applets, you don't need to know anything about how they work. Just read the following section and start exploring.

How To Access Java Applets with Internet Explorer

Nothing is complicated about accessing applets with Internet Explorer. After your browser is set up correctly, you don't need to configure anything to enable Java. To the user, an applet is simply a part of a Web page, just as an image or text can be. In the case that a page contains an image, the browser takes care of getting that image and displaying it. With a Java-compatible browser, the same is true with applets. When you access a Web page with an applet embedded in it, the browser fetches the code and takes care of running it.

Running an applet is not hard. It takes no advanced planning or configuring. As long as your Web browser is Java-compatible, you can just point your Web browser to a page that contains the applet you want. At the end of this chapter is a list of Web sites that have Java applet pages. As long as these Java pages don't tell you that your browser doesn't support Java, you are ready to start exploring Java on the Web.

> **CAUTION**
>
> Some Java applets cannot be accessed by Internet Explorer 3, even though it has Java support, because many Java applets were written while Java was still being developed, and those Java applets are not compatible with the current standard.

How Internet Explorer Runs Java Applets

Now you're ready to look at the technical issues involved in running an applet. When Internet Explorer encounters an HTML page with an <APPLET> tag, it retrieves the compiled Java classes from the remote server in the same way that it retrieves any other object. After the applet has been downloaded across the network onto your machine, it is subjected to various security checks before it is actually loaded and run. These checks are performed by the Java verifier. After the code is checked, the Java class loader loads it into its own place in the Web browser's applet runtime environment. This loading is done in such a way that an applet is kept separate from system resources and other applets.

> **N O T E** In object-oriented languages, classes are the definitions of objects. When a programmer writes a program, he or she writes a class. When the program is run, the computer takes that definition and creates an object. ▪

Because Java code is platform independent, it must be interpreted, or translated, into instructions that your machine can understand. This translation is performed by the Java interpreter built in to Internet Explorer 3. You can think of the Java interpreter as a special viewer application that allows Internet Explorer to run applets inline. One feature of the Internet Explorer implementation of Java is that is uses a "just-in-time" compiler to speed the execution of Java applets. This technology makes Internet Explorer much faster at executing Java applets than the first-generation applet viewers in use until now.

This whole process prevents the applet from harming your computer in any way. It is explained further in the next section on Java and safety.

Why Java Applets Don't Harm Your Computer

The idea of your machine executing code fragments downloaded from a public network most likely makes your stomach a bit uneasy. People often ask if a Java applet can erase their files or propagate a virus into their computers. Luckily, safe execution was a major consideration from the very start of making Java.

The Java language, and the technology Microsoft incorporated into Internet Explorer 3 to run applets, provides many defenses against malicious applets. These strict language security mechanisms, coupled with Internet Explorer's watchful eye, create an environment in which code can be run on your machine with virtually no chance of it accessing your private data or starting a virus.

The Four Layers of Defense

Java contains multiple layers of security, each serving to filter out harmful code. This section provides you with a firm understanding of how Java's security layers serve to protect your machine. At the same time, this section gives you the security background necessary to program your own applets.

The four layers of security built into Java and Internet Explorer are as follows:

- The Java language and compiler
- Java bytecode verification and strong type information
- Java's class loader
- Restrictions on local file system and network access

Safety Layer One: The Java Language's Defenses The first layer of safety in the Java language comes from its lack of the harmful language and compiler features that C and C++ both possess. Java does not allow the programmer to manipulate memory directly. C and C++ do allow direct manipulation of memory, which means that a careless programmer can manipulate memory that the system has reversed for its use. This is the usual cause for a system crash. A malicious programmer can also use this weakness to propagate a virus.

Now let's focus on how the Java applet interacts with Internet Explorer after it is downloaded. The fundamental line of defense is that Internet Explorer keeps the Java applet from dealing with a specific memory address on your computer. Of course, a Java applet does use your computer's memory. It is just that Internet Explorer doesn't let an applet look at or write to a specific memory address. If the applet needs to change something in that data, it hands its changes back to Internet Explorer, which then actually changes the data in memory (see fig. 31.6).

Part
VI

Ch
31

FIG. 31.6
A Java applet can only access memory through Internet Explorer, which prevents it from getting at memory it shouldn't be able to.

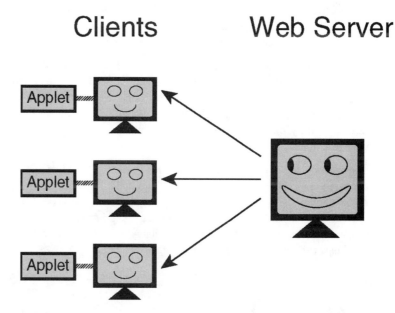

Clients   Web Server

Unlike C and C++, the structure of the Java language requires this interpreter. With a C or C++ program, the programmer might not be malicious or careless, and maybe he or she has used an advanced compiler that doesn't produce evil programs. You don't have to hope that a Java program doesn't harm your computer; the interpreter simply doesn't allow it. Because a Java program must access memory through the interpreter, that interpreter is in complete control. Internet Explorer acts as a firewall between a Java applet and your computer. It does so by isolating the program from the rest of the system and acting as its guardian. By forcing a Java program to obey its guardian, the Java language itself keeps the program from misbehaving and harming your system.

Besides direct memory manipulation, the Java language also deals carefully with casting. *Casting* allows a programmer to change one data type to another, even if changing shouldn't be done. In C++, a programmer can cast a complex object to a much simpler type, like an array of bytes. Generally, doing so causes an error and further causes the program to crash, unless the programmer is very careful. However, a malicious programmer can use this process to change the object itself. He or she can overwrite the individual bytes that make up the object so that it does something that the language doesn't allow. The Java language only allows the programmer to cast between types when it makes sense to cast. It carefully checks all attempts to cast, while C and C++ allow the programmer to cast between literally any two data types. Java's strong checking of casting closes the back door on the type of memory manipulation described previously.

With these capabilities, the Java language itself assures a certain degree of safety for all Java programs. But these features aren't enough to prevent an applet from harming your computer. This layer is just the foundation for the other layers of safety in the Java environment. You now see why this layer means little without the support of the following layers.

Safety Layer Two: Making Sure the Applet Isn't Faking It   After a Java, C, or C++ program is written, the author compiles it. For C and C++, the compilation process produces an executable file. This file can be loaded into your computer's memory and run. Most programs on your desktop have been created through this process.

Java is a semi-compiled language, and its compilation process is different. When Java is compiled, the compiler produces platform-independent machine instructions called *bytecodes*. These bytecodes are what Internet Explorer retrieves from a remote server and then executes on your machine (see fig. 31.7). Because a compiler can easily be altered to bypass the first level of security, these bytecodes must be subjected to strong tests before being executed on your machine.

The second layer of safety accomplishes this process. When Internet Explorer downloads an applet, the bytecode of that applet is examined by its Java verifier. The verifier subjects each code fragment to a sequence of tests before it is allowed to execute. It first looks to see that the bytecode has all the information about the different data types that are going to be used. Actually, more of this type of information is available than strictly necessary. This excess of information helps the verifier analyze the rest of the bytecode.

FIG. 31.7
Java applets are first
compiled into
bytecodes; they are
transmitted across the
Web and executed by a
Java interpreter on the
client computer.

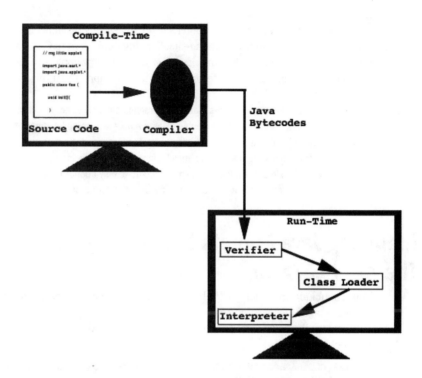

A malicious programmer can try to write a Java compiler that doesn't follow all the rules of the Java language. He or she could write the compiler so that it produces bytecodes that try to trick the Java interpreter into harming your computer. The verifier ensures that no such code ever reaches the interpreter. It checks to make sure that the bytecode plays by the rules of the Java language and protects the integrity of the interpreter.

Safety Layer Three: Keeping an Applet Separate   The class loader offers Java's third line of defense. As independent pieces of code are loaded and executed, the class loader makes sure that different applets can't interfere with each other. It also means that each applet is completely separate from the Java objects already resident that it needs to actually run. Therefore, an applet can't replace the parts of Internet Explorer needed to run applets.

If an applet could replace these parts, all layers of safety could be undermined. All applets depend on the interpreter to provide it with some of the basic constructs of the Java language. If the applets aren't kept strictly separate, an applet can override some of these basic constructs. By doing so, the applet can violate the integrity of the Java language itself and trick the interpreter into hurting your system.

Safety Layer Four: Protecting Your File System   The fourth level of defense against harmful applets comes in the form of file system access protection. Applets are restricted from any access to the local file system, so they cannot read your files, overwrite your existing files, or generate new ones. This restriction not only protects your privacy but also prevents your files from being corrupted or infected by viruses.

The interpreter protects your computer's safety by simply disallowing all Java language calls that deal with files. The Java language itself, being equivalent to C++, can deal with a file system. But the interpreter in Internet Explorer doesn't allow applets to have that capability. If an applet tries to open a file, the interpreter just tells the applet that the file system does not exist.

N O T E   The Java language ensures that a Java program can only affect your system in safe ways. Even if someone takes the trouble to write a fake Java compiler, the verifier in Internet Explorer can figure it out and refuse to run the applet. The class loader makes sure that applets are kept separate from your system and other applets. To top it all off, the interpreter doesn't even allow an applet to access the file system. Therefore, an applet knows only about the Internet Explorer applet runtime environment and can't access any part of your computer beyond that. ■

Including Java Applets in Web Pages: The *<APPLET>* Tag

You can include an applet in a Web document by using an extension to HTML called the <APPLET> tag. This tag, along with the <PARAM> tag, allows you to include and configure executable content in documents. The general syntax for including an applet in a Web page is as follows:

```
<APPLET CODEBASE=codebaseURL CODE=appletFile.class WIDTH=pixels HEIGHT=pixels>
<PARAM NAME=someAttributeName VALUE=1st_attributeValue>
<PARAM NAME=someOtherAttributeName VALUE=Nth_attributeValue>
{Alternate HTML displayed by non-java enabled browsers}
</APPLET>
```

The following are the definitions of the various tags:

- <APPLET>—This tag signifies that an applet is to be included in the document.

- <CODEBASE>—This tag indicates the path to the classes directory containing the Java code. If this field is omitted, then the <CODEBASE> is assumed to be the same as the document's URL.

- <CODE>—This tag is the name of the applet to be included in your page. This file always ends in .class, which indicates that it is a compiled Java class. It should be noted that this variable is relative to the applet's base URL specified with <CODEBASE> and should not be given as absolute.

- <HEIGHT> and <WIDTH>—These tags indicate the dimensions in units of pixels that the applet takes up on your Web page.

- <PARAM>—This tag is used to pass a parameter to an applet.

- <NAME>—This tag is the name of the parameter. This name must be understood by the applet.

- <VALUE>—This tag indicates the value that corresponds to a given name. You can enter your configurations here.

As shown in the preceding list, you can include alternative HTML code between the open and close <APPLET> tags. This code is intended to be displayed if the person who accesses your page is not using a Java-compatible browser. Such a browser ignores the other tags, because it does not understand them, and displays the alternative HTML. A Java-compatible browser such as Internet Explorer 3, on the other hand, knows to instead ignore the alternative HTML included within the <APPLET> and </APPLET> container. The alternative HTML is also used if Internet Explorer 3 can't download the Java applet.

 TIP When you include applets in your Web pages, use alternative HTML inside the <APPLET> tag as a courtesy to people whose browsers are not Java-compatible.

The <PARAM> tag enables you to configure an applet to your special needs. This feature allows you to write applets as generalized tools that can be configured to work in many different situations. If you don't want to learn all the details of programming applets, you can customize other people's Java applets to fit your own needs. For example, a simple animation applet can be told which sequence of images it should load and display. Because such an applet can be configured, many people can run different animations using the same code. You can imagine that, without the <PARAM> tag, using Java would become much more difficult for designers. If applets were not configurable, in the case of the animation applet, individual designers would have to customize their own copies of the program.

Part
VI

Ch
31

Look now at a simple example that shows how to include a configurable applet in a Web page. For simplicity, use the blinking text example from the Java Product Development Team. This applet displays a text string in multiple colors and then blinks each word at random. It takes two parameters: lbl is the text string that is displayed, and speed is the rate at which the text blinks.

To include this applet in one of your Web pages, add the code shown in Listing 31.1.

Listing 31.1 31LST01.HTM How to Configure and Use a Java Applet in Your Web Page

```
<HR>
<APPLET
CODEBASE="http://www.javasoft.com/JDK-prebeta1/applets/Blink/"
CODE="Blink.class" WIDTH=300 HEIGHT=130>
<PARAM NAME=lbl VALUE="Configuring Applets is easy and very useful.
 with Internet Explorer 3, we can make an applet do what WE WANT!">
<PARAM NAME=speed VALUE="4">
</APPLET>
<HR>
```

Figure 31.8 shows the page you should see when you load if you are using Internet Explorer.

FIG. 31.8
You can configure the
blinking text applet to
display any text you
want.

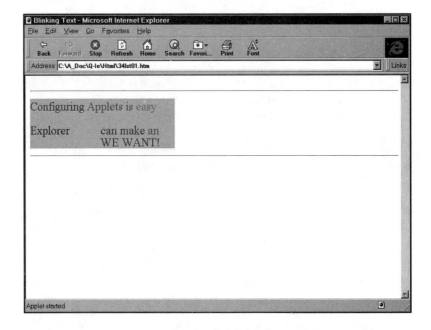

In this example, the blinking text applet is loaded from a remote site—**http://
www.javasoft.com**. As you can see, you are not obligated to download the applet onto your
own machine just to include it on a Web page. As always, when including someone else's work
in your pages, you should make sure you have the permission of the author first.

N O T E Describing how Java applets should be configured is generally impossible. The author of a
Java applet must decide how the applet can be configured and must provide documentation for the applet user. ▓

Examples of Java Applets on the Internet

In the short time that Java has been available, the World Wide Web has come to life with clever
Java programs. The following sections describe a few examples that show the kind of stuff that
Java can do for the Web. Be sure to point Internet Explorer 3 at the URLs to see them in action.

Entertainment and Games on the Web

Because so much of the Web is designed to entertain, it isn't surprising that people have been
writing applets to further the cause. Many applets are designed to spice up Web pages. Probably the most common example is the use of applets to embed animation into a Web page.

Many applets let you play games over the Web. For example, applets for Minesweeper and tic-
tac-toe have been written. The applet shown in figure 31.9 lets you fill in a crossword puzzle. It
has a couple of advantages over the crossword puzzle in your daily newspaper. First, you don't

have to strain to find the clue; you just click the mouse in the box. The clue appears at the top. Second, it gives you feedback. Incorrect responses are displayed in red, while correct ones are shown in black.

FIG. 31.9

The Java crossword puzzle applet is a good example of the quick interactivity Java provides.

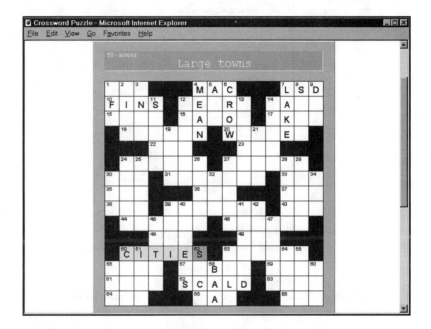

Crossword purists may not consider these improvements, but it is a good example of how applets add interactivity to the Web. It is available at **http://www.starwave.com/people/ haynes/xword.html**.

Educational Java Applets

Java is providing new opportunities in education that were never before possible. Now an educator can write an applet that demonstrates some complex subject. His or her demonstration can be interactive and instantly available to a worldwide audience. A great example of the educational potential of Java is the applet shown in figure 31.10.

This applet shows and demonstrates Pascal's Theorem. In case you're not familiar with it, the Web page also has a hypertext link to where you can find out more about it. The Pascal's Theorem Web page and Java applet are located at **http://www.geom.umn.edu/~krech/java/ pascal/**.

Real-World Business Applications

The ease with which applets can deal with data on a remote computer makes them a good fit with the information needs of companies. Additionally, applets can also provide a good interface to services provided by a company.

FIG. 31.10

Java applets can be used to show examples and guide a user through a difficult idea or process.

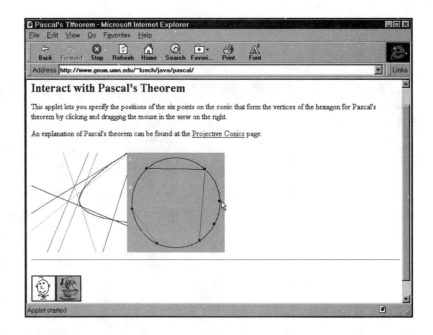

The example shown in figure 31.11 shows what a real-world application of Java might look like. For this particular demo, the information shown is randomly generated by a remote server. It could just as easily come from a server that has real data. You can expect that a service providing real stock prices via Java applets will be available soon from some enterprising Web site.

FIG. 31.11

Java applets can be used to download stock quotes in real time and display them in a variety of ways.

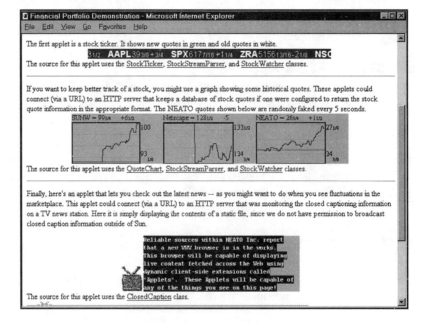

Many companies outside the software industry, including the following, are exploring the usefulness of Java:

- Dow Jones
- Internet Underground Music Archive
- NBC
- Random House

Where To Find More Info on Java

Sun maintains a complete set of documentation on Java at **http://www.javasoft.com**. At this site, you can find everything from language documentation to tutorials. Yahoo has a rather extensive index of pointers to Java resources. You can find this listing at **http://www.yahoo.com/Computers_and_Internet/Languages/Java**.

Part

VI

Ch

31

Finding Java Applets

If you seek Java applets, then check out the Gamelan site at **http://www.gamelan.com/**. This site acts as a registry of applets. It contains links to hundreds of applets, all categorized by subject.

The Java Development Team also maintains their own listing of applets, which you can find at **http://www.javasoft.com/applets**.

▶ **See** "Java Development Resources on the Web," **p. 657**

Language References

The definitive overview of the Java language is the Java Language White Paper, written by the Java Development Team. It is at **http://www.javasoft.com/whitePaper/javawhitepaper_1.html**.

The Java Development Team also has an online overview of the security features inherent to applets. It is available at **http://www.javasoft.com/1.0alpha3/doc/security/security.html**.

Newsgroups and Mailing Lists

For information specific about Java, you should regularly read the newsgroup **comp.lang.java** at **news:comp.lang.java**.

Sun Microsystems, the inventor of Java and applets, also maintains a mailing list concerning Java. To subscribe, send mail to **majordomo@www.javasoft.com**, and enter **subscribe java-interest@www.javasoft.com** *<your email address>* in the body of the message. Replace *<your email address>* with your full Internet e-mail address.

Other Resources

Digital Espresso, produced by Mentor Software Solutions, is a well-formatted, easy-to-read summary of the newsgroups and mailing lists pertaining to Java and Java applets. Information is updated weekly and broken down into categories. You can find Digital Espresso at **http://www.io.org/~mentor/JavaNotes.html**. ●

## CHAPTER 32

Java for C++ Programmers

Java is a new language and set of class libraries developed by Sun Microsystems. In its white paper on the language, Sun defines Java as "a simple, object-oriented, distributed, interpreted, robust, secure, architecture-neutral, portable, high-performance, multithreaded, and dynamic language." That's quite a definition! You look at exactly what Sun means by it in this chapter.

We can't possibly cover every component of the Java language in one chapter. This chapter gives an introduction to the Java language and takes a look at its basic structure and classes. ■

What are the fundamentals of Java?

In this chapter, you learn some of the fundamentals of the Java programming language.

How does Java differ from C++?

Java is very similar to C++. Learn about some of its key differences with that language.

What are some elements of Java syntax?

Learn about the different elements of Java syntax that must be adhered to when programming in Java.

How does Java's class library work?

Find out how you can use Java's class library when developing applications and applets in Java.

The World According to Java

Until now, the various pages on the Web have been fairly static in their ability to interact with the user. With the current conventional Web tools, providing real-time interaction with a user is not easy without performing a lot of CPU processing on your Web server. For example, animation sequences require server push operations to send the new images out to the client browser program.

Another problem with the current paradigm is that you, the user, or your poor system administrator has to keep up with all the different helper applications that you need to really use Netscape to its fullest. Now, how many of you have the latest versions of all your helper applications installed and configured?

Sun Microsystem's Java

Sun Microsystems raised the ante in the Web game when it introduced the Java language and the HotJava Web browser. The goal of Java is to provide a development language that is uniquely suited to developing Web applications. At the same time, Java gives you the ability to deliver both data content and a small application that manipulates the data to the client browser in real time. These small applications, known as *applets*, are downloaded to a user's computer and activated by the user's Web browser transparently whenever the user views a page that contains an applet. This keeps the promise of no longer needing to download and configure helper applications for all the different types of data that you want to view.

Java is uniquely suited for developing Web applications and provides support for parallelism by supporting multithreading. Also, Java is a multiplatform language: any Java applet or application can run directly on any platform that supports the Java runtime system. You look at how this works in the "Java Development" section later in the chapter.

Current Java Information

Because Java is a new language with a lot of new features, getting current information on it can be difficult. The Java Development Kit is in release form from Sun Microsystems for SPARC/Solaris, x86/Solaris, Microsoft Windows NT/95, and the MacOS. Java has gone through alpha, pre-beta, and beta incarnation stages. The methods for building applets and the API for the Java classes have been finalized—but don't be surprised by future changes.

> **N O T E** An API is an Application Programming Interface. It has the complete description and provides the reference for creating applications to conform to a given standard– in this case, for the Java programming language. ■

The best source for up-to-the-minute information on Java and the Java development tools is the Sun Microsystem Java Web site. You can find it on the Web at **http://java.sun.com/**. From this location, you can get the Java Development Kit (JDK), the documentation for the JDK in both HTML and PostScript format, all the documentation for programming the JDK API, and a whole series of lessons on learning to program in Java.

Java Language Features

Java was designed to be an object-oriented language similar to C++ to make it familiar to a large number of programmers. The syntax of Java is similar to C++. Because Java is an object-oriented language, like C++, this chapter assumes that you are familiar with basic object-oriented concepts, such as classes and inheritance.

N O T E In Java, the basic object-oriented programming element is the class. A *class* is a collection of related data members and functions that operate on that data (functions that operate on data as part of objects and classes are known as *methods*). Everything in Java exists within a class—it has no global variables or global functions. ▪

In developing Java, Sun chose to leave out several C++ language features. Specifically, Java does not support multiple inheritance, operator overloading, or extensive automatic coercion of data types. Java also takes steps to make pointer operations much safer. Java's pointer model does not allow memory overwrites and data corruption. In fact, Java does not allow pointer arithmetic at all. It supports true arrays with bounds checking. You cannot change an integer to a pointer via a cast operator. In short, Java eliminates many of the confusing, often misused aspects of C++ and creates a smaller, easier-to-understand language.

Consider some of the new features that Java adds. The language has support for automatic garbage collection, so you no longer have to delete an object explicitly. Objects are automatically deleted whenever they are no longer needed. Java has extensive support for distributed applications. It has native support for the TCP/IP protocols, which allows programmers to work easily with URLs as objects.

Because Java was designed with native support for client/server applications, security is obviously an issue. Java has extensive security support to allow you to create tamper-free systems. Java uses a public-key encryption scheme to provide authentication, and its new pointer model makes it impossible to overwrite secure areas of memory.

If you look back to Sun's definition of Java, you are probably wondering about the architecture-neutral and portable part. Well, Java is really a bytecode-based interpreted language.

Bytecodes are essentially the components of a machine language. They are similar to the object files that you get when you compile a C++ program with your favorite compiler. However, the "machine" language that these bytecodes represent isn't a real machine at all. Bytecodes are really elements of a machine language for an imaginary machine.

Because the Java compiler turns a Java program into bytecodes for an imaginary machine language, the bytecodes are not tied to any one computer hardware platform. In fact, they need a special interpreter program to convert them into actual machine instructions for the destination computer.

Why do it this way? A couple of different reasons. First, by not having the bytecodes represent an actual machine, the compiled Java file is not restricted to any one type of computer. Second, because the bytecode machine language is for an imaginary machine, the designers were able to avoid design problems that are specific to the various types of computers. They were able to design their machine language in a very efficient way. So even though Java files must be run through an interpreter, they are still very efficient.

When a Java program is compiled, it creates a bytecode image that is interpreted by a Java runtime system. Because this bytecode image has nothing to do with the architecture that the Java program was built on, it runs on any platform that has a Java runtime environment. Therefore, you have to write a Java program only once—that one version is portable to any platform with the Java runtime environment.

In addition to being architecture-neutral, Java eliminates all platform-specific data types that have plagued C programmers for years. None of the primitive data types are architecture dependent. All of them have specified sizes and arithmetic operations. For example, a `float` is always an IEEE 754 32-bit floating-point number—on any platform.

A common problem with object-oriented development is that when a company releases a new version of a library, all client software that uses that library has to be recompiled and redistributed. Java was designed to allow classes to add new methods and instance variables without requiring that existing client applications be recompiled.

As you can see, Java truly is an object-oriented distributed language that solves many problems with current object-oriented technology.

Java Development

To develop Java applets and applications, you need a copy of the Java Development Kit (JDK). At the time this book went to press, release version 1.02 of the JDK was available for Windows 95/NT and Sun and Intel Solaris 2.*x* platforms, as well as the MacOS. You can get the JDK from the Sun Microsystems Java Web site at **http://java.sun.com/**.

The process of turning Java source code into compiled Java bytecodes is performed by the Java compiler, javac. To compile a Java program, write your code using your favorite text editor and save it in ASCII text format. The name of the file must have a .JAVA extension. Then compile the file by typing the following:

```
javac filename.java
```

where `filename.java` is the name of your Java source code file. For each class that is defined in your Java source file, the javac compiler generates a file named `classname.class` where `classname` is the name of the particular class. For complete details of the Java compilation process, see the online documentation for Java programmers at **http://java.sun.com/doc/ programmer.html**.

> **N O T E** Java places exactly one class in each bytecode compiled .class file. And the name of the file must be identical to the class name—remember, Java is case-sensitive.

After you have compiled your Java application into a .class file, you can run the file with the Java bytecode interpreter, which is, coincidentally, named java. To do so, you run the java command followed by the name of the .class file that has the main() method for your Java application. For example:

```
java myclass.class
```

This command starts the Java runtime environment and causes it to execute the file myclass.class.

Much of Java's functionality is encapsulated in prewritten collections of classes known as *packages*. These packages are provided with the Java development environment. Each of these packages contains several different classes that are related to a particular topic, and are used during Java development similarly to the dynamic link library (DLL) files used in Windows 95.

Table 32.1 lists the packages in the Java development library at the time this book was written. Packages prefixed with java are actual Java language classes. The other classes are HotJava classes, used in the development of Sun's HotJava browser.

Table 32.1 Java Packages in the Development Library

Package name	Description
java.lang	Basic language support classes
java.util	Utility classes such as encoders and decoders
java.io	Different types of I/O streams
java.awt	A platform-independent windowing system
java.awt.image	Class for handling images in the AWT windowing system
java.applet	Class for building applets to run within Web browsers
java.net	Support for TCP/IP networking

Hello World

You start your exploration of Java with an example that almost all good programming languages use—the Hello World program. In Java, you can use two different types of programs: *applications* and *applets*. An *application* is designed to run directly in the Java runtime environment. An *applet* is designed to run as a component of a network browser, such as Internet Explorer. Of the two, applications are simpler in structure.

The concept of the "Java runtime environment" gets a bit fuzzy here. As you learned in the preceding section, a stand-alone Java interpreter, java, executes a bytecode-compiled file. Applications are executed this way. Applets, on the other hand, are designed to run within the context of a Web browser such as Internet Explorer 3. Applets require more complicated programming than applications because they are actually running within the context of another program. This other program, Internet Explorer 3 in this case, actually has a version of the

Java interpreter embedded within it. Therefore, when Internet Explorer 3 executes a Java applet, it is actually acting as the Java runtime environment for the applet.

The Java code for the Hello World application is shown in Listing 32.1.

Listing 32.1 A Java "Hello World!" Application

```
class HelloApp {
    public static void main(String args[]) {
        System.out.println("Hello World!");
    }
}
```

In Java, all functions and variables exist within a class object; no global functions or variables exist in a Java application. So, the first line of this sample application defines a class named `HelloApp`.

Inside `HelloApp`'s definition is one method called `main`. The `main` method is the method that is invoked when the application's execution is started in the Java runtime environment. Because you have to specify the class that you want to execute in the Java runtime environment, Java invokes the `main` method for that class.

The `main` method is declared to be `public static void`. The `public` keyword means that the `main` method is visible to all other classes outside this class. The `static` keyword indicates that `main` is a *static* method, which means that `main` is associated directly with the class `HelloApp` instead of with an instance of `HelloApp`. Without the `static` keyword, `main` would have been an *instance* method—a method that is associated with an instance of a class.

The next line of code in the `main` method appears to print the `"Hello World"` string as output. So what exactly is `System.out.println`? `System` refers to Java's `System` class. The word `out` is an instance variable in the `System` class, and `println` is one of `out`'s methods. Notice that you don't declare an instance of the `System` class; you just call `out.println` directly. You do so because `out` is a static variable of the `System` class. You can refer to it directly by just referring to the class itself.

Command Line Arguments

Notice that the arguments to `main` are different than they are in a regular C or C++ program. Instead of the traditional `argv` and `argc` arguments, Java gives you an array of strings that contains the command line arguments. It is not an array of pointers as it is under C and C++, but an array of real strings. You can get the length of the array with the `.length` function of the `String` class. For example, the length of the command line argument array is `args.length`.

Another major difference between Java and C++ is that the name of the application program is not passed in the command line argument array. The name of the application program is always the same as the class name where the `main` method is defined. So, while under C++, for example:

```
foo arg1 arg2
```

Running the program `foo` with two arguments would make the first entry in the command line argument array `foo`. While under Java,

```
java foo arg1 arg2
```

the word `java` invokes the runtime environment, and the word `foo` is the class that has `main` defined. Thus, the first argument in the command line arguments array, `args[0]`, is `arg1`.

Introduction to Classes

Classes form the basic program component in Java. Every function and variable must be contained in a class. No global functions or variables are supported by Java. Listing 32.2 shows an example of a Java class declaration.

Listing 32.2   Java Class Declaration

```
/** latitude and longitude of a location **/
public class Location {
    int latitude, longitude;   //latitude and longitude
    ...
}
```

This Java code segment declares a class named `Location`, which contains two instance variables that hold the latitude and longitude of some location.

N O T E   In this example, the ellipses (. . .) just means that additional members or variables could be present. We just didn't write them in the example. ■

You might have noticed that this class doesn't appear to have any parent class. In Java, all classes are subclasses of the class `Object`. So the code sample shown in Listing 32.2 is identical to that shown in Listing 32.3.

Listing 32.3   Java Class Declaration as an Extension of the *Object* Class

```
/** latitude and longitude of a location **/
public class Location extends Object {
    int latitude, longitude;   //latitude and longitude
    ...
}
```

In this example, the `extends` keyword is used to indicate that the new class, `Location`, is a subclass of the class `Object`. In effect, it *extends* the `Object` class by adding new features. You look at this point more in the next section.

Subclassing and Inheritance

A `subclass` is a class that is derived from another class. To create a subclass, you use the `extends` keyword. This way, you can create a new class that adds or changes functionality from its base class. Consider again the example of the `Location` class:

```
/** latitude and longitude of a location **/
public class Location {
    int latitude, longitude;    //latitude and longitude
    ...
}
```

Now create a subclass of `Location` that knows how to print the location. So, you then have the following:

```
/** printable Location **/
public class PrintLocation extends Location {
    void print() {
    ...
    }
}
```

This example simply creates a subclass of `Location` called `PrintLocation` and adds a print method.

Access Specifiers

C++ programmers may, by now, be wondering how Java supports class access specifiers. Java uses the `public`, `private`, and `protected` access specifiers like C++.

An *access specifier* states how visible an entity is during execution. In Java, these specifiers can have different scope—they can be applied to a class, method, or variable. If an entity is declared `public`, it can be accessed from any class. If it is declared `private`, it can be accessed only from within the same class. A declaration of `protected` means that the variable can be accessed by the same class and any of its subclasses but not by any external classes. If no access specifier is given, the entity is given `public` access within the package in which it is defined. You look at packages in more detail later in the "Packages and Interfaces" section later in this chapter.

Using *this* and *super*

Java provides two special variables to a class; they are known as `this` and `super`. The `this` variable is a reference to the current object. It is typically used when an object needs to pass a reference to itself to another method (see Listing 32.4).

Listing 32.4 An Example of Java's *this* Variable

```
/** latitude and longitude of a location **/
public class Location {
    int latitude, longitude;    //latitude and longitude
    ...
```

```
        void Plot(AnotherObject foo) {
            ...
            foo.DoSomething(this);
        }
    }
```

In this example, the `Plot` method of the `Location` class calls the `DoSomething` method of `foo`, an object of class `AnotherObject`. `Location` passes a reference to itself, via the `this` variable, to `foo.DoSomething()`.

The `super` variable works the same way, except that it is a reference to a class's superclass. Remember that Java does not have multiple inheritance, so every class can have only one superclass. Because C++ allows multiple superclasses, you would have no way to know which class you are referring to with a `super` variable in that language. Note that the `super` variable is a special variable and is often referred to as the `super` keyword, because it can only refer to one thing, the superclass.

To recap, in Java, the `Object` class is the ultimate superclass of all other classes. Each class can have, at most, one direct superclass, which can be referred to by the `super` keyword.

Constructors

A *constructor* is a special method that is used to initialize an object. It is indicated by being a method with the same name as the class itself and having no return value. A class can have more than one constructor, as long as they differ in the number or type of parameters. A constructor that takes no parameters is known as the *default* constructor. As in C++, a constructor is automatically called when an object is created.

You can call the constructor of a class's superclass by using the `super` special variable. You can explicitly place the call in your class's constructor. In this way, you initialize the superclass's instance variables, for example. If you don't place an explicit call to a superclass constructor, Java calls the superclass's default constructor for you. Consider the example shown in Listing 32.5.

Listing 32.5   Java Default Superclass Constructor

```
/** latitude and longitude of a location **/
public class Location {
    int latitude, longitude;    //latitude and longitude

    Location(int x, int y) { //constructor with 2 parameters
        latitude = x;
        longitude = y;
    }

    Location() {               // default constructor
        latitude = 0;
        longitude = 0;
```

continues

Listing 32.5   Continued

```
    }
}
/** printablelocation **/
public class PrintLocation extends Location {
    int foo;

    PrintLocation(int x, int y) {
        super(x,y);     // Calls Location(x,y)
        foo = 0;
    }

    PrintLocation() {
        foo = 0;         // implicit call to Location()
    }

    void print() {
    ...
    }
}
```

This example is more complicated than the ones earlier in this chapter. We have expanded the PrintLocation class so that it subclasses the Location class. Both PrintLocation and Location have two different constructors. If you create an instance of PrintLocation so that its default constructor is called, as in

```
blah = new PrintLocation();
```

the default constructor sets the foo instance variable of PrintLocation to be 0. Because no explicit call to PrintLocation's superclass exists, Java calls the superclass's default constructor automatically.

On the other hand, if you create an instance of PrintLocation like the following:

```
blah = new PrintLocation(10,40);
```

the PrintLocation(x,y) constructor is called instead. This constructor makes a call to super(x,y), which calls PrintLocation's superclass constructor that takes two integer parameters. The default constructor of Location is not called in this case.

Comments, Operators, Types, and Identifiers

Now that you've seen how the basic class structure of Java works, you're ready to look at some of the nuts and bolts of the language. You've already seen several of these components in the previous examples.

Types

Java supports five basic data *types*: integers, floating points, characters, and Booleans. You could argue that arrays are really a data type and should be discussed in this section. However, because arrays are also closely linked to Java classes, you look at them in the next section.

Java supports four different sizes of integer data. All Java integers are signed. Unlike integers in other languages, none of the Java integer sizes are platform dependent. In Java, an 8-bit integer value is known as a `byte`, a 16-bit integer is a `short`, a 32-bit integer is an `int`, and a 64-bit integer is a `long`.

For floating-point data types, Java supports both 32-bit single-precision floating point and 64-bit double-precision floating point. To preserve significant digits in floating-point calculations, any operation that has at least one of its floating-point operands as a double gives a result that is a double. Table 32.2 shows the numeric types in Java with their sizes.

Table 32.2   Sizes of the Java Numeric Data Types

Name	Type	Size
byte	integer	8 bits
short	integer	16 bits
int	integer	32 bits
long	integer	64 bits
float	floating point	32 bits
double	floating point	64 bits

The Java character set follows the Unicode standard character set. *Unicode* is an international character set standard that allows for direct support of non-Latin character sets, such as Chinese and Arabic. As such, all Java characters are 16-bit unsigned integers.

The Boolean data type in Java denotes the result of logical Boolean operations. This data type has two values: `true` and `false`.

N O T E   Booleans in Java, unlike C and C++, are not numbers. You cannot cast a Boolean data type to be a number or a string in Java. ▪

Arrays

In some ways, Java *arrays* are similar to the arrays in C and C++, but you will notice significant differences. Java uses arrays to replace pointer arithmetic. You cannot manipulate the pointer to an array and have it point somewhere else. Also, in Java, all arrays have bounds checking enabled, which prevents you from overwriting the end of your array and unintentionally (or intentionally) creating self-modifying code.

N O T E   Under C++, you can create the following:

```
int myarray[10];
myarray[15] = 10;
```

This code segment writes beyond the end of the allocated array and will probably crash your program. Java does not allow you to do this and will throw an exception if you try (see the "Exception Handling" section later in this chapter). ▪

Part
VI

Ch
32

Java arrays are really classes, being a subclass of the `Object` class. As such, arrays are created explicitly with the new operator. For example, the following creates an array of three integers named `myint`:

```
int myint[] = new int[3];
```

N O T E   Java arrays, like those in C and C++, are 0-based. In an array of three integers, therefore, the elements have subscripts: `myint[0]`, `myint[1]`, and `myint[2]`. ■

Java does not allow explicit multidimensional arrays. Instead, you create arrays of arrays. For example, the following is used to simulate a two-dimensional integer array with three rows and five columns:

```
int myint[][] = new int[3][5];
```

Identifiers

An *identifier* is a symbolic indicator, such as a variable, that represents some value. In Java, identifiers must start with an underscore (_), a dollar sign ($), a character in the set *A* to *Z* inclusive, a character in the set *a* to *z* inclusive, or a Unicode character with a value greater than 00C0.

After the first character, the identifier can include digits and any character that is not reserved as a Unicode special character.

Operators

Java has a rich set of operators; they are similar to operators in C++. The order of precedence of operators in Java is as follows from highest to lowest (the meanings of these operators are described in Tables 32.3 and 32.4):

```
. [] ()
++ -- -- ! ~ instanceof
* / %
+ -
<< >> >>>
< > <= >=
== !=
&
^
|
|
&&
||
||
?:
= op=

,
```

Integer Operations   When Java performs operations on integer values, if any element in the operation is a `long`, the result is a `long`. Table 32.3 lists the operations for integers.

Table 32.3   Operations for Integers

Operator	Definition
-	Unary negation
~	Bitwise compliment
++	Increment by one
--	Decrement by one
+	Addition
-	Subtraction
*	Multiplication
/	Division
%	Modulus
<<	Shift left
>>	Shift right
>>>	Shift right with zero fill
&	Bitwise AND
¦	Bitwise OR
^	Bitwise XOR

Boolean Operations   *Boolean*, or logical, operations work virtually identically to those in C and C++. The bitwise logical operators &, ¦, and ^ force evaluation of both sides of a logical expression. You can shortcut the evaluation of the right side of the expression by using the && and ¦¦ operators. Table 32.4 shows the Boolean operations available under Java.

Table 32.4   Boolean Operations in Java

Operator	Definition
&	Bitwise AND; forces evaluation of both sides of operation
¦	Bitwise OR; forces evaluation of both sides of operation
^	Bitwise XOR; forces evaluation of both sides of operation
&&	Shortcut AND; does not force evaluation of both sides of operation
¦¦	Shortcut OR; does not force evaluation of both sides of operation
!	Logical negation
==	Logical equality

continues

Part
VI

Ch

32

Table 32.4   Continued

Operator	Definition
! =	Logical inequality
&=	Logical AND and assignment
¦ =	Logical OR and assignment
^ =	Logical XOR and assignment
? :	If-then-else ternary operator

Comments

In Java, you can specify a comment in a source file in three different ways. You can use the original C syntax of /*   */ to bracket your comments, in which all characters between the two comment indicators are ignored. You can also use the C++-style comments indicated by //. This causes Java to ignore all characters following the // to the end of the current line.

The third style of comments is indicated by bracketing text with the /** and **/ symbols. All text between these symbols is ignored. This style of comment shows there are three different ways to be used immediately before a declaration only. The comments between the /** and **/ symbols are used in automatically generated documentation and are taken to be a description of the immediately following code.

N O T E   Sun provides the javadoc program with their Java Development Kit, which parses the declarations and comments in Java source files and formats them into a set of documentation pages in HTML format. ▨

Literals

A *literal* is an entity that represents the actual value of an integer, Boolean, string, floating point, or character value.

Integer Literals

For *integer literals*, Java supports literals in base-10 (decimal), base-8 (octal), or base-16 (hexadecimal). A decimal literal is a sequence of numbers without a leading 0. If a number has a leading 0 and only the digits 0 through 7, Java interprets it as an octal number. Hexadecimal numbers are prefixed by 0x and can include the digits 0 through 9 and the letters *A* through *F*.

Floating Point Literals

A *floating point literal* uses scientific notation to represent the number. It consists of a decimal integer, a decimal point, another decimal integer representing a fraction, the letter *e* or *E*, an integer exponent that may be signed, and a type suffix. Java supports both single- and double-precision floating point. A *d* or *D* character as the type suffix indicates a double-precision floating-point value. If the type suffix is an *f*, *F*, or is not specified, the number is a single-precision floating-point value.

To simplify this description, here are some examples: 2.0E14, 3.1e3f, and 3.6e-6F are examples of single precision; 3.1e4D and 0.12E3d are examples of double precision.

Character Literals

Java supports *character literals* by enclosing the character in single quotation marks. Like C and C++, Java also has support for a set of special, nongraphical characters. Table 32.5 shows the special characters that you can use in Java.

Table 32.5   Java Special Character Support

Character	Definition
\b	Backspace
\f	Form feed
\n	Newline
\r	Carriage return
\t	Tab character
\ddd	Octal value
\xddd	Hexadecimal value
\udddd	Unicode value

In addition, you can represent the backslash, single quotation mark, and double quotation mark characters as character literals by prefixing the character with a backslash. So, a backslash literal is \\, a single quotation mark literal is \', and a double quotation mark literal is \".

String Literals

A *string literal* is represented as a sequence of characters enclosed in double quotation marks. Every string literal is an instance of the String class. String literals can be continued as multiline strings by using a \ character as a continuation, as in the following example:

```
ans = a + b + c + d + e + f + g + \
      h + i + j;
```

Boolean Literals

Of all the literals, Booleans are the simplest. *Boolean literals* consist of two values, `true` and `false`. For example:

```
boolean flag;
if (a>1) {
    flag = true;
}
```

Statements

Now that you've fought your way through all that information about literals, operators, and identifiers, you're ready to start learning how the various parts of Java work together.

Declarations

A *declaration* is an indicator to the Java compiler that you are going to use a data type. You are declaring that a certain variable is of a particular data type. For example, the following are both declarations for simple data types:

```
int i;
float myFloat;
```

In this case, they declare variables of type `int` and `float`, respectively.

Declarations are also used to define variables that are class objects or arrays. In these cases, the declaration does not allocate any space for these objects. You must use the `new` operator to actually create an object. For example, the following does not actually create an object of type `Location`:

```
Location myLocation;
```

To do that, you need to write the following:

```
Location myLocation;
myLocation = new Location();
```

Similarly, the following does not create an array of integers:

```
int myInt[];
```

To actually create the array, you need to write the following:

```
int myInt[];
myInt = new int[10];
```

Java declarations can appear anywhere that statements can appear, and have a scope that is valid for the duration of the enclosing block. The enclosing block is denoted by the surrounding curly braces { and }.

Control Statements

Java gives you a variety of control structures to specify the flow of control through your program. Most of them are virtually identical to the ones found in C.

The conditional statement structure is identical to the `if` structure in C and C++ (see Listing 32.6).

Listing 32.6   Java *if* Statement Syntax

```
if (a==1) {
    // do something
}
else {
    // do something else
}
```

The Java multiway conditional branch is the `switch` statement. As in C, you switch on a variable and have a `case` entry for each possible value. A `default` label matches if none of the other case labels match. Listing 32.7 shows an example of the `switch` statement.

Listing 32.7   Java *switch* Statement Syntax

```
switch(foo) {
    case 1:
        ...
        break;     // do something
    case 2:
        ...
        break;     // do something else
    case 3:
        ...
        break;     // do something else
    default:
        ...
        break;     // do default action
}
```

Java supports three different looping structures, the syntax of which are identical to C. The Java `for` loop provides loop indices:

```
for (initial condition; while true; each iteration) {
    // loop body
}
```

It looks like the following example:

```
for (i=0; i<5; i++) {
    // do something over and over
}
```

The `while` loop has the following syntax:

```
while (Boolean expression is true) {
    // loop body
}
```

The while loop looks like the following example when implemented:

```
while (i<6) {
    i++;
}
```

The third loop structure is the do-while loop, which has the following syntax:

```
do {
    // loop body
} while (Boolean expression is true);
```

This loop looks like the following example when implemented:

```
do {
    i++;
} while (i<5);
```

N O T E   The primary difference between the while loop and the do-while loop is that in the do-while loop, the loop body is guaranteed to be executed at least once, since the test condition for the loop is at the beginning of a while loop and at the end of a do-while loop. ■

Java also supports the concept of labeled statements and labeled breaks. You saw the break statement in the example of the Java switch statement. The break statement breaks out of the immediately enclosing control structure. If a control structure is marked with a label, and a labeled break is used, control flow can break out of several levels of control structures at once. An example of the break statement is shown in Listing 32.8.

Listing 32.8   Java *break* Statement Syntax

```
escape:
for (i=0; i<10; i++) {
    for (j=5; j<20; j++) {
        ...
        break escape;
    }
}
```

The break statement in the preceding example causes the flow of control to break out of the labeled loop—in this case, the outer loop labeled escape.

To complete the Java control structures, the language includes the continue statement—which, when encountered within a loop, causes the rest of the loop to be skipped and execution to resume on the next iteration—and the return statement—for returning from method calls.

Packages and Interfaces

Java includes two mechanisms for logically grouping and working with classes. They are the interface and the package.

Interfaces

An *interface* is a collection of method definitions without providing the method implementation. A class can implement an interface by providing method bodies for all the methods in the interface definition. Interfaces can be defined to be either public or private. All methods in an interface are public. Java uses interfaces to provide some of the features of multiple inheritance in C++. Interfaces give you an easy way to allow classes from different parts of the class hierarchy to behave in similar ways in a given application or applet.

The code segment shown in Listing 32.9 defines two interfaces.

Listing 32.9   Java Interfaces

```
public interface Test1 {
    Method1();
    Method2(int x);
}
public interface Test2 {
    Foo1(float myFloat);
}
```

A class can then choose to implement either or both of these interfaces (see Listing 32.10).

Listing 32.10   Using Java Interfaces

```
public class IntfExample implements Test1, Test2 {
    Method1() {
        ... // method body
    }
    Method2(int x) {
        ... // method body
    }
    Foo1(float myFloat) {
        ... // method body
    }
}
```

Part
VI

Ch
32

In this example, the class IntfExample implements both the Test1 and Test2 interfaces by providing method bodies for each method defined in the interface.

By using interfaces, you can specify an interface as a data type in a parameter list. This way, you can pass an object in the parameter list, as long as the object implements the specified interface. You don't have to know the exact class details of the object—only that it implements the interface. In this way, for instance, you could create a spreadsheet application or applet that includes an add interface. Then each type of object that you use with that applet—objects containing real number, integers, strings, and other kinds of data—could define an implementation of the add interface appropriate to the type of data. An example is shown in Listing 32.11.

Listing 32.11   More Java Interfaces

```
public class Blah {
    void TestMethod(Test1 x) {
        ...
    }
}
```

In this example, the name of an interface, Test1, is used as a parameter type in the method TestMethod. Therefore, any object that implements the Test1 interface can be passed as a parameter.

Packages

A *package* is a Java construct that is used to manage the program namespace, the complete set of named objects defined. It is a collection of classes and interfaces. Every class is contained in a package. If no package name is explicitly given, the class is contained in the default package. You may remember, from a previous section "Introduction to Classes," that if a class does not give an access specifier to a method, it is considered public for its enclosing package.

To define a package for a compilation unit, you use the package statement. This statement must be the first statement in the file.

N O T E   A *compilation unit* is the basic compiled unit in Java. It is a source code file, as opposed to a class file, that contains one or more classes.

Sun's convention for Java packages is that they be named with period-separated names. You should put the name of the organization that developed the package as the leftmost item in the package name, such as jod.package.

The easiest way to use a class that is in another package is through the use of the import statement. With the import statement, you can import a specific class from a package, or you can import every public class in a package at once.

Assume that you have the package test.package that contains the classes Location and Mapper. If you want to use all the public classes from test.package in your source code file, put the following line at the top of your code, right after the statement defining your current package:

```
import test.package.*
```

The * character tells Java to import all the public classes in test.package. To import just one specific class, such as Location, use the following line instead:

```
import test.package.Location
```

You are now able to create and use objects of the Location class as if it were a local class.

Exception Handling

To manage runtime errors, Java supports runtime exception handling. When a statement causes some type of runtime error, it throws an exception. A special segment of code, called an *exception handler*, is said to catch the exception. Java has many different runtime exceptions defined. You also can define your own exceptions and exception handlers.

Throwing Exceptions

You can define your own exceptions and exception handlers to cope with runtime error conditions in your code. To throw an exception, you must first define an exception class. The `throw` statement takes a class as a parameter. By convention, your custom-defined exception class should be a subclass of `Exception`. For example, you can define your own exception called `PanicCompletely` with the following code segment:

```
class PanicCompletely extends Exception {
}
```

Then you can throw the exception when an error occurs in a class that is subject to a runtime error. An example of throwing an exception is shown in Listing 32.12.

Part

VI

Ch

32

Listing 32.12   Throwing Java Exceptions

```
class CausesErrors {
    void Problem() {
        ...
        if (/* no error occurred */) {
            // do nothing special
        }
        else { /* we have error */
            throw new PanicCompletely();
        }
    }
}
```

Now, when someone executes `CausesErrors.Problem()` and an error occurs, the `PanicCompletely` exception is thrown.

Catching Exceptions

Throwing exceptions is only half the battle. For them to be effective, you must have an exception handler to catch the exception. To create an exception handler, you use the `try-catch` control structure.

To use `try-catch`, bracket the code that is likely to cause an exception with a `try` statement, and then put multiple `catch` statements below it, one for each exception that could be thrown. Consider the example in Listing 32.13.

Listing 32.13   Java Exception Processing

```
try {
    CausesErrors myClass = new CausesErrors();
    myClass.Problem();    // can throw a PanicCompletely exception
}
catch (PanicCompletely exc) {
    // handle the PanicCompletely exception
}
catch (Exception exc) {
    // handle any object of class Exception
}
catch (Object obj) {
    // handle any improperly created exception
}
```

The preceding code contains three catch statements. The first one is for the PanicCompletely exception, which you know that myClass.Problem() can throw. The second catch statement catches all objects of class Exception. It should catch any other exceptions that you didn't explicitly write a catch statement for. The third catch statement catches all objects of type Object. If someone designs an exception that is not a subclass of Exception, it is caught by this catch statement.

N O T E   Remember that all objects, even exceptions, are subclasses of the Object class.   ■

Java also provides another keyword, finally, that is used to mark code in an exception handler that gets executed whether or not an exception occurs. If you add a finally statement to the preceding example, your code looks like that shown in Listing 32.14.

Listing 32.14   Java Exception Processing Using *finally*

```
try {
    CausesErrors myClass = new CausesErrors();
    myClass.Problem();    // can throw a PanicCompletely exception
}
catch (PanicCompletely exc) {
    // handle the PanicCompletely exception
}
catch (Exception exc) {
    // handle any object of class Exception
}
catch (Object obj) {
    // handle any improperly created exception
}
finally {
    // this always gets executed
}
```

The code in the finally block is always executed, no matter what exception is thrown by myClass.Problem() and even if no exception is thrown. ●

Java Tools

Sun Microsystems made a big splash when it released its Java language, which gives Web authors a way of transmitting small applications over the Web to dynamically enhance the capabilities of compatible Web browsers. Java is an object-oriented language similar to C++. Soon after Sun's initial announcement, Netscape jumped on board and released its Java-compatible Netscape Navigator 2 Web browser. Finally, Microsoft announced in December, 1995, that it, too, would license Java technology for its Internet development efforts. Internet Explorer 3 is its first Java-compatible Web browser.

Java is still a very new programming language, however, with its applications, uses, development tools, even the language itself, still changing very quickly. Early Java development tools were relatively crude, and didn't lend themselves to Java development on a large scale. The next generation of Java development tools, however, will bring Java development environments that are much easier to use. ■

Java Development

It's been little more than a year since no one outside of Sun Microsystems had even heard of the Java programming language. With Sun's release of an alpha version of its HotJava Web browser—actually developed with Java itself—and Netscape's release of its Java-compatible Web browser Netscape Navigator 2, a lot of attention has become focused on Java in a very short period of time. Java applets began popping up all over the place.

The early development tools for the Java language, however, were just that—early. And though legions of Java hackers began releasing applets capable of doing anything from playing Hangman or Tetris, to implementing your federal tax form (well, the 1040-EZ, anyway), the development tools used to achieve this were still fairly primitive. Because of the similarity of Java to C++, it was possible to use C++ programming environments, such as Microsoft's Visual C++, for Java development, but it was not an optimal solution.

The next generation of Java development tools and environments is just becoming available. These environments will make the programming of Java applets accessible to more than just the Java hackers. Creating quality Java applets will still require a significant investment of time to develop the expertise in the Java language, but it will now be time spent more productively, developing in Java rather than fighting the development tools.

In this chapter, you'll get a quick overview of some of the commercial Java development environments that are being released. This is not meant to be an exhaustive list of these tools, nor a thorough study of any of the tools in particular. Rather, it is meant to give you an idea of what is available, or what will soon become available, for Java development.

Microsoft Visual J++

On March 12, 1996, Microsoft and Sun Microsystems announced that they had concluded an agreement for Microsoft to license Sun's Java technology to be included in Microsoft's future Internet and Web products.

Microsoft has planned a collection of Java-compatible technologies—with Java as a part of an overall collection—named Visual J++. Included in this is support for Java in its Internet Explorer 3 Web browser using a high-performance Java compiler built into the broswer. Also, the Java language would be integrated into Microsoft's standard component object model (COM) objects using Microsoft's ActiveX Technologies for the Internet.

The final piece of Microsoft's plan for use of Java is to release an integrated, high-productivity Java development tool based on its Developer Studio technology. This technology includes support for multiple developers and will support integrated project management, fast compilation of Java applets and applications, and the full gamut of Microsoft's editors, browsers, wizards, and its graphical debugger.

By integrating the Java language into the COM model, it enables Java to interact with other objects within that model. This means that Java becomes another tool to create a dynamic, continually evolving and improving platform for interacting with the Internet and the World Wide Web. It can be used along with the Web browser built-in capabilties and add-ins, scripting languages such as JavaScript and VBScript, and other ActiveX Controls.

Microsoft's development tool for Java is expected to be available by mid-1996. Additional information on Microsoft Corporation and its Internet and Web strategies is available through its home page at **http://www.microsoft.com**.

Information about Sun Microsystems and the Java language are available at **http://www.sun.com** and **http://java.sun.com**, respectively.

Sun's Java Workshop

As the originators of the Java language, you might imagine that Sun plays an active role in the continued development of the language, and in supporting those programmers who choose to develop applications and applets *in* the language. The alpha, beta, and release versions of Sun's Java Developer's Kit (JDK) formed the foundation for most of the early Java development for their own HotJava browser and the Java-compatible Netscape Navigator 2.

Recently, Sun has announced the release of a new Java developer's environment known as the Java WorkShop (see fig. 33.1).

FIG. 33.1
Java's Java WorkShop is an integrated development environment for creating Java applets and applications.

Part
VI

Ch

33

Java WorkShop Capabilities

The Java WorkShop consists of eight modules for creating an integrated Java development environment for both single developers, as well as teams (see fig. 33.2).

FIG. 33.2
Java WorkShop consists of eight modules, which work in combination to integrate the Java development process.

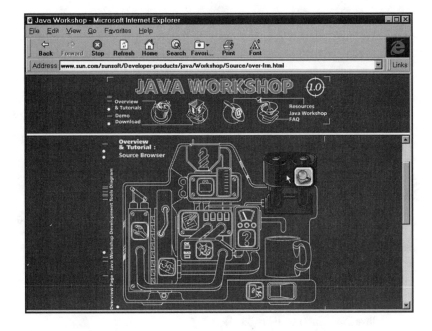

The eight modules are the following:

- Portfolio Manager
- Project Manager
- Source Editor
- Build Manager
- Source Browser
- Debugger
- Applet Tester
- Online Help

Portfolio Manager   Java WorkShop's Portfolio Manager is used to create and customize the portfolios of each of your Java projects. In each individual project you might be working on, the Portfolio Manager allows you to maintain a separate set of objects and Java applets from which to draw.

As each new application, applet, object, and interface is developed for each project, the Portfolio Manager gives you access to the tools that you have developed along the way. As you use each of your new tools and other objects to create further objects of all types, the Portfolio Manager continues to keep track of them.

Project Manager   The Project Manager included in the Java Workshop is used to set and remember the preferences and locations for each of your Java development projects. Because each project may involve a different environment, different tools, and different locations, it's important to be able to keep this information organized to maximize your productivity and that of the other members of your development team.

Rather than you trying to keep all this information straight, however, the Project Manager does it for you. It keeps track of where each path or component leads, and organizes their locations and the environment preferences you have set up for each.

Source Editor The Source Editor brings a point-and-click interface to Java source code creation, editing, and debugging. It is called on by Java WorkShop at many times during the development cycle, allowing you to generate Java code, and debug and correct errors at the touch of the mouse button.

Build Manager As discussed in Chapter 31, "Sun's Java and Internet Explorer," turning Java source code into functioning applets is a two-step process. First, it must be compiled into machine-independent byte codes. It is these that are executed by a Java interpreter—such as that included in Internet Explorer—and perform the function of the applet.

▶ **See** "Sun's Java and Internet Explorer" for information about the way Java works with Internet Explorer, **p. 607**

Java WorkShop's Build Manager performs the first step in this process, compiling Java source into byte codes. It is able to find errors and link back automatically to the Source Editor at the site of the error, to allow easy debugging and correction of coding problems.

Source Browser Because of Java's object oriented nature, it is sometimes easy to lose sight of "the big picture." Each object in Java can inherit properties and methods from other members of its class, and keeping track of all of this is sometimes a problem, particularly for a large project with many objects and applets.

The Source Browser allows you to see the forest, in spite of the trees. By using a tree diagram, it lays out a hierarchical display of all the objects in a project, showing the class inheritance of each. It also lists all methods running in each applet, allowing you to search for strings and symbols. Like the Build Manager, the Source Browser links back to the Source Editor, allowing you to view the code itself.

Part
VI
Ch
33

Debugger Java WorkShop's Debugger provides a collection of tools to manage the debugging process. You are able to run a given project under the control of a control panel, which allows you access to the full gamut of debugging tools. You can suspend and resume threads, set breakpoints, trap exceptions, view threads in alphabetical order, and see messages.

Applet Tester Implementing the final step of the Java development process, the Applet Tester takes the Java byte codes produced by the Build Manager and executes them. As with the rest of the Java WorkShop suite of modules, it is integrated and linked back to the other modules, allowing you to quickly review, debug, and correct problem source code.

Online Help Java WorkShop's Online Help is set up in several main topics that can be accessed directly by clicking HelpBar buttons on the top of each help page. The HelpBar contains the following buttons:

- Contents
- Index
- Getting Started
- Debugging Applets
- Building Applets
- Managing Applets
- Browsing Source

The Online Help system addresses many specifics for each tool not covered in the Java Workshop Tutorial.

SunSoft Internet WorkShop and the Future

A superset of Java WorkShop, the Internet WorkShop includes the Java WorkShop along with the SunSoft Visual WorkShop and NEO development tools—Sun's distributed object application environment. This combination provides a comprehensive development environment at both the client and server levels. Users can use them to develop and administer client and server applications, and convert existing applications into services ready to be integrated into the Web.

Future releases of the Java and Internet WorkShops will include a Visual Java GUI builder, an integrated WYSIWYG HTML editor to ease the publication of applets within Web pages, Apple Macintosh support, and a gateway to allow for easy migration from C++ code to Java.

More information about Sun's Java WorkShop is available from **http://www.sun.com/ sunsoft/Developer-products/java/**.

Symantec Café

Symantec is one of the first companies to announce a commercial development environment meant to bring "visual" tools to Java development. Its Café product, information about which is accessible through its Web site and shown in figure 33.3, provides a highly integrated suite of Visual Java tools for Java development.

Integrated Environment

Symantec Café provides an environment that seeks to seamlessly integrate an open desktop architecture along with a set of individually customizable views. All of the toolbars and palettes with Café are resizable and can be placed where you want them. A tabbed series of virtual desktops allow you to switch rapidly between tasks, with each task being set up with its own layout and toolbar configuration.

FIG. 33.3
Symantec Café is a suite of tools to provide a Visual Java development environment.

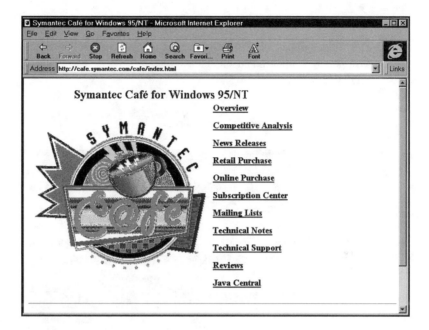

Café Express Agents

Café Express Agents are similar to Windows 95 Wizards. They are visual tools that allow you to quickly generate new files by selecting a few options from a dialog box. Normally, they are used at the beginning of a development effort to set up the environment for that project. The two Express agents are:

- **Project Express**—By using the agent, you can quickly start up a new project into which existing Java source files can be added, or new ones created. The agent is used by specifying the name of the project, the target type, and the existing tools that you want to start out with. This tool is particularly good for starting with an existing Java applet, such as a demo, and using it as the basis upon which to build.

- **App Express**—The App Express agent is a tool to generate a default Java applet, a stand-alone console application, or a Single Document Interface application.

Café Studio

The Café Studio is a visual resource editor for Java applets and objects. Using it, you can create and edit menus and visual form elements such as dialog and alert boxes using simple drag-and-drop (see figs. 33.4 and 33.5). After you have created your interface in this way, the Café Studio takes what you have set up and generates the Java source code and automatically adds it to your project. In addition, the Café Studio is able to create the event handlers to act on the form controls. All Java controls are supported by this, including the following:

Part
VI

Ch
33

- Buttons
- Edit and text controls
- Radio buttons and checkboxes
- List and drop-down boxes
- Panels
- Horizontal and vertical scroll bars

FIG. 33.4
The Café Studio allows for the creation of dialogs and other GUI elements for the inclusion in Java applets via an easy-to-use drag-and-drop interface.

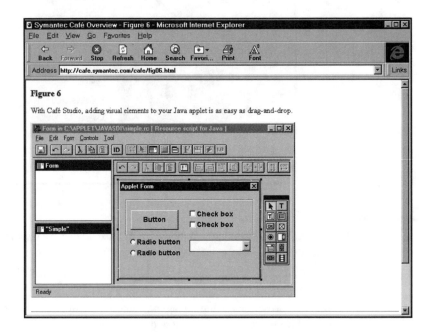

Visual Debugger

Symantec Café provides a GUI-based Java debugger. It is capable of stepping through and inspecting each thread of a multi-threaded application or applet, asserting control over each of them individually, if desired. It has a full set of debugging tools, and is integrated with the other parts of the Symantec Café development environment to allow easy debugging of Java code.

Documentation and Samples

Symantec Café comes with a full set of documentation and tutorials, as well as an extensive set of demonstration Java code and applets. These samples provide a good base from which to develop new Java applets and applications.

More information about Symantec Café can be found at **http://cafe.symantec.com/cafe/index.html**.

FIG. 33.5
Café Studio also allows for the creation of menus and submenus in a very straightforward way.

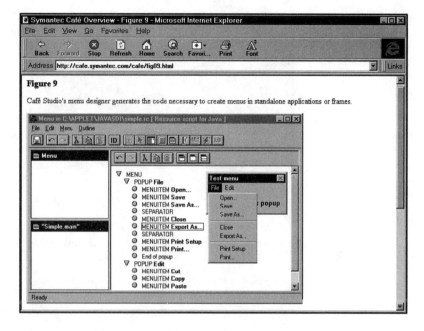

Java Development Resources on the Web

As you might imagine with something so intimately related to the Web as Java, there are many places on the Web to which you can turn for support for Java development. There are certainly too many to name here; but one of the nice features of the Web—and one of the reasons it has the name it has—is that most of these resources tend to be interlinked. And, if you can't find what you're looking for starting at one of these Web sites, you can always hit the Search button on the toolbar, and put one of the Web's many search engines to work for you.

As mentioned previously, information about Microsoft's Java and Visual J++ endeavors can be found through its Web site at **http://www.microsoft.com**.

Sun Microsystems maintains a Developer's Corner which includes information and documentation about Sun's Java development products and can be found at **http://java.sun.com/devcorner.html** (see fig. 33.6).

In addition to the information it maintains on the Web about its own products, Symantec has a Java Central Web site. It is fairly sparse looking, but the links on the page give you access to both a collection of links to other Java resources, both within and outside of Symantec's Web site, as well as Symantec's own mailing lists concerning Java and its Java products (see fig. 33.7). The Java Corner can be found at **http://cafe.symantec.com/javacentral/index.html**.

Finally, there are the many sites that aren't affiliated with a specific company, and probably won't have a slant towards a given company's wares. The Web sites are usually maintained by Java developers both as a collection of links for their own use, and as a service to others out on the Web. One such site can be found at **http://www.nebulex.com/URN/devel.html**, and another is the Gamelan site at **http://www.gamelan.com/** (see figs. 33.8 and 33.9).

Part
VI

Ch
33

FIG. 33.6
Sun Microsystems maintains a Web site devoted to Java developer support.

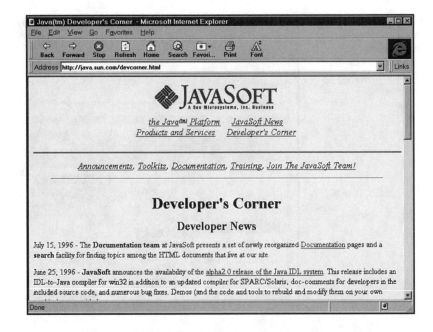

FIG. 33.7
Symantec's Java Central is its clearing-house for links to other Java resources and its own mailing lists.

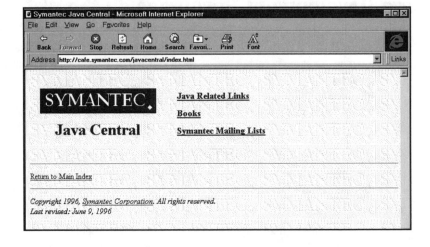

FIG. 33.8

This is one of many Web sites devoted to collecting links to information throughout the Web and the Internet for Java developers.

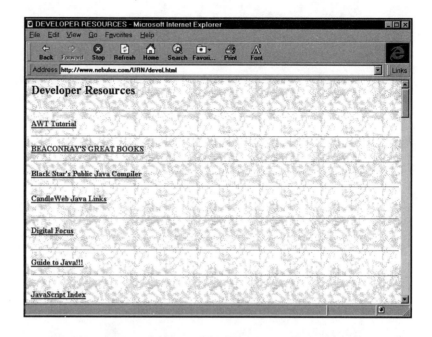

FIG. 33.9

EarthWeb's Gamelan Web site is a clearing-house of Java information. A large list of Java applets is maintained there.

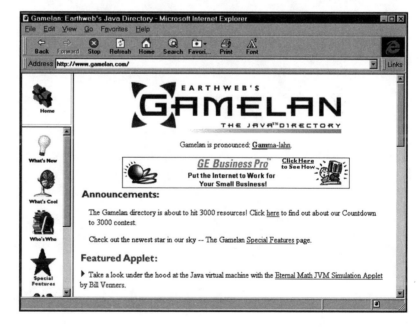

## CHAPTER 34

JavaScript

With the release of Internet Explorer 3, Microsoft has added full support for the JavaScript language. In JavaScript, you can write programs that Internet Explorer 3 executes when users load or browse your pages. The JavaScript language, which was first introduced by Netscape in its Web browser, Netscape Navigator 2, gives Web authors another way to add interactivity and intelligence to their Web pages. And, unlike Java, JavaScript code is included as part of the HTML document and doesn't require any additional compilation or development tools other than a compatible Web browser. In this chapter, you look at JavaScript and get an idea of the sorts of things it can do. ■

What is JavaScript and what can it do?

In this chapter, learn about Internet Explorer's support for Netscape's JavaScript Web browser programming language.

How do you program your Web pages using JavaScript?

Learn about how JavaScript can be used to interact with Web page elements and users.

What does JavaScript consist of?

Find out about the different JavaScript language elements, and how to use them to add functionality to your Web pages.

What do JavaScript programs look like?

Examine sample JavaScript Web browser applications to see what kinds of things JavaScript is capable of doing.

Introduction to JavaScript

JavaScript allows you to embed commands in an HTML page. When an Internet Explorer user downloads the page, your JavaScript commands are loaded by the Web browser as a part of the HTML document. These commands can be triggered when the user clicks on page items, manipulates gadgets and fields in an HTML form, or moves through the page history list.

Some computer languages are *compiled*; you run your program through a compiler, which performs a one-time translation of the human-readable program into a binary that the computer can execute. JavaScript is an *interpreted* language; the computer must evaluate the program every time it's run. You embed your JavaScript commands within an HTML page, and any browser that supports JavaScript can interpret the commands and act on them.

Don't let all these programming terms frighten you—JavaScript is powerful and simple. If you've ever programmed in dBASE or Visual Basic, you'll find JavaScript easy to pick up. If not, don't worry; this chapter will have you working with JavaScript in no time.

N O T E   Java offers a number of C++-like capabilities that were purposefully omitted from JavaScript. For example, you can access only the limited set of objects defined by the browser and its Java applets, and you can't extend those objects yourself. For more details on Java, see Chapter 31, "Sun's Java and Internet Explorer," and Chapter 32, "Java for C++ Programmers." ▇

Why Use a Scripting Language?

HTML provides a good deal of flexibility to page authors, but HTML by itself is static; once written, HTML documents can't interact with the user other than by presenting hyperlinks. Creative use of CGI scripts (which run on Web servers) has made it possible to create more interesting and effective interactive sites, but some applications really demand programs or scripts that are executed by the client.

JavaScript was developed to provide page authors a way to write small scripts that would execute on the users' browsers instead of on the server. For example, an application that collects data from a form then posts it to the server can validate the data for completeness and correctness before sending it to the server. This capability can greatly improve the performance of the browsing session, since users don't have to send data to the server until it's been verified as correct. The following are some other potential applications for JavaScript:

- JavaScripts can verify forms for completeness, like a mailing list registration form that checks to make sure the user has entered a name and e-mail address before the form is posted.

- Pages can display content derived from information stored on the user's computer— without sending that data to the server. For example, a bank can embed JavaScript commands in its pages that look up account data from a Quicken file and display it as part of the bank's pages.

- Because JavaScripts can modify settings for applets written in Java, page authors can control the size, appearance, and behavior of Java applets being run by Internet Explorer. A page that contains an embedded Java animation might use JavaScript to set the Java window size and position before triggering the animation.

CAUTION

If you read this chapter and the next (Chapter 35, "Visual Basic Script"), you will see that they are two very similar languages, with similar syntax and capabilities. Because of this, some of the material presented in this chapter is repeated in the next.

However, JavaScript and Visual Basic (VB) Script are different languages, and you should be careful not to mix them up when you are programming.

▶ **See** "VBScript or JavaScript" for a discussion of the advantages and disadvantages of the two Web browser scripting languages, **p. 733**

What Can JavaScript Do?

JavaScript provides a rich set of built-in functions and commands. Your JavaScripts can display HTML in the browser, do math calculations (like figuring the sales tax or shipping for an order form), play sounds, open new URLs, and even click buttons in forms.

 A *function* is a small program that performs an action; a *method* is a function that belongs to an object. For more lingo, see Chapter 31, "Sun's Java and Internet Explorer."

Code to perform these actions can be embedded in a page and executed when the page is loaded; you can also write *methods* that contain code that's triggered by events you specify. For example, you can write a JavaScript method that is called when the user clicks the Submit button of a form, or one that is activated when the user clicks a hyperlink on the active page.

JavaScript can also set the attributes, or *properties*, of Java applets running in the browser. This makes it easy for you to change the behavior of plug-ins or other objects without having to delve into their innards. For example, your JavaScript code could automatically start playing an embedded QuickTime or .AVI file when the user clicks a button.

What Does JavaScript Look Like?

JavaScript commands are embedded in your HTML documents, either directly or via a URL that tells the browser which scripts to load. Embedding JavaScript in your pages requires only one new HTML element: <SCRIPT> and </SCRIPT>.

The <SCRIPT> element takes two attributes: LANGUAGE, which specifies the scripting language to use when evaluating the script, and SRC, which specifies a URL from which the script can be loaded. The LANGUAGE attribute is always required, unless the SRC attribute's URL specifies a language. LANGUAGE and SRC can both be used, too. Here are some examples:

Part

VI

Ch

34

```
<SCRIPT LANGUAGE="JavaScript">...</SCRIPT>
<SCRIPT SRC="http://www.fairgate.com/scripts/common.JavaScript">...</SCRIPT>
<SCRIPT LANGUAGE="JavaScript"
   SRC="http://www.fairgate.com/scripts/common">...</SCRIPT>
```

JavaScript itself resembles many other computer languages; if you're familiar with C, C++, Pascal, HyperTalk, Visual Basic, or dBASE, you'll recognize the similarities. If not, don't worry; the following are some simple rules that will help you understand how the language is structured:

- JavaScript is case insensitive, so `document.write` and `DOCUMENT.WRITE` are the same.

- JavaScript is pretty flexible about statements. A single statement can cover multiple lines, and you can put multiple short statements on a single line—just make sure to add a semicolon (;) at the end of each statement.

- Curly braces (the { and } characters) group statements into blocks; a *block* may be the body of a function or a section of code that gets executed in a loop or as part of a conditional test.

JavaScript Programming Conventions

Even though JavaScript is a simple language, it's quite expressive. In this section, you learn a small number of simple rules and conventions that will ease your learning process and speed your use of JavaScript.

Hiding Your Scripts   You'll probably be designing pages that may be seen by browsers that don't support JavaScript. To keep those browsers from interpreting your JavaScript commands as HTML—and displaying them—wrap your scripts as follows:

```
<SCRIPT LANGUAGE="JavaScript">
<!-- This line opens an HTML comment
document.write("You can see this script's output, but not its source.")
<!-- This line opens and closes a comment -->
</SCRIPT>
```

The opening `<!--` comment causes Web browsers that do not support JavaScript to disregard all text they encounter until they find a matching `-->`, so they don't display your script. You do have to be careful with the `<SCRIPT>` tag, though; if you put your `<SCRIPT>` and `</SCRIPT>` block inside the comments, Internet Explorer 3 ignores it.

Comments   Including comments in your programs to explain what they do is usually good practice; JavaScript is no exception. The JavaScript interpreter ignores any text marked as comments, so don't be shy about including them. You can use two types of comments: single-line and multiple-line.

Single-line comments start with two slashes (`//`), and they're limited to one line. Multiple-line comments must start with `/*` on the first line and end with `*/` on the last line. Here are a few examples:

```
// this is a legal comment
/ illegal -- comments start with two slashes
/*      Multiple-line comments can
        be spread across more than one line, as long as they end. */
/* illegal -- this comment doesn't have an end!
/// this comment's OK, because extra slashes are ignored //
```

CAUTION

Be careful when using multiple-line comments—remember that these comments don't nest. For instance, if you commented out a section of code in the following way, you would get an error message:

```
/* Comment out the following code
 * document.writeln(DumpURL()) /* write out URL list */
 * document.writeln("End of list.")
 */
```

The preferred way to create single-line comments to avoid this would be as follows:

```
/* Comment out the following code
 * document.writeln(DumpURL()) // write out URL list
 * document.writeln("End of list.")
 */
```

The JavaScript Language

JavaScript was designed to resemble Java, which in turn looks a lot like C and C++. The difference is that Java was built as a general-purpose object language, while JavaScript is intended to provide a quicker and simpler language for enhancing Web pages and servers. In this section, you learn the building blocks of JavaScript and how to combine them into legal JavaScript programs.

N O T E JavaScript was developed by the Netscape Corporation, which maintains a great set of examples and documentation for it at **http://search.netscape.com/comprod/products/ navigator/version_2.0/script/script_info/**. ■

Using Identifiers

An *identifier* is just a unique name that JavaScript uses to identify a variable, method, or object in your program. As with other programming languages, JavaScript imposes some rules on what names you can use. All JavaScript names must start with a letter or the underscore character (_), and they can contain both upper- and lowercase letters and the digits 0 through 9.

N O T E JavaScript does not distinguish between cases, so UserName, username, USERNAME, and any other combination of lower- and uppercase letters spelling out "username" will all refer to the same thing in a JavaScript program. ■

JavaScript supports two different ways for you to represent values in your scripts: literals and variables. As their names imply, *literals* are fixed values that don't change while the script is executing, and *variables* hold data that can change at any time.

Literals and variables have several different types; the type is determined by the kind of data that the literal or variable contains. The following is a list of the types supported in JavaScript:

- **Integers**—Integer literals are made up of a sequence of digits only; integer variables can contain any whole-number value.

- **Floating-point numbers**—The number 10 is an integer, but 10.5 is a floating-point number. Floating-point literals can be positive or negative, and they can contain either positive or negative exponents (which are indicated by an *e* in the number). For example, 3.14159265 is a floating-point literal, as is 6.023e23 (6.02310^{23}, or Avogadro's number).

- **Strings**—Strings can represent words, phrases, or data, and they're set off by either double (") or single (') quotation marks. If you start a string with one type of quotation mark, you must close it with the same type.

- **Booleans**—Boolean literals can have values of either `true` or `false`; other statements in the JavaScript language can return Boolean values.

Using Functions, Objects, and Properties

Before we go any further, let's talk about functions, objects, and properties. A *function* is a piece of code that plays a sound, calculates an equation, or sends a piece of e-mail, and so on. An *object* is a collection of data and functions that have been grouped together. The object's functions are called *methods*, and its data are called its *properties*. The JavaScript programs you write will have properties and methods, and they'll interact with objects provided by Internet Explorer 3 and its plug-ins (as well as any other Java applets you supply to your users).

 TIP Here's a simple guideline: an object's properties are the information it knows; its methods are how it can act on that information.

Using Built-In Objects and Functions   Individual JavaScript elements are *objects*; for example, string literals are string objects, and they have methods that you can use to change their case, and so on. JavaScript also provides a set of useful objects to represent the Internet Explorer 3 browser, the currently displayed page, and other elements of the browsing session.

You access objects by specifying their name. For example, the active document object is named `document`. To use `document`'s properties or methods, you add a period and the name of the method or property you want. For example, `document.title` is the title property of the `document` object, and `"Explorer".length` calls the length member of the string object named `"Explorer"`. Remember, literals are objects, too.

Using Properties   Every object has properties—even literals. To access a property, just use the object name followed by a period and the property name. To get the length of a string object named `address`, you can write the following:

```
address.length
```

You get back an integer that equals the number of characters in the string. If the object you're using has properties that can be modified, you can change them in the same way. To set the color property of a house object, just use the following line:

```
house.color = "blue"
```

You can also create new properties for an object just by naming them. For example, say you define a class called `customer` for one of your pages. You can add new properties to the customer object as follows:

```
customer.name = "Joe Smith"
customer.address = "123 Elm Street"
customer.zip = "90210"
```

Finally, knowing that an object's methods are just properties is important. You can easily add new properties to an object by writing your own function and creating a new object property using your own function name. If you want to add a `Bill` method to your `customer` object, you can do so by writing a function named `BillCustomer` and setting the object's property as follows:

```
customer.Bill = BillCustomer;
```

To call the new method, you use the following:

```
customer.Bill()
```

Array and Object Properties   JavaScript objects store their properties in an internal table that you can access in two ways. You've already seen the first way—just use the properties' names. The second way, *arrays*, allows you to access all of an object's properties in sequence. The following function prints out all the properties of the specified object:

```
function DumpProperties(obj, obj_name) {
    result = ""           // set the result string to blank
    for (i in obj)
        result += obj_name + "." + i + " = " + obj[i] + "\n"
    return result
}
```

You see this code again in the "Sample JavaScript Code" section, and we explain in detail what it does. For now, knowing that you can use two different but related ways to access an object's properties is enough.

HTML Elements Have Properties, Too   Internet Explorer 3 provides properties for HTML forms and some types of form fields. JavaScript is especially valuable for writing scripts that check or change data in forms. Internet Explorer's properties allow you to get and set the form elements' data, as well as specify actions to be taken when something happens to the form element (as when the user clicks in a text field or moves to another field). For more details on using HTML object properties, see the section "HTML Objects and Events."

Part
VI

Ch
34

JavaScript and Internet Explorer 3

Now that you have some idea of how JavaScript works, you're ready to learn about how Internet Explorer 3 supports JavaScript.

When Scripts Get Executed

When you put JavaScript code in a page, Internet Explorer 3 evaluates the code as soon as it's encountered. As Internet Explorer 3 evaluates the code, it converts the code into a more efficient internal format so that the code can be executed later. When you think about this process, it is similar to how HTML is processed—browsers parse and display HTML as they encounter it in the page, not all at once.

Functions don't get executed when they're evaluated, however; they just get stored for later use. You still have to call functions explicitly to make them work. Some functions are attached to objects, like buttons or text fields on forms, and they are called when some event happens on the button or field. You might also have functions that you want to execute during page evaluation; you can do so by putting a call to the function at the appropriate place in the page, as follows:

```
<SCRIPT language="JavaScript">
<!--
myFunction()
<!-- -->
</SCRIPT>
```

Where To Put Your Scripts

You can put scripts anywhere within your HTML page, as long as they're surrounded with the <SCRIPT> and </SCRIPT> tag. Many JavaScript programmers choose to put functions that will be executed more than once into the <HEAD> element of their pages; this element provides a convenient storage place. Since the <HEAD> element is at the beginning of the file, functions and JavaScript code that you put there will be evaluated before the rest of the document is loaded.

Sometimes, though, you have code that shouldn't be evaluated or executed until after all the page's HTML has been parsed and displayed. An example is the DumpURL() function described in the "Sample JavaScript Code" section later in the chapter; it prints out all the URLs referenced in the page. If this function is evaluated before all the HTML on the page has been loaded, it misses some URLs, so the call to the function should come at the page's end.

Internet Explorer 3 Objects and Events

In addition to recognizing JavaScript when it's embedded inside a <SCRIPT> tag, Internet Explorer 3 also exposes some objects (and their methods and properties) that you can use in your JavaScript programs. Also, Internet Explorer can trigger methods you define when the user takes certain actions in the browser.

Browser Objects and Events

Many events that happen in an Internet Explorer browsing session aren't related to items on the page, like buttons or HTML text. Instead, they're related to what's happening in the browser itself, like what page the user is viewing.

The *location* Object   Internet Explorer 3 exposes an object called `location`, which holds the current URL, including the hostname, path, CGI script arguments, and even the protocol. Table 34.1 shows the properties and methods of the `location` object.

Table 34.1   Internet Explorer's *location* Object Containing Information on the Currently Displayed URL

Property	Type	What It Does
href	String	Contains the entire URL, including all the subparts; for example, **http://www.msn.com/products/msprod.htm**
protocol	String	Contains the protocol field of the URL, including the first colon; for example, `http:`
host	String	Contains the hostname and port number; for example, `www.msn.com:80`
hostname	String	Contains only the hostname; for example, `www.msn.com`
port	String	Contains the port, if specified; otherwise, it's blank
path	String	Contains the path to the actual document; for example, `products/msprod.htm`
hash	String	Contains any CGI arguments after the first # in the URL
search	String	Contains any CGI arguments after the first ? in the URL
toString()	Method	Returns `location.href`; you can use this function to easily get the entire URL
assign(x)	Method	Sets `location.href` to the value you specify

The *document* Object   Internet Explorer also exposes an object called `document`; as you might expect, this object exposes useful properties and methods of the active document. The `location` object refers only to the URL of the active document, but `document` refers to the document itself. Table 34.2 shows `document`'s properties and methods.

Part
VI

Ch
34

Table 34.2   Internet Explorer's *document* Object Containing Information on the Currently Loaded and Displayed HTML Page

Property	Type	What It Does
title	String	Contains title of the current page, or Untitled if there's no title
URL or Location	String	Contain the document's address (from its Location history stack entry); these two are synonyms
lastModified	String	Contains the page's last-modified date
forms[]	Array	Contains all the FORMs in the current page
forms[].length	Integer	Contains the number of FORMs in the current page
links[]	Array	Contains all HREF anchors in the current page
links[].length	Integer	Contains the number of HREF anchors in the current page
write(x)	Method	Writes HTML to the current document, in the order in which the script occurs on the page

The *history* Object   Internet Explorer maintains a list of pages you've visited since running the program; this list is called the *history list*, and can be accessed through the Internet Explorer 3 *history* object. Your JavaScript programs can move through pages in the list using the properties and functions shown in Table 34.3.

Table 34.3   Internet Explorer's *history* Object Containing Information on the Browser's History List

Property	Type	What It Does
previous or back	String	Contains the URL of the previous history stack entry (that is, the one before the active page). These properties are synonyms.
next or forward	String	Contains the URL of the next history stack entry (that is, the one after the active page). These properties are synonyms.
go(x)	Method	Goes forward x entries in the history stack if $x > 0$; else, goes backward x entries. x must be a number.
go(x)	Method	Goes to the newest history entry whose title or URL contains x as a substring; the string case doesn't matter. x must be a string.

The *window* Object   Internet Explorer 3 creates a window object for every document. Think of the window object as an actual window, and the document object as the content that appears in the window. Internet Explorer 3 provides the following two methods for working in the window:

- `alert(string)` puts up an alert dialog box and displays the message specified in string. Users must dismiss the dialog box by clicking the OK button before Internet Explorer lets them continue.

- `confirm(string)` puts up a confirmation dialog box with two buttons (OK and Cancel) and displays the message specified in string. Users can dismiss the dialog box by clicking Cancel or OK; the confirm function returns `true` when users click OK and `false` if they click Cancel.

HTML Objects and Events

Internet Explorer 3 represents some individual HTML elements as objects, and these objects have properties and methods attached to them just like every other. You can use these objects to customize your pages' behavior by attaching JavaScript code to the appropriate methods.

Properties for Generic HTML Objects   The methods and properties in this section apply to several HTML tags; note that there are other methods and properties, discussed after the following table, for anchors and form elements. Table 34.4 shows the features that these generic HTML objects provide.

Table 34.4   Properties and Methods That Allow You To Control the Contents and Behavior of HTML Elements

Property	Type	What It Does
onFocus	Function	Called when the user moves the input focus to the field, either via the Tab key or a mouse click
onBlur	Function	Called when the user moves the input focus out of this field
onSelect	Function	Called when the user selects text in the field
onChange	Function	Called only when the field loses focus and the user has modified its text; use this function to validate data in a field
onSubmit	Function	Called when the user submits the form (if the form has a Submit button)
onClick	Function	Called when the button is clicked
focus()	Function	Call to move the input focus to the specified object
blur()	Function	Call to move the input focus away from the specified object
select()	Function	Call to select the specified object
click()	Function	Call to click the specified object, which must be a button
enable()	Function	Call to enable (un-gray) the specified object
disable()	Function	Call to disable (gray out) the specified object

Part
VI

Ch
34

Note that the `focus()`, `blur()`, `select()`, `click()`, `enable()`, and `disable()` functions are methods of objects; to call them, use the name of the object you want to affect. For example, to turn off the button named Search, you type **form.search.disable( )**.

Properties for Anchor Objects   Hypertext anchors don't have all the properties listed in Table 34.4; they have only the `onFocus()`, `onBlur()`, and `onClick()` methods. You modify and set these methods just like the others. Remember that no matter what code you attach, Internet Explorer 3 is still going to follow the clicked link—it executes your code first, though.

Properties for Form Objects   Table 34.5 lists the properties exposed for HTML FORM elements; the section "HTML Objects and Events" also presents several methods that you can override to call JavaScript routines when something happens to an object on the page.

Table 34.5   HTML Forms with Special Properties That You Can Use in Your JavaScript Code

Property	Type	What It Does
name	String	Contains the value of the form's NAME attribute
method	Integer	Contains the value of the form's METHOD attribute: 0 for GET or 1 for POST
action	String	Contains the value of the form's ACTION attribute
target	Window	Window targeted after submit for form response
onSubmit()	Method	Called when the form is submitted; can't stop the submission, though
submit()	Method	Any form element can force the form to be submitted by calling the form's submit() method

Properties for Objects in a Form   One of the best places to use JavaScript is in forms, since you can write scripts that process, check, and perform calculations with the data the user enters. JavaScript provides a useful set of properties and methods for text INPUT elements and buttons.

You use INPUT elements in a form to let the user enter text data; JavaScript provides properties to get string objects that hold the element's contents, as well as methods for doing something when the user moves into or out of a field. Table 34.6 shows the properties and methods that are defined for text INPUT elements.

Table 34.6   Properties and Methods That Allow You To Control the Contents and Behavior of HTML INPUT Elements

Property	Type	What It Does
name	String	Contains the value of the element's NAME attribute
value	String	Contains the field's contents
defaultValue	String	The initial contents of the field; returns "" if blank
onFocus	Method	Called when the user moves the input focus to the field, either via the Tab key or a mouse click
onBlur	Method	Called when the user moves the input focus out of this field
onSelect	Method	Called when the user selects text in the field
onChange	Method	Called only when the field loses focus and the user has modified its text; use this function to validate data in a field

Individual buttons and checkboxes have properties, too; JavaScript provides properties to get string objects containing the buttons' data, as well as methods for doing something when the user selects or deselects a particular button. Table 34.7 shows the properties and methods that are defined for button elements.

Table 34.7   Properties and Methods That Allow You To Control the Contents and Behavior of HTML Button Elements

Property	Type	What It Does
name	String	Contains the value of the button's NAME attribute
value	String	Contains the VALUE attribute
onClick	Method	Called when the button is pressed.
click()	Method	Clicks a button and triggers whatever actions are attached to it

Part
VI

Ch
34

Radio buttons are grouped so that only one button in a group can be selected at a time. Because all radio buttons in a group have the same name, JavaScript has a special property, index, for use in distinguishing radio buttons. Querying the index property returns a number, starting with 0 for the first button, indicating which button in the group was triggered.

For example, you might want to put the user's cursor automatically into the first text field in a form, instead of making the user manually click the field. If your first text field is named UserName, you can add the following in your document's script to get the behavior you want:

```
form.UserName.focus()
```

Programming with JavaScript

As you've learned in the preceding sections, JavaScript has a lot to offer page authors. It's not as flexible as C or C++, but it's quick and simple. Most importantly, it's easily embedded in your WWW pages, so you can maximize their impact with a little JavaScript seasoning. This section covers the gritty details of JavaScript programming, including a detailed explanation of the language's features.

Expressions

An *expression* is anything that can be evaluated to get a single value. Expressions can contain string or numeric literals, variables, operators, and other expressions, and they can range from simple to quite complex. For example, the following is an expression that uses the assignment operator (more on operators in the next section) to assign the result 7 to the variable x:

```
x = 7;
```

By contrast, the following is a more complex expression whose final value depends on the values of the quitFlag and formComplete variables:

```
(quitFlag == TRUE) & (formComplete == FALSE)
```

Operators

Operators do just what their name suggests: they operate on variables or literals. The items that an operator acts on are called its *operands*. Operators come in the two following types:

- **Unary operators**—These operators require only one operand, and the operator can come before or after the operand. The - - operator, which subtracts one from the operand, is a good example. Both - -count and count- - subtract one from the variable count.

- **Binary operators**—These operators need two operands. The four math operators (+ for addition, - for subtraction, * for multiplication, and / for division) are all binary operators, as is the = assignment operator you saw earlier.

Assignment Operators *Assignment operators* take the result of an expression and assign it to a variable. JavaScript doesn't allow you to assign the result of an expression to a literal. One feature that JavaScript has that most other programming languages don't is that you can change a variable's type on-the-fly. Consider the following:

```
function TypeDemo()
{
    var pi = 3.14159265
    document.write("Pi is ", pi, "\n")
    pi = FALSE
    document.write("Pi is ", pi, "\n")
}
```

This short function first prints the (correct) value of Pi. In most other languages, though, trying to set a floating-point variable to a Boolean value would either generate a compiler error or a runtime error. JavaScript and Java happily accept the change and print Pi's new value: `false`.

The most common assignment operator, =, simply assigns the value of an expression's right side to its left side. In the previous example, the variable x got the integer value 7 after the expression was evaluated. For convenience, JavaScript also defines some other operators that combine common math operations with assignment; they're shown in Table 37.8.

Table 34.8   Assignment Operators That Provide Shortcuts To Doing Assignments and Math Operations at the Same Time

Operator	What It Does	Two Equivalent Expressions
+=	Adds two values	x+=y and x=x+y
	Adds two strings	`string = string + "HTML"` and `string += "HTML"`
-=	Subtracts two values	x-=y and x=x-y
*=	Multiplies two values	a*=b and a=a*b
/=	Divides two values	e/=b and e=e/b

Math Operators   The preceding sections gave you a sneak preview of the math operators that JavaScript furnishes. You can either combine math operations with assignments, as shown in Table 34.8, or use them individually. As you would expect, the standard four math functions (addition, subtraction, multiplication, and division) work just as they do on an ordinary calculator.

The negation operator, -, is a unary operator that negates the sign of its operand. To use the negation operator, you must put the operator before the operand.

JavaScript also adds two useful binary operators: -- and ++, called, respectively, the *decrement* and *increment* operators. These two operators modify the value of their operand, and they return the new value. They also share a unique property: they can be used either before or after their operand. If you put the operator after the operand, JavaScript returns the operand's value and then modifies it. If you take the opposite route and put the operator before the operand, JavaScript modifies it and returns the modified value. The following short example might help clarify this seemingly odd behavior:

```
x = 7;    // set x to 7
a = --x;  // set x to x-1, and return the new x; a = 6
b = a++;  // set b to a, so b = 6, then add 1 to a; a = 7
x++;      // add one to x; ignore the returned value
```

Comparison Operators   Comparing the value of two expressions to see whether one is larger, smaller, or equal to another is often necessary. JavaScript supplies several comparison operators that take two operands and return `true` if the comparison is true, and `false` if it's not. (Remember, you can use literals, variables, or expressions with operators that require expressions.) Table 34.9 shows the JavaScript comparison operators.

Part
VI
Ch
34

Table 34.9   Comparison Operators That Allow Two JavaScript Operands To Be Compared in a Variety of Ways

Operator	Read It As	Returns *true* When:
==	Equals	The two operands are equal
!=	Does not equal	The two operands are unequal
<	Less than	The left operand is less than the right operand
<=	Less than or equal to	The left operand is less than or equal to the right operand
>	Greater than	The left operand is greater than the right operand
>=	Greater than or equal to	The left operand is greater than or equal to the right operand

TIP The comparison operators can be used on strings, too; the results depend on standard lexicographic ordering, but comparisons aren't case sensitive.

Thinking of the comparison operators as questions may be helpful; when you write the following:

```
(x >= 10)
```

you're really saying, "Is the value of variable x greater than or equal to 10?" The return value answers the question, true or false.

Logical Operators   Comparison operators compare quantity or content for numeric and string expressions, but sometimes you need to test a logical value—like whether a comparison operator returns true or false. JavaScript's logical operators allow you to compare expressions that return logical values. The following are JavaScript's logical operators:

- &&, read as "and." The && operator returns true if both its input expressions are true. If the first operand evaluates to false, && returns false immediately, without evaluating the second operand. Here's an example:

```
x = TRUE && TRUE;      // x is TRUE
x = FALSE && FALSE;    // x is FALSE
x = FALSE && TRUE;     // x is FALSE
```

- ¦¦, read as "or." This operator returns true if either of its operands is true. If the first operand is true, ¦¦ returns true without evaluating the second operand. Here's an example:

```
x = TRUE ¦¦ TRUE;      // x is TRUE
x = FALSE ¦¦ TRUE;     // x is TRUE
x = FALSE ¦¦ FALSE;    // x is FALSE
```

- !, read as "not." This operator takes only one expression, and it returns the opposite of that expression, so !true returns false, and !false returns true.

Note that the "and" and "or" operators don't evaluate the second operand if the first operand provides enough information for the operator to return a value. This process, called *short-circuit evaluation*, can be significant when the second operand is a function call. For example,

```
keepGoing = (userCancelled == FALSE) && (theForm.Submit())
```

If `userCancelled` is `true`, the second operand—which submits the active form—isn't called.

Controlling Your JavaScripts

Some scripts you write will be simple; they'll execute the same way every time, once per page. For example, if you add a JavaScript to play a sound when users visit your home page, it doesn't need to evaluate any conditions or do anything more than once. More sophisticated scripts might require that you take different actions under different circumstances; you might also want to repeat the execution of a block of code—perhaps by a set number of times, or as long as some condition is true. JavaScript provides constructs for controlling the execution flow of your script based on conditions, as well as repeating a sequence of operations.

Testing Conditions   JavaScript provides a single type of control statement for making decisions: the `if...else` statement. To make a decision, you supply an expression that evaluates to `true` or `false`; which code is executed depends on what your expression evaluates to.

The simplest form of `if...else` uses only the `if` part. If the specified condition is `true`, the code following the condition is executed; if not, it's skipped. For example, in the following code fragment, the message appears only if the condition (that the document's Last Modified field says it was modified before 1995) is `true`:

```
if (document.lastModified.year < 1995)
    document.write("Danger! This is a mighty old document.")
```

You can use any expression as the condition; since expressions can be nested and combined with the logical operators, your tests can be pretty sophisticated. For example:

```
if ((document.lastModified.year >= 1995) && (document.lastModified.month >= 10))
    document.write("This document is reasonably current.")
```

The `else` clause allows you to specify a set of statements to execute when the condition is `false`.

Repeating Actions   If you want to repeat an action more than once, you're in luck. JavaScript provides two different loop constructs that you can use to repeat a set of operations.

The first, called a `for` loop, executes a set of statements some number of times. You specify three expressions: an *initial* expression that sets the values of any variables you need to use, a *condition* that tells the loop how to see when it's done, and an *increment* expression that modifies any variables that need it. Here's a simple example:

```
for (count=0; count < 100; count++)
    document.write("Count is ", count);
```

This loop executes 100 times and prints out a number each time. The initial expression sets the counter, `count`, to zero; the condition tests to see whether `count` is less than 100, and the increment expression increments `count`.

You can use several statements for any of these expressions, as follows:

```
for (count=0, numFound = 0; (count < 100) && (numFound < 3); count++)
    if (someObject.found()) numFound++;
```

This loop either loops 100 times or as many times as it takes to "find" three items—the loop condition terminates when `count >= 100` or when `numFound >= 3`.

The second form of loop is the `while` loop. It executes statements as long as its condition is true. For example, you can rewrite the first `for` loop in the preceding example as follows:

```
count = 0
while (count < 100) {
    if (someObject.found()) numFound++;
    document.write("Count is ", count)
}
```

Which form you use depends on what you're doing; `for` loops are useful when you want to perform an action a set number of times, and `while` loops are best when you want to keep doing something as long as a particular condition remains true. Notice that by using curly braces, you can include more than one command to be executed by the `while` loop (this is also true of `for` loops and `if...else` constructs).

JavaScript Reserved Words

JavaScript reserves some keywords for its own use. You cannot define your own methods or properties with the same name as any of these keywords; if you do, the JavaScript interpreter complains.

TIP Some of these keywords are reserved for future use. JavaScript might allow you to use them, but your scripts may break in the future if you do.

The following are the reserved keywords:

abstract	double	instanceof	super
boolean	else	int	switch
break	extends	interface	synchronized
byte	false	long	this
byvalue	final	native	threadsafe
case	finally	new	throw
catch	float	null	transient
char	for	package	true
class	function	private	try
const	goto	protected	var
continue	if	public	void
default	implements	return	while
delete	import	short	with
do	in	static	

N O T E Because JavaScript is still being developed and refined by Netscape, the list of reserved keywords might change and/or grow over time. Whenever a new version of JavaScript is released, it might be a good idea to look over its new capabilities with an eye toward conflicts with your JavaScript programs. ■

Command Reference

This section provides a quick reference to the JavaScript commands that are implemented in Internet Explorer 3. The commands are listed in alphabetical order; many have examples. Before you dive in, though, here's what the formatting of these entries mean:

- All JavaScript keywords are in monospaced font.
- Words in *italics* represent user-defined names or statements.
- Any portions enclosed in square brackets ([and]) are optional.
- {*statements*} indicates a block of statements, which can consist of a single statement or multiple statements enclosed by curly braces.

The *break* Statement   The break statement terminates the current while or for loop and transfers program control to the statement following the terminated loop.

Syntax:

```
break
```

Example:

The following function scans the list of URLs in the current document and stops when it has seen all URLs or when it finds a URL that matches the input parameter searchName:

```
function findURL(searchName) {
    var i = 0;
    for (I=0; i < document.links.length; i++) {
        if (document.links[i] == searchName)
        {
            document.write(document.links[i])
            break;
        }
}
```

The *continue* Statement   The continue statement stops executing the statements in a while or for loop, and skips to the next iteration of the loop. It doesn't stop the loop altogether like the break statement; instead, in a while loop, it jumps back to the condition, and in a for loop, it jumps to the update expression.

Syntax:

```
continue
```

Example:

The following function prints the odd numbers between 1 and x; it has a continue statement that goes to the next iteration when i is even:

```
function printOddNumbers(x) {
    var i = 0
    while (i < x)
    {
        i++;
        if ((i % 2) == 0)      // the % operator divides & returns the remainder
            continue
        else
            document.write(i, "\n")
    }
}
```

The *for* Loop A for loop consists of three optional expressions, enclosed in parentheses and separated by semicolons, followed by a block of statements executed in the loop. These parts do the following:

- The starting expression, initial_expr, is evaluated before the loop starts. It is most often used to initialize loop counter variables, and you're free to use the var keyword here to declare new variables.

- A *condition* is evaluated on each pass through the loop. If the condition evaluates to true, the statements in the loop body are executed. You can leave the condition out, and it always evaluates to true. If you do so, make sure to use break in your loop when it's time to exit.

- An update expression, update_expr, is usually used to update or increment the counter variable or other variables used in the condition. This expression is optional; you can update variables as needed within the body of the loop if you prefer.

- A block of statements are executed as long as the condition is true. This block can have one or multiple statements in it.

Syntax:

```
for ([initial_expr;] [condition;] [update_expr])
{
    statements
}
```

Example:

This simple for statement prints out the numbers from 0 to 9. It starts by declaring a loop counter variable, i, and initializing it to zero. As long as i is less than 9, the update expression increments i, and the statements in the loop body are executed:

```
for (var i = 0; i <= 9; i++)
{
    document.write(i);
}
```

The *for...in* Loop The for...in loop is a special form of the for loop that iterates the variable variable-name over all the properties of the object-named object-name. For each distinct property, it executes the statements in the loop body.

Syntax:

```
for (var in obj)
{
    statements
}
```

Example:

The following function takes as its arguments an object and the object's name. It then uses the `for...in` loop to iterate through all the object's properties. When done, it returns a string that lists the property names and their values:

```
function dump_props(obj, obj_name) {
    var result = ""
    for (i in obj)
        result += obj_name + "." + i + " = " + obj[i] + "\n"
    return result;
    }
```

The *function* Statement   The `function` statement declares a JavaScript function; the function may optionally accept one or more parameters. To return a value, the function must have a return statement that specifies the value to return. All parameters are passed to functions *by value*—the function gets the value of the parameter but cannot change the original value in the caller.

Syntax:

```
function name([param] [, param] [..., param])
{
    statements
}
```

Example:

```
function PageNameMatches(theString)
{
    return (document.title == theString)
}
```

The *if...else* Statement   The `if...else` statement is a conditional statement that executes the statements in `block1` if `condition` is `true`. In the optional `else` clause, it executes the statements in `block2` if `condition` is `false`. The blocks of statements can contain any JavaScript statements, including further nested `if` statements.

Syntax:

```
if (condition) {
    statements
} [else {
    statements}]
```

Example:

```
if (Message.IsEncrypted()) {
```

```
    Message.Decrypt(SecretKey); }
else {
    Message.Display();
}
```

The *return* Statement   The return statement specifies the value to be returned by a function.

Syntax:

```
return expression;
```

Example:

The following simple function returns the square of its argument, x, where x is any number:

```
function square( x ) {
    return x * x;
}
```

The *this* Statement   You use this to access methods or properties of an object within the object's methods. The this statement always refers to the current object.

Syntax:

```
this.property
```

Example:

If setSize is a method of the document object, then this refers to the specific object whose setSize method is called:

```
function setSize (x, y) {
        this.horizSize = x;
        this.vertSize = y;
}
```

This method sets the size for an object when called as follows:

```
document.setSize (640, 480);
```

The *var* Statement   The var statement declares a variable *varname*, optionally initializing it to have *value*. The variable name *varname* can be any JavaScript identifier, and *value* can be any legal expression (including literals).

Syntax:

```
var varname [= value] [, var varname [= value] ] [..., var varname [= value] ]
```

Example:

```
var num_hits = 0, var cust_no = 0;
```

The *while* Statement   The while statement contains a condition and a block of statements. The while statement evaluates the condition; if *condition* is true, it executes the statements in the loop body. It then re-evaluates *condition* and continues to execute the statement block as long as *condition* is true. When *condition* evaluates to false, execution continues with the next statement following the block.

Syntax:

```
while (condition)
{
    statements
}
```

Example:

The following simple `while` loop iterates until it finds a form in the current document object whose name is `"OrderForm"`, or until it runs out of forms in the document:

```
x = 0;
while ((x < document.forms[].length) && (document.forms[x].name != "OrderForm"))
{ x++; }
```

The *with* Statement   The `with` statement establishes *object* as the default object for the statements in `block`. Any property references without an object are then assumed to be for *object*.

Syntax:

```
with object
{
    statements
}
```

Example:

```
with document {
    write "Inside a with block, you don't need to specify the object.";
    bgColor = gray;
}
```

Sample JavaScript Code

Picking up a new programming language from scratch can be difficult—even for experienced programmers. To make mastering JavaScript easier for you, this section presents some examples of JavaScript code and functions that you can use in your own pages. Each example demonstrates a practical concept.

Dumping an Object's Properties

In the section "Array and Object Properties," you saw a small function, `DumpProperties()`, that gets all the property names and their values. Look at that function again now to see it in light of what you've learned:

```
function DumpProperties (obj, obj_name) {
    var result = ""     // set the result string to blank
    for (i in obj)
        result += obj_name + "." + i + " = " + obj[i] + "\n"
    return result
}
```

Part
VI

Ch
34

As all JavaScript functions should, this one starts by defining its variables using the `var` keyword; it supplies an initial value, too, which is a good habit to start. The meat of the function is the `for...in` loop, which iterates over all the properties of the specified object. For each property, the loop body collects the object name, the property name (provided by the loop counter in the `for...in` loop), and the property's value. You access the properties as an indexed array instead of by name, so you can get them all.

Note that the function itself doesn't print anything out. If you want to see its output, put it in a page (remember to surround it with `<SCRIPT>` and `</SCRIPT>`). Then, at the bottom of the page, use the following where *obj* is the object of interest and *objName* is its name:

```
document.writeln(DumpProperties(obj, objName))
```

Building a Link Table

You might want to have a way to generate a list of all the links in a page automatically, perhaps to display them in a separate section at the end of the page, as shown in figure 34.1. `DumpURL()`, shown in Listing 34.1, does just that; it prints out a nicely formatted numbered list showing the hostname of each link in the page, when called with `document.writeln(DumpURL())`.

Listing 34.1   34LST01.HTM   Using *DumpURL()* To Display a Numbered List of All the URLs on a Page

```
function DumpURL()
{
    // declare the variables we'll use
    var linkCount = document.links.length
    var result = ""

    // build our summary line
    result = "<hr>\nLink summary: this page has links to <b>" +
        linkCount  + "</b> hosts<br>\n"
    result += "<ol>\n"

    // for each link in the document, print a list item with its hostname
    for (i=0; i < linkCount ; i++)
        result += "<li> " + document.links[i].hostname + "\n"

    // add the closing HTML for our list
    result += "</ol><hr>\n"
    return result
}
```

FIG. 34.1

The DumpURL() function creates a list of all the links in a page.

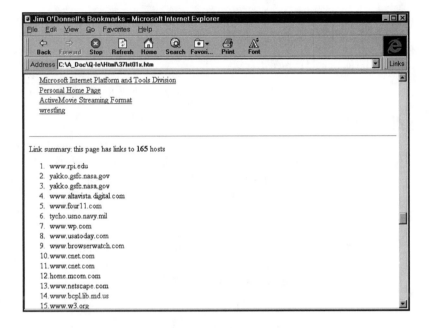

In Listing 34.1, this function starts by declaring the variables used in it. JavaScript requires that you declare most variables before using them, and good programming practice dictates doing so even when JavaScript doesn't require it. Next, you build the summary line for your table by assigning a string literal full of HTML to the result variable. You use a for loop to iterate through all the links in the current document and add a list item for each to the result variable. When you finish, you add the closing HTML for your list to result and return it.

Updating Data in Form Fields

Several times, we have mentioned the benefits of using JavaScript to check and modify data in HTML forms. Now look at an example that dynamically updates the value of a text field based on the user's selection from one of several buttons.

To make this example work, you need two pieces: the first is a simple bit of JavaScript that updates the value property of an object to whatever you pass in. Here's what it looks like:

```
function change(input, newValue)
{
    input.value = newValue
}
```

Then you need to change the onClick method for each button you want to include so that it calls your change() function. Here's a sample button definition:

```
<input type="button" value="Mac"
    onClick="change(this.form.display, 'Macintosh')">
```

Part

VI

Ch

34

When the button is clicked, JavaScript calls the `onClick` method, which happens to point to your function. The `this.form.display` object points to a text field named `display`; `this` refers to the active document, `form` refers to the form in the active document, and `display` refers to the form field named `display`.

Of course, this requires that you have a form `INPUT` gadget named `display`!

Validating Data in Form Fields

Often when you create a form to get data from the user, you need to check that data to see if it's correct and complete before sending mail, or making a database entry, or whatever you collected the data for. Without JavaScript, you have to post the data and let a CGI script on the server decide if all the fields were correctly filled out. You can do better, though, by writing JavaScript functions that check the data in your form *on the client*; by the time the data gets posted, you know it's correct.

For this example, require that the user fill out two fields on the form: ZIP code and area code. Also, present some other fields that are optional. First, you need a function that returns `true` if something appears in a field and `false` if it's empty:

```
function isFilled(input)
{
    return (input.value.length != 0)
}
```

That's simple enough. For each field you want to make the user complete, you override its `onBlur()` method. The `onBlur()` method is triggered when the user moves the focus out of the specified field. Here's what your buttons look like:

```
<input name="ZIP" value=""
    onBlur="if (!isFilled(form.ZIP)) {
                alert('You must put your ZIP code in this field.');
                form.ZIP.focus() }">
```

When the user tries to move the focus out of the ZIP code button, the code attached to the `onBlur()` event is called. That code, in turn, checks to see whether the field is complete; if not, it nags the user and puts the focus back into the ZIP field.

Of course, you could also implement a more gentle validation scheme by attaching a JavaScript to the form's Submit button, as follows:

```
<script language="JavaScript">
function areYouSure()
{
    return confirm("Are you sure you want to submit these answers?")
}
</script>
<input type=button name="doIt" value="Submit form"
    onClick="if (areYouSure()) this.form.submit();">
```

Figure 34.2 shows the Web site at **http://www.resortguide.com/javascript/ FormVerification.html**, which is a great demo of form field validation using JavaScript. You can use Internet Explorer to load this Web site, and select <u>V</u>iew, Sour<u>c</u>e to see how it works.

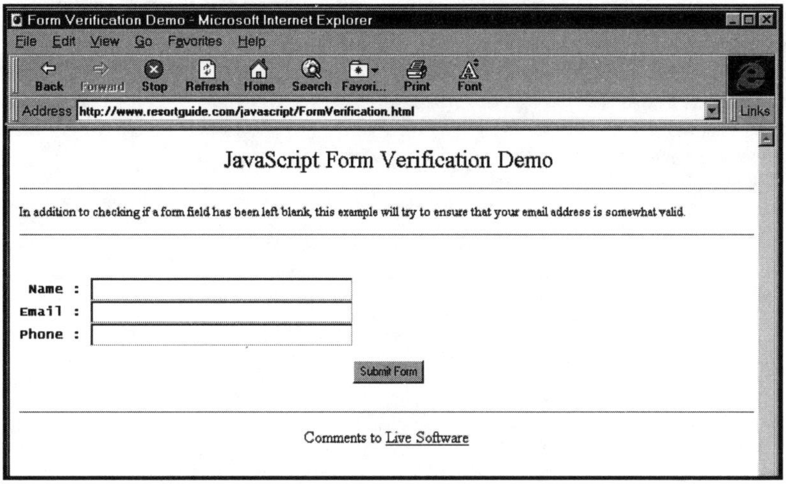

FIG. 34.2

Unless you have entered values in each field, including a valid e-mail address and phone number, JavaScript will not let you submit this form.

An RPN Calculator

If you ask any engineer under a certain age what kind of calculator he or she used in college, the answer is likely to be "a Hewlett Packard." HP calculators are somewhat different from other calculators; you use *reverse Polish notation*, or RPN, to do calculations.

With a regular calculator, you put the operator in between operands. To add 3 and 7, you push 3, then the + key, then 7, and then = to print the answer. With an RPN calculator, you put the operator *after* both operands. To add 3 and 7, you push 3, then Enter (which puts the first operand on the internal stack), then 7, and then +, at which time you see the correct answer. This oddity takes a bit of getting used to, but it makes complex calculations go much faster, since intermediate results get saved on the stack.

Here's a simple RPN example. To compute $((1024 * 768) / 3.14159)^2$, you enter the following:

```
1024, Enter, 768, *, 3.14159, /, x²
```

The correct answer is 6.266475×10^{10}, or about 6.3 billion.

When Netscape introduced JavaScript, they provided an RPN calculator as an example of JavaScript's expressive power—it is still a good example today. Take a detailed look now at how it works. Figure 34.3 shows the calculator as it's displayed in Internet Explorer 3. Listings 34.2 and 34.3 show the HTML document. The HTML code is shown in Listing 34.2, and the JavaScript functions are shown in Listing 34 .3. (Note that they are really in the same file; we've just split them for convenience.)

Part
VI

Ch
34

FIG. 34.3

Internet Explorer 3 displays the RPN calculator as a table of buttons, with the accumulator and the stack at the top.

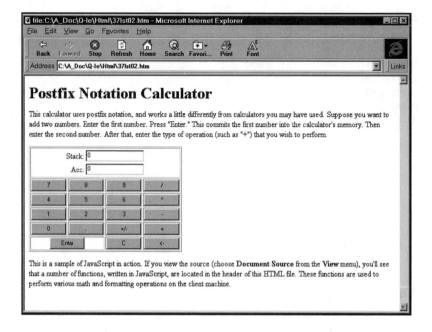

The HTML Page   Listing 34.2 shows the HTML for the calculator's page. For precise alignment, all the buttons are grouped into a table; the *accumulator* (where the answer's displayed) and the *stack* (where operands can be stored) are at the top.

Listing 34.2   34LST02.HTM   The HTML Definition for the RPN Calculator Example

```
<h1>Postfix Notation Calculator</h1>

This calculator uses postfix notation, and works a little differently
from calculators you may have used. Suppose you want to add two
numbers. Enter the first number. Press "Enter." This commits the first
number into the calculator's memory. Then enter the second number.
After that, enter the type of operation (such as "+") that you wish to
perform.

<form method="post">

<table border="1" align=center>
<tr align="center">
<td colspan = 4>

<table border="0">
<tr>
<td align=right>Stack:</td><td><input name="stack" value="0"></td>
</tr>
```

```
<tr>
<td align=right>Acc:</td><td><input name="display" value="0"></td>
</tr>
</table>

</td>
</tr>

<tr align=center>
<td>
<input type="button" value=" 7 "
  onClick="addChar(this.form.display, '7')">
</td>
<td>
<input type="button" value=" 8 "
  onClick="addChar(this.form.display, '8')">
</td>
<td>
<input type="button" value=" 9 "
  onClick="addChar(this.form.display, '9')">
</td>
<td>
<input type="button" value=" / "
  onClick="divide(this.form)">
</td>
</tr>

<tr align=center>
<td>
<input type="button" value=" 4 "
  onClick="addChar(this.form.display, '4')">
</td>
<td>
<input type="button" value=" 5 "
  onClick="addChar(this.form.display, '5')">
</td>
<td>
<input type="button" value=" 6 "
  onClick="addChar(this.form.display, '6')">
</td>
<td>
<input type="button" value=" * "
  onClick="multiply(this.form)">
</td>
</tr>

<tr align=center>
<td>
<input type="button" value=" 1 "
  onClick="addChar(this.form.display, '1')">
</td>
<td>
<input type="button" value=" 2 "
  onClick="addChar(this.form.display, '2')">
</td>
```

Part

VI

Ch

34

continues

Listing 34.2 Continued

```html
<td>
<input type="button" value=" 3 "
  onClick="addChar(this.form.display, '3')">
</td>
<td>
<input type="button" value=" - "
  onClick="subtract(this.form)">
</td>
</tr>

<tr align=center>
<td>
<input type="button" value=" 0 "
  onClick="addChar(this.form.display, '0')">
</td>
<td>
<input type="button" value=" . "
  onClick="addChar(this.form.display, '.')">
</td>
<td>
<input type="button" value="+/-"
  onClick="changeSign(this.form.display)">
</td>
<td>
<input type="button" value=" + "
  onClick="add(this.form)">
</td>
</tr>

<tr align=center>
<td colspan="2">
<input type="button" value=" Enter " name="enter"
  onClick="pushStack(this.form)">
</td>
<td>
<input type="button" value=" C "
  onClick="this.form.display.value = 0 ">
</td>
<td>
<input type="button" value=" <- "
  onClick="deleteChar(this.form.display)">
</td>
</tr>

</table>
</form>
```

This is a sample of JavaScript in action. If you view the source (choose <B>Document Source</B> from the <B>View</B> menu), you'll see that a number of functions, written in JavaScript, are located in the header of this HTML file. These functions are used to perform various math and formatting operations on the client machine.

Notice that each button has an onClick() definition associated with it. The digits 0 through 9 all call the addChar() JavaScript function; the editing keys, C for clear and <- for backspace, call functions that change the value of the accumulator. The Enter key stores the current value on the stack, and the +/- button changes the accumulator's sign.

Of course, the operators themselves call JavaScript functions, too; for example, the * button's definition calls the Multiply() function. The definitions aren't functions themselves; they include function calls (as for the digits) or individual statements (as in the "clear" key).

The JavaScript Of course, all these onClick() triggers need to have JavaScript routines to call. Listing 34.3 shows the JavaScript functions that implement the actual calculator.

Listing 34.3 34LST03.HTM The JavaScript Code That Makes the RPN Calculator Functional

```
<script language="JavaScript">

<!-- hide this script tag's contents from old browsers

// keep track of whether we just computed display.value
var computed = false

function pushStack(form)
{
    form.stack.value = form.display.value
    form.display.value = 0
}

//
// Define a function to add a new character to the display
//
function addChar(input, character)
{
    // auto-push the stack if the last value was computed
    if(computed) {
     pushStack(input.form)
     computed = false
    }

    // make sure input.value is a string
    if(input.value == null || input.value == "0")
        input.value = character
    else
        input.value += character
}

function deleteChar(input)
{
    input.value = input.value.substring(0, input.value.length - 1)
}

function add(form)
```

continues

Listing 34.3   Continued

```
{
    form.display.value = parseFloat(form.stack.value)
                       + parseFloat(form.display.value)
    computed = true
}

function subtract(form)
{
    form.display.value = form.stack.value - form.display.value
    computed = true
}

function multiply(form)
{
    form.display.value = form.stack.value * form.display.value
    computed = true
}

function divide(form)
{
    var divisor = parseFloat(form.display.value)
    if(divisor == 0) {
     alert("Don't divide by zero, pal...");
     return
    }
    form.display.value = form.stack.value / divisor
    computed = true
}

function changeSign(input)
{
    // could use input.value = 0 - input.value, but let's show off substring
    if(input.value.substring(0, 1) == "-")
     input.value = input.value.substring(1, input.value.length)
    else
     input.value = "-" + input.value
}
<!-- done hiding from old browsers -->
</script>
```

As you saw in the HTML shown in Listing 34.2, every button here is connected to some function. The addChar() and deleteChar() functions directly modify the contents of the form field named display—which is the accumulator—as do the operators (add(), subtract(), multiply(), and divide()).

Listing 34.3 shows off some subtle but cool benefits of JavaScript that would be difficult or impossible to do with CGI scripts. First, notice that the divide() function checks for division by zero and presents a warning dialog box to the user.

More important, in this example, all the processing is done on the client—imagine an application like an interactive tax form, where all the calculations are done on the browser and only the completed, verified data gets posted to the server. ●

## CHAPTER 35

Visual Basic Script

In addition to support for Netscape's JavaScript language, Microsoft has given Internet Explorer 3 its own scripting language, Visual Basic Script (VBScript), which is based on the Visual Basic and Visual Basic for Applications languages. Just as those two languages made it much easier to create applications for Windows and within the Microsoft Office suite, respectively, VBScript was designed as a language for easily adding interactivity and dynamic content to Web pages. VBScript gives Web authors the ability to allow Internet Explorer, and other compatible Web browsers and applications, to execute scripts to perform a wide variety of uses, such as verifying and acting on user input, customizing Java applets, interacting with and customizing ActiveX Controls and other OLE-compatible applications, and many other things. ■

What is Visual Basic (VB) Script?

In this chapter, you'll find out about Visual Basic Script, Microsoft's own scripting language for adding interactivity to Internet Explorer and other applications.

How is VBScript related to Visual Basic for Applications and Visual Basic?

Find out how VBScript is related to the Microsoft's Visual Basic for Applications and Visual Basic programming environments.

How does VBScript interact with Internet Explorer?

Learn how to use VBScript to interact with Internet Explorer through the Internet Explorer object model.

What are the VBScript language components?

Learn about the different components of the VBScript programming language.

What is Visual Basic Script?

Like the JavaScript language, first introduced by Netscape and fully supported by Microsoft in Internet Explorer 3, the VBScript scripting language allows you to embed commands into an HTML document. When an Internet Explorer user downloads the page, your VBScript commands are loaded by the Web browser along with the rest of the document and is run in response to any of a series of events. Again, like JavaScript, VBScript is an *interpreted* language; Internet Explorer interprets the VBScript commands when they are loaded and run. They do not first need to be *compiled* into executable form by the Web author who uses them.

VBScript is a fast and flexible subset of Microsoft's Visual Basic and Visual Basic for Applications languages, designed to be easy to program in and for quickly adding active content to HTML documents. The language elements are mainly ones that will be familiar to anyone who has programmed in just about any language, such as If...Then...Else blocks and Do, While, and For...Next loops, and a typical assortment of operators and built-in functions. This chapter attempts to give you an overview of the VBScript language and shows you examples of how to use it to add greater interaction to your Web pages.

N O T E If you are familiar with JavaScript, or have read the previous chapter which discusses it, you will find parts of this chapter to be very similar. That is because JavaScript and VBScript are similar languages, with similar syntax, that can perform many of the same functions.

So, if you know JavaScript, you can probably skip ahead to the "Programming with VBScript" and "Sample VBScript Code" sections later in this chapter, and should probably check out the "VBScript or JavaScript" discussion in the last section. Even if you know JavaScript, unless you have read the previous chapter on JavaScript, you will want to read the "VBScript and Internet Explorer 3" section for information on manipulating elements of the Web browser using VBScript. ■

Why Use a Scripting Language?

HTML provides a good deal of flexibility to page authors, but HTML by itself is static; once written, HTML documents can't interact with the user other than by presenting hyperlinks. Creative use of CGI scripts (which run on Web servers) has made it possible to create more interesting and effective interactive sites, but some applications really demand programs or scripts that are executed by the client.

One of the reasons VBScript was developed was to provide Web authors a way to write small scripts that would execute on the users' browsers instead of on the server. For example, an application that collects data from a form and then posts it to the server can validate the data for completeness and correctness before sending it to the server. This can greatly improve the performance of the browsing session, since users don't have to send data to the server until it's been verified as correct. The following are some other potential applications for VBScript:

■ VB scripts can verify forms for completeness, like a mailing list registration form that checks to make sure the user has entered a name and e-mail address before the form is posted.

■ Pages can display content derived from information stored on the user's computer—without sending that data to the server. For example, a bank can embed VBScript commands in their pages that look up account data from a Quicken file and display it as part of the bank's page.

■ Because VBScript can modify settings for OLE objects and for applets written in Java, page authors can control the size, appearance, and behavior of OLE controls and Java applets being run by Internet Explorer. A page that contains an embedded Java animation might use a VB script to set the Java window size and position before triggering the animation. VBScript can be used to set properties for Internet Explorer 3 itself, since it supports OLE automation.

▶ **See** "Microsoft's ActiveX Technologies" for an overview of the new capabilities that ActiveX can bring to Internet Explorer 3, **p. 591**

▶ **See** "Sun's Java and Internet Explorer" for a description of how Internet Explorer 3 supports Java, **p. 607**

What Can VBScript Do?

VBScript provides a fairly complete set of built-in functions and commands, allowing you to perform math calculations, play sounds, open up new windows and new URLs, and access and verify user input to your Web forms.

Code to perform these actions can be embedded in a page and executed when the page is loaded; you can also write functions that contain code that's triggered by events you specify. For example, you can write a VBScript method that is called when the user clicks the Submit button of a form, or one that is activated when the user clicks a hyperlink on the active page.

VBScript can also set the attributes, or *properties*, of OLE controls or Java applets running in the browser. This way, you can easily change the behavior of plug-ins or other objects without having to delve into their innards. For example, your VBScript code could automatically start playing an embedded .AVI file when the user clicks a button.

How Does VBScript Look in an HTML Document?

VBScript commands are embedded in your HTML documents, either directly or via a URL that tells the browser which scripts to load, just as with JavaScript (and other scripting languages). Embedded VB scripts are enclosed in the HTML container tag <SCRIPT> and </SCRIPT>.

The <SCRIPT> element takes two attributes: LANGUAGE, which specifies the scripting language to use when evaluating the script, and SRC, which specifies a URL from which the script can be loaded. The LANGUAGE attribute is always required, unless the SRC attribute's URL specifies a language. LANGUAGE and SRC can both be used, too. For VBScript, the scripting language is defined as LANGUAGE="VBS". Some examples of valid SCRIPT tags are as follows:

```
<SCRIPT LANGUAGE="VBS">...</SCRIPT>
<SCRIPT SRC="http://www.rpi.edu/~odonnj/scripts/common.VBS">...</SCRIPT>
<SCRIPT LANGUAGE="VBS" SRC="http://www.rpi.edu/~odonnj/scripts/common">...
</SCRIPT>
```

VBScript resembles JavaScript and many other computer languages you may be familiar with. It bears the closest resemblance, as you might imagine, to Visual Basic and Visual Basic for Applications because it is a subset of these two languages. The following are some of the simple rules you need to follow for structuring VB scripts:

- VBScript is case-insensitive, so function, Function, and FUNCTION are all the same. Microsoft has released coding conventions that include a recommended naming and formatting scheme for constants, variables, and other aspects of VB scripts. They are discussed in the "Recommended VBScript Coding Conventions" section in this chapter.

- VBScript is flexible about statements. A single statement can cover multiple lines, if a continuation character, a single underscore (_), is placed at the end of each line to be continued. Also, you can put multiple short statements on a single line by separating each from the next with a colon (:).

VBScript Programming Hints

You should keep in mind a few points when programming with VBScript. These hints will ease your learning process and make your HTML documents that include VB scripts more compatible with a wider range of Web browsers.

Hiding Your Scripts Because VBScript is a new product and is currently supported only by Internet Explorer 3—though Oracle, Spyglass, NetManage, and other companies plan to license the technology for future versions of their Web browsers—you'll probably be designing pages that will be viewed by Web browsers that don't support it. To keep those browsers from misinterpreting your VB script, wrap your scripts as follows:

```
<SCRIPT LANGUAGE="VBS">
<!-- This line opens an HTML comment
VBScript commands...
<!-- This line closes an HTML comment -->
</SCRIPT>
```

The opening <!-- comment causes Web browsers that do not support VBScript to disregard all text they encounter until they find a matching -->, so they don't display your script. Make sure that your <SCRIPT> and </SCRIPT> container elements are outside the comments, though; otherwise, Internet Explorer 3 ignores the whole script.

Comments Including comments in your programs to explain what they do is usually good practice; VBScript is no exception. The VBScript interpreter ignores any text marked as a comment, so don't be shy about including them. Comments in VBScript are set off using the REM statement (short for remark) or by using a single quotation mark (') character. Any text following the REM or single quotation mark, until the end of the line, is ignored. To include a comment on the same line as another VBScript statement, you can use either REM or a single quotation mark. However, if you use REM, you must separate the statement from the REM with a colon (the VBScript multiple-command-per-line separator).

Recommended VBScript Coding Conventions Microsoft has released a whole set of suggestions on how to format and code VBScript programs. The purpose of these suggestions is to standardize the format, structure, and appearance of VBScript programs to make them more readable, understandable, and easier to debug. The full document is available through the Microsoft VBScript home page at **http://www.microsoft.com/vbscript/**.

Some of the major points are summarized as follows:

■ **Variable and Literal Naming**—Because variables and literals are interchangeable and have no fixed data types, distinguish between them by establishing a consistent naming convention.

Literals should be named in all uppercase, with words separated by underscores; for example, MAX_SIZE or END_TIME.

Variables should have descriptive names and be given a prefix indicating the data type they are being used for. Some examples of these prefixes are shown in Table 35.1.

Table 35.1   Recommended Variable Name Prefixes by Data Type

Type	Prefix	Example
Boolean	bln	blnFlag
Single	sng	sngPi
Double	dbl	dblPi
Long	lng	lngPi
Integer	int	intCount
Date (Time)	dtm	dtmToday
String	str	strFilename
Byte	byt	bytCounter
Error	err	errReturn
Object	obj	objForm

■ **Variable Scoping**—VBScript variables may either be scoped at the script level, in which they are accessible by all procedures in the script, or procedure level, in which case they are local to the procedure. It is recommended that variables be given the narrowest scope possible—that is, procedure level—to reduce potential conflicts with variables in other procedures.

■ **Object Naming**—Again, to make code more easily understandable, you should prefix object names to indicate the type of object. Table 35.2 gives a few examples.

Table 35.2   Recommended Object Name Prefixes by Type

Type	Prefix	Example
3D Panel	pnl	pnlGroup
Checkbox	chk	chkReadOnly
Command button	cmd	cmdExitCommon
Dialog	dlg	dlgFileOpen
Frame	fra	fraLanguage
List Box	lst	lstPolicyCodes
Text Box	txt	txtName
Slider	sld	sldScale

 T I P   You may find the suggested naming conventions discussed previously to be cumbersome, and be
tempted to not follow them. If so, you should probably develop a naming convention of your own,
comment it, and follow it.

- **Comments**—Procedures should be commented with a brief description of what they do,
  though not how they do it, since this information may change over time. Comments
  within the procedure should explain how the procedure functions. Arguments should be
  described, if the use isn't obvious.

- **Formatting**—As procedures, conditional statements, and loop structures are used, they
  should be indented to make the structure of the program more easily understood. The
  recommended amount of each level of indent is four spaces.

N O T E   We make an effort to follow most of these coding conventions in the examples presented in
this chapter. However, like all programmers, we are not perfect. ▪

VBScript, Visual Basic, and Visual Basic for Applications

As mentioned previously, VBScript is a subset of the Visual Basic and Visual Basic for Applications languages. If you are familiar with either of these two languages, you will find programming in VBScript very easy. Just as Visual Basic was meant to make the creation of Windows
programs easier and more accessible, and Visual Basic for Applications was meant to do the
same for Microsoft Office applications, VBScript is meant to give an easy-to-learn yet powerful
means for adding interactivity and increased functionality to Web pages.

The VBScript Language

VBScript was designed as a subset of Visual Basic and Visual Basic for Applications. As a subset, it doesn't have as much functionality but was intended to provide a quicker and simpler language for enhancing Web pages and servers. This section discusses some of the building blocks of VBScript and how they are combined into VBScript programs.

Using Identifiers

An *identifier* is just a unique name that VBScript uses to identify a variable, method, or object in your program. As with other programming languages, VBScript imposes some rules on what names you can use. All VBScript names must start with an alphabetic character and can contain both upper- and lowercase letters and the digits 0 through 9. They can be as long as 255 characters, though you probably don't want to go much over 32 or so.

Unlike JavaScript, which supports two different ways for you to represent values in your scripts, literals and variables, VBScript really has only variables. The difference in VBScript, then, is one of usage. You can include literals—constant values—in your VBScript programs by setting a variable equal to a value and not changing it. We will continue to refer to literals and variables as distinct entities, though they are interchangeable.

Literals and variables in VBScript are all of type *variant*, which means that they can contain any type of data that VBScript supports. It is usually a good idea to use a given variable for one type and explicitly convert its value to another type as necessary. The following are some of the types of data that VBScript supports:

- **Integers**—These types can be one, two, or four bytes in length, depending on how big they are.
- **Floating Point**—VBScript supports single- and double-precision floating point numbers.
- **Strings**—Strings can represent words, phrases, or data, and they're set off by double quotation marks.
- **Booleans**—Booleans have a value of either `true` or `false`.

Objects, Properties, Methods, and Events

Before you proceed further, you should take some time to review some terminology that may or may not be familiar to you. VBScript follows much the same object model followed by JavaScript, and uses many of the same terms. In VBScript, just as in JavaScript—and in any object-oriented language for that matter—an *object* is a collection of data and functions that have been grouped together. An object's data is known as its *properties*, and its functions are known as its *methods*. An *event* is a condition to which an object can respond, such as a mouse click or other user input. The VBScript programs that you write make use of properties and methods of objects, both those that you create and objects provided by Internet Explorer 3, its plug-ins, Java applets, and the like.

TIP Here's a simple guideline: an object's properties are the information it knows, its methods are how it can act on that information, and events are what it responds to.

Using Built-In Objects and Functions Individual VBScript elements are objects; for example, literals and variables are objects of type variant, which can be used to hold data of many different types. These objects also have associated methods, ways of acting on the different data types. VBScript also allows you to access a set of useful objects that represent the Internet Explorer browser, the currently displayed page, and other elements of the browsing session.

You access objects by specifying their names. For example, the active document object is named document. To use document's properties or methods, you add a period and the name of the method or property you want. For example, document.title is the title property of the document object.

Using Properties Every object has properties—even literals. To access a property, just use the object name followed by a period and the property name. To get the length of a string object named address, you can write the following:

```
address.length
```

You get back an integer that equals the number of characters in the string. If the object you're using has properties that can be modified, you can change them in the same way. To set the color property of a house object, just write the following:

```
house.color = "blue"
```

You can also create new properties for an object just by naming them. For example, say you define a class called customer for one of your pages. You can add new properties to the customer object as follows:

```
customer.name = "Joe Smith"
customer.address = "123 Elm Street"
customer.zip = "90210"
```

Finally, knowing that an object's methods are just properties is important, so you can easily add new properties to an object by writing your own function and creating a new object property using your own function name. If you want to add a Bill method to your customer object, you can write a function named BillCustomer and set the object's property as follows:

```
customer.Bill = BillCustomer;
```

To call the new method, you just write the following:

```
customer.Bill()
```

HTML Elements Have Properties, Too Internet Explorer provides properties for HTML forms and some types of form fields. VBScript is especially valuable for writing scripts that check or change data in forms. Internet Explorer's properties allow you to get and set the form elements' data, as well as specify actions to be taken when something happens to the form element (as when the user clicks in a text field or moves to another field.) For more details on using HTML object properties, see the section, "HTML Objects and Events."

VBScript and Internet Explorer 3

Now that you have some idea of how VBScript works, you're ready to take a look at how Internet Explorer 3 supports it.

When Scripts Get Executed

When you put VBScript code in a page, Internet Explorer evaluates the code as soon as it's encountered. As Internet Explorer evaluates the code, it converts the code into a more efficient internal format so that the code can be executed later. When you think about this process, it is similar to how HTML is processed; browsers parse and display HTML as they encounter it in the page, not all at once.

Functions, however, don't get executed when they're evaluated; they just get stored for later use. You still have to call functions explicitly to make them work. Some functions are attached to objects, like buttons or text fields on forms, and they are called when some event happens on the button or field. You might also have functions that you want to execute during page evaluation; you can do so by putting a call to the function at the appropriate place in the page, as follows:

```
<SCRIPT language="VBS">
<!--
myFunction()
<!-- -->
</SCRIPT>
```

N O T E   VBScript code to modify the actual HTML contents of a document (as opposed to merely changing the text in a form text input field, for instance) must be executed during page evaluation. ■

Where To Put Your Scripts

You can put scripts anywhere within your HTML page, as long as they're surrounded with the <SCRIPT> and </SCRIPT> tags. One good system is to put functions that will be executed more than once into the <HEAD> element of their pages; this element provides a convenient storage place. Since the <HEAD> element is at the beginning of the file, functions and VBScript code that you put there will be evaluated before the rest of the document is loaded.

Sometimes, though, you have code that shouldn't be evaluated or executed until after all the page's HTML has been parsed and displayed. An example would be a function to print out all the URLs referenced in the page. If this function is evaluated before all the HTML on the page has been loaded, it misses some URLs, so the call to the function should come at the page's end. The function itself can be defined anywhere in the HTML document; it is the function call that should be at the end of the page.

Internet Explorer 3 Objects and Events

In addition to recognizing VBScript when it's embedded inside a <SCRIPT> and </SCRIPT> tag, Internet Explorer 3 also exposes some objects (and their methods and properties) that you can use in your programs. Internet Explorer 3 can also trigger methods you define when the user takes certain actions in the browser.

Browser Objects and Events

Many events that happen in a Internet Explorer browsing session aren't related to items on the page, like buttons or HTML text. Instead, they're related to what's happening in the browser itself, like what page the user is viewing.

> **CAUTION**
>
> Remember that VBScript is a new language, and support for it under Internet Explorer 3 is also very new. As a result, the specifications of the language, as well as the objects, properties, methods, and events supplied by Internet Explorer, may change. Up-to-date information is always available through Microsoft's Internet Explorer Web pages at **http://www.microsoft.com/ie/**.

The *Location* Object   Internet Explorer exposes an object called Location, which holds the current URL, including the hostname, path, CGI script arguments, and even the protocol. Table 35.3 shows the properties of the Location object.

Table 35.3   Internet Explorer's *Location* Object Containing Information on the Currently Displayed URL

Property	What It Contains
href	The entire URL, including all the subparts; for example, **http://www.msn.com/products/msprod.htm**
protocol	The protocol field of the URL, including the first colon; for example, **http:**
host	The hostname and port number; for example, **www.msn.com:80**
hostname	The hostname; for example, **www.msn.com**
port	The port, if specified; otherwise, it's blank
pathname	The path to the actual document; for example, **products/msprod.htm**
hash	Any CGI arguments after the first # in the URL
search	Any CGI arguments after the first ? in the URL

N O T E Internet Explorer object names are not case-sensitive, so references to the following are all equivalent:

```
Location.HREF
location.href
location.Href
LoCaTiOn.HrEf
```

The *Document* Object   Internet Explorer also exposes an object called Document; as you might expect, this object exposes useful properties and methods of the active document. Location refers only to the URL of the active document, but Document refers to the document itself. Table 35.4 shows Document's properties and methods.

Table 35.4   Internet Explorer's *Document* Object Containing Information on the Currently Loaded and Displayed HTML Page

Property	What It Contains
title	Title of the current page, or Untitled if no title exists
location	The document's address (read-only)
lastModified	The page's last-modified date
forms	Array of all the FORMs in the current page
links	Array of all the HREF anchors in the current page
anchors	Array of all the anchors in the current page
linkColor	Link color
alinkColor	Link color
vlinkColor	Visited link color
bgColor	Background color
fgColor	Foreground color
Method	What It Does
write	Writes HTML to the current page
writeln	Writes HTML to the current page, followed by a

The *Window* Object   Internet Explorer creates a Window object for every document. Think of the Window object as an actual window and the Document object as the content that appears in the window. Internet Explorer provides the properties and methods for working in the window shown in Table 35.5.

Part
VI

Ch
35

Table 35.5 Internet Explorer's _Window_ Object Containing Information on the Web Browser Window

Property	What It Contains
name	Current window name (currently set to return Microsoft Internet Explorer")
parent	Window objects parent
self	Current window
top	The topmost window
location	The location object
status	The text in the lower left of the status bar
Method	**What It Does**
alert(_string_)	Puts up an alert dialog box and displays the message given in _string_
confirm(_string_)	Puts up a confirmation dialog box with OK and Cancel buttons, and displays the message given in _string_; this function returns true when users click OK and false otherwise
navigate(_URL_)	Takes the user to the specified _URL_ in the current window

CAUTION

If you have programmed in JavaScript for Netscape Navigator, you will notice that the object model used by Netscape is very similar to the one used by Microsoft Internet Explorer. Be very careful when converting a program from one Web browser to the other and one scripting language to the other, however, to make sure that there aren't any subtle differences that might come back to haunt you.

HTML Objects and Events

Internet Explorer represents some individual HTML elements as objects, and these objects have properties and methods attached to them just like every other. You can use these objects to customize your pages' behavior by attaching VBScript code to the appropriate methods.

Properties for Generic HTML Objects   The methods and properties in this section apply to several HTML tags; note that there are other methods and properties, discussed after the following table, for anchors and form elements. Table 35.6 shows the features that these generic HTML objects provide.

Table 35.6   Methods and Events That Allow You To Control the Contents and Behavior of HTML Elements

Method	What It Does
focus()	Calls to move the input focus to the specified object
blur()	Calls to move the input focus away from the specified object
select()	Calls to select the specified object
click()	Calls to click the specified object, which must be a button
Event	When It Occurs
onFocus	When the user moves the input focus to the field, either via the Tab key or a mouse click
onBlur	When the user moves the input focus out of this field
onSelect	When the user selects text in the field
onChange	Only when the field loses focus and the user has modified its text; use this function to validate data in a field
onSubmit	When the user submits the form (if the form has a Submit button)
onClick	When the button is clicked

Note that focus(), blur(), select(), and click() are methods of objects; to call them, you use the name of the object you want to affect. For example, to turn off the button named Search, you type **form.search.disable( )**.

Properties for *Link* Objects   The Link object is referenced as a read-only property array, consisting of an object for each link that appears in the HTML document. The properties of each of these objects are the same as those for Location objects. The events are onMouseMove, which fires whenever the mouse moves over a link, and onClick, which fires when a link is clicked. You can modify and set these methods just like others. Remember that no matter what code you attach, Internet Explorer 3 is still going to follow the clicked link—it executes your code first, though.

Properties for *Form* Objects   Table 35.7 lists the properties exposed for HTML Form elements.

Part
VI

Ch
35

Table 35.7 HTML Form Special Properties That You Can Use in Your VB Script Code

Property	What It Contains
name	The value of the form's NAME attribute
method	The value of the form's METHOD attribute
action	The value of the form's ACTION attribute
elements	The elements array of the form
encoding	The value if the form's ENCODING attribute
target	Window targeted after submit for form response

Method	What It Does
submit()	Any form element can force the form to be submitted by calling the form's submit() method.

Event	When It Occurs
onSubmit()	When the form is submitted; this method can't stop the submission, though.

Properties for Objects in a Form   A good place to use VBScript is in forms, since you can write scripts that process, check, and perform calculations with the data the user enters. VBScript provides a useful set of properties and methods for text INPUT elements and buttons.

You use INPUT elements in a form to let the user enter text data; VBScript provides properties to get the objects that hold the element's contents, as well as methods for doing something when the user moves into or out of a field. Table 35.8 shows the properties and methods that are defined for text INPUT elements.

Table 35.8 Properties and Methods That Allow You To Control the Contents and Behavior of HTML *INPUT* Elements

Property	What It Contains
name	The value of the element's NAME attribute
value	The field's contents
defaultValue	The initial contents of the field; returns " " if blank.

Method	What It Does
onFocus	Called when the user moves the input focus to the field, either via the Tab key or a mouse click

Method	What It Does
onBlur	Called when the user moves the input focus out of this field
onSelect	Called when the user selects text in the field
onChange	Called only when the field loses focus and the user has modified its text; use this action to validate data in a field

Individual buttons and checkboxes have properties, too; VBScript provides properties to get objects containing the buttons' data, as well as methods for doing something when the user selects or deselects a particular button. Table 35.9 shows some of the properties and methods that are defined for button elements.

Table 35.9 Properties and Methods That Allow You To Control the Contents and Behavior of HTML Button and Checkbox Elements

Property	What It Contains
name	The value of the button's NAME attribute
value	The VALUE attribute
checked	The state of a checkbox
defaultChecked	The initial state of a checkbox
Method	**What It Does**
click()	Clicks a button and triggers whatever actions are attached to it
Event	**When It Occurs**
onClick	Called when the button is pressed.

As an example of what you can do with VBScript and the objects, properties, and methods outlined, you might want to put the user's cursor into the first text field in a form automatically, instead of making the user manually click the field. If your first text field is named UserName, you can put the following in your document's script to get the behavior you want:

```
form.UserName.focus()
```

Programming with VBScript

Part VI · Ch 35

As you've learned in the preceding sections, VBScript has a lot to offer Web page authors. It's not as flexible as C or C++, but it's quick and simple. But, since it is easily embedded in your Web pages, adding interactivity with a little VBScript is easy. This section covers more details about VBScript programming, including a detailed explanation of the language's features.

Variables and Literals

VBScript variables are all of the type *variant*, which means that they can be used for any of the supported data types. Constants in VBScript, called *literals*, are similar to variables and can also be of any type. In fact, VBScript doesn't really have any "constants" in the usual sense of the word, since VBScript treats literals the same as variables. The difference lies in how the programmer uses them. Because of the fact that no differences really exist between literals and variables, and because variables can contain any kind of data, using a naming convention similar to the one described in the section "Recommended VBScript Coding Conventions" to keep track of what is a good idea.

The types of data that VBScript variables and literals can hold are summarized in Table 35.10.

Table 35.10 The Different Data Types That VBScript Variables and Literals Can Contain	
Type	**Description**
Empty	Uninitialized and is treated as 0 or the empty string, depending on the context
Null	Intentionally contains no valid data
Boolean	`true` or `false`
Byte	Integer in the range –128 to 127
Integer	Integer in the range –32,768 to 32,767
Long	Integer in the range –2,147,483,648 to 2,147,483,647
Single	Single-precision floating point number in the range –3.402823E38 to –1.401298E-45 for negative values and 1.401298E-45 to 3.402823E38 for positive values
Double	Double-precision floating point number in the range –1.79769313486232E308 to –4.94065645841247E-324 for negative values; 4.94065645841247E-324 to 1.79769313486232E308 for positive values
Date	Number that represents a date between January 1, 100 to December 31, 9999
String	Variable-length string up to approximately 2 billion characters in length
Object	OLE Automation object
Error	Error number

Expressions

An *expression* is anything that can be evaluated to get a single value. Expressions can contain string or numeric literals, variables, operators, and other expressions, and they can range from simple to quite complex. For example, the following is an expression that uses the assignment operator (more on operators in the next section) to assign the result 3.14159 to the variable x:

```
sngPi = 3.14159
```

By contrast, the following is a more complex expression whose final value depends on the values of the two Boolean variables blnQuit and blnComplete:

```
(blnQuit = TRUE) And (blnComplete = FALSE)
```

Operators

Operators do just what their name suggests: they operate on variables or literals. The items that an operator acts on are called its *operands*. Operators come in the two following types:

- **Unary**—These operators require only one operand, and the operator can come before or after the operand. The Not operator, which performs the logical negation of an expression, is a good example.

- **Binary**—These operators need two operands. The four math operators (+ for addition, – for subtraction, × for multiplication, and / for division) are all binary operators, as is the = assignment operator you saw earlier.

Assignment Operators   *Assignment operators* take the result of an expression and assign it to a variable. One feature that VBScript has that most other programming languages don't is that you can change a variable's type on-the-fly. Consider this example:

```
Sub TypeDemo
    Dim sngPi
    sngPi = 3.14159
    document.write "Pi is " & CStr(sngPi) & "<BR>"
    sngPi = FALSE
    document.write "Pi is " & CStr(sngPi) & "<BR>"
End Sub
```

This short function first prints the (correct) value of *pi*. In most other languages, though, trying to set a floating point variable to a Boolean value either generates a compiler error or a runtime error. Because VBScript variables can be any type, it happily accepts the change and prints Pi's new value: false.

The assignment operator, =, simply assigns the value of an expression's right side to its left side. In the preceding example, the variable sngPi gets the floating point value 3.14159 or the Boolean value false after the expression is evaluated.

Math Operators   The previous sections gave you a sneak preview of the math operators that VBScript furnishes. As you might expect, the standard four math functions (addition, subtraction, multiplication, and division) work just as they do on an ordinary calculator, and use the symbols +, –, ×, and /. The symbol for subtraction (–) also doubles as the negation operator. It is a unary operator that negates the sign of its operand. To use the negation operator, you must put the operator before the operand.

VBScript supplies three other math operators:

- \—The backslash operator divides its first operand by its second, after first rounding floating point operands to the nearest integer, and returns an integer result. For example, 19 \ 6.7 returns 2 (6.7 rounds to 7, which divides evenly into 19 twice).

- Mod—This operator is similar to \ in that it divides the first operand by its second, after again rounding floating point operands to the nearest integer, and returns the integer remainder. So, 19 Mod 6.7 returns 5.

- ^—This exponent operator returns the first operand raised to the power of the second. The first operand can be negative only if the second, the exponent, is an integer.

Comparison Operators   Comparing the value of two expressions to see whether one is larger, smaller, or equal to another is often necessary. VBScript supplies several comparison operators that take two operands and return true if the comparison is true and false if it's not. (Remember, you can use literals, variables, or expressions with operators that require expressions.) Table 35.11 shows the VBScript comparison operators.

Table 35.11   Comparison Operators That Allow Two VBScript Operands To Be Compared

Operator	Read It As	Returns *true* When:
=	Equals	The two operands are equal
<>	Does not equal	The two operands are unequal
<	Less than	The left operand is less than the right operand
<=	Less than or equal to	The left operand is less than or equal to the right operand
>	Greater than	The left operand is greater than the right operand
>=	Greater than or equal to	The left operand is greater than or equal to the right operand

 TIP   The comparison operators can be used on strings, too; the results depend on standard lexicographic ordering.

Thinking of the comparison operators as questions may be helpful. When you write

```
(x >= 10)
```

you're really saying, "Is the value of variable x greater than or equal to 10?" The return value answers the question, true or false.

Logical Operators   Comparison operators compare quantity or content for numeric and string expressions, but sometimes you need to test a logical value—like whether a comparison operator returns true or false. VBScript's logical operators allow you to compare expressions that return logical values. The following are VBScript's logical operators:

- And—The And operator returns true if both its input expressions are true. If the first operand evaluates to false, And returns false immediately, without evaluating the second operand. Here's an example:

```
blnX = TRUE And TRUE      ' blnX is TRUE
blnX = TRUE And FALSE     ' blnX is FALSE
blnX = FALSE And TRUE     ' blnX is FALSE
blnX = FALSE And FALSE    ' blnX is FALSE
```

- Or—This operator returns true if either of its operands is true. If the first operand is true, ¦¦ returns true without evaluating the second operand. Here's an example:

```
blnX = TRUE Or TRUE       ' blnX is TRUE
blnX = TRUE Or FALSE      ' blnX is TRUE
blnX = FALSE Or TRUE      ' blnX is TRUE
blnX = FALSE Or FALSE     ' blnX is FALSE
```

- Not—This operator takes only one expression, and it returns the opposite of that expression, so Not true returns false, and Not false returns true.

- Xor—This operator, which stands for "exclusive or," returns true if either but not both of its input expressions are true, as in the following:

```
blnX = TRUE Xor TRUE      ' blnX is FALSE
blnX = TRUE Xor FALSE     ' blnX is TRUE
blnX = FALSE Xor TRUE     ' blnX is TRUE
blnX = FALSE Xor FALSE    ' blnX is FALSE
```

- Eqv—This operator, which stands for "equivalent," returns true if its two input expressions are the same—either both true or both false. The statement blnX Eqv blnY is equivalent to Not (blnX Xor blnY).

- Imp—This operator, which stands for "implication," returns true according to the following:

```
blnX = TRUE Imp TRUE      ' blnX is TRUE
blnX = FALSE Imp TRUE     ' blnX is TRUE
blnX = TRUE Imp FALSE     ' blnX is FALSE
blnX = FALSE Imp FALSE    ' blnX is TRUE
```

N O T E Note that the logical implication operator, Imp, is the only logical operator for which the order of the operands is important. ■

Note that the And and Or operators don't evaluate the second operand if the first operand provides enough information for the operator to return a value. This process, called *short circuit evaluation*, can be significant when the second operand is a function call.

N O T E Note that all six of the logical operators can also operate on non-Boolean expressions. In this case, the logical operations described previously are performed bitwise, on each bit of the two operands. For instance, for the two integers 19 (00010011 in binary) and 6 (0000110):

```
19 And 6 =    2 (00000010 in binary)
19 Or 6  =   23 (00010111 in binary)
Not 19   = -20 (11101100 in binary) ■
```

String Concatenation   The final VBScript operator is the string concatenation operator, &. While the addition operator, +, can also be used to concatenate strings, using & it is better because it is less ambiguous.

Controlling Your VBScripts

Sometimes the scripts that you write are very simple and execute the same way each time they are loaded—a script to display a graphic animation, for instance. However, in order to write a script that will perform different functions depending on different user inputs or other conditions, you will eventually need to add a little more sophistication. VBScript provides statements and loops for controlling the execution of your programs based on a variety of inputs.

Testing Conditions   VBScript provides one control structure for making decisions—the If...Then...Else structure. To make a decision, you supply one or more expressions that evaluate to true or false; which code is executed depends on what your expressions evaluate to.

The simplest form of If...Then...Else uses only the If...Then part. If the specified condition is true, the code following the condition is executed; if not, that code is skipped. For example, in the following code fragment, the message appears only if the variable sngX is less than sngPi:

```
if (sngX < sngPi) then document.write("X is less that Pi")
```

You can use any expression as the condition; since expressions can be nested and combined with the logical operators, your tests can be pretty sophisticated. Also, using the multiple statement character, you can execute multiple commands, as in the following:

```
if ((blnTest = TRUE) And (sngX > sngMax)) then sngMax = sngX : blnTest = FALSE
```

The else clause allows you to specify a set of statements to execute when the condition is false. In the same single line form as shown in the preceding line, your new line appears as follows:

```
if (sngX > sngPi) then blnTest = TRUE else blnTest = FALSE
```

A more versatile use of the `If...Then...Else` allows multiple lines and multiple actions for each case. It looks something like the following:

```
if (sngX> sngPi) then
    blnTest = TRUE
    intCount = intCount + 1
else
    blnTest = FALSE
    intCount = 0
end if
```

Note that, with this syntax, additional test clauses using the `elseif` statement are permitted.

Repeating Actions   If you want to repeat an action more than once, VBScript provides a variety of constructs for doing so. The first, called a `For...Next` loop, executes a set of statements some number of times. You specify three expressions: an *initial* expression, which sets the values of any variables you need to use; a *condition*, which tells the loop how to see when it's done; and an *increment* expression, which modifies any variables that need it. Here's a simple example:

```
for intCount = 1 to 100
    document.write "Count is " & CStr(intCount) & "<BR>"
next
```

This loop executes 100 times and prints out a number each time.

Related to the `For...Next` loop is the `For Each...Next` loop. You use this construct as follows:

```
Dim intA(3)
intA(0) = 256
intA(1) = 324
intA(2) = 100
for each intI in intA
    document.write "intA element: " & CStr(intI) & "<BR>"
next
```

This `For Each...Next` loop executes the loop once for each element in the array `intA`, each time assigning `intI` to that value.

The third form of loop is the `While...Wend` loop. It executes statements as long as its condition is true. For example, you can rewrite the first `For...Next` loop as follows:

```
intCount = 1
while (intCount <= 100)
    document.write "Count is " & CStr(intCount) & "<BR>"
    intCount = intCount + 1
wend
```

Part

VI

Ch

35

The last type of loop is the `Do...Loop`, which has several forms, either testing the condition at the beginning or the end. When used as `Do While`, the test is at the beginning, and the loop executes as long as the test condition is true, similar to the `While...Wend` loop. Here's an example:

```
intCount = 1
do while (intCount <= 100)
    document.write "Count is " & CStr(intCount) & "<BR>"
    intCount = intCount + 1
loop
```

An example of having the test at the end, as a `Do...Until`, can also yield equivalent results. In that case, the loop looks like the following:

```
intCount = 1
do
    document.write "Count is " & CStr(intCount) & "<BR>"
    intCount = intCount + 1
until (intCount = 101)
```

One other difference between these two forms is that when the test is at the end of the loop, as in the second case, the commands in the loop are executed at least once. If the test is at the beginning, that is not the case.

Which form you prefer depends on what you're doing; `For...Next` and `For Each...Next` loops are useful when you want to perform an action a set number of times, and `While...Wend` and `Do...Loop` loops are best when you want to keep doing something as long as a particular condition remains true.

NOTE Additional options to the `For...Next`, `For Each...Next`, and `Do...Loop` loops are discussed in the the following section. ▓

Command Reference

This section provides a quick reference to many of the VBScript statements. The statements use the following formatting:

- All VBScript keywords are in `monospaced` font.
- Words in *italics* represent user-defined names or statements.
- Any portions enclosed in square brackets ([and]) are optional.
- Portions enclosed in braces ({ and }) and separated by a vertical bar (¦) represent an option, of which one must be selected.
- The word `statements...` indicates a block of one or more statements.

The *Call* Statement   The `Call` statement calls a VBScript `Sub` or `Function` procedure.

Syntax:

```
Call MyProc([arglist])
```

or

```
MyProc [arglist]
```

Note that *arglist* is a comma-delimited list of zero or more arguments to be passed to the procedure. When the second form is used, omitting the Call statement, the parentheses around the argument list, if any, must also be omitted.

The *Dim* Statement   The Dim statement is used to declare variables and also allocate the storage necessary for them. If you specify subscripts, you can also create arrays.

Syntax:

```
Dim varname[([subscripx)][,varname[([subscripx)],...]
```

The *Do...Loop* Construct   The Do...Loop is a flexible structure for building loops for repeated statement execution. It can test the loop condition either at the beginning or the end of the loop, executing either while the condition is true or until it is true.

Syntax:

```
Do [{While¦Until} condition]
    statements...
[Exit Do]
    statements...
Loop
```

or

```
Do
    statements...
[Exit Do]
    statements...
Loop [{While¦Until} condition]
```

Note that if the optional condition is left out, the loop will execute indefinitely unless the Exit Do statement is used. This statement, probably used in conjunction with an If...Then...Else construct, allows execution of the loop to be terminated from within the loop.

The *For...Next* Loop   The For...Next loop allows a block of statements to be executed a fixed number of times.

Syntax:

```
For counter = start To end [Step step]
    statements...
[Exit For]
    statements...
Next
```

Part
VI

Ch
35

As with the `Do...Loop`, `Exit For` in conjunction with an `If...Then...Else` condition, allows the loop to be executed before the counter has run all the way to the end.

The *For Each...Next* Loop   The `For Each...Next` loop is a variant of the `For...Next` that iterates through the values of an array or a collection of objects. For each element in the array, for instance, the loop is executed.

Syntax:

```
For Each element In group
    statements...
[Exit For]
    statements...
Next
```

The *Function* and *Sub* Statements   The `Function` and `Sub` statements declare VBScript procedures. The difference is that a `Function` procedure returns a value, and a `Sub` procedure does not. All parameters are passed to functions by value—the function gets the value of the parameter but cannot change the original value in the caller.

Syntax:

```
[Static] Function funcname([arglist])
    statements...
    funcname = returnvalue
End
```

and

```
[Static] Sub subname([arglist])
    statements...
End
```

Variables can be declared with the `Dim` statement within a `Function` or `Sub` procedure. In this case, those variables are local to that procedure and can only be referenced within it. If the `Static` keyword is used when the procedure is declared, then all local variables retain their value from one procedure call to the next.

The *If...Then...Else* Statement   The `If...Then...Else` statement is a conditional statement that executes statements based on test conditions being true. You can use it in a single- or multiple-line form.

Syntax:

```
If (condition) Then statements... [Else statements...]
```

or

```
If (condition) Then
    statements...
[Elseif (condition) Then
    statements...]...
[Else
    statements...]
End If
```

In the single-line form, multiple statements in either the If...Then or the Else clause must be separated by colons.

The *LSet, Mid,* and *RSet* Statements   The LSet, Mid, and RSet statements are used to manipulate strings. LSet and RSet are used to copy one string into another, left and right aligning it, respectively. If the receiving string is longer, the remainder is padded with spaces; if shorter, the string being copied is truncated. The Mid statement places one string into a specified position within another.

Syntax:

```
LSet string1 = string2
```

or

```
RSet string1 = string2
```

or

```
Mid(string1,start[,length]) = string2
```

The *On Error* Statement   The On Error statement is used to enable error handling.

Syntax:

```
On Error Resume Next
```

On Error Resume Next enables execution to continue immediately after the statement that provokes the runtime error. Or, if the error occurs in a procedure call after the last executed On Error statement, execution commences immediately after that procedure call. This way, execution can continue despite a runtime error, allowing you to build an error-handling routine inline within the procedure. The most recent On Error Resume Next statement is the one that is active, so you should execute one in each procedure in which you want to have inline error handling.

The *While...Wend* Statement   The While...Wend statement is another looping statement, equivalent to one of the ways in which the Do...Loop can be used. Because the Do...Loop is much more versatile, it is recommended that you use that construct.

Syntax:

```
While (condition)
    statements...
Wend
```

Sample VBScript Code

Usually the quickest way to pick up a new programming language is to jump write in and try it—not spend hours studying the reference manual. And the easiest way to get started doing that is to take a look at some examples. In this section, you examine a few examples we found through the Microsoft VBScript Home page at **http://www.microsoft.com/vbscript/**. These examples give you a flavor of what VBScript can add to your Web pages.

Part
VI
Ch
35

The Classic "Hello, World!" Example

The classic first program in any new programming language is one that prints out the familiar "Hello, world!". An HTML document and VBScript for printing this message are shown in Listing 35.1.

Listing 35.1   35LST01.HTM   The HTML Document for the Classic "Hello, World!" Program Using VBScript

```
<HTML>
<TITLE>Hello World</TITLE>
<CENTER>
     <B><I><FONT FACE="Comic Sans MS" SIZE=5 COLOR=navy>My first "Active
document"</B></I><BR><BR>
     <INPUT TYPE=BUTTON VALUE="Click me" NAME="BtnHello">
</CENTER>
<SCRIPT LANGUAGE=VBS>
     Sub BtnHello_OnClick
          MsgBox "Hello, world!", 0, "My first active document"
     End Sub
</SCRIPT>
</HTML>
```

When you view this HTML document using Internet Explorer, you should see the Web page shown in figure 35.1. Clicking the Click me box opens the message box shown in figure 35.2 with this favorite message.

FIG. 35.1
Clicking the Click me
button runs a VBScript.

FIG. 35.2
VBScript responds to the button click event and displays the "Hello, world!" alert box.

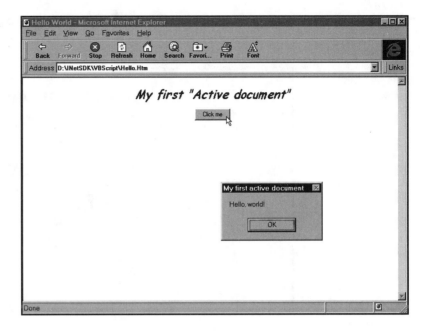

Enhancing Client-Side Imagemaps

With Internet Explorer 3, Microsoft has added support for client-side imagemaps. This example shows how, using a VBScript, you can enhance a page with an imagemap. In this example, as the mouse cursor is moved over different areas of the map, the contents of a text field are changed to give some descriptive information about the corresponding link. This script isn't particularly amazing, but you can imagine the possibilities of being able to take certain actions depending on the position of the user's mouse cursor, without requiring a mouse click.

▶ **See** "Setting Up Client-Side Imagemaps" for an explanation of how to use client-side imagemaps, **p. 466**

Figures 35.3 and 35.4 illustrate how the text field changes depending on the position of the mouse cursor. Listings 35.2 and 35.3 show the two parts of the HTML document for this example; Listing 35.2 shows the HTML code, indicating where the VBScript code should be inserted in the <HEAD> section, and Listing 35.3 shows the VBScript code.

Part
VI

Ch
35

FIG. 35.3
A simple VB script can read the position of the mouse cursor and update information in the page accordingly.

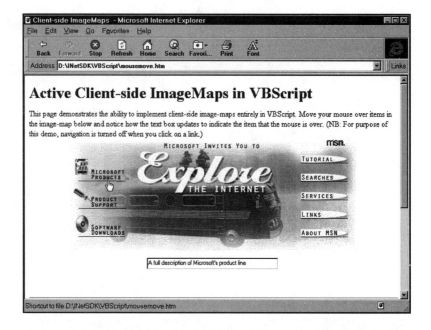

FIG. 35.4
As the mouse moves over different parts of the clickable imagemap, the text field changes to describe the corresponding link

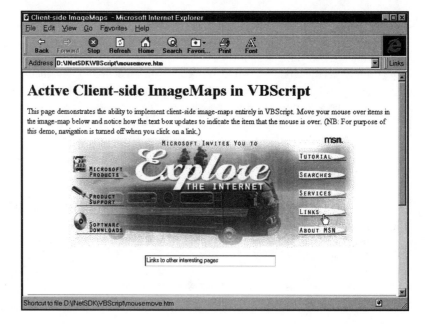

Listing 35.2   *35LST02.HTM*   The HTML Section: the Text in the Input Field is Updated Depending on Where the Mouse Is

```
<html>
<head>
<script language="vbs">
<!-- insert 35lst03.htm -->
</script>
</head>
<body>
<title> Client-side ImageMaps </title>

<H1> Active Client-side ImageMaps in VBScript </em> </H1>

This page demonstrates the ability to implement client-side image-maps
entirely in VBScript. Move your mouse over items in the image-map below
and notice how the text box updates to indicate the item that the
mouse is over. (NB: For purpose of this demo, navigation is turned off
when you click on a link.)

<center>
    <A id="link1" href="">
    <IMG SRC="msn-home.bmp" ALT="Clickable Map Image" WIDTH=590 HEIGHT=224
        BORDER=0>
    </A>
    <br> <br>
    <input type="text" name="text2" size=50>
</center>

<br> <br> <br>

<HR>

<H2> How it's done </H2>

The document contains an anchor named <tt> link1 </tt>. We define a VB
procedure hooked up to the mousemove and test to see what part of the
image the pointer is in, taking actions as appropriate.

<pre>
Sub link1_MouseMove(s,b,x,y)
last_x = x
last_y = y

if (InRect(x, y,  5, 30, 120, 85)=true) then
    DescribeLink "A full description of Microsoft's product line"

Else ...
</pre>
```

continues

Part

VI

Ch

35

Listing 35.2   Continued

```
We remember the last x and y coordinate clicked on so that in the click
event handler (which doesn't take x and y arguments) we can decide where
the user wants to go.

"View Source" on this document for full details on how it's done.
</body>
</html>
```

Listing 35.3   *35LST03.HTM*   The VBScript Commands for Implementing the Enhanced Client-Side Imagemap

```
<SCRIPT for="link1" event="OnClick" language="VBS">
alert "hello world"
</script>

<SCRIPT language="VBS">
' Remember the last location clicked on
DIM last_x
DIM last_y
last_x = 0
last_y = 0

Sub link1_MouseMove(s,b,x,y)
last_x = x
last_y = y
if (InRect(x, y,   5, 30, 120, 85)=true) then
    DescribeLink "A full description of Microsoft's product line"
Elseif (InRect(x, y,   5, 95, 120, 135)=true) then
    DescribeLink "Microsoft's product support options"
Elseif (InRect(x, y,   5, 150, 120, 190)=true) then
    DescribeLink "Download Free Microsoft Software"
Elseif (InRect(x, y,   470, 30, 570, 47)=true) then
    DescribeLink "A Tutorial on how to use MSN"
Elseif (InRect(x, y,   470, 70, 570, 87)=true) then
    DescribeLink "Search the Internet"
Elseif (InRect(x, y,   470, 105, 570, 122)=true) then
    DescribeLink "WWW Services"
Elseif (InRect(x, y,   470, 140, 570, 157)=true) then
    DescribeLink "Links to other interesting pages"
Elseif (InRect(x, y,   470, 175, 570, 192)=true) then
    DescribeLink "About the Microsoft Network"
Else
    DescribeLink ""
End If
End Sub

Sub link1_OnClick
if (InRect(last_x, last_y,   5, 30, 120, 85)=true) then
    Alert "Going to products"
    location.href = "http://www.msn.com/products/msprod.htm"
```

```
Elseif (InRect(last_x, last_y,  5, 95, 120, 135)=true) then
    Alert "Going to support options"
    location.href = "http://www.microsoft.com/support/"
Elseif (InRect(last_x, last_y,  5, 150, 120, 190)=true) then
    Alert "Going to Download Free Microsoft Software"
    location.href = "http://www.msn.com/products/intprod.htm"
Elseif (InRect(last_x, last_y,  470, 30, 570, 47)=true) then
    Alert "Going to A Tutorial on how to use MSN"
    location.href = "http://www.msn.com/tutorial/default.html"
Elseif (InRect(last_x, last_y,  470, 70, 570, 87)=true) then
    Alert "Going to Search the Internet"
    location.href = "http://www.msn.com/access/allinone.hv1"
Elseif (InRect(last_x, last_y,  470, 105, 570, 122)=true) then
    Alert "Going to WWW Services"
    location.href = "http://www.msn.com/access/ref.hv1"
Elseif (InRect(last_x, last_y,  470, 140, 570, 157)=true) then
    Alert "Going to Links to other interesting pages"
    location.href = "http://www.msn.com/access/links/other.htm"
Elseif (InRect(last_x, last_y,  470, 175, 570, 192)=true) then
    Alert "About the Microsoft Network"
    location.href = "http://www.msn.com/about/msn.htm"
End If
End Sub

Function InRect(x, y, rx1, ry1, rx2, ry2)
    InRect =  x>=rx1 AND x<=rx2 AND y>=ry1 AND y<=ry2
End Function

Sub DescribeLink(text)
    text2.value = text
End Sub

</script>
```

Interacting with Form Data

This next example shows a classic use of a client-side scripting language, one that is used to interact with the user when entering data into a form. In this case, the VBScript reads in the current state of a set of radio buttons indicating a choice of pizza, and it sets other elements in the form accordingly.

Figures 35.5 and 35.6 show this example with the pizza type selected, the checkboxes showing the toppings, the text field description, and the cost.

Part
VI

Ch
35

FIG. 35.5
VB scripts can be used to assist in the filling out of forms, depending on user selections of some form elements.

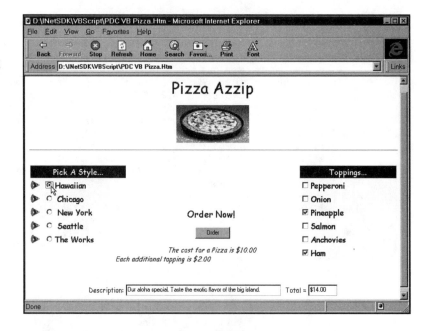

FIG. 35.6
If you use VBScript in this manner, the user is given the choice of a preset selection (for example, a "Hawaiian") or a custom selection of his or her own.

Figure 35.7 shows another function of the VBScript and its use with forms. When the user clicks the Submit button, the script verifies the user's input (including making sure that the user hasn't changed the cost field to get a cheaper pizza) before performing the appropriate action, in this case displaying the message box shown. Performing this verification locally ensures that only valid data is sent back through the Web, decreasing the amount of work that needs to be done by the Web server.

FIG. 35.7

When the user submits his or her order, the VBScript verifies the information and displays this message box.

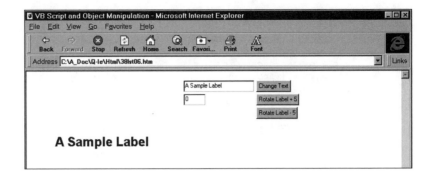

Listings 35.4 and 35.5 show the two parts of the HTML document for this example; Listing 35.4 shows the HTML code, indicating where the VBScript code should be inserted in the <HEAD> section, and Listing 35.5 shows the VBScript code.

Listing 35.4   *35LST04.HTM*   The HTML Section: the Toppings Checkboxes, Text in the Input Field, and Cost Are Updated Depending on Pizza Selection

```
<HTML>
<HEAD>
<SCRIPT LANGUAGE="VBS">
<!-- Insert 38LST05.HTM -->
</SCRIPT>
<TITLE>Pizza Azzip</TITLE></HEAD>

<BODY bgproperties=fixed>

<FONT FACE="Comic Sans MS" SIZE=2>
<FONT COLOR=NAVY>

<CENTER>
    <FONT SIZE=6>Pizza Azzip<P>
    <IMG SRC="THEPIZZA.GIF" ALIGN=MIDDLE width=150 height=75>
</CENTER>

<HR>

<FONT FACE="Comic Sans MS" SIZE=2>
<FONT COLOR=NAVY>

<FORM Name="OrderForm">
<TABLE XBORDER=1 BGCOLOR="#FFFFCC" WIDTH=200 ALIGN=LEFT>
    <TR><TD BGCOLOR=NAVY ALIGN=CENTER><FONT COLOR=FFFFCC>Pick A Style...
        </TD></TR>
    <TR><TD><IMG SRC="SLICE.GIF" ALT="*" ALIGN=CENTER> 
        <INPUT TYPE=RADIO NAME=RadioGroup onClick="DoHawaiian">Hawaiian
        </TD></TR>
    <TR><TD><IMG SRC="SLICE.GIF" ALT="*" ALIGN=CENTER> 
```

continues

Part
VI

Ch
35

Listing 35.4   Continued

```
            <INPUT TYPE=RADIO NAME=RadioGroup onClick="DoChicago">Chicago
            </TD></TR>
      <TR><TD><IMG SRC="SLICE.GIF" ALT="*" ALIGN=CENTER> 
            <INPUT TYPE=RADIO NAME=RadioGroup onClick="DoNewYork">New York
            </TD></TR>
      <TR><TD><IMG SRC="SLICE.GIF" ALT="*" ALIGN=CENTER> 
            <INPUT TYPE=RADIO NAME=RadioGroup onClick="DoSeattle">Seattle
            </TD></TR>
      <TR><TD><IMG SRC="SLICE.GIF" ALT="*" ALIGN=CENTER> 
            <INPUT TYPE=RADIO NAME=RadioGroup onClick="DoTheWorks">The Works
            </TD></TR>
</TABLE>

<TABLE XBORDER=1 BGCOLOR="#FFFFCC" WIDTH=200 ALIGN=RIGHT>
      <TR><TD BGCOLOR=NAVY ALIGN=CENTER><FONT COLOR=FFFFCC>Toppings...
            </TD></TR>
      <TR><TD><INPUT TYPE=CHECKBOX NAME=Pepperoni onClick="SetTotalCost">
            Pepperoni </TD></TR>
      <TR><TD><INPUT TYPE=CHECKBOX NAME=Onion       onClick="SetTotalCost">
            Onion     </TD></TR>
      <TR><TD><INPUT TYPE=CHECKBOX NAME=Pineapple onClick="SetTotalCost">
            Pineapple </TD></TR>
      <TR><TD><INPUT TYPE=CHECKBOX NAME=Salmon      onClick="SetTotalCost">
            Salmon    </TD></TR>
      <TR><TD><INPUT TYPE=CHECKBOX NAME=Anchovies onClick="SetTotalCost">
            Anchovies </TD></TR>
      <TR><TD><INPUT TYPE=CHECKBOX NAME=Ham          onClick="SetTotalCost">
            Ham         </TD></TR>
</TABLE>

<FONT FACE="WINGDINGS" SIZE=6>
      <MARQUEE XWIDTH=100 DIRECTION=RIGHT ALIGN=MIDDLE BGCOLOR=WHITE>F
      </MARQUEE>
</FONT>

<BR>
<CENTER>
      <CENTER>
         <BR><FONT SIZE=4>Order Now!
         <BR><BR>
         <INPUT TYPE=BUTTON VALUE="Order" NAME="Order" onClick="DoOrder">
         <BR><BR>
         <FONT SIZE=2>
         <I> The cost for a Pizza is $10.00 </I> <BR>
         <I> Each additional topping is $2.00 </I>
      </CENTER>

      <BR CLEAR=LEFT>
      <BR CLEAR=RIGHT>
      <BR>
```

```
    Description: <INPUT NAME=Text1 SIZE=60>
    Total = <INPUT NAME=Sum VALUE="$0.00" SIZE=8><BR>
</CENTER>
<BR>
</FORM>
</BODY>
</HTML>
```

Listing 35.5   *35LST05.HTM*   The VBScript Commands for Interacting with Form Data. Form Data is Automatically Updated Depending on User Input

```
<SCRIPT LANGUAGE="VBS">
'-----------------------------------------------
'-- SetTotalCost
'--
'-- This method will set the total cost of the
'-- pizza.
'--
'-----------------------------------------------
SUB SetTotalCost
Dim Form
    Set Form = document.OrderForm
    '----------
    '-- Get total number of toppings.
    '----------
    total = Form.Pepperoni.checked + _
            Form.Onion.checked     + _
            Form.Pineapple.checked + _
            Form.Salmon.checked    + _
            Form.Anchovies.checked + _
            Form.Ham.checked
    '----------
    '-- The price of a pizza is $10... then add the number of
    '-- toppings.
    '----------
    Form.sum.value = "$" + CStr(10 + (total * 2)) + ".00"
END SUB


'-----------------------------------------------
'-- SetDescriptionText
'--
'-- This method will set the description of the pizza.
'--
'-----------------------------------------------
SUB SetDescriptionText(strToSet)
    document.OrderForm.Text1.value = strToSet
END SUB


'-----------------------------------------------
```

Part

VI

Ch

35

continues

Listing 35.5 Continued

```
'-- When the user clicks the order button,
'-- submit the order and alert the user that their
'-- order will be arriving soon...
'-------------------------------------------------
SUB DoOrder
    '----------
    '-- Make sure the total cost is set and
    '-- give the user a nice message.
    '----------

    SetTotalCost
    SetDescriptionText "Thank you, your pizza will arrive piping hot."

    '-- Alert is a method on the window object
    Alert "Thank you, your pizza will arrive piping hot. Your account " + _
          "was billed " + document.OrderForm.sum.value + "."
END SUB


'-------------------------------------------------
'-- SetIngredients
'--
'--    Checks/unchecks the appropriate checkboxes on the page.
'--    Recomputes cost of the pizza.
'-------------------------------------------------
SUB SetIngredients(bPepperoni, bOnion, bPineapple, bSalmon, bAnchovies, bHam)
Dim Form
    Set Form = document.OrderForm

    Form.Pepperoni.checked  = bPepperoni
    Form.Onion.checked      = bOnion
    form.Pineapple.checked  = bPineapple
    Form.Salmon.checked     = bSalmon
    Form.Anchovies.checked  = bAnchovies
    Form.Ham.checked        = bHam

    SetTotalCost
END SUB



'-------------------------------------------------
'-- HAWAIIAN PIZZA
'--
'--    A Hawaiian pizza contains Pineapple and Ham.
'-------------------------------------------------
SUB DoHawaiian
    SetIngredients False, False, True, False, False, True
    SetDescriptionText "Our aloha special. Taste the exotic flavor of the
                        big island."
```

```
END SUB

'----------------------------------------------
'-- CHICAGO PIZZA
'--
'--   A Chicago pizza contains Onion and Pepperoni.
'----------------------------------------------
SUB DoChicago
   SetIngredients True, True, False, False, False, False
   SetDescriptionText "Capone's favorite."
END SUB

'----------------------------------------------
'-- Seattle PIZZA
'--
'--   A Seattle pizza contains Rain... However,
'--   Rain is not a valid choice so the user can
'--   only select Salmon.
'----------------------------------------------
SUB DoSeattle
   SetIngredients False, False, False, True, False, False
   SetDescriptionText "Our best rainy day pizza. For the fish lover in you."
END SUB

'----------------------------------------------
'-- NEWYORK PIZZA
'--
'--   A New York pizza contains Pepperoni.
'----------------------------------------------
Sub DoNewYork
   SetIngredients True, False, False, False, False, False
   SetDescriptionText "For a taste of the Big Apple"
END SUB

'----------------------------------------------
'-- THEWORKS PIZZA
'--
'--   A pizza with the works contains everything.
'----------------------------------------------
SUB DoTheWorks
   SetIngredients True, True, True, True, True, True
   SetDescriptionText "Our most popular"
END SUB

</SCRIPT>
```

Part
VI

Ch
35

Interacting with Objects

This last example shows an example of using VBScript to manipulate another Web browser object, the ActiveX Label Control. The Label Control allows the Web author to place text on the Web page, selecting the text, font, size, and an arbitrary angle of rotation. One of the exciting things about the Label Control is that it can be manipulated in real-time, producing a variety of automated or user-controlled effects.

▶ **See** "Microsoft ActiveX Controls" for an explanation of the Label Control and other ActiveX Controls supplied by Microsoft, **p. 739**

In the following example, text is placed on the Web page using the Label Control, and form input is used to allow the user to change the text used and the angle at which it is displayed. Figure 35.8 shows the default configuration of the label, and figure 35.9 shows it after the text and the rotation angle has been changed.

FIG. 35.8

The ActiveX Label Control allows arbitrary text to be displayed by the Web author in the size, font, position, and orientation desired.

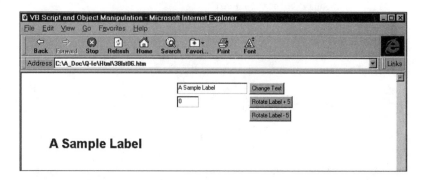

FIG. 35.9

VBScript's ability to manipulate Web browser objects allows the label parameters to be changed dynamically.

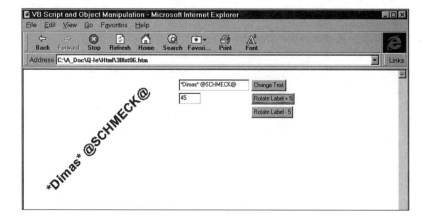

Listing 35.6 shows the code used to produce this example. Some things to note about the example are the following:

- The <OBJECT> and </OBJECT> container tag is where the ActiveX Label Control is included, and its default parameters assigned. The classid attribute must be included exactly as shown. The id attribute is the object name used by VBScript to reference the label control object. The other attributes define the size and placement of the control.

- The <PARAM> tags within the <OBJECT> and </OBJECT> container allow the Web author to define attributes of the ActiveX Label Control. The NAME, VALUE pairs are unique to each ActiveX Control, and should be documented by the ActiveX Control author. For the Label Control, they define various aspects of the appearance of the label. The NAME is also used to manipulate the value with VBScript.

- An HTML form is used to accept input and print output for information about the label control. The first text area is used to set the label text, while the second text area is used to output the current label text angle. The buttons call the appropriate VBScript routine to change the label text or angle.

- One final note about the placement of the VB scripts in this HTML document. The functions are defined in the <HEAD> section—this is not necessary, but it is common practice, so that they will be defined before used. The last <SCRIPT> and </SCRIPT> section, though, which initializes the value of the form text area showing the current angle, is placed at the end of the HTML document to ensure that the object is defined and value set before it is called.

Listing 35.6 *35LST06.HTM* VBScript Can Interact with Objects

```
<HTML>
<HEAD>
<OBJECT
        classid="clsid:{99B42120-6EC7-11CF-A6C7-00AA00A47DD2}"
        id=lblActiveLbl
        width=250
        height=250
        align=left
        hspace=20
        vspace=0
>
<PARAM NAME="_extentX" VALUE="150">
<PARAM NAME="_extentY" VALUE="700">
<PARAM NAME="Angle" VALUE="90">
<PARAM NAME="Alignment" VALUE="2">
<PARAM NAME="BackStyle" VALUE="0">
<PARAM NAME="Caption" VALUE="A Simple Desultory Label">
<PARAM NAME="FontName" VALUE="Arial">
<PARAM NAME="FontSize" VALUE="20">
```

Part VI
Ch 35

continues

Listing 35.6   Continued

```
<PARAM NAME="FontBold" VALUE="1">
<PARAM NAME="FrColor" VALUE="0">
</OBJECT>

<SCRIPT LANGUAGE="VBS">
<!--
Sub cmdChangeIt_onClick
     Dim TheForm
     Set TheForm = Document.LabelControls
     lblActiveLbl.Caption = TheForm.txtNewText.Value
End Sub
Sub cmdRotateP_onClick
     Dim TheForm
     Set TheForm = Document.LabelControls
     lblActiveLbl.Angle = lblActiveLbl.Angle + 5
     Document.LabelControls.sngAngle.Value = lblActiveLbl.Angle
End Sub
Sub cmdRotateM_onClick
     Dim TheForm
     Set TheForm = Document.LabelControls
     lblActiveLbl.Angle = lblActiveLbl.Angle - 5
     Document.LabelControls.sngAngle.Value = lblActiveLbl.Angle
End Sub
-->
</SCRIPT>
<TITLE>VBScript and Object Manipulation</TITLE>
</HEAD>
<BODY>

<FORM NAME="LabelControls">
<TABLE>
<TR><TD><INPUT TYPE="TEXT" NAME="txtNewText" SIZE=25></TD>
    <TD><INPUT TYPE="BUTTON" NAME="cmdChangeIt" VALUE="Change Text">
    </TD></TR>
<TR><TD><INPUT TYPE="TEXT" NAME="sngAngle" SIZE=5></TD>
    <TD><INPUT TYPE="BUTTON" NAME="cmdRotateP" VALUE="Rotate Label + 5">
    </TD></TR>
<TR><TD></TD>
    <TD><INPUT TYPE="BUTTON" NAME="cmdRotateM" VALUE="Rotate Label - 5">
    </TD></TR>
</TABLE>
</FORM>

<SCRIPT LANGUAGE="VBS">
<!--
Document.LabelControls.sngAngle.Value = lblActiveLbl.Angle
-->
</SCRIPT>

</BODY>
</HTML>
```

VBScript or JavaScript?

With a choice of scripting languages supported by Internet Explorer 3, the question of which to use quickly arises. The two languages are similar and have similar capabilities. Also, since they are both relatively new, you don't have a lot of history to rely on for making a choice. The following are a few points to consider:

■ What language are you more comfortable with? JavaScript is based on the Java and C++ languages; VBScript, on Visual Basic and Visual Basic for Applications. If you are proficient at one of these parent languages, using the scripting language that is based on it might be a good idea.

■ What are you trying to do? Both languages are object oriented and can interact with Internet Explorer 3 and other objects that it may have loaded, such as Java applets or OLE Controls. But if you will be primarily working with Internet Explorer 3 using a feature of Microsoft's ActiveX technologies, using VBScript would probably be a good idea, because it is designed with that use in mind.

■ Who is your target audience? For what "general-purpose" interactivity—like processing form inputs of providing simple interactivity—the biggest question to answer is who will be the audience for your Web pages. Though Microsoft has the fastest growing share of the Web browser market, Netscape's Navigator has the lion's share. Unless your Web pages are targeted at a specific audience that will definitely be using Internet Explorer, you will probably want to use JavaScript. At least in the short term, using JavaScript will ensure you maximum compatibility.

## CHAPTER 36

Plug-Ins, Add-Ins, and ActiveX Controls

With the introduction of plug-ins for its Navigator Web browser, Netscape made a quantum leap across the Web's terrain. For the first time, the Web was able to come alive with animation, sophisticated interactivity, and video, all available to a widespread audience, not just in high-tech development labs. Through plug-ins, Netscape users will be able to integrate and access media standards created by other companies, helping to push the Web closer to the envisioned potential of being a truly live, truly real-time, truly interactive conduit to any computer in the world.

Microsoft followed suit with its Internet Explorer Web browsers. Now, with Internet Explorer 3, the company has introduced its ActiveX Technologies. By building on its highly successfuly Object Linking and Embedding (OLE) standard, Microsoft has introduced a standard for adding active content to Web pages, allowing the capabilities of the Web browser to evolve continually, and also allowing data and information from existing applications to be easily accessed. ▪

What are Internet Explorer 3 ActiveX Controls?

In this chapter, learn about Microsoft's ActiveX Controls, and how they are used to increase the capabilities of Internet Explorer 3 and other compatible applications.

What are plug-ins, add-ins, and ActiveX Controls?

Learn about what is meant by Web browser plug-ins, add-ins, and ActiveX Controls, and what the differences are.

What do ActiveX Controls mean for users and programmers?

Find out what the existence of ActiveX Controls mean to the users and developers of World Wide Web software, information, and products.

Does Internet Explorer support Netscape Navigator plug-ins?

Learn about the support within Internet Explorer for Netscape Navigator plug-in modules, and see some examples of these plug-ins in action within the Internet Explorer Web browser window.

What are some of the ActiveX Controls that are available?

Find out which ActiveX Controls are available now, and which ones should be available soon.

What Are Internet Explorer ActiveX Controls?

When Microsoft released the Internet Explorer 2 Web browser, it had the ability to include add-ins, analagous to Netscape Navigator's plug-ins, to extend the capability of the browser. While some add-ins have been produced for Internet Explorer 2, there are nowhere near as many plug-ins for Netscape Navigator.

With Internet Explorer 3, Microsoft has extended the concept of add-ins to that of ActiveX Controls. These controls, formerly known as OLE Controls or OCXs, build on Microsoft's highly successful Object Linking and Embedding (OLE) standard to provide a common framework for extending the capability of its Web browser.

But ActiveX Controls are more than a simple Web browser plug-in or add-in—because of the nature of ActiveX Controls, not only can they be used to extend the functionality of Microsoft's Web browser, but the same controls can be used by any programming language or application that supports the OLE standard. So ActiveX Controls that are used to extend the functionality of Internet Explorer 3 to enable it automatically to search UseNet newsgroups for specific information, for instance, could also be integrated into Microsoft Office products such as Excel or Access to perform a similar function.

As with Netscape Navigator's plug-ins, ActiveX Controls are dynamic code modules that exist as part of Microsoft's Application Programming Interface (API) for extending and integrating third-party software into any OLE-compliant environment. The creation of (and support for) ActiveX Controls by Microsoft is significant primarily because it allows other developers seamlessly to integrate their products into the Web via Internet Explorer or any other OLE application, without having to launch any external helper applications.

For Internet Explorer users, ActiveX Control support allows you to customize Internet Explorer's interaction with third-party products and industry media standards. Microsoft's ActiveX Control API also attempts to address the concerns of programmers, providing a high degree of flexibility and cross-platform support.

What ActiveX Controls Mean for End Users

For most users, integrating ActiveX Controls is transparent. They open up and become active whenever Internet Explorer 3 is opened. Furthermore, because most ActiveX Controls are not activated unless you open up a Web page that initiates them, you may not even see the ActiveX Control at work most of the time. For example, after you install the Shockwave for Macromedia Director ActiveX Control, when it becomes available, you will notice no difference in the way Internet Explorer 3 functions until you come across a Web page that features Shockwave.

Once an ActiveX Control is installed on your machine and initiated by a Web page, it will manifest itself in the following three potential ways:

- Embedded
- Full-screen
- Hidden

An embedded ActiveX Control appears as a visible, rectangular window integrated into a Web page. This window may not appear any differently than a window created by a graphic, such as an embedded GIF or JPEG picture. The main difference between the previous windows supported by Internet Explorer 3 and those created by ActiveX Controls is that ActiveX Control windows can support a much wider range of interactivity and movement, and thereby remain live instead of static. The Surround Video ActiveX Control discussed later in this chapter is an example of this type.

In addition to mouse clicks, embedded ActiveX Controls may also read and take note of mouse location, mouse movement, keyboard input, and input from virtually any other input device. In this way, an ActiveX Control can support the full range of user events required to produce sophisticated applications.

A full-screen plug-in takes over the entire current Internet Explorer 3 window to display its own content. This is necessary when a Web page is designed to display data that is not supported by HTML. An example of this type of ActiveX Control is the ActiveVRML viewer.

If you view an ActiveVRML world using Internet Explorer 3 with the ActiveVRML ActiveX Control, it pulls up just like any other Web page, but it retains the look and functionality of an ActiveVRML world, with three-dimensional objects that you can navigate through and around.

A hidden ActiveX Control doesn't have any visible elements, but works strictly behind the scenes to add some feature to Internet Explorer 3 that is otherwise not available. An example of a hidden plug-in would be the preload control features in Microsoft's ActiveX Gallery, discussed later in the chapter. This ActiveX Control is used to preload a graphic, sound, or other element that will subsequently be viewed by the Internet Explorer 3 user. Since the element is downloaded while the user is browsing through the current Web page, apparent response time is much greater.

Regardless of which ActiveX Controls you are using and whether they are embedded, full-screen, or hidden, the rest of Internet Explorer's user interface should remain relatively constant and available. So even if you have an ActiveVRML world displayed in Internet Explorer 3's main window, you'll still be able to access Internet Explorer 3's menus and navigational controls.

What ActiveX Controls Mean for Programmers

For programmers, ActiveX Controls offer the possibility of creating Internet Explorer 3 add-on products or using development ActiveX Controls to create your own Internet-based applications. Creating a custom ActiveX Control requires much more intensive background, experience, and testing than actually using one. If you are a developer, or are interested in creating an ActiveX Control, the following discussion will be useful.

The current version of the ActiveX Control Application Programming Interface (API) supports four broad areas of functionality. ActiveX Controls can do the following:

■ Draw into, receive events, and interact with objects that are a part of the Internet Explorer 3 object hierarchy.

- Obtain MIME data from the network via URLs.
- Generate data for consumption by Internet Explorer 3, by other ActiveX Controls, or by Java applets.
- Override and implement protocol handlers.

ActiveX Controls are ideally suited to take advantage of platform-independent protocols, architectures, languages, and media types such as Java, VRML, and MPEG. While ActiveX Controls should be functionally equivalent across platforms, they should also be complementary to platform-specific protocols and architectures.

N O T E Microsoft Corporation has a wealth of information online for programmers who want to create their own ActiveX Controls. For starters, you can read the online documentation for the ActiveX Development Kit at **http://www.microsoft.com/intdev/sdk/**.

You can also download the Development Kit itself from this page. ▓

When the Internet Explorer 3 client is launched, it knows of any ActiveX Controls available through the Windows 95 Registry, but does not load any of them into RAM. Because of this, an ActiveX Control is resident in memory only when needed, although many ActiveX Controls may be in use at any one time, so you still need to be aware of memory allocation. ActiveX Controls simply reside on disk until they are needed.

Integration of ActiveX Controls with the Internet Explorer client is quite elegant and flexible, allowing the programmer to make the most of asynchronous processes and multithreaded data. ActiveX Controls may be associated with one or more MIME types, and Internet Explorer 3 may in turn create multiple instances of the same ActiveX Control.

By having many ActiveX Controls readily available without taking up any RAM until just before the time they are needed, the user is seamlessly able to view a tremendous amount of varied data. An ActiveX Control is deleted from RAM as soon as the user moves to another HTML page that does not require it.

At its most fundamental level, an ActiveX Control can access a URL and retrieve MIME data just as a standard Internet Explorer 3 client does. This data is streamed to the ActiveX Control as it arrives from the network, making it possible to implement viewers and other interfaces that can progressively display information.

For instance, an ActiveX Control may draw a simple frame and introductory graphic or text for the user to look at while the bulk of the data is streaming off the network into Internet Explorer 3's existing cache. All the same bandwidth considerations adhered to by good HTML authors need to be accounted for in ActiveX Controls.

Of course, ActiveX Controls can also be file-based, requiring a complete amount of data to be downloaded first before the ActiveX Control can proceed. This type of architecture is not encouraged due to its potential user delays, but it may prove necessary for some data-intensive ActiveX Controls.

If more data is needed by an ActiveX Control than can be supplied through a single data stream, multiple, simultaneous data streams may be requested by the ActiveX Control, so long as the user's system supports this.

While an ActiveX Control is active, if data is needed by another ActiveX Control or by Internet Explorer 3, the ActiveX Control can generate data itself for these purposes. Thus, ActiveX Controls not only process data, but they also generate it. For example, an ActiveX Control can be a data translator or filter.

ActiveX Controls are generally embedded within HTML code and accessed through the OBJECT tag.

N O T E While creating an ActiveX Control is much easier to do than, say, writing a spreadsheet application, it still requires the talents of a professional programmer. Third-party developers offer visual programming tools or BASIC environments that provide ActiveX Control templates, making the actual coding of ActiveX Controls much less tedious. However, most sophisticated ActiveX Controls are, and will be, developed in sophisticated C++ environments, requiring thousands of lines of code. ▪

N O T E Note that, because Microsoft's ActiveX Technologies and ActiveX Controls are so new, at the time of this writing there haven't been that many ActiveX Controls released. As you will see in this chapter, many companies have embraced the technology and are producing ActiveX Controls to enable Internet Explorer 3 to perform many different tasks. This chapter will give an overview of many of these new capabilities, and tell you where to connect to find out more and to download the actual software. ▪

Microsoft ActiveX Controls

Microsoft provides a set of ActiveX Controls with Internet Explorer 3, and hosts an ActiveX Gallery Web site to show them off, as shown in figure 36.1, at **http://www.microsoft.com/activex/controls/.**

The following sections describe some of these controls and demonstrate how they work.

Downloading and Installing ActiveX Controls

As shown in figure 36.1, you can select from the given choices to look at the examples in the ActiveX Gallery. If you attempt to look at an example that uses a component that you have not yet downloaded and installed, this will be done automatically. Some of the components are digitally signed as a security measure and some are not—you need to make sure that your security configuration (under the Security tab of the View, Options menu) allows you to see the examples with signed and/or unsigned software components.

FIG. 36.1

Microsoft maintains an ActiveX Gallery to show off the capabilities of its ActiveX Controls.

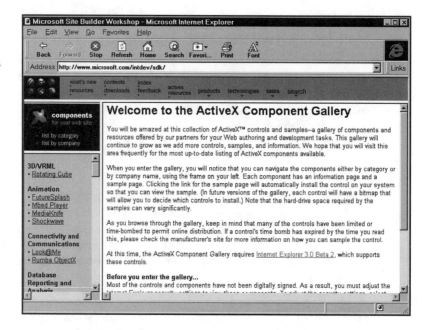

Depending on your security settings, you may get an alert box before a downloaded software component is installed on your system. This box will inform you whether or not the code was digitally signed, and give you the option of installing it. If you are satisfied with this information, click Yes to install the components, and the example will then be able to run.

Chart Controls

An example at the Microsoft ActiveX Gallery Web site shows off the capabilities of the ActiveX Chart Control. A chart can be embedded in a Web page, as shown in figure 36.2.

If the user wants to view the chart in a different format, the Web author can configure the Chart Control to change the format of the chart (see figs. 36.3 and 36.4). Additional controls can define such things as legends and gridlines on the chart. The Chart Control can even be configured using JavaScript or VBScript to dynamically change the format of the chart according to user input.

FIG. 36.2
The chart shown is
created by the ActiveX
Chart Control.

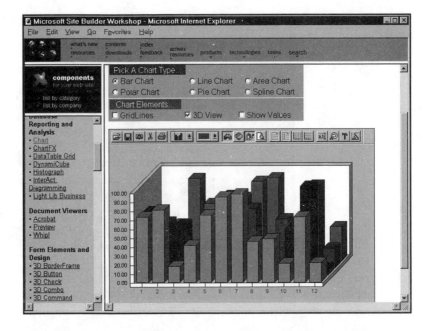

FIG. 36.3
When the chart type is
changed, the chart
shown in the Web page
is updated immediately,
with no need to
communicate with the
Web server.

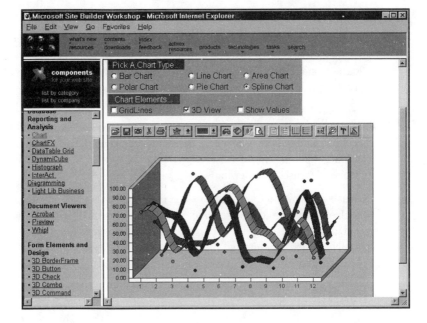

FIG. 36.4
Additional controls can enable or disable gridlines on the chart.

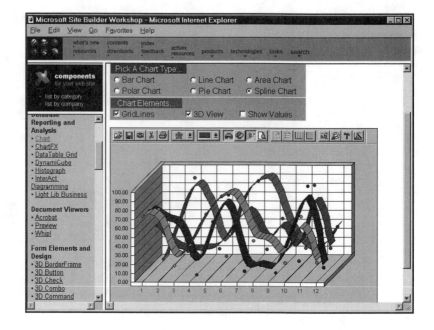

Label Control

The ActiveX Gallery shows an example of the use of the ActiveX Label Control, shown in figure 36.5. Using this control, text can be displayed within a Web page using any installed font, style, and color, and at an arbitrary angle. In the example shown, the two regions change—either color, text, and/or orientation—whenever they are clicked.

Preloader Control

The ActiveX Preloader Control can be used to speed up the apparent throughput of a Web session by allowing Internet Explorer 3 to preload graphics, video, audio, or other HTML elements while a user is reviewing a given page.

Normally, the Web author would use the Preloader Control to quietly preload images or other HTML elements while the users are reading the current Web page. Then, when they want to go on to the next page in the Web site, or when they want to view an image file, hear a sound, or watch a video clip, Internet Explorer has already downloaded it to the cache and they can view it without any further delay.

Timer Control

This example shows the use of the ActiveX Timer Control. This control allows the content of a Web page to be changed dynamically with time. In this example, shown in figures 36.6 and 36.7, the size and color of the two labels (each implemented with the Label Control) changes with time.

FIG. 36.5
The Label Control gives
the Web author the
ability to place text
arbitrarily on the Web
page, without having to
resort to graphics.

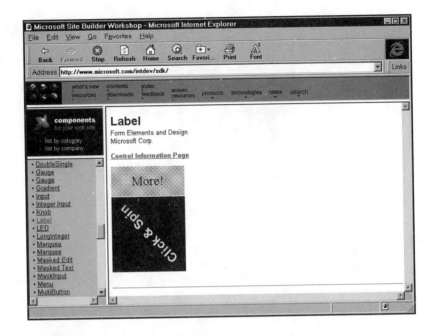

FIG. 36.6
The Timer Control
allows Web page
content to be changed
dynamically over time
as it is being displayed.

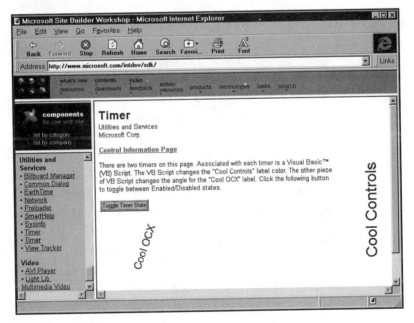

FIG. 36.7
The Timer Control can work with the Label Control and other Web page elements.

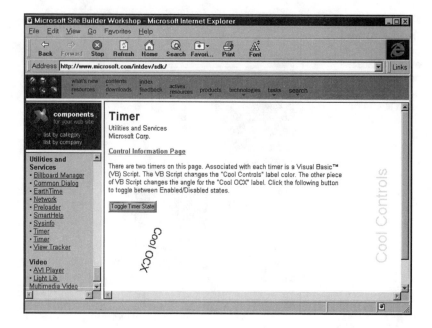

Microsoft Internet Control Pack

Microsoft has supplied a set of ActiveX Controls designed to provide connectivity and functionality over the Internet. The set is designed to work with most of the major Internet data transmission protocols, and is known as the Internet Control Pack. The Web site for the Internet Control Pack can be found at **http://www.microsoft.com/icp/**.

The Internet Control Pack set includes the following:

■ **FTP ActiveX Control**—File Transfer Protocol (FTP) is the standard network protocol used for the transfer of files over networks. This control allows developers to easily implement FTP into Web pages and other applications and take advantage of the large installed base of FTP servers.

■ **HTML ActiveX Control**—This control can be used to provide parsing and layout of HTML data and a scrollable view of the selected HTML page.

■ **HTTP ActiveX Control**—This control implements the HyperText Transfer Protocol (HTTP) client based on the HTTP specification.

■ **NNTP ActiveX Control**—This control allows you to connect to a news server to retrieve lists of newsgroups or articles, and to post new articles.

■ **POP ActiveX Control**—The POP control allows access to mail servers on the Internet that use POP3 protocol. It can be used to retrieve mail from UNIX or any other server that supports the POP3 protocol.

- **SMTP ActiveX Control**—Similar to the POP Control, this control gives Web browsers and applications access to SMTP mail servers for outgoing mail.
- **WinSock TCP ActiveX Control**—The WinSock TCP control can be used to establish a TCP connection with another compatible system for the two-way exchange of data.
- **WinSock UDP ActiveX Control**—This control is similar to the Winsock TCP ActiveX Control, but instead uses the UDP protocol to establish one- or two-way "connectionless" broadcast data exchanges with other Internet systems.

N O T E   Some of these controls—for example, the FTP and HTML Controls—offer capabilities that seem to be redundant in a Web browser that already supports them. Internet Explorer 3 can already establish FTP connections and parse HTML code. The benefits of these controls are twofold, however. First, they can be used to give other applications such as Microsoft Access—and, in the future, all of Microsoft's desktop suite of applications—access to Internet capabilities. Second, they can be used within Internet Explorer 3 to perform more specialized functions. For instance, you could use the FTP Control within a Web page to automatically establish an FTP connection to a site, load a data file from that site, and use the ActiveX Chart Control to display a chart of that data. ■

ActiveX Control Pad

Microsoft has released an ActiveX Control Pad to ease the task of including ActiveX Controls into an HTML document. The task of using an ActiveX Control can be a little daunting, or at least inconvenient, since the controls need to be loaded with a long object classid and configured with a number of parameters (you'll see an example of what this looks like in the following section).

The ActiveX Control Pad eases this task by giving you an interface right into each ActiveX Control. You can insert any of the ActiveX Controls that are loaded into your system anywhere into an HTML document. You can then edit the properties and parameters of the control and see what the actual result will look like in your Web page.

Downloading and Installing the ActiveX Control Pad

The ActiveX Control Pad is a free download available through the Microsoft Internet Explorer Web site at **http://www.microsoft.com/ie/** in the ActiveX Controls section. Downloading and installing it requires only the following few simple steps:

1. Download the self-extracting, self-installing file that contains the ActiveX Control Pad, `Setuppad.exe`, into a temporary directory on your hard drive.
2. Execute `Setuppad.exe`.
3. Answer a few questions that you'll be asked during the installation—primarily your name and where on your hard drive you'd like the ActiveX Control Pad installed.
4. After the installation is complete, read the README file that comes with the software, accessible along with the executable on the Start menu, under Programs, Microsoft ActiveX Control Pad, README. This file will give you up-to-the-minute information you might need to know.

Using the ActiveX Control Pad

Execute the ActiveX Control Pad by selecting Start, Programs, Microsoft ActiveX Control Pad, Microsoft ActiveX Control Pad. The Control Pad will run and start up with a new HTML document, as shown in figure 36.8.

FIG. 36.8

When you start up the ActiveX Control Pad, it starts a new HTML file for you.

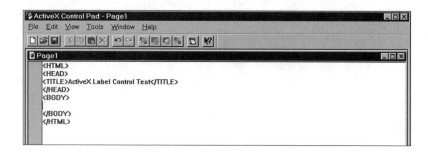

In order to insert an ActiveX Control, position the cursor in the HTML document at the position in which you would like the control to appear. For instance, in the following example I use the Label Control to create a title heading for a Web page, so I position the cursor at the top of the <BODY> section of the file.

To place the desired ActiveX Control at the current position in the HTML document, select Edit, Insert ActiveX Control. The Insert ActiveX Control dialog box appears (see fig. 36.9). Scroll through the list, selecting one of the choices, and clicking OK. Once this has been done, a Properties dialog box such as that shown in figure 36.10 will appear. It is through the Properties dialog that you are given the ability to configure the correct properties for that control.

FIG. 36.9

You can insert any ActiveX Control into your HTML document that has been registered with Windows 95.

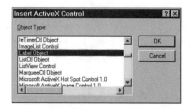

FIG. 36.10

The Properties dialog allows you to configure each ActiveX Control you want to use.

While you are editing the different properties, some of them present you with different options that you can select from by using a drop-down menu (see fig. 36.11). Some properties must be typed in by hand. Along with the Properties dialog, the ActiveX Control Pad also gives you an Edit ActiveX Control window that shows you an actual representation of what your control will look like when placed in your Web page.

FIG. 36.11
As you edit the ActiveX Control properties, the resulting appearance of the control is updated.

drop down window

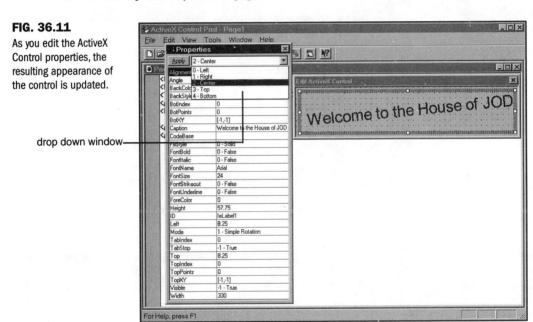

Once you have completed editing the properties of the ActiveX Control, you can close the Properties and Edit ActiveX Control windows, and the necessary HTML code needed to implement the control in your document will be inserted (see fig. 36.12). As you can see, entering all of that information by hand would be a lot more difficult than doing it through the ActiveX Control Pad. When the resulting HTML document is loaded into your Web browser, the configured Label Control is prominently displayed, as intended (see fig. 36.13).

The HTML Layout Control

An ActiveX Control that is currently available from Microsoft along with the ActiveX Control Pad is the HTML Layout Control. This control allows Web authors to precisely position HTML objects and other ActiveX Controls within a Web page. Multiple objects can also be overlapped with full control over the relative vertical placement of each object—for example, images can be placed on top of one another, captions placed right on top of pictures, and HTML forms can be designed with precise layouts of each element.

FIG. 36.12
When you are finished, the resulting HTML code needed to call and configure the ActiveX Control is inserted into your HTML document.

FIG. 36.13
When your HTML document is loaded, the ActiveX Control is there, just as you configured it!

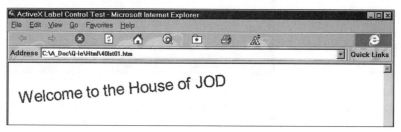

Figure 36.14 shows you an example of a Web page that incorporates the HTML Layout Control—Microsoft's Mr. ActiveX Eggplant Head. This Web page allows viewers to pick up and move the different images on the page to build a face for their own Mr. ActiveX Eggplant Head. The HTML Layout Control is what allows the images to be overlapped (see fig. 36.15).

FIG. 36.14
Microsoft's Mr. ActiveX Eggplant Head uses the HTML Layout Control to allow you to adorn your eggplant.

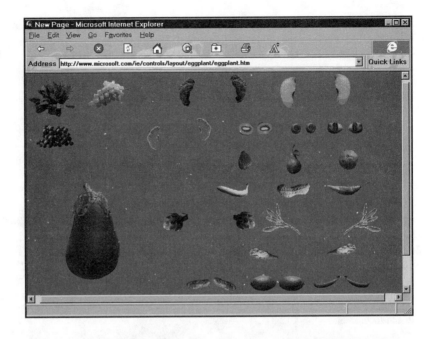

FIG. 36.15
The overlaying of images allows you to create your own creatures from the assorted images you have to work with.

The HTML Layout Control will be fully integrated into the release version of Internet Explorer 3. In the meantime, information about it is available through the Microsoft Internet Explorer Web site.

Surround Video by Black Diamond Consulting

Black Diamond Consulting has developed a Surround Video ActiveX Control to allow 360-degree, panoramic images to be viewed on a computer screen (see fig. 36.16). In addition to the ActiveX Control software that can be downloaded there, Black Diamond Consulting also maintains a few demos available through their Web site at **http://www.bdiamond.com/surround/surround.htm**.

FIG. 36.16

Black Diamond Consulting's Surround Video allows you to embed panoramic images in your Web pages, letting the user pan and zoom around them.

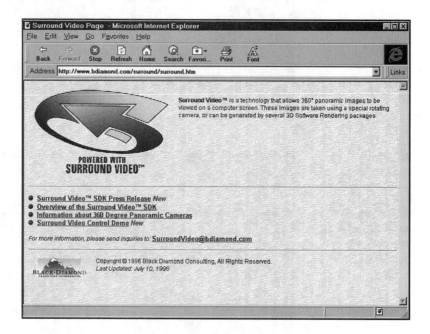

Downloading and Installing the Surround Video ActiveX Control

Just as with the examples in the Microsoft ActiveX Control Gallery, the Surround Video ActiveX Controls will be downloaded and installed onto your computer automatically, whenever you attempt to view a Web page that uses it. If you have already downloaded the current version of the control, of course, it will not be downloaded.

Viewing a Surround Video Web page

There are a couple of Surround Video examples maintained through the Black Diamond Consulting Web site. In each of them, a 360-degree, panoramic image is downloaded. By left-dragging the mouse pointer, you can scan back and forth, up and down, to see all of the image. Figure 36.17 shows a collage of some of the views possible with one of the examples.

FIG. 36.17
The Surround Video ActiveX Control allows you to scan through the 360 degrees of the image.

The Surround Video ActiveX Control also allows you to embed hypertext links into the panoramic images. When the mouse pointer is placed over a hypertext link within the image, it becomes the familiar hand pointer, as shown in figure 36.18.

By right-clicking a completely loaded Surround Video image, a pop-up menu with all of the image's hypertext links is displayed (see fig. 36.19).

FIG. 36.18
The familiar hand pointer signals an embedded hypertext link in the Surround Video images.

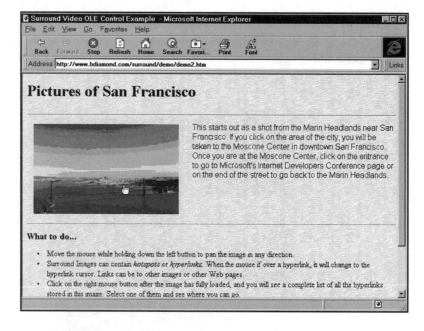

FIG. 36.19
You can either select a hypertext link by clicking it, or access the complete list through this pop-up menu.

Softholic

Softholic maintains a Web site offering a collection of ActiveX Controls at **http://www.internet-express.com/Softoholic/** (see fig. 36.20).

The ActiveX Cards Controls support the playing and display of card games in Web browsers and over the Internet. The ActiveX OpenGL Controls support an interface between ActiveX applications and the OpenGL graphics library. The ActiveX Fountain Fill Controls offer a collection of different fill types, to add exciting, dynamically generated graphics to Web pages, as shown in figure 36.21.

FIG. 36.20
Softholic offers a
collection of ActiveX
Controls.

FIG. 36.21
The ActiveX Fountain Fill
Controls are used to
create a variety of
graphic effects on a
Web page, similar to
GIF images, but
dynamically generated
and more quickly
displayed.

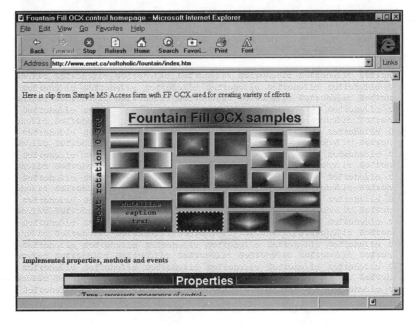

ActiveX Resources

There are many more ActiveX Controls already available, ranging from other offerings from Microsoft—such as the ActiveMovie Control discussed in the audio and video chapters of this book, and the VRML Control discussed in the VRML chapter—to many third-party offerings, such as the streaming video control from VDOLive. As more and more software vendors embrace the ActiveX technology, an increasing number of ActiveX Controls will become available. Microsoft maintains a Web site of many of the third-party ActiveX Controls. This list can be accessed through their ActiveX Controls Web page at **http://www.microsoft.com/activex/ controls/**.

▶ **See** "Microsoft ActiveMovie" for a discussion of using the ActiveMovie control with audio, **p. 271**

▶ **See** "How Internet Explorer Works with Video" to find out how ActiveMovie works with video, **p. 295**

▶ **See** "Microsoft VRML Add-In" for information on Microsoft's VRML ActiveX Control, **p. 344**

Netscape Navigator Plug-Ins

An exciting new capability of Internet Explorer is support for Netscape Navigator plug-ins. By being able to launch and execute Netscape Navigator plug-ins within the Internet Explorer Web browser window, Microsoft has enabled its browser to access many "Netscape-enhanced" Web sites.

Using plug-ins in Internet Explorer is very simple. All of the current plug-ins you may have installed should work without requiring you to do anything. Any new plug-ins you get can be installed in either C:\Program Files\Netscape\Navigator\Program\plugins or C:\Program Files\Plus!\Microsoft Internet\plugins. After that, it becomes available to Internet Explorer.

> **CAUTION**
> Netscape Navigator plug-in compatibility in Internet Explorer is still a pretty new thing, and it's quite likely that all of the bugs haven't been shaken out yet. While early reports indicate that Internet Explorer's plug-in compatibility is good, it is not yet complete. Keep an eye on the Internet Explorer Web site for news and information on further updates, and keep in mind that, for the near future at least, your success with plug-ins in Internet Explorer may vary.

Netscape's Live3D

As discussed in Chapter 18, the Live3D plug-in for Netscape Navigator, providing support for its Moving Worlds VRML standard, can be run within Internet Explorer. Using this plug-in, it is possible to view Moving Worlds VRML worlds, seeing the full three-dimensional structure, movement, and animation of these worlds.

N O T E Keep in mind that you can only have one helper application, plug-in, add-in, or ActiveX Control at a time for a given type of data. If you install the Live3D plug-in to be able to view Moving Worlds VRML worlds, then when you view VRML 1.0 worlds, you will no longer be able to use Microsoft's VRML control (or whatever you happened to be using). Live3D should be compatible with VRML 1.0 worlds, but it is a good idea to keep in mind that the last application installed with Internet Explorer is the one that will be used. ▪

Shockwave by Macromedia, Inc.

Perhaps one of the most significant and awe-inspiring plug-ins that has been supported directly by Netscape Navigator—and will soon be available as an ActiveX Control for Internet Explorer 3—is Shockwave for Macromedia Director, Freehand, and Authorware, which allow you to view Director "movies" and documents from the other applications directly on a Web page. Director movies are created with Macromedia Director (don't confuse Director "movies" with other file types of the same name, such as QuickTime movies), a cross-platform multimedia authoring program that gives multimedia developers the ability to create fully interactive multimedia applications, or "titles." Because of its interactive integration of animation, bitmap, video, and sound media, and its playback compatibility with a variety of computer platforms including Windows, Mac OS, OS/2, and SGI, Director is now the most widely used multimedia authoring tool.

N O T E Macromedia Director was originally designed as an animation tool. When support was added for other media and interactive scripting several years ago, it blossomed into the multimedia authoring program designers craved. Director now supports all major types of multimedia and provides a sophisticated scripting language called Lingo. ▪

Using Shockwave, a Director movie running over the Internet can support the same sort of features as a Director movie running off of a CD-ROM, including animated sequences, sophisticated scripting of interactivity, user input of text right into the Director window (or "stage"), sound playback, and much more. You can find out more information about Shockwave at the Macromedia Shockwave Web site at **http://www.macromedia.com/Tools/Shockwave/ index.html.**

Once the ActiveX Control for Shockwave is available and you have installed it, any Web page that contains a Director movie will automatically play in your Internet Explorer Web browser in the manner prescribed by the Web page. In the meantime, the Netscape Navigator plug-ins for these applications seem to be supported by Internet Explorer. Figure 36.22 shows the Shockwave for Freehand plug-in running in the Internet Explorer window.

FIG. 36.22

Internet Explorer's support for Netscape Navigator plug-ins allows it access to many Web sites previously Netscape-exclusive.

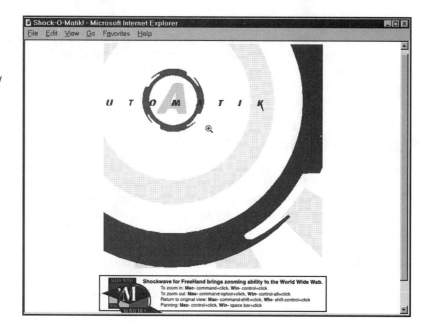

Plug-In Resources

A clearinghouse for information and software for Netscape Navigator plug-ins is available on the Netscape Web site at **http://home.netscape.com/comprod/mirror/navcomponents_download.html.** You should also keep an eye on the Microsoft Internet Explorer Web site, as it will probably be updated regularly with information on the compatibility of Internet Explorer with existing plug-ins. ●

Appendixes

Loading and Configuring Internet Explorer for Windows 3.1

Is Internet Explorer available for Windows 3.1?

In this appendix, learn about Internet Explorer 2.01, the latest release of Microsoft's flagship Web browser for Windows 3.1 and the Macintosh.

How do you download and install Internet Explorer for Windows 3.1?

Find out where to download the latest version of the Web browser, and how to install and configure it on your system.

Microsoft has continued to develop Internet Explorer for other platforms, besides Windows 95. While Internet Explorer 3 is not yet available for anything other than Windows 95, Microsoft has released Internet Explorer 2.01 for both Windows 3.1 and the Macintosh.

This appendix discusses the process for downloading, installing, and running Internet Explorer for Windows 3.1. You also learn a little about Internet Explorer 2.01 for the Macintosh and find out how to get free technical support from Microsoft for these Web browsers. ■

Getting Internet Explorer

Microsoft's Internet Explorer Web browser is available through the Microsoft Internet Explorer Web site, located at **http://www.microsoft.com/ie/** (see fig. A.1). In the version of this Web site available at the time of this writing, all of the different versions of Internet Explorer for different platforms are available by clicking the Get It! hypertext link. Even when the Web site changes, it shouldn't be too hard to find the download area.

FIG. A.1

From the Microsoft Internet Explorer Web site, you can download the latest version of Internet Explorer for Windows 95/NT, Windows 3.1, and the Macintosh.

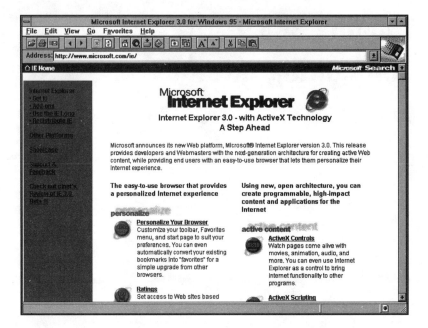

This Web site gives you access to software, support, and information about Microsoft's complete range of Web browser and other Internet products.

> **CAUTION**
>
> To reiterate and make things perfectly clear, Internet Explorer 3, at the time of this writing, is not yet available for either Windows 3.1 or the Macintosh platforms. Microsoft has stated that those platforms will be supported. If Microsoft does in fact produce versions of Internet Explorer 3 for Windows 3.1 and the Macintosh, and if they follow the general schedule that they followed when releasing Internet Explorer 2 for those platforms, you can probably expect to see the new version available roughly six months after the release of Internet Explorer 3 for Windows 95 and NT.

Installing Internet Explorer

Through the Web site listed above, you can download a self-extacting file containing what you need to install Internet Explorer 2.01 for Windows 3.1. Download the file, called DLMINI.EXE, into a temporary directory, and install using the following steps:

1. Run the self-extracting file DLMINI.EXE. This will expand the archive in the temporary directory.

2. Run the program SETUP.EXE in that directory.

3. The first thing you will see is Microsoft's licensing agreement for Internet Explorer. After you have read through it, click the button to agree to its terms, and the installation program will begin (see fig. A.2).

FIG. A.2

The Windows 3.1 version of Internet Explorer 2.0 includes an installation program that makes installation a snap.

4. Enter your name and company affiliation, if applicable.

5. Select the install directory for Internet Explorer, or keep the default directory of C:\IEXPLORE (see fig. A.3).

FIG. A.3

You can install Internet Explorer in the default directory under Windows 3.1, C:\IEXPLORE, or choose another location.

6. Select the Program Manager group in which to install the icons for Internet Explorer. The default is Microsoft Internet Explorer. After you have done this, you should see the dialog box in figure A.4, indicating a successful installation.

FIG. A.4
This alert box tells you that Internet Explorer 2 has successfully been installed on your system.

7. The final step required to complete the installation is for you to reboot your system. When Windows loads a second time, it will be configured to run Internet Explorer, and the icons for doing so will appear in the Program Manager group that you selected in step 6.

8. The Program Manager group will display the icons shown in figure A.5. It's always a good idea to look through the Readme file before using a new program. After you have done that, you're ready to go!

FIG. A.5
You should read the Internet Explorer Readme file before you run it, to see if there are any last-minute things you need to know.

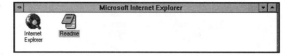

> **N O T E** Microsoft currently offers several different packages for Internet Explorer for Windows 3.1 and the Macintosh. The one just discussed, and packaged in the self-extracting file DLMINI.EXE, includes only the Web browser itself. Another package, packaged as DLBASE.EXE, also includes a TCP/IP stack and dialer program that you can use to establish your connection to the Internet. A third, DLFULL.EXE, also includes a mail client for receiving and sending Internet e-mail. ■

Running Internet Explorer

When you first run Internet Explorer 2.01 for Windows 3.1, you will see the Web page shown in figure A.6. This is a local file that is included with Internet Explorer 2.01, and so will load very quickly when you start up the Web browser. You can click the **www.msn.com** hypertext link to connect to the Microsoft Network Web site, which makes a good entry point to the World Wide Web (see fig. A.7).

FIG. A.6
Your default home page with Internet Explorer for Windows 3.1 is the local file shown; this gives you a link right to the Microsoft Network Home Page.

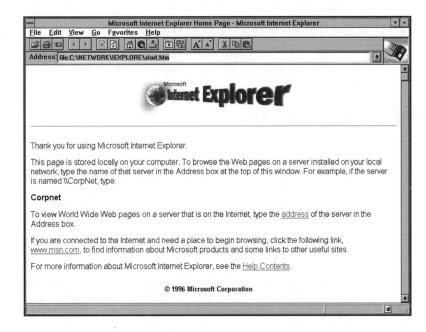

FIG. A.7
The Microsoft Network Home Page is a great jumping off point into the World Wide Web.

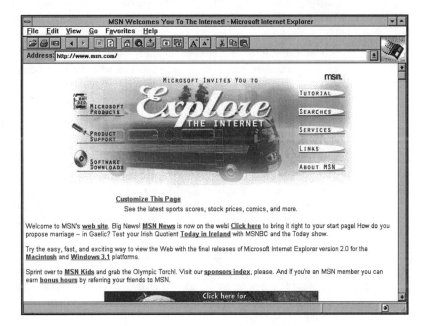

Configuring Internet Explorer

Once you have Internet Explorer up and running, there are a series of options and actions that you can take to configure it for your purposes. Most of these are available under the View, Options menu.

Web Browser Options

The options under the View menu allow you to control many aspects of how the Internet Explorer Web browser window appears, and allow you to customize its behavior in many ways. You can adjust the size of its History list and caches for your system, and set up Internet Explorer helper applications.

▶ **See** "Configuring a Helper Application" for a description of what helper applications are and how they extend the capabilities of your Web browser, **p. 244**

Browser Window   Under the View menu, the first three options allow you to adjust what appears in the Web browser window itself. These options are as follows:

- **Toolbar**—Shows the toolbar across the top of the Internet Explorer window. If you don't need the buttons, turning off this option gives more area within the Internet Explorer window to display images.

- **Address Bar**—The field which displays the URL of the current Web page is optional. You probably want to keep this field visible for use in helping diagnose problematic URLs.

- **Status Bar**—Internet Explorer regularly uses the status bar across the bottom of its window to update you on its progress and on what URLs hypertext links point to. If you don't need this information, you can turn the status bar off and get a little more screen area.

The Appearance Tab   Choose View, Options to open the Options dialog box. Choose the Appearance tab (see fig. A.8).

There are three sections to this tab, each of which control a different aspect of the way Internet Explorer displays Web page information:

- **Page**—The options in this section allow you to automatically Show Pictures, Use Custom Colors in the Web browser window, and select the default Proportional and Fixed-width font.

 TIP If you're in a hurry, or if you don't care about pretty colored buttons, background textures, and the full-page image of the Web page creator's favorite hermit crab, uncheck the Show Pictures checkbox to (often substantially) reduce the amount of time it takes to download a page.

- **Shortcuts**—In this section, you can specify the color that Internet shortcuts (more commonly known as anchors for hypertext links), both Already and Not Yet Viewed, are displayed in. You can also specify if you want to Underline Shortcuts and if you want to Show Shortcut Address in Status Bar.

■ **Addresses**—This determines whether addresses shown are Simplified or Full.

FIG. A.8

The Appearance tab in the Options dialog box gives you control over how Internet Explorer renders different aspects of a Web page.

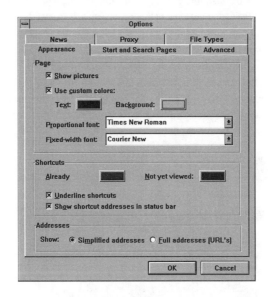

The Start and Search Pages Tab   The Start and Search Pages tab allows you to specify what Web pages Internet Explorer will load when it is first started, and when the Start or Search page toolbar buttons are clicked (see fig. A.9). You can change these pages by clicking the Use Current button when you have the Web page loaded that you want to use, or return to the default page by clicking Use Default.

FIG. A.9

Using the Start and Search Pages tab allows you to set the URL for your Start Page and for the Web page you use to initiate Web searches.

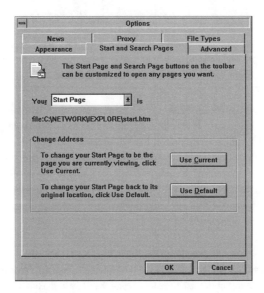

TIP One tip to speed Internet Explorer's startup is to have your start page be a page local to your computer, which doesn't have to be downloaded over your network connection. If you set the startup page to a local HTML file on your hard disk, Internet Explorer typically takes less time to access a hard disk than to download a Web page over its Internet connection.

The Advanced Tab   The Advanced tab screen lets you set the size of the history list and cache that Internet Explorer uses, and where the cache is located on your hard drive (see fig. A.10). The history section allows Internet Explorer to Remember the Places Visited.

FIG. A.10
The Advanced tab
allows you to control
the Internet Explorer
history and cache.

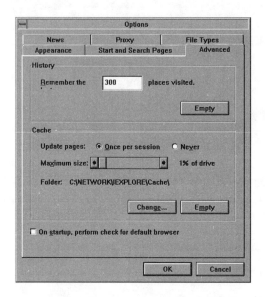

 TIP In addition to using the Back and Forward toolbar buttons to travel through the History list, you can access the most recent items, or a list of all of them, under the File menu.

Internet Explorer's cache does not have to be in the same folder or even the same disk drive where the executable is located. If you decide to go back to a Web page that you've already downloaded, Internet Explorer will look at the version you downloaded five minutes ago instead of reconnecting to the network and downloading the page again (which probably hasn't changed in five minutes). Loading the page from your hard disk will always, except in very special circumstances, be faster than reloading the page from your network connection. You can also select when Internet Explorer will check pages that have been cached for changes—either once per session, or never.

N O T E   If you think the page has changed in the last five minutes (for example, there are several people who have wired digital cameras to their Internet connection and update their Web page every minute with a snapshot of their office), selecting the Refresh toolbar button will always load the page from your network connection, not from the cache. ■

Internet Explorer's cache Maximum Size setting is based on a maximum percentage of your hard drive. The size that you select will, of course, depend on how much space you have on your hard drive, but you should probably set it so that it will be 5 MB or larger.

CAUTION

Reducing the cache size setting so that it is below 1 MB is not recommended, as some individual Web pages and files can exceed 1 MB in size. Reducing the cache too low causes Internet Explorer to act as if it has no cache, which can severely limit performance.

Reading UseNet News: The News Tab   Internet Explorer 2.01 includes a news reader to allow you to access, read, and respond to articles in UseNet newsgroups. The News tab allows you to configure Internet Explorer to connect to the news server provided by your Internet service provider. The information needed, as shown in figure A.11, should be given to you by your provider.

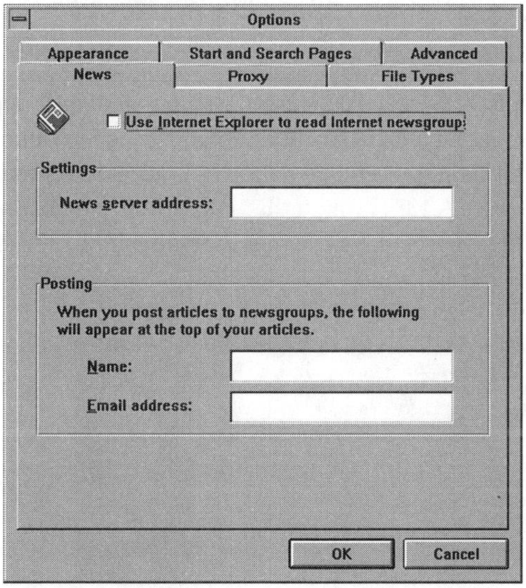

FIG. A.11
Internet Explorer includes an integrated UseNet news reader that allows you to read and respond to news articles right from your browser window.

Web Browser Proxies: The Proxy Tab   The Proxy tab allows you to select proxy applications to be used along with Internet Explorer (see fig. A.12). *Proxies* are applications that are substitutes (that is, they act as a stand-in) for your same type of application. Proxies are rarely present for any other reason than to act as guards on the firewall on a network. You will need to ask your system administrator if there are any proxies present for use across a firewall, and what settings you need to make in Internet Explorer in order to use them.

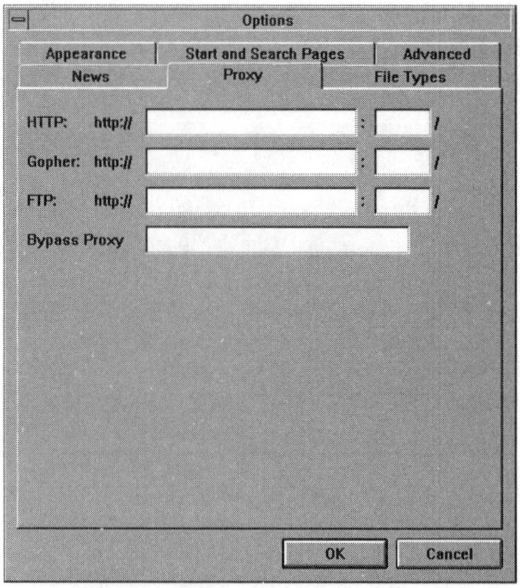

FIG. A.12

Set up Internet Explorer to work through a firewall at a secure Internet site with the Proxy tab.

The File Types Tab   Unlike Netscape Navigator, which maintains a separate list of helper applications it uses for different file types, Internet Explorer uses the same database maintained by Windows 3.1. From Internet Explorer, that database is accessed through the File Types options tab, as shown in figure A.13. Through this, you can see what applications are configured to work with different file types and, by clicking the Add button, set up Internet Explorer to use helper applications for other file types.

FIG. A.13

The File Types tab accesses the Windows default application database to allow you to define helper applications to be used for different file types.

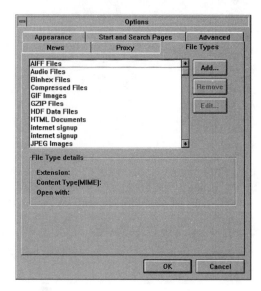

Internet Explorer Updates

Internet Explorer gives you easy access to its Web site which always contains the latest released version of the Web browser for each supported platform. This Web site can be reached by clicking the Internet Explorer Updates toolbar button, or by selecting Go, Internet Explorer Updates. The Web site gives instant access to released versions of Internet Explorer for Windows 95, NT, and 3.1, as well as the Macintosh (see fig. A.14). International versions of Internet Explorer can also be accessed from this page.

FIG. A.14

The Internet Explorer Updates Web page is where you go to obtain the latest released version of Microsoft Internet Explorer.

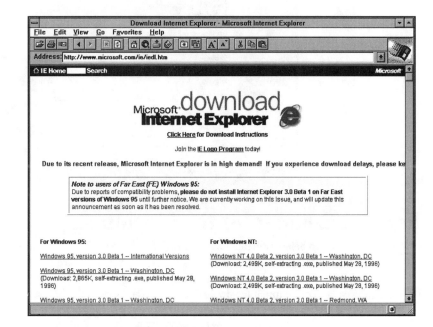

Web Searches

Another capability of Internet Explorer is the Search button that, by default, takes you the search Web site on the Microsoft Network, which is a frontend to many popular Web and Internet search engines (see fig. A.15).

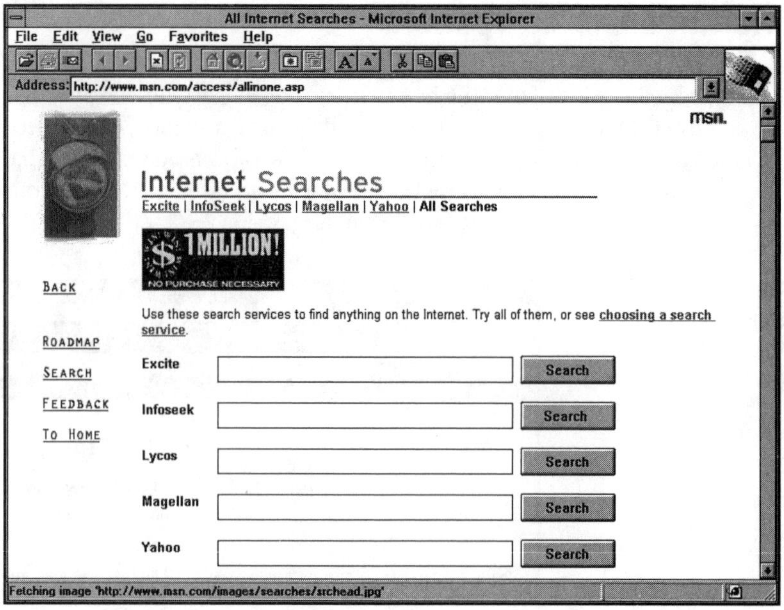

FIG. A.15
The Microsoft Network maintains a handy Web page that acts as an interface to many of the most popular Web search engines.

Internet Explorer for the Macintosh

In addition to being available for Windows 3.1, Microsoft has also released Internet Explorer 2.01 for the Macintosh. The install process is as straightforward as for other platforms (see fig. A.16). The capabilites of the program are similar to those in the other platforms, and shows Microsoft's commitment to supporting them (see fig. A.17).

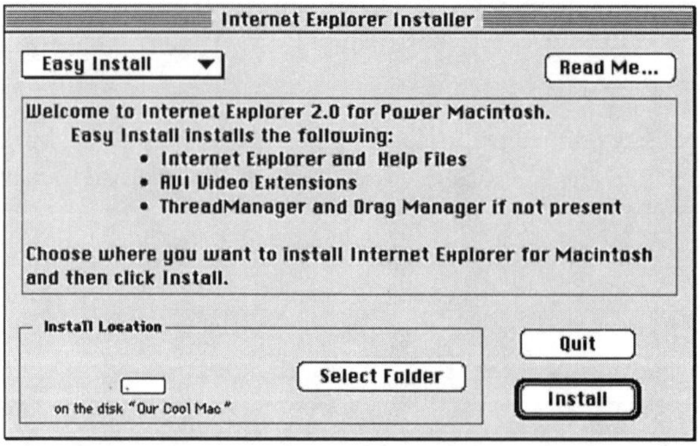

FIG. A.16
Internet Explorer for the Macintosh can be downloaded and installed within a few minutes.

FIG. A.17
Internet Explorer 2.01
brings Microsoft's HTML
and Web enhance-
ments to the
Macintosh.

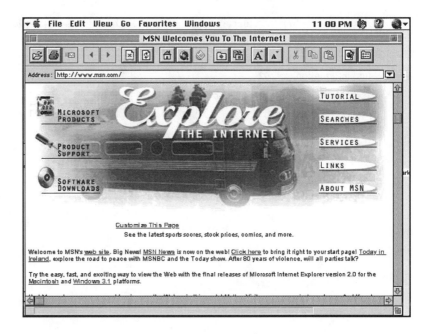

The Future of Internet Explorer for Windows 3.1 and the Macintosh

Microsoft has stated that they intend to continue development of their Internet technologies for Windows 3.1 and the Macintosh platforms. The releases of Internet Explorer 2.01 for each of these platforms can be taken as a sign of this continued support. Microsoft is working to extend their ActiveX Technologies, the cornerstone of Internet Explorer 3, to Windows 3.1 and Macintosh. While they have made no specific statements regarding when Internet Explorer 3 and future versions will be available for these platforms, it has shown by its past performance with Internet Explorer 2.0 that it is committed to the Windows 3.1 and Macintosh platforms. Microsoft's statements about developing ActiveX for these platforms, and the cross-platform support inherent in the ActiveX Technologies, makes it seem likely that Internet Explorer 3 will be available for Windows 3.1 and the Macintosh before too long.

Technical Support for Internet Explorer

Online technical support for Internet Explorer is available from Microsoft through their Internet Explorer Web site at **http://www.microsoft.com/ie** by clicking the After You Install hypertext link. This leads to a Web page with technical information and support.

Another place to get technical support is through the **microsoft.public.internetexplorer** newsgroup that is maintained on Microsoft's news server, **msnews.microsoft.com**.

▶ **See** "The Basics of Using Newsgroups" for a description of how to use UseNet newsgroups to find information, **p. 202**

What's on the CD-ROM?

The CD-ROM included with this book is packed full of valuable programs, utilities, clipart, and online resource links. This appendix gives you a brief overview of the contents of the CD. For a more detailed look at any of these parts, load the CD-ROM and browse the contents. ■

Source Code

Here you'll find examples from the book. Simply click the chapter number of interest and read the code or cut and paste as desired.

Browsers

Here you'll find Internet Explorer 3 as described in this book.

Plug-Ins

Plug-ins are great, but finding and downloading these can be a hassle and is definitely time consuming. We have supplied over a dozen of some of the hottest plug-ins available, which are as follows:

- Acrobat
- Corel CMX
- DWG/DXF
- Envoy Reader
- Fig Leaf Inline
- INSO Word Viewer
- Intercap Inline
- Look@Me
- Scream
- Shockwave for Director
- Sizzler
- VDOLive
- ASAP Web Show
- ASAP Word Power

E-Mail and Newsreaders

Send mail to your friends and follow your favorite newsgroups with the following newsreader:

- News Xpress
- Trumpet Newsreader
- Eudora Lite
- Pegasus Mail

Helpers

The following is a collection of programs to aid you in the creation of multimedia Web pages. You'll find graphics editors, video editors, sound editors, and so on.

Audio

- Cooledit
- Goldwave
- Midigate
- Mod4Win
- WHAM
- WPLANY

Multimedia

- Working Model Macromedia Director 5.0

Video/Image

- ACDSee
- GraphX
- LViewPro
- MPEGPlay
- PolyView
- QuickTime
- SnapCAP
- StreamWorks
- VuePrint
- WebImage
- WinECJ
- WinJPEG

HTML Editors and Utilities

Save yourself the trouble of creating HTML pages with Notepad and take your pick of the following HTML editors or special purpose utilities:

- HotDog
- HTML Assistant
- HTMLed
- HTML Notepad

- HTML Writer
- Live Markup
- WebEdit
- Webber
- Color Manipulation Device
- CrossEye
- EasyHelp/Web
- FrameGang
- Map THIS!
- WebForms
- Webmania

Web Servers

Use the Microsoft Internet Information Server to build your Web site.

Java

Here you'll find Java tools that will help you create animated applets and design scrolling marquees (you'll also get the Java Development Kit):

- Clikette
- Egor
- Ewgie
- Flash
- Swami
- Java Development Kit

VRML

Included here are VRML browsers to enable you to build "home worlds" and navigate 3D worlds:

- NAVFlyer
- Pioneer
- VRScout
- Worldview
- VRML plug-in for Internet Explorer 3

Que Books

- *Special Edition Using HTML*
- *Special Edition Using JavaScript*
- *Special Edition Using Java*

Index

X-Z

Check out Que® Books
on the World Wide Web
http://www.mcp.com/que

As the biggest software release in computer history, Windows 95 continues to redefine the computer industry. Click here for the latest info on our Windows 95 books

Make computing quick and easy with these products designed exclusively for new and casual users

Examine the latest releases in word processing, spreadsheets, operating systems, and suites

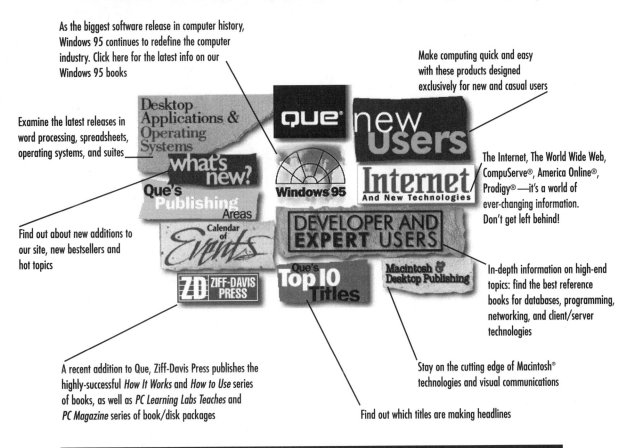

The Internet, The World Wide Web, CompuServe®, America Online®, Prodigy® —it's a world of ever-changing information. Don't get left behind!

Find out about new additions to our site, new bestsellers and hot topics

In-depth information on high-end topics: find the best reference books for databases, programming, networking, and client/server technologies

A recent addition to Que, Ziff-Davis Press publishes the highly-successful *How It Works* and *How to Use* series of books, as well as *PC Learning Labs Teaches* and *PC Magazine* series of book/disk packages

Stay on the cutting edge of Macintosh® technologies and visual communications

Find out which titles are making headlines

With 6 separate publishing groups, Que develops products for many specific market segments and areas of computer technology. Explore our Web Site and you'll find information on best-selling titles, newly published titles, upcoming products, authors, and much more.

- Stay informed on the latest industry trends and products available
- Visit our online bookstore for the latest information and editions
- Download software from Que's library of the best shareware and freeware

QUE® has the right choice for every computer user

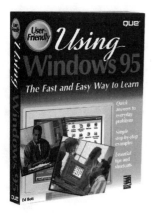

From the new computer user to the advanced programmer, we've got the right computer book for you. Our user-friendly *Using* series offers just the information you need to perform specific tasks quickly and move onto other things. And, for computer users ready to advance to new levels, QUE *Special Edition Using* books, the perfect all-in-one resource—and recognized authority on detailed reference information.

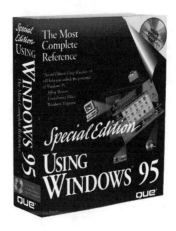

The *Using* series for casual users

Who should use this book?

Everyday users who:

- Work with computers in the office or at home
- Are familiar with computers but not in love with technology
- Just want to "get the job done"
- Don't want to read a lot of material

The user-friendly reference

- The fastest access to the one best way to get things done
- Bite-sized information for quick and easy reference
- Nontechnical approach in plain English
- Real-world analogies to explain new concepts
- Troubleshooting tips to help solve problems
- Visual elements and screen pictures that reinforce topics
- Expert authors who are experienced in training and instruction

Special Edition Using for accomplished users

Who should use this book?

Proficient computer users who:

- Have a more technical understanding of computers
- Are interested in technological trends
- Want in-depth reference information
- Prefer more detailed explanations and examples

The most complete reference

- Thorough explanations of various ways to perform tasks
- In-depth coverage of all topics
- Technical information cross-referenced for easy access
- Professional tips, tricks, and shortcuts for experienced users
- Advanced troubleshooting information with alternative approaches
- Visual elements and screen pictures that reinforce topics
- Technically qualified authors who are experts in their fields
- "Techniques from the Pros" sections with advice from well-known computer professionals

Complete and Return this Card
for a *FREE* Computer Book Catalog

Thank you for purchasing this book! You have purchased a superior computer book written expressly for your needs. To continue to provide the kind of up-to-date, pertinent coverage you've come to expect from us, we need to hear from you. Please take a minute to complete and return this self-addressed, postage-paid form. In return, we'll send you a free catalog of all our computer books on topics ranging from word processing to programming and the internet.

Mr. ☐   Mrs. ☐   Ms. ☐   Dr. ☐

Name (first) ☐☐☐☐☐☐☐☐☐☐ (M.I.) ☐ (last) ☐☐☐☐☐☐☐☐☐☐☐☐☐☐☐☐☐☐

Address ☐☐☐☐☐☐☐☐☐☐☐☐☐☐☐☐☐☐☐☐☐☐☐☐☐☐☐☐☐☐☐☐☐☐☐☐

☐☐☐☐☐☐☐☐☐☐☐☐☐☐☐☐☐☐☐☐☐☐☐☐☐☐☐☐☐☐☐☐☐☐☐☐

City ☐☐☐☐☐☐☐☐☐☐☐☐☐☐☐☐☐☐☐☐ State ☐☐ Zip ☐☐☐☐☐ ☐☐☐☐

Phone ☐☐☐ ☐☐☐ ☐☐☐☐ Fax ☐☐☐ ☐☐☐ ☐☐☐☐

Company Name ☐☐☐☐☐☐☐☐☐☐☐☐☐☐☐☐☐☐☐☐☐☐☐☐☐☐☐☐☐☐☐

E-mail address ☐☐☐☐☐☐☐☐☐☐☐☐☐☐☐☐☐☐☐☐☐☐☐☐☐☐☐☐☐

1. Please check at least (3) influencing factors for purchasing this book.

Front or back cover information on book .... ☐
Special approach to the content .... ☐
Completeness of content .... ☐
Author's reputation .... ☐
Publisher's reputation .... ☐
Book cover design or layout .... ☐
Index or table of contents of book .... ☐
Price of book .... ☐
Special effects, graphics, illustrations .... ☐
Other (Please specify): _____ ☐

2. How did you first learn about this book?

Saw in Macmillan Computer Publishing catalog .... ☐
Recommended by store personnel .... ☐
Saw the book on bookshelf at store .... ☐
Recommended by a friend .... ☐
Received advertisement in the mail .... ☐
Saw an advertisement in: _____ ☐
Read book review in: _____ ☐
Other (Please specify): _____ ☐

3. How many computer books have you purchased in the last six months?

This book only .... ☐   3 to 5 books .... ☐
2 books .... ☐   More than 5 .... ☐

4. Where did you purchase this book?

Bookstore .... ☐
Computer Store .... ☐
Consumer Electronics Store .... ☐
Department Store .... ☐
Office Club .... ☐
Warehouse Club .... ☐
Mail Order .... ☐
Direct from Publisher .... ☐
Internet site .... ☐
Other (Please specify): _____ ☐

5. How long have you been using a computer?

☐ Less than 6 months   ☐ 6 months to a year
☐ 1 to 3 years   ☐ More than 3 years

6. What is your level of experience with personal computers and with the subject of this book?

	With PCs	With subject of book
New	☐	☐
Casual	☐	☐
Accomplished	☐	☐
Expert	☐	☐

Source Code ISBN: 0-7897-0878-7

7. Which of the following best describes your job title?

Administrative Assistant .... ☐
Coordinator .... ☐
Manager/Supervisor .... ☐
Director .... ☐
Vice President .... ☐
President/CEO/COO .... ☐
Lawyer/Doctor/Medical Professional .... ☐
Teacher/Educator/Trainer .... ☐
Engineer/Technician .... ☐
Consultant .... ☐
Not employed/Student/Retired .... ☐
Other (Please specify): _____ ☐

8. Which of the following best describes the area of the company your job title falls under?

Accounting .... ☐
Engineering .... ☐
Manufacturing .... ☐
Operations .... ☐
Marketing .... ☐
Sales .... ☐
Other (Please specify): _____ ☐

9. What is your age?

Under 20 .... ☐
21-29 .... ☐
30-39 .... ☐
40-49 .... ☐
50-59 .... ☐
60-over .... ☐

10. Are you:

Male .... ☐
Female .... ☐

11. Which computer publications do you read regularly? (Please list)

_____
_____
_____
_____
_____
_____
_____
_____
_____
_____

Comments: _____
_____
_____

Fold here and scotch-tape to mail.

Read This Before Opening Software

Before using any of the software on this disc, you need to install the software you plan to use. If you have problems with *Special Edition Using Microsoft Internet Explorer 3*, please contact Macmillan Technical Support at (317) 581-3833. We can be reached by e-mail at **support@mcp.com** or by CompuServe at **GO QUEBOOKS**.

Licensing Agreement

By opening this package, you are agreeing to be bound by the following:

This software is copyrighted and all rights are reserved by the publisher and its licensers. You are licensed to use this software on a single computer. You may copy the software for backup or archival purposes only. Making copies of the software for any other purpose is a violation of United States copyright laws. THIS SOFTWARE IS SOLD AS IS, WITHOUT WARRANTY OF ANY KIND, EITHER EXPRESSED OR IMPLIED, INCLUDING BUT NOT LIMITED TO THE IMPLIED WARRANTIES OF MERCHANTABILITY AND FITNESS FOR A PARTICULAR PURPOSE. Neither the publisher nor its dealers and distributors nor its licensers assume any liability for any alleged or actual damages arising from the use of this software. (Some states do not allow exclusion of implied warranties, so the exclusion may not apply to you.)

The entire contents of this disc and the compilation of the software are copyrighted and protected by United States copyright laws. The individual programs on the disc are copyrighted by the authors or owners of each program. Each program has its own use permissions and limitations. To use each program, you must follow the individual requirements and restrictions detailed for each. Do not use a program if you do not agree to follow its licensing agreement.

These programs—Microsoft Internet Explorer 3.0, ActiveX Control Pad, and HTML Layout Control—were reproduced by Que under a special arrangement with Microsoft Corporation. For this reason, Que is responsible for the product warranty and for support. If your disc is defective, please return it to Que, which will arrange for its replacement. PLEASE DO NOT RETURN IT TO MICROSOFT CORPORATION. Any product support will be provided, if at all, by Que. PLEASE DO NOT CONTACT MICROSOFT CORPORATION FOR PRODUCT SUPPORT. End users of these Microsoft programs shall not be considered "registered owners" of a Microsoft product and therefore shall not be eligible for upgrades, promotions, or other benefits available to "registered owners" of Microsoft products.